Reptiles Do the Strangest Things

For Scott and Tony Shepherd

First paperback edition, 1991
Revised edition

Text copyright © 1970, 1991 by Random House, Inc. Illustrations copyright © 1991 by Jack Graber. All rights reserved under International and Pan-American Copyright Conventions. Published in the United States by Random House, Inc., New York, and simultaneously in Canada by Random House of Canada Limited, Toronto.

Library of Congress Cataloging-in-Publication Data
Hornblow, Leonora, 1920– Reptiles do the strangest things / by Leonora and Arthur Hornblow ; illustrated by Jack Graber.   p.   cm. —(Step-up nature books) Summary: Brief, easy-to-read descriptions of the strange habits of some of the world's more unusual reptiles, including the tuatara, hognose snake, horned toad, basilisk, and Komodo dragon. ISBN 0-679-81158-3 (pbk.) —ISBN 0-679-91158-8 (lib. bdg.) 1. Reptiles—Juvenile literature. [1. Reptiles.] I. Hornblow, Arthur, 1893–   . II. Graber, Jack, ill. III. Title. QL644.2.H67 1991 597.9—dc20 90-8598 CIP AC

Manufactured in the United States of America   1   2   3   4   5   6   7   8   9   10

Reptiles Do the Strangest Things

By Leonora and Arthur Hornblow
Illustrated by Jack Graber

Revised Edition

STEP-UP BOOKS
Random House  New York

CONTENTS

1

THE TIME
OF THE MONSTERS

Millions and millions of years ago there lived a huge animal called Apatosaurus (AP-pat-oh-SOR-uss). He was as long as a line of ten elephants and weighed more than 60,000 pounds. He spent his days eating green plants that grew on land and in the water. He used to be called Brontosaurus (BRONT-uh-SOR-us).

Apatosaurus was a dinosaur. Dinosaurs were reptiles. They ruled the earth for millions of years. There were dinosaurs as small as rabbits. There were dinosaurs as tall as a four-story building.

A terrible kind of dinosaur called Tyrannosaurus rex (tie-RAN-uh-SOR-us REKS) had a huge head and a thousand teeth. He was strong and fierce. He could kill and eat an Apatosaurus.

Tyrannosaurus rex means "king of the lizard tyrants." Dinosaur means "terrible lizard."

These fantastic reptiles all died long before there were any people on earth. So no one ever saw a dinosaur. But today we know about them from their bones.

Dinosaur bones have been found buried in rocks in many parts of the world. You can see these bones in museums. In one museum, there is a giant skeleton of a Tyrannosaurus rex. Even without his skin he is scary.

Today there are only five kinds of reptiles. They are lizards, turtles, snakes, crocodilians, and an odd animal called the tuatara.

2

I'M LEFT OVER

There are many kinds of snakes and turtles. There are many kinds of crocodilians and lizards. But there is only one kind of tuatara.

Over millions of years, all the other reptiles of his kind died away. The small tuatara is a leftover from the days of the dinosaurs.

This strange little leftover breathes very slowly. Sometimes a tuatara may not take a breath for an hour!

And the leathery eggs of the female tuatara hatch very slowly too. The ba-

bies don't come out for at least a year.

Tuataras are found in only one part of
the world. They live on small islands off
New Zealand. On these islands live many
sea birds called petrels. The petrels dig
burrows in the sandy earth. Then a
strange thing happens. The tuataras move
right in with the petrels.

A tuatara can dig his own burrow. Why
does he move in with the petrels? Maybe
even a leftover likes company.

3

THE STRANGE SONG

The largest reptiles on earth are the crocodilians. These are crocodiles, alligators, and their cousins.

Large or small, most reptiles are strangely silent. Some have no voices at all. But the "song of the crocodilian" is one of the loudest sounds in the animal world. The mighty roar of a big crocodile rolls like thunder through the swamp.

Crocodilians live in swamps near rivers and oceans. They love water. All crocodilians are strong swimmers. They catch and eat most of their food right in the water.

A crocodile drifts slowly down the river. He hardly makes a ripple. Only his eyes and the tip of his nose are above the water. He can breathe and see without being seen. He is watching and waiting for his prey. It might be a bug. It might be a fish. Or it might be a big animal.

Often, big crocodiles wait for animals to come to the water to drink. Then the

crocs swing their tails and knock the prey into the water. Or they may grab an animal by the nose with their jaws and pull it in. This is how African crocodiles catch deer, pigs, and sometimes even cows.

The jaws of big crocodilians are so strong they can crush a human being. But some people wrestle with alligators! At "animal farms" in Florida you can see these strange wrestling matches. The terrible teeth of the reptiles look very

frightening. But an alligator cannot bite if his mouth is held shut. So the wrestlers just hold the toothy jaws closed and pretend to wrestle. They may even have to shake the alligators' heads to make the fight look dangerous. The poor 'gators probably just want to get away.

Alligators build wonderful nests for their eggs. First the mother bites off wet leaves and branches from nearby bushes. Then she pushes them into a big pile. With her back feet she digs a hollow in the pile. In the hollow she lays her eggs. Now the mother 'gator covers the pile with mud and damp plants.

With her belly she smooths the top and closes the nest. The mother may have to work for three days and nights to build this nest. But her eggs will be safe and warm.

The mother alligator doesn't forget her eggs. She comes back often to fix the nest.

In about nine weeks she hears little peep-
ing noises. This means the baby alligators are ready to hatch. She tears open
the nest and helps her babies to come out.

The killing of alligators and crocodiles
is against the law. Some people do it any-
way, and sell the animals' skins. Now very
few of these creatures are left in the
swamps. It is sad to think that the thun-
dering "song of the croc" may someday be
heard only at the zoo.

4
THE WONDERFUL
SERPENTS

In old stories and legends you may read about serpents. That is just another name for snakes. There are short snakes and long snakes. There are thin snakes and fat snakes.

There are snakes that can swim a thousand miles out to sea. There are snakes that fly from tree to tree. Some snakes curl themselves up into a ball. One kind of snake can spit poison right in people's eyes. Another kind can catch a bat flying through the air.

Many people don't know that snakes can

do such wonderful things. Some think
that all snakes are dangerous and slimy.
But very few snakes hurt people. And no
snake is slimy. The skin of a snake is clean
and dry and soft.

Some snakes make nice pets. But look
out! Some of the wonderful serpents can
be dangerous.

5
THE DANGEROUS RATTLE

Dogs bark. Birds sing. Pigs grunt. But only one creature on earth can rattle its tail. This is the famous rattlesnake. On his tail he has a built-in rattle. When he is angry or frightened he rattles it.

A baby rattler has no rattle. He has only a tiny button on his tail. But in every other way he is like a grown-up rattlesnake. Baby rattlers can take care of themselves as soon as they are born. Their mother does nothing to help them. Each baby must hunt for his own food.

Rattlesnakes are born with special teeth

called fangs. When a rattler bites, poison comes through these fangs. The poison is called venom. A young rattler has very little venom. His bite cannot kill a human. But it can kill a mouse.

A week or two after he is born, the rattler does a strange thing. He rubs his nose and mouth against a stone. He rubs and rubs until he makes a little hole in his skin. Slowly the young snake pushes himself through the hole. He wriggles right out of his own skin! Under the old skin is a nice new one. The rattler moves away and leaves the old skin on the ground. He will shed his skin about three times a year for the rest of his life.

All snakes shed their skin in this way. Even the clear covering over their eyes comes off. In the old skin this covering looks just like a pair of eyeglasses.

Every time the rattler sheds, a ring of dry skin stays around the button on his tail. As the snake grows, the rattle grows too. The larger the snake, the larger the rattle.

Someday you may hear that rattle. If you do, get away fast! It means a rattle-snake is curled up nearby. He is shaking his tail, ready to strike. But the rattler will not strike unless you come too close and frighten him.

Rattlesnakes are dangerous. But if you don't bother them, they won't bother you. Maybe that is the meaning of the strange rattle.

6

THE GAME OF DEATH

The hognose is a gentle snake. He has no rattle. He has no venom. He never bites. When an enemy is near he does a funny thing. He puffs up his body, hisses loudly, and strikes. If the enemy won't go away, the hognose tries a new trick. He rolls over and plays dead. Then he peeks to see if it is safe to move.

If someone flips him over, he flips right back. He probably thinks he looks more dead upside down.

7

THE GREAT SWALLOW

Many people like to eat eggs. In Africa there is a snake that eats nothing else. It isn't easy. Often the eggs are twice as wide as he is.

The egg-eater opens his mouth very wide. He stretches it over an egg. Slowly the egg slides in. He closes his mouth. For a moment he looks like a little watermelon. Then the egg reaches sharp bones in his throat. These bones cut the shell. The egg slides down. The snake spits out the shell. Nobody, not even an egg-eater, likes to eat eggshells.

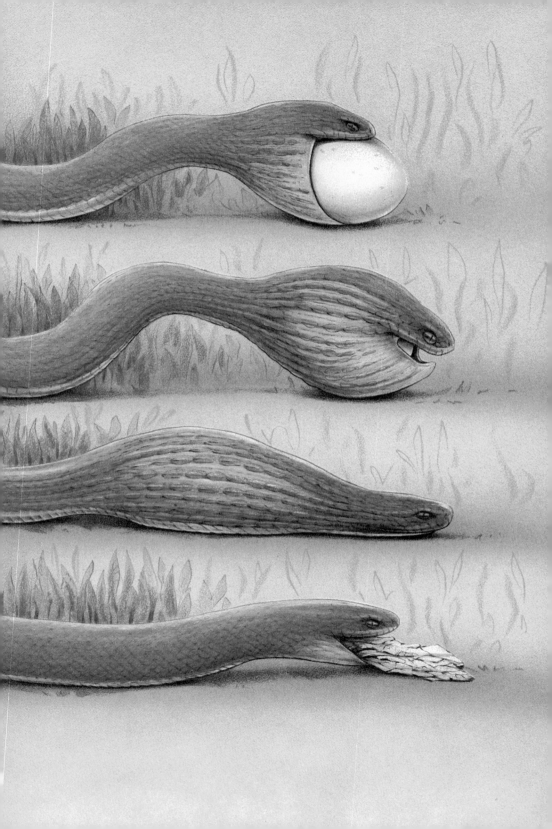

8

THE DANCER IN A BASKET

In India, men called snake charmers make snakes dance. Their favorite dancing snake is the king cobra.

A snake charmer puts a basket down on the street. He sits by it and plays a flute. Suddenly a cobra's head comes up. The big serpent hisses. He leans toward the man. But the wise charmer moves away. He knows that the venom in a cobra's bite could kill him.

The cobra watches as the charmer plays the flute. Soon the skin below the snake's head begins to flatten and spread. This

odd swelling is called the hood of the
cobra. It is a sign that the cobra is angry.
Now the hooded snake sways back and
forth. He seems to be dancing to the music. But he is only following the moving
flute. Like all snakes, the cobra has no
ears. The beautiful dancer can't even hear
the music.

9

THE BIG SQUEEZE

The giants of the snake world are the python and the anaconda. Both can grow to be more than 30 feet long. Some are as big around as a telephone pole.

In the jungles of Asia big pythons live among the trees. They wind their heavy bodies around the branches. They crawl along the jungle trails. Sometimes they crawl into a village and terrify the natives. But they rarely eat people. They eat birds and small animals. The biggest pythons often eat deer and wild pigs.

Pythons and anacondas have no venom.

They have another way of killing. They coil their bodies around their prey. They squeeze and squeeze. Soon the victim stops breathing. Then they eat it.

A python kills a wild pig. Then he grabs its head with his many teeth. Slowly he pulls himself over his prey. Little by little the pig goes in. And soon the python has an enormous middle. After such a big meal he may not eat again for a year.

Pythons and anacondas cannot tear their victims apart. So they must swal-

low them whole. This may seem hard. But all snakes have jaws that open very wide. A giant anaconda can swallow a six-foot crocodilian.

On the banks of the Amazon River, an anaconda wraps himself around a crocodilian. He pins the croc against a tree. Then he squeezes it to death.

Anacondas are great swimmers. They live in rivers. They even give birth to living babies right in the water. The babies are more than three feet long. And they can already swim.

Baby pythons come out of eggs. The mother python does something no other snake does. She coils herself around the eggs until they hatch. But once the babies hatch, the mother does not take care of them. They must take care of themselves. They already know how to hunt. And no one has to teach a python how to use the "big squeeze."

10

A HOUSE ON HIS BACK

Only one kind of reptile carries his house on his back. That is the wonderful turtle. He is born with a soft covering of shell and bone. As he grows, it hardens and grows too. He will wear the shell all his life. It will keep him safe from enemies.

If an enemy comes near, the turtle acts fast. He pulls in his head. He pulls in his tail. He pulls up his legs. And he won't come out until he wants to. No one can make him.

There are turtles that live in the water and turtles that live on land. Water tur-

tles don't always stay in the water. Often
many of them climb up on rocks or logs
to sit in the sun.

Some people have turtles for pets. The
box turtle makes a good pet. He is very
well named. His top shell and bottom shell
fit tightly together. And when he pulls
his legs in, flaps close up each side. But
if he eats too much, he gets too big for
his box. Then his fat legs keep popping
out.

11

THE BIG SNAP

Turtles have no teeth. They have beaks. They use them to catch their food and tear it apart.

One kind of turtle has a very sharp beak. And his strong jaws snap. He is the feisty snapping turtle. Most turtles are gentle. If an enemy is near, they hide in their shells. Not the snapper. He snaps and bites.

If you meet a snapper, don't pick him up. He might think you're an enemy and snap at you.

The biggest and ugliest snappers are the

alligator snapping turtles. They can grow to be more than 200 pounds. They live on muddy river bottoms.

An alligator snapper has a strange way of catching fish. He lies on the riverbed with his mouth wide open. He looks like a lump of mud. Fish may not see him. But they see his tongue. It looks like a tiny pink worm. He wiggles his tongue. A fish swims in to get the bait. The snapper snaps. What a lazy way to get dinner!

12
THE LAND GIANTS

On faraway islands in the Pacific Ocean live the biggest of all the tortoises. These are the Galápagos tortoises. Their thick legs look almost like the legs of an elephant. These huge reptiles live to a very old age. One is known to have lived for more than 152 years.

Some Galápagos tortoises may weigh more than 500 pounds.

13

THE SEA GIANTS

Some of the turtles that live in the sea are giants too. They are the green turtles. They can be as long as a person and five times as heavy.

Sea turtles are fine swimmers. They do not have legs like land turtles. They have flippers. The flippers help them to move through the water. Of all the turtles, the best swimmers are the green giants of the sea.

Sea turtles spend all their lives in the water. They eat and sleep in the water. But there is one thing they have to do on land. The turtles of the sea must come up on beaches to lay their eggs.

On a moonlit night a mother turtle crawls slowly up the sand. It is hard for her to walk on her flippers. She does something very strange. She pushes her flippers through the sand as if she were swimming. It takes her a long time to drag her heavy body up the beach. Sometimes she stops and lets out a huge sigh.

The green turtle waddles along the beach looking for a spot she likes. At last she finds a dry place high above the water. With her front flippers she scoops out a bed for herself. Behind the bed she digs a hole. Now she begins to lay her eggs. Soon there may be as many as 100 eggs in the hole. They look like a pile of Ping-Pong balls. Then the big turtle covers the eggs with sand. Slowly she waddles back to the

sea. She will never see her eggs again.

In two or three months the baby turtles come out of their shells. Now they must get to the sea. No one is there to show them where to go. Somehow they just know. They run right for the water. But many of these little turtles will never reach the sea. Their shells are not yet hard enough to protect them. Birds wait overhead to swoop down and eat them. Animals on the beach run after them. And even if they get to the sea the baby turtles may not be safe. Big fish may eat them. It's lucky for green turtles that the mother turtle lays so many eggs.

14

A PILE OF LEAVES

Some people think a matamata is the oddest looking creature in the world. He surely is the oddest looking turtle. His shell is covered with bumps. Sticking to the bumps are many tiny green plants. The matamata looks like a pile of rubbish and leaves.

On a shallow river bottom in South America, a matamata sits waiting. He stretches his long neck up out of the water. He takes a breath through his strange snorkel nose.

Then he pulls his head back under the

water. He is hungry. His tiny eyes watch for fish. Suddenly a group of fish swim over. The fish try to eat some bits from the rubbish pile. But they don't eat. They get eaten. The matamata just opens his enormous mouth. Swoosh! A great load of water rushes in. A fish gets swept in too. Then the matamata spits out the water. But he doesn't spit out the fish!

15

LITTLE CLOWN

There are almost 3,000 kinds of lizards. They come in many colors and sizes. They do many odd things.

Most lizards have no voices at all. But the merry little gecko squeaks and squeals. And he says "Gecko-gecko." That is how he got his name.

Geckos are found in warm countries. Some kinds like to live in people's houses. The people who have geckos are lucky. Their little lizards will run around eating up roaches, mosquitoes, and many other pests.

It is fun to see geckos running around the house. They are pretty. Their eyes are big and bright. If you talk to them, they seem to listen. But watch out! If you pick up a gecko, you may get a surprise. He might run away—and leave you holding his tail. Geckos can drop off their tails whenever they want to. It doesn't matter. They can grow new ones. Sometimes a tail breaks but doesn't fall off. Then the old tail grows back on again, and a new tail grows beside it. Some geckos even have three tails.

Geckos are great climbers. They can run up and down walls. Some kinds can even run across a ceiling. These geckos have special pads on their feet. On the bottom of each pad are many tiny, tiny hooks. The strange pads are not sticky. But they can cling to almost anything. A gecko with these pads on his feet can walk right up a glass window.

16

THE MAGIC TAIL

Of all the lizards only two kinds have venom. These dangerous reptiles are the Mexican beaded lizard and his cousin, the Gila monster.

The Gila monster doesn't like the heat. He sleeps in the day. When the sun goes down he hunts for eggs and baby animals.

The Gila has an odd way of storing food. When he eats a lot, his tail gets fat. Then he can stop eating. His body slowly uses up the fat. After several months the Gila may still not be hungry. But his tail has grown very thin.

17

THE BLOOD-SQUIRTER

The horned toad looks like a toad. He often acts like a toad. He is called a toad. But he is not a toad. He is a member of the lizard family.

When a horned toad is frightened he will try to run away. But if he is caught, he may do one of the strangest things in all the animal world. From the corner of each eye he may shoot a thin stream of blood. It does not hurt him. And it will not hurt you. But it may give you quite a scare.

Horned toads live in desert country. Most desert animals hide from the sun.

Not the horned toads. They stay out in the blazing sun chasing insects. When the sun goes down, the desert gets cool. To keep warm, the horned toads do another strange thing. They stick their heads in the sand. Then they flip sand over their bodies. Soon they are wrapped in little overcoats of sand. When the big animals come out to hunt in the dark, they won't find any horned toads. The little lizards will be safe in their sandy beds.

18

THE SMOKE-PUFFER

The big marine iguanas are the best swimmers of all the lizards. They spend all their time by the sea.

They live on the beaches and rocks of the Galápagos Islands. There they may lie in the sun for hours. They wait for the water to go down as the tide goes out. Then they crawl slowly down to the water to look for their favorite food—seaweed.

Marine iguanas are angry-looking reptiles. They have tough, flat faces. Along their backs are strange, sharp spines. And when people come near them, they do an

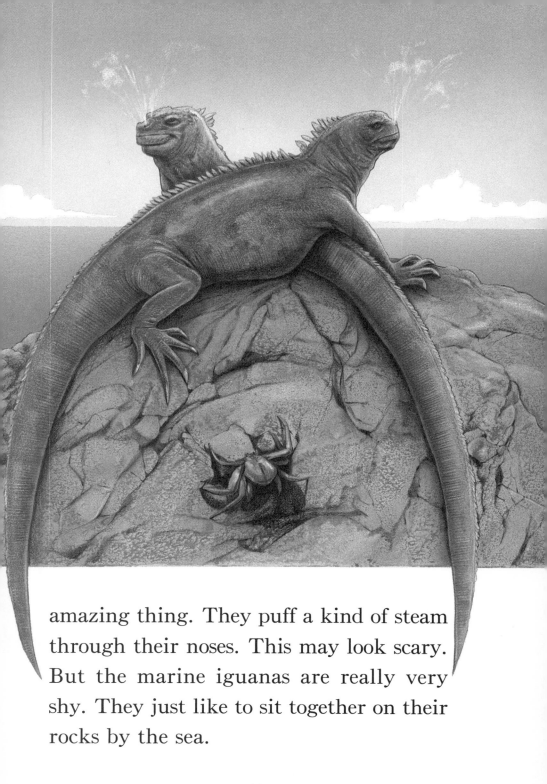

amazing thing. They puff a kind of steam through their noses. This may look scary. But the marine iguanas are really very shy. They just like to sit together on their rocks by the sea.

19

TINY FLYER

The draco is a tiny lizard. He lives where there are lots of trees. He climbs the trees, busily snapping up insects in his path. He is just like lots of other lizards.

But the draco can do something few other lizards can do. At each side of his thin little body are flaps of folded skin. These flaps lie flat against his body when he runs along the ground or climbs a tree. Then the draco looks like a small green twig. But when he reaches the top of a tree, he does something strange. He jumps

off. The brightly colored flaps open out.
They look like beautiful wings. These
beautiful wings work like a little para-
chute. The draco glides from tree to tree.
He steers with his tail. Sometimes he is
called the flying dragon.

20

THE BEAUTIFUL FRILL

In Australia there is a wonderful reptile called the frilled lizard. Around his neck is a fold of loose skin. It lies flat when he isn't using it. But if he sees an enemy, he spreads out the fold. A great frill opens behind his head like a big umbrella. The frilled lizard stands up on his back legs and shows his teeth. Suddenly he looks big and mean. If he's lucky, his act will frighten his enemy away. What a strange way to use a pretty frill!

21

THE WATER-WALKER

The basilisk has no frill. But he has a crest along his back and tail. His tail is long and thin and very strong. And sometimes he uses it to help him run. He can run fast. He can climb trees. He eats small animals and fruit that he finds in the trees.

The basilisk likes to climb trees that hang over lakes and streams. Sometimes he jumps off a branch and into the water. He is a good swimmer. He can hide from an enemy at the bottom of a lake.

But strangest of all, this funny lizard can walk on water. When the basilisk is frightened, he gets up on his back legs and runs. He swings from side to side. His long tail helps him keep his balance. If he comes to a stream, he runs right across the top of it. He may get tired and sink into the water. Then he will swim. But he'd rather run than swim. Running is faster and keeps him safe from enemies that live in the water.

22
THE COLOR-CHANGERS

A little lizard called the "American chameleon" is really a Carolina anole. He does a wonderful thing. He changes color! When he is angry or afraid, he changes. If the air gets colder or warmer, he changes. If the light grows brighter or darker, he changes again. The anole also has a special pouch of skin on his throat. When he spreads it open, it looks like a bright pink fan. Sometimes he uses this fan to show off to a lady anole. More often he uses it to scare away other males.

Wild anoles live in trees. They eat in-

sects and sleep on twigs among the leaves. But people sometimes catch anoles. They sell them at pet shops and fairs. If you ever buy an anole, remember that he is used to living in a tree. He may not know how to drink from a dish. Just sprinkle a few drops of water on a leaf. Then he may feel more at home. And you can watch the nice little color-changer changing color.

Another color-changer is the true chameleon. He is one of the oddest of all the reptiles. He can change from brown to green and back to brown again. Sometimes part of him is in the sun and part in the shade. Then he's two colors at once! This queer lizard has bumpy skin, pop eyes, and a tail that rolls up in a curl. He may have a horn on his head. He might even have three. And his tongue

can be longer than his whole body.

Up in the trees a chameleon watches for insects. He rolls one eye forward and one back. He can see ahead and behind at the same time. Along comes a bug. The chameleon shoots out his fantastic tongue. On its tip is some sticky stuff. The tongue hits the bug. The bug sticks. The chameleon pulls in his tongue. Zip! No more bug.

23

A MONSTER OF TODAY

Far away in the warm Indian Ocean is the island of Komodo. There live the largest lizards on earth. They are the Komodo dragons. These giant lizards can be ten feet long. The biggest ones weigh more than 300 pounds.

Komodo dragons can climb trees. It is strange to see a five-foot dragon sitting up among the branches. But the dragons spend most of their time on the ground.

A Komodo dragon moves slowly through the high grass. His heavy body moves from side to side. His long yellow tongue flicks in and out. He is hunting for food. Like a snake, the dragon picks up smells in the air with his tongue. He looks for a dead animal. If he doesn't find one, he kills a wild pig, a deer, or a goat. Then he has a messy feast. He bites off big chunks of meat and swallows them whole.

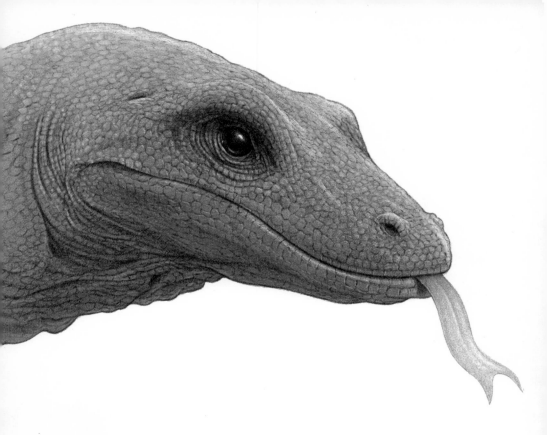

The Komodo dragon is a strange beast indeed. As he flicks his yellow tongue, he looks like the dragon of fairy tales and legends.

We know there are no real dragons. And no one ever saw a live dinosaur. But there are many creatures that are almost as strange. And among the strangest are the remarkable reptiles that still share our earth.

W9-B

Wealth, Health, and Democracy in East Asia and Latin America

Why do some societies fare well, and others poorly, at reducing the risk of early death? This study finds that the public provision of basic health care and of other inexpensive social services has reduced mortality rapidly even in tough economic circumstances, and that political democracy has contributed to the provision and utilization of such services, in a wider range of ways than is sometimes recognized. These conclusions are based on case studies of Argentina, Brazil, Chile, Costa Rica, Indonesia, South Korea, Taiwan, and Thailand, as well as on cross-national comparisons involving these cases and others.

James W. McGuire is professor in the Department of Government at Wesleyan University. He is the author of *Peronism without Perón: Unions, Parties, and Democracy in Argentina*. Professor McGuire specializes in comparative politics with a regional focus on Latin America and East Asia and a topical focus on democracy and public health. He is a recipient of Wesleyan's Binswanger Prize for Excellence in Teaching.

Wealth, Health, and Democracy in East Asia and Latin America

JAMES W. MCGUIRE
Wesleyan University

CAMBRIDGE
UNIVERSITY PRESS

CAMBRIDGE UNIVERSITY PRESS
Cambridge, New York, Melbourne, Madrid, Cape Town, Singapore,
São Paulo, Delhi, Dubai, Tokyo

Cambridge University Press
32 Avenue of the Americas, New York, NY 10013-2473, USA

www.cambridge.org
Information on this title: www.cambridge.org/9780521139342

First published 2010

Printed in the United States of America

A catalog record for this publication is available from the British Library.

Library of Congress Cataloging in Publication data
McGuire, James W. (James William)
  Wealth, health, and democracy in East Asia and Latin America / James W. McGuire.
    p.   cm.
  Includes bibliographical references and index.
  ISBN 978-0-521-51546-7 (hardback)
  ISBN 978-0-521-13934-2 (paperback)
  1. Infants – Mortality – East Asia. 2. Infants – Mortality – Latin America.
  3. East Asia – Social policy. 4. East Asia – Economic policy. 5. Latin America – Social
  policy. 6. Latin America – Economic policy. I. Title.
  HB1323.I42E1863   2010
  304.6'408832095 – dc22   2009047101

ISBN 978-0-521-51546-7 Hardback
ISBN 978-0-521-13934-2 Paperback

Additional resources for this publication at
http://www.cambridge.org/us/catalogue/catalogue.asp?isbn=9780521515467

To
My Family

Contents

Figures and Tables

Preface and Acknowledgments

The goal of this book is to advance the understanding of the nature and causes of national development, and to shed light on policies and circumstances that may promote such development. In contrast to some current and past research, national development is conceptualized in this study as the expansion of human capabilities, rather than in terms of economic achievements alone. The analysis focuses on eight middle-income developing societies, four in Latin America (Argentina, Brazil, Chile, and Costa Rica) and four in East Asia (Indonesia, South Korea, Taiwan, and Thailand). Its main findings are that the public financing or provision of basic social services can produce rapid mortality decline, even in difficult economic circumstances; and that political democracy can expand the provision and utilization of mortality-reducing social services, in a wider range of ways than is sometimes appreciated. The experiences of the societies reviewed in this book suggest that Latin America as well as East Asia has produced development models worth emulating.

Several years ago my father alerted me to Amartya Sen's article "More than 100 Million Women are Missing" (1990). This article led me to other works by Professor Sen, notably the book *Hunger and Public Action* (1989), cowritten with Jean Drèze. Sen argued that development should be interpreted not as the enlargement of incomes, but rather as the growth of human capabilities, our abilities to live the lives that we have reason to choose. Like Professor Sen, I became especially interested in capabilities related to physical survival. I began to teach *Hunger and Public Action* in one of my courses, which already included a unit comparing economic development in East Asia and Latin America. The juxtaposition of these lines of research suggested that scholars of national development had focused heavily on income-related outcomes, neglecting the issue of why some societies do better than others at raising life expectancy and reducing infant mortality. I thus began the research that culminated in this book, which reinterprets development in East Asia and Latin America as being mainly about the expansion of human capabilities, particularly those related to physical survival, rather than about the expansion of peoples' incomes, whether through economic growth or the reduction of income inequality or income poverty.

The love and wisdom of my late father, William J. McGuire, shaped my personal and intellectual development, and his perspectivist epistemology influenced the research in this book. I dedicate this book to his memory, and to the other members of my family. Amartya Sen provided inspiration for the research as well as support and encouragement over the years. My colleagues in Wesleyan's Government Department, as well as other faculty members across the university, made useful comments on parts of the study, as well as on seminars, papers, and journal articles on related topics. Wesleyan students are an inexhaustible fountain of inspiration and insight. Zuleika Arashiro, Bernard Brown, Laura Frankel, and Lily Oster assisted skillfully and graciously in the research. The ideas in this book were developed in dialogue with Eric Bjornlund, Nauro Campos, David Collier, Ruth Berins Collier, Javier Corrales, Margaret Crahan, Jorge Domínguez, Richard Easterlin, Varun Gauri, John Gerring, Stephan Haggard, Evelyne Huber, Wendy Hunter, Robert Kaufman, Abraham Lowenthal, James Mahon, James Mahoney, Joan Nelson, Jeffrey Nugent, Michael Reich, John Seery, Richard Snyder, Judith Tendler, Danny Unger, Stephanie Weber, and Kurt Weyland, and in response to the useful suggestions of the scholars who refereed the manuscript for Cambridge University Press.

For information, commentary, logistical support, and other contributions that helped to improve particular parts of this book, I am indebted to Dararat Anantanasuwong, Maureen Birmingham, Katherine Bliss, Roger Bonilla, Alasdair Bowie, James Brennan, David Cameron, Minja Kim Choe, Mary Clark, Jorge Vargas Cullel, Deon Filmer, Joseph Fins, Fernando Gore, Carol Graham, Donald Green, James Haft, Michael Hansen, Kenneth Hill, Daniel Hojman, Alma Idiart, Joyce Jacobsen, Wen-Hua Kuo, Fabrice Lehoucq, Evan Lieberman, Michael Lovell, Richard Mann, Juliana Martínez Franzoni, Leonardo Mata, Jumroon Mikhanorn, Amy Nunn, Yaa Oppong, Vicente Palermo, Steve Phillips, Kachanasak Phonboon, Sathirakorn Pongpanich, Lant Pritchett, Dietrich Reuschemeyer, Luis Rosero-Bixby, John Ross, Joshua Salomon, Barbara Stallings, Erica Taucher, Michael D. White, and Stanley Zankel.

The Rockefeller Foundation, and separately the Office of Academic Affairs of Wesleyan University, graciously provided publication subventions that permitted Cambridge University Press to issue this book initially in paperback as well as in cloth. Residential fellowships at the Pacific Council on International Policy, at the Woodrow Wilson International Center for Scholars, and at the Harvard Center for Population and Development Studies provided generous support and a friendly environment for research. A Senior Fellowship from the American Council of Learned Societies helped to fund a year of scholarship and writing, and Wesleyan University Project Grants financed research visits to Costa Rica and Thailand. The direction and interpretation of the research were influenced by dialogue at colloquia at Brown University

(Watson Institute of International Studies); Cornell University (Weill College of Medicine); Harvard University (Center for Population and Development Studies, David Rockefeller Center for Latin American Studies); Northern Illinois University (Graduate Colloquium); Stanford University (Asia/Pacific Research Center); the University of California, San Diego (Center for U.S.-Mexican Studies); Wesleyan University (Public Affairs Center); the Woodrow Wilson International Center for Scholars; and Yale University (Council on Latin American Studies), as well as by panel presentations at the meetings of the American Political Science Association, International Studies Association, and Latin American Studies Association.

Anne M. McGuire used her knowledge, wisdom, and vast experience to copyedit the entire manuscript and to produce an excellent index. Claire V. McGuire helped with the index and carefully proofread the text. Eric Crahan of Cambridge University Press was a wise and supportive acquisitions editor, and Suzanna Tamminen of Wesleyan University Press provided sage advice about editorial issues. Bindu Vinod of Newgen Imaging oversaw the production of the book with grace, skill, and good cheer.

Occasional sentences or short passages are taken or adapted from "Development Policy and Its Determinants in East Asia and Latin America," *Journal of Public Policy* 14, No. 2 (April 1995), 205–242; "Labor Union Strength and Human Development in East Asia and Latin America," *Studies in Comparative International Development* 33, No. 4 (Winter 1999), 3–34; "Social Policy and Mortality Decline in East Asia and Latin America," *World Development* 29, No. 10 (October 2001), 1673–1697; "Mortality Decline in Cuba, 1900–1959: Patterns, Comparisons, and Causes" (with Laura Frankel), *Latin American Research Review* 40, No. 2 (June 2005), 84–116; and "Basic Health Care Provision and Under-5 Mortality: A Cross-National Study of Developing Countries," *World Development* 34, No. 3 (March 2006), 405–425.

This research is designed to uncover forces and circumstances that are conducive to human development, and to identify critical points at which policy makers and the public might intervene to redirect the course of events from channels to which historical legacies might otherwise confine them. To the extent that these objectives have been achieved, the individuals and institutions mentioned herein deserve much of the credit. Any errors of fact or interpretation are my own.

Abbreviations

ABRASCO	Associação Brasileira de Saúde Coletiva, Brazilian Collective Health Association
ABRI	Angkatan Bersenjata Republik Indonesia, Armed Forces of the Republic of Indonesia
AIDS	Acquired Immunodeficiency Syndrome
APROFA	Asociación Chilena de Protección de la Familia, Chilean Family Protection Association
ARENA	Aliança Renovadora Nacional, National Renovating Alliance (Brazil)
CAPs	Caixas de Aposentadorias e Pensões, Pension and Retirement Benefits Funds (Brazil)
CARE	Cooperative for Assistance and Relief Everywhere, Inc.
CCSS	Caja Costarricense de Seguro Social, Costa Rican Social Security Fund
CEBES	Centro Brasileiro de Estudos de Saúde, Brazilian Center for Health Studies
CGT	Confederación General del Trabajo, General Labor Confederation (Argentina)
CONTAG	Confederação Nacional dos Trabalhadores na Agricultura, National Confederation of Agricultural Workers (Brazil)
CPT	Communist Party of Thailand
CSO	Caja de Seguro Obligatorio, Mandatory Insurance Fund (Chile)
DTP3	Three doses of the antigen against diphtheria, pertussis, and tetanus
EBAIS	Equipos Basicos de Atención Integral de Salud, Comprehensive Basic Health Care Teams (Costa Rica)
EPH	Encuesta Permanente de Hogares, Ongoing Household Survey (Argentina)
FONASA	Fondo Nacional de Salud, National Health Fund (Chile)

FSESP	Fundação Serviços de Saúde Pública, Special Public Health Service Foundation (Brazil)
FUNASA	Fundação Nacional de Saúde, National Health Foundation (Brazil)
FUNDEF	Fundo de Manutenção e Desenvolvimento do Ensino Fundamental e de Valorização do Magistério, Fund for the Maintenance and Development of Elementary Teaching and for the Valorization of the Teaching Profession (Brazil)
FUNRURAL	Fundo de Assistência ao Trabalhador Rural, Rural Worker Assistance Fund (Brazil)
GDP	Gross Domestic Product
HDI	Human Development Index
HIV	Human Immunodeficiency Virus
HIV/AIDS	Human Immunodeficiency Virus/Acquired Immunodeficiency Syndrome
IAPI	Instituto de Aposentadorias e Pensões dos Industriários, Institute of Pensions and Retirement Benefits for Industrial Workers (Brazil)
IAPs	Institutos de Aposentadorias e Pensões, Pension and Retirement Benefits Institutes (Brazil)
IMAS	Instituto Mixto de Ayuda Social, Mixed Institute of Social Aid (Costa Rica)
IMR	Infant Mortality Rate
INAMPS	Instituto Nacional de Assistência Médica da Previdência Social, National Social Security Medical Assistance Institute (Brazil)
Inpres	Instruksi Presiden, Presidential Instruction Program (Indonesia)
INPS	Instituto Nacional de Previdência Social, National Social Security Institute (Brazil)
ISAPRE	Institución de Salud Previsional, Social Security Health Institution (Chile)
JCRR	Sino-American Joint Commission on Rural Reconstruction (Taiwan)
KMT	Kuomintang, Nationalist Party (Taiwan)
MCV	Measles containing vaccine
MDB	Movimento Democrático Brasileiro, Brazilian Democratic Movement
MPAS	Ministério da Previdência e Assistência Social, Ministry of Social Security and Social Assistance (Brazil)
MPN	Movimiento Popular Neuquino, Neuquén Popular Movement (Argentina)
NHI	National Health Insurance (South Korea)
PAB	Piso de Atenção Básica, Basic Care Grant (Brazil)

PACS	Programa Agentes Comunitários de Saúde, Community Health Agents Program (Brazil)
PAHO	Pan American Health Organization
PIASS	Programa de Interiorização de Ações de Saúde e Saneamento, Program to Expand Health and Sanitation Activities in the Interior (Brazil)
PJ	Partido Justicialista, Justicialist [Peronist] Party (Argentina)
PKI	Partai Komunis Indonesia, Communist Party of Indonesia
PKK	Pemberdayaan Kesejahteraan Keluarga, Family Welfare Movement (Indonesia)
PKMD	Pembangunan Kesehatan Masyarakat Desa, Village Community Health Development Program (Indonesia)
Plan AUGE	Plan de Acceso Universal con Garantías Explícitas, Plan for Universal Access with Explicit Guarantees (Chile)
PLANASA	Plano Nacional de Saneamento, National Sanitation Plan (Brazil)
PLN	Partido Liberación Nacional, National Liberation Party (Costa Rica)
PMDB	Partido do Movimento Democrático Brasileiro, Party of the Brazilian Democratic Movement
PMO	Programa Médico Obligatorio, Mandatory Medical Program (Argentina)
PNAD	Pesquisa Nacional por Amostra de Domicílios, National Household Sample Survey (Brazil)
PNMI	Programa Nacional Materno Infantil, National Mother and Infant Program (Argentina)
PQLI	Physical Quality of Life Index
Prevsaúde	Programa Nacional de Serviços Básicos de Saúde, National Basic Health Service Program (Brazil)
PROMIN	Programa Materno Infantil y Nutrición, Mother and Infant Nutrition Program (Argentina)
PROSANEAR	Programa de Saneamento para Populações em Áreas de Baixa Renda, Low Income Sanitation Technical Assistance Project (Brazil)
PSDB	Partido da Social Democracia Brasileira, Brazilian Social Democratic Party
PSF	Programa Saúde da Família, Family Health Program (Brazil)
PT	Partido dos Trabalhadores, Workers' Party (Brazil)
PUSC	Partido Unidad Social Cristiana, Social Christian Unity Party (Costa Rica)
RGDPCH	Real gross domestic product per capita in international dollars at constant prices according to a chain index
RTG	Royal Thai Government

SERMENA	Servicio Médico Nacional de Empleados, Employees' National Medical Service (Chile)
SESP	Serviço Especial de Saúde Pública, Special Public Health Service (Brazil)
SNIS	Sistema Nacional Integrado de Salud, National Integrated Health System (Argentina)
SNS	Servicio Nacional de Salud, National Health Service (Chile)
SUS	Sistema Único de Saúde, Unified Health System (Brazil)
SUSENAS	Survei Sosial Ekonomi Nasional, National Socioeconomic Survey (Indonesia)
U5MR	Under-5 Mortality Rate
UHS	Universal Health Scheme (Thailand)
UNAIDS	Joint United Nations Programme on HIV/AIDS
UNDP	United Nations Development Programme
UNESCO	United Nations Educational, Scientific and Cultural Organization
UNICEF	United Nations Children's Fund
UPGK	Usaha Perbaikan Gizi Keluarga, Family Nutrition Improvement Program (Indonesia)
U.S. AID	United States Agency for International Development
USOM	United States Operations Mission (Thailand)
WHO	World Health Organization
WIDER	World Institute for Development Economics Research of the United Nations University (Helsinki, Finland)

I

Incomes, Capabilities, and Mortality Decline

Much research has been devoted in recent years to identifying causes of cross-national variation in premature mortality, as measured by such indicators as infant mortality and life expectancy at birth. This research addresses an important topic. Avoidance of early death is a necessary condition for anything else we might wish to achieve. Also, societies with high rates of early death tend to suffer from other sorts of deprivations. Hence, it is well worth identifying reasons why premature mortality is lower, or falls faster, in some societies than in others.

Public health issues are neglected in the literature on the comparative politics of developing countries, and political science issues are neglected in the field of public health. By connecting a public health issue to a political science issue, this book encourages dialogue between the two fields. On the public health side, its aim is to weigh the importance of social service provision on the one hand, and of economic output- and income-related factors on the other, on infant mortality levels and changes in developing countries from 1960 to 2005. On the political science side, the goal of the book is to explain why some developing country governments did better than others at designing and implementing mortality-reducing social services.

The analyses reported in this book challenge some conventional wisdom about economic and social progress in developing countries. Such progress is typically measured according to economic output- and income-related indicators like GDP per capita, income inequality, and income poverty. These measures capture some important inputs into human well-being, but the impact of economic output and income on human capabilities is shaped and constrained by a multitude of antecedent and intervening factors. Avoidance of early death, this analysis will argue, has a more direct relation than any economic factor to an individual's capacity to live the life that he or she has reason to choose. Accordingly, indicators of premature mortality, especially of infant and child mortality, will serve in this analysis as the main criteria of development achievement.

If the literature on development in poor and middle-income countries has been excessively concerned with output- and income-related indicators, the literature on social policy in such countries has been unduly preoccupied with issues of public spending and social insurance coverage. Our concern must be fundamentally with the expansion of human capabilities, particularly those related to physical functioning and survival, and only secondarily with the policy outputs that may facilitate those fundamental outcomes. The analyses reported here find that, at least in the middle-income developing societies on which this book focuses, neither a low level of public health spending, nor a low share of the population covered by contributory health insurance, presents an insurmountable obstacle to rapid mortality decline. From the standpoint of improving survival-related capabilities, the crucial policy output seems to be neither the amount of public health spending, nor the share of the population covered by health insurance, but the existence of government programs that provide, free of charge to the user, inexpensive basic health care to people (including uninsured people) who run a high risk of early death.

The wave of democratization that swept the world in the 1990s raised interest in the issue of whether democracy, whatever its intrinsic merits, improves the well-being of the poor. Exploration of this issue has focused mostly on the proposition that political leaders in democracies, unlike in authoritarian regimes, have an interest in winning votes, and that this interest should encourage them to advocate the provision of social services to the disadvantaged. Less attention has been paid to other dimensions of democracy – the freedom to transmit and receive information; the freedom to associate and organize; and changes in citizen expectations shaped by egalitarian ideals that are reinforced by habituation to democratic practice – that might also contribute to such provision. This study explores these other dimensions of democracy, as well as electoral incentives.

1.1. Economic Affluence, Social Service Provision, and Mortality

Two main hypotheses guide research on the causes of cross-societal variation in premature mortality. The "wealthier is healthier" hypothesis proposes that economic output and purchasing power are crucial.[1] An alternative "social service provision" hypothesis emphasizes government financing or delivery of basic services, including health care, education, family planning, safe water, and sanitation.[2] To the extent that each of these hypotheses is true, important implications follow for public action by citizens and governments. To the extent that economic output and income-related factors influence mortality levels and changes, public action should favor policies aimed at boosting

---

[1] Filmer and Pritchett 1999; Pritchett and Summers 1996.
[2] Caldwell 1986; Drèze and Sen 1989; Ghai ed. 2000; Halstead, Walsh, and Warren eds. 1985; Mehrotra and Jolly eds. 1997; Vallin and López eds. 1985.

economic growth and private incomes.[3] To the extent that the public financing or provision of basic social services influences mortality levels and changes, public action should favor the delivery of such services, accessible to populations at any income level and regardless of insurance coverage, to minimize mortality in high-risk populations. Indeed, insurance coverage, although a central focus of the literature about the welfare state in developing countries (as well as in debates about health care provision in the United States), appears to have had surprisingly limited effects on the pattern or pace of mortality decline in the eight societies studied closely in this book: Argentina, Brazil, Chile, and Costa Rica in Latin America, and Indonesia, South Korea, Taiwan, and Thailand in East Asia.

The wealthier is healthier conjecture comes in three variants that adopt respectively a narrow, intermediate, and broad definition of "wealthier." The narrow variant holds that the higher the level (or the larger the rise) of Gross Domestic Product (GDP) per capita, the lower the level (or the steeper the decline) of premature mortality. At least three mechanisms could mediate these effects. First, a high level or large rise of GDP per capita could create more survival-enhancing physical assets (e.g., roads). Second, a high level or large rise of GDP per capita could generate more private income, allowing households to buy more or better survival-enhancing goods and services (e.g., food, housing, clothing) in private markets. Third, a high level or large rise of GDP per capita could produce more resources for the public financing or provision of survival-enhancing social services.

The narrow version of the wealthier is healthier hypothesis, which focuses only on GDP per capita (setting aside income inequality and income poverty), is useful for depicting how the eight East Asian and Latin American societies studied closely in this book fared, in relation to other developing countries, on GDP per capita and infant mortality at the start of the twenty-first century. In Figure 1.1, infant mortality in 2005 is regressed on GDP per capita in 2005, using a natural log transformation of all values, as is a standard practice in research on this association. In Figure 1.2, the average annual percent decline of infant mortality from 1960 to 2005 is regressed on the average annual percent growth of GDP per capita from 1960 to 2005. In each analysis, the universe of cases consists of the 93 developing countries with information on both infant mortality (World Bank 2008e) and GDP per capita (Maddison 2007) in both 1960 and 2005.

To the extent that the narrow version of the wealthier is healthier hypothesis is supported by the data, we would expect to see regression lines with steep slopes and tightly clustered data points. In other words, to the extent that the

---

[3] Cutler, Deaton, and Lleras Muney (2006: 110) write that "In recent years, a number of authors have followed Pritchett and Summers (1996) and argued from cross-country regressions that income is more important [to health] than any other factors, and have endorsed policies that downplay the role of any deliberate public action in health improvement. According to this view, if countries are growing, the health of their inhabitants will look after itself."

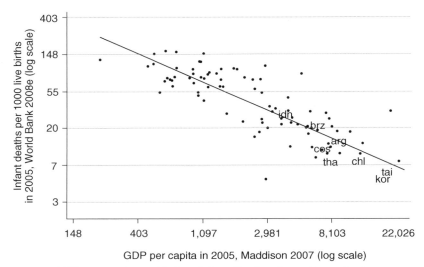

FIGURE 1.1. GDP per capita and Infant Mortality Level, 93 Countries in 2005. R-Square = .69. Output and data in Web Appendices C7 and D1 (McGuire 2009). Symbols: Argentina: arg; Brazil: brz; Chile: chl; Costa Rica: cos; Indonesia: idn; South Korea: kor; Taiwan: tai; Thailand: tha.

narrow version of the hypothesis accords with the evidence, GDP per capita should be a good predictor of the rate of infant mortality at a given point in time ("level"), as well as of the overall amount of infant mortality decline during an extended period of time ("progress").

On these criteria, the evidence for the narrow version of the hypothesis is moderately supportive. The level of GDP per capita in 2005 was a good predictor of the level of infant mortality in 2005. The regression line sloped downward, as expected, and the observations clustered tightly around it (Figure 1.1; R-square = .69). The average annual rate of GDP per capita growth was a weaker predictor of the average annual rate of infant mortality decline from 1960 to 2005. Although the regression line sloped upward, as expected, the observations clustered only loosely around it (Figure 1.2; R-square = .18). In other words, even at similar levels of GDP per capita growth during the period from 1960 to 2005, countries varied widely on the steepness of infant mortality decline – much more widely than was the case when the analysis focused on level.

In cross-national research, the study of variation in infant mortality changes is often more instructive, from both theoretical and practical standpoints, than the study of variation in infant mortality levels. It matters considerably, then, that the narrow variant of the wealthier is healthier hypothesis predicted a country's level of infant mortality much better than it predicted a country's progress at reducing infant mortality. A focus exclusively on cross-national

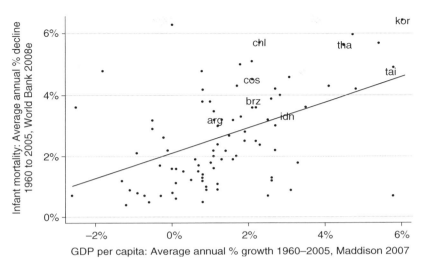

FIGURE 1.2. GDP per capita Growth and Infant Mortality Decline, 93 Countries 1960–2005.
R-Square = .18. Output and data in Web Appendices C7 and D1 (McGuire 2009). Symbols: Argentina: arg; Brazil: brz; Chile: chl; Costa Rica: cos; Indonesia: idn; South Korea: kor; Taiwan: tai; Thailand: tha.

differences in infant mortality levels at a given point in time, neglecting cross-national differences in progress at reducing infant mortality over a particular span of time, would bias findings toward the wealthier is healthier hypothesis and the policy and institutional design recommendations that typically accompany it.

An intermediate version of the wealthier is healthier hypothesis includes under "wealth" not only GDP per capita, but also income inequality and income poverty. Income inequality affects infant mortality partly by increasing income poverty. Higher income poverty, in turn, raises the likelihood of infant death by constraining household purchases of survival-related goods and services in private markets, as well as by making it hard for poor people to utilize ostensibly free public health services (e.g., by taking time away from work or paying for public transport). Even controlling for income poverty, however, higher income inequality seems to be associated with higher mortality.[4] Higher income inequality has been found to raise psychological stress, to deepen feelings of depression, to encourage risk-taking behavior, to reduce social cohesion, and to deter investment in social services.[5] In the cross-national quantitative analysis reported in Chapter 2, higher income inequality

4 Eibner and Evans 2005; Kennedy, Kawachi, and Prothrow-Stith 1996.
5 Lynch et al. 2000; Marmot and Wilkinson 2001; Rojroongwasinkul 2004; Wilkinson 2001.

was associated with higher infant mortality even after controlling for GDP per capita (Table 2.2).

The broad version of the wealthier is healthier hypothesis defines "wealth" to include not only economic output and income, but also "socioeconomic" factors such as ethnic diversity, religion, fertility, urbanization, geographical location, population density, and sometimes educational attainment. Filmer and Pritchett (1999) found that GDP per capita, income inequality, mean years of female schooling, ethnolinguistic fractionalization, and a population more than 90 percent Muslim jointly explained about 95 percent the variance in infant and under-5 mortality across about 100 countries (both developing and industrialized) in 1990. Likewise, the cross-national analysis reported in Chapter 2, which is partly modeled on the Filmer and Pritchett (1999) study, found that an overlapping set of socioeconomic variables – GDP per capita, income inequality, fertility, urbanization, population density, ethnolinguistic fractionalization, and having a population that is more than 90 percent Muslim – jointly explained about 84 percent of the variance in infant and under-5 mortality across about 100 developing countries in 1990.

The quantitative analysis in Chapter 2, the case studies in Chapters 3–10, and the comparative analysis of the eight cases in Chapter 11 juxtapose the intermediate version of the wealthier is healthier hypothesis, which focuses on economic output- and income-related indicators (GDP per capita, income inequality, and income poverty), to an alternative: that mortality rises and falls according to the scope and quality of education, family planning, safe water, sanitation, and basic health care and nutrition services. According to this alternative social service provision conjecture, the state's (and to a lesser extent the private sector's) ability to deliver basic social services of decent quality to most of the disadvantaged population, and the propensity of a country's poor people to utilize those services, has a strong and robust impact on the pattern and pace of infant mortality decline, independent of economic circumstances. The social service provision hypothesis does not directly contradict the wealthier is healthier hypothesis. The basic proposition that wealth promotes health is not questioned. The social service provision conjecture serves rather as a lens through which to try to construct guidelines for public action by extracting policy and institution-building lessons from national and subnational experiences that are anomalous according to the wealthier is healthier conjecture. In Chile in the 1970s, neither slow economic growth, nor high income inequality, nor a repressive authoritarian regime prevented a breathtaking plunge in the infant mortality rate. In Indonesia in the 1970s, neither fast economic growth, nor low income inequality, nor a repressive authoritarian regime produced anything more than a sluggish decline of infant mortality. The social service provision proposition raises the questions of what policies were enacted in Chile, but not in Indonesia, to produce a rapid decline of the infant mortality rate, and why the Chilean government, but not the Indonesian government, designed, approved, and implemented those policies.

Varying combinations of economic achievements and social service provisioning seem to have been at work in the eight cases compared in this book.

In South Korea and Thailand, fast economic growth and stable income inequality contributed significantly to the rapid decline of infant mortality, although public service provision played an underappreciated role in both countries. In Chile and Costa Rica, the effective public provision of basic social services to the poor produced an almost equally steep fall of infant mortality, despite slow economic growth and rising income inequality. The cross-national analysis reported in Chapter 2 confirms that the provision and utilization of basic health, education, family planning, water, and sanitation services is strongly and significantly associated with infant mortality, even controlling for GDP per capita, income inequality, and other socio-economic factors.

The wealthier is healthier and social service provision hypotheses have differing policy implications. Studies whose findings support the wealthier is healthier hypothesis are often taken to imply that policy-makers who wish to accelerate the pace of infant mortality decline would be best advised to focus most of their efforts on economic growth, or perhaps on reducing income inequality. This study finds, on the contrary, that although wealthier is indeed often healthier, the effective provision of basic social services to the poor can lead to sharp declines of infant mortality, even in the face of dramatic failures on the economic front; and that neither fast economic growth nor falling income inequality guarantees a rapid reduction of the infant mortality rate. Moreover, even though it may well be desirable to reduce infant mortality by sharply accelerating economic growth, or by dramatically redistributing income in favor of the poor, such achievements are not always feasible. In such cases, the public financing or provision of basic, and usually quite inexpensive, health, education, family planning, water, and sanitation services often provides a more practical means to the same end.

1.2. Democracy and the Provision of Social Services

Political regime form affects mortality rates primarily, although not exclusively, through its impact on public policies, especially policies concerned with the delivery of basic services to people who run a high risk of early death. A main concern of this book is to explore the hypothesis that governments in democracies tend more than governments in authoritarian regimes to enact mortality-reducing social policies. To this end, a basic definition of democracy is in order. The term democracy will be used in this book to refer to a political regime with fair elections, basic human and civil rights, and autonomy for elected officials. The first criterion means that political leaders must be chosen in fair and periodic competitive elections in which virtually all adult citizens have the right to vote and to stand for office. The second criterion means that citizens must be granted in principle, and not systematically denied in practice, basic rights like freedom from physical abuse by agents of the state, freedom of speech and the press, freedom of association and assembly, and the right to petition the government. The third criterion implies that the decisions of elected officials should not be vetoed or undermined systematically by unelected power-holders (e.g., military leaders, local bosses, guerrilla groups, or foreign governments).[6]

These criteria for democracy are similar to those that Robert Dahl used to define polyarchy, the set of institutions that is necessary, according to Dahl, to achieve the highest feasible attainment of the democratic process in a modern nation-state. Democracy, for Dahl, is not a set of institutions, but rather a process for making binding decisions, that is, decisions that all members of a political community have a duty to obey. A democratic process has criteria of its own (enlightened understanding, effective participation, voting equality at the decisive stage, control of the agenda, enfranchisement of almost all adult citizens), but some of these criteria are very demanding, and full democracy, according to Dahl, is probably unattainable.[7] In principle, it is useful to distinguish an ideal democratic process from the polyarchic institutions required to realize or approximate such a process in a modern nation-state. In conventional language, however, the term "democracy" is usually used to refer to a set of institutions similar to the ones that Dahl subsumes under the rubric of polyarchy. In a concession to conventional language, the term democracy will be used in this book to refer to the three institutional criteria set forth in the preceding paragraph, rather than to the ideal process for making binding decisions that these institutional criteria may approximate.

Democracy may be vindicated instrumentally, by its beneficial consequences for survival or for some other human development outcome; affirmed intrinsically, as a good thing in itself (or at least as immediately necessary for living a good life); or justified constructively, by its role in fostering the discussion and interaction that enables individuals to decide what is desirable and what is possible.[8] This book focuses mainly on the instrumental dimension. On this front, it is notable that among the societies most often cited as having achieved "good health at low cost" (China, Chile, Costa Rica, Cuba, the Indian state of Kerala, Jamaica, and Sri Lanka), all but China had considerable democratic experience during the twentieth century. Costa Rica, Kerala/India, Jamaica, and Sri Lanka were long-standing democracies, Chile was democratic before and after the 1973–1990 military regime, and Cuba in the 1930s and 1940s had competitive elections and an independent press.[9] The average level of democratic experience in these cases is much higher than in most other developing countries. The preponderance of democratic regimes among the good health at low cost societies, as well as cross-national evidence that greater democracy is associated with lower infant mortality,[10] suggest that it is well

---

[6] McGuire 1997: 12–14.

[7] Dahl 1989: Chapter 8; Dahl 1998: 37–38, 85–86.

[8] Sen 1999a: 148.

[9] McGuire and Frankel 2005.

[10] Bhalla 1997: 225–226; Dasgupta 1993: 117–121; Gerring and Thacker 2001; Moon 1991: 142; Przeworski et al. 2000: 228; Zweifel and Navia 2000. Ross (2006), however, finds no effect of democracy on infant mortality.

worth exploring whether democracy might influence the public financing or provision of mortality-reducing social services.

Democracy could affect the utilization of publicly funded or publicly provided social services by changing electoral incentives, by enhancing freedom of expression, by broadening freedom of association and assembly, or by shaping citizen expectations about the proper role for the state in financing or delivering social services. Most studies of the association between democracy and public service provision have focused on electoral incentives, noting that "rulers have the incentive to listen to what people want if they have to face their criticism and seek their support in elections."[11] The median voter hypothesis holds that income under majority rule should be redistributed to those who have less to the extent that democratization (e.g., the extension of the franchise) pulls the income of the voter with the median income below the mean income of all voters.[12] This hypothesis can be transferred from the public redistribution of private incomes to the public provision of social services. As democratization enfranchises a higher share of people inadequately served by public social services, vote-maximizing politicians should try to improve the quality, quantity, and accessibility of such services. Such electoral incentives could result in greater public spending on social services, but they could also produce the reallocation of such spending to uses that politicians believe will win the votes of the previously underserved, or improve the efficiency or effectiveness of public social spending. The latter mechanisms could improve access to and utilization of social services without higher public social spending.

Empirically, however, democratization in poor countries often does not lead to the improved provision of basic social services to the poor. Keefer and Khemani explain this unexpected outcome by noting that some of the assumptions of the median voter hypothesis may not hold in newly democratizing developing countries. In many such countries, Keefer and Khemani point out, voters lack information about incumbent performance; doubt that challengers can deliver what they have promised; or prefer to vote according to religious, regional, or ethnic identity rather than on the basis of a candidate's perceived capacity to deliver basic services.[13] It might be added, moreover, that even when voters in any country cast their ballots on the basis of policy preferences, their preferred policies will not necessarily be conducive to rapid mortality decline. For example, voters in rich and poor countries alike tend to demand curative services excessively and preventive services insufficiently, so politicians who seek their support may well promise and implement policies that are not optimal for mortality decline. A preoccupation with curative at the expense of preventive health services could help to explain

---

[11] Sen 1999a: 152 (quotation); Ghobarah, Huth, and Russett 2004: 78; Lake and Baum 2001: 598.
[12] Meltzer and Richard 1981.
[13] Keefer and Khemani 2005; see also World Bank 2004a: 81–85.

why democratization is sometimes found to be associated with a decline of immunization coverage.[14]

Persuasive arguments thus exist both for and against the hypothesis that electoral incentives promote the public provision or public financing of mortality-reducing social services, or encourage their more widespread or effective utilization. Electoral incentives could even inhibit the public provision of such services, such as by encouraging political leaders to shift resources from preventive to curative health care, as majorities would often prefer. It is unlikely that each of the ways in which democracy could promote the financing, provision, or utilization of mortality-reducing social services is fully operational and effective, whereas none of the ways in which democracy could inhibit such outcomes functions or has an impact on policy. The argument advanced in this book is not that electoral incentives invariably promote the public financing or provision of mortality-reducing social services, but rather that such incentives, along with other forces arising from democratic political regimes, can either promote or inhibit such policy outputs, depending on the context. On balance, the present study finds, democracy does more to promote than to inhibit the delivery of mortality-reducing social services, and to encourage their utilization. That conclusion does not imply, however, that democracy never has any effects that are inimical to such outcomes.[15]

Democracy involves more than elections. Freedom of expression, another aspect of democracy, enables journalists and others to call attention to social problems, including deficiencies in social services. Drèze and Sen argue that democracy reduces the risk of famine, both because it implies freedom of the press, which allows news of a potential famine to spread and encourages elites to take preventive action; and because it involves political competition, which makes the failure to respond to a threatened famine a risky proposition for an incumbent seeking reelection. Drèze and Sen are less optimistic that press freedom will lead to policies that help to reduce chronic poverty. Day-to-day hunger, they point out, is less newsworthy than impending famine, and is also harder to defeat.[16] Although Drèze and Sen make a strong case that democracy is likely to be better at preventing famine than at relieving endemic hunger, they also underscore instances (in Chile, Costa Rica, Sri Lanka, and the Indian state of Kerala) in which a free press and adversarial politics have contributed to the expansion of basic capabilities. The fewer the impediments to the free flow of information, the easier it is to publicize social problems, whether chronic or acute. Calling attention to serious social problems is, in turn, a supportive (but not sufficient) condition for the design, authorization, and implementation of policies conducive to mortality decline.

---

[14] Gauri and Khaleghian 2002: 2124–2125.
[15] This perspectivist epistemology is developed in McGuire, W.J. 1999: 395–432; see also Jost, Banaji, and Prentice, eds. 2004.
[16] Drèze and Sen 1989: 84, 214.

Democracy includes the freedoms of association and assembly, which make it easier for community activists, interest groups, and issue networks (informal groups of experts with interest in, and knowledge about, a particular area of public policy) to pressure for improved social services.[17] Such freedoms also allow more scope for the activities of non-governmental organizations, which may supply as well as demand better social services. Brazil's Pastorate of the Children, which provided maternal and infant health education and monitoring in the 1990s and 2000s, is a case in point. Not all demand-making is good for the poor, however. Schattschneider famously noted that "the flaw in the pluralist heaven is that the heavenly chorus sings with a strong upper-class accent."[18] The empowerment of interest groups and issue networks could impede as well as promote the extension of basic social services to social groups with the highest risk of early death. In Latin America, labor unions have fought for contributory health and retirement insurance schemes, which benefit their leaders and members but rarely include the very poor. The poor nonetheless often pay indirectly for such programs through higher indirect taxes, higher consumer goods prices, and inflationary bailouts from the central bank as population aging, low-yield investments, and often poor administration reduce the solvency of the schemes.[19] The freedoms of assembly and association permit the expression of demands and interests that do not always benefit the poorest.

Evidence throughout this book suggests that long-term democratic experience changes citizen expectations so as to promote the provision of basic social services to the people most vulnerable to premature mortality. Democracy is based on the principle that citizens have equal rights. Over time, this principle tends to produce a perception that the state is obliged to provide social services that are sufficient to enable every citizen, no matter how poor, to live with dignity.[20] The diffusion throughout society, including among the poor, of an expectation that the state will attend to basic social needs is another mechanism by which democracy can promote the extension of basic social services to the poor. Suggesting that this mechanism may be quite important, a quantitative analysis reported in Chapter 2 finds that long-term democratic experience is associated more closely than short-term democratic practice with greater social service provision and with lower infant mortality.

1.3. Research Design and Case Selection

In Chapter 2, associations between indicators of democracy, public service provision, socioeconomic circumstances, and infant mortality are explored using multiple regression analyses involving 105 developing societies in 1990.

---

[17] Issue networks were initially characterized by Heclo (1978: 102–105).
[18] Schattschneider 1960: 35.
[19] McGuire 1999.
[20] Marshall 1950, esp. 53, 77, 82.

In Chapters 3–10, case studies of the eight societies reconstruct the causal processes by which economic factors and the provision of basic social services affected the pattern and pace of mortality decline from 1960 to 2005. The case studies also examine how and to what degree bureaucratic initiative, international factors, political regime form, and the activities of civil society groups encouraged or discouraged the provision of basic health services to the poor. In Chapter 11, the eight societies are compared systematically to extract some general conclusions about the impact of socioeconomic factors and basic social service provision on the pattern and pace of infant mortality decline, and about the impact of democracy and the activities of civil society groups on the implementation and effectiveness of large-scale public primary health care campaigns.

The outcomes to be explained include the *level* of infant mortality that each society attained in 2005; the *progress* that each society made at reducing infant mortality from 1960 to 2005; and the *tempo* of infant mortality decline within each society in the intervening 45 years. Socioeconomic factors go some way toward explaining the level of infant mortality that each society attained in 2005, but social provisioning factors do better at explaining speedups and slowdowns in the tempo of infant mortality decline across the years from 1960 to 2005. Subnational as well as cross-national comparisons are used to identify the causes of public service provision and of infant mortality decline, and the findings of studies using household and individual-level data are incorporated where available. On most dimensions of development, the eight societies selected for study include cases of mediocre or poor performance as well as cases of success. This variation on both the independent and dependent variables provides a better basis for causal inference than does the identification of best practices among "success stories."[21]

The term "nested analysis" describes studies, like this one, that combine large-N quantitative analyses of many societies with small-N studies of a few societies.[22] Large-N analyses permit a more rigorous evaluation of the correlates of outcome variation than is possible using individual case studies or small-N comparisons alone. Case studies and small-N comparisons have their own virtues, however, among which is the ability to identify, through "process-tracing," the causal mechanisms behind the empirical associations detected in the large-N analysis.[23] Another virtue of the case studies is to help to identify variables that may have been omitted from the large-N analysis and

---

[21] Costs of choosing cases that exhibit little or no variation on the outcome to be explained are outlined in Collier and Mahoney 1996; Geddes 1990; Gerring 2001: 185–189; and King, Keohane, and Verba 1994: 129–139. Not all scholars agree that such costs are invariably prohibitive (Collier, Brady, and Seawright 2004: 209–213).

[22] Lieberman 2005. "N" stands for number. Collier, Brady, and Seawright (2004: 249, 260) propose the term "nested inference" for this kind of analysis.

[23] The philosopher David Hume recognized that even the contiguity, succession, and constant conjunction of a hypothesized cause and an observed effect was insufficient to infer causality (Hume 1978 [1740]: 86–94).

to check for reverse causation.[24] Moreover, case-specific (e.g., cross-province or over-time) data, which are often more homogeneous and reliable than cross-national data, can potentially be used to explore the hypotheses evaluated in the large-N analysis.[25]

In nested analyses, case studies and small-N comparisons can be used either to test or to elaborate a model explored initially with a large-N analysis. A model-testing small-N analysis is appropriate if the researcher is confident that (1) all relevant variables are included in the large-N model; (2) all predictor variables are validly and reliably measured; and (3) no significant causal effects flow in reverse, from the outcome to the predictor variables. If each of these conditions is met, the researcher should select for small-N analysis cases that are well predicted by the large-N model, and use historical process-tracing to identify causal mechanisms that account for the associations detected in the large-N analysis.[26] In fact, such conditions are almost never met. Hence, most nested analyses are, or should be, model-building exercises. In a model-building small-N analysis, the researcher should select for small-N analysis cases that are poorly predicted by the large-N model, so as to identify additional variables that will help in building a more persuasive explanation.

The small-N analysis used in the present study is of the model-building variety. Accordingly, some of the eight cases selected for study are "off the line" with respect to the initial model, which is based on the broad variant of the wealthier is healthier hypothesis, whereas others are almost on the line. In a model-building small-N analysis, cases can be chosen either randomly or deliberately. Random selection reduces the chances that biases of the researcher will contaminate the analysis, but suffers from inefficiency.[27] The researcher may get stuck with cases that he or she lacks the expertise to study seriously, that lack the data needed to explore the hypotheses being considered, or that are of limited interest to other researchers. The deliberate selection of cases, by contrast, permits the researcher to choose cases that are intelligible to him or her, that have good data, that have an extensive secondary literature, that have played a central role in previous research, or that are regarded as intrinsically interesting for some other reason. Meanwhile, the large-N component of the nested analysis serves as a check on any researcher bias that may have affected case selection.

The present study uses a modified version of the "diverse case" technique, in which cases are chosen to illustrate the full range of variation on both the independent and dependent variables.[28] The modification is that some range of variation is sacrificed in order to insure that the cases chosen

[24] Collier, Brady, and Seawright 2004: 252–253.
[25] King, Keohane, and Verba 1994: 219–221; Lieberman 2005: 441, 443; Snyder 2001.
[26] Lieberman 2005: 442–448.
[27] Gerring 2007: 87.
[28] Gerring and Seawright 2007.

have adequate data, are treated by a sizable secondary literature, and are familiar to the researcher. Each of the eight cases analyzed was usually categorized as a middle-income society for most of the period from 1960 to 2005.[29] As Appendix Tables A1–A18 show, however, the eight cases vary widely on both the outcomes of interest (infant mortality levels and changes) and the independent variables (democracy, GDP per capita level and growth, income inequality, income poverty, education, family planning effort, access to water and sanitation, and the provision of basic health care and nutrition services). The conclusions drawn from the case studies in Chapters 3–10 and from the comparisons in Chapter 11 are intended to apply to all middle-income developing societies, and some of the findings may pertain to low- and high-income societies as well.

1.4. Development, Capabilities, and Survival

Analyses comparing East Asian to Latin American development have helped to explain why some East Asian "tigers" (South Korea, Taiwan, Hong Kong, and Singapore) have outperformed some Latin American "tortoises" (e.g., Argentina, Brazil, and Mexico) at generating rapid economic growth, avoiding severe income inequality, and reducing the proportion of the population in poverty. Such analyses show consensus on the criteria for development and the facts of the outcome. Debate revolves largely around whether cultural values, finely tuned industrial policy, or market friendliness best explains East Asia's superior development performance.[30]

The criteria such analyses have used to evaluate development progress – mainly economic growth and income distribution – all pertain to production or income. Although output and income can contribute to human development, such economic achievements are only means to a more basic end: the expansion of the capability to lead a thoughtfully chosen life.[31] Rises in output and income are neither necessary nor sufficient for capability expansion. Indeed, to the extent that higher output or income leads to ecological damage, tobacco use, or physical inactivity, such rises can constrict human capabilities. Higher output and income usually facilitate capability expansion, but they are different from, and less important than, the expanded capabilities themselves. The expansion of human capabilities need not mean an increase in human happiness; indeed, an explosion of choice can raise anguish and depression.[32] Capability expansion is stipulated here to be at the core of human development because of philosophical assumptions about the value of freedom

---

[29] None of the eight cases is among the developing countries located in the left-hand (poorer) half of the GDP per capita plane above the log-scaled x-axis in Figure 1.1.

[30] Adams and Davis 1994; Evans 1995; Gereffi and Wyman eds. 1990; Haggard 1990; Harrison 1992; Jenkins 1991; McGuire 1995a.

[31] Nussbaum 2000; Sen 1985; Sen 1993; Sen 1999a.

[32] Lane 2003; Schwartz 2004.

and individual autonomy, not because of any contributions it may make to subjective well-being.[33]

Capabilities are hard to measure directly, but their location at the endpoint of a sequence of causes and facilitating conditions allows them to be measured indirectly. Immediate causes or conditions of choice-making capacity, like physical survival, are reasonable proxies for the degree to which the members of a society enjoy a wide range of very basic capabilities. More remote causes or conditions, like income, are best viewed as determinants or antecedents of such capabilities. From the development-as-capabilities perspective – informed by this notion of a sequence of inputs into capability expansion – the study of human development is largely a matter of examining how more remote inputs into choice-making capacity affect more immediate ones.

To the extent that higher incomes expand capabilities, they do so in part by providing access to basic commodities and services like food, shelter, health care, and schooling. Such goods and services can be purchased in private markets, but they can also be provided free of charge by the state, by a civil society organization, by the community, or by the family. Where basic goods and services can be obtained without recourse to private markets, the failure to command a high income may still restrict capabilities, but no more than a host of other common ills, including war, political repression, social disintegration, gender bias, and race prejudice. Because food, shelter, health care, and schooling are more immediate inputs into choice-making capacity than income, and because they can sometimes be obtained without income (although income usually helps), some indicator of the accessibility and quality of these basic goods and services would be a better measure of aggregate societal choice-making capacity than would income-related criteria. To devise such an indicator was a central concern of some development scholars in the 1970s.[34]

From the development-as-capabilities perspective, the commodities and services that are usually grouped under the heading of "basic needs," including food, shelter, clothing, education, and health care, are themselves only inputs into the expansion of thoughtfully valued capabilities and functionings.[35] As obstacles to one's freedom to choose among these capabilities and functionings, even inadequate food, shelter, clothing, education, and health care are less important than premature mortality. To live the life one chooses, one has to be alive. An adequate income, as well as basic needs satisfaction, can contribute to capability expansion, but the avoidance of early death is indispensable. Survival-related capabilities, as reflected in levels and rates of change of premature mortality indices like life expectancy and the infant mortality rate, are more proximal inputs into one's overall capacity to live the life one chooses than either one's economic entitlement to goods and services through one's

---

[33] Sen 1999a.
[34] Morris 1979; Streeten 1981.
[35] Functionings are states of being or doing; capabilities are the opportunities to achieve such states (Sen 1993: 40 fn. 30).

private income, or one's legal entitlement to publicly provided health care, schooling, and infrastructure, or one's customary entitlement to a share of the resources of the family or community. Even a hedonic perspective would warrant a focus on survival. As one group of writers put it, "the pleasures of life are worth nothing if one is not alive to experience them."[36]

Indicators of premature mortality such as life expectancy and infant mortality measure functionings more directly than capabilities. From the capabilities perspective, however, it is less important to maximize valued functionings, even physical survival, than it is to maximize the advantages, or capabilities, that enable one to achieve those functionings. "It is possible to have genuine advantages and still to 'muff' them. Or to sacrifice one's own well-being for other goals, and not make full use of one's freedom to achieve a high level of well-being... The freedom to achieve well-being is closer to the notion of advantage than well-being itself."[37] One might know, for example, that to engage in a certain voluntary (or initially voluntary) behavior, like smoking tobacco or joining a criminal gang, endangers one's survival, but might still fail to act (or resolve not to act) on this information. In certain circumstances, moreover, one might choose to defend a family, a community, a political system, a religious ideal, or some other valued entity or abstraction, even at the cost of one's life. Nonetheless, as a practical matter, "the assessment of capabilities has to proceed primarily on the basis of observing a person's actual functionings...there is a jump here (from functionings to capabilities), but it need not be a big jump...if a person dies prematurely or suffers from a painful and threatening disease, it would be, in most cases, legitimate to conclude that she did have a capability problem."[38]

Although individuals may knowingly behave in ways that raise the risk of dying prematurely, it is reasonable to assume that mortality indicators such as infant mortality and life expectancy are good proxies for the degree to which some very basic capabilities – to be adequately nourished, to be cared for when sick – have spread throughout a society. Mortality indicators reflect, moreover, the diffusion and robustness of a special sort of functioning – physical survival – whose achievement is necessary for the exercise of any capability. Hence, even if capabilities rather than functionings are taken as the main criteria of development, life expectancy and infant mortality are central to the assessment of development progress. They provide direct insight into a functioning, survival, that is necessary for the exercise of any capability; and indicate indirectly the degree to which a society is meeting basic needs in nutrition, health care, water and sanitation, and education. A society's failure to meet such needs not only raises the risk of early death, but also constricts the capabilities of the living.

---

[36] Cutler, Deaton, and Lleras-Muney 2006: 97.
[37] Sen 1985: 5.
[38] Sen 1999a: 131.

Cross-national comparisons confirm that better performance on income-related indicators is usually associated with better performance on survival-related indicators.[39] Historical studies show, however, that rapid economic growth is neither necessary nor sufficient to achieve a steep decline of premature mortality.[40] Research has also shown that reducing income poverty, although conducive to reducing premature mortality, is neither necessary nor sufficient for the rapid expansion of survival-related capabilities.[41] The present analysis builds on studies showing the partial independence of capability expansion from income expansion,[42] but extends them in two directions: by looking systematically at cases of failure as well as cases of success, and by explaining the origins, as well as consequences, of different types of public service provision.

1.5. The Infant Mortality Rate as an Indicator of Development Progress

To indicate the prevalence of survival-related capabilities in a society, this study focuses on infant mortality: the expected number of deaths before age one per 1000 live births in a given year. Infant mortality is the proxy of a hazard rate, that is, of a probability of death.[43] As a measure of development achievement and development progress, the infant mortality rate, along with the under-5 mortality rate (the expected number of deaths before age five per 1000 live births in a given year), has substantive advantages over alternatives such as the adult mortality rate (the expected number of deaths between the ages of 15 and 60 per 1000 people in that age group) and life expectancy at birth. The death of an infant or under-5 child represents more years of life foregone than does the death of an older person.[44] Moreover, infant mortality and under-5 mortality are more likely than adult mortality to result from preventable causes, and thus to be reducible by appropriate policies.[45] In developing countries in 1988, avoidable deaths comprised 72 percent of adult deaths but 97 percent of child deaths. Under-5 deaths made up 40 percent of all deaths but 50 percent of avoidable deaths and 70 percent of years of potential life lost to avoidable deaths.[46]

Infant mortality and under-5 mortality have practical as well as substantive advantages over alternative indicators of survival-related capabilities. In the many developing countries where vital registration systems are inadequate, censuses and surveys often contain questions that permit infant and under-5 mortality rates to be estimated directly, by analyzing birth histories,

---

[39] Filmer and Pritchett 1999; Pritchett and Summers 1996.
[40] Caldwell 1986; Drèze and Sen 1989; Easterlin 1999.
[41] Mehrotra 1997a: 53–56.
[42] Drèze and Sen 1989; Ghai ed. 2000; Hirschman 1987; Mehrotra and Jolly eds. 1997.
[43] Galiani, Gertler, and Schargrodsky 2005: 95 fn. 3; UNICEF et al. 2007: 12.
[44] Murray 1988: 126.
[45] Filmer and Pritchett 1999: 1312.
[46] Murray, Yang, and Qiao 1992: 28–29.

or indirectly, by analyzing responses to survivorship questions. In such countries adult mortality and life expectancy statistics contain no new information beyond that provided by the under-5 (or under-1 or under-2) mortality estimate from which they are extrapolated using model life tables.[47] Furthermore, the United Nations during the 1990s sponsored a project to identify, evaluate, and reconcile all post-1960 infant and under-5 mortality estimates for 94 developing countries. By 2004 this estimation methodology had been adopted by the World Bank and World Health Organization (WHO).[48] As a result of these initiatives, the public has access to transparently derived estimates of infant and under-5 mortality, but not of adult mortality or life expectancy at birth.

Indirect estimates of mortality based on survivorship questions in censuses and surveys depend on assumptions about fertility and mortality patterns that generally hold better for under-5 mortality than for infant mortality.[49] Estimates of infant mortality go back much farther in time than do estimates of under-5 mortality, however, and the literature on infant mortality is much richer than the literature on under-5 mortality. Empirically, moreover, the correlation across countries of the infant and under-5 mortality rate is very high, so that the practical advantages of using the infant mortality rate outweigh any substantive disadvantages that this indicator may have in relation to under-5 mortality.[50] The case studies reported in Chapters 3–10 will, accordingly, focus mainly on infant mortality, although other mortality indicators will not be neglected where reliable data exist. Among these alternatives are, in addition to under-5 mortality, crude death rates, life expectancy at birth, life expectancy at age one, child (age 1 to 4) mortality, maternal mortality, adult (age 15 to 60) mortality, and the share of the population that is expected to survive to a certain age.

Because infant mortality is such a central concern of this study, the issue of how to measure its rate of change warrants a brief discussion. A society's achieved level of mortality in a certain year reflects its current and past ecological, social, and economic circumstances, as well as its current and past public policies. A main reason for studying mortality, however, is to gain insight into public policies, civic and political institutions, and economic and social circumstances that might reduce the risk of early death. In this light, changes

---

[47] Bos and Saadah 1999: 1; Murray, Yang, and Qiao 1992: 26. Extrapolation is often needed because "countries accounting for 40 percent of global population in 1998 lacked any recent data on adult mortality" (O'Neill and Balk 2001: 9). Infant mortality itself is sometimes extrapolated from the under-5 mortality rate (or vice-versa), but in all but the handful of developing countries with adequate registration of adult deaths, adult mortality and life expectancy are extrapolated from mortality estimates for younger age groups.

[48] Hill et al. 1999; United Nations 1992; UNICEF et al. 2007.

[49] Ahmad, Lopez, and Inoue 2000, 1176–1177.

[50] One study found a correlation of .99 between infant mortality and under-5 mortality across countries in 2000 (Murray 2007: 864). In the vast majority of developing countries with incomplete vital registration statistics, estimates of infant mortality are constructed on the basis of estimates of under-5 mortality (or vice-versa), so a high correlation between the indicators is not surprising.

in mortality levels over time are often more revealing than levels of mortality at a certain point in time. Levels of mortality reflect decades or centuries of heterogeneous policies, institutions, economic and social conditions, and ecological challenges. Changes in mortality do more to help identify policies, institutions, economic achievements, and social circumstances that not only are conducive to mortality decline, but also are amenable to change through public action.

In measuring progress at reducing infant mortality, one must decide what span of time to observe and what metric to use as a basis for comparison. The time span selected should not be so long as to encompass such heterogeneous influences on infant mortality that extracting development lessons becomes impossible. On the other hand, it should not be so short as to create either premature enthusiasm about institutions and policies that may prove impossible to sustain, or premature skepticism about institutions and policies that may take a long time to work. The time period should also be long enough to reduce the noise created by random fluctuation. Because different determinants of infant mortality work their effects over different lengths of time, the choice of a time span is unavoidably arbitrary. In this study, the period chosen for comparative analysis is 1960 to 2005, with the first and last years being the earliest and most recent for which estimates of infant mortality have been derived systematically for a large number of countries.[51]

A metric is required to evaluate national achievement at reducing infant mortality between 1960 and 2005. The absolute decline of infant mortality in a society over a certain period of time says something important about the number of lives saved per thousand infants born, but serves as a poor guide to policy, because using absolute decline as a metric "advantages" countries with high initial levels. With 54 infant deaths per 1000 live births in 1960, Taiwan can hardly be criticized for failing to match Chile's 110-point infant mortality drop over the next 45 years (Table A1). The usual way to correct for this baseline artifact is to use a percent decline indicator, which eliminates the "advantage" that, if measured in absolute terms, a higher initial infant mortality level would give to the steepness of subsequent infant mortality decline.[52] A reduction of infant mortality over a 10-year period from 10 to 8 per 1000 works out, using a compound growth function, to an average annual rate of 2.21 percent, exactly the same as a reduction from 100 to 80 per 1000.

It might be argued that it is "easier" to achieve a 2.21 percent average annual decline of infant mortality by reducing the rate from 100 to 80 per 1000 than by reducing it from 10 to 8 per 1000. Such an argument is hard to sustain. In the first case an absolute decline of 20 per 1000 is required; in the second case the required drop is only 2 per 1000. It is not self-evident that the 100-to-80 reduction can be achieved more cheaply than the 10-to-8 reduction, and even if it could be, "cheaper" is not the same thing as "easier." A society

---

[51] Hill et al. 1999; UNICEF et al. 2007.
[52] Dasgupta 1993: 117; McGuire 2001: 1675–1676; Sen 1981: 292; UNDP 1994: 90–96.

with an infant mortality rate of 100 per 1000 would tend not only to have a lower GDP per capita, but also lower administrative capacity, than a society with an infant mortality rate of 10 per 1000. A program in a rich country to encourage expectant mothers to make prenatal visits might achieve a decline from 10 to 8 per 1000; a program in a poor country to educate traditional midwives might achieve a decline from 100 to 80 per 1000. The latter program would not obviously be cheaper than the former program, and would probably put more strain on available administrative resources.

Empirical evidence corroborates this skepticism about the proposition that it is "harder" for a country to reduce its infant mortality rate (as measured by a percent decline indicator) if it starts from an initially low level than if it starts from an initially high level. To the extent that initial level is related to percent decline, it seems to operate, counterintuitively, *against* societies that started out with higher initial levels of infant mortality. Across 139 countries with infant mortality data for both 1960 and 2005, the 35 countries that started out with the highest levels of infant mortality in 1960 achieved over the next 45 years an average annual rate of infant mortality decline of only 2.24 percent, compared to 2.67, 3.51, and 4.02 percent respectively for the next three groups of 35 (or 34) countries with successively lower initial infant mortality levels. Cross-nationally, then, contrary to expectations, a lower, not a higher, initial level of infant mortality was associated with a steeper subsequent percent decline.[53]

The infant mortality rate cannot fall below 0 per 1000, so the average annual percent decline of infant mortality over a specified time span, as measured by a compound growth function, is suitable for comparing progress across societies that start out at different infant mortality levels. No such compelling limit constrains the maximum attainable national life expectancy. In the late 1980s, a group of demographers estimated that national life expectancy would top out at about 85 years.[54] They assumed that, once infectious diseases were conquered, additional improvement in life expectancy would founder "on the hard rock of the degenerative diseases of older age, especially heart disease and cancer." Casting doubt on this assumption, life expectancy in the 1990s continued to rise at a rapid clip in countries where deaths from infectious diseases had become rare. The improvement was due not only to the decline of infant mortality, but also to the fall of other age-specific death rates because of advances in the prevention and treatment of "diseases previously viewed as the ineluctable result of aging processes, particularly cardiovascular disease."[55] Steady gains in the reduction of mortality at older ages suggest that the maximum human life span may be higher than previously thought.[56]

---

[53] The analysis includes all countries in World Bank (2008e) with infant mortality estimates for both 1960 and 2005. Across the 139 countries, the correlation between the 1960 level of infant mortality and the 1960–2005 percent decline of infant mortality is −.45.

[54] Olshansky, Carnes, and Cassel 1990; see also UNDP 2007: 356.

[55] Both quotations are from Easterlin 2000: 14.

[56] Bongaarts 2006; Olshansky, Carnes, and Désesquelles 2001.

To maintain consistency with other analyses, however, the preferred measure of progress at raising life expectancy will be the total percent rise of life expectancy at birth from its initial level in a chosen year toward a stipulated maximum "goalpost" of 85 years. This indicator may be pictured as the proportion of distance a country has traveled from its initial level of life expectancy at birth, whatever that may have been, toward a stipulated national average maximum of 85 years.

Infant mortality data come from vital registration statistics, national census data, or sample surveys.[57] In the United Nations project to evaluate and reconcile infant mortality data from 94 countries, a knotted regression line was fitted to disparate sources of data (giving less weight to sources deemed less reliable, and no weight to sources deemed unreliable), and projections were made for 1960 and 1995, as well as for every fifth intervening year. In 2004, researchers at UNICEF, the World Health Organization, the World Bank, and the United Populations Division formed the Inter-Agency Group for the Estimation of Child Mortality to combine the data collection resources of each agency and to coordinate and harmonize estimation methodologies, which were modeled closely on those used by the initial United Nations project of the 1990s. The estimates appear in the 2007 or later editions of UNICEF's *State of the World's Children* and the World Bank's *World Development Indicators*.[58] These estimates are used in many of the cross-national analyses in this book, as well as in over-time analysis of infant mortality in Brazil, Indonesia, South Korea, and Thailand, where vital registries were incomplete for most years from 1960 to 2005.

In Argentina, Chile, and Costa Rica, where infant death registration was nearly complete for most of the years analyzed, vital registration statistics are preferred for over-time analyses because they are likely to track the actual trajectory of infant mortality decline better than the Inter-Agency Group estimates, which are statistical reconciliations of alternative estimates from a variety of data sources for several different years. No such infant mortality estimates are available for Taiwan, which is not a member of any of the institutions whose researchers formed the Inter-Agency Group. Until the mid-1990s Taiwanese vital registration statistics were notorious for underreporting infant deaths, so infant mortality estimates for the island have been taken from census data, corrected vital registration statistics, and surveys (Table A1).

1.6. Paths to the Rapid Decline of Infant Mortality

South Korea and Taiwan have long been considered impressive development achievers from which slower-growing, more unequal Latin American countries have much to learn. The financial crisis of 1997 showed some flaws in the

---

[57] McGuire (2009), in Web Appendix A1, reviews the strengths and weaknesses of alternative sources of infant mortality data in developing countries generally and in each of the eight societies studied in Chapters 3–10.

[58] UNICEF et al. 2007; World Bank 2008e.

East Asian model, but Taiwan was barely scathed and South Korea quickly recovered. Indeed, Argentina and Brazil were arguably hit harder by the crisis than either South Korea or Taiwan. The 1997 crisis does not, therefore, seriously challenge the conventional wisdom that development has been more successful in East Asia than in Latin America. The long-term evolution of output- and income-related indicators confirms this view. From 1960 to 2005 Indonesia, South Korea, Taiwan, and Thailand each achieved faster GDP per capita growth and lower income inequality than Argentina, Brazil, Chile, or Costa Rica (Tables A3 and A4).

The East Asian societies did not outperform the Latin American ones in all respects, however. South Korea and Thailand from 1960 to 2005 outpaced Argentina and Brazil at reducing infant mortality, but did not do vastly better than Chile or Costa Rica, and did less well or only equally well at raising life expectancy, despite much faster economic growth and lower income inequality. By 2005, people lived longer on average in Costa Rica than in South Korea, Taiwan, Thailand, or the United States. Infant mortality in 2005 was higher in Chile (7.9 per 1000) than in Thailand (7.7), South Korea (5.5), or Taiwan (4.6), but Chile's infant mortality rate was lower than the rates in 12 of the 50 U.S. states.[59] Moreover, Chile reduced infant mortality more steeply than Indonesia or Taiwan, despite experiencing slower economic growth and higher income inequality. Brazil from 1990 to 2005, as well as Neuquén and some other Argentine provinces in the late 1960s and early 1970s, achieved steep infant mortality decline in challenging economic circumstances. By contrast, neither Indonesia nor Thailand until about 1990 reduced infant mortality as much as their rapid economic growth and stable levels of income inequality would lead one to expect. Some Latin American "tortoises," these examples show, rather than just the more famous East Asian "tigers," provide development models that other countries, including richer ones, might fruitfully investigate.

The evidence reviewed in this book suggests that at least two routes exist to the rapid decline of infant mortality. The route followed by post-1960 Taiwan and South Korea, which Jean Drèze and Amartya Sen call growth-mediated security, involved not only rapid GDP growth and low income inequality, but also the effective provision of education, family planning, and basic maternal and infant health care, as well as the redistribution of assets (via land reform) and employment opportunities (via the promotion of labor-intensive manufacturing). The model followed by post-1960 Chile and Costa Rica, which Drèze and Sen call support-led security, involved the provision of inexpensive basic health services to impoverished mothers and infants, despite slow economic growth and very high (Chile) or moderately high (Costa Rica) income inequality.[60] The first route to infant mortality decline may well be more desirable, but the second route is often more feasible.

---

[59] Mathews and MacDorman 2008: 5.
[60] Drèze and Sen 1989.

2

Democracy, Spending, Services, and Survival

This chapter explores associations involving democracy, public health care spending, the provision and utilization of basic social services, and infant mortality. The universe of cases is the 104 developing countries with populations greater than 500,000 in 1990, plus Taiwan. The analysis is cross-sectional; the technique is ordinary least squares multiple regression using the best data available for a large number of developing countries and employing diverse checks for the robustness of the findings. Most of the variables are measured as close to 1990 as the data permit. The main public health finding is that the provision and utilization of basic social services was associated with lower infant mortality, even taking into account a wide range of economic, demographic, geographic, and cultural factors. The main political science finding is that long-term democratic experience, and to a lesser extent short-term democratic practice, was associated with the more widespread provision and utilization of mortality-reducing basic social services.

The political science part of the analysis suggests that political regime form can affect human development not only intrinsically, by directly shaping and constraining our ability to live the lives we have reason to choose, but also instrumentally, by influencing our ability to survive infancy. The public health part of the analysis has implications for decisions about how to try to reduce the infant mortality rate. As the wealthier is healthier conjecture would predict, a one standard deviation rise in GDP per capita is found in the analyses reported below to "reduce" infant mortality, statistically speaking, more than a one standard deviation rise in any of the social service variables. Such a one standard deviation rise turns out to be hard to achieve, however. Only a small fraction of countries near the median on GDP per capita in 1985 experienced enough economic growth by 1995 to achieve a 5 per 1000 decline of infant mortality. An even smaller fraction reduced income inequality sufficiently to achieve such a decline. By comparison, a large share of developing countries near the median on female schooling and on trained attendance at birth in 1985 improved enough on each indicator by 1995 to achieve a 5 per 1000 decline of infant mortality. Rapid GDP per capita growth and low income

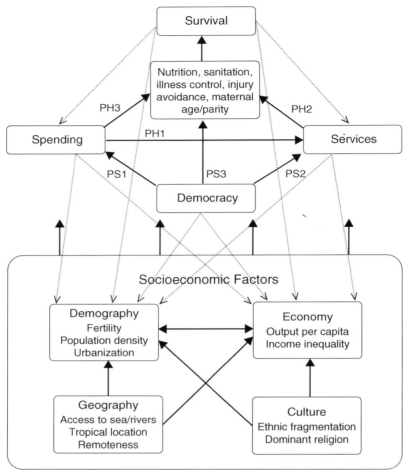

FIGURE 2.1. Model Guiding the Quantitative Analysis.

inequality are desirable development outcomes in many respects, but they are not so easily attained. For many developing countries, improving the provision of basic services is likely to be a more feasible way to reduce the risk of infant death.

Some plausible associations between democratic experience and infant mortality are depicted in Figure 2.1. The model presented in this figure is an extension of one developed by Mosley and Chen (1984), who argue that nutrition, sanitation, illness control, injury avoidance, and maternal characteristics (age, parity, birth spacing) comprise an exhaustive set of five proximate determinants of infant and child health status. More distal "socioeconomic" forces (affluence, education, cultural values, ecological context, governance) operate, in Mosley and Chen's model, through these and only these proximate determinants. Mosley and Chen do not attempt to theorize the hierarchies and relations that structure the socioeconomic forces themselves, so Figure 2.1 reports a preliminary attempt to make sense of some of these hierarchies and relations and to signal some of the main variables that may be involved. Public spending on health care as a share of GDP ("spending") might plausibly be associated with lower infant mortality, as might the public provision and utilization of health, education, family planning, water, and sanitation services ("services"). The dotted lines in Figure 2.1 depict possible reverse causation whereby survival (infant mortality, serving as a proxy for general health status), spending, and services could potentially influence some of the predictor variables. Some of the quantitative analyses are checked for endogeneity (which can result from reverse causation), but otherwise the relations depicted by the dotted lines will not be a major focus of analysis.

The term "socioeconomic" is used differently in this study than in Mosley and Chen's. In Mosley and Chen's study, socioeconomic factors included all causal forces that impinged upon the proximate determinants of child morbidity and mortality. In the present study, socioeconomic factors refer to specific aspects of geography, demography, economy, and culture. These forces are distinguished from the utilization of basic social services, which is stipulated here to have an effect on infant mortality that is distinct from (albeit shaped and constrained by) the effects of the socioeconomic variables. Socioeconomic forces and social services affect the proximate determinants of infant mortality rather than infant mortality itself, but cross-nationally comparable data are unavailable on many of the proximate determinants, so infant mortality will serve as the outcome of interest.

The analysis reported below explores six hypotheses relating democracy, public health care spending, the provision of basic social services, and infant mortality. "Public health" (PH) hypotheses relate public health care spending and basic service utilization to lower infant mortality. "Political science" (PS) hypotheses relate long-term democratic experience and short-term democratic practice to public health care spending, basic service utilization, and infant mortality. The hypotheses are illustrated in Figure 2.1. The main findings of the analysis are reported in Table 2.1.

Pritchett and Summers (1996), in a study of cross-national variation in premature mortality entitled "Wealthier is Healthier," found that GDP per capita is the most important statistical determinant of cross-national variation in mortality rates. Other studies have found that income inequality, tropical location, and ethnolinguistic fractionalization are associated with higher mortality.[1] In the present analysis, such factors taken together comprise the broad variant of the wealthier is healthier claim.

In another study that gave a boost to the wealthier is healthier hypothesis, Filmer and Pritchett (1999) analyzed determinants of infant and under-5

---

[1] Income inequality: Hertzman 2001; Wilkinson 2001; tropical location: Gallup, Gaviria, and Lora 2003; IADB 2000; ethnolinguistic fractionalization: Filmer and Pritchett 1999.

TABLE 2.1. *Main Findings of the Quantitative Analysis*

Hypothesis (see Figure 2.1)	Predictor	Outcome	Models (see Tables 2.2, 2.3, 2.4, 2.5)	Main findings (details below and in text)
PH1	Spending	Services	3–1 to 3–3	+, significant association
PH2	Services	Survival	2–4 to 2–10, 3–8 to 3–10	+, significant association
PH3	Spending	Survival	3–4 to 3–7	No robust association
PS1	Long-term democracy	Spending	4–1	No significant association
PS1	Short-term democracy	Spending	5–1	No significant association
PS2	Long-term democracy	Services	4–2 to 4–6, 4–9	+, significant association
PS2	Short-term democracy	Services	5–2 to 5–6, 5–9	+, significant association
PS3	Long-term democracy	Survival	4–10	+, significant association
PS3	Short-term democracy	Survival	5–10	No significant association

PH1: Public health care spending as a share of GDP was positively associated with trained attendance at birth and with child immunization.

PH2: Provision of basic social services was positively associated with infant survival.

PH3: Public health care spending as a share of GDP was not associated with infant survival, except when the data came from World Bank (2002) rather than World Bank (2001/02) and the two observations with the greatest impact on the parameter vector were discarded.

PS1: Neither long-term democratic experience nor short-term democratic practice was associated significantly with public health care spending as a share of GDP.

PS2: Long-term democratic experience was positively associated with the provision of a wide set of basic social services; short-term democratic practice was positively associated with a narrower set.

PS3: Long-term democratic experience was positively associated with infant survival; short-term democratic practice had no significant association with infant survival.

mortality in 1990 across about 100 countries, both developing and industrialized. They found that GDP per capita, income inequality, mean years of female schooling, ethnolinguistic fractionalization, and having a population that is more than 90 percent Muslim jointly explained almost all variation in infant or under-5 mortality across all countries with available data in 1990. In the presence of these "socioeconomic" variables, the share of GDP devoted to public health care spending explained less than 1 percent of such variation. Other studies have also found health care spending indicators to be remarkably weakly associated with mortality levels or changes.[2] Corruption, weak administrative capacity, misallocation of the funds spent, and redundancy between public and private health care spending may be among the reasons for the apparently weak cross-national association between public health care spending and mortality levels.[3]

In the analyses reported below, GDP per capita was found to have a strong, significant, and robust association with lower infant mortality. Also associated significantly with lower infant mortality were lower income inequality, higher population density, higher urbanization, lower ethnolinguistic fractionalization, lower fertility, and having a population that is less than 90 percent Muslim. Accordingly, the study lends support to the narrow, intermediate, and broad variants of the wealthier is healthier claim. It also confirms that public health care spending is at best tentatively associated with the infant mortality rate. At the same time, however, the analyses reported in this chapter show that the actual utilization of basic, and usually quite inexpensive, social services is strongly associated with lower infant mortality, even after controlling for socioeconomic variables. The analyses also suggest that long-term democratic experience, more than short-term democratic practice, is associated with more widespread social service provision and with lower infant mortality; and that reducing infant mortality by raising GDP per capita or reducing income inequality, however desirable, may not be as feasible as reducing it by extending basic services to those most at risk of infant death.

2.1. Variables

The analyses reported in this chapter are designed to explain cross-national variation in three outcomes: the share of GDP devoted to public health care spending; the widespreadness of the utilization of various types of social services, and the level of infant mortality. The analyses are cross-sectional, comparing countries at a single point in time, rather than over time (good time series are available only for some of the variables). The universe of cases consists of 84 to 105 developing countries observed in, or close to, 1990. The main explanatory variables are long-term democratic experience, short-term democratic practice, the share of GDP devoted to public health care spending, the provision or utilization of various types of social services, and various economic, demographic, cultural, and geographical variables. These socioeconomic factors are used, first, to explore alternative variants of the wealthier

---

[2] Przeworski et al. (2000: 239–240) found an association between more public health care spending and lower infant mortality. Rajkumar and Swaroop (2002) found a similar association, but only in countries with high-quality government institutions. Bidani and Ravallion (1997); Gupta, Verhoeven, and Tiongson (2003); and Wagstaff (2003) identified an association between more public health care spending and lower infant mortality among the poor. Several other studies, however, have found no association between public health care spending and mortality (Barlow and Vissandjée 1999; Kim and Moody 1992; McGuire 2006; Musgrove 1996: 44; Shandra et al. 2004; World Bank 2004a: 37–40).

[3] Filmer, Hammer, and Pritchett 2000; Filmer, Hammer, and Pritchett 2002; Nelson 2007.

is healthier conjecture and, second, to serve as control variables in analyses in which the variables of interest are democracy, public health care spending, social service provisioning, and infant mortality.

This section explains why the predictor variables are expected to affect the outcomes of interest and why specific indicators are chosen to represent both the predictor and the outcome variables. It turns first to infant mortality, which serves only as a dependent variable; second to public health care spending and social service provision and utilization, which serve as both dependent and independent variables; third to democracy, which serves only as an independent variable; and fourth to measures of economic circumstances, demography, culture, and geography, which serve both as independent variables of interest (when exploring the wealthier is healthier hypothesis) and as control variables in analyses of associations involving democracy, health care spending, social service utilization, and infant mortality. Web Appendices associated with this book provide the data, data sources, and statistical output from the analyses.[4]

Infant mortality. Until the late 1990s, estimates of infant mortality levels in developing countries could differ dramatically. Among the first systematic efforts to reconcile this mass of disparate estimates was Hill et al. (1999), who used explicit and transparent methods to produce compromise estimates of infant and under-5 mortality for 94 developing countries in every fifth year from 1960 to 1995 inclusive. Hill et al. (1999) provide 90 of the 105 infant mortality estimates for 1990 used in the analyses in this chapter. The World Bank (2002) is the source of 14 of the other 15 estimates. The remaining estimate, for Taiwan, is taken from a 1989 survey (Table A1). As is usual in cross-national analyses, the natural logarithm of the infant mortality rate is used to linearize its association with the independent variables. As one type of check on the robustness of findings involving the infant mortality rate, all regressions designed to predict the infant mortality level in 1990 are reestimated using an alternative source of infant mortality data (World Bank 2002). All models were also reestimated using under-5 (rather than infant) mortality as the outcome to be explained.

Health care spending. Cross-country analyses designed to unravel the determinants of national mortality levels and changes have used alternative indicators of health care spending. Four of the most widely used are (1) total, public, or private health care spending per capita; (2) total, public, or private health care spending as a share of GDP; (3) public health care spending as a share either of total public spending or total public spending on social services; and (4) the share of public health care spending that is devoted to "basic," "primary," or "local" health care services.

The indicator of health spending used in the present study is *public health care spending as a share of GDP in 1990.* The private sector accounts for a large fraction of health expenditure in many developing countries, but in most

---

[4] McGuire 2009 (Web Appendices C1 and D2).

such countries, and certainly in the eight societies analyzed in this book, the public sector for most of the period from 1960 to 2005 provided the great majority of maternal and infant health services to populations at high risk of infant death. Moreover, using public health care spending as a share of GDP as the appropriate measure of health care spending avoids some of the pitfalls involved in using alternative measures of health care spending. Per capita spending on health care (or on public health care) melds GDP per capita with the share of GDP devoted to health service provision. Hence, a finding that greater health care spending per capita is associated with lower mortality fails to exclude the possibility that the health care spending variable is simply a proxy for affluence, which may affect mortality levels in ways not mediated by health care spending (e.g., by allowing the purchase of more or better food). Data on the share of public spending devoted to social services are often either unreliable or idiosyncratic, and data on the share of public health care spending devoted to basic, primary, or local health care services are available only for a small number of developing countries.

Social service provision and utilization. The indicators of social service provision and utilization include (1) the proportion of births attended by trained personnel, (2) the proportion of children immunized against measles (with the measles-containing vaccine, MCV), (3) the proportion of children receiving three doses of the antigens against diphtheria, tetanus, and pertussis (DTP3), (4) mean years of female schooling, (5) expert ratings of national family planning effort, (6) the share of the population with access to an improved water source, and (7) the share of the population with access to improved sanitation. These social service provision, access, and utilization indicators serve both as dependent variables (i.e., as outcomes hypothetically caused by health care spending, short-term democratic practice, or long-term democratic experience) and as independent variables (as hypothesized causes of cross-national variation in the infant mortality level).

The *share of births attended by trained personnel in 1990* is hypothesized to affect the infant mortality rate not only because such attendance reduces the risk of infant (and maternal) death directly, but also because it serves as a proxy for the quality of, and access to, other aspects of maternal and infant health care. The share of births attended by trained personnel in 1995 is correlated closely with expert ratings of maternal and child health "program effort" across 47 developing countries in 1996. The share of births attended by trained personnel was preferred to an alternative indicator of basic health service provision, the share of expectant mothers utilizing prenatal care, partly because it was more widely available (103 versus 84 countries), and partly because only one prenatal visit, rather than the minimum of four recommended by the World Health Organization (WHO) for women without known pregnancy complications, qualifies an expectant mother as a user of prenatal care, according to the definition employed in the standard cross-national statistical compendia. Trained attendance at birth was also preferred to the share of the population with (geographical) "access" to health services, because trained attendance at birth indicates the actual utilization of a maternal and infant health service, whereas geographical access only facilitates such utilization. Data on geographical access to health services is in any case poor or non-existent for many developing countries.[5]

The higher the *share of children immunized* against specific diseases, the lower the probability that the children will transmit or suffer from such diseases, or from their sometimes mortality-inducing complications. In June 2000, researchers at the WHO and UNICEF started a long-term project to evaluate and reconcile data on immunization coverage around the world, producing for most countries for each year starting in 1980 a "consensus estimate" of the share of a target population (usually children who have survived to age 1) that had been immunized with a specific antigen. To produce these estimates, the WHO and UNICEF researchers reviewed and assessed all available immunization coverage information for as many countries as possible for all available years from 1980 onward.[6] The immunization data in the present study are taken from this WHO/UNICEF (2004) project. Data for 1990 on the share of children immunized with the antigen against measles (MCV), as well as with three doses of the antigens against diphtheria, tetanus, and pertussis (DTP3), are available for 98 of the 105 developing societies included in the present analysis.

The measure of female education employed is the *mean years of schooling in the female population* 15 years or older in 1990. Several mechanisms could mediate the effect of female schooling on infant mortality. More educated women tend to know more about nutrition, sanitation, and health; to be more assertive in demanding food and health care for children; to use modern health facilities; and to care for their children in ways that promote health. Some cross-national studies have classified education as a socioeconomic factor and used it as a control variable in models estimating the impact on infant mortality of health care resources or health care spending.[7] Especially when measured as schooling, however, education is more reasonably viewed as a type of public provisioning than as a feature of the socioeconomic context. Still, educational attainment does influence health service provision and utilization, so there is some justification for treating it as a control variable. Hence, although female education is not included as a control variable in the statistical tests reported in this chapter, the results obtained in those tests are checked for robustness to the inclusion of female education as a control variable.

Mean years of schooling in the female population aged 15 and over in 1990 is highly correlated with female literacy in 1990 ($r = .90$, $N = 81$). For countries with data on both indicators, female schooling is preferred. Female schooling beyond literacy confers not only information that can lower infant mortality,

---

[5] McGuire 2006: 408–410.

[6] WHO 2004: 1–2.

[7] Caldwell and Caldwell 1993. Filmer and Pritchett (1999) treat education as a socioeconomic variable.

but also empowerment that can enable women to contend within the household for a greater share of resources for themselves and for the family's children, and outside of the household for better health services. In Indonesia in the mid-1990s, an extra year of secondary schooling reduced a mother's chances of experiencing the death of an under-5 child by 2.6 percent, whereas an extra year of primary schooling reduced those chances by only 1.9 percent.[8]

Greater *family planning effort* was expected to be associated with lower fertility, which was in turn expected to be associated with lower infant mortality. Expert ratings of national family planning effort correspond to 1989 and were taken from a database of family planning effort scores.[9] These data are based on 359 completed questionnaires filled out by one to twelve family planning experts in each of 98 developing countries. Each expert was asked about family planning effort in four broad areas: service and service-related activities (13 questions), policies and stage-setting activities (8 questions), availability of contraceptive measures (6 questions), and record-keeping and evaluation (3 questions). The experts responded to each question with a rating from "0" to "4," and the scores were added up, with the maximum possible score set to 120. Summary scores for 1989 are available for 88 of the 105 developing societies included in the analysis. China had the highest score (104); Kuwait and Saudi Arabia tied for the lowest (0).[10]

The *share of the population with access to an improved water source* and the *share of the population with access to improved sanitation* are expected to reduce the infant mortality rate by lowering infant deaths from diseases spread by water-borne parasites. Access to safe water and adequate sanitation reduces the risk of disease. In the early 2000s, diarrhea caused mainly by water-borne parasites was implicated in the deaths of 1.8 million under-5 children annually, making it the second-largest cause of death around the world, exceeding AIDS and malaria and trailing only acute respiratory infection.[11] Water data are available for all 105 countries and sanitation data for 102. The figures, taken mostly from United Nations sources, are for circa 1990.[12]

Democracy, which was defined in Chapter 1, is measured both as long-term democratic experience from 1900 to 1990, and as short-term democratic practice from 1980 to 1990. These measures are calculated from the Polity IV

---

[8] Mellington and Cameron 1999: 128–130. For 81 of the 105 developing countries in the analysis, data on mean years of female schooling are taken from Barro and Lee (2000). For the other 24 cases, figures for mean years of female schooling in 1990 were imputed by the Stata impute procedure, using female illiteracy (age 15+) in 1990 as the predictor (World Bank 2002; UNDP 1993; Taiwan. DGBAS 2002). To check whether imputation might be distorting the analyses, each model was reestimated with a dummy variable identifying countries with imputed data (McGuire 2009, Web Appendix C1).

[9] Ross 2001. Summary scores for 1972, 1982, 1989, and 1994 are available in Ross and Mauldin 1996: 146.

[10] Ross and Mauldin 1996: 138.

[11] UNDP 2006: 42.

[12] McGuire 2009 (Web Appendix D2).

dataset, which stands out among large cross-national democracy datasets for its long time frame (data go back to 1800 or to a country's date of independence, whichever is later), for its transparent and detailed coding rules, and for its use of multiple coders and inter-coder reliability tests.[13]

To create the Polity IV database, coders drawing on secondary literature assigned each of the world's independent nations scores on "democracy" and "autocracy" in each year from 1800 to 2005. These annual scores were based on three criteria: (1) "openness and competitiveness of the recruitment of the chief executive"; (2) "constraints on the authority of the chief executive"; and (3) "political participation and opposition." Each criterion had subcomponents. For example, political participation and opposition included "regulation of participation" (how much factionalism and personalism there is in politics) and "competitiveness of participation" (how much incumbents restrict political opposition). The subcomponents and components were scored, weighted, and combined to form a democracy score ranging from +10 to 0, as well as an autocracy score ranging from 0 to –10 (+10 is most democratic, -10 is most autocratic). The two scores were then combined to form a "Polity" score ranging from +10 (most democratic) to –10 (most autocratic).[14] The Polity score is appropriately sensitive to different degrees of autocracy as well as democracy. Autocracy as well as democracy could conceivably affect all three outcomes of interest: the share of GDP devoted to public health care, the provision and utilization of basic social services, and infant and child mortality. Polity scores for the East Asian and Latin American societies compared in this book are shown in Table A18.

Like any effort to quantify the complexities of political life, Polity IV is imperfect. For one thing, "political participation and opposition" gives short shrift to participation.[15] The dimension reflects the degree to which political opposition is personalized, factionalized, or repressed, but a country can score high on "participation" without extending the franchise to the whole adult population, much less achieving high levels of voter turnout, party membership, or affiliation with civic organizations. Polity IV also explicitly neglects civil liberties.[16] The omission of participation (as conventionally understood) and of civil liberties produces some curious ratings. The United States from 1845 to 1849 received the highest possible democracy score of +10, although slavery existed and although women and many free men lacked the right to vote. South Africa under apartheid from 1910 to 1987 received a score of +7, the same as Argentina under Menem from 1990 to 1998 and higher than Chile under Frei Montalva and Allende from 1964 to 1972 (+6).

Despite the questionable validity of the Polity scores for certain countries in certain years, Polity IV is the most systematically and transparently derived

[13] Marshall and Jaggers 2006; Munck and Verkuilen 2002: 28.
[14] Marshall and Jaggers 2000: 22–25.
[15] Munck and Verkuilen 2002: 14.
[16] Marshall and Jaggers 2000: 12.

data set of democracy indicators that covers a large number of cases over a long time span. Long time period coverage is an important virtue of Polity IV, because the impact of most dimensions of democracy on economic and social outcomes is unlikely to be immediate.[17] Writing on democracy and income inequality, the sociologist Edward Muller hypothesized that "a country's accumulated years of democratic experience will have a stronger negative effect on income inequality than the level of democracy that exists at a single point in time," partly because in some new democracies, "sufficient time has not elapsed for the institutions of democracy, operating through mediating variables such as strong trade unions and socialist parties, to have exerted an egalitarian effect on the distribution of income."[18] Analyses reported below explore the hypothesis that, across developing countries in 1990, long-term democratic experience is associated even more strongly than short-term democratic practice with public health care spending, basic social service provision, and infant mortality. Long-term democratic experience is a country's mean Polity (democracy minus autocracy) score over all years from 1900 to 1990 for which data are available. Short-term democratic practice is measured similarly, but only from 1980 to 1990.[19]

Colonies are not included in the Polity IV database, so the main measure of long-term democratic experience used in these analyses (the mean Polity score from 1900 to 1990) fails to penalize a great many subsequently independent developing countries for long and basically authoritarian colonial histories. Semi-democratic experience in these excluded colonies does not seem to have been systematically lower, however, than semi-democratic experience in developing countries that were independent for the entire period from 1900 to 1990. Some colonial experiences included representative institutions (the Volksraad in Indonesia from 1918 to 1941; the legislative councils in some British colonies after World War II), whereas some non-colonized developing countries, such as Afghanistan, Iran, Saudi Arabia, and Thailand, had highly authoritarian political regimes for much of the twentieth century. Hence, the lack of a blanket penalty for colonial experience should not distort the results excessively.

Socioeconomic variables. Such variables are used both to explore the broad variant of the wealthier is healthier conjecture and to serve as control variables

---

[17] Gerring et al. 2005.

[18] Muller 1988: 57, 51.

[19] The results for short-term democratic practice were checked for robustness by replacing the mean Polity score from 1980 to 1990 with, respectively, (a) the country's Polity score in 1990 (Marshall and Jaggers 2006); (b) the country's Freedom House (2007) Civil and Political Liberties score in 1990, and (c) the country's mean Freedom House (2007) Civil and Political Liberties score for 1980 to 1990. The absence of Freedom House data from before 1972 precludes analogous checks for long-term democratic experience, but the results for long-term democratic experience were checked for robustness by replacing the mean Polity score from 1900 to 1990 with, respectively, the mean Polity score from 1970 to 1990 (Marshall and Jaggers 2006) and the mean Freedom House (2007) Civil and Political Liberties score from 1972 to 1990. All findings withstood these checks (Mcguire 2009, Web Appendix C1)

in analyses where the independent variables of interest are democracy, public health care spending, and social service provision. In the analyses designed to predict social service utilization and infant mortality, the socioeconomic factors included as control variables are GDP per capita, income inequality, urbanization, population density, fertility, ethnolinguistic fractionalization, and whether more than 90 percent of the country's population is Muslim. A different set of socioeconomic variables is used in the models predicting public health care spending. That set includes, again, GDP per capita, income inequality, urbanization, and population density; but it also includes the share of the population over age 65, while excluding fertility, ethnic fractionalization, and whether more than 90 percent of the country's population is Muslim.

Higher *GDP per capita* was expected to be associated with higher public health care spending as a share of GDP, higher social service provision/utilization, and lower infant mortality. Higher GDP per capita creates private income that households can spend on food, housing, and other basic needs, and facilitates the construction of roads, clinics, and other assets that reduce the risk of infant death. As societies get richer, moreover, they can afford to spend more on costly medical services, for which the demand is relentless.[20] Richer societies can also afford more and higher quality education, family planning, and water and sanitation services, all of which help to reduce infant mortality. As is typical in such analyses, the natural logarithm of GDP per capita is used in all models because an additional unit of economic output is expected to have less and less impact on the various outcomes as economic output rises.

Lower *income inequality* should be associated with greater social solidarity, with the causality running in both directions. Greater social solidarity, in turn, should contribute to greater public spending on social services and greater provision and utilization of such services. These rises in service provision and utilization should, for their part, reduce infant mortality.[21] Lower income inequality also means that economic growth will translate more readily into a decline of income poverty, which should in turn increase the utilization of social services. Not only does lower income poverty make it easier for a person to purchase private health care services, it also enables the use of nominally free-to-the-consumer public services, which often require the user to leave work or to pay for transport costs. Greater use of basic social services, coupled with a greater capacity to purchase survival-enhancing goods and services in private markets, will tend to reduce the risk of infant death.

Even controlling for income poverty, however, income inequality has been found to raise mortality by increasing psychological stress, deepening feelings of depression, and encouraging risk-taking behavior.[22] If such psychosocial pathways influence the mortality rates of infants (mostly via their caretakers), then income inequality would be associated even more strongly with infant

[20] Newhouse 1977: 123.
[21] Lynch et al. 2000: 1202.
[22] Lynch et al. 2000; Marmot and Wilkinson 2001; Rojroongwasinkul 2004; Wilkinson 2001.

mortality than with public health care spending or with basic social service utilization. In the present analysis that turns out to be the case (Tables 2.2, 2.3, 2.4, and 2.5). Income inequality is measured by the Gini index, which was first proposed in 1912 by an Italian statistician named Corrado Gini. The Gini index ranges in value from 0 (each person or household has the same amount of income) to 100 (one person or household has all the income and all the others have no income). For the purpose of the statistical analyses in this chapter, the value of the Gini index assigned to each country is the mean of its acceptable-quality Gini index estimates from the 1960s to the 1990s.[23]

Cultural variables are included in the models predicting service utilization and infant mortality, but not in the models predicting public health care spending (scholars have yet to turn up robust statistical associations between cultural variables and public health care spending). *Ethnolinguistic fractionalization*, the probability that two persons picked randomly from a society will be from different ethnic groups (defined in linguistic terms), is expected both to reduce social service utilization and to increase infant mortality, because ethnic fragmentation is often associated with discrimination against minority groups. Where ethnic groups are "ranked" rather than "unranked" in respect to one another, ethnic fragmentation has also often resulted in ethnic conflict.[24] Ethnic discrimination and conflict can lead to mortality-increasing violence and can complicate the utilization as well as the provision of mortality-reducing social services.

Countries whose populations are *more than 90 percent Muslim* have been found, all else equal, to have lower social service utilization and higher infant mortality rates than countries in which Muslims are less preponderant.[25] Women in many predominantly Muslim societies face special obstacles in struggling for resources for their children (particularly girl children). In some such societies, moreover, health care and education providers face obstacles to interacting with persons of the opposite sex. Controlling for other potentially relevant variables, infant mortality was higher among Muslim than non-Muslim families in Thailand in 1970 and 1980, as well as in Indonesia in the 1990s.[26]

The higher the *total fertility rate* – the average number of children each woman is expected to bear in her lifetime – the higher, all else equal, the

---

[23] McGuire 2009 (Web Appendix D2).
[24] Horowitz 1985. Data from Easterly and Levine 1996.
[25] Empirically, across the 105 cases analyzed, infant mortality in 1990 was predicted better by a 0–1 dummy variable indicating whether a country's population was more than 90 percent Muslim than by the percentage of the country's population that professed the Muslim faith. Across the cases analyzed here, percent Muslim (La Porta et al. 1998) indeed had no statistical association with the infant mortality rate in the presence of the other six socioeconomic predictor variables.
[26] Thailand: Porapakkham 1986: 22–23. Indonesia: Mellington and Cameron 1999: 131. See Ghuman (2003) for contrasting findings. Filmer and Pritchett (1999: 1312) cite a study by Caldwell (1986) to justify their inclusion of this variable as a predictor of cross-national variation in under-5 mortality.

infant mortality rate.[27] Lower fertility increases birth spacing, lessens the number of higher-order parities, reduces the share of births to very young and very old mothers, and enables parents to devote more attention to each child. All of these effects should reduce infant mortality. Moreover, lower fertility should reduce the burden on obstetric, pediatric, educational, water, and sanitation services, reducing the infant mortality rate by increasing the share of the population with access to such services. Some of these effects of lower fertility could be offset, however, by an increase in the share of first births, which some studies suggest should tend to raise infant mortality.[28] Because the level of infant mortality is sometimes thought to affect the level of fertility, moreover, the findings are checked by excluding fertility as a regressor, as well as by checking for endogeneity using instrumental variables implemented through two-stage least squares.

In Europe until the mid-nineteenth century, *urbanization* was associated with higher mortality, but after the turn of twentieth century, the positive effects of easier health care delivery, better infrastructure, and increased biological resistance began to outweigh the negative effects of crowding and exposure to disease.[29] If urban residence in developing countries today were to confer a similar balance of costs and benefits, urbanization would be associated with greater utilization of social services and with lower infant mortality. *Population density* should also be associated with easier provision and utilization of basic social services, and thereby with lower infant mortality. Both urbanization and population density, which are surprisingly weakly correlated with each other (in 1990, across 105 cases, the correlation coefficient was +.13), make it easier for the population to voice demands for better services. Hence, urbanization and population density were both expected to raise public health care spending. In the models predicting the share of GDP devoted to public health care spending, the *proportion of the population aged 65 or above* is included as a regressor because older people tend to require more frequent and more costly medical treatment than younger people.

Geography, world region, and female educational attainment. No matter what the outcome of interest (public health care spending, social service utilization, or infant mortality), most of the statistical models tested in this chapter include eight predictor variables: one predictor variable of interest (an indicator of democracy, public health care spending, or social service utilization) and seven socioeconomic control variables (GDP per capita, income inequality, fertility, urbanization, population density, ethnolinguistic fractionalization, and whether the population is more than 90 percent Muslim). Conceivably, the results of such tests could be distorted by the omission from the models of

[27] Palloni and Rafalimanana 1999: 41.
[28] Bongaarts 1987; Potter 1988; Trussel 1988. In Chile throughout the 1970s, however, the infant mortality rate for first births was lower than for subsequent births (Raczynski and Oyarzo 1981: 72; Taucher 1996: 296–297).
[29] Easterlin 1996: 73–79.

variables that are also plausibly associated either with the outcome of interest or with one or more of the included predictor variables. To examine the possibility that such omitted variables might be driving the results, the results of each test are checked systematically for robustness to the inclusion, alternatively, of geographic variables, regional dummy variables, and measures of female educational attainment.

In a first such check three geographic variables are added, all at once, to each model. *Proximity to world economic hubs* (the air distance in kilometers of the country centroid from New York, Rotterdam, or Tokyo, whichever is closest) is expected to increase foreign aid, trade, investment, and loans, raising social service utilization and reducing infant mortality. *Coastal access* (the share of the population living within 100 kilometers of the coast or a sea-navigable river) is expected to facilitate the diffusion of health care innovations and of other survival-related technologies, again raising social service utilization and reducing infant mortality. *Tropical location* (the absolute value of the latitude of the country's capital city) is expected, by contrast, to raise the burden of infectious disease on both service providers (reducing social service utilization) and infants (raising infant mortality).[30]

A second check for robustness involves the inclusion as predictors of four *regional dummy variables*, one each for sub-Saharan Africa, Latin America and the Caribbean, South Asia, or East Asia and the Pacific.[31] These variables are included on the right-hand side of each model in order to ascertain whether region-specific cultural factors (in addition to ethnolinguistic fractionalization and having a population that is more than 90 percent Muslim) might be driving the results. In this second set of robustness tests, the four regional dummy variables are included, all at once, alongside the seven socioeconomic factors and the single predictor variable of interest. Their addition to the right-hand side of each model makes a total of twelve predictor variables.

A third robustness test involves the inclusion as a predictor variable of either mean years of female schooling or the literate share of the female population. These indicators of female educational attainment are added separately to the right-hand side of each model, alongside the variable of interest and the seven socioeconomic control variables. (For obvious reasons this robustness check is omitted where female schooling is itself the predictor variable of interest.) As noted above, some scholars have conceptualized educational attainment not as an outcome of social service provision, but as part of the socioeconomic context that needs to be taken into account when exploring the determinants of public health care spending, the provision of social services (apart from education), or infant mortality.

---

[30] Gallup and Sachs 1999; Gallup, Mellinger, and Sachs 2001. Data on these geographical variables for 105 developing countries are provided in McGuire 2009 (Web Appendix D2).

[31] To prevent perfect multicollinearity, and because most analyses already included a dummy variable for whether a country's population was more than 90 percent Muslim in 1990, no dummy variable was included for the Middle East and North Africa.

2.2. Methods

The research design involved (1) creating a baseline model including as predictors seven economic, demographic, and cultural variables; (2) adding an indicator of health care spending, social service utilization, or political democracy to this baseline model as a predictor variable of interest; (3) using multiple regression to explore associations between the eight predictor variables and each outcome of interest across the 105 cases in 1990; (4) checking whether the results could have been influenced by omitted variables, missing data, outlying cases, endogeneity, misspecified functional form, or idiosyncrasies of data source and variable definition; and (5) using the CLARIFY macro for the Stata statistical package to estimate the substantive effects of the socioeconomic, social service utilization, and democracy variables on infant mortality and other outcomes of interest.[32] Except in the checks using two-stage least squares, heteroskedasticity-robust standard errors were used to calculate the statistical significance of the parameter estimates.

The analysis is cross-sectional, although the independent variables include cumulative democratic experience from 1900 to 1990 and from 1980 to 1990. Time-series cross-sectional models have been used to tackle some of the questions raised in this study.[33] Such models take account of temporal sequence, facilitating causal inference. Using fixed effects, moreover, they are less vulnerable than cross-sectional analyses to omitted variable bias. Temporal sequence is a necessary but not sufficient condition for inferring causality, however; and cross-sectional time-series models can suffer from omitted variable bias if changes over time in the omitted variables are correlated with changes over time in the included variables. As a practical matter, moreover, few developing countries have reliable and extended time-series data for all or even many of the factors likely to affect infant mortality. Accordingly, this study uses cross-national analysis at a single point in time (1990) to explore the role of public health spending and of the provision or utilization of basic social services in mediating the association between democracy and infant mortality. The year 1990 was chosen to facilitate comparison of the results with those of Filmer and Pritchett (1999), on which the analysis is modeled, and because 1990 is a year for which data availability is relatively high, in part because it is the starting year for the Millennium Development Goals adopted by the United Nations in 2000. Variables are measured as close to 1990 as data permit.[34]

The restriction of the data set to nations in the developing world deserves some justification, given that some other cross-national studies of the

---

[32] The macro can be used to set the control variables to their means and to calculate how much the outcome would change if a country's value on the independent variable of interest were to rise by a certain amount. The macro was written by Tomz, Wittenberg, and King (2001) and is described in King, Tomz, and Wittenberg (2000).

[33] Gauri and Khaleghian 2002; Gerring, Thacker, and Alfaro 2005; Lake and Baum 2001; Przeworski et al. 2000; Ross 2006; Zweifel and Navia 2000.

[34] In McGuire 2009 (Web Appendix C1) the Filmer and Pritchett (1999) model is replicated using data for developing countries only.

determinants of infant or under-5 mortality have included both developing and industrialized nations. To include industrialized as well as developing nations in the data set lumps together countries at widely differing stages of the demographic transition: the transition from high fertility and high mortality to low fertility and low mortality. In industrialized countries, which have already experienced the demographic transition, the child death toll of infectious diseases is small relative to developing countries, most of which have yet to begin the transition, or are only part way through it. Hence, variation in the share of births attended by trained personnel may have a strong effect on infant mortality in developing countries, but little effect in industrialized countries, which tend to be clustered near the asymptotes of many social service utilization and mortality indicators.[35] Excluding industrialized countries helps to ameliorate this clustering problem.

Also excluded from the data set are developing countries with fewer than 500,000 inhabitants. Such countries are left out of the analysis because many of them lack data on the variables of interest or the control variables, and because idiosyncratic factors (e.g., natural disasters, natural resource booms and busts) are assumed to be more likely to influence the fortunes of small populations than of large ones. Taiwan, on the other hand, is included in the data set of 105 developing societies because it is one of the eight cases analyzed in subsequent chapters, because its population in 1990 was 20 million, and because its government makes policy as a national government would.

By focusing exclusively on developing societies, and by drawing on a careful selection of statistical sources, the data set used in the analyses is more homogeneous than those usually employed in such studies, while managing to maintain a large number of cases with reasonably complete data on the variables explored. A large number of control variables were used; the findings were checked for robustness to alternative model specifications and statistical techniques; and the eight case studies were inspected to identify variables that seemed to have had, historically, an important effect on infant mortality, but were excluded from the initial models developed for the study.[36] A case in point is population density, which was identified as potentially relevant through the case studies in Chapters 3–10. This discovery underscores an advantage of the "nested analysis" research design: the researcher may identify through case studies or through small-N comparisons factors that were initially overlooked,

---

[35] For example, all industrialized countries in the mid-1990s had trained attendants at 98 to 100 percent of births, and all had infant mortality rates below 9 per 1000 (World Bank 2008c). Among developing countries, variance on both indicators was much greater. Hence, the functional form of the equation required to model the association between basic service provision and infant mortality in industrialized countries is likely to differ from the functional form of the equation required to model similar associations in developing countries. Using logarithmic or similar transformations helps, but even these techniques seem too blunt to handle the extreme compression of values among industrialized countries on such indicators as trained attendance at birth and infant mortality, given that standard statistical compendia provide estimates of these indicators only as whole integers.

[36] These initial models were presented in McGuire 2005 and McGuire 2006.

and whose omission from a model could affect its results. The case studies reported in Chapters 3, 5, and 10 showed that attracting health professionals to underserved geographical areas was easier in population-dense Costa Rica than in far-flung Brazil or Indonesia.

The baseline model for the regressions predicting infant mortality and basic service utilization is Model 2–3 (Table 2.2). It includes seven economic, demographic, and cultural variables. Model 4–1 (Table 2.4) and Model 5–1 (Table 2.5) are the baseline models for exploring the association between democracy and the share of GDP devoted to public health spending. These models control for GDP per capita, population density, urbanization, and the share of the population over age 65. Two indicators of democracy are used. Short-term democratic practice is a country's average "Polity" (democracy minus autocracy) score in the 11 years from 1980 to 1990. Long-term democratic experience is a country's average Polity score in the 91 years from 1900 to 1990.[37]

Five sets of checks were used to examine the robustness of the results. First, the models were reestimated using different specifications. It is never possible to rule out definitively that results are being driven by omitted variables, but all findings were tested for robustness to the inclusion of geographic, regional, and educational control variables, as described at the end of Section 2.1. All findings were also checked for robustness to the exclusion of fertility as a control variable. The exclusion of fertility was intended to eliminate possible reverse causation from infant mortality to fertility.

A second check for robustness involved the reestimation of each model with missing data flags – dummy variables indicating whether an observation has been imputed. Dummy variable flags indicating missing data were created for two different measures of GDP per capita (one measure has one imputed observation, the other has five), for the Gini index of income inequality (25 imputed observations), and for two different measures of ethnolinguistic fractionalization (seven and eight imputed observations respectively).[38] Except in the case of the Gini index, then, imputation was needed for only a small number of observations.

A third set of checks for robustness involved reducing the statistical leverage of outlying data points. To check whether outliers might be affecting the results, each of the models that was estimated initially using ordinary least squares regression was reestimated using median regression and again using robust regression. In median regression, the coefficients are estimated by minimizing the sum of the absolute distances between the data points and the median of the data points. This method is less affected by outliers than is the ordinary least squares method of minimizing the sum of the squared distances

---

[37] McGuire 2009 (Web Appendix D2) provides the sources and data set used in all analyses reported in this chapter. McGuire 2009 (Web Appendix C1) previews the research plan, provides the Stata do-file programs that were used to generate the results, and logs the results generated by the Stata statistical package.

[38] Imputation techniques are summarized in the last row of each column of McGuire 2009 (Web Appendix D2).

between the data points and the mean of the data points. Median regression can also be affected by high-leverage values, however.[39] Accordingly, the models were also reestimated using robust regression, which uses iteratively reweighted least squares to estimate regression coefficients and standard errors. The procedure assigns weights to each observation; observations with high leverage or influence receive lower weights.[40] A third procedure used to check for outliers was to exclude the two country observations with the largest impact on the regression line, as measured by the Cook's-D test.[41]

A fourth set of checks for robustness involved checking and correcting for endogeneity, which results when the error term is correlated with the independent variables. Sources of endogeneity may include omitted variables, incorrect functional form, measurement error in the independent variables, or causation flowing from the dependent to the independent variables. To check for omitted variable bias, the study used a wide range of control variables. To check for measurement error, it used (where available) alternative data sources for the same variable. To check for an improperly specified functional form, it experimented with linear transformations of several variables. To check and correct for possible reverse causation, it used instrumental variables implemented through two-stage least squares to ascertain whether (a) lower infant mortality might be reducing fertility; (b) high infant mortality might be encouraging child immunization and trained attendance at birth; and (c) low levels of child immunization and birth attendance might be inducing governments to raise the share of GDP devoted to public health care spending.

As an example of such an analysis, let us consider the use of instrumental variables implemented through two-stage least squares to ascertain whether high infant mortality might be a cause, rather than simply an outcome, of high fertility. As applied to the models explored in this chapter, ordinary least squares assumes that high fertility is causing, but not resulting from, high infant mortality. There are reasons to suspect, however, that high fertility might be a consequence, as well as a cause, of high infant mortality. For example, high infant mortality could cause high fertility through physiological channels (by ending breastfeeding and stimulating ovulation); by raising the incentive for replacement, whereby parents have an additional child to replace one who has died; or by raising the incentive for "hedging" or "hoarding," whereby parents in response to expected mortality keep having children in order to raise the likelihood that a minimum number will survive.[42] If such reverse causation were at work, the magnitude of the coefficient on fertility in models predicting infant mortality would probably be biased upward, because the statistical association would reflect the combined impact of two actual effects. Using the instrumental

---

[39] Chen et al. 2004.

[40] Western 1995.

[41] Filmer and Pritchett (1999) used this procedure to check for robustness to outliers.

[42] Ben-Porath 1980: 152–153. Some research suggests, however, that infant mortality has at most a modest effect on fertility (Palloni and Rafalimanana 1999: 41–43).

variables technique to isolate the effect of fertility on infant mortality, net of the effect of infant mortality on fertility, should attenuate the association.

The procedure used to check for endogeneity bias resulting from infant mortality affecting fertility can be illustrated briefly. (Similar procedures were used to check for the other two sources of hypothesized reverse causation.) The procedure was (1) to find a valid instrument for the total fertility rate; (2) to replace the total fertility rate with the instrument as a regressor; (3) to rerun the regression using two-stage least squares; and (4) to use a Hausman test to check whether the two-stage least squares regression coefficients differed significantly from those in the ordinary least squares analysis. The instrument chosen was the total fertility rate in a neighboring country selected according to a method devised by other scholars.[43] Theoretically, the total fertility rate in the neighboring country is (a) unlikely to be affected directly by the infant mortality rate in the focus country, and (b) unlikely to be associated with the infant mortality rate in the focus country except through its association with the total fertility rate in the focus country, thus meeting two of the three conditions for a valid instrument. Empirically, the first-stage results obtained in such regressions show that the total fertility rate in a neighboring country is a powerful predictor of the total fertility rate in the focus country, so the third condition – that the instrument be a strong predictor of the potentially endogenous variable – is also met.

The hypothesized causal pathways by which higher infant mortality might cause higher fertility seem eminently plausible. Accordingly, it was somewhat surprising to find that the Hausman tests performed to detect possible reverse causation (from infant mortality to fertility) found uniformly that the coefficients produced by the two-stage least squares procedure did not differ significantly from those produced by ordinary least squares. Hausman tests also turned up no evidence of reverse causation from infant mortality to birth attendance, or from birth attendance to health care spending. Because ordinary least squares is the more efficient estimator, its results were preferred.

A fifth set of checks for robustness involved variable definitions and data sources. Models in which infant mortality appeared as the dependent variable were reestimated using under-5 mortality as the outcome to be explained. Models were also reestimated using alternative data sources for infant mortality, for GDP per capita, for ethnolinguistic fractionalization, and for the share of GDP devoted to public health care spending.[44] In Tables 2.4 and 2.5, where democracy served as the predictor variable of interest, long-term democratic experience, which was measured in the basic regressions as a country's average Polity score from 1900 to 1990, was also measured as the mean annual Polity score from 1970 to 1990 and as the mean annual Freedom House Civil and Political Liberties score from 1972 to 1990. Short-term democratic practice, which was measured in most regressions as the country's mean annual Polity score from 1980 to 1990, was also measured as the Polity score in 1990, as the Freedom House score in 1990, and as the mean annual Freedom House score from 1980 to 1990. As is the standard practice, natural log transformations were applied throughout to GDP per capita, infant and under-5 mortality, and population density. Models in which the share of GDP devoted to public health care appeared as a regressor were reestimated using the natural log of that share.

2.3. Results

This section presents the results of statistical analyses designed to explore the three variants of the wealthier is healthier hypothesis (narrow, intermediate, and broad); the three public health hypotheses (spending promotes services, services promote survival, and spending promotes survival); and the three political science hypotheses (democracy promotes spending, democracy promotes services, and democracy promotes survival). Special attention is paid to estimating the magnitude as well as the precision of the associations obtained in the analyses. Some of the more striking or puzzling findings are discussed at the end of this section; their implications are discussed in Section 2.4.

Results pertaining to the wealthier is healthier hypothesis. These results are presented in Table 2.2. The narrow variant of the wealthier is healthier hypothesis, in which the sole predictor variable is GDP per capita, explained 70 percent of the cross-national variance in infant mortality across the 105 developing societies with populations greater than 500,000 in 1990 (Model 2–1). When income inequality was added to the model (the intermediate variant of the wealthier is healthier hypothesis), its coefficient had the expected positive sign and was statistically significant at the .05 level. The addition of income inequality raised the share of variance explained only to 72 percent, however (Model 2–2). The broad variant of the wealthier is healthier hypothesis was operationalized using seven socioeconomic variables: GDP per capita, income inequality, fertility, population density, urbanization, ethnolinguistic fractionalization, and a dummy (0 or 1) variable indicating whether or not the country's population in 1990 was more than 90 percent Muslim (Model 2–3). Each of these socioeconomic variables proved to be statistically significant at the .10 level or better, and Model 2–3 as a whole explained 85 percent of the cross-national variance in infant mortality level in 1990. Model 2–3 serves as the baseline model in all subsequent analyses predicting social service utilization or infant mortality. The baseline models predicting health care spending as a share of GDP (Table 2.4, Model 4–1 and Table 2.5, Model 5–1) exclude three of the independent variables that appear in the models predicting social service provision and infant mortality (fertility, ethnolinguistic fractionalization, and whether a country's population is more than 90 percent Muslim), but include the share of the population over age 65.

TABLE 2.2. *Economy, Culture, Demography, Social Service Utilization, and Infant Mortality*

Dependent variable →	2-1 Infant mortality	2-2 Infant mortality	2-3 Infant mortality	2-4 Infant mortality	2-5 Infant mortality	2-6 Infant mortality	2-7 Infant mortality	2-8 Infant mortality	2-9 Infant mortality	2-10 Infant mortality
GDP per capita	-.742*** (15.50)	-.738*** (15.86)	-.511*** (7.01)	-.454*** (6.63)	-.456*** (6.46)	-.482*** (6.60)	-.439*** (6.01)	-.570*** (8.17)	-.488*** (6.66)	-.393*** (5.09)
Income inequality		.013* (2.35)	.010† (1.70)	.008 (1.35)	.011† (1.80)	.011† (1.75)	.010† (1.82)	.017** (2.71)	.010† (1.73)	.007 (1.15)
Ethnolinguistic fractionalization			.229† (1.90)	.243* (2.19)	.166 (1.43)	.166 (1.42)	.145 (1.24)	.341* (2.55)	.215† (1.80)	.237* (2.10)
Population more than 90% Muslim			.357*** (3.28)	.285* (2.58)	.388*** (3.30)	.370** (3.18)	.208† (1.93)	.498*** (4.79)	.391*** (3.70)	.334** (3.03)
Fertility rate			.088** (2.88)	.049† (1.66)	.061* (2.06)	.068* (2.28)	.025 (0.77)		.070* (2.13)	.071* (2.14)
Population density			-.071* (2.25)	-.089* (2.69)	-.075* (2.04)	-.080* (2.18)	-.088** (2.67)	-.012 (0.45)	-.067* (2.15)	-.074* (1.94)
Urbanization			-.005* (2.06)	-.002 (0.76)	-.006** (2.73)	-.005* (2.37)	-.003 (1.60)	-.007** (2.86)	-.004† (1.78)	-.002 (0.91)
Trained attendant at birth				-.007*** (3.92)						
DTP3 immunization					-.005*** (3.75)					

	(1)	(2)	(3)	(4)	(5)	(6)	(7)	(8)	(9)	(10)
Measles immunization						−.004* (2.57)				
Mean years of female schooling							−.099*** (3.74)			
Family planning effort								−.004* (2.49)		
Access to improved water source									−.003† (1.78)	
Access to improved sanitation										−.007*** (3.68)
N° cases	105	105	105	103	98	98	105	88	105	102
R-squared	.7017	.7236	.8460	.8607	.8403	.8318	.8645	.8354	.8493	.8446

Universe: 105 developing countries in 1990. *Significance:* †10%; *5%; **1%; ***0.1%. All two-tailed. Unstandardized coefficient above; absolute value of t-statistic (using heteroskedasticity-robust standard errors) in parentheses below. Constant term (not shown) included in each model. *Natural log transformation* applied to infant mortality, GDP per capita, and population density. *Data and variable names* in McGuire (2009), Web Appendix D2. *Statistical output* in McGuire (2009), Web Appendix C1.

TABLE 2.3. *Health Care Spending, Public Health Service Utilization, and Infant Mortality*

Dependent variable →	3-1 Trained attendant at birth	3-2 DTP3 immunization	3-3 Measles immunization	3-4 Infant mortality	3-5 3-4 minus 2 outliers	3-6 Infant mortality	3-7 3-6 minus 2 outliers	3-8 3-5 plus attendant at birth	3-9 3-5 plus DTP3 immunization	3-10 3-5 plus measles immunization
GDP per capita	8.25† (1.82)	10.22* (2.60)	7.07† (1.90)	-.517*** (7.12)	-.538*** (7.81)	-.510*** (6.92)	-.530*** (7.71)	-.481*** (7.63)	-.484*** (7.23)	-.510*** (7.31)
Income inequality	-.249 (1.32)	.108 (0.45)	.159 (0.76)	.010† (1.68)	.013* (2.55)	.010† (1.68)	.012* (2.37)	.010* (2.14)	.014** (2.67)	.014* (2.60)
Ethnolinguistic fractionalization	3.32 (0.55)	-7.08 (1.02)	-9.47 (1.53)	.201† (1.70)	.228† (1.98)	.199 (1.66)	.226† (1.92)	.259* (2.44)	.185† (1.67)	.185 (1.64)
Population more than 90% Muslim	-7.28 (1.46)	3.10 (0.50)	-.384 (0.07)	.347** (3.18)	.400*** (4.13)	.345** (3.19)	.391*** (4.05)	.334*** (3.44)	.433*** (4.17)	.416*** (4.06)
Fertility rate	-5.86** (3.05)	-2.74† (1.69)	-2.18 (1.44)	.083** (2.72)	.078** (2.63)	.090** (2.85)	.087** (2.91)	.042 (1.44)	.058† (1.95)	.064* (2.18)
Population density	-1.58 (1.41)	1.54 (1.04)	.845 (0.63)	-.082** (2.65)	-.058* (2.31)	-.077* (2.44)	-.053* (2.15)	-.069* (2.60)	-.051† (1.80)	-.056* (2.00)
Urbanization	.316* (2.51)	-.201† (1.71)	-.103 (0.96)	-.004† (1.80)	-.003 (1.59)	-.004† (1.94)	-.004† (1.80)	-.001 (0.37)	-.005* (2.19)	-.004† (1.79)
Public health spending as % GDP, World Bank 2002	3.82** (3.19)	3.27* (2.25)	3.74** (3.13)	-.043 (1.21)	-.064* (2.39)			-.039 (1.52)	-.045 (1.63)	-.047 (1.61)

						(1)	(2)			
Public health spending as % GDP, World Bank 2001/02						−.038† (1.85)	−.030 (1.21)			
Trained attendant at birth								−.007*** (4.12)		
DTP3 immunization									−.005*** (3.80)	
Measles immunization										−.004** (2.55)
N° cases	103	98	98	105	103	103	105	101	96	96
R-squared	.6729	.3507	.3591	.8497	.8665	.8634	.8487	.8810	.8606	.8523

Universe: 105 developing countries in 1990. *Significance:* †10%; *5%; **1%; ***0.1%. All two-tailed. Unstandardized coefficient above; absolute value of t-statistic (using heteroskedasticity-robust standard errors) in parentheses below. Constant term (not shown) included in each model. *Natural log transformation applied to infant mortality, GDP per capita, and population density. Data and variable names* in McGuire (2009), Web Appendix D2. *Statistical output* in McGuire (2009), Web Appendix C1.

To what extent did a developing country's socioeconomic circumstances in 1990 affect its infant mortality rate? The substantive magnitude of the association between the socioeconomic variables and infant mortality can be conveyed by estimating how much infant mortality would change if the value of a particular socioeconomic variable were to change by one standard deviation, while the values of all others remained at their means. Such quantities of interest can be estimated with the CLARIFY macro written for the Stata statistical package. The simulations run by this macro suggest that a one standard deviation rise in GDP per capita (from the 1990 sample mean of $3,060 to $6,446) would reduce infant mortality by 21 ± 5 per 1000. A one standard deviation decline in the Gini index (from the sample mean of 44.1 to 34.7) would reduce it by 5 ± 5 per 1000. The analogous figures for the other variables are: ethnolinguistic fractionalization 4 ± 4, fertility 8 ± 4, population density 5 ± 4, and urbanization 1 ± 2. Having a population that is more than 90 percent Muslim is associated with a 23 ± 16 per 1000 higher infant mortality rate, controlling for all of the other variables. This estimate is overstated compared to the other variables, however. The 90 percent Muslim indicator is a dichotomous variable; the other six socioeconomic factors are interval variables. Going from 0 to 1 on whether the country's population is more than 90 percent Muslim would be like going from the lowest to the highest value on an interval variable, rather than from the mean to one standard deviation above the mean.

Results pertaining to the public health hypotheses. Hypothesis PH1 holds that the higher the share of GDP devoted to public health care spending, the greater the utilization of basic health services. Two previous studies have found that more public health care spending is associated with a higher share of births attended by trained personnel, but another such study has found that public health care spending is unassociated with the percentage of children immunized.[45] The present study finds that a greater share of GDP devoted to public health spending is associated both with more widespread trained attendance at birth and with more widespread child immunization (Models 3-1, 3-2, and 3-3 in Table 2.3). Controlling for the seven socioeconomic variables, public health spending as a share of GDP was associated significantly with health service utilization at the .01 level in Models 3-1 and 3-3 and at the .05 level in Model 3-2.

To estimate the substantive effect of public health spending on health service utilization, the CLARIFY macro was applied to Models 3-1, 3-2, and 3-3. The results showed that a one standard deviation rise in public health spending as a share of GDP (from the 1990 mean of 2.0 percent to a level of 3.3 percent) would raise the share of births attended by trained personnel by 5 ± 3 percent, the share of children given three doses of the antigen for

---

[45] Birth attendance by trained personnel: Gupta, Verhoeven, and Tiongson 2003: 692; Kruk et al. 2007. Share of children immunized: Gauri and Khaleghian 2002: 2119.

diphtheria, pertussis, and tetanus by 4 ± 4 percent, and the share of children immunized against measles by 5 ± 3 percent. The checks for robustness described in Section 2.2 did not change the results appreciably. Accordingly, a higher share of GDP devoted to public health care spending was associated significantly and robustly with greater, although not much greater, utilization of basic services.

Hypothesis PH2 holds that the greater the utilization of basic social services, the lower the infant mortality rate. Previous studies have found that greater provision and use of maternal and infant health care services, including oral rehydration, infant immunization, the promotion of breastfeeding, and nutritional intervention, is associated at the household level with lower infant and child mortality.[46] Other studies have found that educational attainment, particularly of women, is associated with lower infant and child mortality, and that more widespread access to an improved water source and, especially, to improved sanitation are associated with lower childhood mortality.[47]

The present study confirms that trained attendance at birth, child immunization, female schooling, family planning effort, and access to improved water and sanitation are each associated significantly with lower infant mortality (Table 2.2, Models 2–4 to 2–10). Applying the CLARIFY macro, one standard deviation rises in trained attendance at birth, female schooling, and access to improved sanitation are associated respectively with a 10 ± 5 per 1000 decline of infant mortality. A one standard deviation rise in DTP3 immunization is associated with a 6 ± 4 per 1000 decline of infant mortality, and one standard deviation rises in measles immunization, family planning, and access to safe water are each associated with a 4 ± 4 per 1000 decline of infant mortality. The findings for trained attendance at birth, DTP3 immunization, female schooling, and improved sanitation withstood 18 checks for robustness.[48] The findings for measles immunization also held up well, whereas those for family planning and safe water were a bit less robust.[49] Family planning, however, was strongly associated with lower fertility (Table 2.4, Model 4–8), and lower fertility was associated in turn with lower infant mortality (Table 2.2, Model 2–3).

Hypothesis PH3 holds that the higher the share of GDP spent on public health care, the lower the infant mortality rate. As was noted in Section 2.1, most studies have found a surprisingly weak cross-national association

---

[46] Bryce et al. 2003; Gauri 2002; Jones et al. 2003.

[47] On female educational attainment see Caldwell 1986: 187–191; Mehrotra 1997a; Murthi, Guio, and Drèze 1995; and Schultz 1993: 68–78. On water and sanitation see Esrey 1996; Wood and Carvalho 1988: 90–92; and UNDP 2006: 43–44.

[48] McGuire 2009 (Web Appendix C1).

[49] In Model 2–8, the coefficient on family planning effort was not robust to the use of GDP per capita figures from Maddison (2001) rather than the UNDP (1993). In Model 2–9, the coefficient on access to an improved water source was not robust to the exclusion of outliers.

between various indicators of health care spending and the infant mortality rate. The results of the present analysis tend to confirm such findings (Table 2.3, Models 3–4 to 3–10). The coefficient on public health care spending as a share of GDP attained the .05 level of statistical significance only in Model 3–5, and this result was not robust.[50] To estimate the substantive (as opposed to statistical) significance of raising the share of GDP devoted to public health care spending, the CLARIFY macro was used. Applied to Model 3–5, the CLARIFY macro estimated that a one standard deviation rise in the share of GDP devoted to public health care spending (from the 1990 mean of 2.0 percent to a level of 3.3 percent) would reduce the infant mortality rate by about 4 ± 2 per 1000 – by about the same amount as a one standard deviation rise in measles immunization, family planning, or access to safe water, but by a far smaller amount than a one standard deviation rise in trained attendance at birth, female schooling, or access to improved sanitation. In those cases the estimated effect was 10 ± 5 per 1000; for DTP3 immunization it was 6 ± 4 per 1000.

Surprisingly, the statistical associations between public health care spending and basic health service utilization, and between basic health service utilization and infant survival, were stronger and more robust than the association between public health care spending and infant survival. The low cost and high efficacy of basic health services like trained attendance at birth and child immunization could explain this discrepancy. Even if the vast majority of public health care spending had not the slightest effect on infant mortality, a small share of such spending might improve inexpensive maternal and infant health services that do have the effect of reducing the infant mortality rate. If the (small) absolute amount of public health care spending devoted to improving maternal and infant health services rose in tandem with the share of GDP devoted to all public health care spending, higher spending would be associated indirectly with lower infant mortality.

Does the provision of trained attendance at birth and child immunization really mediate the association between public health care spending as a share of GDP and infant survival? This question is addressed in Models 3–8, 3–9, and 3–10 in Table 2.3. Using Model 3–5 as a baseline, these models each add a different measure of basic health service utilization as a predictor variable. This measure is either the percentage of births attended by trained personnel (Model 3–8), the percentage of children immunized against diphtheria, tetanus, and pertussis (Model 3–9); or the percentage of children immunized against measles (Model 3–10). Each of these additional basic health service utilization variables is hypothesized to intervene between

---

[50] The precision of the coefficient on public health care spending as a share of GDP fell below the conventionally accepted .05 level of statistical significance when the variable was subjected to a natural log transformation, when the statistical technique was changed from ordinary least squares to median regression, and when female illiteracy was present as a control variable (McGuire 2009, Web Appendix C1).

spending and survival. If these basic health service utilization variables really do mediate the association between spending and survival, the addition of any one of them to a model that already includes the antecedent public health care spending variable should cause the coefficient on the public health care spending variable to drop in magnitude. It does, and by a significant amount (Table 2.3). Hence, public health care spending seems to affect the infant mortality rate in significant measure by increasing trained attendance at birth and child immunization.

The data analyzed in the present study suggest that public health care spending is associated somewhat more closely with infant mortality than the Filmer and Pritchett (1999) study implied. Nonetheless, the findings of both studies strongly suggest that infant mortality rates depend mostly on factors other than the share of GDP devoted to public health care spending, including (1) the allocation of public health spending across alternative health services, some of which do more than others to reduce infant mortality; (2) the degree to which money devoted to potentially mortality-reducing health services is spent efficiently, rather than being drained off by corruption or administrative bottlenecks; and (3) the degree to which public spending on infant mortality-reducing health services replaces, rather than augments, private spending – in which case households will retain more money, but health service utilization will stay the same.[51]

Results pertaining to the political science hypotheses. The political science hypotheses relate democracy to public health care spending, to social service utilization, and to infant mortality. Previous studies have found that democracy is associated with higher public health care spending (PS1).[52] Studies have found that democracy is also associated with greater utilization of basic social services (PS2), although the evidence here is weaker for child immunization than for literacy, school enrollment, access to safe water, access to health care, or the share of births attended by trained personnel.[53] Studies exploring the association between democracy and infant mortality (PS3) have also come to mixed conclusions, but most cross-national studies have confirmed the association.[54]

In the present analysis, no evidence is found to support the claim that democracy is associated with higher public health care spending (PS1), but considerable evidence is found to suggest that democracy is associated with the more widespread utilization of a range of basic social services (PS2), and that long-term democratic experience is associated with lower infant mortality (PS3).

---

[51] Filmer, Hammer, and Pritchett 2000; Filmer, Hammer, and Pritchett 2002.
[52] Ghobarah, Huth, and Russett 2004: 81; Kaufman and Segura-Ubiergo 2001: 579, 582; Nooruddin and Simmons 2004; Przeworski et al. 2000: 237.
[53] Gauri and Khalegian 2002: 2124–2125; Lake and Baum 2001.
[54] Gerring, Thacker, and Alfaro 2005; Lake and Baum 2001; McGuire 2005; Przeworski et al. 2000; and Zweifel and Navia 2000 find a positive association between democracy and infant or under-5 survival; Ross 2006 and Shandra et al. 2004 find no association between democracy and infant survival.

The results in the present analysis for long-term democratic experience and short-term democratic practice coincide fairly closely, although they are not identical (Tables 2.4 and 2.5). That is to be expected from two variables whose correlation across the 105 societies in 1990 is 0.84. Still, the two variables measure different phenomena. As of 1990, the Dominican Republic, Ecuador, El Salvador, Thailand, and Venezuela earned much higher scores on short-term democratic practice (1980–1990) than on long-term democratic experience (1900–1990), whereas Chile, Cuba, Guyana, Myanmar, and Syria earned much higher scores on long-term democratic experience than on short-term democratic practice. Controlling for the baseline variables, neither democracy indicator was associated with higher public health care spending (Table 2.4, Model 4–1 and Table 2.5, Model 5–1). Among the social services, neither democracy indicator was associated with child immunization or with access to improved sanitation (not shown), but both democracy indicators were associated strongly and robustly with more access to improved water, greater family planning effort, and lower fertility (Models 6 to 9). Long-term democratic experience had a stronger association than short-term democratic practice with the share of births attended by trained personnel and with mean years of female schooling (Models 2 to 5). Short-term democratic practice had the stronger association with family planning (Model 6). Long-term democratic experience, but not short-term democratic practice, was associated with lower infant mortality (Model 10).

CLARIFY illustrates the size and precision of the statistical effects of the democracy variables on social service utilization, fertility, and infant mortality. Applying the macro, a one standard deviation rise in long-term democratic experience (from the mean of −3.08, near the level in Somalia, to +2.21, near the level in Lebanon) was associated with about 3 ± 2 percent more births attended by trained personnel (Model 4–3); 0.4 ± 0.1 more years of female education (Model 4–5); 6 ± 3 points more family planning effort (Model 4–6);[55] 7 ± 2 percent more of the population with access to an improved water source (Model 4–9); 0.4 ± 0.1 lower fertility (Model 4–7); and 5 ± 2 per 1000 lower infant mortality (Model 4–10). Short-term democratic practice had no statistical association with trained attendance at birth (Models 5–2 and 5–3), but a one standard deviation rise in short-term democratic practice (from the mean of -3.06, near the level in Chile, to +3.06, near the level in Argentina) was associated with 0.3 ± 0.1 more mean years of female schooling (Model 5–5); 8 ± 2 points greater family planning effort (Model 5–6); 0.4 ± 0.1 percent lower fertility (Model 5–7); and 5 ± 2 percent more of the population with access to an improved water source (Model 5–9).

Democracy is hypothesized to affect social policies not only through electoral incentives, but also through freedom of speech and information, through

---

[55] This six-point rise in family planning effort would take a country from the 1989 mean of 54 (approximately the level in Lesotho) to about 60 (approximately the level in the Philippines).

TABLE 2.4. *Long-Term Democratic Experience, Spending, Services, and Mortality*

Dependent variable →	4-1 Public health spending as % GDP	4-2 Trained attendant at birth	4-3 4-2 minus 2 outliers	4-4 Mean years of female schooling	4-5 4-4 minus fertility	4-6 Family planning effort	4-7 Total fertility rate	4-8 Total fertility rate	4-9 Access to an improved water source	4-10 Infant mortality rate
GDP per capita	-.099 (0.43)	7.71† (1.82)	6.68 (1.57)	.685*** (3.11)	1.042*** (3.69)	4.63 (0.81)	-.634* (2.27)	-.582* (2.53)	4.61 (1.45)	-.487*** (6.70)
Income inequality	-.003 (0.16)	-.276 (1.31)	-.233 (1.12)	.000 (0.02)	-.017 (1.10)	.044 (0.14)	.032** (3.02)	.022 (1.62)	-.091 (0.53)	.011† (1.95)
Ethnolinguistic fractionalization		0.24 (0.04)	2.42 (0.39)	-.958† (1.89)	-1.59** (3.07)	-7.06 (0.84)	1.13*** (3.35)	.855* (2.36)	-3.26 (0.60)	.279* (2.28)
Population more than 90% Muslim		-7.44 (1.36)	-6.60 (1.19)	-1.45*** (4.15)	-2.13*** (6.15)	-9.98 (1.16)	1.20*** (3.98)	1.08*** (4.02)	11.25† (1.74)	.327** (2.85)
Fertility rate		-4.88* (2.41)	-5.65** (2.78)	-.563*** (5.26)					-4.21** (2.79)	.056† (1.77)
Population density	-.188 (1.63)	-2.49† (1.90)	-2.60† (1.98)	-.196* (2.14)	-.105 (0.97)	6.64** (3.22)	-.161* (2.06)	-.048 (0.44)	1.62 (1.61)	-.064 (1.91)
Urbanization	.022* (2.33)	.438*** (3.50)	.419*** (3.47)	.014† (1.72)	.023* (2.29)	-.157 (0.79)	-.016† (1.73)	-.020** (2.67)	.298* (2.58)	-.006* (2.50)
Share of population over 65 years of age	.010 (0.10)									

(continued)

TABLE 2.4. (*continued*)

	4-1	4-2	4-3	4-4	4-5	4-6	4-7	4-8	4-9	4-10
Dependent variable →	Public health spending as % GDP	Trained attendant at birth	4-2 *minus 2 outliers*	Mean years of female schooling	4-4 *minus fertility*	Family planning effort	Total fertility rate	Total fertility rate	Access to an improved water source	Infant mortality rate
Family planning effort								-.027*** (4.87)		
Long-term democratic experience	.040 (1.36)	.463 (1.29)	.629* (2.01)	.032 (1.36)	.076** (2.87)	1.22* (2.10)	-.078*** (4.04)		1.00** (2.99)	-.017* (2.30)
N° cases	100	99	97	100	100	86	100	88	100	100
R-squared	.1742	.6492	.6623	.7317	.6739	.3368	.6811	.7296	.7176	.8360

Universe: 105 developing countries in 1990. *Significance:* †10%; *5%; **1%; ***0.1%. All two-tailed. Unstandardized coefficient above; absolute value of t-statistic (using heteroskedasticity-robust standard errors) in parentheses below. Constant term (not shown) included in each model. *Natural log transformation applied to* infant mortality, GDP per capita, and population density. *Data and variable names in* McGuire (2009), Web Appendix D2. *Statistical output in* McGuire (2009), Web Appendix C1.

TABLE 2.5. *Short-Term Democratic Practice, Spending, Services, and Mortality*

Dependent variable →	5-1 Public health spending as % GDP	5-2 Trained attendant at birth	5-3 5-2 minus 2 outliers	5-4 Mean years of female schooling	5-5 5-4 minus fertility	5-6 Family planning effort	5-7 Total fertility rate	5-8 Total fertility rate	5-9 Access to an improved water source	5-10 Infant mortality rate
GDP per capita	-.045 (0.17)	9.49* (2.17)	9.23* (2.34)	.700** (3.03)	1.11*** (3.83)	4.90 (0.97)	-.672** (2.62)	-.582* (2.53)	6.20* (2.01)	-.505*** (6.39)
Income inequality	-.002 (0.13)	-.179 (0.80)	-.185 (0.86)	-.002 (0.14)	-.020 (1.15)	-.102 (0.32)	.037*** (3.28)	.022 (1.62)	-.140 (0.80)	.011* (1.75)
Ethnolinguistic fractionalization		2.08 (0.31)	3.82 (0.57)	-.843 (1.56)	-1.48** (2.63)	-9.08 (1.16)	1.05** (2.93)	.855* (2.36)	-2.92 (0.55)	-.239† (1.79)
Population more than 90% Muslim		-8.88 (1.65)	-9.17 (1.77)	-1.50*** (4.11)	-2.23*** (6.24)	-10.4 (1.27)	1.21*** (4.04)	1.08*** (4.02)	10.83 (1.62)	.349** (2.97)
Fertility rate		-6.21** (2.92)	-6.03** (3.25)	-.606*** (5.38)					-4.22** (3.07)	.074* (2.20)
Population density	-.173 (1.48)	-2.49† (1.92)	-2.38† (1.83)	-.185† (1.94)	-.085 (0.75)	6.35** (3.10)	-.165* (2.06)	-.048 (0.44)	1.51 (1.50)	-.067† (1.94)
Urbanization	.019† (1.78)	.361* (2.59)	.350** (2.67)	.014 (1.50)	.022* (2.01)	-.246 (1.28)	-.013 (1.73)	-.020** (2.67)	.211† (1.93)	-.005† (1.90)
Share of population over 65 years of age	.037 (0.34)									

(continued)

TABLE 2.5. (continued)

Dependent variable →	5-1 Public health spending as % GDP	5-2 Trained attendant at birth	5-3 5-2 minus 2 outliers	5-4 Mean years of female schooling	5-5 5-4 minus fertility	5-6 Family planning effort	5-7 Total fertility rate	5-8 Total fertility rate	5-9 Access to an improved water source	5-10 Infant mortality rate
Family planning effort								-.027*** (4.87)		
Short-term democratic practice	.022 (0.84)	-.297 (0.81)	-.182 (0.51)	.007 (0.33)	.049* (2.06)	1.28** (3.16)	-.069*** (4.20)		.810** (3.20)	-.005 (0.74)
N° cases	98	97	95	98	98	84	98	88	98	98
R-squared	.1536	.6394	.6656	.7274	.6606	.3860	.6792	.7296	.7104	.8270

Universe: 105 developing countries in 1990. Significance: †10%; *5%; **1%; ***0.1%. All two-tailed. Unstandardized coefficient above; absolute value of t-statistic (using heteroskedasticity-robust standard errors) in parentheses below. Constant term (not shown) included in each model. Natural log transformation applied to infant mortality, GDP per capita, and population density. Data and variable names in McGuire (2009), Web Appendix D2. Statistical output in McGuire (2009), Web Appendix C1.

the freedom to assemble and organize, and through the long-term evolution of expectations about the state's obligations to citizens. The operation of the latter mechanism, in addition to the others, is consistent with the finding that long-term democratic experience is associated more closely than short-term democratic practice with mortality-reducing social policies. The long-term evolution of expectations about the state's obligations to citizens also helps to explain how a history of democracy may influence the design and implementation of mortality-reducing social policies even if the regime turns authoritarian, as in Pinochet's Chile (Chapter 4).

In addition to the findings about long-term democratic experience as compared to short-term democratic practice, those for water and sanitation deserve attention. Both democracy indicators were associated with access to improved water, but neither was associated with access to improved sanitation. Could measurement error account for this finding? The water and sanitation indicators embody substantial measurement error: "improved" is not the same thing as "safe" or "adequate," and diverse types of access qualify as "improved."[56] It is unclear, however, that measurement error is systematically worse for sanitation than for water, which would have to be true if measurement error were to account for the finding in question. Democracy is certainly associated more closely with access to improved water than with access to improved sanitation, which is consistent with the hypothesis that the sanitation variable had more measurement error; but infant mortality is associated more closely with access to improved sanitation than with access to improved water, which is consistent with the hypothesis that the water variable had greater measurement error. In short, measurement error does not seem to be systematically worse for sanitation than for water. Hence, it does not take us far toward explaining why democracy is related more strongly to water than to sanitation access.

The tendency of democracies to respond to revealed demand provides a more compelling explanation for why democracy is associated more closely with water than with sanitation access, even though sanitation is more closely associated with lower infant mortality. "Participatory research exercises" reviewed by the United Nations Development Programme show that most people, when asked, place a higher priority on access to an improved water source than on access to improved sanitation. Electoral incentives may also be part of the explanation. The planning frame for sanitation provision in most countries is 10–15 years, compared to 2–3 years for water provision. Hence, a government is more likely win votes if it improves water than if it improves

---

[56] Many people, for example, draw water from standpipes in the rainy season but from streams in the dry season, or from wells on some days but from vendors on others (UNDP 2006: 80–82). Likewise, "improved" sanitation includes everything from pit latrines to flush toilets connected to modern sewerage and sewage treatment systems, even though the health benefits of flush toilets connected to modern sewerage systems are much greater than those of pit latrines (UNDP 2006: 113–115).

sanitation, the electoral benefits of which are likely to accrue to a different government in the distant future. In short, if voters value water more than sanitation, and if incumbents believe that the electoral rewards for improving water are greater than the electoral rewards for improving sanitation, then democracy is likely to be more closely associated with water than with sanitation access.[57] The tendency of democracies to respond to revealed demand could also help to explain why long-term democratic experience was associated with a higher share of births attended by trained personnel, but not with greater child immunization coverage.[58] People tend to demand curative services more intensely than preventive services, and trained attendance at birth has, in the eyes of expectant parents, at least a potential curative component, whereas immunization is purely preventive, and there is always a temptation to ride free on others' immunization.

Another interesting set of findings involves family planning and fertility. Long-term democratic experience, and especially short-term democratic practice, was associated with greater family planning effort, which was associated in turn with lower fertility. Also, long-term democratic experience and short-term democratic practice were each associated with lower fertility (Table 2.4, Models 4–6 to 4–8; Table 2.5, Models 5–6 to 5–8).[59] This finding might be viewed as surprising, because democracy might be expected to limit (rather than augment) the capacity of governments to enact unpopular fertility reduction policies, such as the one-child policy implemented in China in 1979. In India, however, democracy in 1975 failed to prevent Prime Minister Indira Gandhi from enacting what she herself described as "drastic" population control policies, opposition to which contributed to the electoral defeat of her Congress Party in 1977.[60] By other mechanisms, however, democracy might be expected to reduce fertility. Amartya Sen has underscored the critical role of discussion and debate – which democracy facilitates – in making it easier for parents to choose to limit family size.[61] Freedom of organization, another aspect of democracy, could also make it easier for women's groups and others to press for more effective family planning services.

Fertility is also important in that its exclusion as a control variable strengthens the statistical association between long-term democratic experience and the provision of basic social services. When fertility is excluded as a regressor, the t-score of the coefficient on long-term democratic experience in Model 4–2 (predicting trained attendance at birth) rises from 1.29 to 2.34 (p ≤ .05). In Model 4–4 (predicting female schooling) it rises from 1.36 to 2.87

---

[57] The UNDP (2006: 112, 118–120) suggests additional reasons why governments usually do more to raise access to an improved water source than to improved sanitation.

[58] See also Gauri and Khaleghian 2002: 2125–2126.

[59] Przeworski et al. (2000: 244–256) find that democracy is associated with lower fertility. Roberts (2006) produces a similar result and provides evidence that national family planning effort mediates between democracy and fertility.

[60] Klieman 1981: 254–256.

[61] Sen 1999a: 153.

(p ≤ .o1), and in Model 4–9 (predicting access to safe water) it rises from 2.99 to 4.30 (p ≤ .oo1). Excluding fertility as a regressor also raises the t-score of the coefficient on long-term democratic experience in a model predicting DTP3 immunization from 0.98 to 1.76 (p ≤ .10), and in a model predicting access to improved sanitation from 0.46 to 1.21(p ≥ .10).[62] Like those on the coefficients of long-term democratic experience, the t-scores on the coefficients of short-term democratic practice also rise in analogous models when fertility is dropped as a regressor, but only female schooling becomes statistically significant at the .05 level (Model 5–5).

Given these findings, which show a stronger association between democracy and social service utilization in the absence of a control for fertility, an important question is whether, in models designed to assess the association between democracy and service utilization, fertility should be included or excluded as a regressor. The main argument in favor of inclusion is that high fertility rates could raise the demand for education, health, and water and sanitation services. If so, excluding fertility as a regressor could bias estimates of the statistical impact of other variables, including democracy, on service utilization. If democracy is associated with fertility, however, as Models 4–7 and 5–7 suggest, controlling for fertility will reduce democracy's apparent explanatory power, because democracy is in most obvious respects distal to fertility in the causal chain culminating in basic service utilization. Hence, it is advisable to take seriously the results of the models in which fertility is alternatively excluded and included as a control variable. In the former models long-term democratic experience is a powerful predictor of social service utilization. In the latter models the association is somewhat weaker and less robust, but still discernible. More research is needed to unravel the causal mechanisms that link democracy to fertility rates and to conceptualize and quantify the role of fertility in shaping mortality outcomes. Even a conservative interpretation of the findings suggests, however, that long-term democratic experience, although not associated with greater health care spending, is indeed associated with greater social service utilization and with lower infant mortality.

2.4. Implications

As the wealthier is healthier hypothesis would predict, infant mortality in statistical simulations fell much more when GDP per capita rose by one standard deviation than when either trained attendance at birth or female schooling rose by one standard deviation. Applying the CLARIFY macro to Model 2–3 (Table 2.2), a one standard deviation rise in GDP per capita (from the 1990 sample mean of $3,060 to $6,446) would reduce infant mortality by 21 ± 5 per 1000, and a one standard deviation decline in the Gini index (from the

---

[62] These results are not shown in the published tables, but are available in McGuire 2009 (Appendix C1).

sample mean of 44.2 to 35.2) would reduce infant mortality by 5 ± 5 per 1000. Applying the macro to Model 2–4, a one standard deviation rise in trained attendance at birth (from the sample mean of 59.4 percent to 85.3 percent) would reduce infant mortality only by about 10 ± 5 per 1000. Applying the macro to Model 2–7, a one standard deviation rise in mean years of female schooling (from a sample mean of 3.65 to 5.86 years) would likewise reduce infant mortality only by about 10 ± 5 per 1000.

The statistical impact on infant mortality of a one standard deviation rise in the independent variable is thus more than twice as great for GDP per capita as for trained attendance at birth or for female schooling. This result might seem at first to vindicate the narrow version of the wealthier is healthier claim. What such a comparison neglects, however, is an assessment of the feasibility, as opposed to the desirability (from the standpoint of reducing infant mortality), of achieving a one standard deviation rise in each of these independent variables. To gain insight into the feasibility issue, let us use the CLARIFY macro to estimate how much of a rise in each of these independent variables (and how much of a decline of income inequality) would have to occur to reduce infant mortality from 54 to 49 per 1000.[63] We can then calculate what proportion of countries that started out in 1985 around the means of each independent variable managed over the next ten years to improve the requisite amount. Table 2.6 provides these estimates. To achieve this 5 per 1000 reduction of infant mortality, holding other variables at their means, GDP per capita would have to rise $391, the Gini index would have to fall 9.4 points, the share of births attended by trained personnel would have to rise from 59.4 to 72.7 percent, or mean years of female schooling would have to rise 0.94 years.[64]

The requisite rises in trained attendance at birth, as well as in female schooling, seem well within the reach of many developing countries. In the average developing country in 1990, 59.4 percent of births were attended by trained personnel (Table 2.6). Providing trained attendance at an additional 13.3 percent of births would, all else equal, reduce infant mortality by 5 per 1000, assuming that the coefficients in Model 2–4 reflect reality. How feasible is such an increase in trained birth attendance, based on the actual experience of developing countries? Data on trained attendance at birth are sparse before 1980, and are available in most countries only for a scattering of years thereafter. To ameliorate the scattering problem, let us take the five-year mean of the estimates in each country. The first such period for which this mean can be calculated for a large number of developing countries (75) is 1983–1987 (henceforth, "1985"). Among these 75 countries, 9 provided trained

---

[63] 54 per 1000 is an "average" rate of infant mortality for the 105 cases in the study. Specifically, it is the exponential of the mean of the natural logs of the infant mortality rates of the 105 developing societies included in the universe of cases.

[64] The estimates for GDP per capita and the Gini index were derived by applying CLARIFY to Model 2–3. The estimates for trained attendance at birth and mean years of schooling were derived by applying the macro respectively to Models 2–4 and 2–7.

TABLE 2.6. *Changes Required to Reduce Infant Mortality from 54 to 49 per 1000*

Variable of interest	Country closest to actual mean	Actual mean in 1990	Required value	Required change	Uncertainty: Change from actual mean to required value would reduce IMR by 5 per 1000 ± ...	Share of countries achieving the required change, 1985–1995
Infant mortality, natural log	Zimbabwe	(54/1000)	(49/1000)	(−5/1000)	(Dependent variable)	
GDP per capita at PPP, natural log	Ecuador	$1,975	$2,366	+$391	±2.2 per 1000	3 of 12 with $1,500–$2,500 in 1985
Gini index of income inequality	Hong Kong	44.1	34.7	−9.4	±5.8 per 1000	6 of 44 developing countries from late 1950s to late 1980s
Mean years of female schooling	Nicaragua	3.65	4.59	+0.94	±3.0 per 1000	3 of 8 with 3.35 to 3.95 years in 1985
Trained attendant at birth	Peru	59.4%	72.7%	+13.3%	±2.9 per 1000	7 of 9 with 55 to 65 percent in 1985

Output and data in McGuire (2009), Web Appendices C1, D2, D3, D4, D5, and D6. For clarity, the 1990 values of infant mortality and GDP per capita are the exponentials of the means of the natural logs of each variable. Estimations carried out with the CLARIFY macro (Tomz, Wittenberg, and King 2001) for Stata statistical package. An infant mortality rate of 54 per 1000 is the exponential of the mean of the natural logs of the infant mortality rates of the 105 developing countries in the analysis. The *required value* is, in a country with an infant mortality rate of 54 per 1000, the value that the variable of interest would have to attain to reduce the rate to 49 infant deaths per 1000 (± x deaths per 1000), holding all other variables in the model at their means. *GDP per capita, 1985 and 1995:* Heston, Summers, and Aten 2002 (variable RGDPCH). *Gini index:* Deininger and Squire 1998. *Mean years of female schooling, 1985 and 1995:* Barro and Lee 2000 (variables tyrf1585, tyrf1595). *Births attended by trained personnel, 1985 and 1995:* World Bank 2001/02.

attendance at between 55 and 65 percent of births (i.e., near the 1990 average of 59.4 percent). By 1993–1997 (henceforth, "1995"), 7 of those 9 countries had attained or surpassed the 13.3 percent rise in trained attendance at birth estimated to be required, all else equal, to achieve a 5 per 1000 decline in infant mortality.[65]

A similar rough estimate of feasibility can be produced for female schooling. The average developing country in 1990 provided 3.65 years of female schooling (Table 2.6). Providing another 0.94 years, all else equal, would reduce infant mortality by 5 per 1000, assuming the accuracy of the coefficients in Model 2–7. How feasible is such an increase? In 1985, 8 developing countries provided 3.35 to 3.95 mean years of female schooling. By 1995, 3 of those 8 countries had achieved rises of at least 0.94 years of female schooling.[66] From 1985 to 1995, then, almost all of the countries that started out near the average on trained attendance at birth, and nearly half of the countries that started out near the average on female schooling, achieved large enough rises on these indicators to reduce infant mortality, all else equal, by about 5 per 1000 (Table 2.6).

Achieving a comparably efficacious rise in GDP per capita, or decline of income inequality, turned out to be considerably less feasible. In 1990, the average developing country had a GDP per capita of $1,975. Raising GDP per capita by another $391, all else equal, would reduce infant mortality by 5 per 1000, assuming that the coefficients in Model 2–3 reflect reality. How feasible is such an increase? In 1985, 12 developing countries had GDPs per capita in the range between $1,500 and $2,500. By 1995, only 3 of these 12 countries had achieved a GDP per capita rise of more than $391.[67] An even smaller share of countries achieved the requisite decline of income inequality. In 1990, the average developing country had a Gini index of 44.2. Reducing the Gini index by 9.4 points, all else equal, would lower infant mortality by 5 per 1000, assuming that the coefficients in Model 2–3 reflect reality. How feasible is such a reduction? Of 44 developing countries with two or more "good" quality surveys in the Deininger and Squire (1998) database, only 6

[65] The nine countries in which 55–65 percent of deliveries were attended by trained health staff in 1983–1987 were Colombia, El Salvador, Iraq, Myanmar, Oman, Peru, Syria, Tunisia, and Zimbabwe. By 1993–1997, all of the nine except Peru and Zimbabwe had raised the share of births attended by trained personnel by more than 13.3 percent. Botswana, Ethiopia, and Malawi had trained attendance at birth of 55–65 percent of deliveries in 1983–1987, but estimates for circa 1995 were either missing or dubious (in Ethiopia the figure was 58 percent in 1984 but 3 percent in 1993). Data in McGuire 2009 (Web Appendix D3).

[66] The eight countries in which females 15 years of age or older had between 3.35 and 3.95 mean years of schooling in 1985 were Bahrain, Botswana, Brazil, Congo (Brazzaville), Dominican Republic, El Salvador, Indonesia, and Nicaragua. Data in McGuire 2009 (Web Appendix D4).

[67] The twelve countries in which GDP per capita was between $1,500 and $2,500 in 1985 were Angola, Central African Republic, Comoros, Congo (Brazzaville), Cote d'Ivoire, Equatorial Guinea, Guinea, Guyana, Honduras, Indonesia, Mauritania, and Sri Lanka. By 1995, only Guyana, Indonesia, and Sri Lanka had raised their GDPs per capita by $391 or more. Data in McGuire 2009 (Web Appendix D5).

achieved a decline of the Gini index amounting to 9.4 points or more over any span of time from the late 1950s to the late 1980s.[68] These comparisons are only suggestive, but what they suggest is that many developing countries may find it easier to reduce infant mortality by increasing female schooling or trained attendance at birth than by raising GDP per capita or lowering income inequality.

The analysis confirms the utility of calculating "quantities of interest" in assessing the feasibility of alternative ways to reduce infant mortality.[69] To produce an infant mortality decline of 5 per 1000, a country with a rate of 54 per 1000 could, all else equal, either (a) raise GDP per capita by 20 percent, (b) reduce the Gini index by 9.4, (c) give females an extra year of schooling, or (d) give another 13 percent of expectant mothers trained attendance at birth. Only 3 of 12 developing countries that began near the mean of GDP per capita in 1985 managed to achieve the requisite 20 percent rise, and only 6 of 44 developing countries have ever reduced income inequality enough over any recorded span of time to reduce infant mortality by 5 per 1000. By contrast, 3 of 8 developing countries that began near the mean of female schooling, and 7 of 9 such countries that began near the mean of trained attendance at birth, raised the utilization of these services enough over the next ten years to generate a 5 per 1000 infant mortality drop. Achieving fast economic growth or a major reduction of income inequality, however desirable, may be less feasible than improving female schooling or trained attendance at birth.

In the analyses reported in this chapter, democracy was not associated with the share of GDP devoted to public health care spending. Democracy was, however, associated with greater utilization of mortality-reducing social services, even after controlling for economic, demographic, geographic, and cultural factors. Long-term democratic experience was associated more closely than short-term democratic practice with the utilization of mortality-reducing social services, and unlike the short-term indicator, long-term democratic experience was also associated with lower infant mortality. Still, the magnitude and robustness of the associations between democracy and social service utilization, and between democracy and infant mortality, are not overwhelming. That should not be surprising. Democracy does not lead inevitably to the effective provision of social services to people who run a high risk of early death. Democracy creates opportunities; leaders and citizens have to take advantage of them.[70] Only by recognizing that democratic processes

---

[68] The six countries in which the Gini index fell by 9.4 or more points at any time from the late 1950s to the late 1980s are Bahamas, Egypt, Honduras, Panama, Sri Lanka, and Turkey. Guyana and Jamaica also achieved nominal Gini index declines of more than 9.4 points, but in each case the earlier survey was based on income whereas the later survey was based on expenditure. Income-based Gini indices average 6.6 points higher than comparable expenditure-based Gini indices (Deininger and Squire 1996: 581–582). Data in McGuire 2009 (Web Appendix D6).

[69] King, Tomz, and Wittenberg 2000.

[70] Sen 1999a: 147–148, 157–158.

may not provide all of the benefits expected of them, and by identifying the critical points at which the breakdowns occur, is it possible to find ways to improve them. The case studies of Latin American and East Asian societies to which we now turn reveal a range of circumstances in which democracy has, or alternatively has not, contributed in various ways to the design and implementation of major primary health care programs.

3

Costa Rica: A Healthy Democracy

The extension of basic health services to the poor in Costa Rica from 1960 to 2005 made a decisive contribution to the rapid decline of mortality. When governments in the 1970s introduced community-based health care and nutrition programs in impoverished rural and urban areas, mortality rates plummeted. After governments in the mid-1990s made primary care by Comprehensive Basic Health Care Teams (EBAIS) the gateway to the entire health system, mortality decline accelerated after 15 years of slow progress. The public provision of basic health services was not the only reason for the rapid decline of mortality in Costa Rica; other government social policies, particularly family planning programs and the provision of safe water and adequate sanitation, also contributed. In few other nations, however, has the contribution of basic health service provision to the rapid decline of mortality been as conspicuous as in Costa Rica.

This chapter reviews the politics and policies that led to rapid infant mortality decline in late twentieth-century Costa Rica. It reconstructs the tempo of infant mortality decline within Costa Rica over time and compares infant mortality levels and changes in Costa Rica to those in other countries. It finds that these infant mortality levels and changes were associated less closely with GDP per capita, income inequality, and income poverty than with education, family planning, safe water, sanitation, nutrition, and primary health care policies. It also finds that democracy encouraged these mortality-reducing social policies. Costa Rica underscores the limits of the wealthier is healthier conjecture; highlights the importance of publicly provided primary health care for rapid infant mortality decline; and shows that political democracy can shape public policy conducive to rapid infant mortality decline in a variety of ways, not just through short-term electoral incentives.

3.1. Costa Rica: Mortality

Costa Rica in 2005 had an infant mortality rate of 9.8 per 1000, third highest among the eight societies compared in this book, but 53rd lowest among 190 countries for which data are available. Its life expectancy at birth, 78.5 years, was highest among the eight cases, 31st highest among the 187 countries for which data are available, and almost a year higher than in the United States. From 1960 to 2005 Costa Rica ranked only fifth among the eight societies on percent decline of infant mortality, and only third on percent rise of life expectancy. Among all countries for which data are available, however, Costa Rica ranked 25th of 145 on percent decline of infant mortality and 12th of 177 on percent rise of life expectancy.[1] These post-1960 achievements at reducing the risk of early death built on progress made in the preceding 60 years. From 1900 to 1960 life expectancy at birth rose from 32 to 62 years, the third greatest percent rise among the twelve Latin American countries for which data are available. In the same period, infant mortality fell from 208 to 78 per 1000, the fourth greatest percent decline among the eight Latin American countries for which data are available.[2]

Costa Rica's infant mortality rate fell especially rapidly during the 1970s. From 1973, when the Rural Health Plan was introduced, to 1980, when a recession reduced incomes and forced cuts in the primary health care budget, infant mortality fell from 46 to 20 per 1000. For the 1970s as a whole, infant mortality fell from 68 to 20 per 1000 (Table A1), a decline that has been called a world record for a single decade.[3] The percent decline of infant mortality in the first five years of Costa Rica's Rural Health Plan (1973–1978) was greater than the percent decline in the five-year period that followed the introduction of any other nationwide community-based nutrition and health program reviewed in this book (Table 11.2). Infant mortality continued to fall during the 1980s and 1990s, but at a slower pace than during the 1970s (Table A1). To reduce infant mortality from 20 to 10 per 1000 took 23 years in Costa Rica (1980–2003), but only 13 years in Chile (1984–1997).[4]

What needs to be explained, then, is why Costa Rica's infant mortality rate was so low in 2005 (why it attained a certain *level*); why it fell so fast from 1960 to 2005 (why it achieved a certain amount of *progress*), and why it fell faster during the 1970s than at other times within this period (why it evolved at a certain *tempo*). The sustained and effective public provision of basic health services to the poor, this chapter finds, goes a long way toward explaining why Costa Rica from 1960 to 2005 achieved a rapid decline (and, eventually, a low level) of infant mortality, despite registering slow economic growth, high income inequality, and disappointing progress at reducing income poverty.

---

[1] World Bank 2008e. Tables A1 and A2 provide infant mortality and life expectancy data for the eight societies. Costa Rican infant mortality data are from vital registration, which is widely regarded as complete and accurate (McGuire 2009, Web Appendix A1).

[2] McGuire and Frankel 2005: 86.

[3] Data from CCP-UCR 2009. "World record" conjectures in Drèze and Sen 1989: 244 and Garnier et al. 1997: 367.

[4] The infant mortality figures for Costa Rica are from CCP-UCR 2009; those for Chile are from United Nations 1992: 76 (1987–1989) and Chile. Ministerio de Salud 2008 (1990–1997). In both countries the figures are based on vital registration.

3.2. Costa Rica: Affluence, Inequality, and Poverty

Costa Rica's GDP per capita grew slowly but steadily from 1960 to 1980 (Table A3), aided by the growth of traditional agricultural exports (mostly coffee and bananas) and, after it joined the Central American Common Market in 1963, by the growth of small-scale industry. Political stability, which by the late 1970s distinguished Costa Rica from most of its Central American neighbors, also contributed to economic growth. Like many Latin American countries, Costa Rica borrowed heavily abroad during the 1970s, due partly to misguided forays into state-led industrial investment and partly to burgeoning social spending.[5] By 1980 Costa Rica's fiscal deficit was 7.4 percent of GDP, and its foreign debt in per capita terms was among the highest in the world. The rise of interest rates at the end of the 1970s, together with falling coffee prices, soaring oil prices, and the evaporation of foreign loans, triggered an economic crisis. President Rodrigo Carazo (1978–1982) of the Coalición Unidad, one of the country's two major electoral forces at the time, responded to these economic challenges by tightening the money supply, raising taxes and interest rates, cutting public spending, and devaluing the currency.[6] These measures, along with the recessionary effects of the crisis itself, led to a sharp rise in unemployment and a sharp decline in real wages.[7] The worst of the recession ended in 1983, but sustained economic growth did not resume until 1990. From 1980 to 1990, GDP per capita fell at an average annual rate of 1.0 percent (Table A3).

With the help of a tenfold increase in foreign aid from the U.S. Reagan administration, which made ample use of Costa Rican territory in its effort to overthrow the Sandinistas in Nicaragua, the Partido Liberación Nacional (PLN) government of President Luis Alberto Monge (1982–1986) reduced inflation from 90 to 12 percent. The government also enacted import-duty rebates and other policies to stimulate exports of textiles, seafood, pineapple, flowers, and houseplants.[8] Monge's successors maintained these export-promotion policies through the early 1990s, leading to a resumption of steady economic growth. The governments of José María Figueres Olsen (PLN, 1994–1998) and Miguel Ángel Rodríguez (Partido Unidad Social Cristiana/PUSC, 1998–2002) helped to stimulate a boom in manufactured exports, first by wooing foreign-owned clothing plants and then by attracting foreign-owned semiconductor factories. From 1995 to 1999 manufactures rose from 25 to 68 percent of Costa Rican exports.[9] By 2000 Costa Rica's economic model had changed from commodity-financed import substitution to manufactured

---

[5] Clark 2001: 34–42.
[6] Mesa-Lago 2000a: 508.
[7] Mesa-Lago 2000b: 314.
[8] Booth (1998: 162, 216) on Reagan; Wilson (1998: 116, 123) on the Monge government.
[9] World Bank 2008a. Clothing: Mesa-Lago 2000a: 471–472. Semiconductors: World Bank 2006c.

export promotion, some 35 years after South Korea and Taiwan and a decade after Indonesia and Thailand.

Before economic growth accelerated in the 1990s, however, Costa Rica grew slowly. Among the eight cases studied in this book, Costa Rica from 1960 to 2005 ranked seventh on GDP per capita growth (Table A3). In a broader cross-national perspective, Costa Rica from 1960 to 2003 ranked 52nd of 98 countries around the world at GDP per capita growth, and only 47th of 64 countries outside sub-Saharan Africa.[10] Among 93 developing countries for which data are available, Costa Rica did much better than its GDP per capita would predict at achieving both a low level of infant mortality in 2005 and a steep decline of infant mortality from 1960 to 2005 (Figures 1.1 and 1.2). The tempo of infant mortality decline within the interval from 1960 to 2005 was less anomalous from the standpoint of the narrow variant of the wealthier is healthier hypothesis. Across eight five-year periods from 1960 to 2000 (1960–65, ... 1995–2000), the correlation between the average annual rise of GDP per capita and the average annual percent decline of infant mortality was positive, although not strong (Table 11.1).

The intermediate variant of the wealthier is healthier hypothesis incorporates income inequality and income poverty. If levels or changes of income inequality or income poverty could explain why Costa Rica did better on infant mortality than on GDP per capita, Costa Rica's mortality achievements, so anomalous from the standpoint of the narrow variant of the wealthier is healthier hypothesis, could be explained by the intermediate variant of the hypothesis. Close scrutiny, however, shows that even the intermediate variant of the hypothesis falls short of explaining these achievements.

On the income inequality front, Costa Rica has a well-known ethos of egalitarianism. Even the president is expected to live frugally and to be accessible to ordinary people. In the late 1960s, the presidential residence was a cramped, noisy apartment in an industrial zone next to a foul-smelling distillery.[11] While president from 1982 to 1986, Luis Alberto Monge had his pocket picked in San José.[12] In a Latin American perspective, accordingly, Costa Rican income inequality was low. Its Gini index in 2003 of 49.0 (Table A4) was fourth lowest among 19 Latin American countries surveyed in the year 2000 or later.[13] In a global perspective, however, Costa Rican income inequality was high. For 1990–2004 its Gini index averaged 47.6, compared to a mean of 45.5 for 80 countries surveyed at least once during this period.[14]

---

[10] Calculated from Heston, Summers, and Aten 2006, variable RGDPCH.

[11] Denton 1971: 104.

[12] Biesanz, Biesanz, and Biesanz 1999: 77.

[13] This comparison among 19 Latin American Countries is based on each country's mean Gini index recorded in the years 2000–2004 (World Bank 2008a). The Gini indices for Argentina and Uruguay are for urban areas only; the Gini index for Ecuador is for 1998. Costa Rica's Gini index in this series is 48.5.

[14] Calculated from World Bank 2008a.

Costa Rica thus achieved low infant mortality not only despite low GDP per capita, but also despite high income inequality. Moreover, even though the Gini index was about the same in 1960 as in 2003 (Table A4), infant mortality plunged during the intervening years. Within this span of time, the tempo of infant mortality decline was notably inconsistent with the rise and fall of income inequality. From 1971 to 2003, when most of the infant mortality decline took place, the Gini index rose from 43.0 to 49.0. The Gini index apparently declined sharply during the 1960s and again in the early 1980s, when infant mortality fell quite sluggishly, but rose considerably during the 1970s, when infant mortality plunged (Tables A1 and A4).

Turning from income inequality to income poverty, the share of households receiving less than U.S. $3 per day plunged from 65 percent in the early 1960s to 30 percent in the early 1970s. Infant mortality fell slowly during this period, however.[15] Then, from 1970 to 1980, the share of households earning less than U.S. $2 per day rose from 26 to 30 percent, while infant mortality plunged from 68 to 20 per 1000. Next, from 1980 to 1990, $2 per day poverty plummeted from 32 to 16 percent of the population, even though infant mortality dipped only from 20 to 15 per 1000. From 1960 to 1990, then, the tempo of income poverty decline was seriously out of phase with the tempo of infant mortality decline. Only from 1990 to 2005 did the two tempos become more congruent (Tables A1 and A5).

Costa Rica thus provides only weak support for the wealthier is healthier conjecture, regardless of whether comparisons focus on the level of infant mortality in 2005, on the overall amount of infant mortality decline from 1960 to 2005, or on the tempo of infant mortality decline within that period – and regardless of whether "wealthier" is measured in terms of GDP per capita, income inequality, or income poverty. It seems reasonable, then, to explore the possibility that social service provision, more than affluence or income (even among the poor), helps to explain why Costa Rica achieved a low level of infant mortality in 2005, rapidly reduced infant mortality from 1960 to 2005, and recorded faster declines of infant mortality in some years than in others.

3.3. Costa Rica: Education, Family Planning, Safe Water, and Sanitation

In 1995 public social spending per capita was $536 in Costa Rica, compared to $597 in Chile, $932 in Brazil, and $1,532 in Argentina.[16] This $536 represented about 13 percent of GDP. Of this $536, 36 percent went to health care, 27 percent to education, 25 percent to pensions, and 5 percent to housing.[17] Such spending achieved a formidable "bang for the buck," as measured by mortality indicators, in part because it was moderately progressive on both spending and financing. From 1980 to 2000 the poorest fifth of the population received

---

[15] $3 per day poverty: González Vega and Céspedes 1993: 45; infant mortality: Table A1.
[16] CEPAL 2002: 269. These figures are in 1997 U.S. dollars.
[17] Durán-Valverde 2002: 5.

21–23 percent of total public social spending, and 48 percent of such spending came from payroll, income, and property taxes, which are paid mostly by the richest 80 percent of Costa Ricans.[18] In 2000 the most progressive sectors were, in order of progressivity, nutrition programs, non-contributory pensions, income transfers to vulnerable groups, primary health care, and school lunch programs. Among these sectors, the only ones comprising more than 2 percent of social spending were primary health care (5 percent) and income transfers to vulnerable groups (4 percent). The most regressive sectors were contributory pensions (23 percent of social spending), where the richest quintile received 56 percent of benefits and the poorest quintile received 5 percent, and university education (6 percent of social spending), where the richest quintile received 45 percent and the poorest quintile received 3 percent.[19]

Costa Ricans during the nineteenth century are said to have developed a "virtual love affair" with education, making teaching and learning a "virtual civil religion."[20] The 1892 census showed that 42 percent of Costa Ricans were literate, a level not reached in Mexico or elsewhere in Central America until half a century later. Anti-female bias in education was remarkably low,[21] with positive implications for the infant mortality rate. Compared to the seven other cases studied in this book, however, neither Costa Rica's level of educational attainment in 1960, nor its progress at improving education from 1960 to 2005, were exceptional. Gains were especially slow from 1975 to 1995 (Tables A7 and A8), when public education spending fell as a share of both the budget and GDP.[22] During the recession of the 1980s, school buildings crumbled, teacher hiring slowed, the school day and year shrank, and dropout rates rose.[23] High fertility in the 1960s strained educational resources in the 1970s and 1980s, and those resources were not optimally allocated. Administration absorbed an excessive share of the public education budget, and the system subsidized the rich through the public universities. By the late 1990s, "virtually free access to public higher education ha[d] placed a great and growing burden on the state and created a vast and easily mobilized constituency of university students and faculty."[24] Not least because of the political clout of students, faculty members, and university employees, 36 percent of public education spending in Costa Rica went to higher education in the late 1980s. Among the other seven cases compared in this book, only Argentina in the late 1980s allocated more than 20 percent of public education spending to universities.[25] One result of the high level of university spending, however,

[18] Garnier et al. 1997: 374–377.
[19] Trejos 2002: 4, 15.
[20] Booth 1998: 93–94.
[21] Mesa-Lago 2000b: 28; Stycos 1982: 16.
[22] Durán-Valverde 2002: 5–6; Garnier et al. 1997: 372.
[23] Booth 1998: 95; Mesa-Lago 2000a: 498.
[24] Booth 1998: 94–95.
[25] UNDP 1993: 164. By 2000 the Costa Rican share had fallen to 21 percent (Trejos 2002: 4).

was a steady stream of medical and public health graduates on the front lines of the battle against infant mortality.

From 1960 to 2005 total fertility in Costa Rica fell from 7.2 to 2.2 expected births per woman (Table A10). This 70-percent decline was the steepest by far in Latin America during this stretch of time. Taiwan, South Korea, and Thailand each achieved greater fertility decline than Costa Rica from 1960 to 2005, but among 179 countries with data for both years, Costa Rica ranked 11th.[26] In the 1960s modernization rather than family planning was the main force behind fertility decline.[27] In 1968, however, the government began a national family planning program, starting in the poorest areas of the country. By 1974 it was providing contraceptives to 54 percent of women aged 15–49, and by 1981 it served two-thirds of women using contraception, including almost 90 percent of women in agricultural households. By 1970 family planning was the main cause of fertility decline, and by 1972 experts ranked Costa Rica 7th among 94 developing countries in family planning effort.[28] Commitment to family planning fluctuated thereafter (Table A9), but in 2004 Costa Rica again ranked 10th of 82 countries at family planning effort.[29]

Costa Rica's first water treatment plants were built in 1942 during the presidency of Rafael Ángel Calderón Guardia (1940–1944).[30] By 1960, 59 percent of Costa Ricans had access to an improved water source and 69 percent of city dwellers had access to improved sanitation, much higher shares than in any of the other seven societies analyzed in this book. Despite starting from this already high level, Costa Rica made steady progress. By 2005, 97 percent of Costa Ricans had access to improved water and 89 percent of urbanites had access to improved sanitation (Tables A11 and A12). Promoting this progress was the creation in 1961 of the Institute of Aqueducts and Sewers, which helped to raise access in rural areas, especially from 1970 to 1972, when the share of rural households connected to a water supply rose from 39 to 56 percent. The increase in the share of the population with access to improved water and sanitation, particularly from 1965 to 1980, coincided with a spectacular decline in the prevalence of intestinal parasites and in the death rate from diarrhea and parasitic infections.[31]

Costa Rica by the beginning of the twenty-first century thus had progressive financing and allocation of social services, a solid educational system that was not manifestly biased against females, strong family planning, and widespread access to improved water and sanitation. These achievements were

---

[26] Fertility comparisons calculated from figures in World Bank 2008a (except Taiwan, from Table A10).

[27] Reynolds 1973; Stycos 1982.

[28] Contraceptive acceptance: Stycos 1982: 25; use of state family planning: Rosero-Bixby 1986: 60; expert ratings: Ross and Mauldin 1996: 146; main cause of fertility decline after 1970: Reynolds 1973; Stycos 1982: 27–28.

[29] Data from Ross 2008.

[30] Mata 1991: 2.

[31] Mata 1985: 69–70; Rosero-Bixby 1985: 364.

even more impressive given that 38 percent of Costa Ricans lived in rural areas in 2005.[32] All else equal, it is harder to deliver social services in rural than in urban areas. Costa Rica's strong record on social service provision stands in sharp contrast to its sluggish economic growth, high income inequality, and slow decline of income poverty, most conspicuously during the periods when infant mortality fell fastest.

3.4. Costa Rica: Nutrition and Health Care

Total spending on health care in Costa Rica in 2001 was 7.0 percent of GDP, or $567 per capita. Three-quarters of this spending came from the public sector (Table A15), which in 2000 employed 90 percent of Costa Rican doctors (one-third of whom also had private practices) and ran all but six small hospitals.[33] Around 2000, the public sector in Costa Rica dominated health care financing, health risk pooling, and health service delivery to a degree not found in any other society studied in this book.

Gauged by mortality indicators, Costa Rican health care spending was efficient. In 1995 total health care spending per capita in Costa Rica was about average for 20 Latin American countries, but life expectancy was much higher than average and infant mortality was much lower than average.[34] One reason for this efficiency is that public health expenditure was distributed more progressively in Costa Rica than in most other Latin American countries for which data are available. In 2000, 29 percent of public health care spending in Costa Rica benefited the poorest fifth of the population; only 11 percent benefited the richest fifth. Nutrition and primary health care spending were especially progressive. The poorest quintile received 55 percent of public nutrition spending and 38 percent of public primary health care spending, against 2 and 4 percent respectively for the richest quintile.[35]

In 1951 the Ministry of Public Health, in collaboration with UNICEF, began to distribute milk free of charge to infants, school children, pregnant women, and new mothers. By the end of the 1960s the Ministry had set up clinics in San José to rehabilitate seriously malnourished children from around the country, and had opened in the capitals of the 7 provinces and (then) 81 cantons some 124 Nutrition Centers, which provided a mid-morning snack to children aged 2 to 6, gave nutritional aid to pregnant and breastfeeding women, and distributed free food every two weeks to families with undernourished

---

[32] World Bank 2008a. The density of Costa Rica's rural population is rather high, however. Many farmers live in the Central Valley, near the capital city of San José.

[33] Clark 2004: 192.

[34] In 1995 total health care spending per capita in Costa Rica (PAHO 1998a: V. 1, 315) was only 0.2 standard deviations above the mean for 20 Latin American countries, but life expectancy was 1.2 standard deviations above the mean and infant mortality was 1.0 standard deviations below the mean (Hill et al. 1999).

[35] Trejos 2002: 15. On the benefit incidence of public health care spending in other Latin American countries see Suárez-Berenguela 2000: 42.

children. As late as 1966, however, only 10 percent of young children and only 3 percent of expectant mothers were receiving free food at Nutrition Centers.[36] Under President José Figueres Ferrer (1970–1974) of the Partido Liberación Nacional state-run nutrition programs improved dramatically. In 1971 the Figueres Ferrer government created the Mixed Institute of Social Aid (IMAS), which stepped up targeted nutritional aid around the country.[37] The number of Nutrition Centers rose from 124 in 1968 to 471 in 1978, the proportion of schools serving free meals rose from 44 percent in 1975 to 95 percent in 1981, and the share of under-5 children with moderate or severe malnutrition fell from 13.5 percent in 1965 to 6.3 percent in 1982 (Table A14).[38] Rural calorie and protein intake rose little during this period, however, underscoring "the need to relate nourishment and health not to food entitlements as such but to a broader notion of entitlements including command over non-food items" such as health care, clean water, and sanitation.[39] Progress at reducing malnutrition continued during the 1980s and 1990s. From 1982 to 1994 the share of under-6 children with moderate or severe malnourishment fell from 6.3 to 2.2 percent (Table A14). Meanwhile, the share of children aged 6 to 8 who suffered from growth stunting fell from 20 percent in 1979 to 13 percent in 1983 to 10 percent in 1989 and to 7 percent in 1997.[40]

Public health interventions in Costa Rica date back at least to 1805, when traditional healers were mobilized for smallpox vaccination. Lightly trained "town doctors" began to vaccinate children in the 1840s, and by the late 1890s vaccination had become "systematic and effective," aided by "the successful extension of public primary education into many rural communities by the 1880s."[41] The first public assistance hospital opened in 1845, but as of 1900 fewer than 50 doctors practiced in the country.[42] In the first decade of the twentieth century, the United Fruit Company built a hospital in the Atlantic port of Limón and began a program to fight malaria.[43] A general strike by communist-led banana workers in 1934, many of whom were English-speakers of West Indian descent, led to improvement in the quantity and quality of United Fruit's housing, water and sanitation, and medical services.[44] The company's health activities were profit-oriented, racist, and implemented with little consultation, but they improved sanitary and health conditions, and even a critic

[36] Vargas 1995: 98.
[37] Mesa-Lago 2000b: 290.
[38] Vargas 1995: 98 (nutrition centers), 105 (school meals).
[39] Drèze and Sen 1989: 284. On disease causing malnutrition in Costa Rica see Mata 1991: 9 and Mohs 2002: 70.
[40] FAO 1999: 17–18.
[41] Palmer 2003: 37, 60, 71, 106, 111–112 (quotations). On the town doctors see also Mohs 1983: 38.
[42] Casas and Vargas 1980: 264; Rosenberg 1983: 26.
[43] Palmer 2003: 108–109, 116.
[44] Rosenberg 1979: 119; Seligson 1980: 62, 70–77. Two-thirds of the value of the settlement of the 1934 strike involved the United Fruit Company agreeing to improve medical services for workers (Miranda Gutiérrez 2007).

acknowledges that "without United Fruit's sanitation programs, Costa Rica's only Atlantic port [Limón] would have remained the disease-ridden, uninhabitable region it had been since the Spanish conquest."[45]

The government began a nationwide anti-hookworm campaign in 1910 and expanded it after 1915 with the aid of the Rockefeller Foundation. In addition to reducing the incidence of hookworm, the campaign encouraged participation in hygiene activities and contributed to the understanding and acceptance of the germ theory of disease. In 1922 the government's anti-hookworm agency became the Department of Public Health, which in 1927 became the Ministry of Public Health.[46] Anti-tuberculosis measures, along with malaria control involving DDT spraying, began on banana plantations in 1946 and spread throughout the country in the 1950s.[47] In 1940 about 22 percent of Costa Ricans suffered from malaria, and the death rate from the disease was 157 per 100,000. By 1960 malaria prevalence was below 2 percent and the malaria death rate was 2 per 100,000. A new round of malaria control efforts in the late 1960s and early 1970s led to additional progress. In 1967 Costa Rica had 278 cases of malaria per 100,000 inhabitants; by 1973 it had 9 per 100,000. No malaria deaths were recorded from 1975 to 1995, but two occurred in 1996, and prevalence rose in the late 1980s, particularly among undocumented immigrants.[48]

Costa Rica's first rural health post was built in 1928 on the model of the County Health Units developed by the Rockefeller Foundation in the rural United States. The health posts were staffed by a doctor, a nurse, a midwife, and other personnel, who provided vaccinations, sanitary inspection, health education, and other curative and preventive services to the surrounding population.[49] During the 1930s less complex facilities known as Sanitary Units, which were staffed by paraprofessional "village doctors," were established in most cantons. Governments in the 1940s improved health education in schools and instituted a program to provide shoes for all school children, and their successors in the 1950s expanded the number of "healthy child clinics." These advances were partly offset, however, by the newly fashionable practice of bottle-feeding infants in maternity wards, which slowed the decline in diarrhea morbidity and mortality, and by the after-effects of the bloody 1948 civil war between partisans of Calderón Guardia and Figueres Ferrer, in which more than 2,000 people (one out of every 250 people in the country) were killed in a six-week period.[50]

The Costa Rican welfare state took shape mainly during the presidency of Rafael Ángel Calderón Guardia (1940–1944). In 1941 the legislature passed a

---

[45] Morgan 1990: 213.

[46] Palmer 2003: 155–182, 222–224.

[47] PAHO 2000b: 12.

[48] 1967–1973: Mesa-Lago 2000b: 284; 1975–1996: PAHO 1998b: 198.

[49] Palmer 2003: 222–224.

[50] Mata 1991: 3, 6. The 1950 census recorded 800,875 inhabitants.

social insurance law and created the Costa Rican Social Security Fund (CCSS) to administer the resulting health and retirement monies. From this point onward, a single fund controlled contributory pensions and health insurance in Costa Rica. Until the mid-1960s, most of the medical services funded by the CCSS were provided in private or charitable facilities. After the mid-1960s the CCSS began to build its own facilities and to rely more on its own medical personnel.[51] In Argentina and Brazil, by contrast, contributory health insurance during the 1970s and 1980s continued to pay mostly for services delivered by private providers. The vested interests built up under these regimes impeded pro-poor reforms in both countries, especially in Argentina.

Insurance coverage in Costa Rica was initially restricted by a 1943 regulation that limited maternity and medical insurance to workers in six major cities, and that required only low-income wage-earners to contribute to the Social Security Fund. This regulation restricted the resources available to fund the system. Accordingly, in 1944, only about 4 percent of population was covered by health insurance.[52] The welfare state thus initially targeted urban formal-sector workers with relatively low wages, excluding both wealthier people and poorer people who did not receive paychecks. At the end of the 1940s health insurance was extended to contributors' dependents, and some rural residents of the Central Valley were brought into the contributory regime. By the late 1950s about 27 percent of the labor force, and about 18 percent of the total population, was covered by health and maternity insurance.[53] At this time, and throughout the 1960s, the quality of health care received by the insured was enviable enough that those covered by the Social Security Fund were sometimes referred to as the "perfumados." If health services were unavailable in Costa Rica, the insured person might be flown either to Mexico or to the United States for care, even for quite expensive treatments.[54]

In 1961 the legislature passed a constitutional amendment mandating universal health insurance coverage within the next ten years, as well as a law that more than doubled the wage below which Social Security Fund contributions were withheld automatically from paychecks, increasing the amount of money in the fund. Doctors and nurses remained scarce, however. The country's first medical school had just opened, and the Social Security Fund still lacked its own medical facilities. Although health insurance coverage rose to 47 percent of the population by 1970, the mandate of universal coverage by 1971 was not met. In that year, however, a law was passed requiring all wage earners to join the Fund, regardless of salary level. Then, in 1974, self-employed workers were brought into the Social Security Fund and employers became responsible for a higher share of contributions. By putting the system on a stronger financial footing, these reforms allowed health insurance coverage by the Social

[51] Casas and Vargas 1980: 266–269; Clark 2005: 15; Jara Vargas 2002: 20.
[52] Rosenberg 1979: 124; Rosenberg 1981: 287; Yashar 1997: 76–77, 107, 252.
[53] Mohs 1983: 46.
[54] Gutiérrez Góngora 2007.

Security Fund to expand to 76 percent of the total population in 1980, 82 percent in 1990, and 88 percent in 2005.[55] Cross-canton analysis suggests that the expansion of health insurance coverage during the 1970s contributed little, however, to infant mortality decline.[56]

The Rural Health Plan launched in 1973 by the Ministry of Public Health during the PLN government of José Figueres Ferrer gave the poor access to basic health care regardless of whether they had insurance. It started by employing personnel from the anti-malaria program, but the educational level of many such workers proved to be inadequate, so the ministry switched to two-person teams of newly trained auxiliary nurses and rural health assistants with at least 9 years of schooling. The auxiliary nurses, usually female, had 11 months of training, and the health assistants, usually male, had 4. Only rural residents aged 18 to 35 could apply, and trainees were required to sign 3-year contracts.[57] In clinics and through home visits, the auxiliary nurses and health assistants vaccinated children; treated malaria and intestinal parasites; educated villagers about family planning and maternal and child health; dispensed contraceptives; monitored the health and nutritional status of pregnant women, infants, and new mothers; distributed milk; and helped to build sanitation facilities.[58] The program was launched first in "dispersed rural areas," which included communities with 500 or fewer persons, and was later extended to rural communities with up to 2,000 persons. Each team was expected to visit 80 percent of homes in a designated geographical area at least three times per year, and the remaining 20 percent of homes at least three times every two years. These visits inspired many rural women to request long-needed health care for the first time.[59] From 1973 to 1979 the number of rural health posts rose from 27 to 285, the number of rural health workers rose from 43 to 429, and the share of rural residents covered by the Rural Health Plan rose from 11 to 61 percent.[60] After 1976, the Community Health Plan extended similar services to impoverished urban areas.[61]

The implementation of the Rural Health and Community Health plans coincided with rapid gains in health monitoring and health status. Between

---

[55] Figures from Costa Rica. MIDEPLAN 2008: Table 5.1. See also Clark 2005: 4; Mesa-Lago 2000a: 290–291; Miranda Gutiérrez 1995: 48–54; Miranda Gutiérrez 2007; Rosenberg 1979: 123–128; and Sauma and Trejos 1999: 38.

[56] Dow and Schmeer 2003.

[57] Costa Rica. Ministerio de Salud 1976: 61; Vargas 1995: 69–85; Villegas de Olazábal 2005: 29.

[58] Caldwell 1986; Garnier et al. 1997; Mata 1985; Mata 1991; Rosero-Bixby 1985; Rosero-Bixby 1986; Vargas González 1977; Villegas de Olazábal 2004.

[59] Mata 1991: 10–11. The program did not cover rural areas in the Central Valley, where geographical access to health services was already satisfactory (Costa Rica. Ministerio de Salud 1976: 42–43).

[60] Mata 1991: Table 6, p. 31.

[61] Trejos 1995: 189. In 1987 the Health Ministry combined the two programs into an "Integrated Health Program" administered by the Division of Primary Health Care (Costa Rica. Ministerio de Salud 1989: 2; Morgan 1993: 93).

1974 and 1977 the number of children under surveillance rose from 900 to 125,000, and the number of expectant mothers using prenatal clinics rose from 350 to 10,000. Between 1970 and 1980 annual measles deaths fell from 242 to 7, while annual tetanus deaths fell from 217 to 9.[62] In 1973 and 1974 infant and child mortality plunged in two rural cantons in which the Rural Health Plan was introduced, but stayed the same or rose in two rural cantons that had not received the program.[63] An analysis of infant mortality changes in all cantons from 1972 to 1980 found that government health care initiatives accounted for 73 percent of the cross-canton variance in infant mortality decline. Fertility decline accounted for 5 percent and socioeconomic development (a weighted composite of income, urbanization, education, and other variables) accounted for 22 percent.[64] A study of 52 Costa Rican cantons from 1962 to 1977 revealed that "the Rural Health Program, working on a relatively low budget, has done much more to lower infant mortality and malnutrition than the CCSS clinics and regional hospitals."[65]

As noteworthy as the overall drop of infant mortality during the 1970s was the rapid decline of differentials across demographic groups. At the start of the 1970s, the risk of infant death was much lower in rich than in poor cantons, in urban than in rural areas, in the capital city of San José than in the rest of the country, and for well educated than for poorly educated mothers. By 1980 such differentials had shrunk dramatically.[66] The Rural Health Plan was targeted to the cantons with the worst health status indicators, and one study showed "that cantons in which rural and community health coverage was 75 percent or greater experienced a fall in IMR [infant mortality] from 80 to 17 per 1000 in the 1970s, while cantons in which coverage was practically null showed a smaller decline, from 49 to 21 per 1000 in the same period."[67] From 1970 to 1980, thanks mainly to the Rural Health Plan, some of the unhealthiest cantons in the country had become some of the healthiest. Health status equity, so measured, continued to improve from 1980 to 2001. If Costa Rica's 81 cantons are ranked by Human Development Index in 1999 and then partitioned into five quintiles, average infant mortality from 1980 to 2001 fell in the top quintile from 18 to 11 per 1000 and in the bottom quintile from 23 to 12 per 1000.[68]

The role of the Social Security Fund in public health care provision expanded after the mid-1970s, while that of the health ministry shrank. By the mid-1980s the Fund was in charge of most major medical facilities and of

[62] Mata 1985: 70–71.
[63] Vargas González 1977: 360–364.
[64] Rosero-Bixby 1986: 63; Rosero-Bixby 1990: 41; Rosero-Bixby 1996: 171.
[65] Casas and Vargas 1980: 276.
[66] Rosero-Bixby 1985: 349–353. By 1978, the number of medical consultations per inhabitant also varied little by social group or by urban versus rural location (Casas and Vargas 1980: 273).
[67] Rosero-Bixby 1986: 64.
[68] Bortman 2002: 21.

almost all curative care, including for indigents and low-income pensioners, for which it received a subsidy from general revenues. It had also gained control of immunization programs. The health ministry kept responsibility for disease control, food and drug regulation, environmental sanitation, and child nutrition and primary care for the poor.[69] In 1995, however, as part of a fundamental reform of the entire health care system, the government transferred all of the country's primary health care centers from the health ministry to the Social Security Fund.[70] Over the next three years 1,600 health professionals made the switch as well. The Fund took control of the maternal and infant health and nutrition programs that had previously been run by the health ministry and, by placing them under the authority of the EBAIS, integrated them into a strategy of using primary care as a gateway into the entire health system. Owing partly to these changes, the share of public health spending channeled through the Social Security Fund rose from 51 percent in 1976 to 80 percent in 1999.[71] By 2000 the Social Security Fund's budget amounted to fully a quarter of the budget of the entire central government, and the health ministry remained responsible only for policy formulation, regulation, food and water monitoring, coordination of disease control programs, and public health campaigns.[72]

As the Social Security Fund took on new responsibilities in the 1970s it ran into financial problems. Population aging forced it to devote more resources to chronic and degenerative diseases, and as new (often high-cost) medical technology became available, the agency bought it. On the revenue side, employers and state agencies evaded payments to the CCSS, which invested the funds it did receive in low-paying government bonds.[73] The economic crisis of the early 1980s brought these problems to a head. Public health care spending fell sharply during the decade, both in per capita terms and as a share of GDP (Table A15).[74] In 1989, moreover, the government resolved to provide health care and other services to undocumented immigrants, who made up 5 to 8 percent of the population. Foreign aid reduced the cost of such provision, but the commitment was still expensive.[75]

In the early 1990s the PUSC government of Rafael Ángel Calderón Fournier, the son of the former president Rafael Ángel Calderón Guardia, attempted to cope with these financial problems by inviting World Bank representatives to Costa Rica to discuss ways to reform the health care system. In 1993 the World Bank provided a U.S. $22 million loan for health sector reform, in return for which the Calderón Fournier government agreed to undertake a

---

[69] Mesa-Lago 1985: 14.
[70] Rodríguez Herrera 2006: 20.
[71] Clark 2004: 201.
[72] Clark 2005: 4–5.
[73] Clark 2004: 195; Mesa-Lago 1985: 16.
[74] Public health spending from 1980 to 1988 fell almost by half both in per capita terms and as a share of GDP (calculated from Ramírez Rodríguez 1992: 222).
[75] Wiley 1995: 434.

number of efficiency-oriented reforms.[76] The government also made a commitment to reforming primary health care, where services had deteriorated during the 1980s. The Rural Health Plan and Community Health Plan had been partly financed by foreign loans, and excessive foreign borrowing contributed to the economic crisis of the 1980s. These primary health care initiatives were not responsible for more than a tiny fraction of the soaring debt, however. In the mid to late 1970s the Rural Health Plan served about 500,000 people at a cost of somewhere between U.S. $1.70 and $3.50 each.[77] In 1977 the Rural Health Plan and Community Health Plan together absorbed only 2.5 percent of public health spending, perhaps U.S. $8 per capita in then-current dollars.[78] In 1982 the health ministry spent 65 colones per beneficiary on primary health care programs, whereas the Social Security Fund spent 2,180 colones per beneficiary on health insurance benefits. Dr. Juan Jaramillo Antillón, the health minister during the Monge presidency (1982–1986), lamented the high share of public health care spending that was devoted to the purchase of "ultramodern, high-technology equipment whose costs are astronomical and [which] benefit only a small number of patients."[79] In this respect Costa Rica's public health system resembled those of most other Latin American countries in the 1980s. Like Chile, however, Costa Rica also spent a small fraction of its public health care budget on community-based health and nutrition programs that contributed to a sharp decline of infant mortality. By contrast, the governments of Argentina (except in a few sparsely populated provinces) and Brazil (until the Community Health Agents Program was launched in 1991) did much less to provide primary health care to the poor. The more effective public provision of primary health care services to disadvantaged people is one of the main reasons why, from 1960 to 1995, infant mortality declined more steeply in Chile and Costa Rica than in Argentina or Brazil. From 1995 to 2005, however, governments in both Argentina and Brazil stepped up the quantity and quality of public primary health care services in impoverished areas, leading to faster infant mortality decline in those countries as well.

Even if the Costa Rican economy had been healthier in the 1980s, population growth and the expansion of health insurance coverage and health service utilization would have placed a major burden on the health care system. From 1970 to 1980 the share of the population covered by health insurance rose from 47 to 76 percent, while the share of births attended by trained personnel rose from 74 to 92 percent.[80] In the succeeding decade from 1980 to 1990, however, primary health care worsened. The economic crisis brought cuts in health care spending, especially for preventive care. From 1980 to 1990 the

[76] World Bank 2003a; Clark 2004.
[77] Coverage figure pertains to 1976; cost estimates (in then-current US dollars) from Mason et al. 2006: 1062, 1069; Mata 1990; and Vargas González 1977: 356, 365.
[78] Vargas 1995: 85.
[79] Mesa-Lago 1985: 20.
[80] Costa Rica. MIDEPLAN 2008, Tables 5–1 and 5–9.

share of rural and high-risk urban residents served by the health ministry's primary care programs fell from 60 to 40 percent. The quality of services also fell.[81] Some rural health posts closed, others lost staff, and funds for training new health workers dried up. No new primary care workers were trained from 1980 until 1983, when UNICEF stepped in to provide funding. Some cantons reported rises in premature births, low birthweight babies, and infant deaths.[82] The training of paraprofessional health workers began to lag at the beginning of the 1980s, and citizens and Social Security Fund employees began to protest the declining quality of health care, especially for outpatients.

By the early 1990s Costa Ricans were complaining about long waits for appointments and shortages of drugs at public medical facilities. A measles outbreak in the early 1990s added to a perception that a fundamental change in the health care system was required.[83] In 1991 the administration of the PUSC President Rafael Ángel Calderón Fournier appointed a bipartisan group of doctors and public health experts to draft a proposal to restructure the health system.[84] Completed in February 1993, the proposal advocated the formation of Comprehensive Basic Health Care Teams (EBAIS) to deliver primary health care services to geographically delimited populations of about 3,500–4,000 persons each. The Social Security Fund, rather than the health ministry, was given control of the EBAIS program. Separate protocols were designed to meet the health needs of persons in different age groups. In remote places, the teams were expected to travel within their assigned areas. The country was divided into seven health regions and 103 health areas; each health area was then divided into roughly ten health sectors. Each sector was served by a Comprehensive Basic Health Care Team that included a doctor, an auxiliary nurse, and a community health worker. The teams made home visits as well as working in clinics; referred patients to district or national health facilities; and were backed up at the health area level by a support team that included a physician, professional nurse, dentist, social worker, pharmacist, nutritionist, and microbiologist.[85]

The government sent the Comprehensive Basic Health Care Team proposal to the World Bank in 1993 as part of its application for the U.S. $22 million loan for health system restructuring. The World Bank at first resisted the EBAIS part of the proposal, arguing that it would be too expensive. The Costa Ricans stood firm, and the World Bank approved the proposal in 1993.[86] The EBAIS did turn out to be more expensive than the Costa Ricans projected. Instead of the estimated $17 million, the cost wound up being $50 million, of which the World Bank paid U.S. $9 million and the Social Security Fund

---

[81] Budget cuts in preventive versus curative care: Mesa-Lago 2000b: 315. Program coverage and quality: Muñoz Retana and Valverde 1995.

[82] Morgan 1987: 98; Morgan 1989: 214–215; Morgan 1993: 109, 114.

[83] Clark 2004: 197; Marín 2007.

[84] Ayala 2007; Salas 2007.

[85] Costa Rica. CCSS 1998.

[86] Clark 2004: 198–201; IADB 2003: 4; Weyland 2006: 174.

paid $41 million.[87] The Comprehensive Basic Health Care Teams began work in February 1995. As with the family planning program in the late 1960s, the Rural Health Plan in the 1970s, and the Family Health Teams in Brazil in the 1990s, the poorest parts of the country were served first.[88] By mid-1998 there were some 400 EBAIS, about half the number planned, and by December 2001 there were 730, of which 80 percent had the personnel and equipment needed to operate effectively. Together, these teams provided medical services to 81 percent of the population, excluding only a few cantons in the Central Valley. By mid-2006 some 897 EBAIS served almost the entire population.[89] The EBAIS by 2006 had acquired additional personnel and functions (dentistry, mental health, social work), and many worked out of custom-built health centers. Like the family health teams in Brazil, the EBAIS were designed as a gateway to the entire health care system, rather than as an add-on program on the model of the Rural Health Plan and Community Health Plan of the 1970s.

The Comprehensive Basic Health Care Teams raised geographical access to outpatient care, especially among those who had previously lacked it. The appearance of the teams coincided with a sharp rise in prenatal visits.[90] Evidence also suggests that their introduction helped to reduce infant mortality. The average annual rate of infant mortality decline during the first five years of the EBAIS program (1995–2000) was higher than the average annual rate from 1960 to 2005 as a whole (Table 11.3). A 2004 study related age-specific mortality levels in each of Costa Rica's 420 districts in each year from 1985 to 2001 to the presence or absence of EBAIS and to the length of time that EBAIS had operated in the district, controlling for fertility, education, health insurance coverage, asset ownership, and other variables measurable at the county level and likely to affect mortality rates. The study found that districts into which EBAIS had been introduced tended to reduce mortality (1) faster than before the EBAIS appeared; (2) faster than similar districts in which the EBAIS were not (yet) present; and (3) faster according to the length of time that the EBAIS had been operating. The presence of EBAIS in a district, controlling for other relevant factors, was associated with 8 percent lower mortality among children and 2 percent lower mortality among adults, which implied the survival in 2001 of 120 children and 350 adults who would otherwise have died in that year. Having EBAIS in a district was associated with a 14 percent decline in deaths by communicable diseases, compared to a 2 percent decline for chronic diseases and a 0 percent decline for other causes.[91] A World Bank cost-benefit analysis estimated that the health care

[87] World Bank 2003a: 4, 8, 13, 26, 37.

[88] Rosero-Bixby 2004b: 98, 101.

[89] Figures for 1998 from Clark 2004: 202; figures for 2001 from Costa Rica. Ministerio de Salud 2002: 18, 31; figures for 2006 from Marín Camacho 2006.

[90] Outpatient care: Rosero-Bixby 2004a. Prenatal visits: Costa Rica. CCSS 2004: Table 72.

[91] Rosero-Bixby 2004b. See also World Bank 2003a: 7.

reforms averted 919 infant deaths from 1995 to 2002, about 15 percent of all infant deaths in a country that averaged 928 annually during that period.[92]

Evidence thus suggests that the rapid decline of infant mortality in Costa Rica from 1960 to 2005 was due in large measure to the design, adoption, and implementation of effective, low-cost basic health and nutrition programs, particularly during the 1970s and after 1995. This conclusion raises the question of why successive governments implemented these programs.

3.5. Costa Rica: Determinants of Public Health Care Policies

Cultural factors and historical traditions have worked in favor of good public health policies in Costa Rica. In a 1970s survey, respondents in the province of Puntarenas reported more concern about their health than about their incomes.[93] Farmers surveyed in Indonesia in the 1970s and in South Korea in the 1980s, by contrast, were more concerned with income than with health (Sections 8.5 and 10.5). Doctors in Costa Rica have high prestige, and several have served as president.[94] Physicians comprised 39 percent of Costa Rica's national legislators from 1920 to 1948, an exceptional share in relation to other Latin American countries.[95]

Study abroad, international organizations, foreign models, and geopolitical factors shaped the Costa Rican health care system during the first part of the twentieth century. Costa Rica until 1961 lacked a medical school, so all of its doctors studied abroad, where they encountered foreign health systems. Many studied at the Catholic University of Louvain, Belgium, and were influenced by socially progressive teachings of the Catholic Church.[96] The Rockefeller Foundation financed hookworm control as of the 1910s and health posts as of the 1920s; UNICEF financed milk provision as of the 1950s; and the U.S. Alliance for Progress financed twelve mobile medical units in rural areas in the 1960s.[97] The health posts set up in the 1920s and 1930s were modeled on those in the rural United States, and the 1941 Social Insurance Law was modeled closely on Chile's 1924 Workers' Insurance Fund law.[98] The British and Chilean National Health Services, which provided universal coverage from 1948 and 1953 respectively, and the Universal Declaration of Human Rights, which stipulated a right to medical care, influenced legislators who advocated universalizing health insurance in 1961.[99] The desire of Calderón Guardia and

---

[92] World Bank 2003a: 49; average number of infant deaths calculated from Costa Rica. MIDEPLAN 2008: Table 5–13.

[93] Low 1985: 17–18.

[94] Low 1985: 17–18.

[95] Palmer 2003: 216, 228–229.

[96] The Catholic University of Louvain provided good education, had a long history of relations with Latin America, and was relatively inexpensive to attend (Miranda Gutiérrez 2007).

[97] The mobile units encountered logistical problems and did little to reduce infant mortality (Vargas 1995: 64–65).

[98] Rosenberg 1979: 122; Rosenberg 1981: 284–285.

[99] Miranda Gutiérrez 2003: 255.

his allies to take an issue away from the communist left shaped the social security policies of the early 1940s, and worry about contagion from the 1959 Cuban Revolution inspired some Costa Rican legislators to vote for the 1961 constitutional amendment that gave the whole population a right to health insurance.[100]

Political democracy, or semi-democracy, shaped Costa Rican health care policy throughout the twentieth century. Costa Ricans participated in competitive elections from the late 1800s through the early 2000s. If, following Schumpeter, the "democratic method" is defined as a "competitive struggle for the people's vote," Costa Rica would register a long history of democracy.[101] In the Polity IV dataset, which uses a Schumpeterian definition of democracy, Costa Rica received in every year from 1900 to 2005 the highest possible score of "10" on democracy, the same score as the United States received in each year during this period.[102] Under a more demanding definition, however, Costa Rica might not qualify as a democracy until 1975, when the National Assembly amended the constitution to permit the electoral participation of Marxist parties, which had been effectively banned since 1949.[103] The farther back one goes in the twentieth century, the farther Costa Rica strays from a more demanding definition of democracy. Until 1949, women were not allowed to vote, fraud was widespread (although not egregious enough to change the outcomes of presidential elections), and inhabitants of West Indian descent faced various types of legal discrimination.[104] Despite these flaws in its political regime, Costa Rica even before 1975 was one of the least authoritarian developing countries in the world. From 1880 to 2000 it experienced only two years of military rule (1917–1919), and its 1949 constitution prohibited a standing army. Among the eight societies studied in this book, Costa Rica during the second half of the twentieth century was by far the most fully and consistently democratic (Table A18).

Although Costa Rica's political system during the 1930s fell short of full democracy, labor union organizing, even by Marxists, was permitted. A series of strikes by banana workers in 1934 forced the United Fruit Company to improve the health services it provided for workers. The country's main labor confederation resolved in 1943 to pressure the Calderón Guardia government to enact and enforce its newly announced Social Guarantees, among them a nationwide health care system.[105] Labor union influence in the 1940s also

---

[100] Rosenberg 1979: 122, 125.

[101] Schumpeter 1975 [1942]: 269.

[102] Marshall and Jaggers 2000. Costa Rica even received the same scores as the United States (10 on democracy, 0 on autocracy) during the 1917–1919 military dictatorship of General Federico Tinoco Granados.

[103] Hernández Valle 2006: 367–368; Martz 1967: 894; Oconitrillo 1981: 210–211. Under a more demanding definition, the United States might not qualify as a democracy until 1965, when the Voting Rights Act outlawed some of the most conspicuous practical impediments to voting by blacks in many areas of the country.

[104] Molina Jiménez and Lehoucq 1999: 227–228; Harpelle 1993.

[105] Miller 1993: 517–518.

contributed to a change in perceptions whereby "~~government intervention became a socially accepted component of development~~."[106] Pressure from doctors' organizations, on the other hand, worked against the expansion of a welfare state. The National Medical Union, the main professional association of Costa Rican physicians, arose in 1944 to counteract the perceived threat that the newly created CCSS posed to doctors' interests. In 1946 it led a strike against the fund to resist a planned extension of coverage, which was seen as a threat to doctors' private practices.[107] Over time, however, as the CCSS provided employment for physicians and improved their working conditions, the Union's opposition to the CCSS dissipated.[108] By the late 1970s some 95 percent of doctors in Costa Rica worked for the Social Security Fund.[109]

Scholars disagree about the relative weight of bureaucratic initiative on the one hand, and of democracy and interest-group pressure on the other, in encouraging the introduction of contributory social insurance in the 1940s. According to one interpretation, "the decisive leadership in social security was undertaken as if in an authoritarian system, with little mass participation."[110] In this interpretation, neither electoral incentives nor labor union activity contributed significantly to the introduction of contributory pension and health insurance. Rather, autonomous social security officials, authorized by progressive politicians and inspired and advised by experts from the International Labour Office, led the policy-making process.[111] Other scholars have cited Calderón Guardia's need to retain the backing of the Communist Party, together with his courtship of worker support, as motives for his welfare-state policies.[112] Indeed, even scholars associated with the bureaucratic initiative interpretation recognize that "democratic electoral political arrangements and the growing population pressure ma[d]e some measure of elite responsibility mandatory."[113]

Contributory health insurance typically benefits the not-so-poor, among whom infants have a relatively low risk of early death. In Costa Rica, accordingly, analyses have found no association between the expansion of health insurance coverage in the 1970s and the pace of decline of infant mortality rates across cantons, or between the level of health insurance coverage in the 1990s and the level of infant mortality across cantons.[114] More important than

---

[106] Hytrek 1995: 84–85.
[107] Miranda Gutiérrez 2003: 25; Miranda Gutiérrez 2007; Rosenberg 1979: 131 fn. 8; Rosenberg 1983: 87–103.
[108] Jara Vargas 2002: 23–27.
[109] Casas and Vargas 1980: 268.
[110] Rosenberg 1983: 184.
[111] Rosenberg 1979: 126–129; Rosenberg 1983: 151–152, 173–174. Similar arguments have been made by Malloy (1979) for Brazil in the 1940s and by Joo (1999) and Kwon (1999) for South Korea in the 1970s.
[112] Bell 1971: 27; Yashar 1995: 73, 83.
[113] Rosenberg 1979: 130.
[114] On the 1970s see Dow and Schmeer 2003; on the 1990s see Rosero-Bixby 2004b: 99.

contributory health insurance coverage as a determinant of infant mortality, the Costa Rican case suggests, is the delivery of basic health services to vulnerable mothers and infants, regardless of insurance coverage. The widespread delivery of basic health services to the poor began in the 1970s and 1990s, not in the 1940s. A critical analytical task, therefore, is to explain the origins of Costa Rica's major primary health care programs. Special attention is devoted to assessing how and to what degree bureaucratic initiative, democracy, interest group pressure, and international factors contributed to the Rural Health Plan and Community Health Plan of the 1970s and to the EBAIS program of the 1990s.

One interpretation of the political origins of the community-based health and nutrition programs of the 1970s recalls the "bureaucratic initiative" interpretation of the political origins of social insurance. According to this interpretation, the policies that precipitated Costa Rica's infant mortality "breakthrough" in the 1970s were "essentially a bureaucratic achievement. There was no popular crusade."[115] Dr. Edgar Mohs, the vice-minister of health in 1970–1971, recalled that President José Figueres Ferrer wanted to leave a legacy of social achievement as he began his third presidential term (1970–1974).[116] Figueres Ferrer took office in 1970 "with ambitious plans to revamp the health system"[117] and gave strong support to the first National Health Plan, which called for the universalization of social insurance and the extension of primary care to the poor.[118] In a book he wrote while president, Figueres devoted several paragraphs to malnutrition, which Dr. Mohs argued was caused mainly by disease.[119] Francisco Morales, a PLN legislator who worked with Figueres to establish the IMAS, concluded that Figueres Ferrer "may not have won many battles personally in the war against poverty, but he made people aware of it and of the need to act."[120]

The leadership of Figueres Ferrer and his health care team was exercised, however, in a political context marked by factional conflict within the PLN and by competition between the PLN and other parties. In 1968 PLN leftists, many from the Youth Branch of the party, produced the Patio de Agua manifesto calling for major social reforms, including publicly funded and publicly provided health care for the entire population.[121] The backers of the Patio de Agua manifesto believed that the PLN had lost its "social energy" and that it ran the risk of bureaucratic ossification.[122] In addition, they wished to convert the PLN from a highly personalistic organization to a well-institutionalized

[115] Caldwell 1986: 200.
[116] Mohs 1995.
[117] Morgan 1993: 96.
[118] Miranda Gutiérrez 2003: 262.
[119] Figueres Ferrer 1973: 83–84; Mohs 2002: 70.
[120] Ameringer 1978: 257.
[121] PLN 1968: Cap. IV, "La Salud." Patio de Agua was the name of the estate at which the document was written.
[122] Miranda Gutiérrez 2007.

political party with established procedures for choosing leaders and candidates.[123] Figueres Ferrer called the Patio de Agua manifesto "the work of madmen," and most of the PLN members who had signed it soon returned to the fold.[124] The fact that Figueres was pressured within his party more from the left than from the right, however, added impetus to the "war on misery" that he had pledged to fight.[125]

Electoral incentives contributed to the expansion of basic health services in the 1970s. After compulsory voting was introduced in 1959, turnout in presidential elections rose from 65 to 80 percent.[126] By the mid-1960s the rural poor were voting in large numbers. Surveys in the early 1970s showed that peasants, compared to urban residents, were more likely to join community organizations, just as likely to participate in political campaigns, and only slightly less likely to vote.[127] A survey of Costa Rican male peasants in 1972–1973 also showed that political participation, including voting and contacting officials, was higher among poorer than among richer respondents.[128] At the beginning of the twenty-first century class bias in political participation was lower in Costa Rica than in Argentina, Brazil, or Chile, and lower than in most Latin American countries.[129] Costa Rican politicians, then, had good reasons to court the votes of the rural poor.

As in Chile, the major political parties competed for these votes during the 1960s. During the 1950s the PLN enjoyed an electoral advantage among most sectors of the rural poor,[130] partly because of its "programmatic emphasis on social services and extensive assistance of various sorts to the Costa Rican masses." Over time, however, the PLN's margin in rural cantons fell, from 14 percent in 1958 to 7 percent in 1962 to 3 percent in 1966.[131] This decline gave the PLN an incentive to redouble its efforts in rural areas, the more so because political observers anticipated that the 1970 presidential election would be close (it wasn't). Accordingly, between early 1968 and January 1970, Figueres Ferrer took his campaign to a reported 807 towns and villages. In his September 1968 speech accepting the PLN nomination, Figueres announced that he would fight a "war on misery," and reiterated this pledge throughout his campaign. The election results suggested that Figueres attracted a large

---

[123] Gutiérrez Sáenz 2004: 210.

[124] Rosenberg 1983: 152; quotation from English 1971: 54 fn. 10.

[125] Wells 1970–71: 25. Dr. Guido Miranda, a signatory to the Patio de Agua manifesto who served as the medical director of the CCSS from 1970 to 1978, believed that the challenge embodied in the manifesto contributed to the social policies of the 1970–1974 Figueres Ferrer administration (Miranda Gutiérrez 2007).

[126] Voters as a share of the eligible population rose from 65 percent in 1958 to 81 percent in 1962 (Martz 1967: 895), and remained at about 80 percent through 1994 (Seligson 2002: 161–162).

[127] Booth and Seligson 1979: 42; Seligson 2002: 171.

[128] Seligson 1978: 147–152.

[129] Gaviria, Panizza, and Wallack 2003: 17.

[130] English 1971: 107–108.

[131] Martz 1967: 904; quotation from p. 906.

number of swing voters in the provinces of Limón and Puntarenas, which had numerous foreign-owned cacao and banana plantations whose relatively well-off employees often voted for Communist or Social Christian candidates.

The legal framework governing public health care provision was changed under Figueres Ferrer, but the rollout of the Rural Health Plan and Community Health Plan took place mainly during the next presidential term, that of Daniel Oduber (1974–1978).[132] Both Figueres and Oduber belonged to the PLN, but Oduber was to the ideological left of Figueres and was even more identified with support of social and economic policies designed to benefit the poor. Oduber made explicit use of social policies to win votes, arguing that "we [the PLN] must wrest the banner of social security from the *mariachis*" (a colloquialism for the opposition Partido Unificación Nacional).[133]

Rodrigo Carazo of the opposition Coalición Unidad won the presidential election of 1978. Like Figueres Ferrer and Oduber, Carazo had to deal with ideological heterogeneity among his followers. Even as he responded to the debt crisis of 1980 with the austere economic policies and free-market reforms favored by the right wing of his coalition, Carazo used pro-poor social policies to placate its left wing. Moreover, even though the economic crisis had forced him to cut health services, Carazo announced plans to train another 2,000 health care workers in impoverished regions. His government also set up system of citizen health care committees and surveyed 43 rural cantons to identify pressing health problems and to solicit proposals for resolving them. Only about 20 percent of these proposals were eventually implemented, but the surveys, once taken, put pressure on Carazo, as well as on succeeding presidents, to resolve the problems that had been identified.[134]

Carazo used the health care committees to try to win support. The president and his backers viewed community participation in health care as a way of undermining undemocratically chosen local "caciques," often tied to the PLN. The Coalición Unidad leaders also frequently contrasted their "participatory" strategy with the "intervention and paternalism" of the PLN. For its part, the leaders of the PLN, on hearing of Carazo's plans to form the health care committees, accused the president of trying to steal their party's issue. PLN politicians "were obliged by their own sense of partisan rivalry to oppose the community participation program, which Carazo had given top billing."[135] At least in the eyes of the PLN politicians, then, partisan sentiments and electoral incentives deserve some of the credit for perpetuating the Rural Health Plan and Community Health Plan after 1978, when the presidency passed from the PLN to its opponents, and when health care funding was cut.

Carazo's successor, the PLN's Luis Alberto Monge (1982–1986), left the local-level health care committees intact, not least because they helped to

[132] Miranda Gutiérrez 2007.
[133] Gutiérrez Góngora 2007.
[134] Morgan 1990: 216; Morgan 1993: 98.
[135] Morgan 1993: 98–108; quotation from 110.

provide supplies and to pay the expenses of the local health posts. He disbanded higher-level federations of health care committees, however, in part because "some members of the PLN simply wanted no part of the pet program of their opponents" in a context where "organizers from both political parties suspected their opponents of using community participation as a covert way to fortify rural political bases."[136] Electoral incentives thus played into the characteristics as well as the origins and dynamics of the Rural Health Plan. Water provision also was influenced by electoral incentives. One public health expert noted that "water supply has been a political weapon in most presidential campaigns."[137]

No available evidence suggests that interest groups lobbied for the 1970 National Health Plan, which created a framework for the primary health care programs enacted later in the decade. On the contrary, Dr. Rodrigo Gutiérrez Sáenz, who helped to draft the National Health Plan, reported that José Luis Orlich, the health minister from 1970 to 1974, was compelled "to neutralize, tactfully but firmly, pressure from doctors' groups, powerful business executives, and political notables to dismantle the reform program." Progressive doctors from both major parties supported the program; conservative doctors opposed it. The opposition of conservative doctors was based in part on worries that a rapid rise in the number of MDs – a necessary condition for expanding basic health services to the poor – would flood the market, forcing doctors to look for work as "taxi drivers," and that the inclusion of social medicine in the medical school curriculum would turn physicians into Chinese-style "barefoot doctors."[138] Some doctors even sued the administrators of the Rural Health Plan, charging that the handling of medical cases by paraprofessionals amounted to the "illegal practice of medicine."[139] Others opposed the transfer in the 1970s and early 1980s of all of the country's hospitals to the Social Security Fund, worried that bureaucratization and politicization would lead to a deterioration in the quality of medical care.[140] Doctors also voiced opposition to Carazo's plan to expand community participation in health care administration, especially after it was proposed that community members should evaluate physician performance.[141] Other doctors supported the program, however, and those who opposed it lacked the resources to prevent the programs from going forward.

International organizations played a major part in the primary health care programs of the 1970s. The 1972 meeting in Santiago, Chile, of Ministers of Health of the Americas, which was organized by the Pan American Health Organization, provided impetus throughout Latin America for "comprehensive,

---

[136] Morgan 1990: 217.
[137] Mata 1985: 69.
[138] Gutiérrez Sáenz 2004: 214 ("taxi drivers"), 220–221, 225 ("barefoot doctors").
[139] Villegas de Olazábal 2004: 237.
[140] Gutiérrez Góngora 2007.
[141] Morgan 1990: 217; Morgan 1993: 110; Rodríguez Aragones, Mohs, and Evans 1971: 2.

state-sponsored rural health programs of the kind later championed by the
World Health Organization and UNICEF under the banner of primary
health care."[142] In the 1970s, the Inter-American Development Bank helped
to finance the construction of the Social Security Fund's outpatient facilities
and the refurbishing of regional hospitals around the country.[143] During the
1970s, PAHO experts served as the "right hand" of the Costa Rican health
authorities who implemented the primary care programs of the decade.[144] The
World Health Organization/Pan American Health Organization, UNICEF,
the United Nations Development Programme, CARE, and the U.S. Agency
for International Development all helped to fund the Rural Health Plan.[145]
Foreign models, however, do not seem to have been important. The designers of the Rural Health Plan were not "motivated to visit similar programs
in other countries" because "outreach programs targeting rural communities
were practically unknown at the time."[146]

In 1992 the PLN pre-candidate José María Figueres Olsen, the son of the
former president José Figueres Ferrer, asked a group of public health experts
to draw up a health care reform plan. He used it in his campaign for the presidency, which he won in February 1994 by a narrow margin over the PUSC
candidate, Miguel Ángel Rodríguez, who had not drawn up a health care
reform plan.[147] After taking office, Figueres Olsen adopted the Comprehensive
Basic Health Care Team (EBAIS) initiative as a flagship program of his administration. He insisted on fully funding it despite a freeze on overall spending,
and met weekly with Social Security Fund and health ministry officials to
discuss its progress.[148] The EBAIS program encountered resistance. Doctors
worried that the program would reduce their prestige, and possibly their job
security, as health workers with minimal training provided an increasing
share of medical care. Nurses and nursing aides worried that they would be
taken out of urban hospitals and sent to work in remote health posts. Unions
and left parties were suspicious that a program backed by the World Bank
would lead to the "privatization" of health care.[149] Some members of the
PLN "old guard" also resisted the program, arguing that the EBAIS would
be too costly, too curatively oriented, and too inefficient a use of doctors'

---

[142] Morgan 1993: 94 (quotation); PLN 1973: 1, 3; Vargas 1995: 65–66; Vargas González
1977: 355.
[143] Casas and Vargas 1980: 271–272.
[144] Martínez Franzoni 1999: 165.
[145] Costa Rica. Ministerio de Salud 1976: 7.
[146] Vargas 1995: 67. Actually, the SESP in Brazil had been providing basic health care in the
Northeast and the Amazon since 1942 (Section 5.4); and several Argentine provincial governments had launched important primary health care initiatives in the late 1960s and early
1970s (Section 6.4).
[147] Marín 2007.
[148] Ayala 2007.
[149] Ayala 2007; Clark 2005: 13; Marín 2007; Salas 2007; Weyland 2006: 206.

technical training.[150] To handle this resistance Dr. Alvaro Salas, the Director of the Social Security Fund, held as many as 150–200 meetings with academic experts and the leaders of organizations representing health professionals, in part to provide assurance that the CCSS would remain a unified public institution.[151] Dr. Herman Weinstock and Dr. Fernando Marín, meanwhile, negotiated with health ministry unions the transfer of 1,600 employees to the Social Security Fund. Concessions during these negotiations raised the cost of the Comprehensive Basic Health Care Team program but gained the unions' support.[152]

In the Costa Rican electoral system, the 57 National Assembly members are elected by proportional representation, with the country's seven provinces serving as electoral districts. Accordingly, legislators lobbied the government to implement the EBAIS program first in heavily populated areas, where most of the votes are concentrated. The executive branch's health care reform team resisted, insisting the EBAIS be launched first in the poorest areas, which tended to be in more sparsely populated rural areas on the periphery of the country.[153] With the backing of President Figueres Olsen the health care reform team won out, and the program was implemented first in the peripheral regions. In this case, one aspect of democracy, electoral incentives, worked in a manner inimical to the interests of the poor.

Electoral incentives do not, however, exhaust the range of ways in which democracy can influence public health policies. The right of local communities to organize themselves helped to sustain the EBAIS program after the presidency shifted from the PLN's José Figueres Olsen to the PUSC's Miguel Ángel Rodríguez (1998–2002). Rodríguez, an economist, was more concerned about the pension system than about health care reform, which was identified with the preceding governments of Calderón Fournier and especially Figueres Olsen.[154] By 1998, however "the health teams had become popular and communities not yet covered were demanding theirs."[155] When the EBAIS began operating in a certain area, neighboring communities would pressure the government to set up a team in their own region.[156] Democracy thus contributed to the expansion of the EBAIS by permitting community organization, which put pressure on the subsequent PUSC governments of Rodríguez and Pacheco (2002–2006) to keep expanding the program.

The willingness of the Costa Rican medical establishment to cooperate, albeit sometimes grudgingly, with government health care reform efforts in

---

[150] Marín 2007. The "old guard" included health ministry and social security officials prominent in the 1970s.
[151] Clark 2004: 199; Salas 2007.
[152] Marín 2007.
[153] Ayala 2007; Marín 2007; Salas 2007; Weyland 2006: 174; compare to Clark 2004: 201–202.
[154] Salas 2007.
[155] Clark 2004: 204–205.
[156] Rodríguez Herrera 2006: 21.

both the 1970s and 1990s contrasts with the case of Brazil, where associations of doctors, hospitals, drug manufacturers, and health insurers delayed the introduction of the Unified Health System (SUS) from 1988 to 1993. The health insurance systems prevailing in the two countries help to explain why these groups acted differently in each case. In Brazil the contributory health insurance funds mainly purchased medical services from private providers, whereas in Costa Rica the Social Security Fund delivered most medical services through its own facilities and health care professionals. Hence, although doctors, nurses, and other health personnel were among the most strongly unionized sectors of the (weakly unionized) Costa Rican labor force, most of them were ultimately dependent economically on employment by the Social Security Fund.[157] In Costa Rica, moreover, the population is too small to support a major pharmaceutical or medical equipment industry, and it remained illegal through 2006 to sell private health insurance in the country. In Costa Rica, therefore, doctors, medical business, and health insurance companies had less leverage vis-à-vis government health reformers than in Brazil, where resistance to reform efforts in the 1990s was more vigorous and more effective at delaying the restructuring of the health care system.

In Costa Rica, then, the dependence of most health care professionals on salaries paid by the Social Security Fund, coupled with the lack of private health insurers and the scarcity of medical business, facilitated the health care reforms of the 1970s and 1990s, both of which expanded health services among the poor. In Argentina, as in Brazil, unions were stronger than in Costa Rica, and many union members, union leaders, and physicians had vested interests in the continued predominance of contributory health insurance and private-sector health care delivery. Accordingly, pro-poor health care reforms were much harder to implement. Argentine union leaders in charge of huge health insurance funds thwarted efforts by three different governments to combine the resources of those funds with general tax revenues into a single stream of financing for universal health care (Section 5.5). In Costa Rica, by contrast, the Social Security Fund, rather than union leaders, controlled from the outset all funds generated by payroll deductions. With an accordingly diminished stake in the survival of inequities generated by the separation of the contributory from the general revenue-funded health care subsystems, union leaders had fewer incentives in Costa Rica than in Argentina to resist the extension of health services to impoverished groups.

International factors of various sorts contributed to the Comprehensive Basic Health Care Team program of the 1990s, but not as much as such factors shaped the Rural Health Plan and Community Health Plan of the 1970s, or even the social security reform of the 1940s. The World Bank promoted and helped to finance the health care reform of which the EBAIS were a part, but pushed initially for privatization on the model of the Chilean Social Security Health Institutions (ISAPREs) (Section 4.4). The World Bank opposed the

[157] Clark 2004: 202.

EBAIS themselves as too costly, favoring instead a more limited package of health care services targeted to the poorest. The prospective capitation mode of financing by which the EBAIS are supposed to be funded was inspired by the British National Health Service, and the performance contracts by which hospitals and clinics are supposed to be reimbursed were inspired by a system used in Catalonia, Spain.[158] The EBAIS, however, were inspired less by foreign models than by domestic initiatives from the 1970s, including the Rural Health Plan and the Community Health Plan.[159] The EBAIS closely resembled Brazil's Family Health Teams, which were scaled up to the national level in 1994 (a year before the Costa Rican EBAIS), but a Social Security Fund document had proposed the formation of "Equipos Básicos de Atención Integral" as early as 1986, years before the Brazilian program was conceived of.[160] This sequence of events, together with the similarity between the Costa Rican EBAIS and Brazilian Family Health programs, raises the possibility that emulation went in the opposite direction. Members of the team that designed and implemented the EBAIS did not recall having interacted with Brazilian public health officials in the mid-1980s, however, and Jose Serra, the Brazilian health minister from 1998 to 2002, reported that he was unaware of the EBAIS.[161]

Each of the factors analyzed in this section – bureaucratic initiative, political regime form (democracy in the Costa Rican case), interest group pressure (facilitated by democracy), and international influence of various sorts – had intertwined, complex, and sometimes contradictory effects on the social security reform of the 1940s, on the primary health care programs of the 1970s, and on the Comprehensive Basic Health Care Team program of the 1990s. Bureaucratic initiative was the main impetus behind the social security reform in the 1940s, and was also a major force behind the EBAIS program in the 1990s. Electoral incentives and community organization helped the Rural Health Plan and Community Health Plan survive the PLN's loss of the presidency in 1979 and the economic crisis of the 1980s. Health professionals initially opposed each of the three reforms, but their memberships were divided and their bargaining power was limited by their dependence on employment by the Ministry of Health or the Social Security Fund. International organizations supported the primary care programs of the 1970s, but the World Bank initially opposed the EBAIS program of the 1990s. Foreign models were crucial to the social security reform of the 1940s, but not to the primary care programs of the 1970s or to the EBAIS program of the 1990s (except in the case of provider payment schemes whose implementation was delayed).

---

[158] Martínez Franzoni 1999: 170–171; Weyland 2006: 204–206. Capitation as of 2003 had not been implemented (Clark 2004: 207).

[159] Marín 2007.

[160] Costa Rica. CCSS 1986: 11.

[161] Serra 2003a. Neither Norma Ayala (2007), nor Fernando Marín (2007), nor Alvaro Salas (2007), nor Luis Bernardo Sáenz (2007) remembered visits by Brazilians to study the EBAIS, although Salas noted that the head of PAHO from 1982 to 1995, a Brazilian, would have been well aware of the program.

Looking more closely at the impact of democracy, Costa Rica shows that electoral incentives can either promote or impede health care policies that favor the poor. In 1978, when the presidency passed from Oduber to Carazo, competition between the PLN and the Coalición Unidad helped to sustain the Rural Health Plan and Community Health Plan. In 1995, however, PLN legislators pressured the Figueres Olsen government to initiate the Comprehensive Basic Health Care Team program in vote-rich urban areas rather than in sparsely populated but needier rural communities. Community organization, which is facilitated by democracy, put pressure on Carazo's Coalición Unidad government (1978–1982) to preserve the PLN's primary health care initiatives of the 1970s, and encouraged the PUSC government of Miguel Ángel Rodríguez (1998–2002) to preserve the EBAIS program begun under the PLN's José Figueres Olsen (1994–1998). During most of the twentieth century, a free press, along with the right to assemble and organize, has made it easier for Costa Ricans to discover and debate issues related to health care. Perhaps most importantly, the sense of equality and entitlement that all citizens, including those of modest means, acquire in the context of long years of democratic (or semi-democratic) experience, should not be underestimated as a broad policy-conditioning force. This factor also contributed in Chile to the expansion of basic health services to the poor.

4

Chile: The Pinochet Paradox

Chile in 1960 had a fairly high level of overall affluence, one of Latin America's most extensive welfare states, a militant labor movement, and 30 years of political stability and competitive politics. Nevertheless, it had an average life expectancy at birth of only 57 years and an infant mortality rate of 120 per 1000 – higher than the rate of 115 per 1000 in much poorer Brazil (Tables A1 and A3). Behind the high rate of infant mortality in Chile in 1960 was the neglect of basic health services in poor communities, especially in rural areas. Behind this neglect, in turn, were clientelistic ties between the rural poor and landowning elites, which created captive votes for conservative parties.

The next 45 years told a different story. Chile from 1960 to 2005 raised life expectancy and reduced infant mortality more, in percentage terms, than any other Latin American country. By 2005 Chile's infant mortality rate was second lowest (to Cuba's) in Latin America, and only slightly higher than the rate in the United States.[1] From 1960 to 2005 Chile's infant mortality rate went from being nearly twice as high as Argentina's to about half as high, and from being higher than Brazil's to less than half the Brazilian rate (Table A1). Improvement in the public provision of basic health services to the poor bears a large share of responsibility for Chile's success at reducing infant mortality from 1960 to 2005 and at achieving a low level of infant mortality in 2005. Bureaucratic initiative contributed to this improvement, particularly during the military regime that prevailed from 1973 to 1990, but so did the broadening and deepening of democracy from 1958 to 1973 and again from 1990 to 2005.

Rapid infant mortality decline took place not only during eras of competitive politics (1960–1973; 1990–2005), but also under a harsh military regime (1973–1990). The steepest decline occurred from 1973 to 1984, during the most repressive years of military rule. Making this plunge even more remarkable, GDP per capita shrank during those 12 years, while income inequality

[1] Chile (7.9 per 1000): Table A1 (vital registration); USA (6.9 per 1000): Mathews and MacDorman 2008: 3.

and income poverty soared. The sharp drop of infant mortality from 1973 to 1984 raises intriguing questions: did policies of the military government contribute to the plunge? If so, which policies helped, and why did the government enact them? What does Chile's experience tell us about how political democracy affects the public provision of basic social services, and about how the public provision of basic social services affects the decline of infant mortality?

4.1. Chile: Mortality

In 2005, Chile's infant mortality rate according to vital registration statistics was 7.9 per 1000, and its life expectancy at birth was 78.2 years (Tables A1 and A2), six months longer than in the United States (77.7 years).[2] These figures placed Chile in the top 25 percent of the world's countries on each indicator. From 1960 to 2005, Chile ranked in the top 5 percent of countries at reducing infant mortality and raising life expectancy.[3] Compared to other countries around the world, then, Chile from 1960 to 2005 reduced mortality very steeply, to a remarkably low level.

In 1964, when Eduardo Frei Montalva, a Christian Democrat, became president, Chile's infant mortality rate was 104 per 1000, about the same as in 1953 (105 per 1000). By the end of Frei's presidency (1964–1970) the rate had fallen to 82 per 1000, and by the end of Salvador Allende's presidency (1970–1973) it was down to 66 per 1000. Other mortality indicators also improved rapidly under Frei Montalva and under Allende.[4] Although the rapid fall of infant mortality under General Pinochet (1973–1990) has received more attention, Chile made very respectable progress on a wide range of mortality indicators under a competitive political system from 1964 to 1973.

The decline of infant mortality under military rule occurred almost entirely between 1973 and 1984, when the rate fell from 65.2 to 19.6 per 1000, one of the sharpest sustained drops on record in any country ever. From 1985 to 1990, however, despite faster economic growth than in the first decade of the military regime, infant mortality fell only from 19.5 to 16.0 per 1000. Rapid decline resumed after democracy returned in 1990. It took only 11 years, from 1990 to 2000, for Chile to cut its infant mortality rate from 16.0 to 8.9

---

[2] U.S. figure from World Bank 2008c. Experts express confidence in Chilean vital registration statistics from 1960 forward. McGuire (2009), Web Appendix A1, reviews the quality of Chilean infant mortality statistics.

[3] In 2005, Chile ranked 45th of 189 countries on lowness of infant mortality and 34th of 170 countries on life expectancy at birth. From 1960 to 2005, Chile ranked 5th of 145 countries on percent decline of infant mortality and 7th of 178 countries on percent rise of life expectancy (World Bank 2008e, except Taiwan, from Tables A1 and A2).

[4] Infant mortality (vital registration): 1953: Mamalakis 1980: 40. 1970, 1973: United Nations 1992: 76. From 1964 to 1973 maternal mortality fell from 238 to 123 per 100,000 live births, while life expectancy at age 1 rose from 66.0 to 69.3 years (Chile. Banco Central 1989: 405, 424).

per 1000; it took the United States 17 years, from 1975 to 1991, to reduce its own rate from 16.1 to 8.9 per 1000.[5] What needs to be explained, then, is why infant mortality was so high in Chile in 1960, and why a rapid decline began in the mid-1960s, accelerated during the first decade of the military regime, slowed in the late 1980s, and sped up again after democracy returned in 1990.

4.2. Chile: Affluence, Inequality, and Poverty

Chile from 1960 to 2005 did extremely well, in cross-national perspective, at raising life expectancy and reducing infant mortality. By comparison, its performance at GDP per capita growth was an unexceptional 2.0 percent a year from 1960 to 2003, only 46th greatest among 98 countries with available data, and only 41st among 64 countries outside sub-Saharan Africa.[6] From 1960 to 1985, moreover, infant mortality plunged from 120 per 1000 to 20 per 1000, even though GDP per capita rose only from $5,086 to $5,728 (Tables A1 and A3). From 1960 to 1985, accordingly, Chile had fast infant mortality decline despite slow economic growth, whereas from 1985 to 1990 it had slow infant mortality decline despite fast economic growth. After 1985 the tempos coincided more closely, but across eight five-year periods from 1960 to 2000 the tempo of GDP per capita growth was correlated negatively with the tempo of infant mortality decline (Table 11.1).

Chilean governments from the mid-1950s to the early 1970s engaged in the single-minded pursuit of premature heavy import substitution, using revenue mainly from copper exports to finance the import of needed machinery.[7] Economic problems caused by this arrangement, together with expectations generated by promises of land reform and income redistribution, created growing tension by the end of the 1960s.[8] In 1970, Dr. Salvador Allende, a Socialist, won the presidency with only 36 percent of the vote. Undaunted by this frail mandate, Allende announced a transition to socialism and began to nationalize copper companies, raise the minimum wage, expand the scope of land reform, and boost social spending. Transitions from capitalism to socialism (or vice versa) incur huge transitional costs, and this one was no exception. Imports of food and consumer goods rose and foreign exchange dried up, exacerbated by a drop in copper prices. By 1973, the fiscal deficit reached 25 percent of GDP. The United States ended economic aid to Chile, pressured

---

[5] Chile 1973–1989: United Nations 1992: 76. Chile 1990–2000: Chile. Ministerio de Salud 2008. USA 1975–1991: United States. Bureau of the Census 2008a: 62. All figures in both countries are from vital registration data.

[6] Calculated from Heston, Summers, and Aten 2006, variable RGDPCH.

[7] Johnson (1967) describes spectacular inefficiencies of import substitution in the Chilean automobile industry. From 1960 to 1973 copper rose from 68 to 78 percent of Chilean export revenue (Meller 2002: 17).

[8] Cardoso and Helwege 2000.

international financial institutions to stop lending to the Allende government, forced Chilean firms to pay cash for spare parts and other imports, and financed newspapers and organizations opposed to the government. Land seizures, factory occupations, and strikes burgeoned, while inflation rose to 78 percent in 1972 and to 353 percent in 1973.[9] On September 11, 1973, Allende was overthrown in a military coup, ending 42 years of regular elections and continuous civilian rule.

The ensuing military regime under General Pinochet (1973–1990) was one of the harshest in modern Latin American history. Security forces under military rule killed or "disappeared" at least 2,000 persons and arrested and abused many more.[10] The military authorities shut down parties and unions, censored the press, purged universities, and stifled artistic expression. Meanwhile, they replaced the import-substitution model with a new free-market strategy, privatizing 400 state firms, cutting tariffs, weakening laws protecting workers and unions, and selling or returning to former owners most of the land distributed under Frei Montalva and Allende.[11] Cuts in import tariffs and the recessionary impact of other economic policies destroyed hundreds of previously protected industrial firms, contributing to a 16 percent drop in GDP per capita in a single year, 1975. Despite this sharp contraction, the free-market reforms raised confidence among more competitive or otherwise favored entrepreneurs and emboldened them to borrow heavily from foreign banks, which were bursting with petrodollars and eager to lend. Overborrowing led to another economic crisis. In 1982–1983, GDP per capita fell by 18 percent and unemployment rose to 20 percent.[12]

The first crash in 1975 got rid of much of Chile's inefficient industry; the second in 1982–1983 provided some sobering lessons about overborrowing and speculation. Businesses that survived these catastrophes were likely to be viable, given an upturn in the business cycle and an environment of cautious macroeconomic policies, which the government proceeded to enact. As the economy recovered in the mid-1980s, the finance ministry replaced the radical neoliberalism of the 1970s with a more pragmatic variant.[13] To raise revenue, improve the balance of trade, and protect recovering industries, the economic team in 1984 raised import tariffs from 20 to 35 percent.[14] To promote exports, the finance ministry in the mid- and late 1980s kept the peso undervalued (it had been highly overvalued in the late 1970s) and raised subsidies for non-copper exports like timber, fruit, wine, and seafood. To reduce the destabilizing impact of hot money, ministry officials in the late 1980s imposed

---

[9] Cardoso and Helwege 1994: 52–54; Stallings 1978: 125–153. Fiscal deficit from Paus 1994: 37; inflation from Programa de Economía del Trabajo 1992: 37.

[10] Chile. CNVR 1993. Disappearance figure from Appendix II.

[11] Constable and Valenzuela 1991: 166–246; Jarvis 1985: 5, 26.

[12] Graham 1994: 33–42; Roddick 1988: 24–38.

[13] Silva 1996: Chapters 5 and 7.

[14] Mesa-Lago 2000a: 87. In 1987, import tariffs were reduced to 15 percent.

taxes and reserve requirements on short-term foreign capital. These policies, some of which resembled South Korea's and Taiwan's in the 1960s and 1970s, helped to raise Chile's GDP per capita from $5,518 in 1983 (down from $6,115 in 1974) to $7,013 in 1989.[15]

In 1988, with economic growth soaring and under international pressure to step down, General Pinochet called a plebiscite in which Chileans were asked to vote for or against his continuation in office for another eight years. Those voting to reject his continuation won by 55 to 43 percent. In the 1989 elections the Concertación coalition, which included the Christian Democrats, the Socialists, and some smaller left and center parties, won the presidency, a majority in the Chamber of Deputies, and a plurality of elected senators (military-designated senators prevented Concertación from winning a majority in both houses of congress). Concertación also won the 1994, 2000, and 2006 elections, defeating candidates of the right who drew votes from backers of the military regime. The Christian Democrats Patricio Aylwin (1990–1994) and Eduardo Frei Ruiz-Tagle (1994–2000) served the first two terms of the new democracy; the Socialists Ricardo Lagos (2000–2006) and Michelle Bachelet (2006–2010) served the next two.

With the transfer of office in March 1990, the Concertación coalition inherited a growing economy. Macroeconomic indicators were favorable, and conditions were ripe for an inflow of foreign capital. Populist-type policies had failed in the 1980s in Argentina, Brazil, and Peru (as well as in Chile itself in the mid-1960s and early 1970s), and enthusiasm for free-market reform was sweeping the world. In this context, the Concertación leaders decided that the pre-1973 import-substitution model was no longer viable.[16] Accordingly, while discarding the radical free-market orientation of the mid- and late 1970s, they maintained the pragmatic free-market orientation of the mid- and late 1980s, which featured cautious macroeconomic policies, export promotion, and openness to foreign trade and long-term foreign investment. The economy responded with rapid GDP per capita growth, averaging 4.2 percent per year from 1990 to 2004.[17]

Chile achieved rapid infant mortality decline from 1960 to 2005 despite the serious handicap of high and rising income inequality. From 1960 to 1990 Chile's Gini index averaged 51.8, 16th highest among 106 countries with available data.[18] Income inequality in the Santiago metropolitan area, which had remained steady from 1960 to 1973, rose sharply under military rule from 1973 to 1990, when the fastest infant mortality decline occurred.[19] Partly because the Concertación governments maintained a mostly free-market orientation, income inequality changed little from 1990 to 2000, although infant

---

[15] Heston, Summers, and Aten 2006, variable RGDPCH.
[16] Weyland 1997; Weyland 1999.
[17] Heston, Summers, and Aten 2006, variable RGDPCH.
[18] Deininger and Squire 1996: 574–577.
[19] Larrañaga 2001: 305; Marcel and Solimano 1994: 219.

mortality resumed a rapid decline after stagnating in the late 1980s (Tables A1 and A4). In 1996 Chile's Gini Index was 54.8, highest among the top 67 countries on the UNDP's Human Development Index, on which Chile ranked 38th.[20] Accordingly, Chile calls into question such claims as "a society with a highly unequal distribution of income...can never meet the basic needs of many of its people."[21] Despite high income inequality, Chile from 1960 to 2005 did better than most other developing countries at meeting the basic needs of the least advantaged sectors of the population.

A lower income poverty headcount means that a larger share of the population has adequate resources with which to purchase food, housing, health care, and other basic needs, which should reduce the risk of early death, particularly among vulnerable people. From 1960 to 1968 urban poverty fell sharply, and new laws and policies during the late 1960s almost certainly reduced rural poverty as well.[22] Then, from 1970 to 1990, U.S. $2 per day poverty rose from 21 to 31 percent of the population. As was also the case in Costa Rica, then, income poverty and the decline of infant mortality in Chile evolved according to very different tempos. In the 1960s, income poverty fell rapidly while infant mortality fell slowly. In the 1970s and 1980s, infant mortality plunged while income poverty rose. Only from 1990 to 2005 did both poverty and infant mortality decline in rough synchrony (Tables A1 and A5).

To what extent, then, do GDP per capita, income inequality, and income poverty explain Chile's low level of infant mortality in 2005, its steep decline of infant mortality from 1960 to 2005, or the tempo of its infant mortality decline within that period? On level, Chile in 2005 had very low infant mortality for its level of GDP per capita (Figure 1.1). On progress, Chile from 1960 to 2005 achieved one of the fastest infant mortality declines in the world despite sluggish economic growth and rising income inequality. On tempo, the correlation between GDP per capita growth and infant mortality decline across eight five-year periods from 1960 to 2000 (1960–1965,... 1995–2000) was negative (Table 11.1), rather than strongly positive as would be expected if the wealthier is healthier conjecture obtained. Particularly worth noting in this context is that Chile from 1967 to 1983 reduced infant mortality from 95 to 22 per 1000, even though GDP per capita fell from $5,791 to $5,518, the Gini index of income inequality soared from 46 to 55 (1971–1985), and the share of the population receiving less than U.S. $2 per day rose from 21 to 31 percent (1970–1990).[23] The public provision of basic social services does better than income-related indicators at explaining the pattern and pace of infant mortality decline in Chile from 1960 to 2005.

---

[20] UNDP 2002: 194–195.
[21] MacEwan 1999: 149–150.
[22] Altimir 2001: 138; Borzutzky 2002: 110–111.
[23] Infant mortality: sources in Table A1. GDP per capita: source in Table A3. Inequality, poverty: Tables A4, A5.

4.3. Chile: Education, Family Planning, Safe Water, and Sanitation

From 1970, when the Frei Montalva presidency ended, to 1972, in the middle of the Allende years, public spending on social services rose from 20 to 26 percent of GDP.[24] Under military rule from 1973 to 1990, public social service spending plunged to 13 percent of GDP. It remained at this level during the first six years of the democratically elected Concertación governments, then rose to 17 percent in 2000.[25] Even after the return to democracy, however, the allocation of social spending was not particularly progressive. In 1995, "social security" (mostly retirement pensions), which went mostly to those who had held jobs in the urban formal sector, absorbed 43 percent of social spending. Education received 22 percent, health care 18 percent, housing 8 percent, anti-poverty programs 5 percent, and income transfers 4 percent. Chile underscores that a country can make good progress at reducing infant mortality even when social spending absorbs a fairly small proportion of GDP, and even when the allocation of such spending favors the not-so-poor over the poor. The halving of social spending under military rule did not impede a plunge in infant mortality because the military government targeted the spending that remained more effectively than in the past to maternal and infant care, nutritional aid, and the expansion of safe water and sanitation services for the poor. Such programs continued to be emphasized after the return to democracy in 1990, even though total social spending never regained the share of GDP it had absorbed during the Allende years. Infant mortality fell swiftly both during and after the military regime not because the governments of these eras raised the level of social spending, or because they drastically reallocated such spending from certain uses to others, but because they consistently devoted a small amount of social spending to inexpensive, but well designed and implemented, maternal and child health care and nutrition policies.

In 1960 literacy in the 15+ age group was 84 percent in Chile, lower than in Argentina (91 percent), about the same as in Costa Rica, and higher than in Brazil (61 percent).[26] The Christian Democratic government of Eduardo Frei Montalva (1964–1970) doubled spending on scholarships and school loans and raised school enrollment from 1.8 million to 2.9 million.[27] Education thus reinforced advances in health care and access to improved water and sanitation, contributing to rapid infant mortality decline in the late 1960s. Also conducive to infant mortality decline was that Chile, like Argentina and Costa Rica (but unlike Brazil), showed little bias against females in literacy, enrollment rates, or mean years of schooling.[28] As in these other Latin American countries, however, there was plenty of class bias. In the late 1960s

[24] Arellano 1985b: 33.
[25] Chile. MIDEPLAN 2003.
[26] Wilkie and Reich 1978: 118.
[27] Molina Silva 1972: 88.
[28] Barro and Lee 2000; World Bank 2002.

Chilean universities, which enrolled only 3 percent of students (mostly from middle- and upper-class families), received 27 percent of public education spending, whereas primary schools, which enrolled 70 percent of students, received only 36 percent of such spending.[29] Allende's "democratization" of university education, making college tuition-free, produced an 89 percent rise in university enrollments between 1970 and 1973. At the end of this period, only 9 percent of university students were from blue-collar families.[30] Allende, however, also raised secondary enrollment from 38 percent in 1970 to 51 percent in 1974.[31]

Soon after the 1973 coup, "the new rector of the University of Chile parachuted down to the campus, as if landing in enemy territory." Meanwhile, the military government revamped the curricula of primary and secondary schools to reflect the conservative values of its leaders, and in 1980 it began to subsidize tuition-free private schools at the same rate as state-run municipal schools. Mean years of schooling and secondary enrollment rose during the military regime (Tables A7 and A8), but one analysis concluded that "the world's farthest reaching neoliberal experiment in education...did not dramatically improve education."[32] After democratization, the Aylwin government (1990–1994) continued to subsidize tuition-free private institutions, but appealed successfully to Congress to raise education spending and launched a drive to improve the quality of education, resulting in higher test scores.[33] The Aylwin and Frei Ruiz-Tagle (1994–2000) governments also expanded preschool education, improved primary schools in poor areas, gave scholarships to needy students, and introduced work-study programs for impoverished high school students who had to work.[34] Another progressive reform, which was continued from the period of military rule, was to halve the share of public education spending devoted to universities, from 36 percent in 1980 to 18 percent in 1996.[35] Chile thus made fairly good progress on education from 1960 to 2005, and education must be counted as a factor that contributed to Chile's rapid mortality decline under the authoritarian as well as democratic governments of this period.

Between 1960 and 2005 the total fertility rate fell sharply, from 5.5 to 2.0 expected children per woman (Table A10). This 55 percent decline placed Chile 31st among 179 countries for which the World Bank provided data.[36] During this 45-year period modernization contributed to the fall of desired

[29] Raczynski 1994: 41. In 1987, the richest quintile of the population received 43 percent of public spending on university education; the poorest quintile received only 8 percent (Raczynski 1994: 76).

[30] Collins and Lear 1995: 126–27.

[31] Raczynski 1994: 86.

[32] Gauri 1998: 76–77, 103.

[33] Gauri 1998: 84–89; Ruiz-Tagle 2000: 354–355.

[34] Martin 2000: 322–327; Mena and Belleï 2000; Nash 1993; Raczynski 1994: 102–103.

[35] Gauri 1998: 53.

[36] World Bank 2008a.

fertility, while family planning contributed to the decline of unwanted fertility, especially in the late 1960s and early 1970s.[37] In 1962, the private Chilean Family Protection Association (APROFA) launched a family planning program aimed at reducing Chile's high abortion rate. Three years later, APROFA and Ministry of Health began to provide family planning information and services in National Health Service facilities.[38] In 1967 the government launched an integrated national family planning program, again designed mostly to reduce the incidence of abortion and related maternal mortality.[39] The more widespread distribution of contraceptives coincided with a steep decline in the number of women hospitalized for complications of abortion and with a plunge in the estimated maternal mortality ratio from 279 per 100,000 live births in 1965 to 131 per 100,000 in 1970.[40] By 1972 Chile had the third strongest family planning effort rating in Latin America, behind only Costa Rica and Panama. Family planning effort fell after the September 1973 military coup, both in absolute terms (Table A9) and relative to other Latin American countries,[41] but fertility continued to fall swiftly (Table A10), not least because very high unemployment in the mid-1970s and early 1980s persuaded many couples not to have children.[42] Fertility decline contributed appreciably to the sharp reduction of infant mortality during the first decade of military rule. One study found that it accounted for about 25 percent of the infant mortality decline from 1974 to 1982; another found that fertility reduction was responsible for about 30 percent of the infant mortality decline from 1972 to 1982.[43]

Family planning effort as rated by experts rose modestly during the 1980s (Table A9). In 1989, however, just before leaving office, the Pinochet government outlawed abortion even to save the life of the mother. This law stayed on the books through the 1990s, not least because many Christian Democratic legislators, as well as members of the conservative opposition, opposed changing it. During this decade, some 30–36 percent of maternal deaths resulted from abortion-related complications.[44] Despite this law, Chile in the mid-1990s had one of the highest rates of abortion in the world, at least twice as high as that of the United States.[45] Similarly, although divorce remained illegal until 2004, 56 percent of Chilean infants in the late 1990s were born to unwed mothers.[46]

---

[37] Taucher 1996: 289.
[38] Romero 1977; Viel and Campos 1987.
[39] Gall 1972; Livingstone and Raczynski 1974: 31 fn. 1.
[40] Taucher 1996: 289; maternal mortality from FRS/RSMLAC 2003: 24.
[41] Ross and Mauldin 1996: 146.
[42] Hojman 1989: 94, 103; Taucher and Jofre 1997: 1230.
[43] Foxley and Raczynski 1984: 233; Taucher and Jofré 1997: 1229.
[44] CRLP 1999: 18, 24 fn. 85.
[45] Henshaw, Singh, and Haas 1999: S34–S35.
[46] Blofield 2001: 8. To the extent that it served as a deterrent to marriage, the law forbidding divorce might indeed have contributed to the high proportion of births to unwed mothers.

Access to improved water and sanitation rose steadily after the mid-1960s, even during the military regime, when the government sent health workers to build latrines and to improve refuse disposal in the countryside.[47] Pooling annual observations for Chile's 13 regions over the first nine years of the military regime, one study found that the share of households with access to adequate sanitation was among the strongest predictors of the infant mortality level, controlling for other relevant factors.[48] Experts identify the expansion of access to improved water and sanitation as an important contributor to the rapid decline of infant mortality from 1974 to 1983.[49] Progress continued in both areas after the return to democracy in 1990 (Tables A10 and A11).

Like Costa Rica, then, Chile from 1960 to 2005 did very well at expanding access to safe water and sanitation, and moderately well at expanding access to education. Its record on family planning was good until 1973, after which (in contrast to Costa Rica) its progress in this area was reversed. Where Chile really excelled, however, was, again like Costa Rica, in the provision of health care and nutritional assistance to the poor.

4.4. Chile: Nutrition and Health Care

Total health care spending in Chile in 2000 was 6.3 percent of GDP, or $735 per capita. This amount was split evenly between the public and private sectors. In Costa Rica, by contrast, the public sector accounted for almost 80 percent of total health care spending (Table A15). Judged by mortality indicators, health care spending in Chile was efficient, but not as efficient as in Costa Rica. Both countries in 1995 registered infant mortality rates about one standard deviation below the mean for 20 Latin American countries, but whereas total health care spending in Costa Rica was only 0.2 standard deviations above the mean, in Chile it was 0.8 standard deviations above the mean.[50] Still, the comparison of Chile to Costa Rica suggests that what matters for low infant mortality is less the balance of public and private health care spending than a decision by public health authorities to dedicate a small share of public health care spending (whatever its incidence in total health care spending) to inexpensive but well designed and administered basic health care and nutrition programs that include or at least do not exclude the poor. It was these inexpensive public programs, not the oft-heralded privatization of contributory health insurance, that explain the rapid decline of infant mortality during the first decade of military rule in Chile (1974–1984).

Adequate nutrition lowers mortality by increasing resistance to disease and by making it easier for an afflicted person to recover from illness.[51] Most

---

[47] Castañeda 1984: 109; Giaconi, Montesinos, and Schalchli 1988: 74.
[48] Castañeda 1984: 61, 64; see also Raczynski 1991: 80–81.
[49] Raczynski 1994: 81.
[50] Calculated from PAHO 1998a: V. 1, 315 (total health spending) and Hill et al. 1999 (infant mortality).
[51] Fogel 2004: 44–46; Harris 2004; McKeown 1976.

Chileans did well on the nutritional front from 1960 to 2005. Calorie availability was adequate throughout this period, and was actually higher in 1971 than in 1992.[52] Complementing adequate food availability were public milk distribution and school feeding programs that began in 1924 and expanded steadily thereafter, particularly during the mid-1960s, such that by 1967 about 50 percent of under-5 children were receiving milk. From 1960 to 1970 the share of children under six suffering from moderate or severe malnutrition fell from 5.9 to 3.5 percent (Table A14), while the proportion suffering from mild malnutrition fell from 31 to 16 percent.[53] The Popular Unity government of Salvador Allende stepped up the free milk program, tripling the amount distributed by raising eligibility to include children aged 7 to 14 as well as all expectant and nursing mothers. As much as 70 percent of this target population may have been reached under Allende. During Allende's presidency, the proportion of under-6 children with some form of malnutrition fell by 17 percent.[54]

The military government ended the policy of distributing free milk to children aged 7 to 14 and halved the number of meals distributed in schools.[55] Food consumption fell sharply in the years after the 1973 coup, particularly among low-income families, but government food programs offset a part of the difficulty of acquiring food in the private market. The amount of milk provided in 1974, although below the level during the Allende period, was above its 1967 level, and the military government increased the caloric content of the milk.[56] Maintaining the integration of nutrition and health programs, the military government began undernutrition monitoring that put more than one million children under the age of six (70 to 75 percent of such children in Chile) under surveillance at stations set up by the Ministry of Health, and provided intensive care for children with signs of malnutrition.[57] Moderate and severe malnutrition among children under six fell from 3.5 percent in 1970 to 1.6 percent in 1980 (Table A14), while infant mortality plummeted. After the return to democracy the Aylwin government maintained the maternal and infant health care policies inherited from the military regime, while improving school-based nutrition assistance.[58] From 1990 to 2000 the proportion of pregnant women with below-normal weight fell from 16 to 8 percent, while the share of children under six with mild, moderate, or severe malnutrition fell from 8 to 3 percent.[59]

---

[52] Hakim and Solimano 1978: 6–12; Wilkie, Alemán, and Ortega 1999: 200.

[53] Monckeberg 2003: Table 2.

[54] Hakim and Solimano 1978: 37–40, 51–52.

[55] Castañeda 1992: 71; Foxley and Raczynski 1984: 238–239; Hakim and Solimano 1978: 40.

[56] Hakim and Solimano 1978: 40.

[57] Castañeda 1992: 70–79; Foxley and Raczynski 1984: 238–239; Raczynski and Oyarzo 1981: 60–66.

[58] Raczynski 1994: 103.

[59] Expectant mothers from Arellano 2005: 436; infants from Monckeberg 2003: Table 2. The lower figures for under-6 malnutrition in Table A14 refer only to moderate and severe malnutrition.

The year 1924 was a watershed not only for public milk distribution and school feeding, but also for social insurance. In September 1924 the Chilean congress passed legislation giving health, disability, accident, retirement, and burial insurance to blue-collar workers (*obreros*, a category that originally included some peasants, domestic workers, and low-income self-employed), and created a Ministry of Labor, Hygiene, Assistance, and Social Welfare (the Labor Ministry split off in 1938). The Mandatory Insurance Fund (CSO) that administered the blue-collar workers' health insurance was financed by compulsory contributions from workers, employers, and the state, and was modeled on the program introduced in Germany in 1880. The Fund's medical personnel provided outpatient care and home visits for blue-collar workers, their spouses, and their children under two years of age, who also received hospital and maternity care from hospitals run by philanthropies and, as of the late 1920s, from a network of clinics run by the fund itself. The 1924 law also provided for rural health posts staffed by nurses and lay health workers and supervised by a non-resident physician. Doctors in the government and in the legislature were instrumental in promoting the legislation.[60] It took some literal saber-rattling from reformist junior officers seated in the Senate galleries to ensure the passage of the law.[61]

In 1936 doctors associated with the Mandatory Insurance Fund, noting that infant mortality had not declined much since the creation of the rural health posts, created a Mother and Child Department to expand the provision of prenatal, delivery, and postpartum care. The new Department also provided milk for mothers and infants and checkups for babies under age two. To gain access to these services, the mother or her husband had to belong to the Fund. This expanded program of mother and child health care, scholars have argued, helped to reduce infant mortality.[62] The Preventive Medicine Law, passed in 1938, also applied only to persons associated with Fund, but it facilitated the wider distribution of recently invented antibiotics and paved the way for a campaign against tuberculosis, which also accelerated the pace of mortality decline.[63]

A coalition of left and center parties governed Chile from 1938 until 1952, although in 1948, with the cold war heating up, the government shifted to the right and outlawed the Communist Party (as also occurred in Brazil and Costa Rica in the late 1940s). In 1938 congress passed a law requiring the Mandatory Insurance Fund to offer its members an annual medical examination and to treat any illness discovered, and the Fund extended maternal and infant care to female contributors and to male contributors' wives. Four years later, congress passed a law that required the Employees' National Medical

---

[60] Mesa-Lago 1978: 25; Raczynski 1994: 7 fn. 6, 28; Rodríguez 1976: 66.
[61] Nunn 1970: 3, 55; Scully 1995: 107.
[62] Borzutzky 2002: 61–62; Raczynski 1994: 7, 28–29; Rodríguez 1976: 66–68.
[63] Cabello 1956: 245; Hakim and Solimano 1978: 12; Raczynski 1994: 7 fn. 6, 29; Rodríguez 1976: 68.

Service (SERMENA) to provide preventive care to white-collar workers and civil servants. These groups had acquired pensions in 1925, but only minimal medical benefits. In 1952, at the end of the center-left period of government, congress passed a law dividing the Mandatory Insurance Fund into a health insurance (and soon health care) branch (the National Health Service, SNS) and a pension branch (the Social Security Service). The National Health Service centralized control over the various regimes into which the original Mandatory Insurance Fund had disintegrated; took charge of all medical facilities (charity hospitals, outpatient clinics run by the Fund itself, and provincial and local health services); and assumed control of sanitation, epidemiology, and general public health. In so doing it broadened health insurance coverage to a much wider share of the population, including wives of affiliated workers at all times (wives had previously been covered only during pregnancy), children of affiliated workers up to age 15 (previously age two), and the indigent uninsured.[64] The National Health Service also ran orphanages and old-age homes, distributed free milk to all children up to the age of six, and financed school breakfast and lunch programs.[65] With the creation of the National Health Service in 1952, the share of the population covered by health insurance tripled to 65 percent.[66] The National Health Service was funded by both general tax revenues and payroll deductions from blue-collar workers.[67]

Despite the formation of the National Health Service, the infant mortality rate fell only from 122 per 1000 in 1952 to 120 per 1000 in 1960.[68] The slow decline of infant mortality despite the sharp rise in the insured population is consistent with the experience of Costa Rica (Section 3.4), in which the expansion of health insurance coverage seemed to be unrelated to infant mortality levels or changes. The high level and slow decline of infant mortality during the 1950s in Chile "created great consternation among the country's health authorities and within academic public health circles" and "gave special cause for increased concern to maternal and child health services."[69]

In addition to economic stagnation, restricted access to health services slowed the pace of infant mortality decline in the 1950s and early 1960s. In 1966, even agricultural workers who contributed to the National Health Service (some 55 percent of such workers) faced formidable obstacles to obtaining adequate medical care.[70] The SNS was supposed to give medical treatment to very poor people who did not contribute through payroll deductions, but in times of scarcity contributors were given preference, and non-contributors were often physically segregated from people with insurance. National Health Service facilities also suffered from overcrowding, to the point where two

[64] Borzutzky 2002: 48–49, 61–63, 104–105; Mesa-Lago 1978: 25–27; Raczynski 1994: 29–30.
[65] Hakim and Solimano 1978: 28–29.
[66] Raczynski 1994: 30.
[67] Borzutzky 2002: 63.
[68] Mamalakis 1980: 40–41.
[69] First quotation from Taucher 1984: 1–2; second from Hakim and Solimano 1978: 34.
[70] Borzutzky 2002: 51–55; Mesa-Lago 1978: 45.

patients sometimes shared a single bed.[71] One reason for the overcrowding was that 30 percent of white-collar employees, whose payroll deductions went to SERMENA (which paid for preventive care only) rather than to the SNS, are estimated to have used National Health Service facilities for curative care.[72] The SNS was thus financed mainly by blue-collar workers, but was used by many others, both richer (e.g., white-collar employees) and poorer (e.g., the indigent). In this way, the success of the trade union movement in winning health care services may have helped to reduce infant mortality among poorer sectors of the population. At the same time, however, it channeled to union members financial and administrative resources that might otherwise have been devoted to the poor and destitute.

The Frei Montalva government (1964–1970) tried to correct some of these inequities. Soon after taking office it drew up Chile's first national health plan, putting more resources into maternal and child care.[73] Whereas GDP rose only about 30 percent from 1964 to 1970, public spending on health care rose 80 percent.[74] During this period, "the material and resources of the National Health Service...were redistributed clearly in favor of mothers, infants, children, and adolescents." The government created new training programs for doctors in the south; encouraged medical students to become general practitioners; raised incentives to health professionals to serve in rural areas; and promoted the organization of mothers' centers and neighborhood councils.[75] The share of deaths with medical certification, indicating access to medical care during a health crisis, rose from 61 percent in 1964 to 82 percent in 1970. Doctors per capita rose little during this period, but nurses per capita rose by 32 percent, nurse auxiliaries per capita rose by 20 percent, and the number of public outpatient facilities rose from 613 to 918.[76] Meanwhile, the share of births attended by trained health staff rose from 74 to 81 percent (Table A16). Smallholders, tenant farmers, and agricultural laborers began to organize themselves, often with the help of Socialist and Communist activists. Such organization helped them to overcome obstacles to using health insurance benefits to which they were legally entitled.[77] In 1968 congress passed a law giving white-collar employees access to curative care, freeing up National Health Service resources for more impoverished Chileans.

Elected to succeed the Christian Democrat Eduardo Frei Montalva as president of Chile (incumbents were not allowed to run for reelection) was the Socialist Salvador Allende, a senator and physician who had served as health minister from 1939 to 1942, when he wrote a book on Chile's health situation in which he devoted special attention to the high rates of infant and maternal

[71] Mesa-Lago 1978: 37, 65.
[72] Raczynski 1994: 32.
[73] Borzutzky 2002: 104.
[74] Ascher 1984: 125.
[75] Alexander 1978: 116–117; Reichard 1996: 92.
[76] Livingstone and Raczynski 1974: 9, 11, 12, 43.
[77] Borzutzky 2002: 81–87; Mesa-Lago 1978: 29.

mortality prevailing at the time.[78] Allende instructed the National Health Service to shift resources from hospitals to community health centers, whose hours of operation were extended significantly. The government also required public-sector physicians to spend at least a quarter of their time practicing in such centers, and expanded compulsory service in health centers after the receipt of a medical degree from three to five years.[79] During Allende's presidency (1970–1973) the share of births attended by professionals rose from 81 to 85 percent, while infant mortality fell from 82 to 66 per 1000.[80] Allende tried to unify the publicly mandated health insurance system by shifting to the National Health Service a share of the contributions hitherto assigned to the white-collar Employees' National Medical Service. This measure antagonized white-collar workers, who feared that their health services would deteriorate, as well as physicians with private practices, who feared a loss of customers.[81] Doctors were also annoyed by the decision to shift resources from tertiary to primary care, and by a 1971 decree that shifted authority on Community Health Councils from physicians to health worker unions and community associations. In October 1972 about 60 percent of the members of the Medical College went on strike against the government, and in August 1973 the association called a general strike and asked for Allende's resignation as president of Chile. The next month, Allende was overthrown in a military coup.[82]

After the coup, 9 doctors were executed, 11 "disappeared," and hundreds went into exile. The military government cut the budget of the University of Chile's School of Public Health by 75 percent and fired or imprisoned 82 of its 110 faculty members.[83] From 1974 to 1983, when the sharpest infant mortality decline occurred, the government slashed public spending on health care by 28 percent, with the biggest cuts coming in the area of public investment in the health sector.[84] By 1990 Chile's public health care system had lost many of its professionals, half of the country's ambulances had broken down, and many public hospitals lacked sheets and bandages.[85] Crucially, however, the military government allocated a greater share of its reduced health care spending to inexpensive programs designed to improve the health of infants, young children, and expectant and new mothers, using a "map of extreme poverty" to target the poorest areas of the country.[86] From 1973 to 1979 the number of midwives rose sharply, as did the numbers of maternity beds and

[78] Allende Gossens 1939: 77–86.
[79] Navarro 1974: 107.
[80] Chile. Banco Central 1989: 424, 428.
[81] Borzutzky 2002: 143.
[82] Stover 1987: 38–41.
[83] Stover 1987: 42–51.
[84] Foxley and Raczynski 1984: 229; Raczynski 1994: 71.
[85] Collins and Lear 1995: 101–104; Oppenheim 1999: 262; Raczynski 1994: 101; Weyland 1997: 44.
[86] Chile. ODEPLAN 1975; Constable and Valenzuela 1991: 230–231; Foxley and Raczynski 1984.

prenatal visits per live birth. The share of births attended by trained personnel also rose.[87] A time-series analysis suggests that professional attendance at birth, maternity bed availability, and the number of prenatal visits contributed heavily to the decline of infant mortality from 1965 to 1979.[88]

The military government complemented its improvement of mother and child health services with an expansion of mother and child nutrition programs, including weighing and monitoring, supplementary feeding, and nutritional rehabilitation for infants and children. The programs were linked: to receive free milk and food, parents had to bring children to a health center for observation.[89] These local health care facilities gained staff even as overall spending on health personnel fell by 15 percent. In the late 1970s Chile's public health service laid off 300 doctors, but hired 900 nurses, 700 midwives, and 200 nutritionists.[90] These reforms coincided with a steep decline of infant mortality, from 65 per 1000 in 1974 to 22 per 1000 in 1983.[91]

Although the military government targeted health services to mothers and young children, it neglected other basic health-related activities. Cases of hepatitis and typhoid multiplied as the number of food inspections by health officials dropped. By 1983 Chile, with only 2 percent of the Western Hemisphere's population, had 25 percent of its typhoid cases.[92] From 1975 to 1985, as plunging infant mortality generated soaring life expectancy at birth, life expectancy at age one rose only from 70.3 to 71.9, less than half the annual rate for 1965–1975.[93] Neglect of investment in public health care during the earlier years of the military regime may help to explain why infant mortality fell more slowly from 1985 to 1990 than in the previous or subsequent decade (Table A1).

The military government in 1979 replaced both the Employees' National Medical Service (SERMENA) and the funding branch of the National Health Service (SNS) with a single National Health Fund (FONASA), whose revenue stream came from general taxes, payroll deductions from blue-collar and white-collar workers, and copayments from middle- and upper-income clients.[94] It thus managed for the first time to unify the public health insurance system, a project that Frei Montalva and Allende had each attempted and abandoned in the face of resistance from white-collar employees and physicians. The military government also increased the role of the private sector in health care financing and delivery. A government decree in 1981 gave persons subject to payroll deductions for health care the option of channeling their contributions not to the public-sector National Health Fund (FONASA), but rather to private-sector Social Security Health Institutions (ISAPREs), which

---

[87] Chile. Banco Central 1989: 422–424.
[88] Raczynski and Oyarzo 1981: 58–60.
[89] Foxley and Raczynski 1984: 235–236.
[90] Scarpaci 1985: 426.
[91] Chile. Banco Central 1989: 428.
[92] Scarpaci 1985: 427.
[93] Chile. Banco Central 1989: 405.
[94] Mesa-Lago 2000a: 56.

operated like health maintenance organizations in the United States.[95] The proportion of Chileans enrolled in an ISAPRE rose from 2 percent in 1983 to 13 percent in 1989 to 27 percent in 1997.[96] The ISAPREs attracted the rich, young, and healthy, whereas FONASA retained the poor, old, and illness-prone. In addition, many ISAPRE members used the public system for some (often expensive) procedures, draining its scarce resources.[97] In 1987 ISAPREs served only 11 percent of Chileans, but collected more than half of mandatory health care contributions and accounted for almost 38 percent of health care spending.[98] The steep decline of infant mortality between 1974 and 1983 cannot be traced, as has been claimed,[99] to such privatization. In 1983 only 2 percent of Chileans, almost all of them rich, belonged to an ISAPRE, and as the ISAPREs gained members, infant mortality decline slowed. If there is a lesson to be learned from the military government's health care policies, it is not to privatize health insurance, but rather to improve the quality and accessibility of publicly funded primary care.

The democratically elected government of Patricio Aylwin (1990–1994) inherited a public health care system that worked well for the rich and for impoverished mothers and infants, but not for many others. To change this situation, it increased public health spending by 75 percent between 1989 and 1994 and raised the number of doctors employed by the public health service from 5,438 in 1989 to 8,704 in 1993.[100] The Aylwin government also doubled the budget for primary health care in disadvantaged urban and rural areas, built new health posts, increased the staff and operating hours of existing facilities, improved the quality of prenatal and infant care, launched new programs for teenage mothers, and improved school-based nutrition assistance to children.[101] In infant care, public health authorities under Aylwin and his successors established intensive care units for newborns, implemented new protocols for handling respiratory problems, expanded the use of surgery to correct congenital heart defects, and introduced new vaccines.[102] After stagnating from 1984 to 1989, infant mortality fell from 16.0 per 1000 in 1990 to 7.9 per 1000 in 2005 (Table A1). Among 20 Latin American countries, only Peru outpaced Chile at percent decline of infant mortality during this period.[103]

The four perinatal health interventions that contributed to the rapid decline of infant mortality in Chile from 1990 to 2005 were among the 40 initially incorporated into the Plan for Universal Access with Explicit Guarantees (Plan

---

[95] Barrientos 2000.
[96] Barrientos 2002: 447; Miranda et al. 1995: 54.
[97] Barrientos 2000: 103; Barrientos 2002: 452–453; Raczynski 1994: 101; Ruiz-Tagle 2000: 349; Titelman 1999: 273.
[98] Raczynski 1994: 69.
[99] Cifuentes 1991: 88.
[100] Ruiz-Tagle 2000: 348.
[101] Arellano 2005: 434–437; Raczynski 1994: 100, 103; Weyland 1997: 45.
[102] Jiménez and Romero 2007: 462–463.
[103] Calculated from United Nations 2008.

AUGE). The Plan AUGE gave every Chilean citizen as of July 1, 2005, the right to receive timely attention of certified quality at affordable prices (free for the poor) for 40 medical conditions known to produce a significant reduction in disability-adjusted life years. Anyone who was denied such care had the right to legal redress. On July 1, 2006, 16 additional services were added to the list, bringing the total to 56. The number of conditions to be covered was slated to rise to 80 by 2010.[104]

Although 19 constitutions in Latin America and the Caribbean identify health and education as basic rights, and although 15 of 20 Latin American countries (including Argentina and Brazil) have laws requiring insurers to finance a basic package of health services, Chile's Plan AUGE is the most ambitious attempt to date to implement a rights-based approach to health care policy.[105] Such an approach presumes that each citizen has a right to professional attention for certain specified medical conditions; makes the state responsible for providing the financial and administrative resources needed to satisfy that right; devises mechanisms by which citizens can seek redress if that right is denied to them; and is explicitly concerned not only with the cost, efficiency, and efficacy of achieving certain health status outcomes, but also with the process by which health care is provided and utilized, and with public participation in the design and monitoring of health care delivery. No studies of the impact of the Plan AUGE on health status were available at the time of this writing, but a 2007 survey of 1,304 households found that 59 percent of respondents believed that the Plan had improved service quality; 60 percent thought that it had reduced waiting times; and 69 percent thought that it had improved health services in general.[106]

4.5. Chile: Determinants of Public Health Care Policies

In Brazil and Costa Rica, the welfare state emerged mainly through presidential leadership and bureaucratic initiative.[107] In Chile, competition for votes, as well as pressure from unions and other interest groups, were the driving forces behind the creation and expansion of the welfare state.[108] As of 1960, however, the Chilean welfare state had performed poorly at reducing a high level of premature mortality, not least because, before the 1960s, those who ran the highest risk of early death were rarely among those who voted or pressured. Public policies reflected instead the influence of a loose but powerful urban formal-sector coalition that included the rich, the middle classes, and unionized workers, but not destitute people in urban slums or rural areas.

---

[104] Chile. FONASA 2008.
[105] Constitutions: World Bank 2008b: 6; basic package of health services: Mesa-Lago 2008: 217; rights-based health care schemes: Gauri 2004; World Bank 2008b.
[106] World Bank 2008b: 17–18.
[107] See Malloy (1979) on Brazil and Rosenberg (1983) on Costa Rica.
[108] Arellano 1985a; Arellano 1985b; Mesa-Lago 1978: 30–33; Raczynski 2000: 120–121.

Chile in 1960 had a union density (union members divided by the total labor force) of 16 percent,[109] which was high for a developing country at the time. Strong labor unions, along with groups representing the urban middle and upper classes, often induce governments to enact policies that are biased toward the urban formal sector and that contribute to the neglect or even further impoverishment of the very poor.[110] In Chile, organized labor until the late 1960s was reported to be "virtually the exclusive referent" of leftist political parties. A left party leader called the demands of other popular sector groups a "secondary structural contradiction," and union leaders tended to advocate policies and to forge alliances that allowed them to stay in a position of relative privilege.[111] Meanwhile, a large "bottom stratum" of the Chilean population had weak organizational ties and little political clout.[112] This distribution of political resources helps to explain why Chilean economic and social policies at the end of the 1950s were biased toward relatively privileged groups.

The strength of the Chilean labor movement reduced the welfare of the very poor by allowing successive governments to undertake the obligatory gestures toward "the people" by attending to the demands of unionized workers, university students, and middle-class groups, while neglecting the interests of less articulate segments of the population, including the very poor and destitute. On the other hand, payroll taxes paid by blue-collar workers financed health facilities and services that poor people used, especially in cities; and the provision of social services to the urban formal-sector coalition encouraged the evolution of a belief that the state had an obligation to guarantee a minimum level of well-being to all citizens. Union pressure for health and old age insurance thus helped to expand and legitimate the involvement of the state in social welfare activities. Whether this impetus toward the expansion of benefits would overcome countervailing factors (lack of funds, antipathy to "socialism," etc.) depended in part on whether parties and politicians had incentives to court the votes of the poor and destitute.

Although Chile held regular and competitive elections from 1931 to 1973, the political regime was not fully democratic. Women were denied the vote until 1949; the Communist Party was banned from elections from 1948 to 1958 (although it participated in electoral fronts with the Socialists in the presidential elections of 1952 and 1958); no secret ballot existed in the countryside until 1958; and voting was restricted by a literacy clause until 1970 (Allende was elected while the literacy clause was still in effect). The absence of a secret ballot in rural areas was particularly critical to shaping public

---

[109] Calculated from Programa de Economía del Trabajo 1992: 52 (union members in 1960); Goldenberg 1964: 127 (public-sector employees in quasi-union organizations in 1960), and ILO 2002 (labor force in 1960).

[110] McGuire 1999.

[111] Oxhorn 1995: 48–49.

[112] Ascher 1984: 34.

policy. Before 1958, each party in Chile printed its own ballot. To vote, a citizen obtained a ballot from a local party representative and cast it at a place close to the voter's residence. This system permitted some anonymity in cities, but in rural areas it enabled landlords to coerce or cajole many of the poor into voting for their preferred candidates.[113] This system began to break down in 1957, when a Christian Democratic Party was formed. The next year, the Communist Party was legalized and the Australian ballot (a uniform ballot printed and distributed by the government) was introduced in the countryside. These reforms intensified competition among right, center, and left parties, encouraging each to try to attract new or previously "captive" rural voters. The Christian Democrats appealed particularly to sharecroppers and tenant farmers, while the Socialists and Communists courted landless laborers and shanty-town inhabitants. Voter mobilization by the Christian Democratic Party, whose close ties to the Catholic Church helped its militants and doctrines unravel the clientelist networks that bound the rural poor to conservative politicians, helped its candidate, Eduardo Frei Montalva, win the presidency in 1964.

Party competition among Christian Democrats, Socialists, and Communists gave politicians incentives to appeal to previously excluded groups, a process that intensified during the Allende presidency (1970–1973).[114] The resulting "hypermobilization" of the population increased problems of governance, but contributed to the extension of social services to previously ignored Chileans. During the 1970 presidential campaign, for example, each of the three major candidates courted votes by promising to expand nutrition programs. The winner, Salvador Allende, implemented a program to distribute a half-liter of milk per day to expectant and nursing mothers and to every child under 15 (up from the previous age limit of six). A survey after the municipal elections of April 1971 revealed that this initiative was Allende's single most popular program.[115]

After the 1973 coup the military government expanded Chile's health care, nutrition, safe water, and sanitation services in poor areas, contributing heavily to the 70 percent decline of infant mortality from 1974 to 1983. The expansion of such services presents a puzzle. As Drèze and Sen note, "General Pinochet does not have a reputation of being a soft-hearted do-gooder." Government agents killed or "disappeared" more than 2,000 people from 1973 to 1990, and top policy-makers espoused until the mid-1980s a rigidly free-market ideology that stressed a minimal role for the state in the economy and in society. These observations raise "the intriguing question of why a government that had no hesitation in resorting to the most brutal political repression to protect

---

[113] Bauer 1975: 223; Loveman 1979: 293–294; Robinson and Baland 2005: 19–32; Scully 1995: 116–117.
[114] Landsberger and McDaniel 1976; Lewis 2004: 738–739; Torcal and Mainwaring 2003: 67–68.
[115] Hakim and Solimano 1978: 39–40.

the privileges of the dominant classes was so interested in looking after child health and extreme poverty."[116]

A review of available evidence provides at least five answers to Drèze and Sen's question, focusing respectively on international reputation, protest deterrence, state paternalism, market failure, and technocratic leadership. The international reputation and protest deterrence explanations imply that top government policy-makers had no special desire to improve child health or to reduce extreme poverty, but enacted policies dedicated to these goals for instrumental reasons, either to improve the regime's reputation in the international community, or to defuse potential domestic protest. The state paternalism, market failure, and technocratic leadership explanations imply that at least some policy-makers in the military government sincerely wished to improve child health and reduce extreme poverty, and were successful in designing and implementing policies conducive to these goals. The two broad lines of interpretation are not incompatible. That many people serving the military regime were involved in torture and murder does not preclude the possibility that others (or even, conceivably, some of the torturers and murderers) may have been sincerely committed to improving child health and reducing extreme poverty. Even those who did not share such a commitment may have supported policies beneficial to the poor on the grounds that such policies could deter protest or improve the government's international reputation.

Some observers believe that the military government's mother and child health policies were designed in part to win support (or reduce hostility) from foreigners. Collins and Lear observe that "at international conferences, where Pinochet's human rights record invariably came under attack, defensive Chilean officials would boast of Chile's falling infant mortality rate (IMR), which since the 1970s had become internationally recognized as a key indicator of socially positive economic development." Valdés argues that "the reason for the focus on mothers and children is clear: [infant mortality is]...considered internationally to be an indicator of development. It was...an indicator that would show how to evaluate the Pinochet government."[117]

Others stress the role of protest deterrence in motivating the government's mother and child health care policies. Drèze and Sen argue that the policies may be viewed in certain respects as "a strategy for checking popular discontent at a time of political repression, economic instability, and diminished general social provisioning...the expansion of targeted nutrition and health programmes [has a] populist ring in a country where popular expectations of public provisioning are very high...We cannot but observe the part that political pressure and a search for a popular mandate may play even in a country with an authoritarian political atmosphere," especially in a country with "a long tradition of democratic and pluralist politics."[118] Taucher concurs that

---

[116] Drèze and Sen 1989: 230, 238.
[117] Collins and Lear 1995: 93; Valdés 2002.
[118] Drèze and Sen 1989: 238.

one of the reasons why the military government maintained effective mother and child health care policies was that "people had already learned that they had a right to health."[119] Raczynski finds that Chilean mothers before the 1973 coup had built up a "belief in their entitlement to well-baby check-ups and supplementary feeding," and notes that protests from mothers helped to scuttle a 1985 plan to substitute rice for milk as a nutritional supplement.[120] Chile's long history of competitive elections and civil liberties, in this interpretation, along with the expectations generated by decades of welfare-state policies enacted partly in response to electoral competition and interest group pressure, contributed to the military government's mother and child health care policies. A variant on this interpretation would be to view these policies as a "payoff" to the poor: an attempt to deflect criticism about the main health care objectives of the government, which were to privatize health insurance and strengthen the role of the private sector in health service delivery.

The other broad line of interpretation holds that Pinochet and his allies improved mother and child health care not for instrumental reasons, but because of a conviction that such improvements were just and appropriate. One variant of this interpretation focuses on state paternalism. In this perspective, the government improved maternal and child health care because its leaders regarded mothers and infants as helpless and in need of charity. Authoritarian leaders often endorse such views. Italian Fascists, for example, proclaimed that "women were to be wives, mothers, and nurturers," and in 1925 created the National Organization for the Protection of Motherhood and Infancy to improve maternal and child health care, especially in rural areas.[121] In 1974 General Pinochet stated that "a woman should become a mother and expect nothing of the material world; she should seek and discover in her child the culmination of her life, her single treasure, and the goal of all her dreams." According to Molina, "the government exalted the need to protect mothers" and "promoted the image of Pinochet as a stern father, as a protector and a provider. This made sense to many women in terms of their own life experiences, in which these attributes were viewed as the characteristics that a good father should display in the household. It was the most conservative expression of the model of the traditional patriarchal family."[122]

The market failure interpretation focuses not on a paternalistic obligation to help the weak, but on the benefits that such aid may bring to the task of promoting economic growth by making markets more efficient. Top government policy-makers during the Pinochet era embraced the idea of a "subsidiary state" that would "assume only those duties that individuals or intermediate bodies are incapable of carrying out."[123] According to a 1979

---

[119] Taucher 2002.
[120] Raczynski 1991: 35 (quotation); Raczynski 1994: 80 fn. 75. Idiart (2002: 409) makes a similar argument.
[121] Ipsen 1996: 146, 150, 165–173.
[122] Molina 1989: 63 (Pinochet quote), 66.
[123] Vergara 1990: 37.

National Planning Office document, these duties comprised only "national security, the administration of justice, and the implementation of social policy in favor of the most defenseless (*desvalidos*)."[124] Another government document advocated providing nutritional supplements to malnourished mothers and children because their hunger impeded the "socio-economic development possibilities of the country."[125]

The committed technocrat interpretation, like the market failure and state paternalism views, accepts that government policy-makers were sincerely interested in helping the poorest, and focuses on the dedication and efficacy of a small group of government planners in charge of maternal and child health care. A central figure in this interpretation is Miguel Kast, a University of Chicago-trained economist who returned to Chile in 1974 to work in the National Planning Office. Kast headed the team that created the "Map of Extreme Poverty" by which the government targeted health, nutrition, education, and other social policies to the poorest Chileans.[126] According to his biographer, Joaquín Lavín – a conservative politician who narrowly lost the 2000 presidential election to the Socialist Ricardo Lagos – Kast took a special interest in poverty because of "the difficult years his family had spent after arriving in Chile." Kast's father, an officer in the German army who had risen through the ranks during the Nazi era, surrendered to U.S. troops in April 1945, but escaped from custody and made his way back to his home town. Shortly after Miguel Kast's birth in 1948, his parents, "like many other families in post-war Germany, decided to seek out new opportunities in America." The Kast family lived on a small farm outside Santiago in a mud house without electricity or running water, where they grew crops and raised chickens. During this era Miguel Kast not only experienced poverty, but also "developed strong anti-communist feelings," after hearing stories from his father about "what had happened in Germany after the [Soviet] communists came to power...how they took away basic freedoms."[127]

Kast was attracted to Christian Democracy while studying economics at the Universidad Católica, but the dalliance ended with Frei Montalva's agrarian reform, which he opposed. After spending the Allende years at the University of Chicago on a Ford Foundation fellowship earning a master's degree in economics, Kast joined the National Planning Office a few months after the September 1973 coup. A "mystical Catholic who saw his work as a moral mission – and would stop at nothing to achieve it," Kast soon earned a reputation as persuasive, relentless, and hardworking. One of his collaborators noted a "strong sense of teamwork" at the agency, and another reported that "we became part of a crusade to build a modern, efficient economy to

---

[124] Quoted in Raczynski 1983: 6.
[125] Chile. ODEPLAN 1977: 66.
[126] Chile. ODEPLAN 1975.
[127] Lavín 1987, quotations respectively from pp. 47, 9, 25. Lavín did not call attention to the irony of a Nazi officer complaining that the Soviets "took away basic freedoms."

combat poverty...to us, it was a revolution. We had terrible salaries, but a great deal of mystique."[128] In April 1975 Kast became Deputy Director of the National Planning Office, a post that allowed him to meet regularly with General Pinochet, with whom he often spoke about social policies. He received the Directorship, a post with ministerial status, in 1978, and later served as Labor Minister and as president of the Central Bank before dying of cancer in 1983.[129]

More historical research is needed to weigh the various explanations for the expansion of maternal and infant health care during the military regime, and to incorporate other factors as well. The goal here is less to pit the explanations against one another – each provides a plausible account, and none seems inconsistent with any of the others – than to inventory possible motives for the military government's mother and child health care policies. Some of the explanations, especially the one focusing on protest deterrence, suggest ways in which Chile's long history of democracy may have affected policy-making even during the military regime. Democracy may also have influenced the utilization of the services provided (the "demand side") in ways that reduced infant mortality.

The military government in 1980 changed the constitution to allow it to name nine of Chile's 38 senators. Just before exiting in 1990, it juggled electoral districts to overrepresent conservative rural areas and created a two-seat-per-district electoral system for the lower house in which a minority party (presumably of the right in most districts) could win one of the seats with as little as 33 percent of the vote.[130] These amendments made the legislative right strong enough during the 1990s to block efforts to repeal them. The resulting sclerosis constrained social policies after 1990, but the economy continued to grow, the government channeled resources to social services in poor areas, and infant mortality began to fall steeply again after stagnating in the late 1980s.

The abolition of the literacy clause for voting in 1970 and the weakening of unions under military rule made it easier for Concertación governments to favor the very poor without jeopardizing their reelection chances or risking massive protest from the not-so-poor. In 1998, taking into account both financing and expenditure, the poorest quintile of the Chilean population received 56 percent of public health care spending, the next-poorest quintile received 30 percent, and the richest quintile "received" –9 percent (i.e., they paid a subsidy). Public education spending was also progressive: the poorest quintile received 35 percent, the next-poorest quintile received 26 percent, and the richest quintile received 6 percent.[131] Income transfers and public housing expenditures were also distributed progressively around 1990, not as

[128] Quotations respectively from Constable and Valenzuela 1991: 187, Milevcic 2002, and Cristián Larroulet in Constable and Valenzuela 1991: 187.
[129] Lavín 1987: 53.
[130] Constable and Valenzuela 1991: 313–316.
[131] Chile. MIDEPLAN 2003.

progressively as health care spending but more progressively than education expenditure.[132]

Good leadership, learning from past experience, and views prevailing in international agencies like the UNDP, the WHO, and the World Bank enabled and encouraged the Concertación governments to enact policies that worked to the advantage of the very poor as well as the not-so-poor. Democracy also contributed to the design and implementation of such policies.[133] In the mid-1990s, representatives of civil society organizations, political parties, and associations of health professionals organized the National Foundation for Overcoming Poverty, which in 1999 released a document proposing a rights-based approach to health care policy, such as would later inform the Plan for Universal Access with Explicit Guarantees (Plan AUGE).[134] In 1999 the Socialist candidate Ricardo Lagos made health care reform a centerpiece of his presidential campaign. After being elected, Lagos defended the Plan AUGE against pressure from rightist politicians, fiscal conservatives in his own coalition, private health insurance firms, doctors' associations, and labor unions representing health care workers.[135]

What, then, does Chile tell us about how political democracy affects basic health care policies, and about how basic health care policies affect mortality decline? The years of military rule show that inexpensive public health care, nutrition, water, and sanitation programs can produce a steep decline of infant mortality. To design and implement these programs, however, the military government drew on infrastructure, expertise, and expectations that had emerged in the context of a welfare state encompassing an ever-widening share of the population.[136] Electoral competition and interest group activity contributed to the emergence of this welfare state, which popularized the idea that people have a right to social services. From 1964 to 1970 under Frei Montalva and from 1970 to 1973 under Allende, adversarial politics and the mobilization of excluded groups in urban slums and rural areas helped to extend welfare-state programs to the very poor.

The expectations generated by long experience with a welfare state and with a democratic or semi-democratic regime meant that the military had to use harsh repression to silence political parties and labor unions and to withdraw high wages, severance pay, retirement pensions, and other benefits from blue- and white-collar formal-sector workers. Maternal and infant health care

---

[132] Arellano 2005: 420; Marcel and Solimano 1994: 228; PAHO 2007: V. 1, 324.
[133] "The return of democracy [in 1989] allowed for implementation of social policies clearly favourable to the lower income sectors, who were an important segment of the voting population which all parties wanted to attract to their ranks" (Ruiz-Tagle 2000: 342–343).
[134] World Bank 2008b: 12. The name of the organization is Fundación Nacional para la Superación de la Pobreza.
[135] Hanzich 2005: 29–31.
[136] "The success of the health and nutritional intervention programs [under military rule] rested in great measure on the structure and coverage that Chile's public health sector had achieved in the past" (Raczynski 1994: 80).

and nutrition services thrived during the military regime, however, in part because they were much less expensive than most traditional welfare-state benefits, and in part because the paternalism of the military leaders and their civilian allies made it harder for them to withdraw life-preserving services from mothers and children than to slash the wages, benefits, and job security of a largely adult male formal-sector labor force. Moreover, decades of democratic or semi-democratic experience not only generated expectations that militated against the withdrawal of social services, but also helped to produce the expertise and infrastructure on which these services drew, and increased the propensity of impoverished households to utilize services that survived the cutbacks. Even under Pinochet, then, Chile's democratic experience helped in various ways to reduce infant mortality.

Chile under military rule (1973–1990) had an authoritarian government that implemented public maternal and infant health care and nutrition policies that contributed to a rapid decline of infant mortality. It would be unwise, however, to conclude from this experience that authoritarianism systematically encourages social policies that reduce the risk of infant death. First, as the quantitative analysis reported in Chapter 2 found, democracy, especially long-term democratic experience, is associated across countries positively, not negatively, with access to education, family planning, maternal and infant care, and water and sanitation, as well as with lower infant mortality. Second, although infant mortality fell rapidly during the first ten years of the military regime, it fell slowly during the next five years; and even during the first ten years of military rule the pace of infant mortality decline was not radically faster than during the competitive political regimes of 1960–1973 and 1990–2005. Third, life expectancy at age one, an indicator that reflects mortality in all age groups except infants, rose more slowly under military rule than during the elected Frei Montalva and Allende administrations. Fourth, to design and implement their maternal and infant nutrition and health care policies, technocrats in the military regime's Planning Office operated with human and physical resources and popular expectations inherited from the previous democratic era. Such expectations affected not only the provision of basic social services, but also their utilization. No strident demands by destitute rural people or shanty-town inhabitants wrested pro-poor social policies out of the military regime, but expectations that the state would intervene to help the very poor meet their basic needs exerted a quiet and steady pressure on government technocrats whose own worldviews had been shaped in part by democratization and social mobilization from 1958 to 1973. Combined with state paternalism, the goal of making markets more efficient, and the hope of improving the military regime's international reputation, popular expectations and technocratic worldviews originating in more democratic times shaped and constrained the military regime's maternal and infant care policies. Chile thus provides evidence to support, as well as to question, the claim that democracy on balance is conducive to social policies that reduce infant mortality.

5

Argentina: Big Welfare State, Slow Infant Mortality Decline

Of the eight societies compared in this book, Argentina from 1960 to 2005 had not only the slowest GDP per capita growth and the greatest rise of income inequality, but also the smallest rise of life expectancy and the second-smallest decline of infant mortality (Tables A1–A4). Much has been written about Argentina's economic problems, but little attention has been paid to its sluggish progress at reducing the risk of early death. Slow economic growth and soaring income inequality kept mortality rates from falling quickly, but just as important were the failures of successive Argentine governments to provide adequate basic social services, especially maternal and infant health care, to the poor. The precariousness of democratic traditions, the Peronist lock on the votes of the poor, and the strength of interest groups help to explain why the heterogeneous governments that administered Argentina from 1960 to 2005 wound up with uniformly undistinguished records of providing basic social services to the people most in need of them.

To develop these arguments, Argentina will be compared particularly to Chile and to one of its own subnational units, the Patagonian province of Neuquén, which in 2001 had about 475,000 of Argentina's 36 million inhabitants. Chile and Neuquén each did better than Argentina as whole at reducing infant mortality (as well as mortality at older ages). From 1960 to 2005 infant mortality fell from 120 to 8 per 1000 in Chile and from 118 to 9 per 1000 in Neuquén, but only from 62 to 13 per 1000 in Argentina. By 2005, infant mortality was lower in both Chile and Neuquén than in Alabama, Louisiana, Mississippi, South Carolina, or Washington, DC.[1] What Chile and Neuquén had that Argentina as a whole lacked were public maternal and infant health services accessible to the poor. Stronger democratic traditions, more vigorous political party competition for the votes of the poor (especially in the 1960s and early 1970s), and less powerful interest groups representing workers, employers, and professionals help to explain why Chile and Neuquén did more than Argentina to provide such services.

---

[1] Argentina, Chile: Table A1; Neuquén: Neuquén. SS/MDS 2000 (1960); Neuquén. DPEC 2008 (2005); USA: Mathews and MacDorman 2008: 5. All from vital registration.

5.1. Argentina: Mortality

Argentina in 2005 had a life expectancy at birth of 74.8 years and an infant mortality rate of 13.3 per 1000. These levels of premature mortality were about average for the eight societies compared in this book (Tables A1 and A2). Among all countries with available data, Argentina in 2005 ranked in the 70th percentile on average life expectancy and in the 64th percentile on lowness of infant mortality. This moderately good performance was due mostly to progress from 1900 to 1960, when Argentina ranked fourth of twelve Latin American countries on life expectancy rise and third of eight on infant mortality decline. From 1960 to 2005 Argentina lost ground, ranking only in the 47th percentile on percent rise of life expectancy and only in the 49th percentile on percent decline of infant mortality. Outside of sub-Saharan Africa and the former Soviet bloc, few countries made slower progress.[2] From 1960 to 2005 Argentina's infant mortality rate went from being 50 percent below Chile's to almost 70 percent above it, and from being 30 percent below Costa Rica's to almost 40 percent above it (Table A1).

The first year in which vital registration figures can be used to calculate an infant mortality rate for Argentina as a whole is 1938. In that year the infant mortality rate was 104 per 1000, the lowest rate of any of the eight societies compared in this book.[3] This relative position is consistent with the narrow variant of the wealthier is healthier hypothesis; Argentina's GDP per capita in the late 1930s was by far the highest among the eight cases. France, however, which had a GDP per capita only 10 percent higher than Argentina in 1938, had an infant mortality rate of only 60 per 1000.[4] European countries, along with the United States, Australia, and New Zealand, were the main referents for Argentine public health experts writing about infant mortality in the 1930s.[5] The Socialist senator Alfredo Palacios may have had these cases in mind when, in 1936, he called Argentina's infant mortality rate "appalling." Although Socialists were a tiny minority in the conservative-dominated

---

[2] In 2005, Argentina ranked 69th of 190 countries on life expectancy and 56th of 186 countries on lowness of infant mortality. From 1960 to 2005, it ranked 92nd of 174 countries on percent rise of life expectancy at birth and 71st of 140 countries on percent decline of infant mortality. Calculated from World Bank 2008e, except Taiwan, from Tables A1 and A2. Latin American figures for 1900 and 1900–1960: McGuire and Frankel 2005: 85–86.

[3] Vital registration statistics in Argentina, as in Chile and Costa Rica (but not in any of the other societies studied in this book), are complete and accurate enough to be used in the depiction of levels and changes of infant mortality during the period from 1960 to 2005 (McGuire 2009, Web Appendix A1). In 1938, Argentina's infant mortality rate of 104 per 1000 (Somoza, Dehollain, and Salvia 1962) was lower than Costa Rica's 122 per 1000 (Rosero-Bixby 1985: 365); Taiwan's 129–146 per 1000 (Mirzaee 1979: 228; Barclay 1954a: 161); Brazil's 164 per 1000 (Becker and Lechtig 1986: 21); or South Korea's 164 per 1000 (Kwon 1986: 12), and much lower than Chile's 236 per 1000 (Mamalakis 1980: 40). The rates in Indonesia and Thailand were probably close to Chile's (Sections 9.1 and 10.1).

[4] GDP per capita: Maddison 2007; infant mortality: Mitchell 1981: 140–141 (France); Argentina. DGE 1947: 6.

[5] See, for example, Aráoz Alfaro 1936: 157–165.

legislatures of the 1930s, Palacios persuaded his colleagues to create an agency within the Ministry of the Interior to promote maternal and infant care.[6] Between 1938, two years after the agency was created, and 1946, when Perón was elected president, infant mortality fell from 104 to 74 per 1000. Perón detached the Public Health Secretariat from the interior ministry, raised it to cabinet status, and entrusted its operation to Dr. Ramón Carrillo, who presided over rapid growth in the number of nurses, hospitals, and outpatient clinics around the country. By 1955, when Perón was overthrown in a military coup, Argentina's infant mortality rate had fallen to 62 per 1000.[7]

From 1955 to 1971, with Perón in exile and the Peronists banned from electoral participation, Argentina made no progress at reducing infant mortality. Then, from 1971 to 1985, infant mortality plunged from 62 to 26 per 1000, despite a fall in GDP per capita, a rise in income inequality, and no decline in the total fertility rate (Tables A1, A4, and A10). The political climate during this period was also inhospitable to infant mortality decline. Argentina was under military rule from 1971 to 1973, and the ensuing Peronist governments (1973–1976) were hobbled by a revolving door of presidents, a deepening economic crisis, escalating political violence, and shadowy links between government officials and right-wing death squads.[8] Military governments from 1976 to 1983 caused at least 9,000 people to disappear, presided over soaring inflation, and contracted a huge foreign debt. Only during the presidency of Raúl Alfonsín did a stable democracy emerge. Nonetheless, the Argentine military regime, like its Chilean counterpart (1973–1990), did surprisingly well at reducing infant mortality. Between 1976 and 1983 Argentina's infant mortality rate fell from 44 to 30 per 1000 (4.9 percent per year). The decline was particularly steep from 1977 to 1979, when the rate fell from 45 to 35 per 1000 (7.4 percent per year). Paradoxically, the period of fastest infant mortality decline under military rule was, in Argentina as in Chile, a time of especially harsh repression, sluggish or negative economic growth, and soaring income inequality and income poverty.

After democratization the pace of infant mortality decline slowed. During the Alfonsín presidency (1983–1989) infant mortality fell at a rate of only 2.0 percent per year, with almost all of the reduction taking place from 1984 to 1985. The pace of decline rose to 3.4 percent per year during the Menem presidency (1989–1999); then fell to 1.3 percent per year in 1999–2003 (a period that featured a deep economic crisis and the resignation of President Fernando de la Rúa midway through his term); then rose again to 6.0 percent per year from 2003 to 2006, as the economy recovered and the political situation stabilized.[9] These observations invite an exploration of the extent to

[6] Repetto et al. 2001: 9.
[7] Infant mortality rates from vital registration (Somoza, Dehollain, and Salvia 1962).
[8] González Jansen 1986.
[9] Infant mortality rates from the sources for Argentina in Table A1. Average annual rates of decline calculated with the RATE compound growth function in Microsoft Excel.

which income-related factors can explain the level of infant mortality in 2005, the overall amount of infant mortality decline from 1960 to 2005, and the tempo of infant mortality decline within that period.

5.2. Argentina: Affluence, Inequality, and Poverty

From 1960 to 2003 Argentina's GDP per capita rose at an average annual rate of 0.6 percent, slowest by far among the eight societies compared in this book (Table A3), and 79th among 98 countries for which data are available. Growth was erratic as well as slow: in 17 of the 44 years between 1960 and 2003, GDP per capita actually fell.[10] Neglect of agriculture during and after the Peronist period (1946–1955), the single-minded pursuit of capital-intensive import substitution from the mid-1950s to the mid-1970s, struggles among powerful economic interest groups, and economic mismanagement combined to generate this sluggish economic growth.[11] The 1991 convertibility plan, which installed a currency-board exchange rate regime, led to four years of fast economic growth, but also implanted rigidities that later slowed the growth rate (1996–1998) and then precipitated a deep economic crisis (1999–2002). The resulting depressed baseline, combined with soaring prices for grain (Argentina's main export), combined to generate five years of GDP growth averaging 8 percent a year from 2003 to 2008, before a global economic crisis caused GDP growth to plummet again.

Argentina in the early 2000s collected no nationwide data on income inequality or income poverty. Knowledge about these indicators comes mainly from surveys taken in Greater Buenos Aires or, after the mid-1980s, in the country's 28 largest metropolitan areas (which in 1991 held 62 percent of the country's population). These surveys suggest that income inequality changed little during the 1960s and early 1970s and was lower in Greater Buenos Aires than in Brazil, Chile, Costa Rica, Indonesia, or Thailand, although higher than in South Korea or Taiwan. From 1975 to 1995, however, the Gini index rose from 36.8 to 48.1, and by 2003 the Gini index in the country's 28 largest metropolitan areas had reached 52.9, which was higher than the index in Costa Rica and much higher than the Gini indices of any of the Asian cases (Table A4). Argentina is the only Latin American country whose Gini index rose significantly in the 1970s, 1980s, and 1990s alike.[12]

Argentina's income poverty statistics come from the same surveys as its income inequality statistics. The national poverty line applied to these data averaged about U.S. \$150 per month in 1995–2000.[13] From 1980 to 1990 the income poverty headcount in Greater Buenos Aires soared from 8 to 41 percent of the population, peaking at 47 percent in 1989 (a year of hyperinflation).

[10] Heston, Summers, and Aten 2006, variable RGDPCH (see Table A3).
[11] McGuire 1995a; O'Donnell 1978; Waisman 1987.
[12] Morley 2001: 24.
[13] Pessino and Andrés 2002: 74.

After the enactment of the 1991 convertibility law, which stopped inflation and boosted business confidence, economic growth skyrocketed, reducing income poverty to 16 percent in May 1994.[14] The Mexican economic crisis of December 1994, the rising value of the Argentine peso (which was pegged to the rising U.S. dollar), and financial crises in Asia, Russia, and Brazil conspired to slow growth in the late 1990s, raising the poverty headcount to 35 percent in October 2001.[15] When the Argentine peso was finally devalued at the end of 2001, poverty spiked again. In October 2002, an unprecedented 58 percent of individuals in the country's 28 largest metropolitan areas fell below the poverty line. Growth soon picked up again, however, bolstered by the world economic boom and an inflow of foreign investment. By early 2008, the poverty headcount in the 28 areas had fallen to 21 percent and unemployment, which had been 19 percent in late 1994, was down to 8 percent.[16]

Despite this strong finish, Argentina from 1960 to 2005 experienced sluggish and erratic economic growth, a sharp rise in income inequality, and huge fluctuations in income poverty. To what extent do these income-related factors explain the level of infant mortality in 2005, the overall amount of progress at reducing infant mortality from 1960 to 2005, or the tempo of infant mortality decline within that period?

Across a sample of 93 developing countries Argentina's infant mortality level in 2005 was slightly below that predicted by its GDP per capita in 2003 (Figure 1.1). A narrow version of the wealthier is healthier proposition, focusing exclusively on GDP per capita, is thus consistent with the level of infant mortality prevailing in 2005. This consistency can in part be attributed, however, to the depressed level of GDP per capita prevailing in 2003 ($10,170). In 1997, when GDP per capita was higher ($11,605), a bivariate regression model applied to a worldwide sample of countries found that Argentina's infant mortality rate was 55 percent higher than expected on the basis of its level of overall affluence.[17]

Argentina's percent decline of infant mortality from 1960 to 2005 was steeper than predicted by its GDP per capita growth (Figure 1.2), but this overperformance should not be interpreted as a great success. Except for countries in sub-Saharan Africa and in the former Soviet bloc, Argentina from 1960 to 2005 had one of the slowest rates of economic growth in the world. Accordingly, its overperformance on infant mortality decline was as much a result of slow GDP per capita growth as of rapid infant mortality decline.

The tempo of infant mortality decline in Argentina, especially from 1960 to 1985, was also inconsistent with the narrow variant of the wealthier is healthier proposition (according to which "wealth" is measured exclusively

[14] Lee 2000: 18.
[15] Pessino and Andrés 2002: 74.
[16] Argentina. INDEC 2008a, 2008b. 1994 unemployment figure from McGuire 1997: 222.
[17] World Bank 2000b: 65.

by GDP per capita). Across eight five-year periods from 1960 to 2000 (from 1960–1965 to 1995–2000), the correlation between average annual GDP per capita growth and percent decline of infant mortality was -0.14 (Table 11.1), indicating that the pace of infant mortality decline was seriously out of phase with the pace of economic growth. From 1960 to 1985 infant mortality fell fastest when the economy did worst, and fell slowest when the economy did best. GDP per capita grew by 2.1 percent per year from 1960 to 1971, but infant mortality remained at 62 per 1000. GDP per capita then shrank at an average annual rate of -0.8 percent from 1972 to 1985, but infant mortality plunged from 57 to 26 per 1000. The wealthier is healthier proposition fared a bit better in subsequent years. Under Alfonsín (1983–1989), when GDP per capita declined at an average annual rate of 2.3 percent, infant mortality fell at only 2.0 percent per year. Under Menem (1989–1999), when GDP per capita grew at 3.2 percent per year, the pace of infant mortality decline accelerated to 3.4 percent per year.[18] During the economic catastrophe from 1999 to 2002 infant mortality fell at only 1.3 percent per year, whereas during the economic boom from 2003 to 2006 it fell at 6.0 percent per year.

Even in the post-1983 years, however, economic circumstances were not the only determinants of the pace of infant mortality decline. The Alfonsín and Menem years differed more on economic growth than on infant mortality decline, possibly because both governments neglected maternal and infant care for the poor (Section 5.5). After 2004, moreover, it was not only the economic boom, but also the better provision of basic health services to the poor, that raised the pace of infant mortality decline. The Birth Plan (Plan Nacer), which extended basic health services to uninsured mothers and children in impoverished provinces, coincided with a rapid decline of the infant mortality rate. From 2004 to 2006 infant mortality fell 24 percent in the nine provinces where the Birth Plan was initially implemented, but only 8 percent in the other 15 provinces (Section 5.4). Economic conditions shaped the pattern and pace of infant mortality decline in Argentina, but changes in public service provision also mattered.

5.3. Argentina: Education, Family Planning, Safe Water, and Sanitation

Argentina in the mid-1980s spent about 21 percent of GDP on social services. About 8 percent of GDP went to retirement and disability pensions, 5 percent to health care, 5 percent to education, and 1 percent each to housing, family allowances (income transfers to formal-sector wage-earners based on number of family members), and social assistance programs for the poor.[19] Access to many social services, notably pensions and health care, was determined mainly by occupational position, income, and membership in organized

[18] GDP per capita and infant mortality figures from the sources for Argentina in Tables A1 and A3.
[19] Isuani and Tenti 1989: 25.

groups. "Poor sectors [were] excluded because they [did] not qualify to enter the system by any of these doors."[20]

Argentina in 2005 had high rates of literacy, mean years of schooling, and school enrollment (Tables A6, A7, and A8). Among the eight societies compared in this book only South Korea and Taiwan from 1960 to 1999 raised mean years of schooling more, in percentage terms, than Argentina (Table A7). The Argentine educational system had shortcomings, however. Free university education, which mainly benefited higher-income families, drained money from public primary and secondary education, as did state subsidies for private schools.[21] During the 1990s only 60 percent of Argentina's education budget was allocated to teachers, schools, and supplies; the rest went to administration.[22] Teachers earned less than half as much in 1990 as in 1983, and their salaries did not recover much in the first half of the 1990s. These cuts in teachers' salaries contributed to a high level of strike activity that itself disrupted schooling.[23] Children from poor families started school later, had higher rates of truancy and grade repetition, and achieved lower test scores. No school bus system existed, so children who could not afford bus fare could not travel to better schools farther from home. When the opportunity arose, more experienced teachers often migrated toward better schools. One study concluded that schools in the province of Buenos Aires and in the Federal Capital in the early 1990s were "not designed...to avoid the exclusion of poor students, much less to promote their inclusion."[24]

Of the eight societies compared in this book, Argentina in 1960 had the lowest fertility rate. From 1960 to 2005, however, it also had the slowest fertility decline. In a broader perspective, among 179 countries with data for both 1960 and 2005, Argentina ranked 146th at percent decline in fertility.[25] Slow fertility decline contributed to slow infant mortality decline throughout this period, but after about 1970 the tempo of the declines diverged. From 1971 to 1985 fertility remained at 3.1 expected children per woman, but infant mortality plunged from 62 to 26 per 1000, an annual rate of decline of 5.6 percent. From 1985 to 2005 fertility fell from 3.1 to 2.3 expected children per woman, but infant mortality fell only from 26 to 13 per 1000, an annual rate of decline of 3.2 percent (Tables A1 and A10). Stepped-up provision of basic health services during the 1970s, rather than fertility decline (of which there

---

[20] Lo Vuolo 1995: 48.

[21] On universities see González Rozada and Menéndez 2002; on private schools see Fiszbein 1999: 14.

[22] Stillwaggon 1998: 157. Public school facilities were often decrepit (Fiszbein 1999: 13).

[23] On teacher salaries in the 1980s see Lo Vuolo 1995: 15–17, 47; on teacher salaries in the first half of the 1990s see Fiszbein 1999: 28; on teachers' strikes from 1984 to 1993 see McGuire 1996: 139–140.

[24] Fiszbein 1999: 32.

[25] Data from World Bank 2008a. Percent decline is the proportion of distance traveled by 2005 from the total fertility rate in 1960 to a stipulated minimum of zero.

was none, in contrast to Chile during the 1970s), thus appears to be the main reason why infant mortality fell so steeply during the decade.

Weak family planning policies were partly responsible for the glacial pace of fertility decline in Argentina from 1960 to 1985. Tightening previous controls, the 1973–1976 Peronist governments restricted the sale of contraceptives, outlawed the promotion of birth control, and denounced family planning at the 1974 World Population Conference. Behind these pro-natalist policies were both religious conviction and a fear that slow population growth might jeopardize the control of national territory.[26] The 1976–1983 military regime retained these restrictions on family planning, but the elected Alfonsín government (1983–1989) loosened them, and the total fertility rate, which had not declined at all from 1960 to 1985, fell from 3.1 in 1985 to 2.7 in 1995 (Table A10). Still, in both 1989 and 1994, experts ranked Argentina's family planning effort weakest not only among the eight societies analyzed in this book, but also among the 24 Latin American and Caribbean countries for which ratings are available.[27]

By 1998 more than 50 percent of sexually active Argentine women were using contraceptives. Abortion, however, remained illegal, except to preserve the health or life of the mother under certain rarely encountered conditions. With safe, legal abortion virtually impossible to obtain in Argentina in the late 1990s, some 350,000–400,000 annual clandestine abortions occurred, causing about one-third of recorded maternal deaths.[28] President Menem (1989–1999) took a particularly strong stand against legalizing abortion, and family planning initiatives languished in Congress until after Menem left office.[29] In May 2003, however, as one of his first acts as president, Néstor Kirchner (2003–2007) signed a bill allowing the provision of information about family planning, free screening for sexually transmitted infections, and the free distribution of contraceptives.[30] In 2004 Kirchner's health minister, Ginés González García, took a public position in favor of opening dialogue about loosening restrictive abortion laws. Kirchner supported his minister, provoking a serious conflict with the Church and the military by sacking a right-wing military chaplain who stated that the minister should be "thrown into the sea" for his position on abortion.[31]

Argentine governments began to make efforts to improve the quality of urban water supply in 1868, and agencies devoted to this task appeared

---

[26] Argentina. MBS/SESP 1974b: 53–56; Mauldin et al. 1974: 372; Measham 1975: 281; Wood and Carvalho 1988: 161.

[27] Ross and Mauldin 1996: 146.

[28] CRLP 2001: 12–13; Htun 2003: 147–148; World Bank 2003c: 14.

[29] Htun 2003: 161–164.

[30] Rogers 2003: 134.

[31] Valente 2005. The expression evoked images of the "disappeared," many of whom were thrown alive from airplanes into the Rio de la Plata. The chaplain was publicly sympathetic to the 1976–1983 military regime.

shortly after 1900.[32] By 1947, 94 percent of Greater Buenos Aires residents had access to piped water. Perón did little to expand or maintain the water system as the metropolis grew, however, and by 1960 the share with piped water had dropped to 76 percent. Water supply and sewerage systems were allowed to deteriorate in subsequent years, and by 1987 only a minority of households in some impoverished districts of Greater Buenos Aires had access to safe water or adequate sanitation. Water purification and sewage treatment facilities were decrepit even in prosperous districts of the Federal Capital.[33] Outside the Buenos Aires area, conditions were even worse. In 1969, only 55 percent of Argentines had access to safe water and only 34 percent of the urban population had access to adequate sanitation. Argentina in 1998 had a higher GDP per capita than Brazil, Chile, or Costa Rica, but in that year only 79 percent of Argentines had access to safe water, compared to 92–96 percent of Brazilians, Chileans, and Costa Ricans (Tables A11 and A12). Argentines living in rural areas were especially poorly served. In 1998 less than 25 percent of rural dwellers had access to safe water, a proportion lower than in Haiti, and only 39 percent had access to adequate sewage disposal, well below the mean for Latin America.[34] It was not until 2000 that Argentina, according to World Bank statistics, caught up to Brazil, Chile, and Costa Rica on access to improved water sources and improved sanitation.

Argentine governments from 1960 to 2005 thus performed unremarkably at improving primary and secondary education, poorly at providing family planning, and disappointingly at raising access to safe water and adequate sanitation. It is hard to weigh precisely how much deficiencies in the provision of these social services compounded the effects of slow economic growth, rising income inequality, and soaring income poverty, but if one adds in deficiencies in nutritional assistance and health care, and considers that Argentina is a fairly affluent country with very high levels of social spending, it is hard to sustain the argument that income-related factors were the sole or even the main reason why its infant mortality rate fell so slowly from 1960 to 2005.

5.4. Argentina: Nutrition and Health Care

Of 42 countries in the Western Hemisphere, only two in 1996 surpassed Argentina in the share of GDP devoted to health care. The United States spent 15 percent of GDP on health care ($4,296 per capita), Nicaragua spent 13 percent ($59 per capita), and Argentina spent 11 percent ($825 per capita).[35] In 2000, Chile achieved an infant mortality rate of 8.9 per 1000 while spending

---

[32] Isuani and Mercer 1988: 32.

[33] Stillwaggon 1998: 99–110.

[34] PAHO 2000a. The privatization of 138 of the country's 495 municipal water companies from 1990 to 1999 contributed to a sharp decline in under-5 mortality in the affected municipalities, attributable almost entirely to a reduction of deaths due to water-borne diseases (Galiani, Gertler, and Schargrodsky 2005).

[35] Share of GDP spent on health care in 1996, in then-current PPP $US, from PAHO 2000a.

$735 per capita on health care, whereas Argentina registered a rate of 16.6 per 1000 while spending $1,298 per capita on health care (Tables A1 and A15). Compared to Chile, Argentina got less infant mortality bang for its health care buck mainly because its maternal and infant health care and nutrition policies covered a smaller share of the needy population and were less well funded, designed, and coordinated with other policies. General revenue-funded public health care spending was quite progressive in Argentina, with about 31 percent of spending going to the poorest quintile and only 7 percent to the richest, but that was possible mainly because the middle classes and the rich largely abandoned public for private health care providers except for very costly interventions. The distribution of public health care spending in Chile, where the middle classes and the rich also used private health care providers for most services, was almost exactly the same as in Argentina.[36] These cases suggest that the progressivity of public health care spending, like the share of such spending in GDP, may have little to do with infant mortality decline.

Argentina is one of the world's largest exporters of beef and grain. From 1960 to 2005 the country had satisfactory calorie and protein availability,[37] but pockets of malnutrition persisted. A UNICEF survey in the late 1980s in slums around Buenos Aires and La Plata revealed that only 8 percent of children were satisfactorily breastfed, and that 60 percent of mothers who abandoned the practice did so because of insufficient breast milk, a sign of maternal malnutrition.[38] In the mid-1990s, 10 percent of infant deaths in Argentina were attributed to malnutrition.[39] These nutritional deficiencies persisted despite a long history of state-sponsored school lunch and milk provision programs. The first public school to provide milk to children did so in 1906, but it was not until the 1930s that school lunch programs became widespread, and not until the 1960s that Congress passed a law requiring public schools to provide lunches.[40] Public nutrition programs were not always targeted to the people in greatest need of them, and even where they were, the food they provided was often insufficient in quantity or poor in quality. In 1988, only 46 percent of "structurally poor" children in the Greater Buenos Aires area benefited from the school lunch program.[41]

In 1936 Congress passed legislation establishing the National•Mother and Infant Program (PNMI) within the Ministry of the Interior.[42] The PNMI had a primary health care component, but in the late 1990s milk provision absorbed about 90 percent of its budget.[43] The PNMI provided funding and established

---

[36] Suárez-Berenguela 2000: 42.
[37] Wilkie, Alemán, and Ortega 1999: 200.
[38] Stillwaggon 1998: 235.
[39] *El Cronista* February 24, 1995.
[40] Britos et al. 2003: 14–18.
[41] Grassi, Hintze, and Neufield 1994: 191–193.
[42] Repetto et al. 2001: 9.
[43] Calculated from Idiart 2002: 195. In 1964/65, the program spent 49 percent of its budget on powdered milk. Argentina. MASSP 1966: 463.

guidelines for milk distribution; provincial health ministries were in charge of implementation. No baseline surveys were carried out to establish a target population for the milk, and no centralized registry of eligible beneficiaries existed.[44] In 1988 only 25 percent of mothers with children less than four years old in "structurally poor" households in Greater Buenos Aires reported having received milk from the program.[45] The governments of Raúl Alfonsín (1983–1989) and Carlos Menem (1989–1999) sponsored free food programs for the poor, but their impact was limited. Particularly under Menem, the programs were designed as much to cultivate political support as raise the nutritional status of the hungry.[46]

Argentina's health care system was highly fragmented in the early part of the twentieth century. Hospitals and other health facilities were run by ethnic or other philanthropic organizations, religious denominations, or the government. Within the public sector authority over health facilities and personnel was split among municipal governments, provincial governments, and the central government, as well as among various central government agencies.[47] Some better-off people belonged to mutual aid societies that provided or funded health care, and some of the poor belonged to fly-by-night private health insurance schemes, but most citizens had no health insurance at all and relied on "public assistance" hospitals (the government was legally obliged to provide medical services and drugs free of charge to the "solemnly poor," and at low prices to other poor people). Scattered authority and significant inequalities in health insurance coverage and access to health services would characterize the Argentine health care system throughout the twentieth century.[48]

Public health personnel had been involved in primary health care and health education since before 1900,[49] but the first major nationwide initiative dedicated explicitly to improving maternal and infant health care for the poor came in 1937, when the PNMI went into effect. This program funded and oversaw provincial agencies that distributed free milk to poor infants and mothers, but it was also involved in prenatal care, in promoting professional attendance at birth, and in funding and setting general guidelines for the delivery of medicines and treatment to infants, children, and expectant mothers.[50] The PNMI emerged at about the same time that Chile's Mandatory Insurance Fund (CSO) for blue-collar workers introduced a maternal and infant care program for its members and their spouses (Section 4.4). In both countries, the introduction of these maternal and infant health care programs coincided with a sharp decline of infant mortality. From 1938 to 1946 infant

[44] Idiart 2004.
[45] Grassi, Hintze, and Neufield 1994: 194.
[46] Lloyd-Sherlock 1997: 27–28; Midré 1992; Repetto 2000: 605–606.
[47] Escudé 1976: 33–37; Escudé 1989: 63–69.
[48] Lloyd-Sherlock 2000b: 144–146; Munck 1998.
[49] Jankilevich 2003.
[50] Repetto et al. 2001: 16–19.

mortality fell from 104 to 74 per 1000 in Argentina, and from 236 to 160 per 1000 in Chile.[51]

Perón's government from 1946 to 1955 expanded the health ministry's payroll from 7,000 to 35,000 employees, trained thousands of nurses, launched campaigns against infectious diseases (notably malaria in northern provinces), tripled the number of beds in state-run hospitals (favoring poorer provinces), and built 200 health centers in small communities.[52] The Peronist era, according to a health ministry document published in 1985, marked the emergence of a "conception of the health center as a site for the delivery of both preventive and curative services, integrating treatment with monitoring of the environment and serving a defined and limited population."[53]

Under Perón, however, infant mortality fell only about 2 percent per year, from 74 per 1000 in 1946 to 62 per 1000 in 1955.[54] Perón's government did well at placing health personnel and health facilities in previously underserved areas, but otherwise did more to expand health insurance for the not-so-poor than to improve the quality of basic health services for the very poor. The leaders of labor unions, the main beneficiaries of health insurance during this era, were among the groups responsible for this neglect. In 1949, Perón elevated the Health Directorate, which had previously been an agency of the Interior Ministry, to ministerial status, renaming it the National Ministry of Public Health (Ministerio de Salud Pública de la Nación).[55] Dr. Ramón Carrillo, Perón's first health minister, tried to create a "free, revenue-financed universal health system," but after seven years of such efforts he was forced to resign because of "pressure [from] labor union bigwigs" who "did not want a universal system, but rather a plethora of work-centered health social security subsystems, with maximum opportunities for clientelism and graft."[56] For the next 50 years, repeated attempts by post-Perón governments to unify public health care financing foundered under pressure from union leaders who wanted to keep control of the *obras sociales* (the "work-centered health social security subsystems").

The *obras sociales*, which were still operating in the early 2000s, worked like health maintenance organizations in the United States, except that their executives were typically appointed by union leaders. Some of the *obras sociales* traced their roots to mutual aid societies formed in the 1800s by union leaders and European immigrants.[57] In 1944, the military government in which Perón gained recognition granted the union-based *obras sociales* the right to collect payments from employers as well as workers, and established a Social Service

[51] Argentina: Somoza, Dehollain, and Salvia 1962; Chile: Mamalakis 1980: 40–41.
[52] Bermann and Escudero 1978: 534; Escudé 1976: 37, 40; Escudero 1981: 562.
[53] Argentina. MSAS 1985: 240.
[54] Somoza, Dehollain, and Salvia 1962.
[55] Jankilevich 2003; Pérez Yrigoyen 1989: 176.
[56] Escudero 2003: 131.
[57] Munck 1998.

Commission to oversee the funds.[58] After being elected president in 1946 Perón authorized the Labor Ministry to regulate the *obras sociales*, but union leaders retained day-to-day control over the funds.[59] Some *obras sociales* provided health care through their own facilities and personnel, and a few expanded into tourism, recreation, warehousing, legal advice, libraries, discount stores, technical schools, workplace cafeterias, funeral services, and life insurance.[60] Most, however, operated simply as financial intermediaries, obtaining medical services and drugs for their members by signing contracts with federations of private-sector doctors and with private hospitals and pharmacies.[61]

By 1955 the Argentine health care system was already configured much as it would be 50 years later. Its three main components were health care provision (1) in government-run facilities financed by general revenues; (2) in private facilities financed by payroll deductions channeled through the *obras sociales*; and (3) in private facilities financed by out-of-pocket spending or by private health insurance. From the mid-1980s to the mid-1990s, public health care provision in government-run facilities accounted for about 20 percent of total health care spending; the *obras sociales* accounted for about 40 percent; and private sources accounted for the remaining 40 percent.[62] In the late 1990s 47 percent of Argentines depended exclusively on public facilities financed by general tax revenue, 48 percent belonged to an *obra social,* and 7 percent had private insurance.[63] Within the poorest quintile, 67 percent depended only on public facilities, 29 percent belonged to an *obra social*, and 4 percent had private insurance.[64] Hence, about 20 percent of Argentina's total spending on health care served half of the population and about two-thirds of the poor. Among the four Latin American countries compared in this book, Argentina was the only one that entered the twenty-first century without a unified public health care system (with payroll deductions and general revenues funding the same personnel, facilities, and services), and in which the contributory sector remained split into hundreds of separate funds.

After the 1955 coup the military government of General Pedro Aramburu (1955–1958) and the elected government of Arturo Frondizi (1958–1962) each tried to decentralize the general revenue-financed component of the health care system. Both efforts failed, in part because each implied the imposition of an unfunded mandate on provincial governments.[65] The National School of Public Health, which was founded in 1959, trained health administrators and technical personnel, improved the collection and processing of health

[58] Thompson 1985: 35–36.
[59] Lloyd-Sherlock 2000b: 147.
[60] McGuire 1997: 105.
[61] Jankilevich 2003; Pérez Yrigoyen 1989: 178; World Bank 1988: 18.
[62] Castañeda, Beeharry, and Griffin 2000: 256; Lloyd-Sherlock 1997: 29; Lloyd-Sherlock 2004: 97–98; Pérez Yrigoyen 1989: 187–188.
[63] Castañeda, Beeharry, and Griffin 2000: 256.
[64] World Bank 2000b: 126–127.
[65] Pérez Yrigoyen 1989: 176–177.

information, and held educational and training workshops throughout the country. During the elected government of Arturo Illia (1963–1966) the health minister, Arturo Oñativia, strengthened the ministry's branch agencies in interior provinces, asked provincial health authorities to encourage more community participation in the administration of hospitals and other health facilities, opened more than 250 new maternal and infant health care centers around the country, and raised the budget of the National Mother and Infant Program by a factor of five in real terms. Under the military rule of General Juan Carlos Onganía (1966–1970), public health authorities began to take a more technocratic approach to policy-making.[66] Drawing on the expertise and personnel of the fledgling public health school, the Onganía government began to fund federal rural health activities in 1969.[67] Apart from these piecemeal advances, however, little was done at the national level during the 1960s to improve the provision of basic health services. Accordingly, Argentina's infant mortality rate rose from 61.8 per 1000 in 1955 to 62.2 per 1000 in 1971.[68]

A June 1966 coup began seven years of military rule. The government encountered little resistance until June 1969, when students and workers took over 150 square blocks in the center of the city of Córdoba, battling police and army troops. The military government suppressed the cordobazo, as the episode came to be known, but in response to the uprising it stepped up its attempts to mollify civil society organizations, including labor unions.[69] In a decision that vastly expanded the financial resources of union leaders, the military government in 1970 made it legally obligatory for all wage and salary earners to belong to an *obra social*, and permitted dependents of wage and salary earners to join as well. Because of this decision, the proportion of Argentines covered by an *obra social* rose from 35 percent in 1967 to 75 percent in 1984.[70]

Allegations of murky dealing, featherbedding, and corruption have hounded the *obras sociales* for decades.[71] Also, managerial incompetence and malfeasance has caused many *obras sociales* to collapse or to require government bailouts. The *obras sociales* have achieved this woeful record despite shifting a large share of their costs to the already strapped general revenue-funded sector of the health care system. Public health facilities in the early 2000s treated many people who either belonged to an *obra social* or had private insurance.[72] In the 1990s, 30 percent of free consultations in public health care facilities involved patients with some form of health insurance, and as of 2002 "only

---

[66] Argentina. MASSP 1966: 296, 463–464; Belmartino and Bloch 1994: 31–57; Escudé 1976: 41; Neri 1982: 103–108.
[67] Argentina. MSAS 1985: 241; WHO 1980: 56.
[68] Neuquén. SS/MDS 2000.
[69] Brennan 1994; O'Donnell 1988: 177–179; Smith 1989: 153.
[70] Médici 2002: 2–3.
[71] McGuire 1997: 225–226.
[72] Lloyd-Sherlock 1997: 29; Pérez Yrigoyen 1989: 195.

a very small fraction" of these costs were recovered.[73] The public sector also subsidized the private sector and the *obras sociales* by funding almost all of the country's long-term care, health education, preventive and disease control measures, and medical education and training.[74]

Public health care facilities, although nominally free to all, suffered from long delays, poor service, excessive bureaucracy, uneven geographical distribution, administrative fragmentation, and poor coordination.[75] Public health facilities in poor provinces were underutilized, spent too much on salaries and too little on equipment and supplies, and had too many administrators and support staff. Reviewing a public hospital in Tucumán, the World Bank estimated overstaffing to be more than 30 percent, and noted that only half of doctors' time was devoted to patient care.[76] A shortage of nurses exacerbated these problems. To work efficiently, a physician requires the help of two to three nurses. In the mid-1980s, however, Argentina had 69,000 doctors, but only 16,000 nurses.[77] By 1990 Argentina had a doctor-to-nurse ratio of 5.4 to 1, second-highest among 87 countries for which data are available.[78] Nurses' aides were also in short supply.[79] As might be surmised from the top-heavy ratio of doctors to nurses, many doctors performed activities that nurses could have carried out.[80] Hospital administrators were plentiful, however. The city of La Plata had three times as many inhabitants as Madison, Wisconsin, but 30 times as many hospital administrators.[81]

Public health care has long been centralized at the national level in Costa Rica, South Korea, Taiwan, and Thailand, but has been divided among the national, provincial, and municipal levels in Chile since the 1970s, in Brazil since the 1990s, and in Indonesia since the early 2000s. Most decentralized of all is Argentina, where provincial governments have played a major role in public health care provision since the late nineteenth century.[82] In 1970 the Argentine central government still spent more than provincial governments on health care, but by 1988 provincial governments spent more than twice as much as the central government, and by 1995 provincial governments accounted for 70 percent of public health care spending (the central government accounted for only 14 percent, with municipalities making up

---

[73] World Bank 2000b: 124; quotation from World Bank 2003c: 15. See also World Bank 2006a: 31.

[74] Pérez Yrigoyen 1989: 195.

[75] Lloyd-Sherlock 2000a: 112–113; Pérez Yrigoyen 1989: 194; World Bank 1988: 15.

[76] World Bank 2000b: 130–131.

[77] World Bank 1988: 18.

[78] WHO 1993: c12–c19.

[79] PAHO 1988: 80.

[80] World Bank 1988: 17.

[81] Stillwaggon 1998: 157.

[82] Escudé 1976: 35–43. Argentina circa 2000 had the most decentralized political system in Latin America (Jones 2005; Treisman 2002). Its health system was tied with Brazil's for most decentralized (Mesa-Lago 2008: 249–250).

the difference).[83] Of Argentina's 160,000 public health employees in 1980, 53 percent worked for provincial governments, 25 percent worked for municipalities, and only 6 percent worked for the national health ministry. The remaining public health employees worked for other public agencies, such as hospitals associated with public universities.[84] By the mid-1990s the national government was responsible only for funding, priority setting, planning, regulation, coordination, and technical advice; provincial governments were in charge of the hands-on tasks of resource allocation, administration of health care facilities, and implementation of health programs.[85]

Provincial governments have been responsible for many of Argentina's most important primary health care programs. Especially notable was the Provincial Health Plan that was introduced in 1970 in the Patagonian province of Neuquén. This program mobilized Neuquén's public health personnel to monitor the health of school children, to raise the share of professionally attended births, to provide checkups and food to expectant mothers and young children, to conduct vaccination campaigns, to fight tuberculosis and tapeworm, and to educate people about health and hygiene.[86] Between 1970 and 1975 the number of employees in Neuquén's provincial health subsecretariat rose from 550 to 1,427, the number of nursing personnel rose from 250 to 422, and the number of medical consultations rose from 203,000 to 411,000.[87] Between 1970 and 1982 the share of pregnant women receiving care from a physician doubled to 55 percent, the share of births taking place in the home fell from 27 to 6 percent, and the share of children under two receiving checkups rose from 51 to 68 percent.[88]

The introduction of the Provincial Health Plan coincided with a plunge in Neuquén's infant mortality rate, which fell from 108 per 1000 in 1970 to 43 per 1000 in 1975 to 14 per 1000 in 1998. This 87 percent decline of infant mortality from 1970 to 1998 was nearly as great as that of Chile during the same period (89 percent), and was greater than that of Costa Rica (79 percent). By 2005 Neuquén had reduced its infant mortality rate to 9.4 per 1000, just below the rate in Costa Rica in that year (Table A1).[89] The case of Neuquén in Argentina, like that of Kerala in India or Ceará in Brazil, shows that subnational units in decentralized political systems can achieve rapid infant mortality decline through the public provision of maternal and infant

---

[83] 1988: Lo Vuolo 1995: 38–39; 1970 and 1995: González García 1997: 195.

[84] Lo Vuolo 1995: 17.

[85] Espinel et al. 1998: 44. The World Bank (2003c: 15) concluded in 2003 that "the national government level has only limited legal and administrative influence over provincial health sector policy."

[86] Leonfanti and Chiesa 1988: 64; Neuquén. Ministerio de Salud Pública 1990: 32–33.

[87] Moreno 1979: 152–154.

[88] Leonfanti and Chiesa 1988: 65–66.

[89] Neuquén infant mortality rates from Neuquén. SS/MDS 2000 (1970–1998) and Argentina. Ministerio de Salud 2007 (1999–2006); Chilean decline calculated from infant mortality figures in Chile. Banco Central de Chile 1989: 428 and Chile. INE 2002: 53; Costa Rican decline calculated from infant mortality figures in CCP-UCR 2009.

health care even when national policies leave much to be desired.[90] Jujuy, Río Negro, and Salta also implemented vigorous primary health care programs during the 1970s, and each also achieved faster infant mortality decline during the decade than the rest of Argentina.[91] These initiatives in provinces that started out around 1970 with very high rates of infant mortality helped to accelerate infant mortality decline in the country as a whole. Infant mortality fell more steeply in Argentina from 1970 to 1975 than in any other five-year period depicted in Table A1.

The May 1969 cordobazo and the ensuing guerrilla violence shifted support toward a military faction that favored elections and a swift return to civilian rule.[92] As the guerrilla groups grew bolder and as the economy deteriorated, the military let Perón return to Argentina after 18 years of exile. The military did not allow Perón to contest the March 1973 presidential election, but his "personal delegate" ran, won, and resigned after a few weeks in office. In September 1973, with violence escalating, the military allowed Perón to stand for office in a new presidential election, hoping that he could rein in the guerrillas. Perón won and took office in October 1973. In July 1974, however, Juan Perón died, leaving the presidency to his wife and vice-president, María Estela (Isabel) Martínez de Perón. In March 1976, after 21 months of political violence and economic chaos, Isabel Perón's government was overthrown in a military coup.

Despite this tumult, Congress in 1974 established the National Integrated Health System (SNIS), which stipulated a procedure for creating a single, unified health insurance system by merging into a single fund general tax revenue hitherto destined for public health services, the *obras sociales* for civil servants, and the health-related portion of public-sector pensions. Another 1974 law established the National Health Career, which mandated the competitive selection of public sector doctors and nurses, raised wages and benefits, provided higher pay for work in remote areas, and permitted transfer on request from such areas after three years of service. The law also prohibited any participant in the SNIS from working a second job, even as a volunteer.[93] By the time these bills emerged from Congress, however, pressure from union leaders, doctors' associations, and others had watered them down significantly. The military reduced funding for the SNIS after the 1976 coup, and the program disappeared in 1977.[94]

---

[90] On Kerala see Ramachandran 2000; on Ceará see Section 6.4.

[91] Infant mortality from 1970 to 1980 fell 69 percent in Neuquén, 60 percent in Jujuy, 59 percent in Río Negro, and 52 percent in Salta, compared to 47 percent in Argentina as a whole. 1970 figures from Argentina. MSPyMA 1983: 93; 1980 figures from Gore 2000. On the primary health care programs in Jujuy see Argentina. MBS/SESP 1978: 24–26 and Ripoll 2002: 96–97. On Río Negro see Bermann and Escudero 1978: 536; Dal Bo 2000: 89; and Escudero 1981: 564. On Salta see Argentina. MBS/SESP 1978: 26–31; Arce, Katz, and Muñoz 1993: 358; Brett 1984: 117–119, 125; and Vilches and Ibánez 1993: 131–132.

[92] O'Donnell 1988: 173–175; Smith 1989: 154–159.

[93] Argentina. MBS/SESP 1974: 91–102; Neri 1982: 114.

[94] Argentina. MBS/SESP 1974: 86; Belmartino and Bloch 1994: 247–261; González García 1997: 142; Jankilevich 2003.

During the 1976–1983 military regime many public health professionals "disappeared." The government imposed user fees in public health care facilities, exempting only the indigent and those suffering from contagious diseases. It also transferred to the provinces responsibility for the day-to-day operation of most such facilities, saddling the provinces with an unfunded mandate (thus succeeding where the Aramburu and Frondizi governments had failed).[95] From 1975 to 1983 public health care spending (excluding the *obras sociales*) fell from 2.4 to 1.9 percent of GDP.[96] After seizing power in 1976 the military government intervened in the *obras sociales* and replaced their directors with appointed trustees, under whom the expenditures of the *obras sociales* soared from 2.3 percent of GDP in 1975 to 4.4 percent in 1983.[97] Corruption contributed to this rise in expenditure, as did purchases by the *obras sociales* of "high-cost curative health services... designed more to maximise providers' profits than to meet affiliates' basic health needs."[98]

As in Chile under military rule, however, Argentina's 1976–1983 military government also took steps to make basic health care services more accessible to poor people. It gave financial and technical support to rural health services, which expanded their coverage from 500,000 persons in 1976 to 1,400,000 in 1977. The plan was to cover more than 6.8 million inhabitants with "health promotion and protection activities, rural basic sanitation, and medical and dental resources."[99] According to a government document, these activities were designed "to correct failures in the health structures with minimal outlays and personnel requirements." Health agents were to be recruited from local communities, trained to provide medical services, and instructed to make home visits in small towns and in rural areas to collect health information, distribute milk, administer first aid, vaccinate children, provide health and nutrition education, and refer patients to clinics and hospitals. The health agents would be supervised by a nurse and doctor at a nearby hospital, who were themselves expected to make periodic tours of the health zone. Based on these guidelines, provincial health officials were to submit plans to the office of the National Rural Health Program (which in 1978 was renamed the National Primary Health Care Program). If the plans were approved, the federal government would fund the province's rural health agents.[100] Some provincial governments were better prepared than others to carry out these initiatives, and no systematic studies link these activities to health outcomes, but from 1977 to 1979 (the first three years of the National Rural Health Program) Argentina's infant mortality rate fell from 45 to 35

---

[95] Bermann and Escudero 1978: 531–538.
[96] Lo Vuolo 1995: 33–34.
[97] Escudero 1981: 567.
[98] Jankilevich 2003; Neri 1982: 135–136; quotation from Lloyd-Sherlock 2000b: 153.
[99] WHO 1980: 56.
[100] Monsalvo 2003.

per 1000, a greater percent decline than in any other three-year period from 1960 to 2005.[101]

After their ill-fated invasion of the Falkland/Malvinas islands, the military in 1982 returned the *obras sociales* to union control. In 1983 Raúl Alfonsín of the Unión Cívica Radical, Peronism's historical rival, was elected president. One of his first initiatives was to try to unify public health care financing. In 1984 Alfonsín's health minister, Aldo Neri, drew up a National Health Insurance bill that would have extended health insurance coverage to the entire population. The insurance was to have been financed partly by general revenues and partly by a share of the payroll deductions hitherto channeled into the *obras sociales*. Neri's initiative fared no better than previous efforts to unify these revenue streams. Union leaders interpreted Neri's plan as an effort to loosen their control over the *obras sociales*, while the leaders of confederations representing doctors and hospitals wanted to know how, at a time of severe economic crisis, the government was going to fund health insurance for millions of additional patients without cutting back on its payments to health care providers. As the bill worked its way through congress, its main provisions were eroded under pressure from unions and associations of doctors and hospitals, leading to Neri's resignation in April 1986.

Although Neri's initiative failed, both Alfonsín and his democratically elected successor, the Peronist Carlos Menem (1989–1999), attempted to reform the *obras sociales* by reducing employer contributions, by routing contributions through government agencies, by allowing employees to choose freely among the funds, by auditing the funds more rigorously, by removing union leaders from oversight boards, and by introducing competition with private insurers. Protest from the union leaders who controlled the *obras sociales* weakened or thwarted most of these efforts.[102] Two laws at the end of 1988 repealed the *obras sociales* law of 1970 and established a new National Health Insurance System (Sistema Nacional de Seguros de Salud), which was designed in theory to encompass the whole Argentine population. In fact, however, the 1988 laws, whose application was shaped significantly by executive decrees, devised no mechanisms to incorporate the uninsured into the system and did nothing to reduce union leaders' control of the *obras sociales* or to combine payroll deductions with general tax funds in a single revenue stream.[103] Because of these failures to reform the *obras sociales*, contributory health insurance remained highly inequitable in Argentina at the start of the twenty-first century. The quality of service differed widely among the *obras sociales*,

---

[101] Infant mortality figures from the sources for Argentina in Table A1. Primary health care policies under the military regime are less well documented in Argentina than in Chile. The Argentine health ministry lost many of its records during a move in 1992, as well as in a subsequent fire (Idiart 2004: 14).

[102] Epstein 2000; Etchemendy and Palermo 1998: 577–581; Lloyd-Sherlock 2006: 358–359; McGuire 1997: 231–233.

[103] Belmartino and Bloch 1994: 313–358; Pérez Yrigoyen 1989: 179–180; Rossi and Rubilar 2007: 25–26.

and the state did not effectively regulate the *obras sociales* or private health insurance.[104] The fragmentation of the contributory system into hundreds of separate *obras sociales* "reduces the size of risk pools, increases administrative costs and tends to generate persistent deficits that, often, require official bailouts."[105] All taxpayers, including the uninsured, pay for these bailouts.

Among the most ambitious health care reform efforts during the Menem presidency was the Mandatory Medical Program (PMO). Launching this program was a 1996 health ministry decree stipulating that all *obras sociales* and private insurers would henceforth have to provide to each client a minimum set of medical services, including checkups, diagnosis, treatment, dentistry, and drugs. Any *obra social* or private insurer unwilling or unable to guarantee such benefits could be legally obliged to merge with other insurers.[106] The PMO differed fundamentally from Chile's Plan for Universal Access with Explicit Guarantees (Plan AUGE). In the Chilean program, guaranteed minimum services were provided to all citizens as a basic right, with explicit mechanisms for citizens to seek legal redress in case of noncompliance. The Argentine program applied only to insured persons, who comprised only about half of the population, and provided no explicit mechanisms for redress if an insurer failed to fund one of the services included in the basic package. In any case, the economic crisis of 1999–2002 made the Mandatory Medical Program untenable. By January 2002 some 60 to 80 percent of insurers were noncompliant.[107] In response to this crisis, the governments of Eduardo Duhalde (2002–2003) and Néstor Kirchner (2003–2007) declared a national health emergency, raised the health insurance premiums charged to workers and employers, and implemented new public health care programs stressing prevention and primary care, the wider dissemination of birth control counseling and contraceptives, more use of generic drugs, and the provision of medicines to public clinics.[108]

Ginés González García, the health minister who participated in the reforms to the Mandatory Medical Program during the Néstor Kirchner presidency, also devoted renewed attention to the general revenue-funded segment of the health care system. This part of the health care system, which served the families most vulnerable to infant mortality, had been neglected during the 1980s and 1990s, when politicians and state agencies had been preoccupied with the *obras sociales* and with private health insurers. At the beginning of the Alfonsín presidency in 1984, some 3,000 community health agents, working under the auspices of the National Primary Health Care Program, had served 2,000,000 rural Argentines and 200,000 residents of urban and suburban areas. In 1986 the health ministry added a Health Support Program (PAS) to

---

[104] Lloyd-Sherlock 2000b: 155–157; Lloyd-Sherlock 2004: 102–105.
[105] World Bank 2003c: 14.
[106] Acuña and Chudnovsky 2002: 46 fn. 37; Lloyd-Sherlock 2004: 105; Lloyd-Sherlock 2005: 1897; Rossi and Rubilar 2007: 26–31.
[107] Rossi and Rubilar 2007: 30.
[108] Lloyd-Sherlock 2005: 1900; Rossi and Rubilar 2007: 30–31.

fund primary care, maternal and infant care, nutritional aid, measures to fight Chagas disease, and similar public health activities. Both of these initiatives collapsed in the economic crisis of 1989, and even before this breakdown the World Bank had concluded that "health promotion and disease prevention are still not recognized as cost-effective complements to a disease and treatment oriented approach."[109] Despite significant gains during the 1980s in the breadth of childhood immunization (Table A17), the infant mortality rate, which had fallen from 44 to 30 per 1000 under military rule (1976–1983), declined only from 30 to 26 per 1000 under the elected Alfonsín government (1983–1989).[110]

The main national primary health care programs for needy mothers and infants during Carlos Menem's two presidencies (1989–1995; 1995–1999) were the National Mother and Infant Program (PNMI), which had existed since 1937, and the Mother and Infant Nutrition Program (PROMIN), which was launched by presidential decree in March 1993. Designed and funded in close collaboration with the World Bank and UNICEF, the Mother and Infant Nutrition Program operated within the health ministry, but tensions arose between the administrators of the program and other health ministry personnel.[111] Moreover, PNMI and PROMIN were poorly coordinated and competed for employees and beneficiaries.[112] In 1997 PNMI's budget was 57 million pesos and PROMIN's was 41 million pesos.[113] By 2001, in the context of a severe economic crisis, the budgets had fallen to 14 million and 6 million respectively.[114] Even in the relatively flush year of 1997, both programs together accounted for only 2.5 percent of combined national, provincial, and municipal public health care spending.[115] Such spending, in turn, represented only about a quarter of total health care spending. In 1997, accordingly, the two maternal and child health programs together absorbed about one-half of one percent of Argentina's total health expenditure.

Whereas the PNMI picked up recurrent costs of mother and child nutrition and health care, PROMIN provided funds to refurbish and equip health centers and community hospitals, to train health personnel, and to strengthen the system of referrals from primary to secondary and tertiary care. PROMIN targeted urban districts in which more than 30 percent of the population had unsatisfied basic needs.[116] It served about 3 million people, including 110,000 expectant mothers and 510,000 children under the age of six. By 2000, the

---

[109] World Bank 1988: 15.
[110] Neuquén. SS/MDS 2000 (vital registration).
[111] Acuña and Chudnovsky 2002: 2, 10, 32–33.
[112] UNDP 1998: 72; Idiart 2004: 14 fn. 27.
[113] Acuña, Kessler, and Repetto 2002: 21. At the time, one peso was worth one U.S. dollar.
[114] CEDI 2002: 81.
[115] Acuña, Kessler, and Repetto 2002: 20.
[116] Acuña and Chudnovsky 2002: 22; Acuña, Kessler, and Repetto 2002: 20–21; Repetto et al. 2001: 22.

program was operating in 80 municipalities within 16 provinces.[117] The absence of baseline surveys and of nationally aggregated data on beneficiaries make it hard to assess PROMIN's impact on infant mortality, but from 1993, its first full year of operation, to 2000, infant mortality fell from 22.9 to 16.6 per 1000.[118] This decline represented a modest acceleration of the slow pace registered from 1983 to 1993.

The National Mother and Infant Program introduced in 1937 was formally a universalist program, depending on "self-selection" for targeting. Not only did it leak resources to persons who were not very poor; it also did not pro-actively seek out clients, whereas Chilean programs did. Also unlike in Chile, where Miguel Kast's original 1974 "Map of Extreme Poverty" was followed by regular surveys, no systematic studies were conducted in Argentina to identify a target population or to create a baseline against which to measure program effectiveness. Even the Mother and Infant Nutrition Program introduced in 1993, which UNICEF helped to design and which the World Bank helped to fund, persisted for more than ten years without a centralized registry of beneficiaries. Authority over program design, hiring, and day-to-day operations was split between the national and provincial-level health ministries, and neither PNMI nor PROMIN was formally linked to educational or social assistance programs. Potential beneficiaries knew less about maternal and infant care programs in Argentina than in Chile, and beneficiaries in Argentina were less enthusiastic about the programs. Chilean governments stressed the preventive health care part of the program; Argentine governments were preoccupied with the distribution of powdered milk. Accordingly, whereas beneficiaries in Chile referred to the "health and nutrition program for mothers and children," beneficiaries in Argentina described the PNMI as the "milk program." When milk was not available, Argentine mothers tended not to bring their children in for checkups. As far as could be discerned only 30–35 percent of needy Argentine mothers, infants, and children were served by both the health and nutritional components of the PNMI; the proportion in Chile served by comparable programs was 70–95 percent.[119] A main reason, then, why Chile's infant mortality rate went from being almost twice as high as Argentina's in 1960 to being just over half as high in 2005 is that public maternal and infant health care and nutrition programs in Chile covered a higher proportion of needy people and were better designed, targeted, and implemented.

A 1997 survey of 26,000 urban households in Argentina revealed that 38 percent lacked health insurance of any kind.[120] The proportion of people who were uninsured in rural areas was presumably even higher, and rising unemployment and falling wages during the financial crisis of 2001–2002 caused an

---

[117] CEDI 2002: 83.
[118] Argentina. Ministerio de Salud 2007 (vital registration); Idiart 2004: 30, 35 fn. 67; Lloyd-Sherlock 2000b: 158.
[119] Idiart 2002: 189–190, 309, 341–360, 391–417; Idiart 2004 (quotations from pp. 28–29).
[120] Tobar 2001: 6.

additional 12 percent of the insured to reduce or discontinue their coverage.[121] In 2002 public health centers and hospitals ran out of essential supplies and the government cut back on its immunization, tuberculosis, maternal and child health, HIV/AIDS, and nutrition programs. The financial situation eased by the end of the year, but the infant mortality rate stagnated from 2000 to 2003, falling only from 16.6 to 16.5 per 1000. A sharp decline in 2004, to 14.4 per 1000, coincided with soaring economic growth, a plunge in income poverty, and a sharp decline of the unemployment rate.[122] The improvement of these income-related indicators may have affected infant mortality both by increasing the resources available for public service provision and by allowing higher private spending on food, housing, and health services, including ostensibly free public health services, which often require the user to take time off from work or to spend money on transport, lodging for relatives, medications, and informal surcharges.

The coincidence in 2004 of a strong economic recovery with accelerated infant mortality decline does not mean, however, that improved economic circumstances were the only (or even the main) factor causing the speedup. Civil society organizations dedicated to improving government health care and environmental programs also stepped up their activities in 2004.[123] Moreover, the stagnation of the infant mortality rate from 2000 to 2003, the failure during the 1990s to expand the share of the population covered by the *obras sociales,* and a growing recognition that previous health-related initiatives had failed to improve health service delivery in impoverished areas encouraged the Ministry of Health, in collaboration with the World Bank, to introduce the Birth Plan (Plan Nacer) in October 2004. This program was targeted initially to expectant and new mothers and to children under six who lacked health insurance and who lived in any of nine impoverished provinces in the northeast and northwest of the country. Any such person who signed up for the program was eligible to receive, free of charge, a package of 80 basic health interventions (checkups, medications, obstetric services, etc.) aimed at reducing maternal and child mortality and morbidity.[124] The coverage of the Birth Plan expanded rapidly after its introduction in October 2004, from 40,000 beneficiaries in January 2005 to 350,000 in January 2006 to 450,000 in June 2007, representing some 65 percent of the eligible population in the nine provinces in which the program was initially implemented.[125] The Birth Plan was funded jointly by the World Bank and the national Health Ministry, but was implemented by provincial governments, which bought services from public and private providers that independent auditors had certified as being

---

[121] World Bank 2003c: 9; World Bank 2006a: 14.
[122] Infant mortality rates from Argentina. Ministerio de Salud 2007 (vital registration).
[123] Arriagada, Aranda, and Miranda 2005: 42.
[124] World Bank 2006a: 10–11, 17.
[125] World Bank 2006a: 84; World Bank 2007: 27.

capable of providing the various health interventions. The estimated cost of the program was U.S. $10 per beneficiary per month.[126]

The central government funded the Birth Plan on a capitation (per person) basis, releasing 60 percent of the designated funds when the province turned in a registry of enrolled persons and the other 40 percent upon certification every four months by an independent auditor that the provincial government was meeting targets involving prenatal care, immunization, underweight births, and other health care outputs and health status outcomes.[127] In November 2006 the World Bank approved an additional loan to expand the Birth Plan to an additional 1.7 million persons in Argentina's 15 remaining provinces, bringing the projected total targeted to be covered to 2.5 million.[128] Rigorous assessments of the efficacy of the Birth Plan were not available at the time of this writing, but in the nine provinces in which the Plan was implemented, infant mortality fell from 18.7 per 1000 in 2004 to 14.2 per 1000 in 2006 (24 percent), whereas in the fifteen provinces that the Plan had not yet reached, infant mortality fell only from 12.2 to 11.3 per 1000 (8 percent). From 2000 to 2003, by contrast, before the plan was implemented and at a time when infant mortality stagnated, the rate barely budged in either set of provinces.[129] The strong economic recovery from 2003 to 2006 surely helped to accelerate the pace of infant mortality decline throughout the country, but the much greater percent decline in the nine provinces in which the Birth Plan was initially implemented strongly suggests that the improvement of maternal and child health services among the most vulnerable segments of the population contributed significantly to the acceleration over these four years in the pace of infant mortality decline across Argentina as a whole. Observers have suggested that the Néstor Kirchner government, like its predecessors, largely neglected policies aimed at fighting poverty.[130] If so, the Birth Plan was a notable exception.

5.5. Argentina: Determinants of Public Health Care Policies

Argentina has had no shortage of effective health care leaders. The Socialist senator Alfredo Palacios pushed successfully for the law that created the PNMI

---

[126] World Bank 2006a: 17. This cost (U.S. $120 per beneficiary per year) compares to $34–53 for the Brazilian Family Health Program (Section 6.4).

[127] Johannes 2007: 1–2.

[128] World Bank 2006b: 7.

[129] Calculated from absolute numbers of registered births and infant deaths aggregated across the 9 and 15 provinces in 2000 (Argentina. Ministerio de Salud 2001: Table 22, p. 61); 2003 (Argentina. Ministerio de Salud 2004: Table 29, p. 67); 2004 (Argentina. Ministerio de Salud 2005: Table 31, p. 69); and 2006 (Argentina. Ministerio de Salud 2007: Table 32, p. 77). From 2000 to 2003, infant mortality fell only from 21.9 to 21.1 in the nine provinces that would get the Plan Nacer in its initial stage, and from 14.3 to 14.2 in the other 15 provinces.

[130] Levitsky and Murillo 2008: 28.

in 1937; Dr. Ramón Carrillo expanded community hospitals and health centers in interior provinces from 1946 to 1952; Dr. Aldo Neri tried to extend health insurance to the entire population in 1984; Dra. Elsa Moreno mobilized support for the Mother and Infant Nutrition Program in 1991;[131] and Dr. Ginés González García during his terms as health minister (2002–2007) introduced programs that improved primary health care for the poor and strengthened reproductive rights and family planning services. At the provincial level, Dr. Carlos Alberto Alvarado designed and implemented an effective primary health care program in Jujuy in 1967; and Dr. Néstor Perrone and Dra. Elsa Moreno, backed by Governor Felipe Sapag, did the same in Neuquén in 1970.[132] Without such leaders, the Argentine health care system would have been worse off. What constrained the effectiveness of the Argentine health care system was not a shortage of talented leaders, but the power of the social forces that the leaders confronted and the political situation that the people who appointed them faced.

As in Brazil and Costa Rica, and probably more than in Chile, international conferences and organizations have shaped primary health care initiatives in Argentina. The Third Special Meeting of Ministers of Health of the Americas in 1972 gave a boost to both provincial and national primary health care initiatives.[133] The World Bank and UNICEF funded and contributed to the design of the Mother and Infant Nutrition Program, and UNICEF helped to rescue the program after Dra. Moreno stepped down as health subsecretary in mid-1991.[134] The World Bank provided half of the funding, as well as technical advice, for the 2004 Birth Plan.[135]

Democratic traditions are not as deeply rooted in Argentina as in Chile. Argentina's average annual Polity Score from 1900 to 2005 was −0.1, on the autocracy side of the −10 to +10 scale, whereas Chile's average annual score was 2.2, on the democracy side (Table A18). From 1891 to 1925 Chile had a semi-parliamentary form of government, whereas Argentina had a presidential system. By making political power more divisible, parliamentary power reinforced Chile's incipient multiparty system, whereas the predominance of the national executive in Argentina made it easier for a succession of parties, including the Radicals and Peronists, to portray themselves as national "movements" embodying all that was good about the country, rather than as part of a polity in which opposition forces had a rightful (or at least enduring) place. Such "movementism" was not conducive to the consolidation or deepening of democratic practices in Argentina.[136] Argentina, like Chile, suffered long periods of military rule, but in Argentina even civilian governments from

[131] Acuña and Chudnovsky 2002: 24.
[132] Jujuy: Perrone 2000; Ripoll 2002: 95–96. Neuquén: Gore 2000; Perrone 2000.
[133] Bloch 1988: 15; Escudero 1981: 559.
[134] Acuña and Chudnovsky 2002: 9; Idiart 2002: 213.
[135] World Bank 2006b: 7.
[136] Cavarozzi 1984; McGuire 1997; Rock 1987.

1955 to 1973 were delegitimized by the proscription of Peronism, whereas in Chile from 1958 to 1973 Communist, Socialist, Christian Democratic, and conservative parties all competed for the votes of the poor. Even after democracy returned to Argentina in 1983, the Peronist Partido Justicialista had the votes of the very poor locked up. Accordingly, this party and its main rival, the Unión Cívica Radical, focused on enacting policies that catered to the needs of swing groups, including the middle classes and some segments of the working class, rather than to the needs of the very poor.

Argentina in the second half of the twentieth century had the strongest labor movement in Latin America, and one of the strongest in the world.[137] Strong labor unions, along with middle- and upper-class urban residents, often influence state elites to enact policies that benefit urban formal-sector employees while neglecting the rural poor and inhabitants of urban shantytowns. By responding to the demands of unionized workers, university students, and middle-class groups, who have more resources than the destitute to make themselves heard, governments can discharge their obligation to attend to the needs of "the people" while minimizing strikes, demonstrations, and criticism in the mass media. On the other hand, a strong labor movement can also induce a government to provide health facilities and services that some poor people use, and union conquests often set a precedent of state involvement in social service provision that can later be extended to the poor – as long as politicians have incentives to court the votes of the country's least advantaged citizens. In Chile from 1958 to 1973 such incentives existed; in Argentina from 1955 to 1973, where an electoral ban on Peronism (1955–1966) was followed by a military regime (1966–1973), they did not.

In Argentina, union leaders during the period from 1960 to 2005 did more to inhibit than to expand the provision of basic social services to the poor. In particular, they blocked efforts by three different health ministers to combine payroll deductions and general tax revenues into a single revenue stream that would channel funds to a unified public health care system. The first such attempt came in the late 1940s and early 1950s under Perón's health minister, Dr. Ramón Carrillo. The second came in 1974 under Dr. Juan Carlos Liotta, a health minister in the second Peronist government (1973–1976), who tried to implement the National Integrated Health System (SNIS). When Liotta submitted the SNIS legislation to congress, the CGT (General Labor Confederation) announced that it would call a general strike if the legislation were approved.[138] Aldo Neri, Alfonsín's first health minister, reported that "the strongest resistance to the [SNIS] project came from the union leaders," who were worried that merging the contributory and general revenue-financed health care sectors would deprive them of control over the *obras sociales*.[139] A watered-down version of the legislation was finally passed, but the SNIS evaporated shortly

---

[137] McGuire 1997: 265–270; Roberts 2007: 119.
[138] Segundo Foro Social de Salud 2003.
[139] Neri 1982: 114 (quotation); Escudero 1981: 564.

after the 1976 military coup. Neri himself from 1984 to 1986 tried to create a National Health Insurance program under which the entire population would receive health insurance financed by both general revenues and a share of the contributions to the *obras sociales*, but the "fierce opposition of the unions" gutted the bill as it worked its way through congress.[140]

Argentina's most important primary health care programs have been provincial in scope. The most impressive such program was the Provincial Health Plan implemented in 1970 in the province of Neuquén. Bureaucratic initiative was partly responsible for this program, but democratic experience, interest-group pressure, and electoral incentives also contributed. Argentina from 1966 to 1973 was ruled by the military, and the province of Neuquén was administered by military-appointed governors. Hence, the claim that democracy contributed to the Provincial Health Plan gets off to a rough start. Still, democratic experience was involved in the origins of the Plan, interest-group pressure helped to produce the provincial government that enacted it, and electoral competition was involved in its perpetuation. In 1970, in an effort to resolve a major strike by construction workers building a hydroelectric dam in Neuquén, General Onganía, the military president, offered the provincial governorship to Felipe Sapag of the neo-Peronist Movimiento Popular Neuquino (MPN). Created in 1961, the MPN was a neo-Peronist party that endorsed Perón's doctrines and policies but rejected the supervision of the exiled leader. By not taking orders directly from Perón, the neo-Peronist parties (which also existed in other provinces) managed to avoid the electoral ban that the military and its civilian allies imposed on "orthodox" Peronist parties from 1955 to 1973.[141]

Onganía believed that Sapag would be able to resolve the strike because of the popularity that Sapag had gained during a term as elected governor of Neuquén from 1963 to 1966. During his elected term in office, which was cut short by the June 1966 military coup, one of Sapag's achievements had been to reorient the provincial public health secretariat to put more emphasis on primary care and preventive medicine. Shortly after Sapag took office in 1963, the secretariat began to build and restore health care facilities, to create centers for the care of mothers and infants, to vaccinate children, and to expand nutrition programs.[142] Hospital beds in Neuquén per 1000 population rose from 3.0 in 1963 to 5.3 in 1966,[143] and nutritional aid to mothers and infants also increased. From 1964 to 1965, Sapag's two full years as elected governor, provincial health spending rose by 50 percent and the number of persons employed by provincial health centers rose from 288 to 383. According to a health secretariat document, 1965 in the province "marked a turning point at

[140] Pautassi 2001: 25 (quotation); Belmartino and Bloch 1994: 328–341.
[141] On the MPN see Gorosito 2000; Mansilla 1983: 50; Palermo 1988: 25, 111 fn. 4. On neo-Peronist parties see McGuire 1997: 18–20, 84–93.
[142] Bucciarelli, González, and Scuri 1993: 359.
[143] Neuquén. Consejo de Planificación 1968.

which public health activities began to be emphasized."[144] The expansion of primary health care from 1963 to 1966 created infrastructure, expertise, and expectations that contributed to the design, implementation, resilience, and effectiveness of Neuquén's Provincial Health Plan of 1970.

In 1972 the military government lifted the ban on the "orthodox" Peronist Partido Justicialista (PJ) and allowed it to run a presidential candidate in elections scheduled for the following March. As soon as the ban was lifted intense competition, including occasional acts of violence, erupted between Sapag's neo-Peronist MPN and the Neuquén branch of the orthodox Peronist PJ. The provincial PJ accused Sapag and his allies of betraying Perón by collaborating with the military government. The MPN reminded voters of its economic and social achievements and accused the provincial PJ of subordinating the needs of the province to those of national Peronist leaders. One of the ways in which the MPN appealed for votes in the March 1973 election was by highlighting its achievements in health care.[145] It is hard to say how much such appeals increased the popularity of the neo-Peronist party, but the MPN won. Of 65,000 votes for governor, the MPN received 30,000 and the PJ received 21,000.[146] After Sapag took office in May 1973, the Provincial Health Plan expanded in scope and coverage.[147]

Democratic experience (infrastructure, expertise, and expectations built up during Sapag's elected governorship in 1963–1966), popular pressure (the strike that led Onganía to appoint Sapag governor in 1970), and adversarial politics (competition between the MPN and the PJ in 1973) helped to encourage and perpetuate Neuquén's Provincial Health Plan. Pressure groups in Neuquén, however, were relatively weak for Argentina, and moreover confronted a provincial executive in which authority was unusually tightly concentrated.[148] The local doctors' guild (*colegio médico*) failed in its efforts to block the Provincial Health Plan's requirement that doctors employed by the public sector forego private practice of any sort. More broadly, Neuquén never developed "a critical mass of economic interests capable of sustaining a conservative ideological nucleus distinct from and independent of political-statal logic of the Movimiento Popular Neuquino."[149]

Bureaucratic initiative and international influence shaped the provision of basic health services in Argentina, but also important were the country's history of authoritarian or semi-democratic rule, the dearth of party competition for the votes of the poor, and the strength of pressure groups, especially labor unions. In Chile, deeper democratic traditions, greater electoral competition, and weaker pressure groups encouraged or permitted governments to

[144] Neuquén. Ministerio de Salud Pública 1990: 21, 23.
[145] Bucciarelli, González, and Scuri 1993: 377–378; Mansilla 1983: 52–53.
[146] Palermo 1988: 133.
[147] Moreno 1979.
[148] Bucciarelli, González, and Scuri 1993: 357.
[149] Palermo 1988: 120 fn. 1.

implement primary health care policies that were more effective and sustained than Argentina's. Neuquén's democratic traditions were no deeper than those of the rest of Argentina, but the province resembled Chile in the weakness of its pressure groups and in the intensity of electoral competition for the votes of the poor. Political regime form thus helps to explain why governments did more to provide basic health services in Chile and in Neuquén than in Argentina as a whole. The more effective provision of basic health services helps to explain, in turn, why infant mortality fell faster in the former societies than in the latter one.

6

Brazil: From Laggard to Leader in Basic Health Service Provision

From 1960 to 2005 Brazil recorded faster economic growth, but slower infant mortality decline, than Chile or Costa Rica. Brazil's high income inequality helps to explain this disappointing performance, but government neglect of basic social service provision was also important. Such neglect can be traced partly to characteristics of the political regime that prevailed in Brazil for most of the second half of the twentieth century. From 1945 to 1964 Brazil was at best semi-democratic; voting was restricted by a literacy requirement and electoral competition was constrained by a ban on the Communist Party. From 1964 to 1985 the military ruled, although party, electoral, and legislative activity was not entirely shut down. From 1985 to 1990 the regime was again semi-democratic, with a civilian government elected indirectly by a rigged electoral college and subjected to intense military tutelage. Throughout these years, successive Brazilian governments fulfilled their obligations to "the people" partly by expanding the coverage of contributory health insurance, whereby Brazilians who earned a paycheck had a share of their pay deducted as a mandatory contribution to a health insurance fund that paid (usually) private providers for curative health services on a fee-for-service basis. Like Argentina, Brazil from the 1940s until the mid-1990s had a large welfare state (as measured by social spending and by health and old age insurance coverage), but was unsuccessful at providing basic social services to the least advantaged.

A constitutional reform in 1988, followed by full democratization in 1990, marked a turning point after which the Brazilian health care system was unified, decentralized, and focused more energetically than in the past (or in Argentina) on the provision of basic health services to the poor. From 1960 to 1990 infant mortality decline was much slower than GDP per capita growth predicted, and in 1990 infant mortality was much higher than GDP per capita predicted. From 1990 to 2005, however, Brazil began to reduce infant mortality very rapidly, despite anemic GDP per capita growth. By 2005 Brazil's infant mortality rate had fallen to the level predicted by its GDP per capita (which had barely risen for the past 15 years). Argentina also registered catch-up from 1990 to 2005, but not as much as Brazil (Figures 1.1 and 1.2; Tables A1 and A3).

The authoritarianism that contributed to the urban formal-sector bias in Brazilian health care policy began to unravel in 1974, when the military government lifted some restrictions on freedom of association and the press and gave reform-minded health professionals important positions in some municipal, state, and national health agencies. The military leadership undertook this liberalization in part to court allies in a power struggle with one of its own intelligence services,[1] and in part to counter criticism, expressed in part through electoral channels (which the military had not entirely closed), that its policies had failed to benefit the poor. Not until the 1990s, however, after the regime had become fully democratic, did governments implement policies that improved basic health services for the poorest Brazilians. The reactivation of civil society in the 1970s, the return to civilian rule in 1985, and the deepening of democracy in the 1990s empowered networks of academics, health professionals, and others to work more successfully to improve the coverage and quality of health care in poor communities.

6.1. Brazil: Mortality

Vital registration statistics were too incomplete in Brazil from 1960 to 2005 to produce reliable estimates of mortality levels and changes, so estimates have been derived from censuses and surveys, drawing on birth histories and responses to survivorship questions.[2] Among the eight societies compared in this book, Brazil in 2005 had the second-highest infant mortality rate (20 per 1000, below only the rate in Indonesia) and the third-lowest life expectancy (71.8 years, above only the figures in Indonesia and Thailand). Among all countries with available data, however, Brazil's performance looks slightly better. On level achieved, its infant mortality rate in 2005 was 85th lowest among 188 countries, and its life expectancy at birth was 84th highest among 184 countries. Brazil did even better on progress made than at level achieved. From 1960 to 2005 Brazil ranked sixth among the eight cases at both infant mortality decline and life expectancy gain (Tables A1 and A2). Among all countries for which data are available, Brazil ranked in the 66th percentile for infant mortality decline and in the 59th percentile for life expectancy gain.[3]

The earliest estimates of infant mortality in Brazil come from census data and pertain to the period from 1935 to 1940. During these years, infant mortality was estimated to be 163 per 1000. Later estimates, also based on census data, suggest that infant mortality declined steadily to 146 per 1000 in 1945–1950 and to 121 per 1000 in 1955–1960.[4] In 1960, Brazil's infant mortality rate was estimated to be 115 per 1000. Over the next 45 years infant mortality declined at a faster and faster pace, especially after 1990 (Table A1), when

[1] Stepan 1988: 15–44.
[2] McGuire (2009), Web Appendix A1, reviews the quality of Brazilian infant mortality statistics.
[3] Calculated from World Bank 2008e, except Taiwan, from the sources in Tables A1 and A2.
[4] Becker and Lechtig 1986: 21.

innovative primary health care programs were implemented first at the municipal and state levels and then at the national level. These programs contributed to rapid infant mortality decline despite protracted economic stagnation.

6.2. Brazil: Affluence, Inequality, and Poverty

If attention is restricted to its level of infant mortality in 2005, Brazil might appear to be a "poster country" for each of the three variants of the wealthier is healthier conjecture. Brazil's infant mortality rate in 2005 was just about at the level predicted by its GDP per capita alone (Figure 1.1). Likewise, Brazil's infant mortality rate in 2005 was just about at the level predicted by its GDP per capita and income inequality taken together, as well as by its GDP per capita, income inequality, ethnic diversity, fertility, population density, and urbanization taken together (Table 11.2). Such parity was of recent vintage, however. In 1990, controlling for GDP per capita, Brazil recorded the eighth highest infant mortality rate among 105 developing countries with data on both GDP per capita and infant mortality (Table 2.2, Model 2–2). From 1990 to 2005, however, Brazil's infant mortality rate fell precipitously relative to its level of economic affluence. This improvement is attributable in part to anemic GDP per capita growth during this period (Table A3), but it was also due to rapid infant mortality decline (Table A1). Among 188 countries, Brazil ranked 17th at percent decline of infant mortality from 1990 to 2005.[5]

For the Brazilian case, the wealthier is healthier hypothesis predicts the level of infant mortality in 2005 better than it predicts the percent decline of infant mortality from 1960 to 2005 or the tempo of infant mortality decline within that period. Infant mortality fell more steeply in Brazil from 1960 to 2005 than would be expected on the basis of its rate of per capita economic growth (Figure 1.2), and the tempo of infant mortality decline within the period from 1960 to 2000 was radically inconsistent with the wealthier is healthier conjecture. The correlation between the average annual rate of GDP per capita growth and the average annual rate of infant mortality decline across eight five-year periods from 1960 to 2000 (1960–1965,..., 1995–2000) was strongly negative, rather than strongly positive as would be expected if the wealthier is healthier conjecture applied to the case of Brazil (Table 11.1). The negative correlation reflects slow infant mortality decline in a context of fast economic growth at the beginning of the period, and fast infant mortality decline in a context of slow economic growth at the end of the period. From 1960 to 1980 GDP per capita grew at an annual rate of 4.8 percent, but infant mortality fell at an annual rate of only 2.5 percent. From 1990 to 2005 GDP per capita grew at an annual rate of only 0.4 percent, but infant mortality fell at an annual rate of 5.7 percent.[6] Brazil's GDP per capita in 2005 does indeed predict its infant mortality rate in 2005, but its GDP per capita growth from

---

[5] Calculated from World Bank 2008e, except Taiwan, from the sources in Table A1.
[6] Calculated from Brazil sources in Tables A1 and A3.

1960 to 2005 underpredicts its infant mortality decline during this period, and the tempo of its GDP per capita growth within that period was entirely out of phase with the tempo of its infant mortality decline.

Brazil is sometimes called the "world champion" of income inequality. In the mid-1990s researchers at the World Bank assembled all available income distribution surveys for each of 103 countries, constructed a "high-quality" database using only the surveys in each country with national coverage and good documentation, and averaged together (across various years) the Gini indices obtained in these surveys to generate a single number for each country. Brazil's Gini index by this method was 57.3, fourth-highest in the world behind only South Africa (62.3), Gabon, and Sierra Leone.[7] As well as being high throughout the period analyzed, the Gini index rose from 53.0 in 1960 to 57.6 in 2003. Most of the rise took place from 1960 to 1975. From 1975 to 1980 the Gini index fell, and for the next 25 years it moved little (Table A5), although a study using data from successive rounds of Brazil's annual National Household Sample Survey (PNAD) confirms that the Gini index fell modestly from 59.5 in 1993 to 56.4 in 2004. Contributing to this decline of income inequality, according to the study's authors, were the end of hyperinflation and more and better-targeted government cash transfers.[8] In any case, Brazil as of 2004 was no longer the world's, or even Latin America's, champion of income inequality. Its Gini index of 56.4 was below the circa-2000 Gini indices of Guatemala, Paraguay, Colombia, Chile, and eight sub-Saharan African countries.[9]

When infant mortality in 2005 is regressed on GDP per capita in 2005, Brazil's predicted infant mortality rate (19.7) is almost exactly the same as its actual rate (19.8). When the Gini index of income inequality is added as a regressor, the predicted rate rises to 22.9, indicating that Brazil in 2005 had a (slightly) lower infant mortality rate than was expected on the basis of its level of economic affluence and income inequality taken together (Table 11.2). Because high income inequality puts upward pressure on the infant mortality rate, the rise in Brazil's Gini index from 53.0 in 1960 to 57.6 in 2003 might well have offset some of the mortality-reducing effects of Brazil's respectable economic growth during this era. In Chile during the same years, however, an even steeper rise in income inequality (in a context, moreover, of slower GDP per capita growth) did not prevent the country from achieving one of the fastest rates of infant mortality decline in the world. From 1960 to 1980 Brazil's Gini index rose sharply, perhaps offsetting some of the infant mortality-reducing effects of the country's rapid GDP per capita growth. From 1980 to 2005, however, the Gini index also rose, probably compounding the infant mortality-increasing effects of the country's very slow GDP per capita growth, yet infant mortality decline accelerated (Tables A1, A3, and A4). In short, although high income inequality kept Brazilian infant mortality higher

[7] Deininger and Squire 1996: 574–577.
[8] Ferreira, Leite, and Litchfield 2006: 2–3, 6, 31–32.
[9] UNDP 2005: 270–273.

than would otherwise have been the case, its effects on the infant mortality rate should not be overstated.

Income poverty in Brazil from 1980 to 1995 is a matter of contention. According to the World Bank, the share of Brazilian households receiving less than $2 per day fell from 31 percent in 1980 to 22 percent in 1995. According to economists associated with the Inter-American Development Bank, the proportion rose from 28 percent in 1980 to 44 percent in 1995 (Table A5). To adjudicate these discrepant accounts of the trend in income poverty from 1980 to 1995, it is useful to consult data on nutritional status. Because the poor spend a large share of their income on food, undernourishment should be a good proxy for income poverty.[10] Data on nutritional status support the conjecture that the $2 per day poverty headcount fell from 1980 to 1995, as the World Bank data indicate. From 1981 to 1997 the share of Brazilians who lacked adequate nourishment dropped from 15 to 10 percent, and from 1975 to 1995 the share of Brazilian children under the age of five who suffered from moderate or severe malnutrition plunged from 18 to 5 percent (Tables A13 and A14). These data on malnutrition suggest that, despite slow economic growth and a rise in the Gini index, the $2 per day poverty headcount fell surprisingly sharply from 1980 to 1995. The decline of income poverty could help to explain why infant mortality decline accelerated during this 15-year period, but it would be unwise to make too much of this association. From 1995 to 2005, infant mortality plunged even though income poverty stagnated (Tables A1 and A5). Better public provision of basic social services, especially health care, helps to explain this anomaly.

6.3. Brazil: Education, Family Planning, Safe Water, and Sanitation

Spending on social services by federal, state, and municipal governments made up about 21 percent of Brazilian GDP in 1995. About 48 percent of such spending went to pensions. Education received 21 percent, health care 16 percent, housing 5 percent, and other programs 10 percent.[11] Little of this spending reached the poor. Only 18 percent of social spending in the mid-1980s went to the 41 percent of Brazilian households with incomes below two minimum salaries. Pensions, which took up nearly half of social spending in 1995, were especially regressive.[12] To make matters worse, the poor funded a

---

[10] In the 1980s, Brazilian families earning less than $100 per month in then-current U.S. dollars spent an estimated 44 percent of income on food (Draibe, Castro, and Azeredo 1995: 59). In a shantytown near Recife, young families in the 1980s spent an estimated 20 percent of income on powdered milk alone (Scheper-Hughes 1992: 318).

[11] Neri et al. 1999: 19.

[12] In the mid-1980s, 49 percent of employed Brazilians, mostly in the informal sector, were outside the pension system (Draibe, Castro, and Azeredo 1995: 53, 58). In the early 2000s, "less than 1 percent of social security spending reache[d] the poorest 10 percent of Brazilians, while 50 percent [went] to the richest 1 percent" (World Bank 2004b: 197). In 2005, only 3 percent of poor families in Brazil included a pensioner (*Economist* 2006: 33).

large share of these middle-class and upper-class welfare benefits, not only by paying higher indirect taxes to support public-sector pensions (which could exceed U.S. $65,000 per year) and to fund the government share of private pension contributions, but also by paying higher prices for goods and services produced by corporations that passed along to consumers the cost of the payroll taxes that funded the pensions of their employees.[13]

From 1960 to 1995 Brazil had, accordingly, extensive welfare-state benefits for the middle and upper classes, but an undistinguished record of providing basic social services to the poor. As might be expected in a vast federal system, however, certain cities and states had more effective social policies than others. Urban planning in the southern city of Curitiba, as well as primary health care in the Northeastern state of Ceará, became famous for innovative design and effective execution. Even before 1995 some broader government social service initiatives had positive results, including the expansion of elementary school enrollment around the country, the provision of water in central urban zones, and the delivery of primary health care in parts of the Amazon and the rural Northeast. After 1995, moreover, government programs made publicly provided health care and education more favorable to the poor, and from 1999 to 2003 the pension system was reformed to raise contributions, lift the minimum retirement age in the public sector, and cap the maximum benefit. By 2005, although more work remained to be done (particularly in the area of pensions), Brazil had some of the most well-designed, encompassing, innovative, and pro-poor social policies in Latin America.

Among the eight societies compared in this book, Brazil at the beginning of the twenty-first century had the lowest literacy rate and the fewest mean years of schooling, as well as the smallest rises on these indicators from 1960 to 2000 (Tables A6 and A7). Exacerbating the effect of low educational attainment on infant mortality, females trailed males on mean years of schooling from 1970 to 1999. At the turn of the twenty-first century, the gender imbalance amounted to a full year of schooling in a country where the average citizen received five years.[14] Brazilian education was also deficient in quality. From 1970 to 1994 the share of Brazilian primary school students who repeated a grade fell only from 19 to 18 percent, leaving Brazil in 1994 with the highest grade repetition rate among 16 Latin American countries.[15] A 1997 study found that more than half of Brazilian eighth graders were unable to do fourth-grade mathematics exercises.[16]

The sources of this poor educational performance included low per capita public spending on education, inequitable subsidies to university education and

---

[13] Colitt 2003; Draibe, Castro, and Azeredo 1995: 55.

[14] In 1999 females aged 15+ in Brazil had 4.4 mean years of schooling, versus 5.4 years for males. The discrepancy was smaller or absent in Argentina, Chile, and Costa Rica (Barro and Lee 2000).

[15] UNESCO 2001.

[16] Herrán and Rodríguez 2001: xi.

to private schools (both serving mainly the better-heeled), enrollment expansion at the expense of educational quality, excessively short school days and years, inadequate teacher training and pay, reiterated strikes by teachers and other education employees, and the use of schools by political elites more as vehicles for dispensing patronage than as sites for teaching and learning.[17] Not all of the problems of Brazilian education were on the supply side: employers in some parts of Brazil preferred to hire poorly educated workers, whom they considered to be less "uppity" and less likely to leave for a better job.[18] Poverty, meanwhile, kept parents from recognizing some of the potential benefits of schooling, raised the opportunity cost of keeping children out of the labor force, and complicated the acquisition of books, clothing, and transportation. The low quality of education in Brazil in the second half of the twentieth century, coupled with the country's capital-intensive model of economic growth (which created relatively few opportunities for moderately skilled workers), reduced returns to, and thus demand for, schooling.[19]

As with primary health care, the mid-1990s represented a turning point for Brazilian education. Productivity gains increased opportunities for better-educated workers, raising the demand for schooling. On the supply side, the Cardoso administration in January 1998 launched the Fund for the Maintenance and Development of Elementary Teaching and for the Valorization of the Teaching Profession (FUNDEF), which guaranteed that the equivalent of U.S. $300 would be made available each year for the education of each public school student up to the eighth grade. FUNDEF has been credited with raising education spending, enrollments, teacher salaries, and teacher hiring, and with effectively targeting its benefits to the poorest school districts.[20]

Education experiments at the state and municipal levels encouraged policy reforms at the national level. In 1995, three Brazilian cities began to pay mothers a subsidy to keep their children in school. In 2001, after studying these local conditional cash transfer programs, the Cardoso administration introduced the School Stipend (Bolsa Escola), which scaled up these municipal initiatives to the national level. Research suggests that Bolsa Escola was targeted effectively to the needy, and that it helped to reduce poverty.[21] In October 2003, President Lula da Silva combined Bolsa Escola with cash transfer programs designed to help poor families buy food and cooking gas, creating a single conditional cash transfer program called Family Stipend (Bolsa Família). Bolsa Família in 2004 paid U.S. $26 per month to 5.3 million needy Brazilian families.[22] These payments added up to about 2 percent of the Brazilian state's

[17] Birdsall, Bruns, and Sabot 1996; Castro 2000; Plank, Sobrinho, and Xavier 1996.
[18] Tendler 2003.
[19] Birdsall, Bruns, and Sabot 1996.
[20] Castro 2000: 297; Herrán and Rodríguez 2001: Ch. 5, 37–38.
[21] World Bank 2001a: 14–17. Schwartzman (2005) provides a somewhat more skeptical assessment.
[22] Schwartzman 2005: 2.

direct monetary transfers. Pensions, which mainly benefited the middle and upper classes, took 82 percent.[23]

Brazil's total fertility rate fell from 6.2 expected children per woman in 1960 to 2.3 in 2005, an average annual rate of decline of 2.2 percent. This rate of fertility decline was about average for the eight cases compared in this book (Table A10), but was much higher than the average rate of fertility decline around the world (among 180 countries with figures for both 1960 and 2005, Brazil ranked 35th on percent decline of the total fertility rate).[24] Family planning programs cannot be credited with this achievement. Before 1974 the Brazilian government was officially pro-natalist, and it was illegal to distribute birth control information or devices.[25] Some state and munic- ipal governments introduced family planning programs in the late 1970s, but no national-level program was launched before or during the military regime (1964–1985). As late as the 1990s family planning services covered only a small share of the population; abortion and sterilization remained the main methods of fertility control.[26] Expert ratings of family planning effort show a rise in the 1970s (Table A9), possibly due to state and local initiatives toward the end of that decade, but in 2004 Brazil's total family planning effort still ranked in the bottom third of 19 Latin American countries.[27] The main cause of rapid fertility decline in Brazil was not a drop in unwanted fertility, but rather a decline in desired fertility, owing to urbanization, more autonomy for women, and the spread of secular and consumerist values, not least through television.[28] Brazil would be an emblematic case for a "wealthier promotes smaller families" hypothesis analogous to the "wealth- ier is healthier" conjecture.

Across 105 developing countries in 1990, access to an improved water source and especially to improved sanitation was associated with lower infant mortality, controlling for other relevant factors (Table 2.2, Models 2–9 and 2–10). Household studies in Brazil have found similar associations.[29] From 1969 to 2005 the proportion of Brazilians served by water supply systems rose from 30 to 90 percent, while the share of urban residents served by sewer- age or septic systems rose from 25 to 83 percent (Tables A11 and A12). The National Sanitation Plan (PLANASA) introduced in the early 1970s helped to expand access to safe water in central cities, but omitted rural areas and neglected sanitation.[30] Like much else in Brazil, moreover, access to water and sanitation was unevenly distributed. In low-income peripheral urban areas,

---

[23] Hall 2006: 693–694.
[24] Calculated from World Bank 2008a.
[25] Martine 1996: 55; Pitanguy 1994: 112–119; Wood and Carvalho 1988: 160–163.
[26] Martine 1996; Singh and Sedgh 1997: 12.
[27] Calculated from Ross 2008.
[28] Martine 1996; Potter, Schmertmann, and Cavenaghi 2002: 759; Schwartzman 2000: 33–34.
[29] Alves and Belluzzo 2004; Merrick 1985: 19; Terra de Souza et al. 1999: 273; Wood and Carvalho 1988: 90–92.
[30] Heller 2006: 55; Horn 1985: 56; Merrick 1985: 1; Wood and Carvalho 1988: 121.

where the risk of infant death was higher than in the central cities, few families were connected to a water supply system.[31] In the late 1980s only 24 percent of households with per capita incomes below half a minimum wage per household member had safe water in the home.[32] In 1998 only 15 percent of Brazilians in rural areas were served by sewerage or septic systems; the average across 20 Latin American countries was 49 percent.[33]

The provision of water and sewerage services in impoverished areas improved in the early 1990s, when federal agencies, with World Bank financing, began to help install water and sewerage connections in urban shantytowns. Stressing community participation and low-cost appropriate technology, this Low Income Sanitation Technical Assistance Project (PROSANEAR I) had by 1996 linked about a million impoverished households to water and to sewerage systems at a cost of about U.S. $100 per connection.[34] At the state and municipal levels, other promising water and sanitation programs were initiated at about the same time. At the national level, however, much remained to be done. In 2000 only 73 percent of households receiving less than one minimum wage had access to an improved water source, and only 43 percent had access to improved sanitation.[35]

Brazilian governments from 1960 to 2005 thus did moderately well at expanding access to an improved water source, but poorly, at least until the 1990s, at expanding the share of the population with access to education, family planning, or improved sanitation. These deficiencies in social provisioning help to explain why infant mortality fell surprisingly slowly despite moderate GDP per capita growth, a significant drop in the income poverty headcount, and (despite poor family planning services) a rapid decline of the total fertility rate. Deficiencies in nutritional aid and health care also impeded infant mortality decline until the mid-1990s, when both began to improve significantly.

6.4. Brazil: Nutrition and Health Care

Total health care spending in 2000 made up about 8 percent of Brazilian GDP, about U.S. $540 per capita. The public sector contributed slightly less than half of this amount (Table A15). At least until the mid-1990s, this spending, gauged by mortality indicators, was inefficient. In 1995 total health care spending per capita in Brazil was above the mean for 20 Latin American countries, but life expectancy and the infant survival rate were below the mean.[36] As in Argentina until the mid-1990s, the main reason for this inefficiency was the neglect of primary health care for the poor. Even more than in Argentina,

[31] Azevedo 1981: 62; Katakura and Bakalian 1998: 7.
[32] Such households included about 58 percent of Brazilian children (Neri et al. 1999: 6).
[33] PAHO 2000a.
[34] Katakura and Bakalian 1998.
[35] Heller 2006: 19 (statistics), 29–41 (local projects).
[36] Health spending: PAHO 1998a: V. 1, 315; infant mortality: Hill et al. 1999; life expectancy: UNDP 1999.

however, Brazilian governments from 1995 to 2005 made important strides toward improving basic health care and other basic social services.

Although undernourishment at the end of the twentieth century remained a serious problem for the most impoverished Brazilians, Brazil from 1960 to 2005 suffered no overall scarcity of calories and, from about 1970 onward, no overall scarcity of protein.[37] From 1971 to 2004 the proportion of Brazilians with inadequate nourishment fell from 23 to 7 percent (Table A13), a decline that compares favorably to that of the Latin American and Caribbean region as a whole, where the proportion fell from 20 to 10 percent.[38] The percentage of children under five with moderate or severe malnutrition fell even more steeply, from 18 percent in 1975 to 4 percent in 2003 (Table A14). The military government (1964–1985) and the civilian Sarney administration (1985–1990) introduced a succession of food and nutrition programs, but there is little evidence that they helped to reduce infant mortality. In 1989, six such programs run by four different ministries provided few benefits to the poorest families or regions. Many registered "beneficiaries" received nothing, and food distribution was usually separated from health care provision.[39] As of 1989 only about 10 percent of expectant mothers had signed up to receive nutrition assistance, and until the early 1990s school lunch programs, which dated back to the 1950s, were poorly targeted.[40] Accordingly, Brazilians' improved nutritional status in the closing decades of the twentieth century appears to have been driven more by a rise in private income than by government nutrition programs.

Public health interventions in Brazil date back to the 1790s, when the Portuguese Crown encouraged variolation in an attempt to quell outbreaks of smallpox.[41] Most state activities in the health field before 1900 were designed to control infectious diseases, particularly yellow fever, which caused epidemics in major cities after 1849.[42] During the nineteenth century health care was provided, if at all, mainly by the Church, mutual aid societies, and the family.[43] A watershed in public health occurred in the first decade of the twentieth century, when the city of Rio de Janeiro under public health director Oswaldo Cruz began to use vaccination and sanitation campaigns to control epidemic diseases. Cruz's pupil, Carlos Chagas, was the first scientist to identify the insect-borne parasite that causes American trypanosomiasis (also

---

[37] Wilkie, Alemán, and Ortega 1999: 200, but see Scheper-Hughes 1992: 135–163.
[38] "Prevalence of undernourishment" in the Latin American and Caribbean regional aggregate (World Bank 2008e).
[39] Peliano 1992: 113–116.
[40] Nutrition assistance: Draibe, Castro, and Azeredo 1995: 28. School lunch programs: Silva 2000.
[41] Alden and Miller 1987: 209–213. Variolation involved the deliberate infection of an individual with dried smallpox scabs, which transmitted a mild form of the disease and conferred subsequent immunity.
[42] Stepan 1976: 50, 59.
[43] Horn 1985: 48.

known as Chagas disease); he too served as public health minister and helped to organize public health campaigns in the 1920s.[44]

In 1918 doctors, academics, scientists, civil servants, and others formed a Pro-Sanitation League (an early issue network) to urge the federal government to fight malaria, hookworm, Chagas disease, and other endemic illnesses. The League argued, against the prevailing wisdom, that the federal government's neglect, not the tropical climate or the ignorance of the afflicted population, was the main factor perpetuating these diseases. Pro-Sanitation League members encouraged Congress with some success to enact public health legislation and, in general, "to make government more accountable on all levels for the overall health of the population."[45] The goals of the Pro-Sanitation League foreshadowed those of the primary health care and Sanitarian movements of the 1970s and 1980s, whose actions contributed to the unification and universalization of the health care system and to the launch of the Family Health Program in the mid-1990s.

In 1923 the Eloy Chaves Law introduced Brazil's first social insurance program, which provided disability, retirement, burial, and curative medical insurance to railway company employees. The insurance was administered by a Pension and Retirement Benefit Fund (CAP), which collected contributions from railway employees, employers, and the state; invested the money so collected; and paid out benefits to insured persons.[46] Later in the 1920s and thereafter, firms in other industries created CAPs as well. After the 1930 coup that made Getúlio Vargas president, Pension and Retirement Benefit Institutes (IAPs), which served entire occupational sectors rather than individual firms, were inaugurated as well. The largest such fund, the Institute of Pensions and Retirement Benefits for Industrial Workers (IAPI), was set up in 1937 and gained a reputation for administrative competence. By 1938 the contributory health insurance and pension system insured about 3 million Brazilians in 99 CAPs and 5 IAPs. These 3 million Brazilians included most of the country's urban formal-sector workers, but comprised only about 9 percent of the total labor force.[47]

Brazilian social insurance underwent four major reforms from 1940 to 1980. First, in 1953, the Vargas government combined individual firms' Pension and Benefit Funds into a single Pension and Retirement Benefit Institute. Second, in 1966, the military government merged all of the existing Pension and Retirement Benefit Institutes into a single National Social Security Institute (INPS). Third, in 1971, the military government extended health and retirement insurance to rural workers through the Rural Worker Assistance Fund (FUNRURAL). Financed by taxes on agricultural wholesalers and on

---

[44] Stepan 1976: 85–100.

[45] Hochman 1998: 9 (quotation); Lima 2007: 1171–1172.

[46] Malloy 1979: 40–43. In Brazil an aposentadoria is a retirement or disability pension; a pensão is a payment to the survivors of a deceased employee.

[47] Geddes 1994: 75, 77; Malloy 1979: 68, 76, 79, 110.

the payrolls of urban firms, the Rural Worker Assistance Fund was the first Brazilian social insurance program to break with the principle that benefits should depend on contributions. Self-employed and domestic workers gained health and retirement insurance in 1972, and by 1974 some 93 percent of Brazilians were covered by social insurance. Fourth, in 1974, the National Social Security Institute was placed under a new Ministry of Social Security and Social Assistance (MPAS), whose health insurance branch split off in 1977 as the National Social Security Medical Assistance Institute (INAMPS). The INAMPS had some health care facilities of its own, but for the most part, like the Argentine *obras sociales*, it signed contracts with private providers, first on the basis of fee-for-service arrangements and then, after 1991, according to a prospective payment system like that of Medicare in the United States.[48]

These reforms addressed some earlier inequalities of legal entitlement to benefits, but to convert these legal entitlements into services or payments, a claimant usually needed to have a personal connection to a local functionary.[49] Moreover, the retirement and health insurance funds lost solvency as time went on. The aging of the population contributed to this problem, but employers and the government paid less than they owed into the various funds, and during the 1950s and 1960s bad investments, mostly in real estate, eroded the capital base. Meanwhile, except in the top echelons of the Institute of Pensions and Retirement Benefits for Industrial Workers (IAPI), patronage served as the main criterion for hiring the funds' plentiful employees.[50] Because the funds depended on payroll deductions, which fluctuated with economic conditions, their inflows were erratic; and because retirement and disability annuities were fixed, health insurance absorbed the brunt of downturns.[51]

The demand for health services soared with the expansion of health insurance coverage in the early 1970s, and again after a 1975 law granted anyone the right to receive emergency care at National Social Security Institute (INPS) facilities and at INPS-contracted private hospitals and clinics.[52] The National Social Security Medical Assistance Institute (INAMPS) paid private providers on a fee-for-service basis, exercising no control over the kind of care provided and providing little oversight of the services delivered. In 1980, mounting foreign debt and a sharp rise in oil prices triggered a recession, drastically reducing contributions to INAMPS. The government responded by reducing payments to private sector health care providers, who countered by presenting fraudulent bills, by going on strike, and by refusing to handle certain types of patients and cases.[53]

---

[48] Draibe, Castro, and Azeredo 1995: 19; Lobato 2000: 13, 15; Lobato and Burlandy 2000: 3, 4; Malloy 1979: 32, 68, 128–134; Malloy 1991: 30, 35; World Bank 1994: 21.

[49] Huber 1996: 171; Mainwaring 1999: 183.

[50] Malloy 1979: 72–73.

[51] Lobato and Burlandy 2000: 5; Weyland 1995: 1707; Weyland 1996: 171.

[52] World Bank 1994: 21.

[53] Lobato 2000: 13–15; Weyland 1996: 159; World Bank 1994: 62.

Over time, financial problems led to a decline in the quality and quantity of health care. As funds grew scarcer at the end of the 1970s, *de facto* rationing emerged. Top civil servants and military personnel, and to a lesser extent employees of large firms, tended to receive better care than the more recently insured rural workers, domestic workers, and self-employed people.[54] The INAMPS practice of reimbursing office visits at a lower rate, relative to cost, than diagnostic tests or hospital stays contributed to inadequate provision of health education and preventive care.[55] Higher INAMPS fees for cesarean births led to an estimated 186,000 unnecessary cesarean deliveries in the late 1970s.[56] In 1986 cesarean births made up 32 percent of all births, more than double the 10–15 percent share recommended by the World Health Organization (among high-income groups in São Paulo, the share was 64 percent). Hospital stays were themselves a major cause of death: at least 53,000 and perhaps as many as 100,000 Brazilians died of hospital-acquired infections in 1990, a rate much higher than in industrialized countries.[57]

Military governments from 1964 to 1985 promoted the expansion of the private sector in health care provision, believing that state-provided services were inefficient.[58] The promise of guaranteed INAMPS contracts encouraged the construction of new private hospitals; the share of hospital beds in private-sector facilities rose from 14 percent in 1960 to 73 percent in 1976. Although the private sector in 1976 accounted for only 2 percent of local health posts and 38 percent of outpatient visits, it included 53 percent of doctors, 57 percent of nurses, and 84 percent of hospitalizations. By the early 1970s INAMPS, which funded 90 percent of Brazil's health services, allocated only 21 percent of its expenditures to its own facilities. Private hospitals took 61 percent; the rest went to businesses, associations, universities, non-profits, and other government agencies.[59] Such policies resulted in a high-cost, specialized, curative, hospital-based health care concentrated in profitable regions of the country. Private medical personnel and facilities were located mainly in middle-class neighborhoods in big cities, mostly out of reach of the urban and rural poor.[60]

At the national level, as health services deteriorated in the 1970s, the quality of health care became a salient social issue. In 1976, leftist health professionals and academics in universities, research institutions, and health service organizations formed an issue network known as the Sanitarian Movement to

---

[54] Lobato 2000: 15; Malloy 1991: 35.
[55] Among 14 countries in the Americas circa 1980, Brazil had the lowest ratio of office visits to hospital stays (McGreevy, Piola, and Vianna 1989: 324–325). In the mid-1970s, health professionals ordered 130 diagnostic tests for every 100 office visits, much higher than the international norm of 25 per 100 (Horn 1985: 60).
[56] McGreevy, Piola, and Vianna 1989: 325.
[57] World Bank 1994: 111.
[58] Weyland 1995: 1701.
[59] Cordeiro 1980: 162; Lobato 2000: 10, 13–14; Lobato and Burlandy 2000: 4–5.
[60] Lobato and Burlandy 2000: 4–5; Weyland 1995: 1701.

press for change in public health care provision. Recalling the Pro-Sanitation League of the 1920s, the Sanitarian Movement criticized the health care available to the rural and urban poor. It also denounced the dependence of government-funded health care on the private sector and protested the system's excessive reliance on curative as opposed to preventive medicine.[61] Leaders of the movement formed academic research institutes such as the Brazilian Center for Health Studies (CEBES) in 1976 and the Brazilian Collective Health Association (ABRASCO) in 1979, and won support from national and international scientific agencies for research projects, graduate fellowships, seminars, conferences, and the convening of working groups.[62] Despite being the main target of the Sanitarian Movement's criticisms, the military government, in an effort to dispel its image as insensitive to the poor, began from the late 1970s onward to appoint Sanitarians to top posts in INAMPS as well as in the ministries of health and social welfare.[63]

The Sanitarian Movement, like its namesake in nineteenth-century England and like the Pro-Sanitation League of the 1920s, was formed to pressure the state to protect the health of all citizens. It fought mainly for big changes in health care financing and administration, such as decentralization, provider reimbursement reforms, and serious oversight of private medicine. Many Sanitarians criticized the preoccupation of some of their colleagues with improving the provision of basic health services to the poor as "poor medicine for the poor." Unpersuaded on this last point, public health advocates from around the country, including a large contingent of nurses, formed a loose alliance in the early 1990s that came to be known as the Primary Care Movement. This alternative issue network put top priority on the immediate improvement of basic health services in poor areas, using a variety of municipal and state experiments as pilot projects. The Primary Care Movement played an important role in persuading the Ministry of Health in 1991 to scale up to the national level the State Community Health Agents Program that had been introduced in Ceará in 1987.[64] A few years later, the national Community Health Agents Program (PACS) was folded into the Family Health Program (PSF), which was designed not only to deliver basic health services to the poor in all parts of the country, but also to serve as a gateway into the entire health care system. In this respect, the Sanitarian position against "poor medicine for the poor" won out.

The Sanitarians helped in other ways to transform the Brazilian health care system. The Federal Constitution of 1988 stipulated a universal right to health (Article 6) and required the state to actualize that right by creating a Unified Health System (SUS) (Articles 196–200). Introduced in 1990, the Unified Health System was financed both by payroll deductions and by general tax

[61] Arretche 2005: 167; Cornwall and Shankland 2008: 2175; Weyland 1995: 1702.
[62] Abrantes Pêgo and Almeida 2002: 17–18, 21–22.
[63] Abrantes Pêgo and Almeida 2002: 10; Vasconcelos 1999: 15; Weyland 1995: 1701.
[64] Weyland 2006: 174–175, 207–209.

funds, ending the formal distinction in health service provision between those eligible for usually higher-quality health care funded by contributory health insurance, and those eligible only for the usually lower-quality health care funded by general tax revenue. A coalition of private-sector health providers, clientelist politicians, and civil servants with a stake in the old system delayed the constitutionally mandated transition toward health system unification,[65] but in 1993 the INAMPS was finally dissolved into the Ministry of Health, ending the last vestiges of legal privilege for contributors to the social insurance system. Under the Unified Health System, administrative control of public health service provision was decentralized to state and municipal governments, but the funding for public health services still came mostly through the federal Ministry of Health, which also made the main strategic decisions and exercised oversight over local health care administration. Initially, then, "decentralization" was just deconcentration, the transfer of administrative but not political authority.[66]

Operating alongside health services available to those enrolled in contributory health insurance schemes were the general revenue-funded programs of line ministries headed by members of the president's cabinet. The first government agency devoted to disease control and public health was created in 1920.[67] A Ministry of Education and Health was created in 1930, from which a separate Ministry of Health split off in 1953.[68] The Ministry of Health was responsible for health education, long-term care, health policy coordination, and the provision of basic health services to the poor, especially in rural areas.[69] In the first half of the twentieth century, the line ministries accounted for most public health spending. In 1949, when the central government spent about 1 percent of GNP on health care, 87 percent of this spending passed through the National Health Department and only 13 percent through the contributory health insurance system. During the next three decades the contributory system rose enormously in relative importance. By 1978, 81 percent of public health care spending passed through the contributory system, and only 19 percent passed through the Ministry of Health.[70]

In 1927 the government began to build health centers to give inhabitants of less densely populated areas better access to curative medical care, health education, maternal and child health care, and sanitary inspection. By 1942 Brazil had 54 health centers, 194 health posts, and 340 health subposts, all administered by state health departments under the supervision of the National

---

[65] Araújo 1997: 118–119; Arretche 2005: 166–174; Haggard and Kaufman 2008: 285; Weyland 1995; Weyland 1996: Ch. 7.
[66] Araújo 1997.
[67] Lima 2007: 1172.
[68] Ruffino-Netto and Souza 1999: 41.
[69] Lobato and Burlandy 2000: 4.
[70] McGreevy 1984: 14.

Department of Health.[71] In 1942 the Special Public Health Service (SESP), an agency within the Ministry of Education and Health, launched Brazil's first major primary health care program. The SESP was organized mainly to control malaria near U.S. military bases in northeast Brazil, in rubber tapping areas of the Amazon, and in mining areas of Goiás and Minas Gerais. In some of these areas, SESP personnel also delivered other medical services, including simple curative care. The larger purpose of the program was to facilitate the export of natural rubber, iron ore, quartz, and mica, which were important to the Allied effort in World War II.[72] The U.S. Institute of Inter-American Affairs supplied most of the SESP's initial funding, nearly half of its technical personnel, and its first two directors, one of whom was the noted U.S. anthropologist Charles Wagley. When U.S. aid ended in 1960, the Brazilian government put SESP under the authority of the Ministry of Health and renamed it the Special Public Health Service Foundation (FSESP).[73]

The agency's payroll rose from 1,398 in 1946 to 10,330 in 1986. During this period it conducted medical research, initiated water and sanitation projects, and began to operate in additional areas of the country. By 1986 about half of the agency's employees worked in the Northeast and about a quarter worked in the Amazon. During the 1970s the FSESP employed female *visitadoras* (community health workers) to make home visits to deliver immunizations, nutrition education, oral rehydration, pre- and postnatal care, checkups for infants and children, first aid, and simple curative care. The agency's personnel offices selected the *visitadoras* according to merit criteria from an applicant pool made up of women aged 19 to 25 who resided in the community being served and who had completed at least six years of schooling. The FSESP trained the *visitadoras* for five months, paid them regularly and relatively well, and granted them a degree of job security. As many as 100 candidates might apply for a single position.[74] By 1969 the agency had become a pocket of efficiency in the Brazilian state. The FSESP acquired a "reputation for honesty, efficiency, and effectiveness in public health," won "great respect from national and international technical personnel," and radiated "a certain public health 'mystique'."[75] After the health ministry was reorganized in 1970, however, FSESP lost some of its responsibilities for medical research and for water and sanitation projects, demoralizing some of its leaders. When Brazil returned to civilian rule in 1985 the agency became plagued by partisan and ideological conflict, patronage appointments, and strikes.[76] These

[71] Campos 1997: 270–271.
[72] Bastos 1993: 26–30, 59–115; Campos 1998.
[73] Bastos 1993: 141–142, 471, 479; Campos 1997: 15–34, 123; Horn 1985: 49.
[74] Campos 1997: 256–260; Rice-Márquez, Baker, and Fischer 1988: 89–91.
[75] First quotation from Horn 1985: 49; second and third from Azevedo 1981: 90. Miguel Kast's collaborators in Chile also reported feeling a sense of "mystique" (Section 4.5), and Tendler (1997a: 14, 28–31) cites employee dedication and morale as a key to the success of the Community Health Agents Program in the state of Ceará. On "pockets of efficiency" in the Brazilian state see Evans 1995: 61–62 and Geddes 1994: 61–69.
[76] Bastos 1993: 485–491.

problems, together with the introduction of the Unified Health System, led the demise of the FSESP in 1990, when it was incorporated into the National Health Foundation (FUNASA), an autonomous agency within the Ministry of Health, which consolidated responsibility for disease control, vaccinations, basic sanitation, and epidemiological surveillance, especially in indigenous communities.

Despite the obstacles it faced, FSESP contributed significantly to disease control and health care in some of the poorest regions of Brazil. Its main limitation was its lack of scale. FSESP was too small to produce major improvements in the health status of tens of millions of impoverished Brazilians. Although its personnel carried out about 2 million medical consultations per year during the 1960s and 1970s,[77] Brazil's rural areas in 1980 included nearly 22 million people with incomes insufficient to meet basic needs.[78] In 1989, FSESP's 10,905 employees included 939 doctors, 337 nurses, 356 nurses' aides, and 1,852 community health workers (now known as *atendentes* rather than *visitadoras*). In 2000, by comparison, the Community Health Agents Program employed 118,960 community health workers, while the Family Health Program employed 5,957 health care teams, each of which included a doctor, a nurse, a nurse auxiliary, and four to six community health workers.[79] In the Northeastern state of Ceará in 1986 FSESP had 713 employees, from security guards to doctors to administrators.[80] By comparison, the State Community Health Agents Program in Ceará in 1987 employed 7,300 health agents.[81]

In 1976 the military government launched another primary health care initiative, the Program to Expand Health and Sanitation Activities in the Interior (PIASS). This program focused on the Northeast. Funding for the program came from the National Social Security Medical Assistance Institute (INAMPS), from the national Ministry of Health, and from state health secretariats. PIASS got off to a quick start, building 2,280 health posts and centers in 1978 and 1979. The health workers who staffed these facilities were usually young people selected by local leaders, given three months of training, and paid a monthly salary of one minimum wage. They distributed food, provided simple curative care, immunized children, and referred clients to health centers for inpatient care. They were poorly supervised, however, and rarely came from the part of the country in which they worked. These factors, combined with the limited range and sometimes poor quality of the services they provided, led to the underutilization of the newly-built facilities.[82]

After 1979 PIASS began to spread beyond the Northeast. According to its own administrators, however, the program suffered from inflexibility,

[77] Brasil. Ministério da Saúde 1972: 4.
[78] David et al. 2000.
[79] Brasil. Ministério da Saúde 2000a: 5, 32; Brasil. Ministério da Saúde 2000b: 6, 30.
[80] Bastos 1993: 473.
[81] Tendler 1997a: 42.
[82] Pinto 1984; Scheper-Hughes 1992: 201–210.

disorganization, poor recruitment, underfunding, and problems in acquiring land for facilities. It never covered more than 25 percent of its initial target population.[83] Moreover, the PIASS health workers were selected by local and regional leaders, often according to political rather than technical criteria.[84] In 1980 the government folded PIASS into the National Basic Health Service Program (Prevsaúde), which was supposed to extend basic health service coverage to the entire population under the joint administration of the Ministry of Health and the Ministry of Social Welfare.[85] The social welfare ministry was reluctant to fund the initiative, however, and this reluctance, coupled with hard economic times and opposition to the expansion of health insurance coverage from physician, hospital, and insurance associations (whose leaders criticized Prevsaúde as "statizing"), gutted the program in 1981 and 1982.[86] PIASS built a large number of health centers and health posts in the late 1970s and early 1980s, but their patronage hiring, poor service quality, and underutilization attenuated their benefits for the poor.

In 1983 the National Conference of Bishops of Brazil launched the Pastorate of the Children (Pastoral da Criança), a volunteer organization that delivered basic health care in poor communities. The organization's personnel worked closely with the Ministry of Health, which funded at least 70 percent of its expenditures from 1987 to 2000, as well as with UNICEF and other national and international agencies. Staffed in 2000 by some 145,000 volunteers, the Pastorate of the Children provided immunizations, prenatal care, checkups for infants and children, nutrition education, and oral rehydration therapy. It also collected health statistics, promoted literacy and breastfeeding, fought child abuse, and worked to combat HIV/AIDS and other diseases. About 90 percent of its volunteers were women, and most of its activities involved home visits.[87] In 2004 the Pastorate of the Children served a monthly average of 90,000 expectant mothers and 1,800,000 children under the age of six.[88] The organization reported that infant mortality in the communities in which it worked – which tended to be poorer than the national average – fell from 52 per 1000 in 1991 to 15 per 1000 in 2003.[89] By comparison, infant mortality in Brazil as a whole fell only from 48 per 1000 in 1990 to 20 per 1000 in 2003 (Table A1). A 1996 study in Criciúma, Santa Catarina, showed that mothers assisted by the Pastorate of the Children had greater health knowledge, and their infants better health status, than mothers who did not receive such assistance.[90] Other studies have come to mixed conclusions about the program's coverage, targeting, and efficacy.[91]

---

[83] Atwood 1990: 157.
[84] Pinto 1984: 179; compare Tendler (1997: 28–37) on the state of Ceará.
[85] Brasil. Ministério da Saúde e Ministério da Previdência e Asistência Social 1981: 6, 42–60.
[86] Atwood 1990: 158; Cordeiro 1982: 90; Pinto 1984: 176; World Bank 1994: 21–22.
[87] Pastoral da Criança 2000; Serra 2001: 22; UNICEF 2001: 17.
[88] Cesar et al. 2005: 1845.
[89] Pastoral da Criança 2006.
[90] Neumann et al. 1999.
[91] Barros et al. 2005; Cesar et al. 2005; Neumann et al. 2002.

As in Argentina, individual states and municipalities in Brazil have under-taken important public primary health care initiatives, particularly since the late 1980s.[92] None is more famous than the State Community Health Agents Program (Programa Estadual de Agentes Comunitários de Saúde) that was launched in 1987 in Ceará, an impoverished state in the Northeast. In 1993 this program won UNICEF's Maurice Pate Award for promoting the well-being of children. When a drought hit the Northeast in 1987, Ceará's state government began to hire community health agents, mostly women, as part of a job creation program. After three months of training, each of the new health agents made monthly visits to 50–250 households to provide prenatal care, vaccinations, and checkups, as well as to promote breastfeeding and oral rehydration therapy. By 1992 the state government had hired 7,300 community health agents and 235 half-time nurse supervisors who served 65 percent of Ceará's population at a cost of less than U.S. $8,000,000 per year, or about U.S. $1.50 for each person served.[93] Ceará's State Community Health Agents Program lasted until 1994, when it was incorporated into the nation-wide Family Health Program.[94]

The utilization of maternal and infant health services rose sharply after Ceará's program began. From 1987 to 1990 the share of births in institutions rose only from 70 to 78 percent, but the proportion of children under three years old who visited a doctor at least once a month rose from 5 to 47 percent, while the proportion of such children who received oral rehydration therapy after suffering a bout of diarrhea rose from 23 to 56 percent.[95] In the first five years of the program, from 1987 to 1992, Ceará's infant mortality rate fell, according to one source, from 102 to 65 per 1000 or, according to another, from 77 to 44 per 1000.[96] Economic growth in Ceará from 1987 to 1992 was higher than the national average, and a milk distribution program initiated in 1987 may also have raised the pace of infant mortality decline, but nei-ther life expectancy, nor the literacy rate, nor the income poverty headcount improved comparably during this five-year period.[97] Evidence thus suggests that the State Community Health Agents Program accelerated infant mortal-ity decline in Ceará.

Under the Unified Health System, municipalities, overseen by state gov-ernments, had administrative responsibility for primary health care. Using a capitation (per person) financing system, the federal government as of 1998

---

[92] Azevedo 1981: 90; Goulart 2002: 100–101, 108–109; Jatene 2001; Viana and Dal Poz 1998: 18, 20.

[93] Tendler 1997a: 11, 22, 35; Terra de Souza et al. 1999: 268.

[94] Svitone et al. 2000: 300.

[95] Svitone et al. 2000: 297.

[96] Tendler 1997a: 22; Tendler 1997b: 110. Svitone et al. (2000: 297) report a 1987–1990 decline of 32 percent in Ceará (95 to 65 per 1000), compared to 10 percent in Brazil as a whole (52 to 47 per 1000). Terra de Souza et al. (1999) report a less impressive decline in Ceará over a longer period from 1986 to 1994, from 102 to 80 per 1000.

[97] Tendler 1997b: 111–113.

transferred to each municipality U.S. $6–10 per month per inhabitant to fund primary care, raising the contribution if the municipal government was willing and able to undertake initiatives promoted by the federal government.[98] This transfer, known as the Basic Care Grant (PAB), involved a minimum benefits package along the lines of Argentina's Mandatory Medical Program (PMO) or Chile's Plan for Universal Access with Explicit Guarantees (Plan AUGE). The Basic Care Grant was consistent with the rights-based approach to health care embodied in Articles 6 and 196 of the Brazilian Constitution of 1988.[99] Funding for public health care in general, and especially for primary care, rose substantially during Fernando Henrique Cardoso's presidency (1995–2002). Federal spending on health care grew about 30 percent in real terms from 1994 to 2000, while the proportion spent on primary health care rose from 17 to 25 percent.[100] In absolute terms, federal spending on primary health care doubled from 1996 to 1999 and tripled in the poorest municipalities.[101] The main vehicles for the delivery of such care were the Community Health Agents Program (PACS), which began in 1991, and the Family Health Program (PSF), which began in 1994.

   Like the program in Ceará, the nationwide Community Health Agents Program began as an emergency response, in this case, to a cholera epidemic in the Amazon in 1991. Had it not been for the eruption of another cholera epidemic in the Northeast in 1992, the program might have been abandoned.[102] Unlike the Program to Expand Health and Sanitation Activities in the Interior (PIASS) in the late 1970s, but like the Special Public Health Service (SESP) after the 1940s and the Pastorate of the Children in the 1980s, the Community Health Agents used proactive outreach rather than passive, facility-based care. The Community Health Agents Program employed modestly trained health agents to make home visits once a month to 50–200 households in a geographically delimited area. The agents identified health risks; recorded health information; monitored the health of infants, children, the elderly, and people with chronic diseases; promoted prenatal care, vaccinations, breastfeeding, oral hygiene, sanitary precautions, school attendance, and cancer screening; and provided education about family planning, oral rehydration, nutrition, and sexually transmitted infections. Each agent was given 80 hours of classroom instruction and 400 hours of on-the-job training, and each was supervised by a salaried nurse, who was responsible for no more than 30 agents. Municipal officials chose the agents, statutorily according to merit criteria. Candidates had to be over 18 years old, literate, and resident for at least two years in the community to be served. The agents were paid the equivalent of

---

[98] Gauri 2002: 37.
[99] World Bank 1993a: 106–107; Mesa-Lago 2008: 217–219; Cornwall and Shankland 2008.
[100] Serra 2001: 15; Serra 2002a: 25. In the health ministry in particular, the proportion of spending devoted to primary care rose from 10.5 percent in 1995 to 17.3 percent in 2002 (Weyland 2007: 178–179).
[101] Negri 2000: 5–6.
[102] Brasil. Ministério da Saúde 2002: 8–9.

about $100 per month (in 2000 U.S. dollars) from federal, state, and municipal revenues.[103]

The Family Health Program, which began in 1994, eventually subsumed the Community Health Agents Program.[104] The Family Health Program incorporated four to six health agents into a team alongside a doctor, a nurse, one or two nurse auxiliaries, and other personnel (e.g., a dentist or a nutritionist) according to local resources and needs. Each team identified major health problems and health risks among the population for which it was responsible, developed a plan to improve the health status of the population, submitted the plan for evaluation by a municipal health council, and delivered basic health care, mostly through a program of home visits. The Family Health Teams were selected by municipalities in cooperation with community associations, trained at university-based facilities, and funded by federal, state, and municipal revenues.[105] Members of the teams were hired to full-time contracts and earned salaries that were at least twice as high as those paid to other municipal employees with equivalent professional training.[106] In June 2000, the annual cost of the Family Health Program per person attended was between U.S. $34 and $53, depending on region and team composition.[107] The Family Health Program was designed as a universal program: it was intended to serve the entire population as the main port of entry into the Unified Health System, rather than to be an add-on program like SESP or PIASS.[108]

Along with this new model of primary health care delivery came new mechanisms for financing (per capita payments partly replaced fee-for-service), administration (state governments supervised municipal governments), and community participation (elected health councils oversaw the family health teams).[109] The scale of the Community Health Agents and Family Health programs dwarfed all preceding public primary health care programs in Brazil. In 1994, 29,000 health agents attended 17 million people; by March 2006, 211,266 agents attended more than 78 million people, about 41 percent of the Brazilian population.[110] Both programs operated throughout the country, but were implemented first in the poorest municipalities, as measured by a

[103] Brasil. Ministério da Saúde 2000a; Mishima et al. 1992: 71; Viana and Dal Poz 1998: 18–19.

[104] Dal Poz 2002: 82; FGV-EPOS 2001: 12.

[105] Brasil. Ministério da Saúde 2000a; Dal Poz 2002; Dal Poz and Viana 1999; Gauri 2002: 45–48.

[106] Gauri 2002: 45; Viana and Dal Poz 1998: 29 fn. 24.

[107] FGV-EPOS 2001: 55. The monthly cost per capita was between 5.11 and 7.99 reais. The annual U.S. $34 and $53 figures assume the exchange rate prevailing in June 2000 (RS $1.81 = U.S. $1.00). Macinko et al. (2007: 2079) estimate the annual cost of the program to be about U.S. $30 per person served.

[108] Viana and Dal Poz 1998: 20, 27–28.

[109] Collins, Araújo, and Barbosa 2000; Gauri 2002: 45–48; Viana and Dal Poz 1998.

[110] 1994 figure from Brasil. Ministério da Saúde 2000a; 2006 figure from Brasil. Ministério da Saúde 2006.

Mapa da Fome (Hunger Map) like the one in Chile (Section 4.4).[111] In 2000, community health workers served about 80 percent of the population in the Northeast, but only about 20 percent in the wealthier Southeast. The Family Health Program, which required more financial and administrative resources than the Community Health Agents Program, had more scattered coverage in poor states.[112] Federal transfers covered only about 40 percent of the costs of the Family Health Program, so local resources were important. In some municipalities, including in the state of Tocantins, doctors from Cuba were hired to participate in the family health teams until Brazilian doctors could be recruited and trained.[113]

Although better designed and much wider in scope than previous government initiatives, the Family Health Program was not an unqualified success. Unlike Cuba (which provided an initial model for the program) or Costa Rica (whose Comprehensive Basic Health Care Teams operated in a fashion similar to the family health teams), Brazil is a huge country, and it was hard to find doctors and nurses who lived in, or were willing to relocate to, remote areas. A similar problem plagued the far-flung archipelago of Indonesia (Section 10.4). Brazilian medical schools were not set up to train generalists, so many doctors in family health teams lacked appropriate skills. Many doctors and nurses were hired on temporary (albeit full-time) contracts, leading to high turnover. Referral upward to higher levels of care, and downward to the family health teams themselves, functioned poorly. Teams were often made responsible for more families than guidelines suggested, and medicines (e.g., for tuberculosis and hypertension) were often scarce. The quality of the health data collected by the teams was inconsistent. People whose port of entry into the health system was supposed to be a family health team often bypassed the team and went straight to a hospital for basic health services.[114]

Despite these defects in the Family Health Program, the weight of the evidence suggests that its implementation helped to reduce infant mortality significantly. One study comparing municipalities in Ceará during the period from 1994 to 1998 found that the introduction of the program was not related to faster infant mortality decline, but another comparing municipalities in Pernambuco during the period from 1995 to 1998 found that infant mortality declined by 13 percent in the 33 municipalities in which the Family Health Program operated, but increased by nearly 17 percent in the 98 municipalities in which the program did not operate.[115] A study of Camaragibe, an impoverished municipality of 119,000 on the outskirts of Recife, obtained evidence of a dramatic decline of infant mortality from 1994, when family health teams began to function, to 1999, by which time the teams served 90 percent of

---

[111] Peliano 1993.
[112] Brasil. Ministério da Saúde 2003: 15.
[113] Dal Poz 2002: 87; Gauri 2002: 47; Viana and Dal Poz 1998: 46.
[114] Brasil. TCU 2003; Gauri 2002: 46–48.
[115] On Ceará see Morsch et al. 2001; on Pernambuco see Gauri 2002: 77.

Camaragibe's population. Camaragibe in 1993 had 153 public health workers, of whom 7 percent were community health agents. By 1999 it had 782 public health workers, of whom 360 were community health agents. Infant mortality in Camaragibe reportedly fell from 112 per 1000 in 1993 to 16 per 1000 in 1999.[116] In Cabo de San Agostinho, another city of about 150,000 a short distance from Recife, infant mortality fell from 49 per 1000 in 1994 to 11 per 1000 in 2006, "due in no small part to the reorganization of the delivery of primary care services and the introduction of a hugely successful national primary care programme, the Programa Saúde da Família (PSF)."[117] In Brazil as a whole, a time-series cross-sectional analysis of the 26 Brazilian states plus the Federal District from 1990 to 2002 found that a 10 percent rise in Family Health Program coverage was associated with a 4.6 percent decline in infant mortality, controlling for other relevant factors.[118] Much evidence suggests, then, that Brazil by the turn of the twenty-first century was a leader rather than a laggard in the provision of basic health services to the poor.

6.5. Brazil: Determinants of Public Health Care Policies

Health care policies in Brazil from 1960 to 2005 were shaped and constrained by bureaucratic initiative, international influence, the activities of interest groups and issue networks, and political regime form. Although bureaucratic initiative and international influence should have a place in any comprehensive account of Brazilian health policies during this era, this book is concerned primarily with political regime form, interest groups, and issue networks. After the mid-1970s, political liberalization made it easier for labor unions, business groups, and professional associations to try to influence the health care system, sometimes in ways inimical to the improvement of health services for the very poor. On the other hand, liberalization also facilitated the rise of social movements and issue networks that encouraged the universalization and unification of the public health care system. Electoral incentives shaped some of the most successful health care policies from 1990 to 2005, notably the Cardoso government's HIV/AIDS and primary health care policies and the Lula government's streamlining and expansion of the Family Stipend (Bolsa Família), a conditional cash transfer program that included a primary health care component. Brazil is thus a case in which democracy and democratization were especially conspicuous in encouraging mortality-reducing social policies.

Like the other societies studied in this book, Brazil has produced renowned public health leaders. In the early twentieth century, Oswaldo Cruz and Carlos Chagas organized successful disease-prevention campaigns and made Brazil a world leader in infectious disease research. In 1918, Belisario Penna,

---

[116] Levcovitz et al. 2000.
[117] Cornwall and Shankland 2008: 2175.
[118] Macinko, Guanais, and Marinho de Souza 2006; see also Macinko et al. 2007.

a future Director of the National Department of Health, founded the Pro-Sanitation League, an issue network dedicated to improving the health of the poor. During Vargas's presidency in the late 1930s and early 1940s, Gustavo Capanema, the minister of education and health, and João de Barros Barreto, the director of the National Department of Health, organized campaigns against infectious diseases and built public hospitals and other health facilities in the interior of the country.[119] In 1976, Sérgio Arouca, Hésio Cordeiro, and Cecília Donnangelo helped to form the Sanitarian Movement, which pushed for the unification and decentralization of the public health care system and for the more effective public provision of basic care, particularly to those without contributory insurance. Dom Paulo Evaristo Arns, the Archbishop of São Paulo, founded the Pastorate of the Children in 1983. His sister, Zilda Arns Neumann, headed the organization and was recognized by the Pan American Health Organization in 2006 as one of eleven "Public Health Heroes of the Americas." Jamil Haddad, who had ties to the Sanitarian Movement and who served as minister of health under president Itamar Franco (1992–1994), presided over the introduction of the Unified Health System and the Family Health Program and gave leftist health reformers important responsibilities.[120]

Jose Serra, the health minister under President Cardoso from 1998 to 2002, was an economist rather than a health professional.[121] Nevertheless, Serra's personal ties to Cardoso, his previous experience as planning minister (1995–1996), and his careful attention to the mass media made him an effective advocate for the health ministry's budget and programs.[122] Serra fought for and oversaw Brazil's successful HIV/AIDS treatment and drug procurement policies.[123] He also sustained and expanded the Community Health Agents and Family Health programs, which might otherwise have been abandoned (like PIASS and Prevsaúde) or remained small in scale (like FSESP). It was argued persuasively in the mid-1990s that prospects for improving Brazil's health system were grim.[124] Few would make such an assessment after Serra's administration.

International influence has shaped Brazilian health care policy throughout the twentieth century. The Rockefeller Foundation began to work in Brazil in 1916 and collaborated closely with the Pro-Sanitation League in the 1920s. By the 1940s most top Brazilian health officials had been trained abroad, and from 1942 to 1959 the U.S. government funded more than 200 scholarships for doctors, nurses, and other health professionals to advance

---

[119] Hochman 2005.

[120] Arretche 2005: 175.

[121] Accordingly, he was initially reluctant to take charge of the ministry (Serra 2002b: 225). At the time of his appointment, Serra was not sure that he knew the difference between a virus and a bacterium (Serra 2003b).

[122] Arretche 2005: 156, 178; Nunn 2009: 105–106.

[123] Cohen 2006; Gauri and Lieberman 2006; Nunn 2009.

[124] Weyland 1995; Weyland 1996.

their education in the United States.[125] World War II provided the impetus for the creation of the SESP, Brazil's first major primary health care program; and the United States Institute of Inter-American Affairs provided much of its funding, many of its technical personnel, and its first two directors. From 1945 to 1960, U.S. government officials continued to support the SESP financially, albeit with progressively smaller sums, because they regarded the control of disease in Brazil as beneficial to health in the United States, to U.S. exports, and to winning hearts and minds in the cold war struggle with communism.[126]

After 1960, the main source of international influence on Brazilian health policy shifted from the United States government to multilateral organizations. Officials in the Pan American Health Organization (PAHO) gave strong support to the Sanitarian Movement in the late 1970s, and other international agencies funded research projects, graduate fellowships, seminars, conferences, and working groups for Sanitarians.[127] The World Bank from 1993 to 2003 provided three loans worth a total of U.S. $425 million to help finance HIV/AIDS prevention. The World Bank did not directly fund treatment, calling it cost-ineffective, but supported prevention and institutional infrastructure.[128] PAHO and UNICEF experts helped to design the Family Health Program. Halim Antônio Girade of UNICEF facilitated dialogue among health care experts, administrators, and the health ministry, and encouraged the United Nations Development Programme (UNDP) to support the Family Health Program financially. Personnel under contract with the UNDP, rather than career officials, coordinated the program within the health ministry.[129]

The design and implementation of the Family Health Program was informed by foreign models, including Cuba's Family Doctor and Nurse Program (initiated in 1984) and programs in Britain, Quebec, and Switzerland.[130] Subnational models were also important in Brazil. The designers of the national Community Health Agents Program, initiated in 1991, drew on the experiences of health agent programs previously implemented in the states of Ceará, Mato Grosso, and Paraná. The designers of the national Family Health Program, initiated in 1994, drew on innovations in basic health care provision in the states of Ceará, Goiás, and São Paulo and in the municipalities of Campinas, Londrina, Niterói, and Porto Alegre.[131] State-level HIV/AIDS programs in São Paulo and elsewhere put pressure on the national government to enact a nationwide program, and provided a group of experienced professionals to

---

[125] Campos 1997: 245, 247, 300; Faria 1995: 122; Hochman 2005: 138–139.
[126] Campos 1997: 209–221.
[127] Abrantes Pêgo and Almeida 2002: 18, 21.
[128] Nunn 2009: 64–68, 102, 176.
[129] Viana and Dal Poz 1998: 18.
[130] Vasconcelos 1999: 15; Viana and Dal Poz 1998: 29.
[131] Bertone 2002: 15–16; Goulart 2002: 100–101, 108–109; Jatene 2001; Viana and Dal Poz 1998: 18, 20.

help implement it.[132] Despite similarities between the Family Health Program and the Comprehensive Basic Health Care Teams (EBAIS) initiative launched in 1995 in Costa Rica, Jose Serra reported never having heard of the Costa Rican program, and Costa Rican health officials, when asked whether Brazilian colleagues had inquired about the EBAIS, replied that they had not.[133]

The Brazilian welfare state took shape during the presidency of Getúlio Vargas, who came to office in 1930 as a result of a coup. Vargas began his 15-year presidency by introducing the secret ballot, by extending the vote to women, by calling an assembly to reform the constitution, and by extending pension and curative medical care benefits to some urban workers. After being elected by a constituent assembly in 1934, Vargas scheduled direct elections for 1938. In 1937, however, as fascism gained momentum in Europe, Vargas, with the support of the army and the coffee elite, canceled the elections, closed congress, disbanded political parties, introduced press censorship, and imprisoned his political opponents. He then announced a new political system called the New State (Estado Nôvo), in which society was to be organized, as in fascist doctrine, around corporatist lines, with a legislature composed of occupationally based interests rather than of territorially based representatives. Democracy thus had little to do with the initial creation of the Brazilian welfare state. By all accounts, the system of pensions and limited health care for urban-formal sector workers was imposed from above, partly as a means of controlling potential labor opposition.[134]

The Estado Nôvo's corporatist design was never fully implemented, and as the Allies gained the upper hand in World War II, corporatism under authoritarian auspices fell out of favor. In 1943 Vargas allowed political parties to resume operations, permitted wage hikes, restricted foreign investment, and freed leftist political leaders from prison, with an eye toward mobilizing support for his candidacy in a presidential election scheduled for 1945. Partly in response to this policy shift to the left, the military made a preemptive coup in 1945 and oversaw a presidential election in which Vargas was barred from running. The winner of this election was General Eurico Dutra, who served from 1946 to 1951. Vargas himself served as an elected president from 1951 to 1954, when he was ousted by the military amid a scandal implicating one of his aides in a murder (Vargas subsequently committed suicide). After a succession of interim governments, Juscelino Kubitschek was elected president in late 1955. Promising "fifty years of progress in five," Kubitschek oversaw rapid industrialization and the building of a new federal capital in Brasília. His successor, Jânio Quadros, resigned after seven months in office, possibly in a failed effort to create a political crisis that would result in congress granting him enhanced powers. He was replaced by the vice-president, João Goulart (1961–1964), who was serving as president when the military intervened in 1964.

[132] Gauri and Lieberman 2004: 25–26.
[133] Ayala 2007; Marín 2007; Salas 2007; Serra 2003a.
[134] Collier and Collier 1991; Huber 1996; Malloy 1979.

Although four presidential elections were held from 1945 to 1964, Brazil during this period was not fully democratic. Illiterate people were denied the vote, the Partido Comunista Brasileiro (which won 8–10 percent of the vote in 1945 and 1947) was banned from 1947 to 1985, and the military exercised growing influence in the political system. By the early 1960s, military leaders were urging congress to curb presidential power and hinting that Goulart's goals of agrarian reform, rural unionization, enfranchisement of illiterate people, and legalization of the Communist Party might provoke a coup. During the period from 1945 to 1964, moreover, politicians frequently switched parties and formed unlikely electoral alliances to gain access to government funds. These politicians had few incentives to court the electoral support of poor people, whose votes, as in rural Chile before 1958, were largely under the control of clientelistic politicians.

Clientelism, a set of social relations characterized by inequality, reciprocity, and informality, was pervasive in Brazil throughout the twentieth century. In addition to diminishing the quality of democracy, not least by detracting from the autonomy of individual political participation, clientelism made policy less responsive to the interests of the poor. It biased social programs toward conspicuous public works projects with opportunities for construction and supply contracts, personnel hiring, and ribbon-cutting ceremonies. Lots of school buildings and health clinics were built, and lots of teachers and health care providers were hired, but the health and education facilities were often poorly equipped, and the teachers and health care workers were often poorly qualified and supervised. A place in a public school or admission to a public health facility might be legally available to poor people in a certain area, but in practice such access often depended on the intervention of an intermediary, who might also grant benefits (e.g., rural pensions) to persons who were not formally entitled to them. Spending on pork-barrel projects tended to make the state inefficient and, ultimately, insolvent, while at the same time discrediting parties, politicians, and electoral activity itself. By taking advantage of vertical clientelist ties, individual poor people could win small favors from local politicians, discouraging the formation of class consciousness or other horizontal solidarities. In the absence of such solidarities among the disadvantaged, the political system responded mainly to economic elites, who had better access to politicians at the state and national levels.[135]

In October 1965 the military government abolished the previously existing political parties, but instead of ending all party and electoral activity it organized a new pro-government party, the Aliança Renovadora Nacional (ARENA), and an officially sanctioned "opposition" party, the Movimento Democrático Brasileiro (MDB). Most of the pre-1964 politicians joined one or the other of these parties, which contested only legislative and some mayoral elections (military leaders chose the president, state governors, and the mayors of state capitals, seaports, and border towns). The persistence of elections

[135] Mainwaring 1999: 178–185, 208–214.

under the military regime in post-1964 Brazil, in contrast to post-1976 Argentina, is attributable in part to the lower perception by Brazilian elites of a threat from the left before the 1964 coup.[136] The persistence of elections was also due, however, to Brazilians' more weakly held political identities and to the more clientelistic character of interactions between citizens (especially the poor) and politicians.[137] The followers of Getúlio Vargas in Brazil were never as fervent in their allegiance as were the followers of Juan Perón in Argentina. In Brazil under military rule, national leaders could use elections and legislatures to help legitimate the authoritarian regime without opening the way to a powerful opposition.[138] Under the 1976–1983 military regime in Argentina, permitting electoral or legislative activity would have been perceived as risky, given that mobilization behind Peronist banners had contributed to the demise of the 1966–1973 military regime. ~~Facing a less mobilized population, the Brazilian military could afford to be less repressive~~. Per capita, 400 times as many Argentines as Brazilians died of state repression during the military regimes of 1976–1983 and 1964–1985 respectively.[139] Argentina and Brazil had similar average levels of democracy from 1900 to 2005 (Table A18), but authoritarianism could be less authoritarian in Brazil than in Argentina in part because democracy had been less democratic.

The Brazilian military returned to the barracks in 1985, but Jose Sarney, the first civilian president (1985–1990), owed his office not to a popular vote but to a military-devised electoral college. During Sarney's five years in office, the army retained decisive influence over a wide range of policy areas and serious human rights violations persisted around the country.[140] The literacy clause was abolished and the Communist Party was legalized in 1985, but it was not until the early 1990s that military influence in politics diminished significantly. Patronage and clientelism, moreover, expanded toward the end of the military regime, and continued unabated during the presidencies of Fernando Collor de Mello (1990–1992) and Itamar Franco (1992–1994).[141] Clientelism did not disappear during the presidencies of Fernando Henrique Cardoso (1995–2002) or Lula da Silva (2002–), but it began to erode as democracy became better institutionalized, as urbanization continued, as educational levels rose, and as anti-clientelist politicians in the Partido da Social Democracia Brasileira (PSDB) and Partido dos Trabalhadores (PT) won more popular support.[142]

Until the mid-1970s, Brazilian interest groups were legally and financially more beholden to the state than were interest groups in Argentina, Chile, or

---

[136] O'Donnell 1988: 161, 174n.
[137] Da Matta 1991: 137–170; Mainwaring 1999: 175–218; O'Donnell 1984.
[138] Mainwaring 1999: 84.
[139] King 1989: 1062.
[140] McGuire 1995b: 203.
[141] Literacy clause abolished: Schneider 1991: 317. Communist Party legalized: Skidmore 1988: 263. Erosion of military influence in the 1990s: Hunter 1997. Clientelism after 1995: Mainwaring 1999: 200–214.
[142] Weyland 2005.

Costa Rica. In Brazil it was bureaucratic initiative, rather than interest-group pressure, that brought urban workers limited curative health insurance in the 1920s, 1930s, and 1940s. As in Bismarck's Germany, Brazilian state policymakers viewed the extension of health insurance to urban workers as a way to diminish potential labor opposition.[143] The exigencies of World War II and of U.S. foreign policy, rather than pressure by poor people in the countryside, gave rise to the SESP in the Amazon and the Northeast. During the 1980s the National Confederation of Agricultural Workers (CONTAG) lobbied the military government to extend to its members the same type of health insurance as urban workers received, but did not demand that the government restructure the health care system to provide better primary care for the poor.[144] The Sanitarian Movement contributed to the founding of the Unified Health System and to the initiation of the Family Health Program, but it was not really an interest group: it never acquired a mass base and exercised its influence more as an issue network within the state than as a pressure group operating mainly in civil society.

To argue that democracy on balance contributes to social policies conducive to steeper infant mortality decline does not require one to maintain that democracy never has any effect inimical to that outcome. By permitting the activities of interest groups whose interests were not immediately aligned with the improvement of basic social services in poor areas, democracy and democratization may in some respects have impeded infant mortality decline in Brazil. As Lula noted in his 2006 campaign, "the poor...don't have the money to go protest in Brasília, to organize marches."[145] Labor unions, business organizations, and professional associations do have such resources. Labor unions representing employees of the National Social Security Medical Assistance Institute (INAMPS) resisted the unification and decentralization of the health care system in the late 1980s, and state and municipal health worker unions made salary demands whose satisfaction required resources that might have been spent more effectively to improve health.[146] Associations of doctors, hospitals, drug manufacturers, and health insurers opposed the introduction of the Unified Health System and managed to delay it effectively for five years, from 1988 to 1993.[147]

Although political liberalization after 1974 increased the freedom of action of interest groups whose aims did not involve the expansion of basic health services to the poor, it also allowed the formation of an issue network, the Sanitarian Movement, which had precisely this goal. In 1974, the pro-military ARENA party suffered its first defeat in elections for the Brazilian Senate. This defeat forced the military to take more seriously mounting criticism that

[143] Collier and Collier 1991: 173, 187; Malloy 1977.
[144] Weyland 1996: 158.
[145] Rohter 2006: A8.
[146] Weyland 1996: 165.
[147] Weyland 1995: 1700, 1704–1708.

the poor had been left out of the economic "miracle." Partly in response to this concern, the military's Second National Development Plan, published in 1976, took special note of the "persistent problems" of health, education, and poverty. The allocation of more resources to the health field, the holding of mayoral elections in many cities, and the growing emphasis on primary health care in UNICEF and in the World Health Organization opened up space in public health institutions, particularly at the municipal level, for medical professionals and health experts from the Sanitarian Movement.[148]

In 1976, newly elected mayors from the official opposition party, the Movimento Democrático Brasileiro (MDB), began to appoint Sanitarians, especially recent medical graduates, to positions in municipal health secretariats, where they had an opportunity to try out some of their ideas. The alliance between the Sanitarians and some MDB mayors solidified in 1978 during the First Municipal Meeting of the Health Sector, which brought Sérgio Arouca and Hésio Cordeiro, prominent leaders of the Sanitarian Movement, into closer dialogue with municipal health officials in the southern cities of Campinas, Londrina, and Niterói.[149] The Sanitarian Movement provided strong support for the unification and decentralization of the health care system, which was enshrined in the 1988 constitution and fully implemented in 1993. Politicians with ties to the Sanitarian Movement, supported by representatives of UNICEF and other international agencies, also helped to design and implement the Community Health Agents and Family Health programs.

Liberalization and democratization facilitated the activities of the Pastorate of the Children, which used volunteer networks connected to neighborhood religious committees to provide basic health services directly in poor communities. The opening of the political regime also allowed the convocation of National Health Conferences. According to a 1937 law such conferences were supposed to be held every two years, but only three took place between 1937 and 1964. Four were convened under military rule, and the last one, in 1980, focused on basic health care, discussing the recently designed National Basic Health Service Program (Prevsaúde), which the government never implemented.[150] In 1979, a year after legislative elections in which the opposition MDB did well, the Brazilian Chamber of Deputies organized a Health Policy Symposium whose resolutions foreshadowed the formal proposal for a Unified Health System that was presented seven years later at the Eighth National Health Conference. In 1982, when direct gubernatorial elections permitted the newly renamed PMDB (Partido Movimento Democrático Brasilero) to win the governorships of ten states (including the three most heavily populated ones), health policy experts who had attended the 1979 conference were appointed as state health secretaries.[151]

[148] Abrantes Pêgo and Almeida 2002: 10.
[149] Bertone 2002: 24–25.
[150] Cesaltina 2004.
[151] Bertone 2002: 68.

Electoral incentives, the aspect of democracy on which political scientists usually focus, influenced several public health initiatives that proved to be beneficial for the poor. A quantitative study found no association between the competitiveness of municipal elections and a municipality's propensity to adopt either the Bolsa Escola or Family Health programs.[152] Qualitative evidence suggests, however, that electoral incentives were among the factors that triggered several changes in health care policy that ultimately helped the poor. In the mid-1980s, "the center-left politicians who headed the MPAS [Ministry of Social Security and Social Assistance] supported health care reform in order to increase the electoral appeal of their party, the PMDB."[153] By 1998, when president Cardoso appointed him to lead the health ministry, Jose Serra was already being discussed as a possible presidential candidate in 2002. After Serra became health minister, Community Health Agents and Family Health Program team members began to wear uniforms and to mark the materials they distributed with a distinctive logo. Some health ministry officials attributed these policy changes to Serra's presidential aspirations, and Serra invoked the Family Health Program in his 2002 presidential campaign.[154] Serra also stressed the health ministry's HIV/AIDS policies in his run for president.[155]

Serra lost the 2002 presidential election to Lula, but did surprisingly well in the Northeast, an outcome he attributed partly to the expansion of the Community Health Agents and Family Health programs in the region.[156] Electoral incentives also informed Lula's decision in October 2003 to unify conditional cash transfer programs for schooling (Bolsa Escola), food, and cooking gas into a single Family Stipend (Bolsa Família), and to expand the reach of this unified conditional cash transfer program to a greater share of the Brazilian poor.[157] Bolsa Família is likely to improve the health status of impoverished Brazilians, not just by raising private incomes, but also because, to receive the cash transfer, expectant mothers must obtain prenatal checkups and take classes on maternal and child health, while parents of children below the age of seven must take their toddlers for regular checkups and immunizations. By the end of 2006 Bolsa Família covered 11.1 million families, nearly 100 percent of households earning less than the eligibility threshold of about U.S. $2 per day. The unification and expansion of these programs contributed to Lula's reelection as president in 2006.[158]

The case of Brazil highlights the multiplicity of ways in which democracy can work its effects on policies that influence that pattern and pace of infant mortality decline. These mechanisms include, but are not limited to, electoral incentives. The expansion of political participation and competition from the

---

[152] Sugiyama 2008: 207, 211.
[153] Weyland 1996: 159.
[154] Information provided by a pre-publication reviewer of the manuscript for this book.
[155] Nunn 2009: 125–126, 141.
[156] Serra 2003a.
[157] Hall 2006: 704–706.
[158] Hunter and Power 2007: 1819.

late 1970s onward made it easier for labor unions, business organizations, and professional associations to operate, not always in ways that improved the provision of basic health services to the poor. At the same time, however, these processes opened the way for social movements (like the Pastorate of the Children) and issue networks (like the Sanitarian and Primary Care movements) that contributed substantially to interventions that improved the health status of the poor. They also opened the way for the holding of conferences and symposia at which progressive social policy ideas were introduced and debated. Meanwhile, electoral incentives encouraged politicians like Jose Serra and Lula da Silva to advocate the expansion of such initiatives as the Family Health Program and Bolsa Família. These programs, in turn, improved the quality of democracy by giving poor Brazilians more resources with which to take advantage of their legal rights. By reaching out to poor people and by encouraging them to regard health services as rights, rather than as privileges requiring the intervention of a patron, the Family Health Program itself contributed to the further erosion of clientelistic practices,[159] raising the quality of democracy by this avenue as well. In Brazil, then, pro-poor health policies and the deepening of democracy became mutually reinforcing in the 1990s.

[159] Serra 2003a.

7

Taiwan: From Poor but Healthy to Wealthy and Healthy

Taiwan achieved a rapid decline of infant mortality, from 54 per 1000 in 1960 to less than 6 per 1000 in 2005, in part through what the World Bank has termed "shared growth," a process that involves a rapid rise of GDP per capita in a context of low income inequality.[1] Less widely appreciated is the role of the public provision of basic social services in reducing infant mortality on the island, before as well as after 1960. Infant mortality fell rapidly from 1947 to 1960 not only because of economic recovery from World War II, as the wealthier is healthier conjecture would lead one to expect, but also because of the activities of the Sino-American Joint Commission on Rural Reconstruction (JCRR), which built and staffed health clinics across the island and developed programs to control malaria and other infectious diseases.

Before 1995, the year in which national health insurance was introduced, Taiwan had a small welfare state in terms of social spending, health insurance coverage, and pension eligibility. The ruling Kuomintang (Nationalist Party) nevertheless did well at providing basic social services, notably primary and secondary education, but also basic health care as of the late 1940s and early 1950s, disease control as of the 1950s, and family planning as of 1964. Such inexpensive programs were fully compatible with a small welfare state, and Taiwan could implement them despite a low GDP per capita. In 1965, when Taiwan had a GDP per capita of only U.S. $2,001 (much lower than in any of the four Latin American cases), infant mortality was only 44 per 1000 (which was also much lower than in any of the four Latin American cases) (Tables A1 and A3). State provision of basic health services also improved in the 1970s and (to a lesser extent) the 1980s, particularly in rural areas. In 1995, when the National Health Insurance plan was implemented, the infant mortality rate had already fallen to 8 per 1000. Hence, Taiwan's low infant mortality rate in 2005 should be attributed not to the advent of universal health insurance coverage, which happened when the infant mortality rate was already very low, but rather to fast economic growth and low income inequality, together with

[1] Campos and Root 1996: 1–2, 50–75; World Bank 1993b: 4, 157–189.

the effective public provision of basic social services to poor people – not just education, but also family planning and, especially in the late 1940s, 1950s, and 1970s, health services.

Democracy is a supportive, rather than necessary, condition for public policies that contribute to rapid infant mortality decline. China, Cuba, Vietnam, and other countries with leftist authoritarian governments have enacted social policies that have led to the rapid decline of infant mortality.[2] Like Chile under military rule, Taiwan had a rightist authoritarian government, and also enacted policies that reduced the risk of infant death. In Chile and Taiwan respectively, rightist authoritarian leaders committed to outshining leftist predecessors (Allende) or rivals (the People's Republic of China) improved health care services for the poor. Similarly, infant mortality fell rapidly under right-wing personalist dictatorships in Cuba in the 1950s and in Nicaragua in the 1970s, as well as under military-fist-in-civilian glove rule in El Salvador in the 1980s.[3] In each of these cases, leftist insurgencies improved health services in occupied zones and provoked right-wing authoritarian or semi-authoritarian governments to improve health services in impoverished rural areas in an effort to win hearts and minds.

From 1947 to 1986 the Kuomintang held a monopoly on executive power, and martial law prevailed until 1987. The first glimmer of democratization appeared in 1972, when the government allowed opposition candidates to run for legislative seats. Political liberalization during the 1970s coincided with greater attention to basic health service provision, especially in rural areas. In the 1980s and 1990s, as liberalization and democratization deepened, electoral incentives, the pressures of issue networks and social movements, and the activities of empowered neighborhoods and villages encouraged the expansion of health insurance to new sectors of the population, until a universal National Health Insurance program was adopted in 1995.[4] Even in Taiwan, then, as in South Korea, adversarial politics and political liberalization contributed to the design and implementation of health policies, despite a political context that was basically authoritarian.

7.1. Taiwan: Mortality

Taiwan in the late nineteenth century was not a healthy place. Malaria was endemic, outbreaks of cholera and bubonic plague were frequent, and gastrointestinal afflictions, venereal disease, and tuberculosis were rampant.[5] Female infanticide was common, and the custom of foot-binding contributed to circulatory and other problems that may have raised female mortality.[6] In 1874,

[2] Caldwell 1986; Drèze and Sen 1989; Moon 1991.
[3] Cuba: McGuire and Frankel 2005. Nicaragua: Sandiford et al. 1991. El Salvador: Smith-Nonini 1997; Ugalde et al. 2000.
[4] Wong 2004.
[5] Barclay 1954a: 133–136; Mirzaee 1979: 44–46; Riggs 1952: 132.
[6] Barclay 1954a: 159n; Taeuber 1961: 108.

547 of 5,990 Japanese troops involved in a six-month military expedition to Taiwan died of disease; only 20 died of battle wounds or other injuries.[7] After the Japanese occupied the island in 1895, health conditions improved. The crude death rate fell from 38 per 1000 in 1906 to 20 per 1000 in 1940; life expectancy at age one rose from 34 in 1906 to 50 in 1936–40; and reported maternal mortality fell from 55 per 100,000 in 1920 to 28 per 100,000 in 1941.[8] Officially registered infant mortality declined fitfully from about 175 per 1000 in 1906 to about 125 per 1000 in 1943.[9]

Infant mortality rates in Taiwan are hard to establish definitively. The rate fell from at least 130 per 1000 in 1940 to about 54 per 1000 in 1960, but the tempo of the decline is uncertain. If we take at face value the trends in depicted in vital registration statistics, infant mortality fell precipitously from 77 per 1000 in 1947 to 35 per 1000 in 1950, then only to 31 per 1000 in 1960.[10] A sharp decline in the late 1940s followed by almost no decline in the 1950s seems implausible. Taiwan was bombed heavily during World War II, resulting in the destruction of many hospitals. Most trained Japanese doctors left in 1945; cholera, smallpox, and bubonic plague epidemics broke out in 1946 and 1947; and the Chen Yi government from 1945 to 1948 was a kleptocracy. Many Taiwanese who fled to rural areas during World War II contracted malaria in the countryside and then brought it back to the cities.[11] The quarantine system broke down, garbage piled up in cities, and hundreds of thousands of mainland refugees camped out in the streets, creating a sanitation crisis.[12] In 1947 the Kuomintang, in response to mild expressions of protest, unleashed more than ten thousand soldiers against the native Taiwanese, killing some eight thousand people and sending many others into the hills.[13]

These contextual factors cast doubt on the hypothesis that infant mortality fell rapidly from 1945 to 1947, but it would be unwise to discount this possibility entirely: Latin America is rife with periods of unlikely success, as in Cuba in the 1950s, Argentina and Chile in the 1970s, and El Salvador in the 1980s. Some evidence suggests, however, that infant mortality did fall steeply from 1947 to 1950. The uncorrected vital registration rates of 77 per 1000 in 1947 and 35 per 1000 in 1950 are probably understated, but the trend they depict may not be misleading. Corrected vital registration statistics, as would be expected, show a similarly sharp decline from 179 per 1000 in 1947 to 110 per 1000 in 1950, with almost all of the drop occurring in 1948.[14] These

[7] Katz 1996: 202.

[8] Crude death rate from Mirzaee 1979: 47; life expectancy at age one from Barclay 1954a: 154; maternal mortality from Mirzaee 1979: 184. Even if the reported maternal mortality ratio is understated, the trend may be accurate.

[9] Barclay 1954a: 161–162.

[10] 1947–1950: United Nations 1952: 322–323; figures exclude "tribal aborigines." 1952–1960: United Nations 1961. These figures, by all accounts, suffer from underregistration.

[11] Han 1956: 47; Riggs 1952: 133–134; Yen 1973a: 8.

[12] Kuo 2002: 2–4.

[13] Deaths estimate from Lai, Myers, and Wou 1991: 160.

[14] Barclay 1954b: 24–27.

corrected figures leave room for a substantial decline in the 1950s to about 54 per 1000 in 1960, an estimate that is also based on corrected vital registration figures (Table A1).

Underregistration of infant deaths continued to complicate the assessment of infant mortality levels and changes from 1960 to 1995. In Table A1, estimates for 1960 to 1985 are taken from vital registration statistics corrected by reported death rates at other ages; estimates for 1990 and 1995 are taken from island-wide surveys; and estimates for 2000 and 2005 are taken from uncorrected vital registration statistics.[15] These figures suggest that infant mortality fell from 54 per 1000 in 1960 to 5.5 per 1000 in 2005, the second-lowest level among the eight cases compared in this book. Taiwan's life expectancy at birth in 2005, 77.8 years, although only fourth highest among the eight societies (Table A2), was only a year shorter than in Costa Rica (the leader), and was slightly longer than in the United States.[16] Taiwan's percent decline of infant mortality and percent rise in life expectancy from 1960 to 2005 were likewise only fourth-greatest among the eight societies (Tables A1 and A2), but this is tough competition. Had it been a country, Taiwan would have ranked in the top 25 percent of the world's nations at infant survival and life expectancy in 2005, and in the top 15 percent at infant mortality decline and life expectancy rise from 1960 to 2005.[17]

Infant mortality fell modestly from 1960 to 1980 (4.0 percent per year), steeply from 1980 to 1990 (8.2 percent per year), and then modestly again from 1990 to 2005 (4.0 percent per year) (Table A1). Neither measurement error, nor socioeconomic modernization, nor social provisioning alone explains the acceleration of infant mortality decline during the 1980s. As for measurement error, the infant mortality estimates for 1980 and 1985 are based on corrected vital registration records, whereas the estimate for 1990 (actually 1989) comes from an island-wide survey. The 1980 and 1985 estimates are more likely than the 1989 estimate to understate the true infant mortality rate, so the actual rate of decline during the 1980s was, if anything, even greater than 8.2 percent. As for socioeconomic modernization, the 1980s indeed saw fast GDP per capita growth (albeit a slight rise of income inequality), a 25 percent rise in the share of households with a washing machine (suggesting a rapid decline of income poverty), and a plunge in the total fertility rate (Tables A3, A4, A5, and A10). During the 1970s, however, when infant mortality fell only 3.7 percent per year, GDP per capita grew even faster, income inequality declined, the share of households owning a washing machine rose by 60 percent, and fertility fell even more steeply. As for social provisioning, the 1980s was a decade of

[15] The quality of these estimates is discussed in McGuire (2009), Web Appendix A1.

[16] U.S. life expectancy at birth in 2005 was 77.7 years (World Bank 2008e).

[17] In 2005, Taiwan would have ranked 36th of 189 countries at lowness of infant mortality and 39th of 181 at life expectancy at birth. From 1960 to 2005, Taiwan would have ranked 17th of 145 countries at percent decline of infant mortality and 23rd of 170 at percent rise of life expectancy. Source: World Bank 2008e, except Taiwan (Tables A1 and A2).

sharp rises in access to tap water; rapid growth in the per capita availability of doctors, nurses, and hospital beds; better staffing of rural health stations; and vastly expanded hepatitis B immunization. The 1970s, however, saw even greater gains in access to tap water and in the per capita availability of health personnel and health facilities, as well as a four-year program to improve rural health and a law requiring new medical graduates to practice for a time in underserved areas.[18] Like socioeconomic modernization, then, social provisioning improved at least as much during the 1970s as during the 1980s, leaving unclear why infant mortality fell faster during the 1980s.

Synergies between social provisioning and socioeconomic modernization, together with the lagged effects of prior achievements, probably account for this perplexing outcome. In general, socioeconomic modernization provides a fairly persuasive explanation of infant mortality outcomes in Taiwan. Socioeconomic factors did well at explaining both the steep decline of infant mortality from 1960 to 2005 and the low level of infant mortality prevailing in 2005 (5.5 per 1000, below the U.S. rate of 6.9 per 1000). Across eight five-year periods from 1960 to 2000, moreover, the correlation between economic growth and infant mortality decline was positive, although not very strong (Table 11.1). At the outset in 1960, however, infant mortality was lower in Taiwan than in any of the other seven societies, even though GDP per capita was also lower than in all of the other cases except Indonesia and Thailand. The public provision of primary health care, disease control, and water and sanitation during the late 1940s and 1950s, as well as expanded food production and land reform (leading to higher incomes among the poor), account for Taiwan's remarkably low infant mortality rate in 1960.

7.2. Taiwan: Affluence, Inequality, and Poverty

GDP per capita in Taiwan in 1960 was $1,444, higher than in Indonesia or Thailand but lower than in South Korea and vastly lower than in any of the four Latin American cases. By 2003 Taiwan had a GDP per capita of $19,885, highest among the eight cases. From 1960 to 2003, accordingly, Taiwan turned in the fastest annual GDP per capita growth among the eight societies compared in this book (Table A3). Indeed, Taiwan's annual GDP per capita growth rate of 6.3 percent from 1960 to 2003 was the greatest among the 98 societies with data for both years.[19] Four sets of policies help to explain this rapid economic growth: land reform (in the late 1940s and early 1950s), public investment in basic education (from the 1950s onward), the promotion of labor-intensive manufactured exports (from the 1960s onward), and cautious macroeconomic policies (throughout the period). Contributing to the design and implementation of these policies were Taiwan's meager natural

---

[18] Tap water: Table A11. Doctors, nurses, and hospital beds: Taiwan. CEPD 2007: 24, 293, 303. Other information: Section 7.4.

[19] Heston, Summers, and Aten 2006, variable RGDPCH (see Table A3).

resource endowment, its small domestic market, its low levels of class cohesion and organization, and its geopolitical situation.[20] Rapid fertility decline, due partly to strong family planning policies, contributed to economic growth by increasing the working-age share of the population, while rising life expectancy contributed by raising savings rates.[21]

Taiwan from 1960 to 1990 had the world's lowest level of income inequality outside Europe.[22] Simon Kuznets hypothesized that income inequality would be low at low levels of GDP per capita (when almost everyone is poor), high at medium levels of GDP per capita (when the benefits of growth accrue mainly to an elite in a small modern sector), and low again at high levels of GDP per capita (after modern-sector growth had created opportunities for non-elites).[23] From 1964 to 2003, however, even though Taiwan's GDP per capita rose nearly tenfold, its income inequality barely budged (Tables A3 and A4). The policies that contributed to low inequality were similar to those that promoted rapid economic growth: land reform, investment in basic education, and the promotion of labor-intensive manufactured exports. Low income inequality may also have encouraged fast GDP growth by reducing pressure for market-distorting income-redistributive policies; by diminishing political instability; by raising the supply of and demand for education; and by expanding the internal market.[24] Low inflation, which was due in part to cautious macroeconomic policies, also helped to keep income inequality low. Inflation tends to hurt the poor, who carry money around, more than the rich, who can often find ways to insulate their savings against price rises.

Fast economic growth in the context of stable income inequality should result in rapid income poverty decline. The nearest thing Taiwan has to a poverty line is a cutoff for public income assistance. Until a new limit was legislated in 1997, this cutoff was set very low so as to minimize the burden on state revenue.[25] The share of the population receiving such assistance fell steeply, from 12 percent in 1960 to less than 1 percent from 1975 onward.[26] Other studies using higher poverty lines have found sharp drops in the poverty headcount from 1964 to 1972 and again from 1980 to 1987.[27] These data coincide with the evolution of the share of households owning durable consumer goods of various types (Table A5). In 1960, fewer than 2 percent of Taiwanese households had a telephone, a refrigerator, or a washing machine.

---

[20] Taiwan and South Korea shared each of these policies and policy determinants (McGuire 1995a).

[21] Bloom, Canning, and Malaney 2000; Kinugasa and Mason 2007.

[22] Data from Deininger and Squire 1996: 574–577.

[23] Kuznets 1955.

[24] On these hypothesized mediating mechanisms see, respectively, Persson and Tabellini 1994 and Alesina and Rodrik 1994; Alesina and Perotti 1996; Birdsall, Ross, and Sabot 1995; and Murphy, Schleifer, and Vishny 1989.

[25] Fields 1992: 398; Lee, Parish, and Willis 1994: 1025.

[26] Aspalter 2002: 74.

[27] Fields 1992: 397.

By 1995, almost every household owned each item. Television ownership rose even faster: TV sets per 1,000 households rose from 14 in 1964 to 931 in 1976.[28]

Income-related achievements go some way toward explaining why Taiwan's infant mortality fell so steeply from 1960 to 2005, to such a low level. Although Taiwan in 2005 had a much lower infant mortality level than was predicted by its GDP per capita, the discrepancy shrank when income inequality was added as a predictor, and vanished when seven economic, demographic, and cultural variables were also added as predictors (Table 11.2). Accordingly, Taiwan might well be regarded as a "poster society" for the broad variant of the wealthier is healthier hypothesis. Still, Taiwan's infant mortality rate was low in 2005 not only because it fell fairly rapidly from 1960 to 2005 (although not as rapidly as in Thailand, South Korea, Chile, or Costa Rica), but also because it was already remarkably low in 1960. Social provisioning, particularly the expansion of public health services and disease control initiatives in the late 1940s and 1950s, helps to explain why Taiwan started out in 1960 with such a low infant mortality rate. After 1960, social provisioning continued to work together with fast economic growth and low income inequality to produce a low rate of infant mortality. Moreover, social provisioning contributed to these economic achievements themselves. Family planning encouraged fertility decline, which contributed to faster economic growth (by reducing the dependent share of the population for a few decades) and lower income inequality. Likewise, the expansion of basic education and of basic health services had beneficial effects on income-related as well as survival-related outcomes.

7.3. Taiwan: Education, Family Planning, Safe Water, and Sanitation

In 1995 social spending at all levels of government made up about 21 percent of GDP in Argentina and Brazil and about 13 percent of GDP in Costa Rica and Chile.[29] Social spending in Taiwan was much lower: 6.7 percent of GDP, more than half of which (3.4 percent of GDP) went to "education, science, and technology."[30] In 1990, however, only half of such spending was controlled by the education ministry; the other half went to national defense and economic development. A more realistic figure for the education part of the spending might be 2 percent of GDP, which would put total social spending in Taiwan in 1995 at about 5.3 percent of GDP.

Public social spending in areas apart from education went mostly to pension and health insurance benefits for veterans, military personnel, and government employees. In 1991, the government spent almost exactly the same amount on welfare benefits (including pensions, excluding education) for 275

---

[28] Taiwan: DGBAS 2001: 38–39; Thornton and Lin 1994: 85.
[29] See Sections 3.3, 4.3, 5.3, and 6.3. The figure for Argentina is from the mid-1980s.
[30] Taiwan. DGBAS 2002: 148, 239.

retired legislators as for 4,407,406 children – about 0.65 percent of welfare spending in each case.[31] Social spending in Taiwan was thus even more regressive than in Argentina or Brazil, but its effects were less inequitable because it consumed a much smaller share of GDP. The case of Taiwan confirms that the scope of social assistance and contributory social insurance programs is one thing, whereas the public provision of mortality-reducing social services is quite another. Despite the underdevelopment of its welfare state, Taiwan's governments during the era of rapid economic growth and low income inequality from 1960 to 2005 did well at providing most basic social services to most of the poor. A notable exception was safe water and adequate sanitation, where a dense population, a huge industrial base, and millions of livestock presented formidable technical challenges.

Social insurance in Taiwan dates back to 1950, when the government established health, retirement, and disability plans for military personnel. During the next 15 years the government mandated contributory social insurance schemes for manufacturing, fishing, and sugar workers and for active and retired civil servants. In nearly three decades from 1952 to 1980, however, health insurance and pension coverage rose only from 2 to 17 percent of the population. New groups gained coverage during the 1980s, and by 1990 some 47 percent of Taiwanese were eligible for health insurance and 38 percent for pensions.[32] In 1995, by which time health insurance coverage had risen to about 60 percent of the adult population,[33] the government merged the main health insurance schemes (for government employees, private-sector workers, and farmers), as well as some smaller ones (e.g., for private school employees), into a compulsory, contributory, single-payer National Health Insurance plan that by 1998 covered 96 percent of the civilian population.[34]

The roots of Taiwan's strong educational performance date back to the colonial era. Under Japanese rule from 1907 to 1944, the share of primary school-aged children in school rose from 5 to 74 percent. By providing such education, the Japanese intended mainly to train the labor force and to create loyal subjects by exposing the locals to Japanese language and culture. Primary schooling contributed to lower infant mortality in part by improving hygiene and sanitation, which were taught assiduously.[35] Because the colonial authorities were also wary of producing restive students and educated unemployed people, however, they did not provide much secondary education. In 1939, only nine middle schools enrolled significant numbers of Taiwanese.[36]

---

[31] Ku 1997: 58, 61.
[32] Aspalter 2002: 51–57; Chan and Yang 2001: 154; Chiang 1997: 227–228; Chow 2001: 23–25; Deyo 1992: 53; Goodman and Peng 1996: 205; Ku 1997: 46, 52; Tang 2000: 72; Wong 2004: 45, 52.
[33] Liu and Lee 1998: 15.
[34] Chow 2001: 34, 37; Liu and Lee 1998: 12, 18; Wong 2004: 76–86.
[35] Tsurumi 1977: 148, 213–214, 224.
[36] Woo 1991: 1030.

Article 160 of the Taiwanese constitution, which took effect in 1947, made education at state expense mandatory for all children aged 6 to 12 and committed the government to provide free textbooks for poor children. Adults without an elementary education also gained the right to acquire it at state expense. The number of years of free and mandatory education was raised to nine in 1968, a policy change that a group of economists has credited with reducing infant mortality by 9–13 percent.[37] By the mid-1990s the last three years of high school were also free, although not mandatory.[38] To reduce the cultural distance between persons of Taiwanese and mainlander ancestry, Mandarin was used in the schools and emphasis was placed on a common Chinese heritage.[39] From 1952 to 1960 public spending on education amounted only to about 2 percent of a low GDP, yet the literate share of the population aged six or older rose from 58 to 73 percent. Classes were conducted in two shifts, parents were asked to make in-kind contributions to schooling, and educated soldiers with six months of training were sent to teach in remote rural areas.[40] Rapid gains in educational attainment continued from 1960 to 2005. Literacy in the population aged 15 and older rose from 54 to 97 percent during this period, and mean years of schooling more than doubled (Tables A6 and A7).

In the mid-1960s the Taiwanese government, in close collaboration with business interests, shifted resources from general to vocational education. From 1963 to 1980 the proportion of ninth graders who went on to vocational school rose from 40 to 66 percent, while the share going on to general education senior high schools fell from 60 to 34 percent. At the tertiary level, the government promoted two-year degrees in vocational fields while discouraging general university education by making entrance exams hard to pass. It also allowed the fee-charging private sector to take a dominant role in university education, keeping state subsidies low. The government subsidized private universities, but students in the late 1980s paid about 50 percent of educational costs in such institutions, compared to 7 percent in public universities. In both public and private universities, the government encouraged the study of science and engineering while de-emphasizing humanities and fine arts.[41] Over time, moreover, the government shifted spending from university to primary education. Per-student public spending at the university level exceeded that at the primary level by 8:1 in 1976; by 1995 the ratio had fallen to 3:1. From 1976 to 1995 universities absorbed from 20 to 24 percent of public education spending, about the same as in many Latin American countries, but the benefits of such spending accrued to a much higher proportion of students. In 1997 about 90 percent of Taiwanese junior high students went on to senior

[37] Chou et al. 2007: 49.
[38] Baraka 1999: 5.
[39] Gold 1986: 112–113.
[40] Rao 1998: 687.
[41] Woo 1991: 1032–1039.

high school, and nearly 60 percent of high school graduates went directly to university, about the same share as in the United States.[42]

Several factors help to explain the government's emphasis on education. Traditional Confucian concern for teaching and learning, a desire to catch up with Western science and technology, and the legacy of Japanese colonialism fostered an emphasis on schooling. The Kuomintang attributed their loss of the mainland in part to failures of the educational system, and stressed that education was critical to national reconstruction.[43] Concern for regime stability may also have played a role. Many teenagers by the mid-1990s spent more than 60 hours per week under instruction, thanks to long school days and weeks and extra lessons to prepare for high school and college entrance examinations. Because of the hours they spent in the classroom, "Taiwan's young people [did] not [have] time for casual fun, crime, drugs, or dissident political thoughts."[44]

Taiwan's total fertility rate fell from 5.8 in 1960 to 1.1 in 2005 (Table A10), the greatest percent decline of any society compared in this book. In a broader comparative perspective, Taiwan from 1960 to 2005 had the second-greatest percent decline of fertility among the 179 societies for which data are available, trailing only Macao.[45] Rapid fertility decline contributed to fast GDP per capita growth by slowing the rise in population; to fast GDP growth by expanding the working-age share of the population; and to low individual income inequality by reducing family size more in poor households than in rich households. Fertility decline began in the mid-1950s, well before the national family planning program in 1964, and would have continued even in the absence of the initiative, but without the family planning program, "it is likely that the fertility decline would have proceeded more slowly, less equitably, and with greater costs in human suffering."[46]

In 1950 the Kuomintang denounced a Sino-American Joint Commission on Rural Reconstruction (JCRR) booklet promoting family planning by the rhythm method as a communist plot to weaken the military. The JCRR soon gained ground, however, with the argument that unchecked population growth could divert resources from industrialization and create destabilizing unemployment. In 1959, government officials added traditional methods of family planning to a maternal and child health care program that dated back to 1952.[47] In 1963, the government launched in Taichung, Taiwan's third-largest city, "the largest intensive program for family planning ever carried out in a limited geographical area."[48] In previous years, contraceptive use had been largely confined to more educated women, mostly in urban areas, who

[42] Chow 2001: 7, 10, 11.
[43] Chow 2001: 7–11.
[44] Wade 1990: 241.
[45] Figures from World Bank 2008a, except Taiwan, from Table A10.
[46] Freedman et al. 1994: 302–303.
[47] Hsu 1970: 3, 6–8; Yen 1973b: 32.
[48] Freedman and Takeshita 1969: 3.

wanted no more children.[49] The Taichung program was successful in extending birth control to lower economic status couples who had not previously engaged in the practice, and available evidence suggests that it reduced the birth rate significantly among those who participated in it.[50] The perceived success of the Taichung program led to the initiation of an island-wide program in 1964. By 1972 experts judged Taiwan's family planning effort, along with South Korea's, to be the third-strongest in the world, behind only Singapore's and China's.[51] A program of similar intensity was maintained through 1999 (Table A9).

Taiwan as of 2005 faced serious water supply and sanitation problems. After Hong Kong, Singapore, and Bangladesh, Taiwan had the highest population density of any society in the world with a population of more than one million. Twenty-one million inhabitants shared the island with tens of thousands of manufacturing plants and seven million hogs (the sanitary equivalent of 30 million humans). Overall, domestic sewage produced 44 percent of water pollution, industrial waste produced 33 percent, and hog farms produced 22 percent.[52] From 1946 to 1965 the proportion of the population "served by tap water" rose from 18 to 38 percent. By 1971 major urban water supply systems were sanitized with chlorine, and more than 36,000 covered wells had been dug. The custom of tea-drinking, which requires boiled water, made the intake of initially contaminated water safer than it would otherwise have been.[53] Access to "tap water" rose steadily from 31 percent of households in 1960 to 91 percent in 2005 (Table A11). The main problem with the water supply was its poor quality, which was related to deficient household sewage disposal, industrial waste pollution, and intensive hog raising. Boiling of household water and the purchasing of bottled water remained common practice throughout the country in the 1990s.[54]

Minimally adequate sewer systems were "non-existent" in 1955, even for urban residents. United States agencies in cooperation with the Taiwanese government set up some village water supply and sanitation projects in the early 1950s, but the scale of such endeavors was modest.[55] In 1963 only 7 percent of dwellings had a sewerage connection, and little progress was made during the rest of the 1960s.[56] As late as the early 1990s only 25 percent of homes and businesses in the capital city of Taipei, with the highest connection rate in the country, were linked to a sewerage network that led to a treatment

---

[49] Freedman et al. 1994: 289, 292.
[50] Freedman and Takeshita 1969: 292–310.
[51] Ross and Mauldin 1996: 146.
[52] Taiwan. EPA 2006.
[53] Baker and Perlman 1967: 107; Yen 1973b: 33.
[54] Edmonds 1996: 1233.
[55] United States. MSMC 1956: 66. In 1962, a cholera outbreak killed 24 people and infected more than 350 others (Taiwan. CDC 2000: 1).
[56] Yen 1973b: 33. Figure for 1963 from Baker and Perlman 1967: 107.

facility.[57] By 2004 the connection rate in Taipei had reportedly risen to 69 percent, but across the island it was still only 27 percent.[58]

In view of these failings on the water and sanitation front, it is remarkable that Taiwan achieved such a steep decline and low level of infant mortality. Rapidly expanding incomes and educational levels may have enabled parents to offset at the household level the risk of potentially fatal water-borne infections to which infants were exposed because of unsafe water supplies and inadequate sanitary arrangements. Plummeting fertility, encouraged by one of the world's most effective family planning programs, meanwhile reduced burdens on obstetric and pediatric services and allowed parents to devote more attention to each child. Improvements in nutrition and in the provision of basic health services also contributed to infant survival in Taiwan.

7.4. Taiwan: Nutrition and Health Care

Food was scarce in Taiwan in the aftermath of World War II. In 1945, Taiwanese farmers produced only 639 metric tons of rice (down from 1,402 tons in 1940), and only 1,277 calories per person per day were available on the island. By 1960, farmers were producing 1,912 metric tons of rice and 2,361 calories per person per day were available. Protein, vitamin, and mineral availability was also judged to be adequate by 1960.[59] Recovery from World War II, land reforms in the late 1940s and early 1950s, and U.S. foreign aid each contributed to a rise in agricultural output. From 1946 to 1951 agricultural production rose at an annual rate of 10.3 percent, and from 1951 to 1967 it rose at a rate of 5.6 percent, thanks in part to the expansion of multiple cropping. The government squeezed agriculture to finance industry during the 1950s and 1960s, but rising farm productivity allowed the real income and consumption of farmers to grow as well. Farmers' associations created during the colonial era helped the government to deliver credit, agricultural inputs, marketing help, and extension services to agriculturalists.[60] In 1964, moreover, the government introduced a school lunch program for pupils in indigent areas that provided free meals to about 10 percent of the primary school population.[61] Apart from this measure, however, and sanitary inspection of markets and restaurants, the Kuomintang left the population to fend for itself on the food and nutrition front.

Presbyterian missionaries introduced Western medicine to Taiwan in the 1860s and 1870s. Chinese-style medicine flourished until 1895, when the Japanese colonial rulers suppressed folk healers and imposed strict limits on the practice of Chinese medicine. Repression was lifted after 1945, and

---

[57] Edmonds 1996: 1234.
[58] Taiwan. Ministry of the Interior 2005. Section VII, Part 1.
[59] Rice production: Taiwan. AREC 1972: 31; other figures: Hsu 1972: 8.
[60] Dorner and Thiesenhusen 1990: 76.
[61] Hsu 1972: 11.

Chinese and Western medical practitioners and facilities have since coexisted. Surveys in the 1980s found that about one-third of Taiwanese used Chinese medicine in a given year, and the 1995 National Health Insurance program covered visits to Chinese-style as well as Western-style doctors and clinics. Many Chinese medicine doctors had no formal medical education, however, and licensing procedures were loose, making it difficult for the consumer to assess the qualifications of such practitioners.[62]

The Japanese took a quick interest in disease control and sanitation in Taiwan, not least because 4,642 Japanese died of disease in the first few months of occupation, compared to the 164 who died in combat during the invasion.[63] As one Japanese colonial health authority noted, "the prevention of infectious diseases is a prerequisite for our residence [in Taiwan] and our utilization of its plentiful natural resources."[64] Also contributing to the emphasis on health and hygiene was that Goto Shimpei, the Chief of Home Affairs in Taiwan from 1896 to 1918, had served in Japan's sanitation bureau, had authored a handbook on epidemic prevention, and had written a doctoral dissertation in Germany on enforcement of medical and sanitary laws.[65]

The colonial administration in Taiwan put the police in charge of sanitation.[66] To deal with plague the police exterminated rats and inspected ships from infested areas. To fight cholera they improved sewage and garbage disposal, drained gutters, launched a campaign against the house fly, and strictly regulated food handling and distribution. In urban areas they dug wells, insisted that residents keep them covered, piped in water from mountain streams, supervised the construction of sewers and septic tanks, and systematized the process of removing sewage. Sanitation rules were strictly enforced, and Taiwanese were required to clean their houses and streets twice a year. A vaccination campaign wiped out smallpox, although it reappeared briefly in 1946. Efforts to control malaria by cleaning up mosquito breeding grounds were hampered by the island's dependence on irrigation, but the colonial authorities drained swamps and stocked ponds and rivers with larva-eating fish. The Japanese insisted that Taiwanese take action to reduce the risk of contracting malaria, and all individuals suspected of having been infected were forced to undergo blood tests, more than 3 million of which were carried out annually by the 1930s. Those who tested positive were forced to take quinine. The colonial government's draconian measures in preventive and curative medicine produced a substantial reduction in deaths from epidemic diseases.[67] The Taiwanese, who were used to Chinese-style medicine, resisted some of these initiatives, particularly vaccination, and the Japanese practice of

[62] Chi 1994: 310–315; Chiang 1997: 230; Kleinman 1980: 16.
[63] Barclay 1954a: 138; Katz 1996.
[64] Quoted in Chin 1998: 327.
[65] Johnston 1995: 176, 181; Yip 2000: 118.
[66] Chin 1998: 328; Johnston 1995: 179–181, 184.
[67] Barclay 1954a: 136–138; Ku 1997: 154; Riggs 1952: 132; Taeuber 1944: 153; Yip 2000: 119.

"often relying on the police to carry forward technical advancements" generated resentment among the population.[68]

The colonial authorities also trained medical personnel and established hospitals and clinics. By 1940 there were 249 medical facilities in Taiwan, including 33 public hospitals and 216 private clinics with 10 to 50 beds each. The number of persons receiving medical treatment rose from 64,000 in 1897 to 726,000 in 1907 to more than 1,000,000 by 1938, and facilities were set up to care for patients with tuberculosis, leprosy, venereal disease, and mental illness. The 2,000 medical personnel on the island in 1940 included both highly trained Japanese doctors and a much larger number of Taiwanese who had taken a course that entitled them to provide limited health care in rural areas and towns in exchange for a small stipend from the colonial administrators. In an effort to reduce infant mortality, the Japanese also trained more than 1,500 women to serve as midwives. All told, although "behind contemporary Western practice, the medical and public health facilities of [Taiwan during the era of Japanese colonialism] were in advance of anything realized on the south and east Asian mainland."[69] Because of these initiatives, Taiwan entered the postwar era with a sizable number of physicians, midwives, nurses, and public health specialists. These trained health personnel played important roles in the rural health care and disease control initiatives of the 1950s.[70]

After the end of World War II, the Kuomintang government under Chen Yi (1945–1948) destroyed many of the Japanese colonial social welfare institutions, but retained a number of programs with precolonial roots, including financial aid and medical care for the poor and famine and disaster relief.[71] Under Chen Yi, however, corruption soared and health service administration deteriorated. The public health system was entrusted to a pharmacologist who had little experience in health care administration, and who was accused of neglecting his duties in order to profiteer from drug sales. School-based health services, anti-malaria measures, and vaccinations all ceased, and the government stopped subsidizing rural health practitioners who could not support their practices independently.[72] The number of health stations rose from 15 in 1945 to 101 in 1948, but only about 50 were fully functioning at the end of 1948.[73] From 1954 to 1971, international organizations operating in Taiwan spent six times as much as the Kuomintang government on health care.[74] One reason for the Kuomintang's reluctance to invest in health care and disease control is that they initially viewed Taiwan as a transitory military base from which they would eventually regain control of the whole of China.

[68] Chin 1998: 330; Raper 1953: 4 (quotation).
[69] Riggs 1952: 132–133.
[70] Kuo 2002: 19.
[71] Ku 1997: 37.
[72] Riggs 1952: 134.
[73] Raper 1953: 225; number of health stations from Yen 1973a: 9.
[74] Kuo 2002: 4–11.

In April 1949 the Sino-American Joint Commission on Rural Reconstruction (JCRR) began to operate intensively in rural Taiwan. Its "challenge from the beginning was to find things to do, and ways to do them, that would help the most people in the most lasting ways in the shortest time."[75] The JCRR helped to restore 77 rural water supply plants, aiding about 200,000 rural people; supported the training of rural public health nurses and midwives; and funded malaria research and subsidized malaria prevention stations.[76] It also opened village and town health stations, one of which in 1952 was staffed by a doctor, two midwives, two assistant nurses, one sanitation inspector and malaria technician, and one clerk. The health station midwives delivered about 75 babies per year, carried out regular postnatal home visits (prenatal calls were rarer), and taught new skills and sanitary practices to other midwives in the township. Health station personnel also educated the populace, especially teachers, about health and hygiene. They operated clinics, dispensed medicine, administered inoculations, inspected food shops and restaurants, and examined school children twice a year.[77] By early 1953, 366 health stations were operating.[78] Most were initially placed in houses, temples, or malaria control units, but by 1960 about half of such stations had been replaced by new free-standing facilities.[79] In late 1952, the JCRR asked inhabitants in 16 rural towns whether they thought that "present medical care is better" than in either 1937 or 1948. Fully 66 percent replied that it was better than in 1937, and 75 percent replied that it was better than in 1948.[80]

The government and JCRR sponsored pilot malaria control projects in the early 1950s, and followed them up with an island-wide DDT-spraying program from 1953 to 1957. Program leaders mobilized school teachers and principals to explain and popularize the initiative and to teach residents how to avoid the chemical. Between 1952 and 1957, the share of 2 to 7 year-old children testing positive for the malaria plasmodium fell from 10 percent to a small fraction of 1 percent, while the number of reported malaria cases fell from more than 1.2 million in 1950 to 558 in 1958. Surveillance continued until 1965, when the World Health Organization certified that Taiwan was free of malaria.[81] By the 1950s, however, malaria, which had been the leading cause of death in Taiwan before World War I, was no longer among the top ten causes.[82] As significant for public health were immunization campaigns by the government, in collaboration with international organizations, against tuberculosis, smallpox, polio, diphtheria, pertussis, tetanus, and cholera.[83]

---

[75] Raper 1953: 63.
[76] Riggs 1952: 135–136.
[77] Raper 1953: 224–233; see also Kirby 1960: 128.
[78] Raper 1953: 225.
[79] Kuo 2002: 11.
[80] Raper 1953: 224.
[81] Kirby 1960: 27; Yip 2000: 122–124.
[82] Kuo 2002: 14.
[83] Taiwan. CDC 2000.

A study of health station records in the mid-1960s found deficiencies in these campaigns, but the incidence of vaccine-preventable diseases fell rapidly after immunization programs were implemented throughout the island.[84] The disease control initiatives of the 1950s contributed to a significant decline of infant mortality, from about 110 per 1000 at the beginning of the decade to 54 per 1000 in 1960 (Section 7.2).

Public health care initiatives lost momentum in the 1960s. From 1964 to 1970 the government limited health spending to 3.5 percent of the budget, and no cabinet-level health ministry existed until 1972.[85] Nurses and hospital beds per 10,000 population stagnated during the 1960s, while the ratio of doctors to population declined.[86] The health stations depended heavily on funding from international sources, and when U.S. aid ended in 1965, the rural health system deteriorated. In the early 1970s, however, international setbacks and a limited political opening provided the impetus for renewed emphasis on public health (Section 7.5). In 1972 the government created a cabinet-level Ministry of Health and doubled first-year medical enrollment from 600 to 1200, and in 1973 the Kuomintang launched a four-year program to improve rural health.[87] In 1975, the government began to require medical graduates who had received state scholarships to serve for six years in remote areas or understaffed medical branches.[88] The number of nurses per 10,000 inhabitants quadrupled during the 1970s and tripled again in the 1980s.[89] Meanwhile, the government in 1984 launched a program to immunize infants against hepatitis B, reducing its prevalence in children under six years old from 11 to 2 percent.[90] Health station staffing and equipment also improved after 1980. By 2000 each station averaged one to two doctors, and health stations had X-ray machines and similar equipment even in remote areas. In 1997, 99.7 percent of Taiwanese births were assisted by trained personnel, and expectant mothers received an average of nine prenatal checkups for each childbirth.[91]

Total spending on health care in Taiwan in 2005 was 5.9 percent of GDP, up from 3.3 percent in 1980 (Table A15). Until 1995, when National Health Insurance raised the public share to 64 percent, private sources contributed about 50 percent of such spending.[92] Many Taiwanese, especially the uninsured, relied on private-sector pharmacists for medical advice, and most of the island's outpatient clinics, which numbered more than 15,000 by 1995,

---

[84] Shen 1970: 219–220; Taiwan. CDC 2000. On deficiencies in the immunization programs see Yen 1971: 163.

[85] Kuo 2002: 7.

[86] Calculated from Taiwan. CEPD 2007: 24, 293, 303.

[87] Chiang 1997: 227–228 (enrollment); Kuo 2002: 18–20.

[88] Taiwan. GIO 2003a.

[89] Calculated from Taiwan: CEPD 2007: 24, 293.

[90] 15–20 percent of Taiwanese test positive for hepatitis B, one of the world's highest rates. Taiwan. GIO 2003b.

[91] Lee 2001; Taiwan. GIO 2002.

[92] Chow 2001: 31.

were privately run.[93] The government oversaw these facilities closely, however. Private clinics had to be authorized by the local health station, which inspected them periodically and required them to maintain high standards in order to have their licenses renewed.[94] More than in Chile or Costa Rica, primary health care in Taiwan often required out-of-pocket expenditures for user fees in public hospitals and clinics as well as for private services, and even the 1995 National Health Insurance plan required significant co-payments.[95] Rapidly rising and evenly distributed incomes gave the Taiwanese the money they needed to access primary health care services. In the mid-1990s Taiwanese averaged more than 12 physician visits per year, one of the highest rates in the world.[96]

By the 1990s, however, health care provision and health insurance were encountering financial problems. Health care spending rose faster than GDP in the 1980s (Tables A3 and A15), and contributory health insurance schemes for government employees, private-sector workers, and farmers ran large deficits, partly because these insurance plans required no co-payments for doctor visits. In the early 1990s, nearly half of total health spending went to drugs and injections, which doctors were allowed to sell. Doctors derived most of their income from the sale of these medicines, which were heavily over-prescribed. Health personnel and facilities were insufficient in rural areas; the multiple-payer system with decentralized administration detracted from the economies of scale and volume purchasing advantages typically enjoyed by single-payer systems; the multiplicity of insurance schemes with different modes of funding and levels of benefits impeded the goals of equity and social solidarity; and many patients sought routine care at hospitals rather than primary care facilities.[97]

The National Health Insurance program introduced in 1995 was designed to make health care provision more equitable by covering the 40 percent of Taiwanese who were still uninsured. The other goals of the program were to reduce the burden of health expenditures on individuals and families; to strengthen the financial condition of the public health system; and to improve health care and health status.[98] Two-thirds of the program's funding came from payroll taxes; the remainder came from public revenue generated partly by lottery, wine, and cigarette taxes. The insured had free choice of providers, including practitioners of Chinese as well as Western medicine.[99] All of the insured were entitled to similar benefits, which included expensive services like organ transplants, anti-retroviral therapy for HIV-positive patients, care for

---

[93] Chi 1994: 313–314; Liu and Lee 1998: 5–6.
[94] Taiwan. GIO 2003a.
[95] Chen, Wen, and Li 2001: 37; Chen, Liu, and Chen 2003: 110; Chiang 1997: 229–232.
[96] Chiang 1997: 237.
[97] Cheng 2003: 62–63; Chiang 1997: 230–237; Chow 2001: 32–33; Lin 1994: 3–5; Lu and Hsiao 2003: 78.
[98] Liu and Lee 1998: 15.
[99] Chiang 1997: 229–230; Chow 2001: 35.

premature infants, and treatment for serious or terminal illnesses.[100] Premiums varied by income status and occupation: low income households paid nothing; most wage and salary earners paid 30 percent; teachers and government employees paid 40 percent; and the self-employed paid 100 percent.[101]

The introduction of National Health Insurance had several positive consequences. Its cost was initially put at U.S. $9.6 billion per year, or about $500 per capita, a remarkably low level given that life expectancy and infant mortality were about the same in Taiwan as in the United States, which in 1996 spent about $4,300 per capita on health care.[102] Only 2.6 percent of Taiwan's total health care spending went to administration, a lower share than in most other industrialized economies.[103] After the National Health Insurance plan was introduced, health facility usage rose much faster among the previously uninsured than among the previously insured, suggesting that the program satisfied unmet demand for health services.[104] The new insurance plan signed contracts with a much higher proportion of hospitals (97 percent) and clinics (90 percent) than had previous insurance schemes, giving patients more choice. Surveys show that the plan expanded medical care in aboriginal areas and in outlying islands, where many of the poorest Taiwanese lived.[105] Reported satisfaction with National Health Insurance rose from just over 30 percent in April 1995 (soon after it was introduced) to nearly 80 percent in January 1998.[106]

National Health Insurance was not a panacea. In 1995, 32 percent of Taiwanese mothers gave birth by cesarean section, much higher than the 10–15 percent recommended by the World Health Organization.[107] The rate rose even higher after the advent of National Health Insurance, which reduced the out-of-pocket costs of the procedure and reimbursed cesarean births at twice the rate of ordinary births. Use of expensive prenatal services like ultrasound rose sharply after National Health Insurance began, above the levels regarded as necessary for adequate care.[108] One consequence of the widespread use of ultrasound, given the preexisting son preference among many Taiwanese, was a rise in the ratio of male to female births (especially among higher-order parities), although the increase was not as dramatic as in contemporary South Korea.[109] Health care costs rose sharply after 1995 because of a rapid rise in the demand for health services and because National Health Insurance reimbursed providers for most services at a higher rate than previous health

100 Taiwan. GIO 2003a.
101 Liu and Lee 1998: 28.
102 Taiwan: Liu 1998: 9; USA: PAHO 2000a.
103 Chow 2001: 34.
104 Chen, Wen, and Li 2001: 41.
105 Chen, Liu, and Chen 2003: 111.
106 Chiang 1997: 233; Chow 2001: 36.
107 Liu 1998: 9.
108 Chen, Wen, and Li 2001: 37–38, 41.
109 Croll 2001: 231.

insurance schemes had.[110] More resources devoted to health care, however, resulted in better access to health care for the previously uninsured.

7.5. Taiwan: Determinants of Public Health Care Policies

Contributing to rapid infant mortality decline in Taiwan from 1960 to 2005 were not only fast economic growth and low income inequality, but also the public provision of basic health services. Encouraging the provision of such services were international agencies, especially in the 1950s; competition between communism and anti-communism; efforts to defuse tension between recent migrants from the mainland and Taiwan-born Chinese; and the Kuomintang's search for expanded popular support, especially after political opposition emerged in the 1970s.

International agencies and personnel were critical to Taiwanese health care initiatives during the late 1940s and throughout the 1950s. From 1954 to 1971 the Kuomintang reportedly devoted to health care only one-sixth as much money as was earmarked for this purpose by various international aid organizations, including the Sino-American Joint Commission on Rural Reconstruction (JCRR), the World Health Organization, UNICEF, and the Rockefeller Foundation. Representatives from these groups "were not just consultants. They decided which policies should be incorporated in this plan and be given priority." The JCRR provided much of the impetus and most of the financing for the rural health stations set up in the late 1940s and early 1950s. Dr. Harold W. Brown, on sabbatical from the Columbia University College of Physicians and Surgeons, founded a health station in Taipei in 1958 that helped to modernize public health education on the island. The Rockefeller Foundation, World Health Organization, JCRR, and United States International Cooperation Administration (a precursor of the United States Agency for International Development) organized the malaria eradication campaign that began in 1952. At this time the chief of Taiwan's Health Department, an agency within the Ministry of the Interior, was "not a director in the traditional sense of politics, but functioned more like a liaison person between the U.S. Aid institutes and the ruling KMT [Kuomintang] in Taiwan." The purpose of these health interventions, from the U.S. government point of view, was mainly to contribute to the island's economic development and thus to further U.S. strategic objectives in the cold war.[111]

A major challenge for the Kuomintang after its retreat to Taiwan in the mid-1940s, and especially after its army's February 1947 massacre of some 8,000 Taiwanese, was to gain acceptance from the locals.[112] Another of its challenges, shared by the JCRR, was to dissuade peasants from turning to

[110] Chiang 1997: 235.
[111] Kuo 2002: 9–11, 18–20. Quotations from pp. 9 and 20 respectively.
[112] Wong 2004: 56.

communism, as had recently happened on the mainland.[113] The initial wave
of contributory insurance programs in the 1950s, particularly the labor insurance scheme, "was widely regarded in Taiwan as an appeasement measure to
avoid potential worker revolts."[114] A comparative analysis of labor and social
welfare policies in the East Asian newly industrializing countries finds that
Taiwan developed a more "proactive" social policy than South Korea in the
second half of the twentieth century in part because of "the Kuomintang's
desire to achieve political legitimacy in its new insular home and, thus, to
avoid the political catastrophe it had suffered on the mainland."[115] During
the 1960s, however, particularly after U.S. foreign aid ended in 1965, public
health care initiatives declined. Because the Kuomintang continued to perceive
Taiwan as a way-station from which to retake the mainland, its leaders continued to pay limited attention to public health care on the island itself.[116] To the
extent that inhabitants exerted any pressure for health service improvement,
authoritarianism made it easier for the government to ignore them.[117]

From 1949 to 1996, when Taiwan held its first direct presidential election, the island had only four rulers: General Chiang Kai-shek until his death
in 1975, interim President Yen Chia-kan from 1975 to 1978; Chiang's son
Chiang Ching-kuo until his death in 1988, and Lee Teng-hui from 1988 to
1996 (Lee also won the direct presidential election of 1996 and served until
2000). Each of these presidents came from the Kuomintang, which dominated the island's political system. The Kuomintang permitted "satellite"
parties to operate and let their candidates compete in certain local elections,
but suppressed any vocal opposition and tightly controlled interest groups.[118]
Internally, despite its intense anti-communism, the Kuomintang retained until
the late 1980s the Leninist organization imparted to it in 1923 by an agent of
the Comintern.[119] Martial law was in effect from 1949 to 1987. The national
executive, particularly the president (who under the Chiangs was also the head
of the Kuomintang), dominated the legislative and judicial branches.

During the 1970s, the Kuomintang transited from "hard" to "soft"
authoritarianism.[120] Taiwan lost its seat at the United Nations in 1971; the
United States acknowledged that "Taiwan is a part of China" in 1972, and
the U.S. government broke diplomatic ties in 1978. As these international
setbacks mounted, authoritarianism became less harsh. After 1972, when
President Chiang Kai-shek appointed his son Chiang Ching-kuo as prime
minister, growing numbers of Taiwanese joined the Kuomintang, which had
previously been dominated by mainlanders; the press gained more freedom;

[113] Raper 1953: 63; Shen 1970: 13.
[114] Goodman and Peng 1996: 205.
[115] Deyo 1992: 53.
[116] Kuo 2002: 4–5, 8, 21; Goodman and Peng 1996: 206.
[117] Chow 2001: 5; Deyo 1992: 53.
[118] Tien 1992: 5–7.
[119] Spence 1990: 337–338; Tien 1992: 5, 10–11.
[120] Winckler 1984.

non-Kuomintang candidates began to win legislative seats; and public protest (e.g., against local electoral fraud) became more frequent.[121] As opposition mounted, government officials began to worry that families facing rising
health care costs – public hospitals and health stations imposed fees – might
turn against the regime.[122] In response to these concerns, the government in
the early and mid-1970s created a ministry of health, stepped up the training
of medical personnel, launched a four-year program to improve rural health,
and required beneficiaries of medical scholarships to work for six years in
underserved areas or in understaffed medical branches (Section 7.4). Further
regime liberalization took place in the 1980s, which saw the growth of social
movements, civic groups, and opposition periodicals. In 1986 the Democratic
Progressive Party was established as the Kuomintang's chief rival, and in 1987
martial law was lifted. The Kuomintang democratized internally in the late
1980s and early 1990s, when legislators formally representing mainland provinces were forced to resign.[123] Taiwan held its first fully competitive legislative
election in 1992, and its first free direct presidential election in 1996. The winner of the 1996 contest was the incumbent President Lee Teng-hui. In 2000
Chen Shui-ban, the candidate of the opposition Democratic Progressive Party,
became Taiwan's first non-Kuomintang president.

Cultural changes associated with modernization, including a fall in average
family size and a decline in the propensity of middle-aged Taiwanese to support their elderly relatives, contributed to the decision by the Kuomintang to
expand social insurance in the 1980s and 1990s.[124] Still, the rise of electoral
competition and the lifting of restrictions on interest-group activity in the late
1970s and early 1980s also created incentives for such expansion. In the early
1980s, the Kuomintang created a health insurance scheme for government
employees, in part to maintain the support of village heads and city council
members who delivered votes in local elections.[125] Vote-seeking by incumbent
politicians contributed to the rapid rise in the coverage of this scheme from
1.0 million in 1989 to 1.7 million in 1992. The health insurance program for
farmers, established in 1989, has been linked to the Kuomintang's efforts "to
enhance its support among the crucial, forthcoming electorate of the masses
of farmers," as well as to compete more effectively in elections against the
newly formed Democratic Progressive Party. An intense lobbying campaign
by farmers themselves also played a role.[126]

The Democratic Progressive Party formed in 1986 criticized the Kuomintang
for neglecting social policies and advocated national health insurance "as
a critical indicator of a 'good' government and a modernized nation." The

---

[121] Omestad 1988: 185.
[122] Chiang 1997: 227–228.
[123] Tien 1992.
[124] Chow 2001: 26.
[125] Chow 2001: 23.
[126] Aspalter 2002: 60–62, 63 (quotation); Goodman and Peng 1996: 218 fn. 28; Son
2003: 470–471.

Kuomintang initially resisted, but soon acquiesced and even advanced the target year for the plan from 2000 to 1995, hoping "that the chaos resulting from the implementation might fade away prior to the elections" of March 1996.[127] One observer has argued that Taiwan would have introduced National Health Insurance earlier had democratization occurred sooner, and that "social welfare programs were speeded up by partisan competition for voter support during the periodic elections" of the late 1980s and early 1990s.[128] Another observer has noted that employed people who were not wage-earners, who made up 42 percent of the population, gained health insurance coverage shortly before the first direct presidential election in 1996, and argues that vote-seeking provided a major incentive for the extension.[129] Moreover, the absence of private health insurance facilitated the introduction of the National Health Insurance scheme by relieving the government of the need to "fight against an entrenched private health insurance industry,"[130] as in Argentina or Brazil.

Democratization encouraged the expansion of health insurance coverage in the 1980s and 1990s, but the tempo of this insurance expansion was out of phase with the tempo of infant mortality decline (Table A1). Taiwan in 1980 already had an infant mortality rate of only 24 per 1000, even though social insurance still covered no more than 16 percent of the population. Moreover, mothers who were still uninsured in 1995 were likely to have run a higher risk of infant death than mothers who gained coverage during the 1980s, so if health insurance had influenced infant mortality decline, such decline should have been steeper from 1995 to 2005 than from 1980 to 1990 (it was not). Contributing more significantly to infant mortality decline seem to have been the opening of rural health stations and the control of infectious diseases in the 1950s; the sharp decline of income poverty in the 1960s and 1970s (which allowed many of the initially poor to pay for either public or private health care); public provision of primary and secondary education; a strong family planning program as of 1964; and improved rural health services during the 1970s. International influences and national security concerns encouraged these policies, but the Kuomintang's search for a popular mandate was also involved, particularly in the 1970s. After Indonesia, Taiwan from 1960 to 2005 was the most deeply and persistently authoritarian of the eight cases studied in this book (Table A18). Even so, the Kuomintang recognized that the extension of basic health services could help to produce acquiescence to the regime, without which the exercise of authoritarian rule would have been more costly.

---

[127] Chiang 1997: 228–229.
[128] Chow 2001: 6 (quotation), 18, 34, 42. Cheng (2003) makes a similar argument.
[129] Son 2003: 463–464.
[130] Lin 1994: 4.

8

South Korea: Small Welfare State, Fast Infant Mortality Decline

South Korea and Taiwan fared differently on mortality in the 1950s. In Taiwan, the Sino-American Joint Commission on Rural Reconstruction introduced primary health care and disease control initiatives that contributed to rapid mortality decline. In Korea, war in the early 1950s cost nearly 3 million lives, including nearly a million civilian dead in South Korea. The stark difference in the fortunes of the two societies helps to explain why, in 1960, infant mortality was 54 per 1000 in Taiwan, but 90 per 1000 in South Korea.

After recovering from the Korean War, South Korean governments, which were semi-democratic during the 1950s and 1960s but highly authoritarian from 1972 to 1986, relied in their efforts to improve the well-being of the population not only on "shared growth" – a rapid rise in GDP per capita coupled with an even distribution of income – but also on the provision of basic social services. Working together to improve the well-being of the initially poor were the public provision of primary and secondary education after the late 1950s, family planning after the mid-1960s, water and sanitation after the early 1970s, and maternal and infant care after the late 1970s. A combination of shared growth and social provisioning, rather than shared growth alone, explains why, from 1960 to 2005, South Korea had the steepest infant mortality decline and the lowest 2005 infant mortality level among the eight societies compared in this book.

Relative to shared growth, the public provision of basic social services was even more important to reducing infant mortality in South Korea than in Taiwan. In South Korea in 2005 infant mortality was 27 percent lower than predicted by GDP per capita, income inequality, ethnic homogeneity, fertility, population density, and urbanization taken together; in Taiwan infant mortality was 5 percent higher (Table 11.2). South Korea's low infant mortality rate, relative to its socioeconomic circumstances, was due not to high public spending on health care or to broad social insurance coverage, but to the effective public provision of basic social services – not just education, whose contribution to South Korea's development achievements is widely recognized, but also family planning, water and sanitation, and maternal and infant health care and nutrition.

South Korea was highly authoritarian from 1972 to 1986, but it was semi-democratic in the 1950s and in some respects from 1963 to 1972 (Table A18). Indeed, General Park's near defeat in a 1971 presidential election contributed to his government's decision, after imposing martial law in 1972, to expand the public provision of maternal and infant health care and nutritional assistance in rural areas. Even in South Korea, then, which might seem at first thought to be a poster society for the conjectures that wealthier is healthier and that authoritarianism promotes mortality decline, democratic aspects of the political regime before 1972 encouraged effective social provisioning, which in turn contributed significantly to the rapid decline of infant mortality.

8.1. South Korea: Mortality

South Korea among the eight societies compared in this book had the lowest infant mortality level in 2005. At 4.6 per 1000 it was 30th lowest among the 189 countries for which the World Bank provided an infant mortality estimate, and was 30 percent below the rate in the United States (6.9 per 1000). In 2005 life expectancy at birth, at 78.4 years, was second-highest among the eight cases, 37th among 181 countries for which the World Bank provided a life expectancy estimate, and almost a year longer than in the United States (77.7 years). On progress at reducing mortality from 1960 to 2005, South Korea ranked first among the eight cases at both infant mortality decline and life expectancy rise (Tables A1 and A2). Among all countries with data South Korea turned in one of the world's best performances over this 46-year period, ranking third of 145 on percent decline of infant mortality and sixth of 170 at percent rise of life expectancy.[1]

From 1940 to 1960 infant mortality fell from 156 to 90 per 1000 in South Korea (the 1940 figure is for Korea before partition), but from 129 to 54 per 1000 in Taiwan.[2] Infant mortality fell less steeply during this era in South Korea than in Taiwan in part because of the Korean War, which killed 5 percent of the civilian population and destroyed 25 percent of physical capital,[3] and in part because of the sanitation, disease control, and primary care programs enacted in Taiwan by the Sino-American Joint Commission on Rural Reconstruction (Section 7.4), which had no counterpart in South Korea. In South Korea after 1960, infant mortality fell steeply in the 1960s, very steeply in the 1970s, steeply again in the 1980s and early 1990s, and slowly from 1995 to 2005 (Table A1).[4] Fast economic growth and low income inequality, along with demographic and cultural factors, help to explain South Korea's low level of infant mortality in 2005, its steep fall of infant mortality from 1960

[1] Calculated from World Bank 2008e, except Taiwan (Tables A1 and A2). Change calculated as in Tables A1 and A2.
[2] 1960 figures: Table A1. 1940 figures: Korea from Kwon 1986: 12 (interpolated from life table estimates for 1935–1939 and 1940–1944); Taiwan from Mirzaee 1979: 228.
[3] Adelman 1996: 4.
[4] Web Appendix A1 (McGuire 2009) evaluates South Korean infant mortality data.

to 2005, and the tempo of its infant mortality decline within that period, but South Korea, it will be argued, outdid even the very successful performance that would be expected on the basis of these income-related factors alone.

8.2. South Korea: Affluence, Inequality, and Poverty

Economic growth was slow in South Korea from the end of World War II to the end of the Korean War, due not only to the devastation of the war itself, but also to the need to incorporate 6 million migrants, mostly from the North, into a part of the country that had previously included no more than 20 million inhabitants. South Korea's population density doubled from 1944 to 1955.[5] Economic growth remained sluggish from 1953 to 1961, averaging only about 1 percent per year. Much of this growth was financed by U.S. foreign aid, which contributed 7–12 percent of GNP during this era.[6] By 1960, South Korea had attained a GDP per capita of $1,458. Although highest among the four Asian cases, this figure was below the GDPs per capita of Guinea and Senegal and far below the GDP per capita of each of the four Latin American societies (Table A3).

From 1960 to 2003 South Korean GDP per capita grew at an average annual rate of 6.0 percent, second-fastest (after Taiwan) among 98 societies for which data are available.[7] By 2003 South Korea's GDP per capita was $17,597, second only to Taiwan's among the eight societies compared in this book (Table A3). The reasons for this spectacular economic growth were similar in both places: land reform in the early 1950s, investment in basic education from the 1950s onward, the promotion of labor-intensive manufactured exports in the 1960s, and the maintenance throughout the period of cautious economic policies. (South Korea, it must be conceded, fell a bit short on the latter front, devoting enormous resources to building expensive heavy and chemical industries in the 1970s, and later opening capital markets too abruptly to massive and skittish foreign portfolio investment in the 1990s.) Shaping and constraining these policies in South Korea were, as in Taiwan, a dearth of natural resources, the weakness of class organizations, aspects of the legacy of Japanese colonialism, and a strong perceived communist threat after the end of World War II.[8]

The infant mortality rate in South Korea in 2005 was far below the level predicted by the country's GDP per capita, and the decline of infant mortality from 1960 to 2005 was even steeper than predicted by the country's strong GDP per capita growth (Figures 1.1 and 1.2). Within the period from 1960 to 2005 the tempo of GDP per capita growth was correlated with the tempo of infant mortality decline, but not strongly (Table 11.1). In particular,

[5] Chung 1979: 496.
[6] Adelman 1996: 4.
[7] Heston, Summers, and Aten 2006, variable RGDPCH (see Table A3).
[8] McGuire 1995a.

infant mortality fell more steeply during the 1970s, when economic growth was moderately fast and income inequality rose, than during the 1980s, when economic growth was very fast and income inequality fell (Tables A3 and A4). GDP per capita growth and changes in income inequality affected the steepness and tempo of infant mortality decline from 1960 to 2005, as well as the level of infant mortality in 2005, but do not provide a complete explanation for any of these outcomes.

South Korea from 1960 to 2005 had, after Taiwan, the second-lowest level of income inequality among the eight cases examined in this book (Table A4). Low income inequality in South Korea, as in Taiwan, resulted partly from land reform in the decade after World War II, and partly from the transfer to state control of properties previously owned by colonialists. In South Korea alone, however, massive destruction during the Korean War in the early 1950s resulted in "a very substantial leveling of real asset ownership."[9] In the 1960s, moreover, the Park Chung Hee government spent heavily on public works projects and on subsidies for manufactured exports. Both of these areas of economic activity employed large numbers of workers per unit of capital invested. Such labor-intensive production, along with the expansion of education during the previous decade, helped to keep inequality low in the 1960s.[10] Income inequality rose significantly during the 1970s, when land tenancy increased and industrialization became more capital-intensive. Even during the 1970s, however, income inequality was far lower in South Korea than in most other countries.[11] Rapid economic growth in the context of low income inequality produced a swift decline of income poverty. According to one study, the share of South Koreans below the national income poverty line fell from 41 percent in 1965 to 16 percent in 1975.[12] Another study estimated that the poverty headcount had declined from 20 percent in 1975 to 7 percent in 1995 (Table A5). Corroborating these rapid declines of income poverty, the share of household expenditure devoted to food purchases fell from 56 percent in 1966 to 27 percent in 1993.[13]

From 1960 to 2005, then, South Korea enjoyed fast economic growth, low income inequality, and plummeting income poverty. Even together, however, these factors do not entirely explain why South Korea ended up in 2005 with such a low level of infant mortality. When infant mortality is regressed on GDP per capita and income inequality across 102 developing countries with available data for 2005, South Korea's predicted infant mortality level is 9.0 per 1000 – almost twice as high as its observed level of 4.6 per 1000. When

[9] Haggard 1990: 225.
[10] Adelman 1996: 3–8.
[11] Averaging the Gini indices obtained from "good" quality surveys in the period from roughly 1960 to 1990, Deininger and Squire (1996: 574–577) estimated that South Korea had a Gini index of 34.2, 26th lowest among 116 countries. Only Nepal, Taiwan, and 24 communist or rich capitalist countries had lower average Gini indices.
[12] Kwon 1993.
[13] Adelman 1996: Table 3.

five cultural, geographical, and demographic variables are added to the right-hand side of the model as predictors, the predicted rate is still 6.8 per 1000 (Table 11.2). Economic factors alone do no better at explaining the progress or tempo of infant mortality decline from 1960 to 2005 than they do at explaining the level of infant mortality in 2005. From 1960 to 2005, infant mortality fell 38 percent more steeply than was predicted by the rise of GDP per capita during this era (Table 11.1). Within this period, the tempo of infant mortality decline was often inconsistent with the tempo of economic growth: infant mortality fell most steeply in the 1970s, when GDP per capita growth was slower than in the 1980s. A more complete explanation for the level of infant mortality in South Korea in 2005, as well as for the pace and tempo of infant mortality decline from 1960 to 2005, requires an analysis of the scope and quality of the public provision of social services during this period.

8.3. South Korea: Education, Family Planning, Safe Water, and Sanitation

The South Korean government in 1997 spent about 6.1 percent of GDP on "education, health, social security and welfare, housing and community amenities, recreation, culture, and religious affairs."[14] This share was about the same as in Taiwan, but only about half as large as the proportion expended in Chile or Costa Rica, and only about a quarter as large as the share spent in Argentina or Brazil. From 1960 onward, state policy-makers in South Korea provided social services mainly to complement and promote economic development, rather than to redistribute resources or to improve the well-being of the poor.[15] The subordination of social welfare to economic growth was especially pronounced from 1960 to 1977, when governments relied mostly on rising incomes and on the extended family to take care of the needy. By the late 1970s, however, discontent among the relatively deprived had induced the government, despite its imposition of martial law in 1972, to spend more on social welfare, using the resources generated by higher tax revenue. A brief but sharp recession in 1980–1981 curtailed social spending for the next few years,[16] but by the end of the 1980s, thanks in part to democratization and associated electoral incentives, almost all South Koreans had government-mandated health insurance, and most had government-mandated retirement pensions.

Although frugal in total amount, South Korean social spending was targeted heavily to the poor and destitute. In December 1961, the military government of General Park Chung Hee introduced the Livelihood Protection Act, which created a means-tested social assistance program covering the working poor and those unable to work due to age or disability.[17] From its inception in

---

[14] UNESCAP 2003: 230–231.
[15] Ramesh 1995b: 50, 56–57; Tang 2000: 95–98.
[16] Suh 1985: 16–17; Yeon 1989: 3.
[17] Haggard and Kaufman 2008: 136.

1961 to the early 1990s, this program provided food, cash for fuel, and tuition exemptions for junior high school to about 5 percent of the population, with 60 to 80 percent of recipients living in rural areas. The whole package was worth about two-thirds of a poverty-line income per month. Not all of the poor were covered, budgetary constraints limited participation, and residency requirements made it hard for migrants to receive benefits, but the program probably improved the nutrition, schooling, and health of some of the most impoverished Koreans.[18] In October 2000 the Livelihood Protection Act was effectively supplanted by the Minimum Living Standards Security Act, which tripled the share of the population eligible for assistance.[19]

Reinforcing the progressivity of South Korean social spending, few citizens before the late 1970s had contributory social insurance, which is often regressive. In 1976 state-subsidized contributory medical insurance covered only 67,000 people, and before democratization in the late 1980s only civil servants (as of 1961), military personnel (as of 1963), and private school teachers (as of 1975) had state-mandated pensions.[20] Health insurance in the late 1970s was mildly redistributive, and retirement insurance in the late 1980s had "a small income-equalizing component favouring lower-income pensioners."[21] Universities, which catered mostly to the upper middle classes and the rich, absorbed less than 10 percent of public education spending in both 1980 and 1995, a much lower share than in any of the four Latin American cases.[22] Public spending on housing, however, was regressive. So was the tax system, which depended heavily on value-added and other indirect taxes and suffered from widespread evasion.[23]

The Confucian emphasis on education and the adoption from China of the examination system for civil service posts encouraged schooling in premodern Korea. Public education dates back at least to the Koryo dynasty (918–1392). A national academy was founded in 982, and King Injon in 1127 ordered every prefecture in the country to establish a school. Schooling was confined mainly to the upper classes and almost exclusively to males, but literacy was probably higher in premodern Korea than in most other premodern societies.[24] After 1910, the Japanese colonial rulers expanded primary education in an effort to win the allegiance of young people and to teach them "how to live in modern society."[25] Accordingly, the number of students enrolled at all levels rose from 111,000 in 1910 to 1,777,000 in 1945. By the end of World War II about 45 percent of the population in the southern half of the country was literate – about the same share as in Brazil, which at the time was a much

---

[18] Friedman and Hausman 1993: 148–152; Ramesh 1995a: 232; Yi 2003: 31–32.
[19] Moon and Yang 2002: 148.
[20] On medical insurance see Son 1998: 21; on pensions see Kwon 1993: 159.
[21] Kwon 1993: 300–305 (on health insurance); Ramesh 1995a: 230 (quotation).
[22] UNESCAP 2003: 232. For the Latin American shares, see UNDP 1993: 164.
[23] On housing see Tang 2000: 97–98; on the tax system see Kwon 1993: 221–228.
[24] Seth 2002: 9–12.
[25] Tsurumi 1977: 160.

richer society.[26] A 1938 survey of 1,225 farm families in eight provinces of present-day South Korea revealed that 91 percent of such families had at least one member who could read and write.[27] Only about 5 percent of children received more than a primary education, however, and at the end of colonial rule only 14 percent of Koreans had any formal schooling whatsoever.[28]

Schooling and literacy increased dramatically in Korea during the U.S. occupation from 1945 to 1948. One estimate suggests that elementary school enrollment as a share of the appropriate age group rose from 40 to 70 percent during this period, while secondary enrollment rose sixfold from 1945 to 1947. During the same period a series of literacy campaigns, organized mostly by the leftist People's Enlightenment Movement, reportedly raised the literacy rate from 23 to 71 percent of the adult population – until being halted by political purges carried out by the U.S. Army Military Government in Korea.[29] The 71 percent literacy figure for 1947 may well be overstated (Table A6 gives an identical figure for literacy in 1960), but this unheralded Korean literacy campaign may have been even more effective than Castro's far more widely touted campaign in Cuba in 1961.[30]

Education received a major setback during the Korean War, when enrollments fell at all levels and when some 80 percent of educational facilities were damaged or destroyed. After the war, however, progress continued. From 1954 to 1959 the Rhee government implemented a major primary and lower-secondary school-building program.[31] The South Korean constitution of 1949 made elementary education free and compulsory, and both elementary and junior high school enrollment rose by 62 percent from 1953 to 1960. Moreover, whereas the number of boys in elementary school doubled from 1945 to 1960, the number of girls quadrupled, reducing gender bias at the primary level and contributing to lower fertility and infant mortality rates during the 1960s and 1970s. Targeting scarce educational resources to non-elites, the government focused public spending on elementary and junior high schools, leaving senior high school and university education mainly to the private sector. Indeed, worried that the country was producing more college graduates than the economy could absorb, the Rhee government in the late 1950s tightened accreditation standards and revoked a rule exempting college students from military service.[32]

---

[26] Korean enrollment and literacy figures from Henderson 1968: 89; Brazilian figure interpolated from Astorga and Fitzgerald 1998: 32.

[27] Ban, Moon, and Perkins 1980: 312.

[28] Kim 1980: 240.

[29] Seth 2002: 45–46, 91.

[30] On the Cuban literacy campaign see Fagen 1969: 32–68. That campaign reportedly raised literacy (defined as the attainment of a first grade level, against the UNESCO definition of a fourth grade level) from 74 to 97 percent of the adult population (Benglesdorf 1994: 86).

[31] Haggard and Kaufman 2008: 138.

[32] Seth 2002: 78, 83, 105, 115.

Partly because of these initiatives in the 1950s, South Korea by 1960 had a very high level of educational attainment for its level of GDP per capita.[33] Progress continued from 1960 to 2005, when literacy rose from 71 to 98 percent, mean years of schooling rose from 4.3 to 10.8, and gross secondary enrollment rose from 27 to 93 percent (Tables A6, A7, and A8). From 1960 to 1973 junior high enrollment rose from 36 to 71 percent of the age-appropriate population and high school enrollment rose from 20 to 39 percent, while university enrollment remained at only 8 percent.[34] The government of General Park Chung Hee (1961–1979), like that of Syngman Rhee in the 1950s, limited access to higher education in order to preserve its quality and to reduce the supply of university graduates in the labor market. As industrialization progressed, however, the demand for college-educated employees rose, and university enrollment was allowed to expand. By 2005 the number of South Koreans enrolled in post-secondary education added up to 90 percent of 18–22 year-olds, giving South Korea the second-highest gross tertiary enrollment ratio in the world.[35]

One reason for rising school enrollment was the population's "zeal for education." The Park Chung Hee government and its successors were able to keep public spending on education low in part because parents, siblings, and students were willing to shoulder much of the cost. Poor families made extraordinary sacrifices to educate their children. Young female factory workers in the mid-1970s reported in a survey that the single most important motive they had for taking a factory job was to earn money for their siblings' education. Accordingly, public spending on education in 1995 was about 4 percent of GDP, lower than in most rich countries, but total spending on education was about 12 percent of GDP, higher than in most rich countries.[36] Quality lagged quantity, however. A government report in 1987 highlighted a range of major problems in Korean education, including excessively large schools, overcrowded classrooms, inadequate facilities, rote learning, and low teacher morale.[37] "Examination hell," notorious in Japan, was just as infernal in South Korea. Fifty high school students committed suicide in 1987 after failing college entrance exams, and a 1990 study found that 5 percent of high school students had attempted suicide and that 20 percent had contemplated it. Until democratization in 1987, schooling was pervaded by military drills and heavy-handed political indoctrination, with special emphasis on anti-communism.[38]

From 1960 to 2005 the total fertility rate in South Korea fell from 5.7 to 1.1. Much of the decline took place from 1960 to 1985, by which time fertility had dropped below the replacement level of 2.1. The average annual percent

[33] Rodrik 1994: 17; World Bank 1993b: 45.
[34] Chung 1979: 524.
[35] World Bank 2008a. The figure in the United States was 82 percent.
[36] Seth 2002: 98–101, 187.
[37] Adams and Gottlieb 1993: 216.
[38] Seth 2002: 166, 244–247.

decline of the total fertility rate in South Korea from 1960 to 2005 trailed only that of Macao and Taiwan among 179 societies for which data are available.[39] By reducing the youth dependency ratio, rapid fertility decline made an important contribution to economic growth, which in turn contributed to fertility decline "in a virtuous cycle of cumulative causation."[40] At the household level, studies in the 1980s found a close association between lower fertility and lower infant mortality, mediated in part by longer intervals between births.[41]

Rapid modernization contributed to the steep decline of desired fertility in South Korea. Economic growth, the rising age of marriage, changing norms and values conducive to smaller family size, parents' growing desire to educate their children, and a rapid rise in employment opportunities for urban women encouraged parents to want fewer children.[42] A national family planning program, meanwhile, permitted a plunge in unwanted fertility. After the Korean War, the Rhee government sponsored some 400 small-scale rural development projects, several of which included a family planning component.[43] In 1957, Methodist agencies opened family planning clinics in cities. In general, however, the Rhee government took a pronatalist stance, rejecting more systematic family planning and ratifying Japanese laws against abortion and contraceptive distribution. Nevertheless, social scientists in the late 1950s began to advocate a national family planning program and private doctors began to provide family planning services.[44] After seizing power in a 1961 military coup, General Park and his collaborators proved more receptive than their predecessors to the argument that unchecked population growth could threaten long-term economic development. In December 1961 they launched a national family planning program.[45]

The government approached the family planning program "much like a military campaign," setting numerical objectives for the distribution of various types of contraceptives and monitoring whether the goals had been met.[46] Men as well as women were targeted. Military reservists were urged to consider vasectomy, and condoms were distributed in factories. The government bolstered family planning in 1973 by legalizing abortion and by authorizing medical personnel other than physicians to perform fertility-related medical procedures that had previously been reserved for licensed doctors. Despite administrative fragmentation, high field worker turnover, and a bonus scheme that encouraged the overreporting of the number of contraceptives distributed,[47] the program achieved remarkable success. From 1964 to 1988

---

[39] Calculated from World Bank 2008a, except Taiwan, from Table A10.
[40] Bloom, Canning, and Malaney 2000: 283.
[41] Choe 1987; Kwon 1986.
[42] Cho and Seo 1992: 29; Mason et al. 1980: 389–390.
[43] Boyer and Ahn 1991: 30.
[44] Mason et al. 1980: 386; World Bank 1979: 120–121.
[45] Yang et al. 1965: 237.
[46] Mason et al. 1980: 390.
[47] World Bank 1979: 122–126.

the share of married couples aged 15 to 44 who used birth control rose from 9 to 77 percent,[48] and from 1962 to 1975 the practice of contraception resulted in an estimated 1.5 million births averted, a number equivalent to 45 percent of the births that took place during this period.[49] By 1980 the South Korean program was acclaimed as one of the most successful large-scale family planning initiatives ever launched.[50] This evaluation is corroborated by expert ratings. From 1972 to 1989, only China among 104 developing countries regularly ranked above South Korea in family planning effort.[51] Family planning effort tailed off after 1990, appropriately enough, considering that by 2005 the total fertility rate, as in Taiwan, had reached 1.1, barely half the replacement level (Table A10).

In 1970 only 33 percent of South Korean dwellings had piped water (Table A11), and in 1973 only about 10 percent of rural dwellers were served by centralized piped water supplies. Sanitation was no better. The practice of using untreated night soil as fertilizer was outlawed in 1968, but the law was widely flouted, particularly in impoverished areas.[52] In one rural district in 1973, 75 percent of the population was found to be suffering from enteric parasites, and in another rural district in 1974, more than half of vegetable samples were found to contain parasitic eggs.[53] In 1973–1974 there were still 600–800 cases of typhoid in South Korea, although this number was down from several thousand in the mid-1960s. Parasitic infections (as well as tuberculosis) remained widespread in rural areas in the mid-1970s, almost as prevalent as in the mid-1950s.[54] Sanitary conditions in urban areas also left much to be desired. In the early 1960s the capital city of Seoul had "poor environmental sanitation," especially in shantytowns lining the Han River, which were "unsanitary" and "overcrowded." Rapid migration from rural areas into such conditions in the cities, particularly Seoul, is said to have been responsible for a 40 percent rise in the death rate from epidemic diseases from 1962 to 1966.[55] As late as 1980, health and sanitation conditions were often better in rural areas than in the Seoul slums to which rural people often migrated.[56]

In the early 1970s the government-led New Village (Saemaul Undong) movement began to improve drainage, water supply, and sanitation in rural areas.[57] The government gave road building top priority, but villagers were also encouraged to keep streets, ditches, and gutters clean; to dig a community well; to exterminate rats; and to set up a village laundry.[58] Government

[48] Cho and Seo 1992: 27; UNFPA 1982: 35.
[49] Foreit, Koh, and Suh 1980: 79; Mason et al. 1980: 387.
[50] UNFPA 1982: 31.
[51] Ross and Mauldin 1996: 146.
[52] World Bank 1979: 138–139.
[53] Mason et al. 1980: 401.
[54] Ban, Moon, and Perkins 1980: 311.
[55] Adelman 1996: 10.
[56] Suh 1985: 6.
[57] Kwon 1986: 59; Mason et al. 1980: 400–401; Turner et al. 1993: 73–89.
[58] Boyer and Ahn 1991: 33–35; Park 1998: 55.

investment in water supply and sewerage tripled in real terms between the Third and Fourth Economic Development Plans (1972–1976, 1977–1981), and rose from 0.5 to 1.0 percent of total public investment.[59] Rural electrification also expanded rapidly. In 1970 only 27 percent of villages had electricity; by 1977 the proportion was 98 percent. Electrification was critical for water supply, because many families used electric pumps to bring water from wells into the house.[60] These water and sanitation improvements contributed to a sharp decline in cases of typhoid and parasitic infection from 1970 to 1989.[61] Nonetheless, South Korea's overall record at providing safe water and adequate sanitation was weaker than that of some of the other societies studied in this book. In 2000 only 63 percent of South Koreans had "access to improved sanitation," a proportion lower than in much poorer Brazil, Costa Rica, or Thailand.[62] In 2005 Argentina, Chile, and Costa Rica were much poorer than South Korea, but had higher shares of the population with access to an improved water source (Table A11).

From 1960 to 1980 South Korea reduced infant mortality from 90 to 16 per 1000, whereas Taiwan reduced it only from 54 to 24 per 1000. In 1980 South Korea's infant mortality rate was 33 percent lower than Taiwan's, even though its GDP per capita was much lower ($4,497 versus $5,963) and even though its Gini index was much higher (38.6 versus 27.2) (Tables A1, A3, and A4). Better public provision of basic social services, the evidence suggests, contributed significantly to the spectacular decline of infant mortality in South Korea during this period. In the 1960s the Park government markedly improved the public provision of education and family planning, and in the 1970s it made more limited progress in expanding access to safe water and adequate sanitation. As the next section will show, the Park government also improved basic health services in the 1970s, especially in rural areas. Shared growth helped the Park government reduce infant mortality steeply, to a remarkably low level, but South Korea is not simply a poster society for the wealthier is healthier conjecture.

8.4. South Korea: Nutrition and Health Care

From 1970 to 2005 total health care spending in South Korea rose from 2.5 to 5.9 percent of GDP. After adjustment for inflation, the $727 per capita that South Koreans spent on health care in 2000 was more than ten times as high as in 1970 (Table A15), although it was still fairly low in comparison to such countries as Argentina (as well as the United States, which in 2005 spent more than five times as much as South Korea on health care, but had a higher infant mortality rate). Health care spending and provision from 1960 to 1995

[59] World Bank 1979: 136.
[60] Park 1998: 104, 135.
[61] Bark 1994: 436.
[62] UNDP 2003: 254.

came more from private than from public sources,[63] but the total amount of private health care spending was low. In 1975, South Korean consumers spent 112 won on cigarettes for every 100 won they spent on health care.[64] Public health care spending was still lower: in 1973 South Korea spent less than one-fifth as much as Malaysia on public health care, even though both countries were at similar levels of affluence.[65] The public sector share rose sharply from 1977 to 1989, as the coverage of government-mandated, compulsory affiliation, not-for-profit health insurance societies rose from 15 to 96 percent of the population. The government subsidized the administrative costs of the health insurance societies and paid a share of the premiums for public employees and the self-employed. From 1970 to 2005, accordingly, the public share of health care spending rose from 20 to 55 percent of the total (Table A15). In the late 1990s, however, public facilities still provided only about 10 percent of medical services.[66]

The nutritional status of South Koreans depended in part on the production of food grains, which soared from 1945 to 1983, thanks in part to the introduction of higher-yielding rice varieties and to other technological improvements. By the mid-1960s South Korea was self-sufficient in rice. Nutritional status also depended on the acquisition by households of sufficient income to buy food. Per capita spending on food rose by 50 percent from 1960 to 1973, and by the end of the 1960s the "spring hunger" had vanished in rural areas.[67] Public food assistance also influenced the nutritional status of South Koreans, especially those in poverty. In 1953 the Rhee government introduced a national school meal program, obtaining the financial support of UNICEF, CARE, and U.S. AID. In 1973 the Park administration took full financial responsibility for the program, and by 1997 meals were offered in 89 percent of primary schools.[68] In 1961, under the Livelihood Protection Act, the state began to give free food to a small number of poor people who were unable to work.[69] In 1968 the government launched in rural areas a multidimensional Applied Nutrition Project that persisted to the end of the century.[70] Nutritional status depended, finally, on the public provision of education, health, water, and sanitation services, which affect the ability to turn food into nourishment. All of these services improved during the period analyzed, raising the nutritional status of the population. From 1960 to 2000, accordingly, calorie, protein, and micronutrient supply rose swiftly, and the height and weight of

---

[63] Chung 1979: 518; Roemer 1991: 304; World Bank 1979: 139.

[64] Park 1980: 115.

[65] Mason et al. 1980: 405. GDP per capita in 1975 was $3,384 in South Korea, compared to $3,704 in Malaysia. Heston, Summers, and Aten 2006, variable RGDPCH.

[66] Lee 2003: 50.

[67] Food production and spending: Mason et al. 1980: 398. Spring hunger: Chung 1979: 502–503. Agricultural technology: Kwon 1986: 62.

[68] Ju 2000: S196.

[69] Friedman and Hausman 1993: 150.

[70] Ju 2000: S196.

schoolchildren increased markedly.[71] Better nutrition from the 1960s onward has been credited with "improving health status, despite the limited public health services."[72]

Private herb doctors provided most medical care in traditional Korea. Western-trained Japanese military doctors began to work in Korean cities in the 1870s, and missionary doctors from the United States and Canada arrived in the 1880s. King Kojong, the last ruler of the Chosun dynasty (1392–1910), founded a medical school and a few public hospitals around 1900. In 1894 pro-Japanese reformers reorganized the public administration and created government agencies to oversee disease control, vaccination, and the licensing of physicians and pharmacists. At the end of the 1800s, however, Western medicine reached only a small fraction of the population. Most Koreans continued to obtain medical care from traditional practitioners, or to do without treatment.

After annexing Korea in 1910, the Japanese colonial authorities tried to suppress traditional medicine, in part because it was associated with nationalism. Many traditional health care providers continued their practices, however, and a shortage of Western-trained doctors forced the colonial government to incorporate traditional practitioners into the health care delivery system. Meanwhile, the colonial government licensed medical personnel, established quarantines to control infectious diseases, forced the population to be vaccinated against smallpox, placed a public hospital in each province, regulated private hospitals (which rose rapidly in number), urged doctors to make traveling visits to the countryside, and founded six new medical schools and a dental college.[73]

In the early 1950s the Rhee government submitted a bill to outlaw traditional medicine, but it failed to pass the National Assembly. For the next several decades traditional practitioners, trained in their own educational institutions and working under their own legal regime, continued to provide the bulk of medical care to the rural population and to others with limited access to the modern health care system. In the late 1980s, when health insurance was extended to the whole population, it covered traditional as well as Western medicine, and from 1987 to 1990 the number of patients reportedly treated by traditional practitioners rose from 459,000 to 1,408,000. In 1990, however, herbal doctors made up only about 10 percent of medical practitioners, and the two medical traditions remained isolated from each other.[74] In the early 2000s, the incipient single-payer national health insurance scheme covered acupuncture and traditional drugs for treatment, but did not cover traditional medicines when used for prevention or for health promotion.[75]

---

[71] Chung 1979: 501; Kwon 1986: 63–74; Mehrotra, Park, and Baek 1997: 282; Pak 2004: 516.
[72] Mehrotra, Park, and Baek 1997: 281–283.
[73] Kwon et al. 1975: 20–21; Kwon 1986: 47; Kwon 1993: 244; Lee and Kee 1996; Son 1999: 544.
[74] Son 1999: 545–549.
[75] Kwon 2003d: 535.

In 1945 the U.S. Army Military Government in Korea introduced new drugs and pesticides that reduced the incidence of pneumonia, typhus, and other infectious diseases. In the 1950s, after the end of the Korean War, physicians were required to spend six months in an area without doctors in order to get a specialist's license. From 1952 to 1960 the proportion of townships without a doctor fell from 48 to 30 percent, and from 1955 to 1965 the number of government-run health centers rose from 16 to 189.[76] In 1962 alone, coincident with the implementation of a major family planning program, the government opened 102 health centers and 1,473 health subcenters. By 1962 every city and county had a health center, and by 1964 every township had a health subcenter.[77] In 1963, a Maternal and Child Health Section was established within the Bureau of Public Health.[78]

The health center was designed to be led by a physician. Its staff was responsible for family planning, immunization, tuberculosis control, food inspection, sanitation initiatives, the collection of vital statistics, and the provision of basic health services, including mother and child care, to the poor. The health subcenter was designed to be led by a local private physician who would receive a small salary, as well as the right to practice privately in the facility, in exchange for administering the subcenter and providing free medical services to the poor. The doctors in charge of subcenters were assisted as of 1967 by three field workers, always female. One was responsible for family planning, another for tuberculosis control, and the third for mother and child health services.[79]

The expansion of health centers and subcenters in rural areas during the 1960s, together with the increase of their staffs in the late 1960s and early 1970s, had some positive effects on access to health care. The share of townships without a doctor fell from 30 percent in 1960 to 17 percent in 1974, and the proportion of rural people who consulted a physician in time of illness rose from 13 percent in 1966 to 37 percent in 1971.[80] Nevertheless, health services still failed to reach many households with a high risk of infant death. In 1970 the share of births attended by a doctor or a qualified midwife was still about 10 percent, and a study in one rural area found that unsterilized instruments were used in more than 75 percent of births, causing a high incidence of tetanus.[81] In the mid-1970s, 40 percent of rural dwellers received no medical treatment when ill.[82] In the late 1970s health services remained "limited and maldistributed," and more than 50 percent of the country's doctors and nurses served the 20 percent of the population living in Seoul.[83] The public

[76] Kwon 1986: 47–48; number of government health centers from Mason et al. 1980: 402.

[77] Kwon 1986: 48. "Counties" are *guns*, "townships" are *eups* or *myuns*.

[78] Kwon et al. 1975: 112.

[79] Cho and Seo 1992: 23–24; Kwon 1986: 48–49; Kwon 1993: 247–248.

[80] Townships without doctors: Kwon 1986: 48. Physician consultations: Chung 1979: 523.

[81] Mason et al. 1980: 396.

[82] Park 1980: 106–108.

[83] Mason et al. 1980: 382, 404.

sector provided mainly preventive and promotive health services; the private sector, which provided most curative care, remained financially or geographically inaccessible to many poor people.[84] Hospitals were poorly funded and, especially in rural areas, underutilized.[85]

The county health centers and township health subcenters operating during the 1960s were deficient not only in accessibility, but also often in quality. Many health centers had inadequate equipment and personnel,[86] and most maintained "no official relationship, either administrative or medical, with the hospitals or clinics in their area."[87] In the late 1970s about half of the doctors who ran township subcenters were young residents doing compulsory service. The others were mostly "limited area doctors," underqualified practitioners whom the government had licensed to practice in an area that would otherwise not have a doctor.[88] The field workers involved in family planning and tuberculosis control had poor training, supervision, and motivation, while professional nurses with the skills needed to contribute to a significant improvement in maternal and child care were hard to recruit.[89] In 1981, accordingly, the health subcenters employed 2,461 family planning workers and 2,101 tuberculosis workers, but only 916 mother and child health workers.[90] Because of these problems, the mother and child health care functions of the health centers and subcenters were judged in 1980 to have been "totally unsuccessful."[91]

In the late 1970s researchers reported that the "government has given very low priority over the years to provision of health services, effective implementation of mass inoculation programs, improvement of water supply, and sanitation." These problems, they noted, raised a question: "why are the death and infant mortality rates so low, when the health services are so limited and maldistributed?"[92] A World Bank report provides a partial answer, noting that health status rose in South Korea from 1960 to the mid-1970s "despite the modest scale of government initiatives" because rapid economic growth, and the accompanying decline of income poverty, helped to improve nutrition, housing, sanitation, and access to private health services.[93] Still, some of the infant mortality decline during the 1960s and 1970s was surely attributable to the public primary health care infrastructure set up during this era, even if the rise of private incomes, along with more effective government provision of education and family planning, also contributed.

---

[84] Yeon 1981: 21–22.
[85] Park 1980: 106–108.
[86] Roemer 1991: 306.
[87] World Bank 1979: 139.
[88] Roemer 1991: 306.
[89] Cho and Seo 1992: 23–24, 27; Kwon 1986: 51; Yeon 1981: 21–22.
[90] Cho and Seo 1992: 23–24.
[91] Kwon 1986: 51.
[92] Mason et al. 1980 (first quotation p. 396; second p. 382).
[93] World Bank 1979: 137.

The fragmentation of public health administration was partly responsible for deficiencies in South Korea's health care system during the 1960s and 1970s. From 1962 to 1977, "although the health network grew rapidly, no vigorous, congruent health policy evolved."[94] The Ministry of Health and Social Affairs was supposed to be responsible for coordinating health policy, but until 1974 it lacked an administrative unit or staff person in charge of health planning.[95] The Ministry of Home Affairs controlled health centers, water supply, sanitation, pollution control, and provincial and municipal hospitals; the Ministry of Education and other public agencies operated other public hospitals.[96] In the mid-1970s, according to a World Bank study, the health ministry's "lack of authority and its inability to provide leadership and coordinate health activities has perhaps been the greatest impediment to the effective delivery of health services in Korea."[97] The poor performance of the public health care systems of Argentina and, until the mid-1990s, Brazil, has also been attributed to administrative fragmentation.[98]

Underfunding was another major impediment to the effective operation of public health care services in South Korea through the 1970s. In 1973, when GDP per capita was $3,059 in South Korea but only $1,925 in Thailand,[99] South Korea spent only $1.33 per capita on public health care, compared to $2.45 in Thailand.[100] One review of ten high development achievers reported that "of all the countries examined...Korea is unique in being the only one which did not have a government-financed public health system worth the name – except a family planning programme – till thirty years after independence [in 1945]."[101] Other assessments concur that South Korea's record at public health care financing and delivery was, at best, undistinguished during the 1960s and 1970s.[102]

Provision of basic health services improved considerably after 1978, when the government enacted the Special Law for National Health Service. This law gave new medical graduates the option of practicing for three years in a doctorless area instead of signing up for three years of otherwise compulsory military service. In 1984, 67 percent of the 1,202 doctors staffing the country's 1,303 health subcenters were newly licensed physicians on three-year tours of duty; another 22 percent were "limited area doctors" whose qualifications were lower than those of credentialed physicians. Permanently employed, fully credentialed physicians comprised only 10 percent of doctors

[94] Kwon 1986: 48.
[95] Yeon 1988: 7.
[96] Park 1980: 109; World Bank 1979: 139.
[97] World Bank 1979: 150.
[98] On Argentina see Lloyd-Sherlock 2000b; on Brazil see Weyland 1996.
[99] Heston, Summers, and Aten 2006, variable RGDPCH (see Table A3).
[100] In 1973 US dollars at then-current market rates; Mason et al. 1980: 405.
[101] Mehrotra, Park, and Baek 1997: 276.
[102] Ban, Moon, and Perkins 1980; Bark 1994; Eberstadt and Banister 1992.

practicing in the health subcenters.[103] Still, the new medical graduates went some way toward ameliorating the chronic undersupply of doctors in rural areas. In 1985, moreover, the health ministry began to hire salaried health workers to serve alongside the doctors in the health subcenters, replacing the lightly trained field workers on temporary contracts.[104]

In December 1980, a Special Act for Rural Health funded the construction of community-administered primary health care posts in agricultural and fishing villages with more than 500 residents, as long as they were located more than 30 minutes by public transport from the nearest medical facility. A typical primary health care post served three to five villages and 500 to 700 persons. By the end of 1984 there were 1,404 such posts serving 6,349 villages and 2.9 million people, about 20 percent of the 14.4 million rural dwellers at the time. Nurses who had signed contracts to work for at least two years, and who had received 24 weeks of additional on-the-job training, were designated "community health practitioners" and placed in charge of the new primary health care posts. The number of such practitioners rose from 1,477 in 1984 to 2,034 in 1996. Assisting each community health practitioner were three village health care workers, who had briefer training but closer ties to villagers. The relation of community health practitioners to village health care workers was analogous to that of Village Health Volunteers to Village Health Communicators in Thailand in the early 1980s (Section 9.4). Local management boards, which often included village heads and New Village (Saemaul Undong) leaders, were responsible for stocking and equipping the primary health care posts and for deciding on user fees. The government envisioned the primary health care posts as being used mainly for sanitation, family planning, and health education, but their personnel were legally allowed to provide vaccinations, first aid, simple medical tests, referrals, and other basic services.[105] The expansion of the village health posts coincided with a sharp rise in the utilization of maternal health services. From 1977 to 1986 the proportion of expectant mothers who visited health care facilities rose from 57 to 94 percent, and the share of births attended by trained personnel rose from 36 to 77 percent (Table A16).[106] The average annual decline of infant mortality from 1980 to 1985, 7.2 percent, was faster than the annual average for 1960–2005 as a whole (6.4 percent) (Table A1).

Despite improvements in maternal health service utilization during the 1980s, the geographical maldistribution of health personnel remained a problem. In 1989, the year that medical insurance coverage expanded to the entire population, only 5 percent of doctors served the 21 percent of South Koreans in rural areas, and some rural townships still lacked adequate health personnel

---

[103] Whang 1985: 18.
[104] Cho and Seo 1992: 24.
[105] Kwon 1986: 51; Kwon 1993: 250–251; Lee and Kim 2002: 15, 35; Whang 1985: 19–21, 28–29.
[106] Prenatal care statistics from Bark 1994: 437 and Kwon 1986: 59.

or facilities. Also, poor transport and ambulance services plagued many rural communities, making it hard for their residents to use health services in urban areas.[107] Another barrier to basic health care provision was that medical schools churned out specialists four times as fast as general practitioners.[108] The fragmentation and ossification of public health care administration posed additional problems. Health centers, health subcenters, community health care stations, and village health workers remained poorly coordinated with one another. Local governments, rather than the national health ministry, were formally in charge of the county health centers and township subcenters, and all of these facilities operated in a bureaucratic, top-down manner, making it hard to adapt rural health services to local needs and encouraging imperious behavior toward patients.[109] Referral systems and medical record-keeping were weak.[110] Local councils in rural areas, which typically included the village chief, New Village leaders, and other influential members of the community, showed more concern for income-generation and infrastructure projects than for health care initiatives.[111]

Closely related to these administrative deficiencies were problems at the point of service, notably long waits, unfriendly treatment, poorly maintained facilities, and rising costs.[112] Many people viewed the new medical graduates on three-year tours of duty as unmotivated, inadequately skilled, and unsure of their own abilities, and regarded the public system as having worse facilities, more cumbersome bureaucracies, and less congenial staffs than private clinics or hospitals.[113] Accordingly, health subcenters were "meagerly utilized, because people had little confidence in them."[114] Many patients preferred to obtain routine care at large urban hospitals rather than at primary care clinics even though co-payments were higher at the hospitals.[115]

Health centers around the year 2000 were used mainly by low income and elderly people in urban areas, but by 30 to 40 percent of the population in rural areas. In some remote rural areas, up to 90 percent of the population used the community health post.[116] Despite their reputation for low-quality service (and for being places where mainly poor people go), demand for health center services rose sharply after the 1997 financial crisis, seriously overburdening them.[117] Meanwhile, as part of the austerity plan that the government enacted to cope with the effects of the crisis, layoffs reduced the number of community health practitioners. Accordingly, the number of primary health

[107] Bark 1994: 438–439.
[108] Kwon 1993: 274–278; Kwon 2003b: 174; Lee 2003: 50.
[109] Whang 1985: 21–22, 26, 32.
[110] Kwon 1993: 274–278.
[111] Whang 1985: 29.
[112] Kwon 1993: 274–278.
[113] Whang 1985: 21–22.
[114] Roemer 1991: 306.
[115] Peabody, Lee, and Bickel 1995: 37–38.
[116] Lee and Kim 2002: 17.
[117] Yang, Prescott, and Bae 2001: 377–378.

care posts fell from 2,034 in 1996 to 1,750 in 2001.[118] At the turn of the twenty-first century, then, South Korean primary health care facilities were overburdened and understaffed, but continued to play an important role in delivering basic health services to the poor, particularly in rural areas.

8.5. South Korea: Determinants of Public Health Care Policies

The rapid rise of private incomes facilitated the steep drop of infant mortality in South Korea from 1960 to 2005, but the public provision of basic social services, including health services, contributed more than is sometimes appreciated. Accordingly, it is useful to try to identify the political factors that shaped and constrained major government decisions about social service provision. Five sets of decisions were particularly pivotal: (1) to raise the number of rural health centers, to provide social assistance to the poor, and to expand family planning in the early 1960s; (2) to improve rural water supply and sanitation through the New Village (Saemaul Undong) movement in the early 1970s; (3) to build primary health care facilities and train primary health care personnel in the late 1970s and early 1980s; (4) to universalize health insurance coverage from 1977 to 1989; and (5) to unify the multiple health insurance societies into a single-payer system in 2000. There is little to suggest that adversarial politics contributed to the first three decisions, which were more important than the last two from the standpoint of reducing the infant mortality rate. There is plenty of evidence that electoral competition contributed to the fourth and fifth decisions, but not much to support the proposition that the resulting changes to the health insurance system accelerated the pace of infant mortality decline.

South Korea from 1961 to 1987 had an authoritarian political regime (Table A18). General Park, the president from 1961 to 1979, allowed restricted elections from 1963 to 1971, but in October 1972, citing "security threats," he imposed martial law and installed himself indefinitely in the presidency, where he remained until the head of the Korean Central Intelligence Agency assassinated him in 1979. In 1981 General Chun Doo Hwan made himself president, banned his political opponents, and announced that he would stay in office until February 1988.[119] From 1961 to 1987 South Koreans toiled under the watchful eye and heavy hand of a militarized state. In 1964, when the population was 28 million, the Korean Central Intelligence Agency had 370,000 employees.[120] In May 1980, an army division assigned to quell student protest in the city of Kwangju killed an estimated 2,000 people.[121] In 1988 intra-military conflict, strikes, and renewed student protest led Chun's anointed successor, the former general Roh Tae Woo, to call a direct presidential election. The opposition,

---

[118] Lee and Kim 2002: 35.
[119] Eckert et al. 1990: 362–384.
[120] Johnson 1987: 157.
[121] Eckert et al. 1990: 375.

led by the leftist Kim Dae Jung and the centrist Kim Young Sam, ran divided, allowing Roh to win the election (which was tainted by reported vote-buying, fraud, and intimidation). Kim Young Sam won the December 1992 election after merging his party with that of Roh Tae Woo, marking the first time since 1960 that a civilian had been elected president, and Kim Dae Jung won the December 1997 election amid the Asian financial crisis, marking the first time that an opposition candidate had won the office.

A perplexing feature of South Korean public service provision from the 1960s onward involves the discrepancy between the government's strong investment in basic education and family planning on the one hand, and its relatively weak investment in primary health care on the other. Cultural factors may account for part of this discrepancy. Whereas Koreans are said to have a "zeal" for education,[122] rural survey respondents in South Korea, as in Indonesia (Section 10.5), showed less interest in better health services than in higher farm prices and other income-generating policies.[123] Also important in explaining the discrepancy in attention to the various types of social services may have been the Park government's intense commitment to economic growth. Basic education and family planning contribute visibly to economic growth; primary health care makes a less conspicuous contribution. A desire to promote economic growth and to institutionalize social control was behind the Park government's energetic measures to expand access to basic schooling in the 1960s and 1970s.[124] The family planning program introduced in 1961 was launched explicitly to ameliorate the drag that unchecked population growth might otherwise place on economic development.[125] Rural health center construction in the early 1960s was motivated principally by a perceived need to promote economic growth through family planning, and only secondarily to respond to the other basic health needs of the rural population.[126]

In December 1961, the same month in which it launched the nationwide family planning program, the Park government also introduced the Livelihood Protection Act, which provided subsidized fuel, food, and education to poor people in rural areas. According to one interpretation, the Livelihood Protection Act was "part of a political strategy aimed at enhancing the legitimacy of the political regime."[127] Political leadership, and in particular General Park's predilections, may also have inspired the Livelihood Protection Act. Even before he assumed the presidency in 1963, General Park was "at the heart of all the decision-making processes" in the military government that seized power in July 1961.[128] Like Suharto in Indonesia (Section 10.5), General Park grew up in a poor rural environment and was "sympathetic to the problems of

[122] Seth 2002: 98.
[123] Whang 1985: 23, 29.
[124] Haggard and Kaufman 2008: 138.
[125] Mehrotra, Park, and Baek 1997: 273; World Bank 1979: 121; Yang et al. 1965: 237.
[126] Kwon 1986: 48.
[127] Kwon 1999: 132 (quotation); Yi 2003: 31–32.
[128] Yi 2003: 32.

the farmers."[129] Park's leadership seems also to have contributed to the New Village movement's rural development policies in the early 1970s. The president mobilized other government officials to support the movement by inviting farmers to Seoul and asking them to speak to government officials and on television about the hardships they faced. The sessions provided "an opportunity for farmers to convey the critical need for medical services to high officials." As a result of these encounters, "leaders of the National Assembly were deeply moved by the need for rural electrification, rural communication, and medical services in rural areas." General Park recommended that medical services be delivered free to very poor families, and that rural health subcenters be established at the subcounty level and staffed by a junior doctor and nurse. Facilitating the recruitment of doctors was the 1978 law that exempted new medical graduates from military conscription in exchange for three years of service in a rural health center.[130]

Two years after seizing power in a 1961 coup, General Park restored elections. At the same time, however, his government banned thousands of prominent politicians from competing for office and biased the electoral system toward its allies in congress, who manipulated legislative rules to push through a constitutional amendment that allowed the president to run for a third consecutive term in April 1971.[131] In this contest, opposition candidate Kim Dae Jung nearly defeated General Park. Attributing his near defeat in part to "failing support from rural areas...Park – himself from a rural background – undertook a concerted effort for rural transformation in the 1970s."[132] Other scholars concur that "the fact that [Park's] traditional political support in the countryside showed signs of fading in his third term election probably did not go unnoticed. A hidden objective may have been the development of a stronger base of agrarian support through the use of subsidies and mass crusades." Accordingly, the enthusiastic response of many villages to a government decision to distribute surplus cement in 1971 "pointed the way to a more organized program [the New Village movement] that would help to dispel the disenchantment of rural voters."[133] The introduction of income support for farmers and the expansion of pension and health insurance coverage during the 1970s have also been attributed to Park's near loss of the 1971 election.[134]

Recalling the debates over the origins of social insurance in Costa Rica (Section 3.5) and Brazil (Section 5.5), some scholars have attributed the post-1977 extension of contributory health insurance in South Korea to bureaucratic initiative, whereas others have put more emphasis on the role of social

---

[129] Turner et al. 1993: 75.
[130] Park 1998: 130–131, 141.
[131] Eckert et al. 1990: 362–365.
[132] Boyer and Ahn 1991: 27.
[133] Turner et al. 1993: 75–76.
[134] Ramesh 1995a: 236.

protest or anticipated protest.[135] Each of the main candidates in the South Korea's first direct presidential election in 1987 promised to expand national health insurance, and the "highly competitive atmosphere" surrounding this election has been credited with the expansion of health insurance to the entire population.[136] One scholar argues that Roh Tae Woo's victory in this election with a scant 37 percent of the vote motivated the new president to extend health insurance to the self-employed as a way of bolstering his political legitimacy.[137]

International factors of various sorts have been credited with a major role in shaping health care policies in South Korea. The December 1980 Special Act for Rural Health that launched a major nationwide primary health care program has been characterized as "an official response by the Korean government" to the primary health care declaration at the WHO/UNICEF Alma Ata conference in September 1978.[138] The extension of health insurance in 1977 and 1978 to public employees, private school teachers, and employees of large firms has been traced to the Park Chung Hee government's desire to "save face in international society."[139] Pressure from the United States has also been cited as a motivation for this reform.[140] One scholar argues that Roh Tae Woo extended health insurance in 1987 to most of the self-employed population not only to shore up his domestic legitimacy, but also to improve his international reputation.[141] Competition between the South Korean and North Korean leaderships to see which one could achieve more impressive social and economic indicators may also have encouraged leaders in the South to do at least the minimum needed to avoid high rates of infant mortality, at least until the 1980s, when it became clear that the North was heading for social and economic disaster. North Korean criticism of South Korean health care is reported to have encouraged the South Korean government to extend health insurance coverage to a broader share of the population in the late 1970s.[142]

The Park government's decision in the mid-1970s to reject a single-payer health insurance system in favor of multiple noncompeting funds based on occupation or place of residence was influenced by the model of Japan, whose Medical Insurance Law had also provided a legal framework for South Korea's first health insurance program in 1963. Japan also had multiple noncompeting health insurance funds. In the 1970s, legislators drafting South Korea's national health insurance law invited a group of Japanese doctors to Seoul

---

[135] In the bureaucratic initiative camp is Son 1998; in the protest camp is Joo 1999.
[136] Kwon 1999: 61–62, 135.
[137] Son 2003: 470.
[138] Whang 1985: 19.
[139] Joo 1999: 397.
[140] Wong 2004: 46.
[141] Son 2003: 470.
[142] Wong 2004: 46.

to describe Japan's health insurance system.[143] The fee-for-service payment scheme that South Korea eventually adopted was "copied verbatim from the Japanese model."[144] Other considerations also favored a fragmented health insurance system. The Park government worried that a single-payer system would run a chronic deficit, forcing the state to provide subsidies that would slow economic growth.[145] Also, the state in the late 1970s may have lacked the capacity to administer a single-payer system.[146] Furthermore, top government and health ministry officials used the health insurance societies to provide generous incomes for their retired colleagues. Many executives of the health insurance societies were retired military officers, government officials, or persons close to the ruling party.[147]

Political leadership, electoral considerations, interest group pressure, and the activities of issue networks all influenced the decision by the Kim Dae Jung government in the late 1990s to move from multiple-payer to single-payer health insurance. Kim Dae Jung had a progressive political ideology, a strong belief in social solidarity, and a special interest in social policy. Kim viewed a single-payer system as more equitable than a multiple-payer system, and had advocated a transition to a single-payer system during his presidential campaign. "Without the strong will of the president," noted a student of the health insurance reform process, "the political resources to implement the structural reform in health care financing would not have been mobilized."[148]

President Kim may have supported the reform not only out of conviction, but also in an effort to expand political support for his government. One analyst has argued that "Kim Dae-Jung...used the issue of NHI [National Health Insurance] administration to consolidate his power. President Kim chose unification [of the health insurance societies] not because he agreed with its policy objectives, but because he felt that it would more effectively empower the political base of his government."[149] Whatever the influence of such political considerations in Kim's own decision-making process (the analyst may have been overstating the case; the South Korean president in the late 1990s was limited to a single five-year term in office), electoral incentives may have influenced legislative approval of the reform. In particular, "politicians with constituents in rural areas supported the merger of insurance societies to maximize votes."[150] A desire to win votes in rural areas is also said to have motivated President Roh Tae Woo's decision to extend health insurance to farmers in 1987 and 1988.[151]

[143] Son 1998: 17, 20, 25; Lee 2003: 48; Kwon 2003a: 90.
[144] Wong 2004: 47.
[145] Kwon 2003b: 175.
[146] Lee 2003: 49.
[147] Kwon 2003a: 81, 86.
[148] Kwon 2003a: 85–86 (quotation); Kwon and Reich 2003: 9–11.
[149] Lee 2003: 49.
[150] Kwon 2003a: 85. Unlike the president, members of the National Assembly were eligible for reelection.
[151] Wong 2004: 70–71.

In the 1960s and 1970s, issue networks and interest groups did little to influence South Korean social policy.[152] One observer stressed that "the policy process that resulted in the 1976 Health Insurance Act was insulated from outside influence." In the late 1980s, this situation began to change. Demonstrations by farmers contributed to a decision by the Roh Tae Woo government to reduce the share of the health insurance premium that farmers were required to pay.[153] In the early 1990s, issue networks led by progressive doctors, academics, and former prodemocracy activists began to press for the introduction of a single-payer National Health Insurance system. As late as 1998, health insurance in South Korea was administered by 370 noncompeting, mandatory membership, not-for-profit insurance societies. During the presidency of Kim Dae Jung (1998–2003), these societies were merged into a single-payer system.[154] Like the Sanitarian Movement in Brazil (Section 6.5), issue networks in South Korea served as "policy entrepreneurs" for the introduction of a single-payer system. In contrast to previous years, when top civil servants, sometimes in consultation with physicians' associations, had dominated health care policymaking, President Kim Dae Jung actively incorporated these issue networks into the policy process.[155]

Farmers favored the single-payer system because they believed that their premiums to regional health insurance societies were too high relative to the services available in their areas. Labor unions were divided over the issue, but they united to resist layoffs after the merger. The active role of unions in the creation of the single-payer system represented "their first involvement in the social policy process apart from the unemployment issue."[156] Unlike in Brazil, where doctors' associations fiercely opposed the unification of health insurance (Section 6.5), medical providers in South Korea cooperated with the introduction of the single-payer system. Physicians who might have been expected to worry that a single-payer system would enable the government to use its monopsony power to drive down reimbursement fees could recognize that the uniform fee schedule under the multiple-payer system already gave the government such power. In addition, the new system promised to relieve doctors of bad debts incurred by the less solvent societies.[157] By contrast, doctors' strikes in 2000 forced the government to raise the fees it paid for medical services, to exclude many injectable drugs from a law separating drug prescription from drug sales, and to postpone the introduction of a prospective payment system for nine common medical diagnoses.[158]

---

[152] Kwon 1999: 133.

[153] Wong 2004: 46 (quotation), 71.

[154] On the merger see Korea NHIC 2002; Kwon 2003a; Kwon and Reich 2003; and Wong 2004: 88–111.

[155] Kwon 2003a: 85–88; Kwon and Reich 2003: 11; Wong 2004: 71, 146.

[156] Kwon 2003a: 90; see also Wong 2004: 100–101, 148.

[157] Kwon 2003a: 82–89.

[158] Kwon 2003c; Kwon 2003d.

Democracy had a starkly important influence on the expansion of health insurance from the late 1980s onward, as well as on the transition to a single-payer national health insurance system in 2000. Little evidence exists, however, that either of these insurance-related changes had a significant impact on the infant mortality rate. Most of the infant mortality decline took place from 1960 to 1990, when the rate fell from 90 to 8 per 1000. South Korea was at best a semi-democracy from 1961 to 1972, and it remained under martial law from 1972 to 1987. Accordingly, it is not easy to make the case that electoral incentives, a free press, interest group pressure, or issue network activities encouraged policies that contributed to South Korea's rapid infant mortality decline from 1960 to 1990. Moreover, none of these democracy-related factors seem to have shaped government decisions in the early 1960s to promote labor-intensive manufactured exports, to raise access to primary and secondary education, or to expand family planning, all of which contributed to rapid infant mortality decline, in part by stimulating economic growth and reducing income inequality.

Still, among the reasons why General Park's government in December 1961 implemented the Livelihood Protection Act, which contributed to infant mortality decline by transferring income to the destitute, were a search for legitimacy and a desire to deflect public criticism for its seizure of power six months earlier. Moreover, General Park's near defeat in the April 1971 presidential election gave him a strong incentive to try to shore up his support via the New Village movement, which improved the provision of roads, electricity, water, and sanitation in rural areas in the early 1970s. It also encouraged General Park to court support by increasing the supply of rural doctors, by placing better-qualified health personnel in rural health subcenters, and by raising access to prenatal care and to trained attendance at birth. Other factors, including the international primary health care movement, also shaped these infant mortality-reducing social policies during the 1970s, but the case of South Korea, like that of Chile, underscores that democracy-related factors can have an influence on social policy even after an authoritarian regime has been imposed.

9

Thailand: Democratization Speeds
Infant Mortality Decline

Thailand from 1960 to 2005 achieved fast economic growth and a rapid decline of income poverty. It also did well at raising educational attainment, improving family planning, expanding access to safe water and adequate sanitation, and delivering basic health services and nutritional assistance to the poor. Not surprisingly, then, Thailand from 1960 to 2005 had one of the steepest infant mortality declines in the world, ranking by one measure eighth of 140 countries for which data are available.[1] At older ages, however, the spread of HIV infection and AIDS deaths from the mid-1980s onward caused the risk of dying between ages 15 and 60 to rise sharply (few AIDS deaths occur among infants, so the epidemic had only a small direct effect on infant mortality). Mainly as a result of these AIDS deaths, Thailand's level of life expectancy in 2005, as well as its percent rise of life expectancy from 1960 to 2005, ranked below the median of the world's countries. A broad consensus exists, however, that Thailand's policies to fight HIV/AIDS were among the most successful in the world. By 2000 the rate of adult mortality had begun to fall again.

Because Thailand from 1960 to 2005 achieved one of the world's fastest rates of economic growth and income poverty decline, it is tempting to attribute its success at reducing infant mortality mainly to economic factors. Thailand, however, did even better at reducing infant mortality, and at achieving a low level of infant mortality, than its strong performance on GDP per capita predicted (Figures 1.1 and 1.2). Moreover, infant mortality fell faster after the 1997 Asian financial crisis, when GDP per capita initially plummeted and then resumed a slower rate of growth, than during earlier decades, when GDP per capita grew at a rapid or very rapid pace. Improvements in family planning after 1970; in water, sanitation, and health care provision after 1980; and in education after 1990 help to explain these anomalies.

These improvements in social policy originated from a range of sources, notably bureaucratic initiative, international factors of various kinds, and the nature of the political regime (in particular, the extent to which the regime

---

[1] Percent decline of infant mortality from 1960 to 2005. Data: World Bank 2008e, except Taiwan, from Table A1.

was authoritarian or democratic). The focus here will be on ways in which the character of the political regime may have shaped and constrained the public provision of basic health services to the poor. The most democratic years in modern Thai history (1992–2005) coincided both with better health service provision and with faster infant mortality decline, so it is well worth exploring whether democracy might have contributed to these outcomes.

9.1. Thailand: Mortality

Vital registration statistics were incomplete in Thailand from 1960 to 2005, so mortality estimates must be derived from censuses and surveys.[2] A Multiple Indicator Cluster Survey taken from December 2005 to April 2006 by Thailand's National Statistical Office (assisted by UNICEF and other national and United Nations agencies) was "the largest survey on the situation of women and children ever carried out in Thailand."[3] On the basis of child survivorship questions asked in this survey, researchers estimated that Thailand in mid-2003 had an infant mortality rate of 9 per 1000. Reconciling these figures with estimates derived for earlier years from census and survey data, a group of experts from United Nations organizations assigned Thailand in 2005 an infant mortality rate of 7.7 per 1000 (Table A1).[4] Among the eight societies compared in this book, only South Korea and Taiwan had lower 2005 infant mortality rates than Thailand, although Chile's rate was about the same as Thailand's. Nonetheless, Thailand's 2005 infant mortality rate was lower than that of 15 of the 50 U.S. states, a remarkably low level for a country whose GDP per capita in 2003 was $7,274, compared to $34,875 in the United States.[5] Thailand ranked only third among the eight societies at percent decline of infant mortality from 1960 to 2005 (Table A1), but among 140 countries for which data are available it ranked eighth, just behind South Korea (second) and Chile (sixth). Because of the rising prevalence of HIV/AIDS after the mid-1980s, Thailand was less successful at raising life expectancy. Estimated life expectancy at birth in 2005 was 69.9 years, higher only than in Indonesia among the eight cases studied in this book. Moreover, Thailand's 50 percent rise of life expectancy from 1960 to 2005 was second smallest among the eight cases (Table A1). Among all countries with available data, Thailand ranked below the median on both life expectancy level in 2005 and life expectancy increase from 1960 to 2005.[6]

---

[2] Hill et al. 2007b. McGuire (2009), Web Appendix A1, reviews alternative sources of mortality data for Thailand.
[3] UNICEF Office for Thailand 2007: 4.
[4] World Bank 2008c (Country Data Sheet for Thailand).
[5] Infant mortality in the 50 U.S. states in 2005: Mathews and MacDorman 2008: 5. U.S. and Thai GDP per capita in 2005: Heston, Summers, and Aten 2006, variable RGDPCH (see Table A3).
[6] Thailand's life expectancy at birth in 2005 ranked 107th among 186 countries, and its percent rise of life expectancy from 1960 to 2005 (toward a stipulated maximum of 85 years) ranked 89th among 174 countries (World Bank 2008e).

Data on Thai mortality rates before 1960 are sparser than for most of the other cases, but evidence suggests that the country in the first half of the twentieth century had a very high rate of infant death. In the 1920s, registered infant mortality in the Bangkok area averaged 234 per 1000, comparable to the rate reported in Batavia (Jakarta), Indonesia.[7] Estimates of infant mortality in the whole country during the 1920s range from 300 per 1000 up.[8] By comparison, infant mortality in the 1920s averaged 253 per 1000 in Chile, 224 in Taiwan, 187 in Costa Rica, 186 in South Korea, and 117 in Argentina.[9] Life expectancy at birth in Thailand was estimated to be about 40 years in 1937 and about 42 years in 1947, slightly lower than the Brazilian figures for those decades. From 1947 to 1960, however, life expectancy at birth reportedly rose from 42 to 53 years.[10] Most of the rise seems to have occurred between 1948 and 1955, when the estimated crude death rate fell from 27 to 18 per 1000.[11] Japan, Sri Lanka, and Taiwan also experienced sharp drops in mortality in the decade after World War II. Better control of infectious diseases, particularly malaria and tuberculosis, contributed heavily to mortality decline in each of the four cases.[12]

After 1960, the average annual rate of infant mortality decline was moderate from 1960 to 1975 (3.4 percent), fast from 1975 to 1990 (5.6 percent), and very fast from 1990 to 2005 (7.7 percent) (Table A1). This tempo was distinctly out of phase with the ebb and flow of GDP per capita growth (Tables 11.1 and A3). The tempo of life expectancy rise, by contrast, was stable from 1960 to 1990, when it slowed because of the AIDS epidemic. It resumed the previous rate of decline from 2000 to 2005, as the epidemic was brought under control. Mortality per 1000 adults aged 15 to 60, after soaring from 165 in 1990 to 250 in 2000, fell back to 226 by 2005.[13]

9.2. Thailand: Affluence, Inequality, and Poverty

In 1960, Thailand's GDP per capita of $1,059 was lowest among the eight societies compared in this book. By 2005 it had risen to $7,274, surpassing per capita economic output in Indonesia and Brazil. Thailand's 4.6 percent annual rise in GDP per capita from 1960 to 2003 trailed those of South Korea and Taiwan (Table A3), but ranked sixth among the 98 countries for which data are available for both years (Taiwan and South Korea ranked first and second respectively). The Asian financial crisis of 1997, which was triggered by the devaluation of the Thai baht, caused GDP per capita to fall from $6,965

---

[7] Bangkok: Varavarn 2000 [1930]: 217. Batavia: De Haas 1939: 16–17, 21.

[8] Varavarn 2000 [1930]: 228; Rungpitarangsi 1974: 69.

[9] See the first sections of the chapters pertaining to these other cases.

[10] Thailand: Rungpitarangsi 1974: 57–64, 179. Brazil: Wood and Carvalho 1988: 87.

[11] Muscat 1994: 122.

[12] Thailand: Section 9.4. Japan: Taeuber 1958: 289–290. Sri Lanka: Livi-Bacci 2001: 138. Taiwan: Section 7.4.

[13] World Bank 2008e.

in 1996 to $6,159 in 1998, but the economy soon recovered: GDP per capita grew at an average annual rate of 3.4 percent from 1999 to 2003.[14] Economic growth from 1960 to 2003 provided a strong foundation for the reduction of infant mortality in Thailand.

Thailand shared some, but not all, of the policy orientations that encouraged rapid economic growth in South Korea and Taiwan.[15] From 1960 to 1995 Thai leaders enacted macroeconomic policies that were at least as cautious as those in South Korea or Taiwan.[16] Thailand had no land reform comparable to those in these other societies, but in 1983 some 83 percent of Thai landholdings were already owner-occupied.[17] Land was abundant in most parts of the North and Northeast until about 1980, and farmers who wished to homestead new frontier land faced few obstacles.[18] Tenancy rates were fairly high in the Center region, however, as well as in the Northern provinces of Chiang Mai and Lampang. In the early 1970s some tenants in the Center began to protest both high rents and the insecurity of tenancy contracts, prompting a short-lived democratic government to pass a land reform law in 1975.[19] Little action was taken, however, until the early 1990s, when the government distributed some 1.76 million hectares, mostly degraded forest land, to nearly 600,000 land-poor families (as well as to some rich developers in the province of Phuket, causing a scandal that resulted in the collapse of the Chuan Leekpai government in 1995). This reform distributed three times as much land as in the previous 17 years combined.[20]

After 1960, Thailand made good progress at expanding primary education, especially from 1975 to 1980, when gross primary enrollment surged from 84 to 99 percent.[21] As late as 1995, however, only 9 percent of Thais aged 25 and over had any secondary education, and only 4 percent had completed it.[22] These proportions were much lower than in South Korea or Taiwan, and help to explain why Thailand took longer than its East Asian neighbors to achieve sustained economic growth by moving up through the product cycle to export increasingly elaborate manufactured goods. Thai officials announced a shift from import substitution to export promotion as early as 1970, but it was not until 1984, nearly 25 years after South Korea or Taiwan, that the government began (with a significant currency devaluation) to promote manufactured exports aggressively.[23] Similarities in economic policy between Thailand on the one hand, and South Korea and Taiwan on the other, help to explain why

[14] Heston, Summers, and Aten 2006, variable RGDPCH (see Table A3).
[15] On such development policies in South Korea and Taiwan see McGuire 1995a.
[16] Bowie and Unger 1997: 187–188; Muscat 1994: 228–232.
[17] Siamwalla, Setboonsarng, and Patamasiriwat 1993: 101.
[18] Krongkaew 1995: 40.
[19] Phongpaichit and Baker 2002: 315.
[20] *Economist* 1995; Rattanabirabongse et al. 1998: 7.
[21] World Bank 2001c.
[22] Barro and Lee 2000.
[23] Muscat 1994: 108; Unger 1998: 73.

the Thai economy grew rapidly from 1960 to 2003. The differences in policy help to explain why Thailand's economic growth, although impressive in a global perspective, did not quite reach the pace of economic growth in South Korea or Taiwan.

The mean Gini index obtained in eight "good" quality surveys in Thailand from 1962 to 1992 was 45.5, placing Thailand 67th of 107 countries on income inequality (the country with the lowest income inequality is ranked first in this comparison).[24] Behind this moderately high level of income inequality from the 1960s to the 1980s were low access to secondary schooling and low agricultural productivity.[25] The change in income inequality during the period analyzed was minimal, however (Table A4). Fast economic growth in the context of stable income inequality should result in a rapid decline of income poverty, and surveys confirm that such a decline took place. From 1960 to 2002, the share of the population below the national poverty line fell from 57 to 10 percent (Table A5). Income inequality is sometimes found to boost mortality not only by raising income poverty, but also by elevating psychological stress, deepening feelings of depression, encouraging risk-taking behavior, reducing social cohesion, and discouraging investment in social services (Section 2.2). In Thailand, such mediating mechanisms seem to have been weak. A study of 76 Thai provinces in 2000 found that provinces with high levels of inequality had lower, not higher, mortality, controlling for other factors likely to affect mortality levels.[26] In short, income inequality did not change much in Thailand during the period from 1960 to 2005, and a cross-province study finds no evidence in any case that higher income inequality is linked to higher infant mortality.

In South Korea and Taiwan, fast economic growth in a context of low income inequality provided strong support for rapid infant mortality decline from 1960 to 2005, although the public provision of social services (itself facilitated by rapid economic growth) helped more than is sometimes recognized. In Chile and Costa Rica, economic growth was slow and erratic until the 1990s and income inequality climbed steadily. In these countries, the public provision of social services played a preponderant role in contributing to an equally rapid decline of infant mortality. In terms of the main driving force behind infant mortality decline, Thailand occupies a position between South Korea and Taiwan on the one hand, and Chile and Costa Rica on the other. Fast economic growth and stable (although not low) income inequality contributed to Thailand's strong performance at infant mortality decline, but Thailand's estimated 2005 infant mortality rate of 7.7 per 1000 was much lower than its GDP per capita would predict (Figure 1.1). Also, Thailand's

---

[24] Deininger and Squire 1996: 574–577; 6.6 added to consumption-based Ginis (Deininger and Squire 1996: 582).
[25] *Economist* 1996: 30; Lewis and Kapur 1990: 1373; World Bank Thailand Office 2001: 28–31.
[26] Rojroongwasinkul 2004: 50–54.

progress at reducing infant mortality over the entire period from 1960 to 2005 was much greater than its GDP per capita growth would lead one to expect (Figure 1.2). Furthermore, the correlation between infant mortality decline and GDP per capita growth across eight five-year periods from 1960 to 2000 (1960–1965 ... 1995–2000) was negative (Table 11.1). The tempo of infant mortality decline from 1960 to 2005 was more consistent with public service provision than with GDP per capita growth.

9.3. Thailand: Education, Family Planning, Safe Water, and Sanitation

By conventional measures, Thailand in the second half of the twentieth century had a small welfare state. From 1972 to 1995 public spending on social services, including education, amounted to less than 6 percent of GDP. This share was about the same as in South Korea and Taiwan, about half as large as in Chile or Costa Rica, and about a quarter as large as in Argentina or Brazil. In 1995, about 60 percent of the Thai government's social services budget went to education. Health care received 20 percent and housing and pensions received 10 percent each.[27] Compared to the Latin American cases, public social spending in Thailand was much lower as a share of GDP and flowed much more into education (where it tends to be progressive, except for university education) than into contributory pensions or health insurance (where it tends to be regressive).

These differences in social spending reflect in part the weakness of the Thai labor movement. In Argentina, Brazil, Chile, and Costa Rica, labor movements in the first half of the twentieth century fought successfully for pensions and contributory health insurance. Labor unions were weaker in Thailand, where industrialization was less advanced and where labor union activity was more relentlessly repressed.[28] It was not until 1991 that private firms became legally obliged to enroll their workers in a social security plan funded by employees, employers, and the government, and as late as 1997 the social security system for private-sector workers insured only 18 percent of the labor force against sickness, maternity, invalidity, disability, and death (but not retirement).[29]

One reason why Thailand from 1960 to 2005 had faster economic growth than the Latin American countries was that its less burdensome welfare state made it easier to sustain more cautious and orthodox economic policies. To the extent that social insurance emerged, however, it was no less inequitable in Thailand than in Latin America. Beneficiary contributions to social insurance funds are almost always withheld from paychecks, so many smallholders, tenant farmers, and urban informal sector workers are ineligible to participate. Members of these usually impoverished social groups do, however, pay direct and indirect taxes that help to fund insurance plans for state and military

[27] Ramesh 2000: 27.
[28] Phongpaichit and Baker 2002: 187–222; Unger 1996: 28–30.
[29] Ramesh 2000: 60–63.

employees, as well as to finance government contributions to insurance plans for relatively privileged private-sector workers. Also, social insurance contributions in Thailand during the period analyzed were tax-exempt, raising the tax burden on non-contributors. Public sector pensions were excessively generous, and lower-paid employees received smaller pensions than higher-paid ones, because pension benefits were tied to contributions.[30] From an equity point of view, the low coverage of Thai social insurance was both its greatest defect (it benefited only a small share of the population) and its saving grace (it absorbed only a small share of resources).

Thailand in the decades leading up to 1990 achieved good progress at raising literacy and primary schooling, among girls as well as boys. The literacy rate among females aged 15 to 24 rose from 92 percent in 1970 to 98 percent in 2000, and in most years from 1980 forward girls as well as boys had gross primary enrollment ratios of about 100 percent.[31] Before 1990, progress at improving secondary schooling was not as impressive (Table A8). A scarcity of high schools in poor areas, the poor quality of primary education, and opportunities for work in agriculture combined to reduce the secondary enrollment rate.[32] In 1990, however, the Thai cabinet raised the length of compulsory education from six to nine years, and in 1991 the government began to train teachers in primary schools (the only schools in the vast majority of villages) to offer free lower secondary courses. The number of primary schools offering such courses rose from 119 in 1990 to 6,281 in 1994.[33] Gross secondary enrollment from 1990 to 2005 rose from 30 to 77 percent (Table A8). According to a World Bank study, "the poor quintiles...increased their share of lower secondary students impressively during the decade of the 1990s."[34] A few years are likely to intervene between the expansion of secondary enrollment and the decline of infant mortality, but the impressive expansion of such enrollment in the early 1990s probably contributed to the decline of fertility and infant mortality in subsequent years.

Thailand, like the Latin American countries, devoted a large share of education spending to universities, exacerbating educational inequities. In part, however, this spending went to fund physical infrastructure, which was previously non-existent. In 1938, among roughly 15 million Thais, only 872 had received a university education.[35] Gross tertiary enrollment was only 3 percent in 1975, but jumped to 22 percent in 1983,[36] thanks mainly to the expansion of Ramkamhaeng and Sukothai universities, which charged no fees and had open admissions. In 1989, 88 percent of Thai university students attended one of these two institutions. Universities served mainly the better-heeled. In 1983,

[30] Ramesh 2000: 74–75.
[31] World Bank 2001c.
[32] Khoman 1995: 305–306.
[33] Jones 2003: 11–15.
[34] World Bank Thailand Office 2001: 34.
[35] Bresnan 1993: 75.
[36] World Bank 2001c.

the mean family income of a Thai public university student was nearly five times the national average.[37] A 1991 study reported that less than 2 percent of farmers' university-aged children were studying.[38] As in Costa Rica, however, the expansion of university education produced a steady stream of medical graduates capable of leading public health initiatives.

Thailand's total fertility rate fell from 6.4 in 1960 to 1.8 in 2005 (Table A10), the seventh-greatest decline among 179 societies with available data. Thailand's fertility rate in 2005 was lower than that of the United States (where fertility stood at the replacement level of 2.1).[39] Already in 1990, Thailand's fertility decline was being described as "breathtaking – sweeping everyone in its path in a fertility transition that must be one of the most rapid ever recorded."[40] Making this plunge even more impressive, urbanization, which was critical to fertility decline in Brazil, made only a small contribution in Thailand, where the population in 1990 was still 81 percent rural. Helping to keep Thai families small were the relatively high status of women in the household, elevated levels of female literacy and female labor force participation, the absence of a strong son preference, and the autonomy of couples in making childbearing decisions. Moreover, Theravada Buddhism, the religion practiced by 95 percent of Thais, includes no ban on contraception; teaches that individuals, rather than God, control their own fate; and restricts the jurisdiction of religious authorities in secular matters.[41] These cultural factors were already present in 1960, however, so they cannot fully explain why Thailand achieved such rapid fertility decline in the subsequent 45 years.

Modernization encouraged a decline of desired fertility in Thailand after 1960, while family planning contributed to a drop in unwanted fertility. Thailand's military-dominated governments during the 1950s and 1960s followed pronatalist policies, arguing that a big population would contribute to national security. In the early 1960s, however, some government officials began to worry that unchecked population growth would soon overwhelm the education budget and the remaining frontier land. In 1964 the government launched pilot family planning projects in the provinces of Ratchaburi and Chiang Mai. Judging them to be successful, it introduced a National Family Planning Program in 1970.[42] From 1972 to 2004 experts rated Thailand's family planning effort among the strongest in the world (Table A9). Research suggests that the National Family Planning Program contributed significantly to fertility decline during this era.[43]

The first major effort to improve access to safe water and adequate sanitation came in the late 1950s, when the government, with funding from

---

[37] Khoman 1993: 331, 334.
[38] Jones 2003: 8.
[39] Data from World Bank 2008a.
[40] Hirschman and Guest 1990: 149.
[41] Knodel, Chamratrithirong, and Debavalya 1986.
[42] Muscat 1994: 121–123; Reisman 1999: 611; Thailand. MoPH 1988: 27.
[43] Knodel, Chamratrithirong, and Debavalya 1986.

the United States Operations Mission, introduced the Village Health and Sanitation Program. The main activities of the program were well-digging, outhouse construction, and the creation of sanitation committees in villages. The program represented an attempt to come to terms with a major health problem, for gastrointestinal diseases by 1960 accounted for 80 percent of morbidity and 40 percent of mortality in rural Thailand. In the end, however, the program was modest in scope, and its effectiveness was limited by a lack of coordination among projects and by problems in maintaining the hand pumps used to draw water from wells.[44] In 1960, hardly anyone in Thailand had access to safe water or adequate sanitation. As late as 1980 only 23 percent of households had access to an improved water source, and only 43 percent of urban households had access to improved sanitation. In response to this situation, the government designated 1981–1990 as the "Safe Water and Environmental Sanitation Decade." Villagers were encouraged to store rain-water, and the government supplied materials to build latrines, with the villagers contributing the labor.[45] The results were impressive. During the 1980s, the share of the population with access to an improved water source rose from 23 to 74 percent, and the share of city-dwellers with access to improved sanitation rose from 43 to 74 percent (Tables A11 and A12). This increase might well have contributed to faster infant mortality decline during the 1980s, and an additional sharp rise from 1990 to 1995 may have contributed to even faster decline in the 1990s.

Thailand thus developed from 1960 to 2005 a number of social policies conducive to reducing infant mortality. A strong family planning program dates from 1970, ambitious rural water and sanitation policies date from 1981, and secondary schooling expanded markedly in the 1990s. Hence, a fairly strong performance on education, family planning, and water and sanitation worked together with fast economic growth and plummeting income poverty to reduce the infant mortality rate. Improvements in the public provision of basic health services to the rural poor also contributed to a steady acceleration of the pace of infant mortality decline as the years progressed.

9.4. Thailand: Nutrition and Health Care

Total health care spending in Thailand in 2000 was about 6 percent of GDP, up from 4 percent in 1980. The private sector accounted for more than two-thirds of total health care spending (Table A15). In rural areas, however, where the vast majority of Thais lived, public health services predominated. A 1996 survey showed that 70 percent of rural respondents went to a public health facility when sick; only 12 percent sought treatment at a private hospital or clinic. A 1998 survey showed that in rural areas, public facilities provided

[44] USOM 1969: 6–7, 9.
[45] Mikhanorn 1991: 42, 127; Muscat 1994: 238; Sepúlveda 1994: 54; Thailand. MoPH 1988: 34.

prenatal care to 82 percent of pregnant women and obstetric care to 78 percent. Only 9 percent received prenatal care from private facilities, and less than 2 percent gave birth in such facilities.[46] Hence, even though the private sector absorbed more health care spending, the public sector provided most of the health services that were critical to infant survival.

Thailand since 1980 has produced more than enough food to feed its population, and has been among the world's largest exporters of rice, which is also the main domestic staple. In 1982, however, a national survey showed that 51 percent of preschoolers were malnourished, and that the problem was even worse in the impoverished Northeast.[47] The survey provided evidence that malnutrition was causing 55,000 child deaths per year, a figure that "sent a shock wave through the government." The Fifth Five-Year Plan (1982–1986) included a nutrition plan targeted to children, pregnant women, and new mothers. It focused on nutrition education, production of more nutritious foods, growth monitoring, supplementary feeding, rehabilitation for malnourished children, and school lunches in 5,000 impoverished areas.[48] From 1986 to 1995 the proportion of children under five years of age who suffered from severe or moderate malnutrition fell from 26 to 15 percent. By 2005 the share was 9 percent (Table A14). The rate of decline of child malnourishment from 1986 to 1995 was about twice as high as would have been expected from overall modernization in the absence of a nutrition program.[49]

Until an American Presbyterian Mission introduced Western medicine in 1828, Thais relied for medical care on traditional healers, many of whom used methods derived from Indian Ayurvedic medicine. Some Thais continued to use traditional healers and remedies throughout the twentieth century, and legislation in 1937 and 1953 established registries for traditional practitioners who passed an examination.[50] By 1999, however, fewer than one in twenty survey respondents reported using traditional practitioners or medicines in response to illness, and respondents rated the quality of care given by traditional practitioners below that of mainstream ones.[51]

Under the absolute monarchy, which fell to a military coup in 1932, King Chulalongkorn (1868–1910) improved urban sanitation and founded Thailand's first school of Western medicine in 1889. His son, Prince Mahidol, the father of the future King Bhumipol Adulyadej (1946–), received an MD from Harvard in 1928 and helped to persuade the Rockefeller Foundation to fund hospitals and medical training.[52] Between 1909 and 1936 the monarchy

---

[46] Nitayarumphong et al. 2001: 69, 138.
[47] Chutikul 1986: 19; Krongkaew 1982: 73–74.
[48] Heaver and Kachondam 2002; Kiranandana and Tontisirin 1992: 22 (quotation), 27–28; Mikhanorn 1991: 168; Muscat 1994: 238; Porapakkham 1986: 56–59; Sepúlveda 1994: 53; Thailand. MoPH 1988: 31–32.
[49] Heaver and Kachondam 2002: 49.
[50] Cohen 1989: 165.
[51] Nitayarumphong et al. 2001: 132–133, 146.
[52] Muangman 1987.

and its military-dominated successor opened 136 health centers in rural towns, paying the salaries of the health workers and nurse-midwives but asking communities to provide materials, labor, and funding for building construction. Also during the 1920s, the monarchy launched a health education campaign featuring films, slide shows, pamphlets, handbills, and exhibits at fairs and pilgrimages.[53]

It was proposed during the 1920s that "junior doctors" be trained for two to three years to work in rural areas, without going through the longer training of fully credentialed physicians. The scheme was finally launched in 1934 under the slogan "if you can't wear silk, wear cotton." The junior doctor program expanded in the early 1940s, when a four-year training course was established in the town of Lopburi. In the 1950s, however, partly because of pressure exerted by doctors in the Thai Medical Association, junior doctors were confined mainly to disease control programs.[54] Little was done during the 1950s to relieve the shortage of health care providers in rural areas. The outgoing head of the U.S. Operations Mission lamented this deficiency in 1959, and encouraged the government to give rural doctors, nurses, and other health personnel higher pay, faster promotion, more responsibility, and better housing.[55]

In other respects, however, the 1950s was a decade of significant progress in the health field. The military government of Field Marshal Plaek Pibulsonggram (1948–1957), an anti-communist (and one-time pro-fascist) who won U.S. backing after World War II, took action to improve disease control. In 1951 the government launched an anti-malaria campaign, whose cornerstone was the application of insecticides to the homes of some 14 million people.[56] In the late 1940s malaria had been Thailand's leading cause of death, taking some 47,000 lives annually. By 1958 it was in fifth place with about 10,000 annual fatalities; by 1968 it was in eighth place with some 5,000 yearly deaths.[57] In 1995 Thailand recorded just over 800 malaria fatalities, compared to 16,727 traffic deaths.[58] The anti-malaria program, along with campaigns against leprosy, plague, smallpox, tuberculosis, and yaws, coincided with a sharp plunge in mortality from 1947 to 1960.[59] The Pibul government also established programs to immunize infants and children against diphtheria, pertussis, tetanus, tuberculosis, and polio; to train traditional birth attendants and other health care providers; to expand health education; and to increase access to safe water and adequate sanitation in rural areas, especially in the Northeast. Many of these programs received financial support from UNICEF

[53] Haynal 1959: 3; Thailand. MoPH 1988: 4; Varavarn 2000 [1930]: 186–207, 211–212.
[54] Cohen 1989: 160–161, 165; Goldstein and Donaldson 1979: 326–329.
[55] Haynal 1959: 4–5, 19–20, 25.
[56] Muscat 1990: 87–89.
[57] USOM 1969: 3.
[58] Malaria fatalities: Thailand. MoPH 2000. Traffic deaths: Thailand. NSO 2001: Table 5.17.
[59] Muscat 1994: 122; Porapakkham 1986: 15, 69–70; Rungpitarangsi 1974: 69.

or the U.S. Operations Mission.[60] The Pibul government also built hospitals and health centers in outlying provinces in the 1950s.[61]

In 1966 the Village Health and Sanitation Program set up in cooperation with U.S. AID was folded into a Comprehensive Rural Health initiative, which focused additionally on maternal and child health, nutrition, and public health, concentrating on the Northeast where rural insurgency was on the rise.[62] Successive governments also initiated pilot primary health care projects in the provinces of Phitsanulok (1964–1968), Chiang Mai (1968–1971), and Lampang (1974–1979).[63] In 1967, concerned that nearly 50 percent of new medical graduates had emigrated in 1965, the Thanom Kittikachorn government began to provide medical scholarships if the newly trained physician agreed to work for three years in an underserved rural area. The program became compulsory in 1971, although graduates could buy their way out by paying a fine. Compulsory service programs were later enacted for nurses, midwives, and other health personnel.[64]

In 1978 the Ministry of Public Health launched the Rural Primary Health Care Expansion Project, complementing an expanded National Food and Nutrition Plan, a Rural Development Plan, and a Poverty Alleviation Program.[65] The Rural Primary Health Care Expansion Project recruited volunteer villagers, trained them for a few days or weeks, and assigned them to help government health personnel, usually based in health centers, to provide health education, family planning, nutrition, sanitation, disease control, simple curative care, immunization, and maternal and child health services in the villages in which they lived.[66] Village Health Volunteers linked government health officials to villagers, and Village Health Communicators linked Volunteers to 8–15 households. About 80 percent of Volunteers and Communicators were women. From 1977 to 1986 the number of Volunteers rose from 1,900 to 43,000, while the number of Communicators rose from 16,700 to 419,300.[67]

The government redoubled its primary health care efforts in the early 1980s, forming an interministerial committee to coordinate primary health care policy and programs.[68] Spending on primary health care by the Ministry of Public Health tripled in real terms from 1977 to 1987. From 1981 to 1985

[60] Mikhanorn 1991: 14–15, 23–24, 69–70, 128; Muscat 1994: 92, 120, 122; Thailand. MoPH 1988: 35.

[61] Mikhanorn 1991: 23; Muscat 1990: 92.

[62] USOM 1969: 6–13.

[63] Krongkaew 1982: 92–97; Mikhanorn 1991: 196; Sepúlveda 1994: 32.

[64] Nitayarumphong et al. 2001: 57–58; Wibulpolprasert and Pengpaibon 2003: 3.

[65] Other programs implemented in conjunction with the Rural Primary Health Care Expansion Project included literacy expansion, infrastructure projects, agricultural production schemes, and emergency employment activities (Heaver and Kachondam 2002: 5).

[66] Heaver and Kachondam 2002: 6–8, 13–14; Mikhanorn 1991: 128, 196.

[67] Cohen 1989: 166; Sepúlveda 1994: 32, 48. The estimate that 80 percent of these personnel were female comes from Heaver and Kachondam 2002: 7.

[68] Chandarasorn 1990: 45–46; Kiranandana and Tontisirin 1992: 2; Thailand. MoPH 1988: 6.

the share of the health budget devoted to rural areas rose from 41 to 56 percent, and from 1981 to 1986 the proportion of villages with health volunteers rose from 47 to 99 percent. The ratio of doctors per capita in Bangkok to doctors per capita in the impoverished Northeast fell from 21:1 in 1979 to 9:1 in 1986.[69] Meanwhile, "some communities with poor health indicators were targeted for special programmes, and many more health-care facilities were constructed and staffed. In short, health-care policy was realigned in favor of the rural poor during the 1980s."[70] In 1993 the Village Health Volunteers and Village Health Communicators were merged into a single category called the Health Volunteer, who was empowered to treat minor illnesses.[71] By 1990 there were 679,000 Health Volunteers, and by 2002 there were 759,000.[72] Thailand thus managed to sustain its primary health care efforts well beyond 1986, when the Rural Primary Health Care Expansion Project formally ended and when the services it had provided were tranferred to the health ministry.

In terms of health spending, facilities, and personnel, rural health care improved significantly in Thailand from 1975 to 1985. In terms of the quality of care provided, however, the gains were less impressive. Village Health Volunteers received only 15 days of training; Village Health Communicators received only 5 days. Both categories of volunteers participated in occasional refresher programs, but these courses were judged to be "weak."[73] Moreover, "in the final analysis volunteers will always be volunteers, so it is impossible to expect them to dedicate more to community work than to their own occupations." At the end of 1986, the country's 7,432 health centers averaged only two health personnel, well below the prescribed level of five.[74] District health officials, partly because of competing demands on their time, tended to "stay in the office...and devote not much time to health promotion and health prevention activities...community visitation, [or the] supervision of Village Health Communicator and Village Health Volunteer activities." The Ministry of Public Health gave district health centers as little as U.S. $40–60 annually for motorcycle repairs and gasoline, constraining their outreach activities, and monitored the quantity but not the quality of services provided. The will and capacity of provincial governors to implement the program varied, and the agencies involved in supervising the initiative often suffered from poor information and from overworked or disinterested personnel. The National Committee on Primary Health Care met only a few times during the 1980s and did little to coordinate the activities of its associated ministries.[75] Doctors

---

[69] Budget: Sepúlveda 1994: 32. Villages with volunteers: Mikhanorn 1991: 125. Doctors per capita: Wibulpolprasert and Pengpaibon 2003: 5.

[70] Kiranandana and Tontisirin 1992: 38.

[71] Heaver and Kachondam 2002: 7 fn. 2.

[72] Thailand. MoPH 2007: 48.

[73] Heaver and Kachondam 2002: 13.

[74] Mikhanorn 1991: 74, 76, 154.

[75] Chandarasorn 1990: 48–54.

and other personnel in district hospitals were often reluctant to cooperate with primary care initiatives.[76]

Compounding these problems was an overall shortage of doctors, especially in rural areas. Thailand in 1995 had only 2.4 doctors per 10,000 inhabitants, only one-fifth to one-tenth the ratio in South Korea, Taiwan, and the four Latin American cases (the ratio in Indonesia, however, was even lower than in Thailand). The situation was better for nurses, where Thailand's ratio in 1995 was 8.7 per 10,000, just below Costa Rica's and twice that of Chile.[77] Both doctors and nurses were geographically maldistributed, however. In 1981 Bangkok had 17 times as many doctors and 18 times as many nurses per capita as the Northeast. By 1995 the figures had fallen to 11 times as many doctors and 6 times as many nurses, but more than 50 percent of the doctors were fledgling degree recipients doing temporary compulsory service. To deal with the shortage of doctors and nurses, a technical team proposed that more students from rural areas be admitted to medical school and that rural health personnel receive better pay and perquisites.[78] In 1995, the government began to finance the training of doctors from rural areas who agreed to work for three or more years in their regions of origin. In 2002 this program accepted 293 students. In 1994 only 23 percent of Thailand's doctors came from rural areas; by 2001 the share had risen to 32 percent.[79]

Thailand had little health insurance before 1975, when a Low Income Card Scheme was introduced.[80] Under this program, households below an income poverty line were given a free health card entitling them to access to drugs, examinations, obstetric care, and medical treatment at public health facilities, provided that they followed a referral system that encouraged the use of local health centers. About 68 percent of the population met the income cutoff in 1976, but many who were entitled to a health card did not obtain one, either because they were unaware of their entitlement, or because they could not afford transport to health facilities, or because they preferred to use the private sector, or because they did not like to be classified as "low income." In 1978, when the Thai population was about 45 million, the cards were used only 9.3 million times. Bangkok received much higher per capita funding than the impoverished Northeast,[81] and in the early 1990s the aged, school children, primary health care volunteers, village headmen, veterans, the disabled, and Buddhist monks became entitled to a free card. In 1991, when only the poor and war veterans could participate, the Low Income Card Scheme had covered only 17 percent of the population, with the poor making up 98 percent of

[76] Cohen 1989: 166; Mikhanorn 1991: 150.
[77] WHO 2003.
[78] Charoenparij et al. 1999: 13–15.
[79] Wibulpolprasert ed. 2002: 428–429; figures from Wibulpolprasert and Pengpaibon 2003: 9–10.
[80] Ramesh 2000: 166.
[81] Kiranandana and Tontisirin 1992: 14–15, 36; Mills 1991: 1242–1247; Reisman 1999: 638; World Bank Thailand Office 1999: 21, 26.

beneficiaries. By 1998 the scheme covered 45 percent of the population, with the poor accounting for only 42 percent of beneficiaries.[82]

In 1984 the government began to allow persons with higher incomes to purchase health cards through a separate plan called the Voluntary Health Card Scheme. During the 1990s, a card that would provide a family of up to five free medical care for three years cost 500 baht, about U.S. $20 before 1997.[83] The purpose of this plan was to improve access to health care and to encourage people to use basic, close-to-home services before major hospitals.[84] Although aimed at the "near poor," many falling into this category did not buy the cards, whereas many of the wealthy did. The program also suffered from adverse selection: people tended to buy the card after noticing a health problem, raising the cost of the program.[85] People from Bangkok were excluded from the scheme until 1995, when the program was scaled up to the national level. Accordingly, the share of the population covered by the voluntary cards rose from 2 percent in 1991 to 14 percent in 1998.[86]

In 1983 the government introduced the Civil Service Medical Benefit Scheme, which provided health insurance for public employees and their dependents. By 1998 it covered 11 percent of the population. The Civil Service Scheme was funded by general revenues, making it regressive from the financing perspective, but its payments improved the finances of providers who also delivered free medical care to the poor. In 1991 the government launched the Social Security Scheme, which made health insurance mandatory for private-sector workers in firms with at least 20 employees (10 as of 1993, 5 as of 2001, and 1 as of 2002). Workers, employers, and the government each contributed 1.5 percent of the worker's gross salary to the Scheme. In 1995, self-employed and unemployed workers were admitted if they paid both the employer's and employee's share. From 1992 to 1998, the coverage of the Social Security Scheme rose from 4 to 9 percent of the population.[87]

By 1998, then, Thailand had four health insurance programs: the free health card scheme, covering about 45 percent of the population; the voluntary health card scheme, covering 14 percent; the civil service scheme, covering 11 percent; and the social security scheme, covering 9 percent. In 2001 the newly elected government of Thaksin Shinawatra replaced the two health card schemes with the Universal Coverage ("30 baht") program, which was open to any citizen who did not already belong to the civil service or social security schemes. After registering with a network of health care providers, beneficiaries of the Universal Coverage program were entitled to receive health services from a clinic or hospital for a flat fee of 30 baht (about U.S. $0.75 in

[82] Nitayarumphong et al. 2001: 64, 84; Reisman 1999: 637.

[83] Mills 1991: 1247; Reisman 1999: 633–634.

[84] Thailand. MoPH 1988: 49–50.

[85] Charoenparij et al. 1999: 23.

[86] Nitayarumphong et al. 2001: 84.

[87] Charoenparij et al. 1999: 23–24; Ramesh 2000: 60–62; Reisman 1999: 627; coverage figures from Nitayarumphong et al. 2001: 84.

2001). The very poor were exempt from the 30 baht fee. Each beneficiary registered with a chosen provider or network of providers; the government then paid each provider on a capitation basis (i.e., a set amount determined by the number of persons who had registered with it). The Universal Coverage program was financed by general revenues. In urban areas patients could choose their own providers; in rural areas the scarcity of private providers effectively restricted choice to public hospitals and their affiliated health centers.[88] The Universal Coverage program transformed publicly funded health insurance for the poor from a means-tested program to a legal entitlement.[89]

Because the Universal Coverage program excluded the 20 percent of Thais who belonged to the civil servants and social security schemes, it did not go as far toward the unification of publicly mandated health insurance programs as did the analogous programs in Brazil (1990–1993), Taiwan (1995), or South Korea (1998–2003). Among the eight societies considered in this book, the degree of unification in Thailand's Universal Coverage scheme was most similar to the National Health Fund (FONASA) in Chile (1979). FONASA unified Chile's preexisting blue-collar and white-collar schemes and used general revenues to cover the uninsured, but gave wage and salary earners the option of channeling their payroll deductions into privately run Social Security Health Institutions (ISAPREs) instead of into FONASA. In the late 1990s some 27 percent of Chileans used the ISAPREs rather than FONASA. Analogously, some 20 percent of Thais in the early 2000s remained in the civil servants or social security schemes rather than opting for Universal Coverage. In both Thailand and Chile, those who belonged to the narrower programs tended to be richer, younger, and healthier than those who belonged to the broader schemes.

The Universal Coverage program was among the Thaksin government's most popular policies, and the minuscule co-payment of 30 baht generated a huge rise in health service utilization. Soon after the program was implemented, hospitals in Bangkok began to receive numerous out-of-towners who, bypassing community hospitals and rural health centers, arrived in pursuit of "the country's best, and highest-paid, specialists."[90] Many public hospitals went deeply into debt, and many public-sector doctors and other professionals, finding that their workloads had soared, resigned to work full-time in the private sector.[91] In 2004 the Universal Coverage program covered 74 percent of the population, compared to 12 percent in the Civil Service Medical Benefit Scheme and 10 percent in the Social Security Scheme. An additional 4 percent were eligible to register under the Universal Coverage Program but had not done so.[92] The Universal Coverage program served mainly the poor; the

---

[88] Tangcharoensathien et al. 2002: 59–63.
[89] Haggard and Kaufman 2008: 254.
[90] Montlake 2002.
[91] *Bangkok Post* 2006; Kittikanya 2005; Pongpanich 2003.
[92] Hughes and Leethongdee 2007: 1001.

other two schemes served mainly the better-off.[93] In 2005 the government funded the Universal Coverage program at a level of 1,396 baht per person, about 2 percent of which came from the 30 baht co-payment.[94] After the September 2006 coup the new military-backed government abolished the co-payment because it cost more in bookkeeping than it generated in revenue.

Despite its financial imbalances, the Thai health system at the close of the twentieth century had several positive features. By 1998 the vast majority of the rural population lived within half an hour of a health clinic, and waiting times at rural health facilities averaged less than half an hour. A 1999 survey found that more than 90 percent of pregnant women used prenatal care, more than 90 percent gave birth attended by a doctor or a nurse, and more than 90 percent of new mothers rated these prenatal and obstetric services as satisfactory or better. Access to health services varied only slightly with rural versus urban location, and hardly at all with socioeconomic status. During the 1980s and 1990s, more and more patients made their first contact with the health system at a local health center rather than at a more sophisticated facility.[95] By 2002, thousands of "medical tourists" from the United States and elsewhere were flocking to such institutions as Bangkok's Bumrungrad Hospital for high-quality, inexpensive elective surgery. In 2003, 973,532 foreigners received medical treatment in Thailand, spending a total of U.S. $660 million. Thirty percent of these foreigners came to Thailand specifically to receive such treatment.[96] The downside of this phenomenon is that doctors are extremely scarce in Thailand, particularly in rural areas, and foreigners seeking medical treatment were expected to raise the demand for doctors by about 10 percent from 2005 to 2015.[97]

Another triumph of the Thai health system was its resilience in the face of the 1997 financial crisis, which forced the Ministry of Public Health to reduce its budget by 17 percent in real terms between 1997 and 1998. Although spending for disease control and health promotion fell, planned investments bore most of the cuts. Use of public health centers in the rural Northeast increased significantly as patients switched from private services and as migrants from the area returned. Overall, the use of health centers and district hospitals by health card holders rose 272 percent between 1997 and 1998. A World Bank report found that "two years after the onset of the 1997 economic crisis, most of the pessimistic expectations did not materialize. There is little if any evidence of a crisis impact on health needs and outcomes."[98] In one way the crisis actually improved access to health care in rural areas. As the Thai economy went into a tailspin, recent medical graduates found themselves both unable to

---

[93] Thailand. IHPP 2006: 7, 11.
[94] Tangcharoensathien et al. 2007: 13–14.
[95] Nitayarumphong et al. 2001: 84, 133, 138, 141, 187; Tangcharoensathien et al. 2007: 6.
[96] Bombardieri 2002; Kittikanya 2005; Pachanee and Wibulpolprasert 2006: 313.
[97] Aongsonwang 2005: 1–7; Pachanee and Wibulpolprasert 2006: 313.
[98] World Bank Thailand Office 1999: 15–23.

find a job in Bangkok and unable to buy their way out of the compulsory three years of service in a doctorless area. Hence, a higher share remained in the rural posts to which they had been assigned.[99] In 1997 more than 30 percent of new medical graduates failed to complete their compulsory three years of service; in 1998 the proportion was 4 percent.[100]

The greatest challenge to the Thai health system at the end of the twentieth century was HIV/AIDS. Thailand's first documented case of AIDS occurred in 1984. The number of reported HIV infections rose from 191 in 1987 to 10,764 in 1989, but the actual number was thought to be higher.[101] UNAIDS and the World Health Organization estimated that, in 2007, 610,000 Thais were living with HIV and 31,000 died of AIDS.[102] Sexual transmission accounted for about 88 percent of AIDS cases whose mode of transmission was known; intravenous drug use and mother-to-child transmission made up about 5 percent each.[103]

Public education about HIV/AIDS prevention began in the late 1980s, but it was mainly in the printed press and was thus not available to many rural people. In 1990, however, Mechai Viravaidya, a politician who had been an early leader in family planning and who had strong ties to non-governmental organizations, joined forces with the Ministry of Public Health, members of the Royal Family, and non-governmental organizations to launch a major television campaign to warn people about the dangers of HIV infection.[104] Another critical component of the campaign against AIDS was the promotion of condom use. In 1989, the government began a pilot program in the province of Ratchaburi to demand the use of condoms in 100 percent of sexual encounters in brothels. The program was extended to the rest of the country in 1991. The government gave brothel-based sex workers free condoms, and as a way of determining compliance with the "100 percent condom" policy, it monitored the incidence of sexually transmitted diseases among both the sex workers and their clients (anyone requesting treatment for a sexually transmitted disease fell under suspicion of noncompliance).[105] From 1988 to 1992 condom use in brothels rose from 14 percent to more than 90 percent. In a 1997 survey, 97 percent of commercial sex workers reported always using condoms with casual customers, and 93 percent reported always using them with regular clients.[106]

Thailand's campaign against HIV/AIDS achieved notable success. From 1991 to 2003 the annual number of new HIV infections fell from 143,000 to

---

[99] Pongpanich 2003.
[100] Wibulpolprasert ed. 2002: 429.
[101] Ford and Koetsawang 1991: 405.
[102] UNAIDS/WHO 2008: 5–6.
[103] UNAIDS/WHO 2004: 2.
[104] Lyttleton 2000: 48, 60, 109.
[105] Lyttleton 2000: 257; Nitayarumphong et al. 2001: 89; World Bank Thailand Office 2000: 10.
[106] World Bank Thailand Office 2000: 10.

21,000. The campaign was estimated to have prevented about 200,000 new infections during the 1990s. HIV prevalence among new army conscripts fell from 4 percent in 1993 to 0.5 percent in 2003. The number of new AIDS cases peaked in 1998 at 27,500; by 2003 it had fallen to 13,600.[107] The proportion of patients requiring anti-retroviral therapy who actually received it rose from 21 percent in 2004 to 61 percent in 2007.[108] These achievements notwithstanding, major challenges remained. Although HIV transmission fell sharply in brothels, it did not decline not among intravenous drug users or casual sex partners. Commercial sex was unregulated in neighboring countries, and any decline in condom use in Thai brothels held out the possibility of a renewed spike in HIV transmission.[109]

From 1978 to 2005 the rural poor in Thailand benefited from a significant improvement in public health services. This improvement worked together with the growth of GDP per capita and the reduction of income poverty, as well as with the improvements in other basic social services, to produce a rapid decline of infant mortality. Because of AIDS, progress at reducing mortality rates at older ages was not as impressive. In the end, however, the Thai health care system was remarkably effective at fighting AIDS, as well as in reducing infant mortality. The Rural Primary Health Care Expansion Project (1978–1986), which introduced Village Health Volunteers on a large scale, was a turning point in the provision of basic health and nutrition services to the rural poor. The quality of the services initially left something to be desired, partly because it was hard to persuade trained health personnel to practice in remote rural areas (this was also a major problem in Indonesia, and to a lesser extent in Brazil). Thereafter, however, the quality of services improved. Accordingly, the pace of infant mortality decline accelerated not only after 1975, but again after 1990 (Table A1).

From 1980 onward the Thai government allocated an increasing share of revenue to the health ministry, whose officials channeled the money increasingly to community hospitals, rural health centers, and various primary care providers. Health Volunteers linked villagers to public health authorities throughout this period. Also, the technical competency of health ministry personnel, which was high to begin with, increased even more during the 1980s and 1990s. By the early 2000s Thai health ministry officials were publishing prodigiously in the world's top public health journals. These officials also devised solutions to the problem of getting doctors and nurses to practice in rural areas, making the health system less biased toward cities. As a result of these improvements, the share of births attended by trained personnel, perhaps single best indicator of the quality of maternal and infant care in the standard cross-national statistical compendia, rose from 41 percent in

---

[107] UNAIDS/WHO 2004: 2, 6. Estimate of number of HIV infections averted in the 1990s: World Bank Thailand Office 2000: 12.

[108] UNAIDS/WHO 2008: 13.

[109] World Bank Thailand Office 2000: 17–22.

1983 to 97 percent in 2005, while child immunization rose from less than 50 percent in 1980 to nearly 100 percent in 2005 (Tables A16 and A17). Because the Rural Primary Health Care Expansion Project helped to set in motion these significant improvements in health service utilization from 1980 onward, it is well worth understanding the forces and conditions that led to its implementation.

9.5. Thailand: Determinants of Public Health Care Policies

The Rural Primary Health Care Expansion Project built upon Thailand's extensive experience with disease control and health service provision in poor areas, which produced expertise and infrastructure upon which the Project drew. Thailand until 1932 was an absolute monarchy, but King Chulalongkorn (1868–1910) took an interest in health-related issues and encouraged the expansion of Western medicine. The parents of King Bhumipol Adulyadej (1946–), who exercised enormous influence under the constitutional monarchy, were a doctor and a nurse. Junior doctor schemes were implemented in the 1930s, disease control and rural health facility construction expanded in the 1950s, and compulsory service in underserved areas for new medical graduates was introduced in the 1970s. Pilot primary health care programs started in 1964, nationwide family planning commenced in 1970, and the Low Income Card Scheme began in 1975. The Rural Primary Health Care Expansion Project thus emerged from a long historical process and drew heavily on expertise and infrastructure built up in previous decades.

The international primary health care movement, which culminated in the WHO/UNICEF conference in Alma Ata in September 1978, had special resonance in Thailand because of the country's long history of involvement with international public health organizations. In 1976 the government consulted the World Health Organization before including the Rural Primary Health Care Expansion Project in its Five-Year Development Plan.[110] The Thai delegation took an active part in the Alma Ata conference itself, sharing accounts of its pilot primary health care programs with officials from other countries. Dr. Jumroon Mikhanorn, a leader of the Rural Primary Health Care Expansion Project, stressed the role of the international public health community in giving impetus to the initiative.[111]

As early as the 1950s the Thai government was targeting social and economic programs to the Northeast because of concern for the security situation in the region.[112] The upheavals in Vietnam, Laos, and Cambodia, as well as the rural insurgency in Thailand itself, heightened such concerns in the 1960s. As the U.S. Operations Mission (USOM) noted, "while health needs have always been more acute in the poorer Northeast region of Thailand, the middle 60s

---

[110] Cohen 1989: 166.
[111] Mikhanorn 2003.
[112] Muscat 1994: 139–140.

saw new emphasis focused on the northeast provinces by the RTG [Royal Thai Government] and USOM because of the growing insurgency."[113] In the 1970s the Asia Foundation, a U.S. non-governmental organization, funded training, transport, and supplies for village health workers in the province of Nongkhai, on the border with Laos, hoping that "through the program, the remote villages would feel support and linkage with the rest of Thailand, improve their solidarity as a group, and be able to resist some of the border movements."[114] The wars in Southeast Asia also made a more direct contribution to the expansion of health services in rural areas. Particularly near the borders of Laos and Cambodia, the Thai government in the 1970s and early 1980s built or expanded small community hospitals to treat battle injuries. These hospitals were also used to deliver basic health services to the poor.[115]

The conflict between communism and anti-communism also contributed to the implementation of the Rural Primary Health Care Expansion Project through its influence on the military. In the mid-1970s insurgents from the Communist Party of Thailand (CPT) used medical treatment in remote rural areas as a way to win political support. U.S. analysts lamented that "the problem is compounded because medical service is inadequate for the present population, something the CPT is quick to exploit."[116] In response to this challenge, the Democratic Soldiers, a group of middle-ranking army officers that emerged in the mid-1970s, made improving material conditions in the villages the centerpiece of their counterinsurgency strategy. The army high command rejected these ideas, but General Prem Tinsulanonda, operating in the Northeast in the mid-1970s, adopted them and trained villagers in simple health care techniques in order to help win the hearts and minds of the rural poor. Shortly after Prem became prime minister in March 1980, the government officially adopted a policy of fighting communism by political as well as military means. Among those who drafted the order instituting this policy were members of the Democratic Soldiers.[117]

Thailand was an absolute monarchy until 1932, when a heterogeneous group of civilians and military officers launched a bloodless coup that forced the monarchy to accept a constitution and to relinquish most of its power to a cabinet and legislature. The next 75 years saw 18 more coups (mostly to overthrow existing military leaders), 54 governments, and 16 constitutions.[118] From 1932 to 1969 the country remained under military or military-dominated governments. A brief democratic opening in the late 1960s was followed by another coup. In October 1973 student demonstrations against a widely disliked military government ushered in three years of civilian rule.

---

[113] USOM 1969: 13.
[114] Stark 1985: 270–271.
[115] Zankel 2003.
[116] Randolph and Thompson 1981: 45.
[117] Phongpaichit and Baker 2002: 345–347; Tinsulanonda 1995.
[118] *Economist* 2002: 5. The September 2006 coup and the Surayud Chulanont government have been added to the totals in this source.

From October 1973 to October 1976, Thailand came closer to democracy than ever before (Table A18). Taking advantage of the political opening, medical students and health professionals mobilized in support of rural primary health care and other health-related activities.[119] Some of the students and doctors who participated in the "Return to the Countryside" and "Public Health for the Masses" campaigns of 1973 and 1974 collaborated with the Communist Party of Thailand.[120] These activities put pressure on the government to show that it too could deliver health benefits to the poor. The democratic opening of the early 1970s also led to the proliferation of non-governmental organizations (NGOs) involved in health care.[121]

After the rural insurgency died down in the late 1970s, some of the doctors who had worked with communists were threatened or blackballed. Nonetheless, primary health care "provided an important bridge between NGOs and Government agencies, with doctors playing an intermediary role" and "provided a legitimate means for members of the medical profession to re-engage themselves in some of the reform activities which had previously led to accusations of being 'communist'."[122] The Rural Doctors Forum, an issue network that traced its origins to the student demonstrations of October 1973, spearheaded the push by progressive health professionals in support of primary care. This organization remained politically influential throughout the last quarter of the twentieth century, designing activities to support rural doctors (awards, newsletters, handbooks, training programs), advocating tobacco control, lobbying for the formulation of an essential drugs list, promoting democratization, and fighting corruption.[123]

To the extent that the democratic opening of 1973–1976 contributed to the expansion of primary health care in Thailand, it did so not so much by triggering electoral competition for the votes of the rural poor, as by creating a "groundswell of social demands from newly mobilized labor and farmer organizations, some with policy leadership from sympathetic academics and students."[124] In particular, the democratic opening made space for the organization of progressive health professionals in the Rural Doctors Forum, which contributed materially to the improvement of health services for decades thereafter. In terms of the particular mechanisms by which democracy promoted mortality-reducing social policies, Thailand in the 1970s resembled Brazil in the 1980s more than Chile in the 1960s or Costa Rica in the 1970s. By organizing health professionals in support of primary health care, and by serving as a link between government health officials and left-leaning groups in civil society and non-governmental organizations, the Rural Doctors Forum

---

[119] Bamber 1997: 236–237; Cohen 1989: 167; Trirat 2001: 13–15.
[120] Bamber 1997: 237.
[121] Cohen 1989: 167–168.
[122] Bamber 1997: 239.
[123] Green 2000: 53; Trirat 2001; Wibulpolprasert and Pengpaibon 2003: 13.
[124] Haggard and Kaufman 2008: 134.

in Thailand in the 1970s played a role analogous to that of the Primary Care Movement in Brazil.

Although the period during which the Rural Primary Health Care Expansion Project was implemented saw faster infant mortality decline than in previous years, deficiencies in the quality of care made this decline slower than it would otherwise have been. These quality deficiencies were partly rooted in Thailand's social structure. Thailand is one of the world's least urbanized countries. In 2005, Thailand ranked 164th among 207 countries on urbanization. From 1960 to 2005, moreover, the proportion of Thais living in urban areas rose only from 20 to 32 percent. By comparison, the urban share of the population in the other Asian cases rose during the same period from 15 to 48 percent in Indonesia, from 28 to 81 percent in South Korea, and from 64 to 95 percent in Taiwan.[125] Thailand's low level of urbanization facilitated growth by weakening class organization and reducing overt class conflict, giving the state more "steering capacity." On the other hand, low urbanization was an obstacle to health service delivery. It is hard to recruit health personnel to remote rural areas, and it is difficult to monitor the performance (or even the presence) of those who undertake such service.[126] Tellingly, a shortage of highly skilled medical personnel in rural areas was cited as a major flaw in the Thai health care system by the outgoing head of the USOM in the late 1950s, by the editor of the official study assessing the impact of the Rural Primary Health Care Expansion Project in the 1980s, and by a technical team making recommendations for health sector reform at the end of the 1990s.[127] Some progress was made in this area at the end of the 1990s, but as long as Thailand remains predominantly rural, sustained effort will be needed to recruit rural people as doctors and nurses and to make service in rural areas attractive to a wider range of health care professionals.

The roots of the unification and universalization of health insurance in Thailand lie in the political liberalization of the mid-1970s, when the Rural Doctors Forum emerged and began to exert pressure in this direction, mostly inside executive-branch agencies. In the 1980s and 1990s, pressure from labor unions and other groups led to a modest rise in the share of the population covered by health insurance. The 1997 constitutional reform, by stipulating a basic right to health, gave juridical support to those who advocated unifying existing health insurance schemes into a single-payer system and who favored making basic health services more accessible to the poor.

Proponents of health insurance unification in Thailand in the late 1990s initially advocated substituting Universal Coverage for all existing publicly mandated health insurance schemes. That is what happened in Taiwan after 1995, when National Health Insurance replaced ten extant publicly mandated

---

[125] World Bank 2008a; Taiwan. DGBAS 1975: 12 and Taiwan. DGBAS 2007: 26 (cities of 20,000+).

[126] Chomitz et al. 1997; Filmer, Hammer, and Pritchett 2002: 60–61.

[127] Haynal 1959: 25; Mikhanorn 1991: 149; Charoenparij et al. 1999: 13–15.

health insurance schemes, and in South Korea after 1998, when National Health Insurance replaced hundreds of such schemes. This initial plan, however, "met resistance from government departments running the other schemes and from civil servants and trades unionists benefiting from the two employment-based schemes." Resistance from similar groups delayed Brazil's Unified Health System, whose launch had been scheduled for 1990, for three years. In Thailand such resistance succeeded in preserving the civil servants and social security schemes, although the November 2002 National Health Security Act (the law that created the Universal Coverage scheme) permitted the Universal Coverage Scheme to absorb these other health insurance programs by executive decree rather than by legislation.[128]

Democracy contributed to the expansion of health insurance coverage and to the unification of health insurance schemes in Thailand, just as it did in Brazil in the 1980s and in Taiwan and South Korea in the 1990s. Thailand's Social Security Act of 1990, which introduced health insurance coverage for private-sector wage earners, emerged during the Prime Ministership of Chatichai Choonhavan (1988–1991), which saw an elected parliament, renewed labor organization and peasant protest, the erosion of military influence, challenges by elected ministers to career bureaucrats, and "the re-emergence of many of the radical and dissident elements which had first surfaced after 1973, and which had been repressed since 1976." Employers opposed the Social Security Act, but labor unions supported it, as did many non-governmental organizations and media outlets. The bill passed, and the military-dominated governments immediately after the 1992 coup enforced it.[129]

Initial discussion of Universal Coverage involved only academics and policymakers, some of whom had "gone to the countryside" as medical graduates in the early and mid-1970s.[130] Wider support emerged in 1999, however, when the Foundation for Consumers, which grew out of the Coordinating Committee for Primary Health Care of Thai NGOs, issued a booklet summarizing the findings of its research into the health care system. The booklet revealed serious deficiencies and included 15 case studies of persons whom the system had dramatically wronged. The booklet's findings were picked up by the mass media, enabling a dozen non-governmental organizations to band together to collect the 50,000 signatures required to submit to Parliament a bill for universal health insurance coverage. Appropriately, given the organization's emphasis, the bill introduced by the Foundation for Consumers included a provision to empower non-governmental organizations to monitor health service delivery. Despite "intense lobbying from the medical profession and the private sector to derail the passing of the Bill," Parliament approved it in November 2002.[131]

---

[128] Towse, Mills, and Tangcharoensathien 2004: 103.

[129] Phongpaichit and Baker 2002: 370, 380 (quotation); Green 2000: 50.

[130] Pannarunothai, Patmasiriwat, and Srithamrongsawat 2004: 18; Tangcharoensathien et al. 2007: 8.

[131] Consumers International 2005: 32–33. NGOs stands for non-governmental organizations.

In 2001, however, well before the bill was introduced, a supporter of Universal Coverage in the Ministry of Public Health had discussed the proposal with leaders of the Thai Rak Thai party, which had been organized in 1998 by Thaksin Shinawatra, a prominent and wealthy business executive. Thai Rak Thai endorsed the Universal Coverage plan and promoted the scheme in its 2001 electoral campaign, along with other programs designed to appeal to the rural poor. The party won and the program was enacted well in advance of the November 2002 National Health Security Act. Universal Coverage became one of Thaksin's most popular policies. The government's top leaders were "keenly aware that the UHS [Universal Health Scheme] [was] a significant element in [the government's] popularity," and the program served again as a centerpiece of Thai Rak Thai's 2005 campaign, which the party won in a landslide.[132] Despite the scale of the victory, especially in rural areas, protest mounted in Bangkok against Thaksin's autocratic style and his family's tax-exempt sale of a U.S. \$2 billion stake in a communications conglomerate. A perception that the prime minister had criticized the monarchy while defending himself against the charges of the protesters brought matters to a head, and Thaksin was ousted in a September 2006 coup.

Democracy was thus important not only to the expansion of basic health care services in the late 1970s and early 1980s, but even more directly and saliently to the universalization of health insurance coverage in the early 2000s. It is not clear, however, that broader health insurance coverage led to steeper infant mortality decline. The expansion of coverage failed to accelerate infant mortality decline in Chile in the 1950s, in Costa Rica in the 1970s, in Taiwan in the 1990s, or in South Korea in the 1990s. To expand health insurance coverage is to reduce financial barriers to medical care. Without a large rise in the number of doctors and nurses in rural areas, the resulting increased demand will simply increase the workloads of those already working in the countryside, giving them an incentive to resign to work full-time in the private sector, as happened in Thailand after 2001. In Indonesia, where health professionals are even scarcer, the Askeskin health insurance plan of 2005 ran a similar risk.

Universal health insurance is likely eventually to encourage policies conducive to better health status, but its short-term impact may differ. By allowing the previously uninsured to retain income that they would otherwise have to spend on health services, universal coverage makes them richer, but not necessarily healthier. Universal coverage is more an anti-poverty program than a way to improve health. In Thailand, moreover, the Universal Coverage Plan was introduced in 2001, when the infant mortality rate had already fallen to 10 per 1000.[133] Accordingly, it cannot explain the country's remarkable decline of infant mortality from 103 per 1000 in 1960 to 8 per 1000 in 2005.

[132] Hewison 2004: 517 (quote); Pachanee and Wibulpolprasert 2006: 311–314; Tangcharoensathien et al. 2007: 7–8.
[133] World Bank 2008c (Country Data Sheet for Thailand).

The roots of this rapid decline can be traced more persuasively to the Rural Primary Health Care Expansion Project of 1978, which was introduced when the infant mortality rate was still about 79 per 1000.

Electoral incentives contributed to universal coverage, but other aspects of democracy did more to encourage earlier policies with more important implications for the infant mortality rate. From 1973 to 1976, as citizens gained more freedom to associate, the Rural Doctors Forum was able to coalesce, make contacts and gain influence within the health ministry, and institutionalize itself sufficiently to withstand a return to authoritarian rule. The Rural Doctors Forum promoted both the 1978 Rural Primary Health Care Expansion Project and the 2001 Universal Coverage Scheme. Just as importantly, periods of liberalization and democratization in Thailand in 1973–1976 and in 1992–2005 encouraged political mobilization in general, which can improve the quality of social services from the demand side. In Indonesia, the New Order regime went to great lengths to try to secure the political quiescence of the population. Partly as a result of Indonesia's more persistent and thoroughgoing authoritarianism, political mobilization after the 1965 coup was lower in Indonesia than in Thailand, so demand-based improvements in health service quality were harder to achieve. This difference in political mobilization helps to explain why Indonesia's primary health care policies were less successful than Thailand's at reducing infant mortality.

Indonesia: Authoritarianism Slows Infant Mortality Decline

Indonesia from 1960 to 1990 achieved fast economic growth, low income inequality, and a steep decline of income poverty. It also improved primary education and introduced a major family planning program, which contributed to a rapid decline of the total fertility rate. Despite these advantages, Indonesia in 1990 had a high infant mortality rate for its level of GDP per capita, a very high infant mortality rate for its level of GDP per capita and income inequality taken together, and an extremely high infant mortality rate relative to that predicted by a broader range of socioeconomic variables.[1] From 1990 to 2005, however, infant mortality decline sped up even though GDP per capita growth slowed down. The acceleration may have been due in part to the lagged effects of previous GDP per capita growth and social service provision, but it also resulted from more effective public service provision after 1990. A good record at public service provision after 1990 offset a poor record in earlier years, such that Indonesia wound up with an infant mortality rate that was just at the level predicted by its GDP per capita in 2005, and with a decline of infant mortality that was almost precisely the amount predicted by its GDP per capita growth from 1960 to 2005 (Figures 1.1 and 1.2). Given its achievements in education, family planning, and fertility, however, Indonesia's record might well have been better. Among the eight cases compared in this book, Indonesia ranked last on the average annual percent decline of infant mortality from 1960 to 2005 (Table A1).

Slow progress at expanding secondary school enrollment, at raising access to improved water and sanitation, and at improving basic health services contributed to the unimpressive decline of infant mortality in Indonesia. From 1960 to 2005 Indonesia had two major primary health care programs: the Village Community Health Development Program, which began in 1978 (just after the meeting at Alma Ata, in the same year as Thailand's Rural Primary Health Care Expansion Project), and the village midwife program, which began in 1989. The Village Community Health Development Program was

[1] In Table 2.2, Indonesia's residuals were +0.22 in Model 2–1, +0.37 in Model 2–2, and +0.38 in Model 2–3. These residuals were, respectively, 67th, 85th, and 94th highest among the residuals produced by the 105 developing countries in the analysis.

successful in raising the number of local health centers and subcenters, and the village midwife program was successful in raising the number of health workers who were capable of providing trained assistance at birth. The 1989 village midwife program coincided with a sharper acceleration of infant mortality decline than did the broader 1978 initiative.

Deficiencies in the 1978 Village Community Health Development Program can be traced in part to the authoritarian character of Suharto's New Order regime (1967–1998), coupled with the weakness of democratic traditions in a country which, like South Korea and Taiwan, was under colonial rule until 1945. Without effective electoral competition, politicians had few incentives to try to win or retain votes by promising or delivering better health services. The Suharto administration, moreover, controlled most interest groups, reducing their ability to shape public service provision (for better or worse). When rural health personnel tried in the 1970s to organize an autonomous issue network similar to Thailand's Rural Doctors Forum, the Suharto government repressed the initiative. Moreover, three decades of authoritarian rule discouraged demand-based improvements in public health services.

10.1. Indonesia: Mortality

Indonesia's vital registration statistics are too incomplete to be used to estimate infant mortality levels and changes from 1960 to 2005.[2] Accordingly, such estimates come from censuses and surveys. The most recent available estimates of infant mortality are for 2000, and are derived from birth histories and survivorship questions in the Demographic and Health Survey of 2002–2003.[3] The infant mortality estimate for 2005 in Table A1 is a projection based on data from 2000 and earlier. That is not prohibitively troublesome for cross-national comparisons of infant mortality in 2005, but the projection precludes any meaningful assertion about infant mortality decline from 2000 to 2005.

In 1960 as in 2005, Indonesia had the highest rate of infant mortality and the lowest level of life expectancy among the eight cases compared in this book. In a broader perspective, Indonesia's 2005 infant mortality rate of 28 per 1000 placed it 108th of 190 countries with available data (the country with the lowest infant mortality rate is ranked first). Its 2005 life expectancy at birth of 67.8 years also placed it below the median, at 118th of 186 countries with available data (the country with the highest life expectancy is ranked first). From 1960 to 2005, Indonesia among the eight cases ranked fifth on life expectancy rise and eighth on infant mortality decline (Table A1), but among all countries with available data it performed more impressively, ranking 52nd of 174 countries at life expectancy rise and 64th of 140 countries at infant mortality decline.[4] Thus, Indonesia reduced mortality a bit more steeply than

---

[2] McGuire 2009 (Web Appendix A1) analyzes the quality of mortality data in Indonesia.
[3] World Bank 2008c (Country Data Sheet for Indonesia).
[4] Calculated from World Bank 2008e.

most other countries from 1960 to 2005, but ended at a higher level because it began with a much higher level.

Until 1900, birth and death records in Indonesia existed only on the island of Java and were seriously incomplete. A few localities in Java improved their vital records in the late 1930s, but the Japanese occupation (1942–1945) and subsequent hostilities with the Dutch (1945–1949) halted this progress. No censuses were taken between 1931 and 1960, and political conflict during the 1961 census led to the loss of information for most provinces. Hence, not much can be said about the tempo of infant mortality decline in the period before 1960.[5] In subsequent years, infant mortality fell at a faster and faster pace (Table A1). Infant mortality fell slowly under Sukarno in the early 1960s, which were years of political and economic turmoil. It fell a bit faster under Suharto from 1967 to 1990, especially in the late 1970s, although the overall pace of decline was still quite slow. From 1990 to 2000, however, a decade that featured the Asian financial crisis, Suharto's fall, and renewed political turmoil, infant mortality decline accelerated considerably (the pace of decline from 2000 to 2005 is not yet known). What needs to be explained, then, is why infant mortality was so high in 1990; why it fell surprisingly slowly from 1960 to 1990; and why the pace of decline picked up in the 1990s.

10.2. Indonesia: Affluence, Inequality, and Poverty

Indonesia in 1960 was extremely poor. Its GDP per capita, $1,071, ranked just above Thailand's, but this ranking was reversed two years later, and Indonesia in subsequent years fell even farther behind Thailand on economic output per capita. From 1960 to 2005 GDP per capita growth in Indonesia averaged 3.2 percent per year, higher than in any of the four Latin American cases but lower than in any of the other three Asian cases (Table A3). Still, among 98 countries with data for both years, Indonesia ranked 16th on GDP per capita growth from 1960 to 2005.[6] In a broad cross-national perspective, then, Indonesia did well at raising the level of overall affluence.

The years from 1961 to 1967 included the chaotic final throes of Sukarno's presidency, a military coup, and the devastating upheaval of 1965–1966, when hundreds of thousands died in political violence. GDP per capita shrank slightly during this turbulent period. From 1967 to 1978, however, political stability, U.S. foreign aid, and an oil price hike contributed to GDP per capita growth averaging 6.7 percent per year.[7] Also encouraging economic growth, and defying some hypothesized effects of natural resource booms, were cautious macroeconomic policies, to which Suharto's economic team

---

[5] McGuire 2009, Web Appendix A1.
[6] Calculated from Heston, Summers, and Aten 2006, variable RGDPCH. Taiwan ranked first, Korea ranked second, and Thailand ranked sixth.
[7] Calculated from Heston, Summers, and Aten 2006, variable RGDPCH.

adhered rigorously.[8] Indonesia had followed loose macroeconomic policies in the waning years of the Sukarno presidency, leading to hyperinflation in the mid-1960s. After Sukarno's fall, however, the government implemented a stabilization plan featuring budget cuts, unification of the exchange rate regime, higher interest rates, and a tighter money supply.[9] Somewhat less cautious policies coincided with the oil boom of the 1970s, but on the whole, "Indonesia displayed generally sound macroeconomic policies during the 1970s as well as the 1980s."[10] From 1966 to 1996 the budget was mostly in balance, inflation was low, and the exchange rate was not greatly overvalued. The financial sector, as in other Asian countries, was "under-regulated and over-guaranteed," but the 1997 crisis stemmed less from any underlying economic imbalance than from poor management of the repercussions of the devaluation of the Thai baht, exacerbated by a "fragile political system and...escalating social and ethnic tensions."[11]

More than other oil producers, Indonesia in the 1970s invested a large share of its windfall earnings in rural development, building roads and irrigation works, subsidizing fertilizer and high-yielding rice seed, extending farm credit, financing agricultural extension services, and promoting rubber, palm oil, timber, and other export crops.[12] Repression allowed the government to make such investments rather than spending revenue on pensions and health insurance for the middle classes and the not-so-poor (as in Latin America), and also helped to suppress wages, which facilitated the turn to manufactured export-led development from the late 1980s onward. Also, by lowering the birth rate, a strong family planning program raised overall affluence, not just by raising GDP in per capita terms, but also by reducing the share of the population below working age.

A plunge in oil prices caused a brief recession in 1982, but economic growth resumed quickly. From 1983 to 1996 GDP per capita grew at an average annual rate of just under 5 percent. Currency devaluations in 1983 and 1986, export subsidies, customs and banking reforms, import liberalization, and the lifting of some restrictions on direct foreign investment produced a surge in labor-intensive manufactured exports that drove the rapid economic growth of the late 1980s and early 1990s.[13] The Asian financial crisis caused growth to slow sharply in 1997, and in 1998 GDP per capita declined by 9 percent. The crisis precipitated the collapse of Suharto's New Order regime and triggered a return to civilian rule. Growth soon recovered, but not to the levels of

---

[8] Bowie and Unger 1997: 187–188; Gelb et al. 1988: 223–224; MacIntyre 1994: 17; Muscat 1994: 228–229. Cautious macroeconomic policies mean, at a minimum, not letting budget deficits, currency overvaluation, or interest rate subsidies get too large for too long.

[9] Bresnan 1993: 65–67; Hill 2000: 3; Prawiro 1998: 21–57.

[10] MacIntyre 1994: 17.

[11] Hill 2000: 276–279.

[12] Bevan, Collier, and Gunning 1999: 256, 264–265, 417; Bresnan 1993: 191.

[13] Hill 2000: 164.

previous years. From 1999 to 2004, GDP per capita grew at an average annual rate of only 2.5 percent.[14]

Indonesia's infant mortality levels and changes are, at first glance, well explained by a narrow version of the wealthier is healthier hypothesis. In 2005 Indonesia's infant mortality level was well predicted from its GDP per capita level, and from 1960 to 2005 its infant mortality decline was well predicted from its GDP per capita growth (Figures 1.1 and 1.2). As noted earlier, however, this performance was the product of worse-than-expected progress from 1960 to 1990 followed by catch-up from 1990 to 2005, due to a slowdown of economic growth and a speedup of infant mortality decline in the 1990s (Brazil and Thailand displayed a similar pattern even more vividly). GDP per capita did less well at predicting the tempo of infant mortality decline within the period from 1960 to 2000. Across the eight five-year intervals in this time span, infant mortality decline had almost no correlation with GDP per capita growth (Table 11.1). The narrow version of the wealthier is healthier hypothesis would have predicted a strong positive correlation.

Most standard statistical compendia report a Gini index for Indonesia that is based on reported household consumption expenditure, rather than on reported household income (as with the other seven societies compared in this book). Income-based Gini indices are available for Indonesia, however, and four are presented in Table A4, alongside consumption-based estimates for the same years. Each is calculated from responses to questions in the periodic National Socioeconomic Survey (SUSENAS). The income-based estimates are, respectively, about 3, 4, 7, and 9 Gini index points higher than the corresponding consumption-based estimates, a result that is consistent with a previous finding that Gini indices based on consumption expenditure average 6 to 7 points lower than Gini indices based on income.[15] For cross-societal comparisons, the income-based estimates are used. For changes over time, the expenditure-based estimates are used because they have a longer time series. Measured according to income, Indonesia's level of economic inequality from the 1960s to the 1990s was low by international standards – lower than Thailand's, and much lower than the level of economic inequality in any of the four Latin American cases.

From 1976 to 1996 Indonesia's income poverty headcount plunged from 69 to 33 percent of the population (Table A5). Income poverty rose in 1997–1999 as the Asian financial crisis forced a currency devaluation, which raised poverty by causing inflation to spike. By the second half of 2000 the economy was recovering and the poverty headcount had fallen back to the precrisis level.[16] The pace of decline of income poverty was notably out of step with the pace

---

[14] Heston, Summers, and Aten 2006, variable RGDPCH.

[15] Deininger and Squire (1996: 581) found that consumption expenditure-based Gini indices were lower than income-based Gini indices in 46 of 47 cases where contemporaneous estimates were available, by an average of 6.6 Gini index points.

[16] Suryahadi, Sumarto, and Pritchett 2003: 21–22.

of decline of infant mortality. From 1975 to 1990 income poverty fell rapidly but infant mortality fell slowly, whereas from 1990 to 2000 income poverty fell slowly but infant mortality fell rapidly (Tables A1 and A5).

Infant mortality outcomes in Indonesia were thus consistent with the wealthier is healthier hypothesis in 2005, but not in earlier years. In 1990 the level of infant mortality was higher than would have been predicted from the level of GDP per capita, and from 1960 to 1995 the decline of infant mortality was smaller than would have been predicted from the rise of GDP per capita.[17] Moreover, across successive five-year periods within the era from 1960 to 2000, the tempo of GDP per capita growth had a near-zero correlation with the tempo of infant mortality decline (Table 11.1), rather than a strongly positive correlation as would be expected if the wealthier is healthier expectation obtained. Strengths and weaknesses in the public provision of basic social services help to explain these findings.

10.3. Indonesia: Education, Family Planning, Safe Water, and Sanitation

In the early 1990s the Suharto administration spent only 4.2 percent of GDP on education, health care, housing, and social security combined, an even lower share than in Thailand (Section 9.3). Education in the early 1990s took 37 percent of the social services budget; housing 30 percent; and retirement, disability, and survivor pensions 22 percent. Health care absorbed only 9 percent.[18]

Contributory social insurance in Indonesia dates back to 1963, when civil servants began to receive retirement, survivor, and disability pensions. Post-retirement health care was added in 1968. Government-mandated private-sector retirement, survivor, and disability pensions date from 1977; health care was added in 1992.[19] These contributory programs in 2000 covered about 8 percent of the population. If private health insurance is added, about 15 percent of Indonesians were covered by some form of health insurance.[20] At the end of the twentieth century, then, contributory social insurance covered a smaller share of the population in Indonesia than in any of the other cases studied in this book. Indonesia therefore suffered less than the other countries from the inequities that typify most contribution-based, non-universal social insurance programs, but the small scope of such social insurance left urban formal sector workers without protection against basic risks; stunted the development of a secondary and tertiary treatment infrastructure; and

---

[17] 1990 level: See fn. 1 of this chapter. 1960–1995 change: bivariate regression analogous to the one for 1960–2005 that produced Figure 1.2. GDP per capita from Heston, Summers, and Aten 2002, variable RGDPCH; infant mortality from World Bank 2002. Universe of cases for 1960–1995: the 85 developing countries with data in both 1960 and 1995 on both infant mortality and GDP per capita.

[18] Ramesh 2000: 27.

[19] Djamin and Kertonegoro 1998: 15–23.

[20] Callison 2002: 9–10.

deprived poorer Indonesians of the hope and expectation that someday they too, or their children, might be covered.

Under the Ethical Policy implemented by the Dutch from 1900 to 1930, the number of Indonesians in school rose from 0.3 million to 1.7 million, but the latter figure still amounted only to 8 percent of the school-age population. Although 40 percent of Indonesians by the 1930s had attended school at some time, the 1930 census found that only 7 percent of adults were literate. Education above the primary level barely existed.[21] Accordingly, Indonesia in 1960 had by far the lowest levels of literacy, mean years of schooling, and secondary enrollment among the eight societies compared in this book. From 1960 to 2005, however, educational attainment improved markedly; Indonesia passed Brazil on level of literacy and mean years of schooling and achieved a greater percent gain on literacy than did Thailand or any of the Latin American cases (Tables A6, A7, and A8). Contributing to these enrollment gains were the decline of fertility, which diminished the number of children needing education; and the rise in oil revenues after the OPEC price hikes of 1973, together with the government's decision to invest part of the windfall in schooling. Public spending on education rose at an annual rate of 45 percent from 1971 to 1978, and the Suharto government committed itself in 1974 to establishing a primary school in every village. In 1977 and 1978, education officials removed a major obstacle to primary enrollment by abolishing primary school fees for transport, lunch, books, and uniforms.[22]

Despite these gains, school enrollment at the end of the 1980s was nearly universal only for younger children. Of 5.4 million children who completed in Grade 1 in 1988, only 89 percent completed Grade 3, only 66 percent completed Grade 6, and only 39 percent completed Grade 9. The low quality of schooling helps to explain these high dropout rates. Many teachers were poorly trained, and many sought outside employment because of low pay and short hours. The government spent little on facilities or supplies, forcing many schools to rely on parental donations. Textbooks were scarce and often poor in quality. Student performance was assessed mostly by multiple-choice tests, discouraging analytical and writing skills. Lower secondary education cost about three times as much as primary education, and the returns to lower secondary schooling could be low in places where teaching was poor and few work opportunities existed apart from low-skilled agricultural or construction labor.[23] Secondary schooling suffered from similar problems in Brazil and Thailand.

High dropout rates were an obstacle to the reduction of infant and child mortality. A probit analysis of 6,620 respondents in the 1994 Demographic

---

[21] In 1930 fewer than 85,000 Indonesians attended secondary school (Ricklefs 1993: 159), and in 1938 only 1,101 of 68 million Indonesians had received a university education (Bresnan 1993: 75).

[22] Jones and Hagul 2001: 215; Leinbach 1984: 305; Oey-Gardiner 1997: 139–140.

[23] Jones and Hagul 2001: 208, 215, 228; Oey-Gardiner 1997: 142.

and Health Survey showed that a mother's chances of experiencing the death of a child under five years of age fell by 1.9 percentage points for each extra year of primary schooling the mother had attained, but by 2.6 percentage points for each extra year of secondary schooling, controlling for other factors likely to influence under-5 mortality. When literacy was added to models that already included schooling, it had no additional statistical effect on the chances of under-5 mortality. These findings show that a mother's "involvement in formal education, even beyond the years in which literacy skills are acquired, is an important factor" in reducing the risk of child death.[24] To explain the counterintuitive finding that the risk of under-5 mortality is predicted better by secondary than by primary schooling, it may be hypothesized that primary education contributes mostly to the store of information needed to reduce the risk of infant and child mortality, whereas secondary education promotes (or reflects) greater female autonomy and empowerment, which enables mothers to contend more effectively (in the household as well as in the community) for the resources needed to keep infants and children alive.

The island of Java, which in 2005 was home to more than half of Indonesia's 235 million inhabitants, is one of the most densely populated places on earth. In 1960 its population was growing rapidly. Believing that a large population meant a strong country, Sukarno in the 1950s adopted a pronatalist policy, just like his contemporaries in South Korea, Taiwan, and Thailand. In the late 1960s, however, Sukarno's successor, Suharto, began to worry that unchecked population growth might undermine the economy and environment, and introduced a family planning program in the first five-year development plan Repelita I (1969–1974). The mainstays of the program were volunteer fieldworkers who led public education campaigns, advocated later marriage, provided contraceptives at subsidized prices, and even operated microcredit programs for the program's clients. The result was one of the world's strongest family planning initiatives. Between 1971 and 1985 the proportion of eligible couples practicing family planning rose from 3 to 63 percent.[25] Meanwhile, Indonesia's family planning effort index rose from 47 in 1972 to 84 in 1994 (second highest in the world after China),[26] before dropping back as fertility approached the replacement rate (Tables A9 and A10). The program worked because modernization raised the demand for contraceptives; because the volunteers were closely supervised; and because the government considered family planning to be crucial to national security and economic development, and was therefore willing to fund it (in contrast to other areas of social policy, like health care, which the government deemed less essential).[27]

[24] Mellington and Cameron 1999: 128–130; see also Hobcraft 1993.
[25] Elson 2001: 173; Prawiro 1998: 191–194, 199–201 (family planning practice figures); Shiffman 2002: 1207.
[26] Ross and Mauldin 1996: 146.
[27] Achmad 1999: 140; Caldwell 1997: 64; Hull 1987; Leinbach 1984: 303.

Family planning worked together with modernization to produce a rapid decline in fertility. From 1960 to 1970, when the nationwide family planning program began, the total fertility rate fell only from 5.5 to 5.3. From 1970 to 1990, however, it fell from 5.3 to 3.1 (Table A10). One scholar attributes the post-1970 acceleration in the pace of fertility decline to "a highly organised family planning program from the late 1960s," and notes that fertility decline in Indonesia during this period was "steeper than anything known in the Western experience." Another agrees that "the family planning program in Java and Bali has produced results which mark it as a success story which is unrivaled in family planning history."[28]As modernization reduced desired fertility and as the family planning program reduced unwanted fertility, total fertility fell rapidly. Indonesia ranked 59th of 179 countries on percent decline in the total fertility rate from 1960 to 2005.[29]

From 1970 to 2005 the proportion of Indonesians with access to an improved water source rose only from 35 to 77 percent, the smallest rise among the eight cases. Meanwhile, the proportion of the urban population with access to improved sanitation rose only from 47 to 55 percent (Tables A11 and A12), the smallest rise among the six cases with available data. After the 1974 oil price hikes the Suharto government began to fund hygiene education, the distribution of hand pumps, and the construction of wells, rain cisterns, and latrines, but an observer in the mid-1990s concluded that "hygiene behaviour at the family and community level has changed little over the past decades."[30]

After the political turmoil of the 1960s, Indonesia from 1970 to 2005 experienced fast economic growth, low income inequality, and plummeting income poverty. The government also improved literacy, mean years of schooling, primary school enrollment, family planning and, to a lesser extent, access to safe water. Why, then, was Indonesia's progress on infant, child, and maternal mortality so unremarkable, and why did the country wind up in 2005 with levels of infant mortality no lower than would be predicted on the basis of its GDP per capita? Slow progress at expanding access to sanitation, combined with ongoing deficiencies in nutritional status and secondary school enrollment, help to explain the discrepancy, but problems in the health care system also contributed. Improvements in the public provision of basic health services also help to explain why infant mortality fell faster during the 1990s, which was a decade of relatively slow economic growth, than during the 1970s or 1980s, which were decades of faster economic growth (Tables A1 and A3).

---

[28] First quotation from Caldwell 1997: 61; second from Leinbach 1984: 302. These claims may be somewhat overstated. From 1970 to 1995 Thailand, which also had a well-regarded family planning program, reduced fertility even more than Indonesia. During the same period Brazil, which had no family planning programs at all until the late 1970s, and which had only relatively weak programs from 1980 to 1995, reduced fertility about as much as Indonesia.

[29] Calculated from World Bank 2008a.

[30] Prawiro 1998: 185; Betke 2001: 3 (quotation).

10.4. Indonesia: Nutrition and Health Care

Total spending on health care in Indonesia in 2005 made up only 2.1 percent of GDP, and public spending on health care accounted for only 1.0 percent of GDP (Table A15). In addition to having the lowest GDP per capita among the eight cases, then, Indonesia also devoted the smallest share of GDP to total spending on health care, as well as to public spending on health care. Accordingly, spending per capita on health care and on public health care was minuscule. In 1998, only three countries in the world ranked below Indonesia on the share of GDP devoted to public health care, and only eight had lower per capita health care expenditure.[31] Research has found a surprisingly weak relation between health care spending, however measured, and infant and under-5 mortality.[32] In Indonesia, however, such spending has been so low that even a small rise in its absolute level might make more of a difference to mortality levels than would a similar rise in a country that started out with a higher absolute level of health care spending.

Exacerbating the low level of public spending on health care in Indonesia was its inequitable allocation, which "heavily [favored] upper income groups and urban areas with a bias toward big hospital services."[33] In Argentina, Brazil, Chile, and Costa Rica in 1986–1994, the poorest 20 percent of the population received 27–31 percent of public health care spending.[34] In Indonesia, the share fell from 12 percent in 1987 to less than 10 percent in 2001.[35] In absolute terms, however, public health care spending per capita rose from about $32 in 1990 to about $69 in 2000 (Table A15). This hefty gain could help to explain why infant mortality decline sped up during the 1990s even though the allocation of public health care spending grew even more regressive.

In the early and mid-1960s, food availability in Indonesia was "desperately low" and hunger was "endemic and widespread."[36] The food and nutrition situation began to improve in the late 1960s, and progress continued through 1995 and beyond. Calorie availability per person per day rose from 1,800 in 1965 to 2,132 in 1969 to 3,151 in 1996.[37] Rice, fish, and meat consumption each rose by about 40 percent from the late 1960s to the late 1980s, while the share of income that the average household spent on food fell from 77 percent in 1970 to 55 percent in 1993.[38] One factor behind the improvement in food availability was the oil windfall of 1974–1986, most of which accrued to the state because of its ownership of Pertamina, the national oil monopoly. The Suharto government, as noted earlier, dedicated part of this windfall to

---

[31] UNDP 2002: 166–169.
[32] Filmer and Pritchett 1999; McGuire 2006.
[33] Achmad 1999: 9.
[34] PAHO 2007: V. 1, 324.
[35] 1987: Van de Walle 1994; 2001: World Bank 2005: 2.
[36] Hill 2000: 203.
[37] Friend 2003: 147; Prawiro 1998: 183.
[38] Hill 2000: 203–205.

agriculture and rural development, contributing to a rapid expansion of food production, especially of rice.[39] From 1970 to 1995 the share of the population estimated to be suffering from undernourishment fell from 47 to 6 percent (Table A13).

Hunger declined after the mid-1970s not only because of the rise in food production, but also because of the activities of female volunteers in the Family Welfare Movement (PKK), the state-sanctioned women's organization under the New Order regime. Founded in 1967 and controlled by the interior ministry, the Family Welfare Movement had 4 million members by the mid-1990s. Its purpose was to educate mothers and other villagers about nutrition, hygiene, health care, and related topics. In the late 1970s and early 1980s, Family Welfare Movement volunteers distributed vitamins and supplements and urged mothers to bring their children to health centers.[40] These nutrition programs combined with rising food availability to cause a swift decline in child malnutrition. In 1973, according to a government survey, "more than two thirds of Indonesia's 20 million children under five years old were undernourished."[41] By 1987 the figure had dropped to 40 percent, and by 2005 it was 28 percent. Despite this progress, Indonesia in 2005 had a child malnutrition rate three times as high as Thailand's, which in turn was higher than that of any of the four Latin American countries (Table A14).

Public health interventions in Indonesia date back at least to 1780, when the Dutch introduced variolation in an effort to curb smallpox. Vaccination followed in 1804, but its extent is unclear. An 1829 law in Java requiring daily yard-cleaning may have reduced the spread of disease.[42] Medical training of Indonesians, including birth attendants and village doctors, began around 1850. The colonial authorities built several hospitals during the 1800s,[43] but most of them were controlled by the colonial military apparatus, and as late as 1870 a majority of Java's 53 doctors were employed in military facilities. A medical historian concluded in 1935 that the Dutch did almost nothing, except for smallpox vaccination, to improve public health in the 1800s.[44]

During the Ethical Policy period (1900–1930) the colonial authorities raised health spending tenfold and started campaigns to provide safe water, latrines, and vaccinations, as well as to control pests, distribute mosquito nets, and isolate patients with contagious diseases.[45] Like the Japanese in

---

[39] Prawiro 1998: 130–144.
[40] In 1988, the Family Welfare Movement won the World Health Organization's Sasakawa Health Prize and UNICEF's Maurice Pate Award for dedication to child survival (Achmad 1999: 29; Prawiro 1998: 184–185, 189–190).
[41] UNICEF 1996: Panel 9.
[42] Hull 1989: 142. On vaccination, Boomgaard (1987: 62–63) and Hugo et al. (1987: 135 fn. 1) give a more positive assessment than Widjojo (1970: 40–41).
[43] Boomgaard 1986: 72. Village or "Javanese" doctors with three years of training assisted Dutch doctors in some localities. After independence, Sukarno called this practice a "national insult" (Achmad 1999: 162).
[44] Cited in Widjojo 1970: 41.
[45] Boomgaard 1986: 72–75; Hugo et al. 1987: 108–109; Ricklefs 1993: 155.

Taiwan, the Dutch implemented these programs in an authoritarian manner. After an outbreak of bubonic plague in 1910, for example, the colonial government evicted thousands of people and burned their houses and clothing.[46] To facilitate delivery of social services the Dutch amalgamated Javanese villages, whose number fell from 30,500 in 1897 to 18,500 in 1927. As in the Tanzanian villagization program of the 1970s, which President Julius Nyerere likewise designed in part to facilitate the delivery of social services, the new settlements "often had no indigenous basis" and rarely improved the lives of their inhabitants.[47] In Indonesia under Dutch colonial rule, much as in Korea and Taiwan under Japanese colonial rule, few people came to believe that they had a right to public (or publicly funded) health services. In Argentina, Brazil, and Chile, by contrast, strong labor movements and populist political leaders organized social insurance schemes whose expansion to new sectors of the population helped to establish a perception of a right to social services.

In rural areas during the Ethical Policy period some cash crop plantations provided medical care to resident workers. Those on the east coast of Sumatra "conducted a well-organized health campaign" to retain scarce labor, and some in Java provided free clinics and immunization.[48] Some observers are skeptical that colonial public health policies from 1900 to 1930 did much to reduce mortality, but smallpox immunization, vector control, and health education were not totally ineffective. Even a critic concedes that the public health infrastructure built by the Dutch was fairly good by the standards of the rest of Asia.[49] In 1924, moreover, the Rockefeller Foundation sponsored in West Java a hookworm control campaign that was "based on the premise that people should be taught about germ theories so they would adopt behaviours which prevented disease."[50] In 1933 the Foundation set up in Purwokerto, Central Java, a primary health care project featuring health education, training for traditional midwives, the collection of health and mortality statistics, and improvements to water supply and sanitation facilities. This Hygiene Program left a legacy of health-promoting sanitation practices that persisted in Central Java through the 1980s, and "provided an exemplary model of community health care which would be difficult to match even today."[51] In the rest of Indonesia, however, the program had little effect.[52] Any progress made under the Dutch ended, moreover, with the Japanese invasion of 1942, which created "serious set-backs...in all aspects of health care."[53] These setbacks, combined with harsh policies of labor conscription and food requisitioning,

[46] Hull 1989: 144.
[47] Nyerere 1969: 261–262. Quotation and statistics on number of villages: Ricklefs 1993: 156.
[48] Sumatra: Widjojo 1970: 113. Java: Hugo et al. 1987: 109.
[49] Hugo et al. 1987: 109. Another skeptic is Ricklefs (1993: 155–156). Gardiner and Oey (1983: 23–26) provide a more positive evaluation.
[50] Hull 1989: 144.
[51] Hugo et al. 1987: 109, 127.
[52] Hull 1989: 145.
[53] Hugo et al. 1987: 109.

caused a sharp rise in mortality. During the ensuing war of independence (1945–1949), the Dutch imposed a naval blockade that kept medical supplies from reaching areas controlled by nationalist forces. Life expectancy reportedly fell from 35 years in the late 1930s to 28 years in the late 1940s.[54]

After independence in 1949, health care officials in Sukarno's government, supported by UNICEF, began to build maternal and child health centers in villages around the country.[55] They also launched campaigns to fight malaria, yaws, and smallpox; raised the number of hospital beds and doctors; and doubled the number of nurses and other health personnel.[56] In 1960, however, health care providers were still extremely scarce, particularly in rural areas. Hyperinflation and political violence halted most progress in health care from 1960 to 1967, when General Suharto became president and established his New Order regime, which remained in power until 1998.

From 1968 to 1970 the Suharto government built more than 2,300 health centers (puskesmas) in villages and towns around the country.[57] The health centers were designed to provide "medical care, maternal and child health, family planning, communicable disease control, environmental health and sanitation, nutrition, health education, dental health, simple laboratory services, mental health, and community health nursing," as well as to record medical and mortality data.[58] By 1979 each of Indonesia's 3,500 subdistricts had at least one health center.[59] To staff these facilities, the Suharto government in 1974 instituted a rule that medical graduates, to obtain a physician's license, would henceforth have to work for one to five years in an underserved area, with the duration dependent on the remoteness of the posting.[60] This requirement remained in effect until 2001, when public health care administration was decentralized to district governments. By the late 1990s, staffing at a typical health center ranged from 5 to 10 in some of the Outer Islands to 28 in Java and Bali.[61] The health centers were designed to be headed by a physician, but in 1980 only about half of them actually had a doctor in residence.[62] As late as 1998, 12 provinces averaged fewer than one doctor per health center, and doctors were missing from more than 40 percent of health

---

[54] Widjojo 1970: 158.

[55] Gunawan 2001: 6–8.

[56] Hugo et al. 1987: 110–111.

[57] Gunawan 2001: 8; Hugo et al. 1987: 110; Kristiansen and Santoso 2006: 248; Thabrany 2000: 1–2.

[58] Thabrany 2000: 2.

[59] Hull 1989: 146.

[60] Achmad 1999: 85; Chomitz et al. 1997: 3; Prawiro 1998: 189; Thabrany 2000: 3. As in Thailand, however (Zankel 2003), "many newly graduated doctors can bribe their way to work in the big cities" (Achmad 1999: 175).

[61] Lieberman and Marzoeki 2000: 13. These numbers suggest more extended operations than a decade earlier, when the average number of staff in a health center was 15 in Java and "a fraction of that number" in the Outer Islands (Van de Walle 1994: 282).

[62] Hugo et al. 1987: 110; Peterson 2000: 77.

centers in several impoverished provinces.[63] Health center physicians were typically recent medical graduates doing compulsory service; most saw few patients and spent much of their time on administrative work.[64]

In 1970 Suharto created the Presidential Instruction (Inpres) program to improve social and physical infrastructure in rural areas. Its "allocations grew in step with Indonesia's rising oil revenues."[65] Presidential Instruction funds were used to raise the number of health centers and to complement them with health subcenters, which had regular opening hours and were usually run by a nurse or midwife, assisted by one or two other staffers. By the 1980s the government required that one health center be built for every 30,000 persons and one health subcenter for every 10,000 persons.[66] All told, the government during the 1970s built more than 2,000 health centers and 7,000 health subcenters.[67] Supporting these facilities were health posts, which were staffed by paramedics and were open only on certain days; and mobile medical units, which made periodic visits to designated sites and were staffed by personnel based at health centers. Better-off patients tended to use health centers or private health care providers, whereas poorer clients were more likely to use health subcenters or health posts.[68] Many people also used traditional practitioners or self-treatment.

Supporting these primary health care facilities were volunteer village health workers. The first such workers appeared in the early 1970s, but it was not until 1976 that they began to be recruited systematically, first in the context of the Program to Improve Family Nutrition (UPGK), and then, in 1978, in the context of the Village Community Health Development Program (PKMD), which was Indonesia's first major nationwide rural primary health care initiative. These health care volunteers were typically village members who were nominated by neighbors, given a few days or weeks of training, and assigned to work with 10–15 households apiece. The health care volunteers delivered simple curative care, referred serious cases to health centers, weighed infants, distributed dietary supplements, provided health education, encouraged the maintenance of home gardens, and organized village health insurance programs. A survey in Java showed that the health care volunteers reached a high share of the target population, and that their services, in contrast to those provided in health clinics, showed no bias against the poor.[69] In 1987 more than 70 percent of villages had at least one health care volunteer, and 21 percent of villages had ten or more such volunteers.[70] By the mid-1990s village health volunteers numbered about a million.[71]

---

[63] Indonesia. MoH 2000.
[64] Berman, Sisler, and Habicht 1989: 787–788; Peterson 2000: 76; World Bank 2003b: 5.
[65] Prawiro 1998: 175.
[66] Prawiro 1998: 186; Thabrany 2000: 2–3.
[67] Thabrany 2000: 2.
[68] Berman, Sisler, and Habicht 1989: 784–785, 800.
[69] Berman 1984; Hugo et al. 1987: 112–113.
[70] Frankenberg 1995: 159.
[71] UNICEF 1996: Panel 9.

The number of health centers and subcenters rose steadily during the 1980s, and the proportion of Indonesians living within five kilometers of a health facility rose from about 25 percent in the 1970s to 89 percent in 1995.[72] In 1984, village health volunteers began to participate in monthly maternal and child health care sessions called integrated service posts (posyandus). The posyandu was "an activity rather than a location." Once a month volunteer workers, supervised by health center staff, converged at a site, often a room in the home of a villager, to provide to their neighbors family planning services, maternal and child health care, nutritional supplements, immunizations, and medications to control diarrhea. The volunteers typically had three to six days of training. Their supervisors provided family planning supplies, packets of oral rehydration salts, and growth-monitoring cards.[73] Between 1985 and 1995 the monthly number of posyandu sessions rose from 25,000 to 245,000.[74]

The health facilities that proliferated from the late 1970s onward suffered from underutilization, especially by the poor.[75] High costs, poor service quality, and cultural factors, more than any lack of geographical proximity, were behind this underutilization. User fees and other expenses (e.g., informal surcharges, drug costs, transport fees, and lost work time) kept many away from public health facilities.[76] Many health centers in remote rural areas lacked doctors, and many health professionals with ostensibly full-time public-sector jobs also had private practices, and sometimes shirked their health center duties to treat fee-paying patients privately. Many rural Indonesians preferred traditional to modern practitioners for certain types of health care services.[77] In general, "findings from interviews and field observation depict a passive and ineffective [public health sector] labor force, which seems disconnected from outcomes including the costs of their activities and distracted by the lure of private practice." A comparison in March 1999 of health centers on the island of Borneo, some in West Kalimantan (Indonesia) and the others in adjoining Sarawak (Malaysia), showed that the facilities in Sarawak were far superior.[78] Surprise visits to primary health care clinics in 2002–2003 showed that 40 percent of health workers were absent at times when they were supposed to be present.[79]

---

[72] Health facilities: Thabrany 2000: 2; proximity: Leinbach 1984: 302 (1970s); UNDP-Indonesia 2001: 39 (1995).

[73] Peterson 2000: 78.

[74] Prawiro 1998: 187.

[75] Chernichovsky and Meesook 1986: 613–616; Hugo et al. 1987: 111; Leinbach 1984: 302; Lieberman and Marzoeki 2000: 4, 31; World Bank 2003b: 3.

[76] Achmad 1999: 75–76; Chernichovsky and Meesook 1986: 612; Cholil 1997: 10–11; Hugo et al. 1987: 112; Leinbach 1984: 302; Lieberman and Marzoeki 2000: 6; UNDP 1996: 31; Van de Walle 1994: 283.

[77] Chernichovsky and Meesook 1986: 615; Hugo et al. 1987: 111–112; Leinbach 1984: 302.

[78] Lieberman and Marzoeki 2000: 9, 12 (quotation), 17.

[79] Absenteeism was even higher in remote areas (Chaudhury et al. 2006: 92, 94–95, 109).

In 1987, two years after a survey found that Indonesia's maternal mortality ratio was an extremely high 450 deaths per 100,000 births, a conference in Nairobi focused world attention on the issue of safe motherhood. Together, these events inspired Indonesian health officials to inaugurate the village midwife program in 1989.[80] Arguing that the lack of trained attendance at birth, especially among the rural poor, was a main reason for Indonesia's high level of maternal mortality, health officials resolved to place a trained midwife in each of the country's villages. Between 1989 and 1996 the village midwife program gave some 54,000 trainees a year-long course to provide assistance at birth, preventive interventions, nutrition education, child immunization, basic curative care, oral rehydration, and the distribution of micronutrients. The share of rural villages and townships with such midwives rose from 10 percent in 1993 to 46 percent in 1997.[81]

The village midwife program helped to boost the share of births attended by trained personnel from 36 percent in 1990 to 64 percent in 2000 (Table A16). The greatest gains were in the poorest fifth of the population, where the figure rose from 13 percent in 1990 to 30 percent in 2000; and in the next-poorest fifth, where trained attendance at birth rose from 25 to 51 percent over the same period.[82] Cross-nationally, trained attendance at birth is closely associated with lower infant mortality.[83] In Indonesia in the 1990s the presence of a trained attendant at delivery was associated significantly at the household level with a reduced risk of infant death.[84] From 1990 to 2000, the sharp rise in the share of new mothers in Indonesia who received trained attendance at birth worked together with continued fertility decline and with the expansion of secondary education to accelerate the pace of infant mortality decline (Table A1).

The main goal of the village midwife program was, however, to reduce the risk of maternal death, and in this respect it may have been less successful. The 1994 Demographic and Health Survey found that Indonesia's maternal mortality ratio rose from 360 per 100,000 in the mid-1980s to 390 per 100,000 in the early 1990s. Like the Village Community Health Development Program of 1978, the village midwife program of 1989 did better at expanding the number of health personnel than at assuring the quality of health services provided. In its rush to place the midwives in the villages, the government compromised on candidate selection, training, supervision, and mentoring. These compromises had particularly deleterious implications for the ability

---

[80] Shiffman 2003: 1200. Estimates by Hill, Abou-Zahr, and Wardlaw (2001) for 1995, adjusted for underreporting, found maternal mortality ratios per 100,000 of 472 in Indonesia, 262 in Brazil, and 44 in Thailand.

[81] Frankenberg, Suriastini, and Thomas 2005: 5–8; Hatt et al. 2007: 774; Shankar et al. 2008: 1227.

[82] Hatt et al. 2007: 778.

[83] McGuire 2006; Taghreed et al. 2005.

[84] Frankenberg and Thomas 2001: 263–264; Titaley et al. 2008: 12.

of the newly trained midwives to handle delivery complications.[85] A critical factor in maternal survival is access to emergency obstetric care.[86] In the 1990s, 30–40 percent of deliveries in Brazil, South Korea, and Taiwan were by cesarean section.[87] These levels were about three times the 10–15 percent rates that the World Health Organization regards as likely to be medically necessary. The Indonesian poor suffered from the opposite problem. From 1987 to 2003, the share of births by cesarean section among the poorest 40 percent of Indonesians remained at about 1 percent.[88] In the mid to late 1990s, although 5 percent of expectant mothers needed emergency operations, and although 15 percent were at risk for pregnancy complications, only 30 percent of district hospitals had equipment for emergency obstetric surgery, and only about 50 percent had obstetricians, who were typically on call only for about a quarter of the work day.[89] Abortion, which was illegal during the period being studied, was also a major cause of maternal death.[90]

In response to the finding that the village midwife program, however beneficial for infant survival, had failed to reduce the maternal mortality ratio, Dr. Abdullah Cholil, the Minister of Women's Roles, launched the Mother-Friendly Movement in 1996. This program focused directly on the lack of access to emergency obstetric care.[91] It involved monitoring expectant mothers for signs of risk, encouraging ambulance cooperatives, identifying waiting homes near main roads and medical facilities, producing written protocols for emergency treatment, training men to identify and act upon danger signs in pregnancy, and recognizing explicitly a link between the low status of women and a high level of maternal mortality.[92] Meanwhile, the government improved the village midwife program by providing better pay, longer training, refresher courses, clinical audits, and more continuous supervision.[93] In the second half of the 1990s the share of births attended by trained personnel rose more, and the infant mortality rate fell more steeply, than in the first half of the 1990s (Tables A1 and A16). Not so for maternal mortality. According to two rounds of the Demographic and Health Survey in Indonesia, the maternal mortality ratio apparently fell from about 334 per 1000 in 1993–1997 to about 307 per 1000 in 2002–2003.[94] A revised estimate using an improved methodology, however, put the maternal mortality ratio as high as 420 per 100,000 in 1998–2003.[95]

---

[85] Shankar et al. 2008: 1227.
[86] Bulatao and Ross 2003; Shiffman 2003: 1198.
[87] Sections 6.4, 7.4, and 8.4.
[88] Hatt et al. 2007: 779.
[89] Need and risk: Parsell 1998; equipment: Iskandar 1997: 214; obstetricians: Achmad 1999: 162, 175.
[90] Iskandar 1997: 216.
[91] Shiffman 2003: 1201.
[92] Cholil 1997; Parsell 1998; Shiffman 2002; Shiffman 2003: 1202.
[93] Shankar et al. 2008: 1228.
[94] Indonesia. BPS and ORC Macro 2003: 190.
[95] Hill et al. 2007a: 1314.

The financial crisis of 1997 led to short-term cuts in public health care spending, including for primary care; and to sharp downturns in immunization coverage and in utilization of the health centers (puskesmas) and integrated service posts (posyandus).[96] On the whole, however, the impact of the financial crisis on health care delivery and on health status outcomes was, as in Thailand, modest and short-lived. Emergency programs dedicated to maternal and infant care, communicable disease control, and hospital care for the poor helped to ameliorate the impact of the crisis.[97] Particularly notable was the health card program enacted in late 1998, which entitled impoverished recipients to free health care at public facilities. By February 1998 some 22 million people, more than 10 percent of the Indonesian population, had received a card. The health card program was hindered by leakage to the non-poor and by the indirect costs (transport, etc.) of using the nominally free public services.[98] From 1995 to 2000, however, most health care indicators registered notable improvement (Tables A16 and A17). Attendance at birth by trained personnel in the poorest 40 percent of the population rose faster from 1996 to 1999 than from 1993 to 1996 or from 1999 to 2002.[99] The infant mortality rate fell more steeply from 1995 to 2000 than during any other five-year interval since 1960 (Table A1).

Even more challenging than the financial crisis to the provision of basic health services was the decision in 1999 by the initial post-Suharto government under B.J. Habibie to decentralize public administration. Under pressure from separatist movements and international financial institutions, the legislature passed decentralization laws in 1999. These laws went into effect on January 1, 2001. In the health sector, responsibility for funding health care facilities and personnel passed from the central government to the country's 440 cities and rural districts (regencies). One consequence of decentralization for the delivery of basic health services was that the central government could no longer require newly credentialed health professionals to practice for a time in underserved areas. It was now up to the district governments to staff their own health facilities, and not all of them had the money or administrative resources to meet this obligation.[100] Moreover, although the central government continued to transfer funds to the district governments, the latter became responsible for generating a rising share of their own revenue. The health centers and public hospitals, which had always imposed user fees (except on those with health cards), raised their charges, and the doctors who staffed these facilities increasingly used contacts with patients to recruit clients for their fee-paying private practices. Meanwhile, because curative care generated more revenue than preventive interventions, public health and sanitation were neglected.[101]

[96] Simms and Rowson 2003; Waters, Saadah, and Prabhan 2003.
[97] Lieberman and Marzoeki 2000: 18–19; World Bank 2001b: 70.
[98] Sparrow 2008: 198.
[99] Hatt et al. 2007: 778.
[100] Thabrany 2006: 76, 79–80.
[101] Kristiansen and Santoso 2006: 255.

In an effort to rectify these deficiencies, the health ministry in 2004 issued a decree stipulating that district governments must provide 26 types of essential services, 18 of which involved disease surveillance, preventive measures, and maternal and child health care.[102] This measure was formally similar to the basic minimum services packages enacted in Argentina, Brazil, and Chile during the 1990s and early 2000s. In Indonesia, however, revenue transfers to the districts were not contingent on the provision of the essential services, as in Brazil, nor did citizens acquire the right to legal redress in cases were the essential services were denied to them, as in Chile. As basic health care provision deteriorated, the utilization of health facilities declined. The proportion of Indonesians who reported going to a health facility when ill fell from 51 percent in 1997 to 34 percent in 2006.[103] Meanwhile, reduced attention to disease control contributed to a resurgence of polio and leprosy and to a rise in the number of cases of avian influenza.[104]

On January 1, 2005, the newly elected government of Susilo Bambang Yudhoyono launched the Askeskin program, which was designed to become a universal health insurance coverage scheme, but which for the moment entitled any Indonesian who could produce a letter from a local political leader certifying the holder as "poor" to receive a card that was good for free health care at a public health center or a district-level public hospital. The government initially anticipated that some 36.5 million Indonesians would qualify for a card, but later estimates put the figure as high as 76.4 million.[105] The central government funded the Askeskin program through PT Askes, the company that handled health insurance finances for private-sector workers. It paid health centers according to capitation (about U.S. $1 per health card per month) and district hospitals prospectively whereby each patient condition was assigned to a diagnostic-related group with a specified level of reimbursement, much as in the post-1983 U.S. Medicare system. The Askeskin health insurance program increased health facility utilization, but was seriously underfunded. Many who were not poor qualified for a health card, and health facilities and personnel had a hard time keeping up with demand. Meanwhile, another 2005 initiative called Vigilant Village (Desa Siaga) built on the village midwife program by recruiting a nutritionist and a sanitation specialist, as well as a nurse or midwife, to practice in each village.[106] A total of 70,000 health professionals were slated to be hired under this program.

The effect of the 1998 health card scheme and of the 2002 decentralization of public health administration on the infant mortality rate is not yet known, but initial signs are discouraging. The use of public health care facilities declined from 2000 to 2005; treatment overshadowed sanitation, disease

---

[102] Thabrany 2006: 77.
[103] World Bank 2008d: 19.
[104] Thabrany 2006: 79.
[105] World Bank 2008d: 14, 19.
[106] Thabrany 2006: 83.

control, and prevention; and the government ended the requirement that newly trained health personnel work for a time in underserved areas. On the positive side, the number of integrated service post (posyandu) sessions rose after falling during the Asian financial crisis.[107] Whether the Askeskin health insurance scheme or the Vigilant Village program will help the country meet some of the resulting challenges remains to be seen. Indonesia was democratic from 1999 to 2005, but it lacked the long-term democratic experience that the Latin American cases had. Even Thailand had more experience than Indonesia with adversarial politics and with basic human and civil rights, and patron-client relations were well entrenched in many rural areas of Indonesia, preventing impoverished rural people from exerting more pressure for health care policies conducive to a more rapid decline of infant mortality.

10.5. Indonesia: Determinants of Public Health Care Policies

The Suharto government, as noted in Section 10.2, enacted policies designed to raise the incomes of the rural poor. Expectations generated by Sukarno's populist promises in the 1950s and early 1960s encouraged these policies.[108] So did Suharto's personal history, combined with his power within the regime. Suharto left junior high school because his family could not afford to buy him proper pants and shoes, and wrote that "in my childhood I had to endure such suffering which perhaps others could not imagine...I have become a person who can really think about and feel what hardship means."[109] Suharto's childhood may have been a bit less impoverished than he portrayed it,[110] but it was not privileged. At any rate, the president reportedly "was sympathetic to every program aimed at serving the interests of the Javanese rice farmers among whom he had lived as a boy."[111] As with Chiang Kai-Shek in Taiwan and Park Chung Hee in South Korea, Suharto's personal views were a crucial determinant of policy. By the late 1980s Suharto "was unchallengeable in his position as paramount power in the state," and in 1996 *Asiaweek* considered him to be "the most powerful leader in Asia."[112] The only institution potentially capable of challenging him was the army (ABRI), but by the early 1990s a retired general lamented that "only Soeharto has the power to get anything done in Indonesia...Abri is very weak, and subservient to Soeharto. We just implement what he wants us to do."[113] Given that Suharto wanted to raise the incomes of the rural poor, why did he not do more to improve the public provision of basic health services?

---

[107] Prawiro 1998: 187; World Bank 2008d: 30.
[108] Bevan, Collier, and Gunning 1999: 420.
[109] Schwarz 1994: 27.
[110] Elson 2001: 1–5.
[111] Bresnan 1993: 281.
[112] Elson 2001: 253, 297; Friend 2003: 160.
[113] Schwarz 1994: 284.

The preferences of rural dwellers may provide a partial answer to this question. In the district of Banjarnegara, Central Java, in 1971, a young doctor who tried to start a community health insurance scheme found that people were "more interested in increasing their meager incomes than in paying for health care." Likewise, a community survey conducted in the early 1970s found that people in Banjarnegara were "much more concerned about agriculture than health."[114] Suharto and his allies might thus defensibly claim that their policies were designed more to raise rural incomes than to improve rural health care because the people wanted it that way.

Indonesia's geography exacerbated the Suharto government's neglect of public health services. Particularly across a far-flung archipelago, it is hard to persuade adequate numbers of doctors and nurses to staff health facilities in remote rural areas, especially when pay is poor, localities are devoid of basic amenities, supplies are erratic, and hospitals are hard to reach. Accordingly, health personnel in Indonesia work disproportionately in cities and in Java, where the rural population is dense. In 1999, per 100,000 inhabitants, Jakarta and Yogyakarta had a mean of 31 doctors working at health centers or hospitals, whereas four provinces in the outer islands each had an average of fewer than seven.[115] In the early 1990s family members were the main attendants at birth in 67 percent of deliveries in Irian Jaya, 34 percent in East Timor, and 22 percent in East Nusa Tenggara, but in less than 1 percent in any of the Javanese provinces.[116] In Thailand infant mortality decline was relatively sluggish until the government, in the late 1980s, redoubled its efforts to recruit health professionals to rural areas (Section 9.4). In Chile and Costa Rica, which produced two of the most successful primary health care programs reviewed in this book (Table 11.3), most rural people lived fairly close to population centers. Indonesia was thus disadvantaged by the sparse populations and remote geographical locations of several of its provinces.

Institutional arrangements also contributed to deficiencies in basic health care provision during and after the New Order regime. Some of the negative effects of decentralization from 2001 forward have already been noted. Institutional arrangements had also damaged health policy in earlier years. Under Suharto, the health ministry controlled policy-making but the interior ministry, through provincial and district governments, controlled implementation. Because health ministry officials lacked the political or bureaucratic resources needed to control provincial governors or district regents or mayors, and because interior ministry officials did not suffer if health policy performed poorly, policies designed in the health ministry often unraveled during implementation. Moreover, local governments used health facilities as cash cows. Health centers retained only about 25 percent of the revenue they obtained from user fees, drug sales, and other operations; the rest went to

---

[114] First quotation from Haliman and Williams 1983: 1450; second from Gunawan 2001: 7.
[115] Indonesia. MoH 2000: 38.
[116] Indonesia. CBS 1995: 160.

local governments, which typically used the funds to buy land and construct buildings rather than reinvesting them in the health sector. Dr. Adhyatma, the health minister from 1988 to 1993, asked the association representing obstetricians and gynecologists to reduce from four to two years the period of study required for an obstetric license, so as to facilitate the growth of the profession. Partly because the health ministry had no influence with the education ministry, the initiative failed.[117]

Oil windfalls helped to finance the expansion of health centers and integrated service post sessions in the 1970s and 1980s. One problem with such windfalls is that too much investment suddenly finds itself chasing too few well-designed projects. A study of how six major oil exporters handled the oil windfalls of the 1970s found that "because of the desire to spend rapidly, public investment favored large projects that minimized decision time and did not require laborious and controversial institutional and political changes."[118] An analogous problem seems to have impeded the public provision of high-quality health services in Indonesia during the 1970s and into the 1980s. The government expanded the number of health centers too rapidly, constructed them on too homogeneous a model, overburdened them with responsibilities, failed to monitor their performance adequately, and focused too much on producing a rise in the number of integrated service post sessions. These design and implementation problems resulted in poorly trained health workers, over-standardized service delivery, inadequate community participation, and the underutilization of health facilities.[119]

Of the eight countries compared in this book, Indonesia was the most autocratic (Table A18). Some 44 years elapsed between September 1955, when the country held its first free parliamentary election, and June 1999, when it held its second. Elections were held under Suharto, but from 1973 onward the governing Golkar grouping, which loyally supported Suharto, permitted only two opposition parties, which were not allowed to open an office below the district level, nor to reject the government's ideology, nor to present candidates whom the government considered to be politically or professionally unqualified. Moreover, many legislators were appointed rather than elected, and elections were plagued by fraud and violence. Accordingly, Golkar won every election by a huge majority, and Suharto held the presidency for 31 consecutive years, from 1967 to 1998. Security forces repeatedly committed serious human rights abuses, notably against persons accused of belonging to separatist movements, and the government regularly violated the freedoms of speech, press, assembly, and association.

Democratization in the late 1990s did not produce any discernible short-term improvement in the provision of maternal and infant health services in Indonesia. Indeed, democratization was associated with decentralization,

[117] Achmad 1999: 69, 90, 156, 170.
[118] Gelb et al. 1988: 137.
[119] Lieberman and Marzoeki 2000: 9, 31.

which placed more power in the hands of local elected officials. These politicians were less interested in promoting intangible objectives like maternal and child health than in spending money on policies with visible results, such as road construction.[120] Still, decentralization might also have been problematic under authoritarianism. The impact of democracy on the provision of basic health services has to be evaluated in a wider perspective. Democracy can contribute to better basic health care services by creating electoral incentives for their provision, by promoting free discussion and debate about the strengths and weaknesses of existing services, by permitting the formation of interest groups and issue networks that capable of exerting pressure on health care policy, or by producing a populace that expects more of public officials. None of these factors was present in Indonesia. The government thoroughly controlled village political life, and was grimly determined to avoid a resurgence of the political violence of 1965–1966, in which hundreds of thousands of followers of the Communist Party of Indonesia (PKI) and others died.[121] District political leaders, although nominally chosen by district assemblies, were in practice appointed by provincial governors, giving them "no incentive to win the poor farmers' votes... by improving the health services to the local population." Moreover, because the New Order regime prohibited open discussion of public health policies not only in the press and in academic circles, but also among members of parliament and executive branch officials, health ministers found it impossible to persuade central planners of the urgency of improving health services for the rural poor. By the end of his regime, Suharto had so monopolized power that "none of his subordinates dared to tell him bad news, such as problems in the health system."[122]

A more open political regime than Suharto's might have created a political climate more propitious for the emergence of issue networks by which health professionals and others could organize behind the goal of raising the quality and quantity of primary health care for the poor. In Thailand during the democratic opening of 1973–1976, progressive physicians organized the Rural Doctors' Forum. In Brazil during the late 1970s, as the military regime lifted controls on civil society, academics, public health specialists, and health professionals organized the Primary Care and Sanitarian movements. No comparable process occurred in authoritarian Indonesia. On the contrary, the Suharto government outlawed an effort by rural health center doctors to set up an association in the 1970s.[123]

Critical to understanding the deficiencies in Indonesian health care, according to a doctor who served for ten years as the director of a rural health clinic, is that "a rural population, still with little educational background

---

[120] Shiffman 2007: 801.
[121] Achmad 1999: 30. On the causes and dimensions of the massacres see Friend 2003: 113–115.
[122] Achmad 1999: 157, 172–173.
[123] Achmad 1999: 89.

and with a traditional respect for authority, is unused to insisting on service quality." Henry Mosley has argued that "a passive approach of only making services available will not succeed in most situations unless the population has a heightened consciousness of their political rights."[124] In Indonesia, colonial rule through the late 1940s, and authoritarianism for most of the second half of the twentieth century, precluded the emergence of such a consciousness. In the Indian state of Kerala, by contrast, competition between the Congress and Communist parties from 1957 onward encouraged an awareness of political rights that helped to raise the quality of health care provision above that found in other Indian states. In Kerala, unlike in other states, "a literate, politically conscious population ensure[d] that government health personnel [were] actually at their posts."[125] Jose Serra, the health minister of Brazil from 1998 to 2002, argued that an important effect of democracy is to contribute to a "sense of equality": a generalized perception that no citizen, no matter how poor, lacks a right to basic social services.[126] The lack of such a perception among many impoverished Indonesians helps to explain why public primary health care services remained deficient in quality and underutilized, reducing their impact on infant, child, and maternal mortality.

[124] Achmad 1999: 10 (first quotation), 21 (Mosely quotation), 142.
[125] Mehrotra 1997b: 71.
[126] Serra 2003a.

11

Wealth, Health, Democracy, and Mortality

In the eight cases just reviewed, as well as in the quantitative analysis reported in Chapter 2, democracy, especially long-term democratic experience, generally did promote the public provision and expanded utilization of basic health care, education, family planning, water, and sanitation services, in more diverse ways than is often recognized. These social services, in turn, were associated with lower infant mortality, even after economic, demographic, geographic, and cultural circumstances were taken into account. Democracy, then, can be vindicated on the basis of its beneficial consequences for policies that promote the expansion of important human capabilities, as well as defended both on the basis of its intrinsic importance and by virtue of the role it plays in encouraging discussion and debate in which wants and needs originate.[1]

In particular, democracy encouraged large-scale primary health care programs. Even in cases where authoritarian governments implemented such programs, as occurred in Chile under Pinochet, the expectations that encouraged the programs, the expertise and infrastructure on which the programs drew, and the propensity of poor people to use the services provided by the programs was influenced by many decades of previous democratic or semi-democratic experience. The success of many such programs at accelerating infant mortality decline, even in the context of unfavorable economic circumstances, suggests that improving economic output- and income-related indicators is not the only way for a society to reduce the risk of early death. Just as effective, and often more feasible, is for governments to finance or provide, and for citizens to demand and utilize, a well-known set of inexpensive health, education, family planning, water, and sanitation services that are accessible to the poor.

The case studies in Chapters 3–10 traced the pattern and pace of infant mortality decline in four East Asian and four Latin American societies from 1960 to 2005. Each of these case studies explored how and to what extent

[1] Sen 1999a: 148, 152–154.

economic factors on the one hand, and the provision of education, family planning, water and sanitation, and health and nutrition services on the other, affected infant mortality decline. Each case study also examined the ways in which, and degree to which, bureaucratic initiative, international factors, political regime form, and the activities of civil society groups encouraged or discouraged large-scale primary health care programs. This chapter will draw together the findings of the eight case studies and reinterpret them in the light of quantitative analyses involving a large number of developing countries worldwide.

11.1. Economic Output, Income, and Infant Survival: Was Wealthier Healthier?

The narrow variant of the wealthier is healthier proposition has three testable implications: (1) that societies with higher levels of GDP per capita will achieve lower levels of infant mortality; (2) that societies with steeper rises of GDP per capita will achieve steeper declines of infant mortality; and (3) that societies will reduce infant mortality more during periods of high GDP per capita growth than during periods of slow or negative GDP per capita growth. These implications pertain respectively to the *level* of infant mortality at a particular point in time; to *progress* at reducing infant mortality over a particular span of time; and to the *tempo* of infant mortality decline within that span of time.

As regards the level of infant mortality, the large-scale cross-national analyses reported in Chapters 1 and 2 generally confirmed the wealthier is healthier claim. Across countries, a higher level of GDP per capita was associated with a lower level of infant mortality. Regression of the infant mortality rate on GDP per capita across 93 developing countries in 2005 produced a downward sloping regression line around which observations clustered tightly (Figure 1.1). Similarly, in a regression of the infant mortality rate on GDP per capita across 105 developing countries in 1990, GDP per capita took on a negative, high-magnitude, and statistically significant coefficient. Even after income inequality and five demographic, geographic, and cultural variables were added as predictors, the coefficient on GDP per capita remained negative, large, and statistically significant (Table 2.2, Models 2–1, 2–2, and 2–3). In short, the narrow, intermediate, and broad variants of the wealthier is healthier hypothesis were each consistent with the results of the analyses reported in Chapter 2.

As regards progress over time in reducing infant mortality, the evidence for the wealthier is healthier claim was a bit weaker. A steeper rise in a country's GDP per capita from 1960 to 2005 was indeed associated with a steeper decline in its infant mortality rate, but the association was not as strong as it was for the level of infant mortality. Across the same 93 developing countries included in the level analysis reported in Figure 1.1, those with greater GDP per capita growth also had greater infant mortality decline, but the observations clustered less cozily around the regression line (Figure 1.2).

TABLE 11.1. *Infant Mortality Decline and Economic Growth in Eight Societies, 1960–2005*

[handwritten annotation: narrow ↓ GDP/capita]

	1. Level	2. Progress	3. Tempo
	Actual infant mortality level in 2005 as a proportion of the level predicted by GDP per capita in 2005	Actual average annual percent decline of infant mortality 1960–2005 as a proportion of the decline predicted by average annual GDP per capita growth 1960–2005	Correlation between average annual GDP per capita growth and average annual infant mortality decline across eight five-year periods, 1960–2000
Thailand	0.51	1.41	−0.22
South Korea	0.58	1.38	+0.28
Costa Rica	0.64	1.52	+0.26
Chile	0.71	1.87	−0.15
Taiwan	0.75	1.08	+0.27
Argentina	0.98	1.26	−0.14
Brazil	1.02	1.28	−0.64
Indonesia	1.04	0.99	+0.05

Output and data in McGuire 2009, Web Appendices C2 and D7. Columns 1 and 2: data identical to those in Figure 1.1 and Figure 1.2 respectively. For Argentina, Chile, and Costa Rica, the infant mortality estimates used in this table (World Bank 2008e) differ slightly from those in Table A1 (vital registration). Column 3: Calculated from data in Tables A1 and A3.

As for the tempo of infant mortality decline, evidence to support the wealthier is healthier conjecture was scarce. Indeed, the case study chapters turned up time periods in several countries in which slow or negative GDP per capita growth coincided with fast infant mortality decline, and several others in which fast GDP per capita growth coincided with slow infant mortality decline. The surprising scarcity of time periods in which fast GDP per capita growth was associated with fast infant mortality decline, and in which slow GDP per capita growth was associated with slow infant mortality decline, provides perhaps the strongest evidence that factors other than wealth are important to explaining changes in infant mortality rates. Evidence for the wealthier is healthier proposition was thus strongest for level, next strongest for progress, and weakest for tempo. Table 11.1 shows how each of the eight cases fared on each of these dimensions of infant mortality relative to GDP per capita achievement.

Turning first to the level of infant mortality, Thailand, South Korea, Costa Rica, Chile, and Taiwan each achieved a much lower level of infant mortality in 2005 than would be expected on the basis of its GDP per capita (Table 11.1, Column 1). As for progress, Thailand, South Korea, Costa Rica, and Chile each achieved a much steeper reduction of infant mortality from 1960 to 2005 than would be expected on the basis of its GDP per capita growth, and Taiwan achieved a slightly steeper reduction (Table 11.1, Column 2).

Indonesia performed about as expected on both level and progress, whereas Argentina and Brazil did about as expected on level but overperformed moderately on progress (due mainly to fast infant mortality decline in the context of slow GDP per capita growth from 1990 to 2005). As for tempo, the indicator chosen is the correlation within each society between its average annual GDP per capita growth and its average annual infant mortality decline across eight successive five-year time intervals from 1960 to 2000 (1960–1965, 1965–1970 ... 1995–2000).[2] To the extent that the narrow variant of the wealthier is healthier hypothesis is consistent with the data, infant mortality would tend to fall more during intervals of greater economic growth, and to fall less during intervals of modest or negative economic growth. Hence, if the tempo of GDP per capita growth were a good predictor of the tempo of infant mortality decline, one would expect to find a high positive correlation coefficient in each row, indicating a close association within each five-year period between GDP per capita growth and infant mortality decline.

In fact, the tempo of GDP per capita growth proved to be a poor predictor of the tempo of infant mortality decline (Table 11.1, Column 3). In Argentina, Brazil, Chile, and Thailand the correlation was negative, indicating that intervals of greater GDP per capita growth tended to be intervals of slower infant mortality decline, and vice versa. In Brazil, the mismatch between changes in GDP per capita and in infant mortality was extreme (the negative correlation was a whopping –0.64). This mismatch reflected very little infant mortality decline during intervals of rapid economic growth from 1960 to 1975, followed by impressive infant mortality decline during intervals of negligible economic growth from 1990 to 2000 (Tables A1 and A3). In Indonesia, the tempo of infant mortality decline was apparently independent of the tempo of economic growth across the eight five-year intervals (the correlation coefficient for Indonesia in Table 11.1, Column 3, was close to zero). In Costa Rica, South Korea, and Taiwan, the pace of infant mortality decline was only weakly associated with the change in GDP per capita across the eight five-year intervals (the correlations, although positive, were small).

In response to these findings it could plausibly be argued that changes in GDP per capita could have had delayed as well as immediate effects on infant mortality levels, such that a change in GDP per capita in one period might affect the pace of infant mortality decline in a later period. One would expect, however, that a fair proportion of such effects would materialize at some point within a five-year interval. Had the tempo of GDP per capita growth exercised a powerful influence on the tempo of infant mortality decline, as the narrow variant of the wealthier is healthier conjecture would lead one to expect, the correlation coefficients in Table 11.1, Column 3, would have been higher and more uniformly positive than the coefficients actually obtained.

[2] At the time of this writing Heston, Summers, and Aten (2006) provided GDP per capita data only through 2003, so no 2000–2005 interval was included in the analysis.

Level criteria can be used to compare the performances of the eight societies not only in relation to the narrow variant of the wealthier is healthier hypothesis, but also in relation to the intermediate and broad variants. In relation to the narrow variant, when GDP per capita is the only predictor of the infant mortality level in 2005 (Table 11.2, Model 1), the measured infant mortality rate is below the expected rate in seven of the eight societies compared in this book (in Brazil the infant mortality rate was 2 percent above the expected level). This finding does not disconfirm the narrow variant of the wealthier is healthier hypothesis, but it underscores that GDP per capita is not the only determinant of country's possibilities for achieving a certain level of infant mortality.

To explore the intermediate variant of the wealthier is healthier hypothesis, income inequality was added to GDP per capita as a second predictor of the infant mortality level in 2005 (Table 11.2, Model 2). The addition of income inequality as a predictor moved some countries closer to their expected infant mortality rates, but left others farther away. When GDP per capita was the only predictor in the analysis (Model 1), Indonesia's measured infant mortality level in 2005, 28 per 1000, was 25 percent lower than its expected level of 37.5 per 1000. When income inequality was added as a predictor (Model 2), Indonesia's expected infant mortality level dropped to 28.8 per 1000 – almost exactly the same as its measured level. In other words, Indonesia's low level of income inequality fully explained, in a statistical sense, the 25 percent gap between its measured infant mortality level and the infant mortality level that would be expected on the basis of its GDP per capita alone. In contrast, adding income inequality as a predictor moved Brazil farther away from the 2005 infant mortality level that would be expected on the basis of its GDP per capita alone. Brazil's measured infant mortality level in 2005, 20 per 1000, was 2 percent higher than its GDP per capita predicted (Model 1). This measured infant mortality level of 20 per 1000 was, however, 12 percent lower than the rate predicted by Brazil's GDP per capita and (high) income inequality taken together (Model 2).

The broad variant of the wealthier is healthier hypothesis (Table 11.2, Model 3) adds five geographic, demographic, and cultural variables to GDP per capita and income inequality as predictors of the infant mortality level in 2005.[3] In Models 1 and 2, which operationalize respectively the narrow and intermediate variants of the wealthier is healthier hypothesis, seven of the eight societies had lower infant mortality than their levels of economic affluence predicted. In Model 3, which operationalizes the broad variant of the hypothesis, only five of the eight societies had lower infant mortality than their socioeconomic circumstances predicted. South Korea's overperformance on infant mortality, which was striking in relation to GDP per capita alone,

---

[3] These five geographic, demographic, and cultural variables are identical to those in Table 2.2, Model 2–3, the "baseline regression" in the cross-national quantitative analyses reported in Chapter 2, except that they pertain to 2005 rather than to 1990.

TABLE 11.2. *Infant Mortality and Socioeconomic Circumstances in Eight Societies, 2005*

Actual infant mortality level in 2005 as a proportion of the level predicted by GDP per capita across 102 developing countries		Actual infant mortality level in 2005 as a proportion of the level predicted by GDP per capita and income inequality across 102 developing countries		Actual infant mortality level in 2005 as a proportion of the level predicted by GDP per capita, income inequality, ethnic diversity, whether 90+% Muslim, fertility, population density, and urbanization across 102 developing countries	
MODEL 1 $limrwba_i = b_i + lgdpwbai_i + e_i$		MODEL 2 $limrwba_i = b_i + lgdpwbai_i + ginipci_i + e_i$		MODEL 3 $limrwba_i = b_i + lgdpwbai_i + ginipci_i + ethf_i + musl_i + fert_i + ldens_i + urb_i + e_i$	
Country	*Ratio*	*Country*	*Ratio*	*Country*	*Ratio*
Thailand	0.36	Thailand	0.41	Thailand	0.38
S. Korea	0.47	Chile	0.46	Chile	0.54
Chile	0.52	S. Korea	0.56	Costa Rica	0.66
Costa Rica	0.57	Costa Rica	0.58	S. Korea	0.73
Taiwan	0.64	Taiwan	0.80	Argentina	0.83
Indonesia	0.75	Argentina	0.80	Taiwan	1.05
Argentina	0.84	Brazil	0.88	Brazil	1.06
Brazil	1.02	Indonesia	0.97	Indonesia	1.09

Output and data in McGuire 2009, Web Appendices C3 and D8. Models identical to Table 2.2, Models 2–1, 2–2, and 2–3, but use data for 2005 rather than 1990. The 2005 data set has 102 cases (versus 105 for 1990) because GDP per capita was unavailable for Afghanistan, Iraq, or Somalia in 2005. The figures in Table 11.2, Model 1 differ from those in Table 11.1, Column 1 because the GDP per capita figures pertain to 2005 rather than to 2003 and come from World Bank 2008e rather than from Heston, Summers, and Aten 2006. *limrwba*: Natural log of the infant mortality rate in 2005. World Bank 2008e, except Hong Kong (World Bank 2008a) and Taiwan (Taiwan. DGBAS 2007: 28). *lgdpwbai*. Natural log of GDP per capita at PPP (in 2000 international dollars) in 2005. World Bank 2008e. Figures for Cuba, North Korea, and Zimbabwe were imputed with the Stata impute procedure using as a predictor variable the 2003 GDP per capita figures (RGDPCH) in Heston, Summers, and Aten 2006. *ginipci*: Gini index of income inequality, observation closest to 2005. 81 of the 102 observations are taken from WIDER 2007. The observation for Benin is from UNDP 2007. The observation for Cuba is from Brundenius 2002: 342. Each of the 19 countries without a Gini estimate was assigned that of its nearest neighbor (Rajkumar and Swaroop 2002: 26–27) with a Gini estimate. McGuire 2009, Web Appendix D9, explains how this variable was constructed. *ethf*: Ethnolinguistic fractionalization in 1979–2001. Data associated with Alesina et al. 2003. Sudan is assigned Ethiopia's level; Yemen is assigned Saudi Arabia's level. *musl*: Whether the country's population was (1) or was not (0) more than 90 percent Muslim in 1980. Based on percent Muslim in 1980 according to data associated with La Porta et al. 1998. *fert*: total fertility rate in 2005 (or in five cases 2002). World Bank 2008a, except Taiwan (Taiwan. DGBAS 2007: 27). *ldens*: Natural log of population density (inhabitants per square kilometer) in 2005. World Bank 2008a, except Taiwan (Taiwan. DGBAS 2007: 11). *urb*: Urban population as a share of total population in 2005. World Bank 2008a, except Taiwan (Taiwan. DGBAS 2007: 26, share in cities with 20,000+).

was attenuated in the presence of six other socioeconomic variables, and Taiwan's overperformance vanished. In other words, low income inequality, low ethnic diversity, low fertility, high population density, high urbanization, and the absence of an overwhelmingly Muslim population seem to "explain" (statistically) all of Taiwan's overperformance on infant mortality relative to GDP per capita, as well as a fair share of South Korea's.

South Korea and Taiwan support the broad variant of the wealthier is healthier proposition, in that their infant mortality levels in 2005 are explained wholly (Taiwan) or mostly (South Korea) by seven socioeconomic variables. The 2005 infant mortality levels in Brazil and Indonesia, and to a lesser extent Argentina, are also consistent with the broad variant of the wealthier is healthier proposition. Far less consistent with the wealthier is healthier conjecture were the 2005 infant mortality levels in Chile, Costa Rica, and Thailand. These cases provide the strongest support among the eight for social provisioning-focused explanations of cross-national variation of infant mortality levels. Each of these countries had much lower infant mortality in 2005 than would be expected on the basis of any variant of the wealthier is healthier hypothesis (Table 11.2). In Chile and Costa Rica (especially after about 1970), as well as in Thailand (especially after about 1990), governments provided unusually good education, family planning, water, sanitation, nutrition, and health care services in the context of the socioeconomic circumstances they inherited and/or created. These cases underscore that a fairly low GDP per capita, even when exacerbated by high income inequality, does not present an insurmountable obstacle to achieving a low level of infant mortality.

In Chile and Costa Rica, effective nationwide primary health care programs made up for low GDP per capita (especially in Costa Rica) and high income inequality (especially in Chile). In South Korea and Taiwan, nationwide primary health care programs either received mixed reviews for quality (South Korea in 1978) or began before the period over which mortality decline is measured (Taiwan in 1949). From the 1960s onward, however, both societies excelled at the public provision of education and family planning services, so their infant mortality achievements cannot be credited to shared growth alone. Indonesia and Thailand each enacted a major primary health care program in 1978, but these programs during their initial years suffered from quality and utilization problems that reduced their effects on infant mortality. Meanwhile, economic growth in Indonesia and in Thailand, although rapid during the 1970s and 1980s, was not quite fast enough to make up for these deficiencies in the quality of the basic health services provided. In Argentina (except in a few small provinces) and in Brazil (until the early 1990s), the neglect of primary health care for the poor kept infant mortality rates high during the years from 1960 to 1990, compounding the effects of slow economic growth (especially in Argentina) and high income inequality (especially in Brazil).

Infant mortality outcomes in Thailand, Brazil, and Indonesia deserve closer inspection, because each of these countries in 1990 had an infant mortality rate that was at (Thailand) or above (Brazil, Indonesia) the level expected on the basis of its GDP per capita. From 1990 to 2005, however, each of the three societies registered significant progress in reducing infant mortality. Among 188 countries with available data, Thailand ranked 2nd, Brazil ranked 17th, and Indonesia ranked 30th at percent decline of infant mortality from 1990 to 2005.[4] Accordingly, Thailand went from having an expected level of infant mortality in 1990, given its GDP per capita, to having a much lower-than-expected infant mortality level in 2005. Brazil, and less spectacularly Indonesia, went from being underperformers on infant mortality in 1990 to being expected performers in 2005. Argentina remained an expected performer (with an infant mortality rate in both 1990 and 2005 that was close to the rate predicted by its GDP per capita), while Chile, Costa Rica, South Korea, and Taiwan remained overperformers (with infant mortality rates in both years that were much lower than predicted by GDP per capita).

Thailand, Brazil, and Indonesia each achieved rapid infant mortality decline from 1990 to 2005 even though each suffered a serious economic crisis in the late 1990s. In each case governments made significant advances in the public provision of basic health services to the poor, through post-1990 improvements to primary health care in Thailand, through the village midwives program in Indonesia (1989), and through the Community Health Agents (1991) and Family Health (1994) programs in Brazil. Costa Rica also implemented a major primary health care program in 1995 (the Comprehensive Basic Health Care Teams), and infant mortality fell rapidly during the first five years of the program's operation. The tempo of infant mortality decline in each of these cases was inconsistent with the narrow variant of the wealthier is healthier conjecture.

By contrast, South Korea and Taiwan from 1960 to 2005, consistent with the intermediate variant of the wealthier is healthier proposition, achieved rapid declines of infant mortality in a context of fast economic growth and low income inequality. Moreover, while the Latin American countries were building large welfare states, neither South Korea nor Taiwan from 1960 to 1990 spent a large share of GDP on social services or covered a large share of the population with health insurance. Even in the East Asian cases, however, the rapid rise of GDP per capita and the low level of income inequality were not the only reasons for the rapid decline of infant mortality from 1960 to 2005. The provision of basic social services – which is not the same as the construction of a huge welfare state – also contributed. It is widely recognized that, from the 1960s forward, the governments of South Korea and Taiwan were among the most successful in the world at providing education and family planning services. The literature on the "East Asian miracle" has tended, however, to overlook the contributions of family planning services, although fertility decline is gaining recognition for its contribution to economic growth.[5]

---

[4] Data from World Bank 2008e, except Taiwan, from Table A1.
[5] Bloom, Canning, and Malaney 2000; McNicoll 2006.

South Korean and Taiwanese governments from 1960 to 2005 did more to promote basic education and family planning than to deliver or finance health care, nutrition, or water and sanitation services. Still, South Korea remained an overperformer on infant mortality even when seven socioeconomic factors were taken into account (Table 11.2, Model 3). A share of its overperformance may well have been due to improved provision of safe water, sanitation, and basic health services during the 1970s, which was a decade of particularly fast infant mortality decline (Table A1). Taiwan's overperformance on infant mortality in 2005 vanished when seven socioeconomic factors were included as predictors, but the most spectacular advances in primary health care services on the island occurred in the late 1940s and early 1950s. In 1960, accordingly, despite being desperately poor, Taiwan had the lowest infant mortality rate among the eight societies reviewed in this book (Tables A1 and A3).

It might be argued that the improvement of basic social services in South Korea and Taiwan, as well as in other societies, was a predictable consequence of the rise in overall affluence, and should therefore not be accorded independent causal status. GDP per capita growth certainly facilitated service provision. It raised the resources available to build schools, hospitals, clinics, and water systems, as well as to pay teachers, doctors, nurses, and family planning workers. Also, the rapid growth of GDP per capita, especially when accompanied by a rapid decline of income poverty, raised access to both private and public services (by making it easier to buy clothing and supplies for public-school children, to pay for transport to public health care facilities, and so on). On the other hand, the provision of basic social services also contributed to growth in economic output per head. Improved education, health care, water, and sanitation boosted labor productivity, while family planning reduced birth rates, raising the working-age share of the population and thus encouraging economic growth for the next several decades.[6] Rising life expectancy promoted saving, which boosted economic growth.[7] Social provisioning reinforced income-related achievements, not just vice versa.

In evaluating the wealthier is healthier hypothesis, and especially in considering its implications for public policy, one observation that is well worth underscoring is the low economic cost of the primary health care programs that were found in the case study chapters to have reduced infant mortality significantly. From an economic point of view, many countries that are poorer than the middle-income developing societies analyzed in this book are certainly capable, even before attaining even a moderately high level of overall affluence, of launching primary health care programs with a good chance of reducing the infant mortality rate appreciably.

Countries that attain a low infant mortality rate despite a low GDP per capita, or rapid infant mortality decline despite sluggish economic growth, are not in every respect desirable development models. Higher incomes usually

---

[6] Bloom, Canning, and Malaney 2000.
[7] Bloom, Canning, and Graham 2003; Kinugasa and Mason 2007.

contribute to capability expansion, even when they are not associated with lower levels or faster declines of infant mortality. Still, countries whose performance on survival-related indicators is better than their performance on income-related indicators, and vice versa, can provide useful examples to be emulated or avoided respectively, with due consideration of the particularities of national context. The analysis in Chapter 2 showed that, in the short run (10 years), it has been hard for developing countries to raise GDP per capita or to reduce income inequality in an amount sufficient to achieve a significant decline of infant mortality. By identifying societies that have played their economic hands well, by observing their provision of basic social services, and by exploring the forces and circumstances that influenced their provision of such services, lessons can be drawn as to what types of provision might be desirable and feasible to adapt to other societies. Conversely, societies that have played their economic hands poorly can provide useful lessons about what to avoid in the areas of social service provision and mortality reduction.

11.2. Social Service Provision and Infant Survival: Did Primary Health Care Help?

Within the area of service provision, the case studies in Chapters 3–10 devoted special attention to nationwide primary health care programs. A comparison of the experiences of the eight cases over time will permit some tentative conclusions as to whether these campaigns were associated with accelerated infant mortality decline during their initial years of operation, when their impact is likely to have been strongest.

The major primary health care programs reviewed in the case study chapters are ranked in Table 11.3 according to the average annual percent decline of infant mortality achieved in the first five years after the program began (or, if data are unavailable for those years, during the nearest five-year period for which acceptable infant mortality data are available). A steep decline of infant mortality during such an interval does not provide conclusive evidence of program success. For one thing, such a decline cannot be attributed conclusively to the program. For another, the assessment of infant mortality decline over the first five years of a program's operation (rather than over some other period) is partly arbitrary and partly imposed by the inadequacy of annual vital registration data in five of the eight cases. Also, conclusions drawn from this type of assessment could be affected by the delayed effects of previous levels and changes of socioeconomic factors, as well as of social service provision.

Some societies, for whatever reasons, reduce infant mortality more quickly than others. From 1960 to 2005 the average annual decline of infant mortality was 6.4 percent in South Korea, but only 3.3 percent in Indonesia (Table A1). To minimize the distortion imposed by such "fixed effects," the average annual percent decline of infant mortality during the first five years of a program's operation may be considered in the light of the average annual percent decline of infant mortality within each society from 1960 to 2005. Controlling for fixed effects in this way, eight of the eleven programs for which data were available (Taiwan, 1949–1954, is excluded for lack of data) were associated with greater declines of infant mortality than their societies achieved over the longer period from 1960 to 2005. In five of the eight cases the increment exceeded 1 percent per year.

The three programs that were not followed by an accelerated decline of infant mortality were those introduced in Chile in 1967, in Brazil in 1976, and in Indonesia in 1978. The qualitative analyses in Chapters 6 and 10 respectively found that the basic health services provided by Brazil's 1976 Program to Expand Health and Sanitation Activities in the Interior (PIASS) and by Indonesia's 1978 Village Community Health Development Program (PKMD) were often poor in quality and, partly as a result of this deficiency, often under-utilized by the people that the programs were designed to serve. No evidence suggests, however, that similar quality or utilization problems afflicted the primary health care initiatives in post-1967 Chile. Indeed, the annual percent decline of infant mortality in Chile in the five years after 1967 was a respectable 5.1 percent (Table 11.3). Chile reduced infant mortality even faster during other intervals, however, so its 5.1 percent pace of decline for 1967–1972 was slightly behind its 5.7 percent pace for the entire period from 1960 to 2005. Still, the cases of post-1976 Brazil and post-1978 Indonesia suggest that the introduction of a nationwide primary health care program will be associated with accelerated infant mortality decline if and only if the health services it provides are high enough in quality that people decide to utilize them.

In the other eight cases, the introduction of a primary health care program was followed by an acceleration of the pace of infant mortality decline. In four of these eight cases – post-1973 Costa Rica, post-1980 South Korea, post-1989 Indonesia, and post-1995 Costa Rica – GDP per capita growth in the first five years of a primary health care program's operation was also faster than the country's historical average (Table 11.3). These four cases are thus consistent with the hypothesis that wealthier is healthier, as well as with the conjecture that primary health care helps. In the other four cases, however, GDP per capita growth was slower than the country's historical average. The second-greatest percent decline of infant mortality in the first five years of a program's operation, in Chile from 1974 to 1979, took place in a context of very slow GDP per capita growth, skyrocketing income inequality, and soaring income poverty. The third-greatest decline, in Argentina from 1977 to 1982, happened in the context of falling GDP per capita, a sharp rise in income inequality, and a pronounced increase in income poverty. The fifth-greatest decline, in Brazil from 1994 to 1999, occurred in a context of very slow GDP per capita growth, albeit without any appreciable worsening of income inequality or income poverty. In these three cases, the percent decline of infant mortality during the first five years of the program's operation was much higher than the country's historical average. In each case, state policy-makers – in the military government in Argentina, in the Pinochet dictatorship in Chile, or in the elected Collor, Franco, and Cardoso governments in Brazil – implemented a

TABLE 11.3. *Major National Primary Health Care Programs in Eight Societies*

Country	Primary health care program	First five years of program	Average annual infant mortality decline in the first five years of program	Average annual infant mortality decline in country 1960–2005	Average annual GDP per capita growth in the first five years of program	Average annual GDP per capita growth in country 1960–2003
Costa Rica	Rural Health Plan, Community Health Plan	1973–1978	12.3%	4.5%	2.7%	1.5%
Chile	Maternal and child health care and nutrition programs	1974–1979	10.2%	5.9%	0.9%	2.0%
Argentina	National Rural Health Program	1977–1982	7.3%	3.4%	-2.2%	0.6%
South Korea	Special Act for Rural Health	1980–1985	7.2%	6.4%	6.4%	6.0%
Brazil	Family Health Program	1994–1999	5.7% (1995–00)	3.8%	0.9% (1995–00)	2.4%
Thailand	Rural Primary Health Care Expansion Project	1978–1983	5.7% (1980–85)	5.6%	4.4% (1980–85)	4.6%
Costa Rica	Comprehensive Basic Health Care Teams	1995–2000	5.1%	4.5%	2.8%	1.5%
Chile	Maternal and child health care and nutrition programs	1967–1972	5.1%	5.9%	2.2%	2.0%
Indonesia	Village Midwife Program	1989–1994	4.4% (1990–95)	3.3%	4.9%	3.2%
Brazil	Program to Expand Health and Sanitation Activities in the Interior	1976–1981	3.3% (1975–80)	3.8%	3.9% (1975–80)	2.4%
Indonesia	Village Community Health Development Program	1978–1983	2.4% (1980–85)	3.3%	1.3% (1980–85)	3.2%
Taiwan	Joint Commission on Rural Reconstruction	1949–1954	Data discrepant	4.9%	No data	6.3%

Infant mortality decline in first five years of program: Average annual percent decline of infant mortality in the first five years of the program (or years with infant mortality data). Data sources: as in Table A1. *GDP per capita growth in first five years of program:* Average annual percent rise of GDP at PPP (in 2000 international dollars) in the first five years of the program (or in the nearest five years with infant mortality data). Data sources: as highly effective maternal and infant health care program targeted to impoverished areas. These three experiences underscore the limits to the explanatory power of the wealthier is healthier hypothesis, and provide especially compelling evidence that primary health care helped to reduce infant mortality.

One of the advantages of country case studies is that they can generate time series or subnational data with which to test hypotheses designed initially for cross-national analysis.[8] Time-series cross-sectional analyses show that the primary health care programs introduced in 79 Costa Rican cantons in 1972–1980, in 420 Costa Rican districts in 1995–2001, and in 26 Brazilian states in 1990–2000 were each associated with a lower infant mortality rate than would be expected on the basis of control variables.[9] Case studies of individual subnational units also provide evidence that primary health care helps. After the initiation of a province-wide primary health care program in Neuquén, Argentina, in 1970, infant mortality plunged. Steep declines of infant mortality also followed the introduction of provincial primary health care programs in the Argentine provinces of Jujuy, Rio Negro, and Salta from 1967 to 1973. The Community Health Agents program launched in the Brazilian state of Ceará in 1987 achieved, according to most studies, a rapid reduction of infant mortality. In 1978 Yogyakarta, one of Indonesia's poorest provinces, had the lowest infant mortality in the country, partly because of a midwife training program in the 1950s.[10] Scholars interested in public service provision and infant mortality often bring up the Indian state of Kerala, which has done better than other Indian states on both service provision and mortality decline, despite a disappointing performance on income-related indicators.[11] To maximize analytic leverage on the problem, research on such cases should be complemented by research on provinces or other subnational units which, despite favorable economic circumstances, have experienced sluggish declines of infant mortality.

Just as the evidence in Section 11.1 did not show irrefutably that GDP per capita and income distribution are the most important factors behind infant mortality levels and changes, the evidence in this section does not demonstrate conclusively that the public provision of basic social services is the most critical determinant of the pattern and pace of infant mortality decline. The evidence in this section shows only that the public provision of basic social services, particularly primary health care, can reduce infant mortality significantly – provided that the quality of such services is reasonably good – even in the context of difficult economic circumstances. The modesty of this claim belies its significance. Countries do not have to wait to get rich, or to achieve low income inequality, in order to achieve a rapid fall in the infant mortality rate.

[8] Gerring 2007: 205; King, Keohane, and Verba 1994: 219–223.
[9] Costa Rica 1970s: Rosero-Bixby 1986: 63; Rosero-Bixby 1990: 41. Costa Rica 1990s: Rosero-Bixby 2004b; World Bank 2003a: 49. Brazil 1990s: Macinko, Guanais, and Marinho de Souza 2006; Macinko et al. 2007.
[10] Gunawan 2001: 6–8.
[11] Drèze and Sen 1995; Ramachandran 2000.

Steep declines of infant mortality can be achieved, and have been achieved, through the provision of inexpensive public health services. This finding raises the question of what determines whether and when a society will provide such services.

11.3. Political Origins of Large-Scale Primary Health Care Programs

The political origins of large-scale primary health care programs lie in bureaucratic initiative, international factors, interest group pressures, issue network activities, and political regime form. In unraveling the origins and operation of such programs, the preceding chapters have focused on the activities of interest groups and issue networks, and especially on the democratic or authoritarian character of the political regime. These factors are interrelated, in that interest groups and issue networks are usually freer to act under democracy than under authoritarianism. They need to be distinguished, however, because interest groups and issue networks can also be influential under authoritarian regimes. For example, interest groups representing landowners, business, and labor shaped and constrained economic policy in Argentina under military rule in the late 1960s, and issue networks advocating better health services for the poor influenced public health policy in Brazil and Thailand under military rule in the late 1970s and early 1980s.

Political regime form, interest group influence, and issue network activity are the hypothesized policy determinants of primary interest in this book. Bureaucratic initiative and international factors are also analyzed, but they are treated in a fashion analogous to control variables in a multivariate statistical analysis. These factors, in other words, need to be taken into account in any comprehensive explanation of the making and operation of social policies. Moreover, their omission from the analysis could bias conclusions about the magnitude and direction of the impact exerted by political regime form and by the activities of civil society organizations. Accordingly, this section will begin by summarizing how and to what degree bureaucratic initiative and international factors shaped and constrained the primary health care initiatives on which this book has focused. This summary will prepare the way for an analysis of the effects of interest group influence, issue network activity, and political regime form.

Bureaucratic initiative is responsible for a large-scale primary health care program to the extent that officials in an executive-branch agency (a health ministry, a social security institute, etc.), acting with a degree of autonomy from pressures from outside the executive branch, propose, design, approve, or implement such a program. Officials may get involved with national primary health care programs at the behest of top political authorities; but more often, and usually in accordance with broader policy orientations outlined by such authorities, they propose and design the programs on their own, and then seek political approval after having done so. Bureaucratic initiative had a particularly conspicuous impact on the origins of national primary health care programs in Costa Rica, Chile, and Thailand. John Caldwell argued that Costa Rica's Rural Health and Community Health plans in the 1970s were "essentially a bureaucratic achievement. There was no popular crusade."[12] In Chile under military rule, Miguel Kast and his collaborators in the National Planning Office, to whom Pinochet had delegated significant policy autonomy, were largely responsible for expanding maternal and infant care services in rural areas in the mid-1970s. Dr. Stanley Zankel, the U.S.-born Project Coordinator for Thailand's Hill Tribe Health and Family Planning program in the 1980s, attributed to Dr. Jumroon Mikhanorn and his colleagues in the health ministry most of the responsibility for originating the Rural Primary Health Care Expansion Project in the late 1970s.[13]

A national primary health care program always originates, in an immediate sense, from some sort of bureaucratic initiative. Nevertheless, explanations that highlight bureaucratic initiative, political will, and political leadership raise the questions of where the political will originated and what determined whether and how it influenced policy.[14] Government policy-makers always have some freedom of choice. Political will is not an unmoved mover, however, and is shaped and constrained by the environment in which it is exercised. In the case of public health care, political will in the eight societies studied in this book was shaped and constrained particularly by foreign influence, political regime form, and the activities of civil society organizations.

Foreign influence on social policies, including national primary health care programs, spreads through diverse mechanisms.[15] Among the most important are missionary activities, occupation and colonization, the operations of multinational corporations, foreign study and training, war and the threat of war, international ideological conflict, bilateral and multilateral financial aid, the activities of agencies like the World Bank and World Health Organization, international conferences, prevailing international norms about public health care, competition between nations for status and prestige, and foreign models of public health care provision.

Each of these mechanisms was at work in several of the societies analyzed. Protestant missionaries helped to introduce Western medicine to Korea, Taiwan, and Thailand. Japanese colonial authorities improved health care, disease control, and sanitation in Korea and Taiwan. The Dutch made health-related improvements in Indonesia. Foreign plantation owners in Costa Rica and Indonesia gave farm workers health care and fought yellow fever, malaria, tuberculosis, and other diseases. Before a medical school was opened in 1961, aspiring doctors in Costa Rica often studied at the Catholic University of Louvain, Belgium, where many instructors were committed to the social teachings of the Catholic Church, particularly as expressed in the 1891 *Rerum*

---

[12] Caldwell 1986: 200.
[13] Zankel 2003.
[14] Reich 1994.
[15] Nelson 2004a: 45.

Novarum encyclical.[16] Many such medical graduates returned to Costa Rica with a strengthened commitment to public service. By the early 1940s most senior Brazilian health officials had studied in the United States, and by 1960 more than 200 additional Brazilian health professionals had won scholarships to study there.[17] In the early 1970s, Thai health ministry officials studied at the Johns Hopkins School of Public Health on World Health Organization scholarships. Returning to Thailand, they streamlined the ministry's operations and improved its planning and implementation capacities.[18]

During and after World War II the U.S. government funded disease control and primary health care programs in several of the societies analyzed, partly in response to national security interests. In Brazil from 1942 onward, the U.S. government funded and helped to staff the Special Public Health Service in an effort to facilitate the extraction and transport of raw materials critical to the Allied war effort. In southern Korea in the late 1940s, the U.S. Army Military Government introduced drugs and vector controls that reduced the incidence of infectious diseases. In Taiwan as of 1949, the Sino-American Joint Commission on Rural Reconstruction built and repaired hundreds of rural health stations and launched programs to control tuberculosis and malaria. During the 1950s, the United States Operations Mission in Thailand engaged in health education, sanitation promotion, and disease control activities in rural areas.

The global conflict between communism and anti-communism, which encouraged both land reform and labor repression in South Korea and Taiwan, also contributed to the expansion of basic health services in many societies. In Brazil after World War II, U.S. governments continued to fund the Special Public Health Service in the Amazon and in the Northeast with an eye toward winning hearts and minds in the cold war. In Costa Rica, worries about the spread of the Cuban Revolution encouraged some legislators to vote for the 1961 constitutional amendment that mandated the extension of health insurance to the entire population. In Taiwan, the Sino-American Joint Commission on Rural Reconstruction built rural health clinics and implemented disease control measures in the late 1940s and early 1950s in part to keep the poor from turning to the left. The Thai government in the early 1950s targeted social programs to the impoverished Northeast because of concern for the security situation in the region, and in the 1960s and 1970s the United States Operations Mission in Thailand built roads, financed health posts, and funded the training of health workers in the North and Northeast in response to the growing insurgency. Battle injuries in these areas in the 1970s led to the expansion of community hospitals, which became important sites of primary health care delivery in rural areas on the periphery of the country.[19]

[16] Miranda Gutiérrez 2007.
[17] Campos 1997: 245, 247.
[18] Muscat 1990: 222.
[19] Zankel 2003.

International organizations shaped health policy in each of the eight societies and provided inspiration, financing, and expertise for disease control and primary care. In the first few decades of the twentieth century the Rockefeller Foundation funded hospitals and medical training in Thailand, as well as disease control and primary health care in Brazil, Costa Rica, and Indonesia. In the 1950s UNICEF financed maternal and child health centers in Indonesia and nutrition programs in Costa Rica and South Korea. In the early 1970s seven international organizations funded the Rural Health Plan in Costa Rica, and later in the decade the U.S. Agency for International Development sponsored pilot primary health care programs in South Korea. In Indonesia, a World Health Organization study helped to persuade the government to implement the Village Community Health Development Program in 1978. The Pan American Health Organization supported Brazil's Sanitarian Movement in the late 1970s, and other international agencies funded research and study opportunities for its members. In the early 1990s, the World Bank and UNICEF funded Argentina's Mother and Infant Nutrition Program. At the same time, Pan American Health Organization and UNICEF experts helped to design Brazil's Family Health Program, and personnel contracted by the United Nations Development Programme coordinated it. The World Bank's 1993 World Development Report, *Investing in Health,* and the Inter-American Development Bank's 1996 report on *Economic and Social Progress in Latin America: Making Social Services Work,* have been credited with influencing international norms about the public provision of health, education, and water and sanitation services.[20]

Such norms have also been diffused and reinforced at major international conferences. In 1972, the Third Special Meeting of Ministers of Health of the Americas encouraged the Rural Health Plan in Costa Rica, as well as a series of provincial primary care programs in Argentina. The international primary health care movement, which culminated in the WHO/UNICEF conference in Alma Ata, USSR, in September 1978, had particular resonance in Thailand because of the long history of interchange between Thai health officials and international public health organizations. In South Korea, the 1980 Special Act for Rural Health has been called "an official response by the Korean government" to the primary health care declaration at the Alma Ata conference.[21] Seven of the twelve nationwide primary health care programs reviewed in this study started between 1973 and 1980 (Table 11.3). It was precisely during this period that the World Health Organization began to emphasize primary health care.[22] Between 1971 and 1976, Taiwan, South Korea, Thailand, and Indonesia each introduced compulsory (or strongly incentivized) service in underserved areas for new medical graduates. In 1970, President Allende of Chile extended the length of such service from three to five years. Even

[20] Kaufman and Nelson 2004: 488.
[21] Whang 1985: 19.
[22] Litsios 2002.

in Taiwan, whose major primary health care initiative took place in the late 1940s, the Kuomintang in 1973 introduced a four-year program to improve rural health. Averaging the eight cases compared in this book, infant mortality fell more steeply from 1975 to 1980 than in any other five-year period from 1960 to 2005. The runners-up were the two adjoining periods (Table A1).

Considerations of international prestige contributed to the introduction of several of the health care initiatives reviewed in this book. Scholars have argued that military governments in Argentina and Chile in the 1970s stepped up the public provision of maternal and child health services in an effort to expand support (or reduce hostility) from foreigners. An observer of public health care policies in Argentina during the 1976–1983 military regime asserted that the goal of "extending health service coverage with a special emphasis on primary care and maternal and infant health…was aimed at securing internal legitimacy and improving the tarnished image of the military government abroad."[23] Others have contended that officials in the Pinochet government expanded maternal and infant care services for the poor in the 1970s in an effort to improve the military regime's dismal international reputation.[24] The North Korean government's remarkable criticism of the inadequacy of health care in South Korea has been cited as a motivation for the expansion of health insurance coverage in South Korea in the late 1970s. One writer attributed this expansion of coverage to the Park Chung Hee government's wish to "save face in international society."[25]

The international diffusion of policy models has been accorded a critical role in the origins and evolution of social insurance in Latin America.[26] Foreign models have also influenced the design of national primary health care programs. Health posts in the rural United States served as a model for those set up in Costa Rica in the 1920s and 1930s. The Brazilian Family Health Program, introduced in 1994, was modeled on Cuba's Family Doctor and Nurse Program, introduced in 1984, and on primary health care programs in Britain, Quebec, and Switzerland. These diverse sources of international influence to varying degrees shaped and constrained health and other social policies in each of the eight societies analyzed. No attempt to explain the origins and evolution of such policies would be complete without taking these international factors into account.

Like international influence, democracy works through several channels to influence health care policies and mortality outcomes. These channels include electoral incentives, freedom of expression (especially through the mass media), freedom of association (especially the freedom to organize), and citizens' expectations. Democracy could also conceivably affect mortality outcomes either by boosting economic growth or by lowering income inequality,

---

[23] Belmartino 1991: 23.
[24] Collins and Lear 1995: 93; Valdés 2002.
[25] Joo 1999: 397.
[26] Weyland ed. 2004; Weyland 2006.

but scholarly work on these hypothesized relations has not shown conclusively that political regime form, controlling for other relevant variables, is related either to economic growth or to income inequality.[27] Accordingly, it is well worth exploring the possibility that democracy might also reduce infant mortality by creating incentives, sustaining freedoms, and generating expectations that induce governments to initiate primary health care programs, and that encourage poor people to support and utilize such programs once they have gotten under way.

The policy-making process for health and education reforms can usefully be divided into four stages: agenda-setting, design, authorization, and implementation.[28] Democracy might improve the provision of social services at each of these stages. At the agenda-setting stage democracy could call attention to problems in existing services. At the design stage democracy could affect the participation of issue networks or individual experts in the formulation, monitoring, or reform of public health services, as well as influence the appointment of public health officials. At the approval stage democracy could create incentives for executives or legislatures to authorize or reject improvements to public health services. At the implementation stage democracy could generate habits and expectations that could encourage citizens to support and utilize public health services.

In several of the cases reviewed in this book, politicians acted as if they believed that voters would reward them for expanding basic social services to the poor. In Chile in 1970, in Costa Rica in 1970 and 1974, in the Argentine province of Neuquén in 1973, and in Brazil in 2002 and 2006, presidential or gubernatorial candidates courted votes by expanding or promising to expand the delivery of basic health care and food assistance programs. Such electoral incentives seem to have been at work "even in some authoritarian or only semidemocratic systems, where heightened electoral competition...increased politicians' interest in providing those kinds of social service that are immediately popular." After closing down congress and the courts in 1992, Alberto Fujimori, the president of Peru, accelerated school-building in poor areas with an eye toward running for reelection in a contest scheduled for 1995.[29] Similarly in Taiwan, as opposition candidates began to win legislative seats in the early 1970s, the government created a Ministry of Health, stepped up the training of medical personnel, launched a four-year program to improve rural health, and began to require medical scholarship recipients to work for six years in underserved areas or in understaffed parts of the health care system. Even intraparty competition has encouraged the

---

[27] In a review of the literature on democracy and economic growth, Kurzman, Werum, and Burkhart (2002) find no systematic relation between the two variables. On democracy and inequality, Muller (1988) and Huber et al. (2006) find an inverse relation; Bollen and Jackman (1985) find no relation.

[28] Kaufman and Nelson 2004: 474. Grindle (2004: 17) adds a fifth stage of sustainability.

[29] Kaufman and Nelson 2004: 484.

public provision of mortality-reducing social services. In Costa Rica in 1970, President José Figueres Ferrer of the Partido de Liberación Nacional declared a "war on misery" partly to heal a rift in his party, in which he had recently been challenged from the left. In the early 1980s, President Rodrigo Carazo of the Partido Unidad expanded Figures Ferrer's primary health care programs partly because he was trying to induce the left wing of his own party to agree to an economic austerity plan.

The analyses in Chapter 2 showed that short-term democratic practice was not associated with trained attendance at birth, and that neither short-term democratic practice nor long-term democratic experience was associated with child immunization. Clearly, electoral incentives do not provide an automatic, fail-safe mechanism leading to improved provision of basic health services. Voters in many developing countries are often unable to hold their elected leaders accountable for failures in service provision, either because they lack information about incumbent performance; or doubt that challengers will be able to do better; or vote on the basis of religious, regional, or ethnic identity, rather than on the basis of a candidate's perceived ability to deliver services.[30] Moreover, voters themselves often demand curative services more aggressively than preventive services, and often prefer policies aimed at expanding private incomes to policies aimed at improving public health services. Aspects of democracy that take a longer time to work, rather than short-term electoral incentives, may well be the main mechanisms by which democracy encourages the provision of basic social services to the poor. Electoral incentives affect mainly the authorization stage of the policy-making process; other aspects of democracy may be more critical at the agenda-setting, design, and implementation stages.

One such aspect of democracy involves the freedom of expression. The cases reviewed in this book reveal several instances in which news reports of acute health crises or the publication of unfavorable social statistics – which could never have come to light in the absence of a modicum of press freedom – put deficiencies in social service provision on the political agenda. In Chile in the 1930s, and again in the 1950s, the publication of studies revealing a high level of infant mortality induced government policy-makers to try to do something about the problem. In Brazil in the early 1990s, highly publicized cholera epidemics in the Amazon and the Northeast contributed to the health ministry's decision to introduce Community Health Agents at the national level. In Costa Rica, news coverage of a measles epidemic in 1992 added a sense of urgency to the design and implementation of the Comprehensive Basic Health Care Team program. The publication of unflattering statistics has catapulted the provision of basic health and nutrition services onto the political agenda even in authoritarian regimes that have not entirely silenced their mass media. In Thailand in the early 1980s, the publication of a survey showing that half of the country's children were malnourished encouraged the government to

[30] Keefer and Khemani 2005; World Bank 2004a: 81–85.

introduce a successful nutrition program. In Indonesia in the 1990s, publication of the results of the 1994 Demographic and Health survey showed that an already high rate of maternal mortality had risen even higher, galvanizing support for the Mother-Friendly Movement. In each case, mass media attention gave politicians stronger incentives to attend to health issues.

Democracy can also contribute to the introduction of national primary health care programs, or to other basic health services, by protecting freedoms and extending legal rights that raise the capacity of groups of poor people and others to demand such programs. In several cases reviewed in this book, constitutional reforms in the context of democratization gave new legal resources to those who favored making health services more accessible. In Brazil, the constitution of 1988 included a basic right to health and outlined the major features of a Unified Health System (SUS). In Thailand, the 1997 constitution also included a basic right to health, strengthening the arguments of the advocates of Universal Coverage. In Indonesia, the amendment of the constitution in 1999 to include rights to medical care and to a healthy environment provided a legal foundation for the 2005 Askeskin program, which gave free medical care to tens of millions of poor people.

People who are motivated to demand basic social services usually face higher costs in acting on this motivation in authoritarian than in democratic regimes. Hence, authoritarian incumbents are more likely than democratic incumbents to risk not providing such services.[31] In Chile and Costa Rica, poor people organized themselves to demand improvements in basic health services. In 1958, the Chilean government introduced the Australian ballot in the countryside. Once this reform was implemented, smallholders, tenant farmers, and landless agricultural laborers began to organize themselves, often with the aid of Communist or Socialist activists. Such organization helped them to overcome obstacles to using health insurance benefits to which they were legally entitled. In Costa Rica, the government of Miguel Ángel Rodríguez (1998–2002) was less committed than the government of José Figueres Olsen (1994–1998) to the Comprehensive Basic Health Care Team (EBAIS) strategy. When Rodríguez took office in early 1998, only about half of the planned EBAIS were operating. The perceived success of the teams that were already up and running, however, induced communities without EBAIS to organize themselves to demand teams in their own areas.

Another way in which democracy can encourage national primary health care programs involves the formation of citizen expectations. Jose Serra, the health minister of Brazil from 1998 to 2002, regarded the emergence of such a "sense of equality" in the 1980s and 1990s as the main way in which democracy encouraged the expansion of health services during his administration.[32] Chile provided an even more fertile environment than Brazil for the emergence of such expectations. From 1931 to 1973 Chileans had competitive electoral

[31] Lake and Baum 2001: 594–596, 618.
[32] Serra 2003a.

politics, a free press, and substantial freedom of association. The expectations that evolved during these years continued to shape government policies even after the 1973 coup.

Chile, with its many years of democratic experience, may usefully be juxtaposed to Indonesia, which was a colony until the late 1940s and had an authoritarian regime for most of the post-independence period. In 1933, nine years after Chile introduced its milk distribution program, the Rockefeller Foundation launched the Hygiene Program in Indonesia, which was then under Dutch colonial rule. As Terence Hull explains, "because the Hygiene Program had been an enclave activity, a sub-theme in what was essentially an authoritarian colonial health structure, many of its principles and practices were lost after Independence. Even as the Indonesian Government embraced the notion of a primary health care approach [in the 1970s], it did so with reference to rhetoric based on [communist] Chinese experience rather than reference to its own colonial heritage."[33] A similar fate befell the health initiatives carried out by the Japanese in Korea and Taiwan before 1945. The authoritarian character of public health policies enacted by colonial governments in Indonesia, Korea, and Taiwan, and by the monarchy and military in Thailand, as compared to the greater democratic experience of the Latin American countries, particularly Costa Rica but also Argentina, Brazil, and Chile (Table A18), helps to explain why national primary health care programs in the Asian countries were often less effective than similar programs in Latin America.

In Argentina, Brazil, Chile, and Costa Rica, long years of democratic or semi-democratic experience created citizens who were more inclined than the inhabitants of the East Asian societies, which had emerged only recently from colonial rule (or, in the Thai case, absolute monarchy), to regard publicly provided social services as rights. Such a perception encouraged not only the public financing or provision of basic social services, but also their utilization. In countries with significant democratic experience a higher propensity of citizens, particularly poor citizens, to utilize whatever services the government does provide, could help to explain why national primary health care programs generally achieved sharper infant mortality declines in Latin America than in East Asia (Table 11.3). The quantitative analysis in Chapter 2 found that long-term democratic experience was associated more closely than short-term democratic practice with trained attendance at birth and with female schooling. Such a finding is consistent with the hypothesis that democracy promotes the public provision of basic social services, not only through the short-term mechanism of electoral incentives, but also through long-term effects like the ratcheting up of legal rights, the empowerment of communities, and the evolution of expectations.

Democratic regimes, as well as some soft authoritarian regimes, also permit the formation and influence of interest groups and issue networks. Interest groups include labor unions, professional associations, and business

[33] Hull 1989: 145.

organizations; issue networks are informal groups of experts with interest in and knowledge about a particular area of public policy.[34] Interest groups and issue networks influence health care policy making in a variety of ways, including strikes, protests, lobbying, and the provision of information and technical personnel to state agencies. The effect of such influence may be either to promote or to impede pro-poor health reforms, including national primary health care programs.

Interest groups and issue networks had little input into policy making in South Korea or Taiwan until the political liberalization of the late 1980s. In South Korea during the 1960s and 1970s, top civil servants made social policy with a great deal of autonomy. In the early 1990s, however, an issue network led by progressive doctors, academics, and former prodemocracy activists lobbied successfully for the introduction of single-payer National Health Insurance. In Taiwan, there is little evidence of interest groups affecting social policy until the authoritarian regime began to liberalize in late 1980s, at which point farmers launched a successful campaign for health insurance. Indonesia, which was under Suharto's authoritarian rule from the late 1960s to the late 1990s, was nearly devoid of autonomous interest groups and issue networks during this period. The interior ministry administered the Family Welfare Movement (PKK), which provided nutritional aid and health education in villages from the late 1960s onward. When rural health center doctors tried to set up an autonomous organization in the 1970s, Suharto shut it down.

Doctors in Latin America, as in Thailand, have been active participants in the proposal, design, implementation, evaluation, and maintenance of large-scale primary health care programs. Dr. Elsa Moreno in the Argentine province of Neuquén, Dr. Zilda Arns Neumann in Brazil, Dr. Fernando Marín in Costa Rica, and Dr. Jumroon Mikhanorn in Thailand were among the many physicians who made notable contributions to the design and implementation of large-scale primary health care programs. In two cases, moreover, issue networks involving doctors pushed quite successfully for national primary health care programs. In Thailand after 1973, students, researchers, and health professionals organized the Rural Doctors' Forum to try to improve health care in impoverished rural communities. The Forum continued to operate into the twenty-first century, organizing support for primary health care, placing sympathizers in top health ministry posts, and lobbying government health officials. In Brazil in 1976, shortly after the military government began to liberalize, leftist health professionals and health care experts in universities, research institutions, and health care agencies formed the Sanitarian Movement to press for better health care for the poor, as well as to oppose the growing influence of private health care and to protest the military government's preoccupation with curative medicine. The Sanitarians formed academic research institutes, sponsored seminars and conferences, and placed supporters in top positions in the health and welfare ministries and in the social security agencies.

---

[34] Heclo 1978: 102–103.

In contrast to these issue networks, formal associations representing the professional interests of physicians were often unsympathetic to pro-poor health care reforms, including large-scale primary health care programs. For doctors, shifting resources to such programs often means "lower salaries, less sophisticated equipment, pressures to serve where living conditions and career prospects are unattractive, and the substitution of less highly trained health workers (nurses, public health workers, midwives) for doctors in performing certain services."[35] Consequently, although many individual doctors, along with some issue networks involving physicians, have been enthusiastic supporters of major primary health care programs, organizations representing the professional interests of physicians have often opposed such programs.

Doctors' associations opposed pro-poor health reforms, including national primary health care programs, in several of the cases considered in this book. In Thailand, physicians in the Thai Medical Association, worried about competition from paraprofessional health workers, lobbied successfully in the 1950s to confine "junior doctors" to disease control activities. In Chile in the early 1970s, about 60 percent of the members of the Chilean Medical Association went on strike to protest decisions by the Allende government to devote more health spending to primary care, as well as to shift authority on Community Health Councils from doctors to health worker unions and community groups. In Costa Rica in the early 1970s, doctors' groups unsuccessfully resisted the Rural Health Plan on the grounds that raising the number of physicians would flood the market and reduce incomes, that revamping the medical school curriculum to emphasize general practice would turn physicians into Chinese-style "barefoot doctors," that paraprofessionals lacked the expertise to handle the medical tasks assigned to them, and that community councils had no right to evaluate physician performance. In the province of Neuquén, Argentina, in the early 1970s, the provincial doctors' guild lobbied unsuccessfully against the Provincial Health Plan's mandate that public sector doctors forego private practice of any sort. A similar proposal to restrict publicly paid physicians from engaging simultaneously in private practice foundered at the national level in 1974, however, partly as a result of tenacious resistance by national-level doctors' associations. In the mid-1980s, physicians' associations in Argentina successfully fought an effort by Aldo Neri, President Alfonsín's first health minister, to pass legislation to expand health insurance coverage to the poor. The associations contended that the expense of absorbing the new beneficiaries would force existing insurers to reduce payments to providers.

Opposition to pro-poor health care reforms has often also come from associations of hospital directors, manufacturers of medical equipment and drugs, private health insurance firms, and state agencies with a stake in the pre-reform model of health care financing and delivery. In Brazil, opposition from such groups managed to delay from 1988 to 1993 the implementation

[35] Nelson 2004b: 33.

of the Unified Health System. In Thailand, employees of the civil servants' and private sector workers' health insurance schemes thwarted a plan in the late 1990s to provide universal health insurance coverage under a single-payer system. In Costa Rica, by contrast, the population is too small to support a major pharmaceutical or medical equipment industry, and the domestic sale of private health insurance was illegal during the latter part of the twentieth century. These characteristics of the health care system facilitated the national primary health care programs of the 1970s and 1990s. Similarly, it has been argued that the small role played by the purely private sector in the provision of health care in pre-1959 Cuba, where many doctors worked for large mutualist associations that had evolved from ethnically based mutual aid societies in the nineteenth century, made it easier for the revolutionary government to socialize the medical system in the 1960s.[36]

In rich countries, strong labor unions are associated statistically with faster economic growth, lower unemployment, more redistributive government policies, lower wage inequality, and lower infant mortality.[37] In Latin American countries, however, strong labor unions tended to complicate export promotion and cautious macroeconomic policies. In such countries as Argentina, Brazil, and Chile, particularly from the 1950s to the 1970s, labor unions pressured for heavy import substitution and for social welfare and industrial promotion policies that implied large budget deficits, persistently low real interest rates, and overvalued currencies. The resulting trade deficits and macroeconomic imbalances contributed to slower economic growth and higher income inequality, and thereby to slower declines and higher levels of infant mortality.[38] In the Asian societies reviewed in this book, labor unions were weaker than in Latin America. Consequently, export promotion and cautious macroeconomic policies were more feasible options. Once implemented, these policies led to faster economic growth and lower income inequality.

Labor union strength could affect infant mortality not only through its impact on economic policies and outcomes, but also through other channels, such as the provision of basic health services to the poor. If stronger labor movements encouraged the provision of such services, the resulting gain in terms of infant mortality decline could offset, at least partly, the loss suffered as a result of slower economic growth or higher income inequality. Hence, it is well worth exploring the impact of labor union resources and activities on national primary health care policies and programs. This exploration of labor union influence on the public provision of basic health services to the poor is necessarily confined to the four Latin American cases. The four Asian cases, with the exception of South Korea after 1988, had weak labor movements, and little available evidence suggests that unionists as such weighed

---

[36] Danielson 1979: 121.
[37] Growth and employment: Cameron 1984; redistributive policies: Hicks and Swank 1984; wage inequality: Freeman and Medoff 1984; infant mortality: Wennemo 1993.
[38] McGuire 1999.

in much, via either lobbying or protest, on national health policy. In the four Latin American cases, unions often were influential in shaping national health policy. Whether this role worked in favor of or against the expansion of basic health services to the poor depended on each country's long-term democratic experience and on its short-term political circumstances in the 1960s.

In Argentina, Brazil, Chile, and Costa Rica during the first half of the twentieth century, the initiatives of forward-looking presidents and civil servants, party competition for the votes of the urban working and middle classes, and pressures exerted by civil society groups, notably labor, encouraged the state to provide pensions, medical care, and other social insurance programs to substantial sectors of the population.[39] These programs were particularly helpful to the military, civil servants, and a white- and blue-collar labor aristocracy, but they also served as a source of infrastructure, expertise, and expectations that facilitated, in principle, their expansion to poor people in rural areas and urban slums. Such expansion occurred in the mid-1960s and early 1970s in Chile and Costa Rica, which had been democratic (or semi-democratic) for a long time; but not in Argentina or Brazil, which had somewhat less long-term democratic experience (Table A18). In the Latin American cases, long-term democratic experience and the degree of political competition in the 1960s shaped how labor movement strength and the buildup of a large welfare state would affect the public provision of basic health services to the poor. In Chile and Costa Rica, where democracy was more deeply rooted and where it persisted through the 1960s and early 1970s, governments extended basic health services to the poor and destitute, and rapid declines of infant mortality ensued. In Brazil and Argentina, where civilian rule was cut short by military coups in 1964 and 1966, welfare states continued to be biased toward the middle classes and the organized working classes, and slow declines of premature mortality persisted.

By wresting concessions from the state and employers, labor unions in each of the four Latin American countries set a precedent of state involvement in social welfare that could later be extended to the poor – provided that politicians had incentives to court the votes of impoverished citizens. Unions also contributed to better health services for the poor in other ways. In Chile, health facilities financed mainly by contributory insurance were often used by the non-contributing poor, creating a cross-subsidy from union members to poor people. In Costa Rica, a banana workers' strike in 1934 forced the United Fruit Company to improve health services and sanitation on its plantations. In Argentina, a strike by construction workers in Neuquén induced General Onganía in 1970 to appoint a governor who oversaw the implementation throughout the province of a remarkably effective primary health care program. In Costa Rica in 1995 health worker unions, after initial reservations, supported the EBAIS primary health care initiative. In each case, union resources and activities encouraged the provision of health services to the poor.

[39] Collier and Collier 1991; Huber 1996; Mesa-Lago 1978.

In other ways, however, union resources and activities thwarted such provision. In Argentina, union leaders helped to scuttle the efforts of health ministers in the 1950s, 1970s, and 1980s to unify and universalize the public health care system. Strong unions, moreover, together with actors representing better-off urban groups, often induced governments to enact health care policies that reached neither the rural poor nor urban shantytown inhabitants, and that contributed to the further impoverishment of the very poor by encouraging governments to impose higher indirect taxes and to run inflationary budget deficits. The bias of government policy-makers toward health care policies that benefited primarily the not-so-poor was exacerbated when elected politicians (as well as authoritarian leaders) found that the quickest way to reduce protest about neglect of "the people" was not to expand primary health care services in urban slums and rural communities, where many people are politically disengaged, but rather to leave health insurance funds in the hands of union leaders or to forego fee hikes for university students. The not-so-poor tend to be more politically articulate than the very poor, and elected and unelected government officials alike respond more readily to manifest demands than to latent needs.[40]

Union members are not the only, or even major, group to pressure for, or benefit from, a skewing of public social services away from the very poor, who live mainly in rural areas and urban shantytowns. The main actor behind this skewing is, rather, an urban formal-sector coalition that includes owners, managers, civil servants, professionals, government officials, and university faculty and students, as well as union leaders and members. In Latin America and elsewhere, the non-union members of the urban formal-sector coalition have pressured for, and delivered, the trade protection and state subsidies that have made urban formal-sector wages higher, employment more secure, and unions stronger than one might expect in the context of an underlying labor surplus. Labor movement strength is thus itself in part the outcome of pressures exerted, and policies enacted, by non-union participants in the urban formal-sector coalition.[41]

The main actor blocking human development progress in Argentina and Brazil for much of the period analyzed was this broader urban formal-sector coalition, not the labor movement alone. Still, union leaders and members have interests that can clash not only with those of more advantaged groups, like employers; but also with those of less advantaged groups, like the rural poor and shantytown dwellers. Some scholars have drawn attention to these conflicts of interest,[42] but there is still a widespread perception that the interests

[40] Thiesenhusen (1995: 176, 179) makes a similar argument about Latin American land reform, which, he argues, benefited mostly better-off peasants rather than "the most stubbornly rural poor who were less organized." Governments would then "overpublicize" the gains of the beneficiaries. Thiesenhusen concludes that "the standard of living of the unorganized masses may have been hurt each time a smattering of better-off peers was advanced."

[41] Nugent 1991: 24.

[42] Campos and Root 1996: 70–71; Haggard and Kaufman 2008: 22–23; McGuire 1999; Moon 1991: 48; Nelson 1992: 232–233.

of such groups as union leaders and university students invariably coincide
with those of the poor and destitute. Until conflicts between the poor and
the not-so-poor are taken seriously and studied systematically, it will be hard
to develop policies that serve the interests of both sectors of the population.
Further research, appropriately designed, should identify the contexts in which
these groups are locked in a zero-sum game, and other contexts in which they,
and perhaps the more affluent as well, decline or flourish together.

11.4. Implications for Development Theory and Development Policy

The reduction of premature mortality, and especially of infant and child mortality, should be given more priority as a criterion of development success.
Mortality is central both to the wealthier is healthier literature and to the public service provisioning literature. It is neglected in studies of East Asian and
Latin American development, however, which have focused instead on economic output- and income-related indicators like GDP per capita and income
inequality. Such factors, as noted in Chapter 1, are no more than distal inputs
into the expansion of human capabilities, whereas survival is a precondition
for the exercise of any capability.

It might well be argued that there is more to life than survival, and that
research should go beyond mortality indicators to focus on a wider range of
development outcomes incorporated into a composite index. Several such indices have been devised, including the Physical Quality of Life Index (PQLI) in the
1970s and the United Nations Development Programme's Human Development
Index (HDI) in the 1990s. Composite indices like the HDI, however, include
phenomena at widely disparate points in the causal chains leading to capability
expansion. The HDI incorporates measures of economic output, educational
attainment, and life expectancy. This amalgamation has the pragmatic virtue
of creating a single number to serve as an alternative to GDP per capita,[43] but
the multifaceted composition of the HDI makes it hard to interpret, and tends
to obscure important lessons that might otherwise be learned from societies
that perform well on some of its dimensions (e.g., economic output per capita)
but poorly on others (e.g., life expectancy) – as is often the case.

Unlike composite indices, measures of premature mortality are both intrinsically important and readily intelligible. More comprehensive measures of
physical well-being exist, such as disability-adjusted life years, but few developing countries have records that are adequate to reconstruct such indicators
for extended historical time periods. To recognize that there is more to life
than survival does not entail rejecting infant mortality and life expectancy
as important indicators of development. A high level of premature mortality
usually signals serious deprivations in the lives of the living.

The quantitative analysis reported in Chapter 2 found a strong cross-
national association between GDP per capita and infant mortality. Four of the
eight case studies in Chapters 3–10 were also consistent with the wealthier is

[43] Sen 1999b: 23.

healthier hypothesis. In South Korea and Taiwan, infant mortality fell rapidly in the context of fast economic growth; in Argentina and Brazil, at least until the 1990s, infant mortality fell slowly in the context of sluggish economic growth. Higher output facilitates the construction of mortality-reducing physical assets (roads, power plants), tends to raise private incomes that permit individuals to purchase mortality-reducing goods and services in private markets, and generates resources that the state can tax to finance or provide social services. Hence, a society experiencing fast economic growth is likely also to do well on mortality decline.

A comprehensive explanation of why some societies do better than others at reducing infant mortality requires, accordingly, an account of why some societies outperform others at achieving economic affluence. Among the eight East Asian and Latin American cases compared in this book, policies in the areas of land tenure, basic education, export promotion, and macroeconomic management go a long way toward explaining why some did better than others at achieving rapid economic growth, low levels of income inequality, and rapid declines of income poverty. The historical and social-structural factors that affected the will and capacity of government officials to design and implement such policies include colonial heritage, the post-World War II geopolitical situation, natural resource endowment, and the cohesion and organization of landowners, industrialists, and urban workers. A full account of the mortality differences among the eight societies would have to take account of a wider range of policies and policy determinants than those on which this book has been able to focus.[44]

Although wealthier was generally healthier, economic factors (GDP per capita, income inequality, income poverty) should not be oversold as contributors to infant mortality decline. Neither fast economic growth nor low income inequality guaranteed rapid mortality decline, and neither slow economic growth nor high income inequality precluded it. The evidence reviewed in this book strongly suggests that a society's success at reducing mortality depends crucially, in the absence of an extraordinary performance on income-related indicators, on the public provision of basic social services. A focus on survival, moreover, rather than just on economic output and private income, underscores some Latin American development achievements and qualifies some East Asian ones, particularly during the period from 1960 to 1990. In Costa Rica and Chile during this era, the public provision of basic social services promoted rapid infant mortality decline despite a poor performance on income-related indicators. In Indonesia and Thailand, inadequate public service provision slowed the pace of infant mortality decline despite a good performance on income-related indicators. In Argentina and Brazil not only economic problems, but also deficiencies in public service provision, impeded rapid infant mortality decline. In South Korea and Taiwan, public

---

[44] McGuire (1995a) explores some of these policies and policy determinants in Argentina, Brazil, Mexico, South Korea, and Taiwan.

service provision – not just education, but also family planning and maternal and infant care – did more than is often recognized to promote infant mortality decline, notwithstanding the contribution of rapid economic growth, low income inequality, and a steep decline of income poverty.

Health care spending and health insurance coverage, the usual outcomes to be explained in the literature on the welfare state in developing countries (and the main topics of current debates about health care policy in the United States), had no more than modest effects on infant mortality in the eight societies compared in this book. Public health care spending, it would seem, is often misallocated, inefficient, or redundant with private health care spending. Health insurance, for its part, ameliorates financial but not other barriers to the effective utilization of health services, and has no direct effect on the quantity or quality of the health services provided. Even when the poor have health insurance, it tends to make them richer rather than healthier, as the insurance replaces out-of-pocket spending on health care.[45] Studies of the determinants of cross-national differences in public health care spending, or in health insurance coverage, provide important insight into forces shaping government priorities, casting light on the perennial political science question of "who gets what, when, and how."[46] Such studies have been less successful, however, in explaining why some societies do better than others at reducing infant death.

What does seem to matter for reducing infant mortality is, in addition to economic factors, access to primary and secondary education, particularly for girls, along with trained attendance at birth, child immunization, family planning, and access to improved water and sanitation. A small fraction of the public resources spent on expensive medical procedures, university education, and middle-class and upper-class pensions in many developing countries would suffice to extend access to these basic mortality-reducing services to the vast majority of the population. Mortality decline depends much less on the overall level of public social spending, or even on the share of such spending that goes to health, education, and pensions, than on the allocation of public spending within these areas, on the quality of the services provided, and on propensity of the poor to utilize whatever services the government may offer.

If the grinding inadequacy of basic health services in many poor countries is heart-wrenching, their persistent inadequacy in some rich nations is astonishing. In the U.S. state of Mississippi, the state government from 1990 to 2005 closed a number of public health clinics and cut the opening hours of others. During this period, infant mortality for non-whites rose from 15.9 to 17.0 per 1000. Had non-white Mississippi been a nation, from 1990 to 2005 it would have ranked 187th of 190 countries at percent change of infant mortality – just above Equatorial Guinea (where infant mortality also rose). In Sharkey County, however, in the Mississippi Delta, where the population

[45] Filmer, Hammer, and Pritchett 2000; Filmer, Hammer, and Pritchett 2002.
[46] Quotation from Lasswell 1936. On the impact of democracy and globalization on public social spending see Avelino, Brown, and Hunter 2005; Kaufman and Segura-Ubiergo 2001; and Rudra and Haggard 2005.

was 32 percent poor and 69 percent black, infant mortality for non-whites in 2001–2005 was 5.2 per 1000. A steep decline of infant mortality had begun in the county during the early 1990s, when the Cary Christian Center, a local religious organization subsisting on private donations and building on work done by a single physician, organized a group of volunteers with minimal medical training to make home visits to pregnant women. At the same time, it began to offer prenatal classes for expectant mothers and postnatal classes for new mothers, providing free transport to the women taking the classes.[47]

Had a similar program been launched in Mississippi's many other impoverished counties, backed by a modest amount of state government funding, many hundreds of lives might have been saved. Instead, one of the candidates for governor contested the November 2003 election on a platform of imposing much more burdensome requirements on applicants for Medicaid and the state's Children's Health Insurance Program. He won, providing a stark reminder that democracy need not always lead to the public provision of mortality-reducing social services, even in places like Mississippi where large numbers of eligible voters are poor. As soon as the newly elected governor took office, the state government cut funding for the office that informed people about their eligibility for these programs. After these policy changes the infant mortality rate for non-whites in Mississippi rose from 14.2 per 1000 in 2004 to 17.0 per 1000 in 2005, almost as high as the overall rate in Brazil.

The state Medicaid director dismissed as "conjecture" a claim that cuts in the Medicaid and Children's Health Insurance Programs had caused the spike in the infant mortality rate.[48] Possibly no such causation existed. The activities of the Cary Christian Center had nothing to do with health insurance, and health insurance coverage was not closely associated with infant mortality levels or changes in any of the eight societies reviewed in this book. More perplexing to a political scientist specializing in the public health policies of developing countries is that a candidate for elective office would actually appeal (successfully) for popular support by promising to cut health insurance for the poor. It is hard to imagine a similar appeal coming from any vote-seeking political leader in any of the eight societies analyzed in this book at any time from 1960 to 2005.

The kinds of interventions that can dramatically reduce the infant mortality rate are neither particularly hard to identify nor particularly burdensome to pay for. Why such interventions are not implemented almost everywhere, despite being technically, administratively, financially, and even in many respects politically quite feasible, is more a question for political science than for public health research. By 2005 Chile, Costa Rica, South Korea, and

[47] Infant mortality statistics from Mississippi. SDH 2008: 124, 170 and World Bank 2008e; poverty (2004) and percent black (2006) statistics from United States. Bureau of the Census 2008b; other information from Eckholm 2007.

[48] Eckholm 2007. See also http://carychristiancenter.org/ Infant mortality from Mississippi. SDH 2008: 124, 170.

Taiwan had surpassed the United States in life expectancy, despite being less affluent than the United Sates in GDP per capita terms. What gave these societies higher life expectancy than the United States was (surely) not a higher level of health care spending, nor even universal health insurance coverage (although by 2005 such coverage existed in each of the four societies), but the effective public provision – free of charge to the user, and regardless of insurance coverage – of inexpensive basic health services to people experiencing a high risk of early death.

The cross-national analyses and case studies reviewed in this book suggest that democracy often has a significant beneficial impact on the provision of basic health services to the poor – and, partly because of such provision, on the expansion of survival-related capabilities. As the example of Mississippi underscores, however, democracy's impact on these policy and mortality outcomes is neither invariably powerful nor invariably beneficial. It has been argued here, moreover, that the mechanisms through which democracy exerts its effects on social service provision and on mortality go well beyond electoral incentives. These mechanisms also include freedom of information, freedom to organize, freedom of action for issue networks, and changes in political culture. Suggesting that the latter factor is particularly important, long-term democratic experience was associated more closely than short-term democratic practice with the provision of many infant mortality-reducing social services and with lower infant mortality (Tables 2.4 and 2.5). Over the long term, democracy tends to give rise to a presumption that the poor as well as the rich have needs that the state is obliged to try to meet. Such a presumption can influence the provision of basic health services even after democracy gives way to authoritarianism, as happened in Chile after 1973.

Interest group pressure, which is also facilitated by democratic political institutions, had a mixed effect on policies conducive to the reduction of premature mortality. In the Latin American countries, where labor was stronger than in the East Asian societies, union pressure helped to build an infrastructure of health care institutions which, although designed for people in contributory social insurance programs, often (but not reliably) provided medical treatment to uninsured people. In some Latin American countries, however, notably Argentina, labor union pressure also delayed or derailed economic reforms (such as trade liberalization) and social policy reforms (such as the unification of public health care financing and the universalization of public health care delivery) that might have done more to help the very poor. Associations of physicians, health insurers, hospital administrators, and drug and medical equipment firms also blocked pro-poor health reforms, notably in Brazil. Still, even where strong unions exerted pressures that, on balance, inhibited the provision of basic social services to the poor, they also usually acted directly to promote more rewarding labor, more dignity and control for workers, and more humane relations between employers and employees. A full evaluation of the impact of labor union strength on human development would have to take into account a wide range of effects, positive as well as negative.

Robert Lucas wrote that "advising a society to 'follow the Korean model' is a little like advising an aspiring basketball player to 'follow the Michael Jordan model.'"[49] Policies that worked well in one context may be unfeasible or ineffective in another. Contributing to the rapid economic development of South Korea and Taiwan were, for example, aspects of the Japanese colonial legacy, a military threat from a powerful neighbor, scarce natural resources, and weakly organized social classes. Other countries will not share this policy environment, so the presence of two routes to rapid mortality decline – the one followed by Chile and by Costa Rica, which emphasized the direct provision of basic public services, and the one followed by South Korea and by Taiwan, which stressed the redistribution of land, skills, and jobs – raises the likelihood that other societies will be able to learn useful lessons from at least one of the models. Chile and Costa Rica show that a strong performance on human development is possible even in countries that struggle with slow economic growth, high income inequality, and prevalent income poverty. Rapid economic growth and low income inequality are nice work, but only if you can get it. Many developing countries may find it more feasible to reduce the risk of early death not by achieving East Asian levels of economic growth or income distribution, but rather, like Chile or Costa Rica, by providing basic, and usually quite inexpensive, health, education, family planning, water, and sanitation services.

If, as has been argued in this book, political institutions and social policies can have important effects on mortality outcomes, then that is good news for proponents of public action to reduce the risk of early death. But if, as has also been noted throughout the work, political institutions and social policies are heavily shaped and constrained by historical legacies and social-structural factors over which contemporary actors have little control, then such action faces serious limitations. From the assertion that a given set of conditions favored a policy in one context, however, it does not follow that the same set of conditions is necessary to apply that policy in another context. Policy choices matter, and will matter even more if political actors understand the opportunities and constraints that others have faced. A grasp of these opportunities and constraints can help such actors identify, and hence more easily overcome, historical legacies and social-structural conditions that might otherwise confine them. Social science research can best contribute to human development by identifying which institutions and policies were beneficial (or harmful) in certain contexts, by specifying why they were conducive (or destructive) to development in those contexts, and by illuminating forces and conditions that helped to bring them about. Such research gives actors in new contexts a better grasp of the costs and benefits of alternative institutions and policies, as well as a better appreciation of the opportunities for, and constraints upon, their operation.

[49] Lucas 1993: 252.

Appendix Tables

TABLE A1. *Infant Mortality, 1960–2005*

PANEL A1.1. *Infant deaths per 1000 live births in the indicated year*

Year	South Korea	Chile	Thailand	Taiwan	Costa Rica	Brazil	Argentina	Indonesia	Mean
1960	90	119.5	103	54	77.9	115	62.4	128	92
1965	64	97.3	86	44	75.5	106	56.9	121	81
1970	43	82.2	74	35	68.4	95	61.2	104	70
1975	24	57.6	61	29	40.1	83	43.2	94	54
1980	16	33.0	46	24	19.9	70	33.2	79	40
1985	11	19.5	34	17	18.5	60	26.2	70	32
1990	8	16.0	25.7	10.2	15.0	48.1	25.6	60	26
1995	5.8	11.1	17	8.0	13.3	36.1	22.2	48	20
2000		8.9	11.4	7.5	10.3	26.9	16.6	36	15
2005	4.6	7.9	7.7	5.5	9.8	19.8	13.3	28	12

PANEL A1.2. *Average annual percent decline of infant mortality during the indicated interval*

Interval	South Korea	Chile	Thailand	Taiwan	Costa Rica	Brazil	Argentina	Indonesia	Mean
1960–1965	-6.6	-4.0	-3.5	-4.0	-0.6	-1.7	-1.8	-1.1	-3.3
1965–1970	-7.6	-3.3	-2.9	-4.5	-1.9	-2.1	+1.5	-3.0	-3.6
1970–1975	-11.0	-6.9	-3.7	-3.7	-10.1	-2.8	-6.7	-2.0	-5.5
1975–1980	-7.8	-10.5	-5.7	-3.7	-13.0	-3.3	-5.1	-3.4	-6.5
1980–1985	-7.2	-10.0	-5.7	-6.7	-1.5	-3.2	-4.6	-2.4	-5.8
1985–1990	-6.2	-3.9	-5.4	-9.7	-4.1	-4.2	-0.5	-3.0	-5.4
1990–1995	-6.2	-7.1	-7.9	-4.7	-2.4	-5.6	-2.8	-4.4	-5.2
1995–2000	-2.9	-4.3	-7.7	-2.6	-5.1	-5.7	-5.6	-5.6	-4.4
2000–2005	-1.7	-2.4	-7.5	-4.7	-1.0	-5.9	-4.3	-4.9	-4.1
1960–2005	-6.4	-5.9	-5.6	-4.9	-4.5	-3.8	-3.4	-3.3	-4.9

Average annual percent decline calculated by the compound growth formula = RATE (5,,–IMR60, IMR65), and so on for successive periods, in Microsoft Excel.

Sources: Brazil, Indonesia, South Korea, and Thailand: World Bank 2008e (based on census and survey estimates). *Taiwan:* 1960–1975: Mirzaee 1979: 233–240, from life tables based on vital statistics corrected for underreporting of neonatal deaths and for the misclassification of infant deaths as deaths at the age of 1. 1980–1985: Vital registration from Taiwan. DGBAS 2001: 28, corrected by the Sullivan (1972) method that Mirzaee (1979: 34) used for previous years. "1990" (=1989), "1995" (=1996): Wen et al. 2002: 149 (1989 and 1996 island-wide surveys). 2000, 2005: Taiwan. DGBAS 2007: 28 (uncorrected vital registration). *Argentina* (vital registration): 1960–1975: Neuquén. SS/MDS 2000. 1980–2005: Argentina. Ministerio de Salud 2007. *Chile* (vital registration): 1960–1985: United Nations 1992: 76. 1990–2005: Chile. Ministerio de Salud 2008. *Costa Rica* (vital registration): CCP-UCR 2008. See McGuire (2009), Web Appendix A1, for a discussion of the quality of these and alternative infant mortality estimates.

TABLE A2. *Life Expectancy at Birth, 1960–2005*

PANEL A2.1. *Life expectancy at birth in the indicated year*

Year	South Korea	Chile	Costa Rica	Taiwan	Indonesia	Brazil	Thailand	Argentina	Mean
1960	54.2	57.3	61.9	64.4	41.5	54.8	55.1	65.2	56.8
1965	56.7	59.6	64.6	67.4	44.6	56.9	57.5	65.8	59.1
1970	61.2	62.4	67.1	69.1	47.9	58.9	59.7	66.8	61.6
1975	64.0	65.7	69.9	70.8	51.3	60.8	61.8	68.2	64.1
1980	65.8	69.3	72.7	72.1	54.8	62.8	63.9	69.6	66.4
1985	68.5	71.9	74.6	73.3	58.6	64.7	65.7	70.7	68.5
1990	71.3	73.7	75.8	74.0	61.7	66.6	67.0	71.7	70.2
1995	73.4	75.1	76.9	74.9	64.0	68.6	67.6	72.8	71.7
2000	75.9	76.9	77.8	76.7	65.8	70.4	68.3	73.8	73.2
2005	78.4	78.2	78.5	77.6	67.8	71.8	69.9	74.8	74.6

PANEL A2.2. *Percent rise of life expectancy at birth during the indicated interval*

Interval	South Korea	Chile	Costa Rica	Taiwan	Indonesia	Brazil	Thailand	Argentina	Mean
1960–1965	8.1	8.3	11.7	14.6	7.1	7.0	8.0	3.0	8.5
1965–1970	15.9	11.0	12.3	9.7	8.2	7.1	8.0	5.2	9.7
1970–1975	11.8	14.6	15.6	10.7	9.2	7.3	8.3	7.7	10.6
1975–1980	8.6	18.7	18.5	9.2	10.4	8.3	9.1	8.3	11.4
1980–1985	14.1	16.6	15.4	9.3	12.6	8.6	8.5	7.1	11.5
1985–1990	17.0	13.7	11.5	6.0	11.7	9.4	6.7	7.0	10.4
1990–1995	15.3	12.4	12.0	8.2	9.9	10.9	3.3	8.3	10.0
1995–2000	21.6	18.2	11.1	17.8	8.6	11.0	4.0	8.2	12.6
2000–2005	27.5	16.0	9.7	10.8	10.4	9.6	9.6	8.9	12.8
1960–2005	78.6	75.5	71.9	64.1	60.5	56.3	49.5	48.5	63.1

Total percent rise during the indicated period, stipulating a "goalpost" of 85 years. Formula: (LifeExpEndYr–LifeExpStartYr)/(85–LifeExpStartYr). The result of this quotient may be pictured as the proportion of distance traveled by the last year in the period from the life expectancy in the initial year of the period toward 85 years.

Source: World Bank 2008e, except Taiwan, from Taiwan. Ministry of the Interior 2008 (mean of male and female life expectancies).

TABLE A3. *GDP per capita, 1960–2003*

PANEL A3.1. *GDP per capita in the indicated year*

Year	Taiwan	South Korea	Thailand	Indonesia	Brazil	Chile	Costa Rica	Argentina	Mean
1960	1,444	1,458	1,059	1,071	2,644	5,086	4,513	7,838	3,139
1965	2,001	1,727	1,292	1,016	3,219	5,331	4,920	8,769	3,534
1970	2,846	2,552	1,734	1,273	4,026	6,157	5,653	9,821	4,258
1975	3,982	3,384	2,047	1,732	5,601	5,141	6,342	10,440	4,834
1980	5,963	4,497	2,708	2,084	6,776	6,675	6,990	10,921	5,827
1985	7,617	6,136	3,360	2,218	6,531	5,728	6,115	8,960	5,833
1990	11,248	9,593	4,864	2,918	6,831	7,120	6,349	8,195	7,140
1995	15,169	13,297	6,729	3,704	6,894	9,916	7,265	10,565	9,192
2000	19,184	15,702	6,474	3,772	7,194	11,430	8,341	11,332	10,429
2003	19,885	17,597	7,274	4,122	7,205	12,141	8,586	10,170	10,873

PANEL A3.2. *GDP per capita, average annual percent growth during the indicated interval*

Interval	Taiwan	South Korea	Thailand	Indonesia	Brazil	Chile	Costa Rica	Argentina	Mean
1960–1965	6.7	3.4	4.1	-1.0	4.0	0.9	1.7	2.3	2.8
1965–1970	7.3	8.1	6.1	4.6	4.6	2.9	2.8	2.3	4.8
1970–1975	6.9	5.8	3.4	6.4	6.8	-3.5	2.3	1.2	3.7
1975–1980	8.4	5.9	5.8	3.8	3.9	5.4	2.0	0.9	4.5
1980–1985	5.0	6.4	4.4	1.3	-0.7	-3.0	-2.6	-3.9	0.9
1985–1990	8.1	9.3	7.7	5.6	0.9	4.4	0.8	-1.8	4.4
1990–1995	6.2	6.7	6.7	4.9	0.2	6.8	2.7	5.2	4.9
1995–2000	4.8	3.4	-0.8	0.4	0.9	2.9	2.8	1.4	2.0
2000–2003	1.2	3.9	4.0	3.0	0.1	2.0	1.0	-3.5	1.4
1960–2003	6.3	6.0	4.6	3.2	2.4	2.0	1.5	0.6	3.3

GDP per capita in purchasing power parity international dollars at 2000 constant prices, according to a chain index. From Heston, Summers, and Aten 2006, variable RGDPCH. GDP per capita, average annual percent growth calculated by the compound growth formula = RATE (5,,–GDP60, GDP65), and so on for successive periods, in Microsoft Excel. Number of periods is 3 rather than 5 for 2000–2003 and 43 rather than 5 for 1960–2003.

TABLE A4. *Gini Index of Income Inequality, 1960–2003*

Year	Brazil	Chile	Costa Rica	Thailand	Argentina	Indonesia	Indonesia	South Korea	Taiwan
	income	income	income	income	income	income	cnsmp.	income	income
1960	53.0		50.0	43.7				32.0	
1965					36.0		33.3	35.2	32.8
1970	59.0	46.0	43.0	43.8	36.4		30.7	33.3	29.9
1975	63.5	53.2	46.4	42.8	36.8	43.3	34.0	39.1	28.1
1980	56.0	54.9	47.6	45.1	42.5		34.2	38.6	27.7
1985	58.9	55.1	43.2	43.6		40.4	35.7	34.5	29.0
1990	60.5	54.8	47.9	43.7	44.4	38.7	31.9	33.6	30.9
1995	59.1	55.2	47.5		48.1	39.6	36.5	33.5	31.5
2000	58.9	54.6	45.8	44.8	50.4		30.8	37.2	31.9
2003	57.6		49.0		52.9				33.9
Mean	58.5	53.4	46.7	43.9	43.4	40.5	33.4	35.2	30.6
Change, c. 1970-latest	-1.4	8.6	6.0	1.0	16.5	-3.7	2.7	3.9	4.0

Source: WIDER 2007. Selection criteria: McGuire 2009, Web Appendices B1 and B2. The quantity surveyed is income, except in Indonesia, where income and consumption expenditure Ginis are given separately (for income, change is calculated from 1976 rather than 1970). "Argentina" is Greater Buenos Aires (1965–1990); 15 metropolitan areas (1995); or 28 metropolitan areas (2000, 2003). In 2003, the three sets of metropolitan areas had similar income distributions (Gasparini 2004: 33). Surveys are from the indicated year or from a nearby year as follows: *Costa Rica:* 1961, 1971, 1974, 1986; *Chile:* 1971, 1976, 1996; *Brazil:* 1976, 1999; *Taiwan:* 1964, 1976, 1999; *South Korea:* 1961, 1976, 1988, 1998; *Thailand:* 1962, 1969, 1981, 1996; *Indonesia, income:* 1976, 1984, 1996; *Indonesia, consumption:* 1964, 1976, 1984, 1996, 1999.

TABLE A5. *Percent of Population in Poverty, 1960–2005*

	Costa Rica U.S. $2 per day		Chile U.S. $2 per day		Argentina EPH: national line WB: U.S. $2		Brazil U.S. $2 per day		Taiwan no washing machine	South Korea national line	Thailand national line	Indonesia national line
	LS	WB	LS	WB	EPH	WB	LS	WB				
1960											57	
1965									99.6			
1970	26.0		20.6				49.4		93.0		39	
1975	29.0						36.0		61.4	20.0	31	68.9
1980	29.6	32.0	23.5		8.0		28.2	31.1	35.3	14.5	23	60.8
1985	22.7	18.1		24.1	16.0	<2	31.5	37.0	22.2	14.2	30	51.1
1990	24.7	16.1	31.0	25.0	41.0	5.8	46.3	32.3	11.2	10.5	27	42.8
1995	22.1	13.3	23.5	9.7	23.7	9.8	43.5	21.7	7.2	7.4	14	32.5
2000		9.5		9.6	30.6	14.3		23.0			14	
2005		9.8		5.6	51.9	17.4		21.7			10	

Costa Rica. LS: Londoño and Székely 1997, percent of population receiving less than $2 per day ($U.S. 1995, PPP). Projection for indicated year; surveys in various years. WB: World Bank 2008a, surveys 1981, 1986, 1990, 1996, 2000, 2003; *Chile:* As in Costa Rica except WB surveys 1987, 1989, 1994, 2000, 2003; *Argentina.* EPH: percent of population in poverty in Greater Buenos Aires. 1980–1995: October Encuesta Permanente de Hogares (EPH). In 1996, the poverty line was about U.S. $5 per day (Lee 2000: 11, 18). 2000 and 2003; Ciocchini and Molteni 2007: 25, May EPH. WB: World Bank 2008a, surveys 1986, 1992, 1996, 2001, 2004. *Brazil:* as in Costa Rica except WB surveys 1981, 1984, 1990, 1996, 1999, 2003. *Taiwan:* percent of households lacking a washing machine. 1966, 1970: Thornton and Lin 1994: 87. 1975(=1976)–1995: Taiwan. DGBAS 2001: 38–39. *South Korea:* national poverty line (about U.S. $6 per day in 1990). Park and Kim 1998. *Thailand:* National poverty line (about U.S. $0.75 per day in 2002). 1960–1990: Thailand. MoPH 2000, Table 3.2. Surveys: 1962/63, 1968/69, 1975/76, 1981, 1986, 1990. 1995–2003: Thailand. NESDB 2004a: 10, 11. Surveys: 1995 (avg. 1994, 1996), 2000, 2002. *Indonesia:* National poverty line adjusted by Dhanani and Islam (2002). Surveys 1976, 1981, 1984, 1990, 1996.

TABLE A6. *Literacy in the Population Aged 15 and Older, 1960–2005*

Year	Taiwan	South Korea	Indonesia	Thailand	Chile	Costa Rica	Argentina	Brazil
1960	54.0	71.0	39.0	68.0	84.0	84.0	91.0	61.0
1965								
1970		86.8	56.3	80.3	88.2	88.2	92.3	64.5
1975	85.0	90.2	63.1	84.5	90.0	90.1	93.2	69.0
1980	87.7	92.9	69.3	87.6	91.6	91.7	94.0	73.5
1985	90.4	94.5	74.8	90.3	93.0	92.9	94.8	77.1
1990	92.4	95.9	79.7	92.4	94.1	93.9	95.6	80.2
1995	94.0	97.0	83.7	94.2	94.9	94.8	96.3	83.0
2000	95.5	97.8	86.8	92.6	95.7	94.9	97.2	86.4
2005	97.3	98.4	89.5	93.7	96.3	95.7	97.5	88.6
Percent rise 1960–2005	94.1%	94.5%	82.8%	80.3%	76.9%	73.1%	72.2%	70.8%

Sources: 1960: World Bank 1980: 154–155, except Costa Rica (Wilkie and Reich 1978: 118). 1970–1995: World Bank 2001c, except Taiwan. 2000–2005 (estimate): UNESCO Institute for Statistics 2008, except Taiwan (for Chile, 2000=2002). Taiwan: 1965, 1970, 1975 (=1976): Taiwan. CEPD 2001: 24. 1980–2005: Taiwan. CEPD 2007. Percent rise in literacy 1960–2005 formula: (lit05-lit60)/(100-lit60).

TABLE A7. *Mean Years of Schooling in the Population Aged 15 and Older, 1960–2005*

Year	South Korea	Taiwan	Argentina	Indonesia	Chile	Thailand	Costa Rica	Brazil
1960	4.25	3.88	5.25	1.55	5.21	4.30	4.03	2.85
1965	5.39	4.61	5.45	1.83	5.04	3.80	4.16	2.96
1970	4.91	5.31	6.21	2.87	5.65	4.09	3.94	3.31
1975	6.60	6.41	6.30	2.98	5.61	4.03	5.14	2.99
1980	7.91	7.61	7.04	3.67	6.42	4.43	5.19	3.11
1985	8.68	7.62	7.09	4.00	6.69	5.18	5.39	3.48
1990	9.94	7.98	8.13	4.01	6.97	5.58	5.55	4.02
1995	10.56	8.37	8.46	4.55	7.25	6.08	5.77	4.45
1999	10.84	8.76	8.83	4.99	7.55	6.50	6.05	4.88
Percent rise 1960–1999	56.1%	40.3%	33.3%	23.8%	21.7%	18.8%	16.9%	15.4%

Source: Barro and Lee 2000, variables tyr1560…tyr1599. Percent rise in mean years of schooling 1960–1999 formula: (mys99-mys60)/(16-mys60).

TABLE A8. *Secondary School Enrollment, Gross, 1960–2005*

Year	Taiwan	South Korea	Chile	Argentina	Brazil	Thailand	Costa Rica	Indonesia
1960		27	24	23		13	21	6
1965		35	34	28		14	24	12
1970		42	37	44	18	17	28	16
1975		56	47	54	9	25	43	20
1980		78	53	56	14	29	48	29
1985		92	67	70	14	31	40	41
1990	95	90	74	71	16	30	42	44
1995	96	101	70	73	20	54	48	52
2000	99	97	83	97	68	67	61	55
2005	98	93	91	86	78	77	79	62
Percent rise 1960–2005		90.4%	88.2%	81.8%	78.0%	73.6%	73.4%	59.6%

Source: Taiwan: Taiwan. DGBAS 2007: 86: All others: 1960–1995: World Bank 2001c; 2000–2005: World Bank 2008a. For Brazil, 1995=1994 and 2005=2004. Percent rise in gross secondary enrollment 1960–2005 formula: (enrl05-enrl60)/(100-enrl60).

TABLE A9. *Family Planning Effort Rated by Experts, 1972–2004*

Year	Costa Rica	Chile	Argentina	Brazil	Taiwan	South Korea	Thailand	Indonesia	Mean for 83–104 countries
1972	70	53		0	80	80	37	47	20
1982	33	44		43	79	79	61	75	29
1989	55	58	21	32	81	81	80	80	46
1994	46	55	21	43	77	71	75	84	48
1999	32	61	30	59	79	55	75	82	54
2004	60	60	39	37			66	56	47

Mean expert rating of family planning effort, expressed as a percent of the maximum attainable score.

Sources: 1972–1994: Ross and Mauldin 1996: 146; 1999: Ross 2001; 2004: Ross 2008. The 1972 and 2004 data are not strictly comparable to data for other years, but comparisons to the mean for 83–104 countries are valid for all years (Ross and Mauldin 1996: 146; Ross 2008).

TABLE A10. *Total Fertility Rate, 1960–2005*

Year	Taiwan	South Korea	Thailand	Costa Rica	Chile	Brazil	Indonesia	Argentina	Mean
1960	5.8	5.7	6.4	7.2	5.5	6.2	5.5	3.1	5.7
1965	4.8	4.9	6.1	6.4	4.8	5.7	5.5	3.1	5.4
1970	4.0	4.5	5.3	4.9	4.0	5.0	5.3	3.1	4.8
1975	2.8	3.5	4.2	4.0	3.1	4.5	5.0	3.3	4.2
1980	2.5	2.8	3.2	3.6	2.7	4.0	4.4	3.3	3.6
1985	1.9	1.7	2.5	3.4	2.7	3.4	3.7	3.1	3.1
1990	1.8	1.6	2.1	3.1	2.6	2.8	3.1	3.0	2.7
1995	1.8	1.7	1.9	2.7	2.3	2.5	2.7	2.7	2.4
2000	1.7	1.5	1.9	2.4	2.1	2.4	2.4	2.5	2.2
2005	1.1	1.1	1.8	2.2	2.0	2.3	2.3	2.3	2.0
Mean annual percent decline 1960–2005	−3.6%	−3.6%	−2.8%	−2.6%	−2.2%	−2.2%	−1.9%	−0.7%	−2.3%

Number of children each woman would bear in her lifetime if she bore children at the rate prevailing in the indicated year.

Sources: World Bank 2008a, except South Korea 1965 and Indonesia 1965 and 1975 (World Bank 2001c) and Taiwan (1960–1970 from Taiwan. DGBAS 1975: 27; 1975 from Taiwan. DGBAS 2001: 27; 1980–2005 from Taiwan. DGBAS 2007: 27). 1960–2005: average annual percent decline toward a stipulated minimum of zero, calculated in Microsoft Excel by the compound growth formula = RATE(45,,-TFR60,TFR05).

TABLE A11. *Percent of Population with Access to an Improved Water Source, 1960–2005*

Year	Thailand	Argentina	Costa Rica	South Korea	Chile	Brazil	Taiwan	Indonesia
1960	0		59	18			31	
1965	2		63	22			38	
1970	9	55	72	33	42	30	44	35
1975	14		78	43	59		50	
1980	23		82	55	68		67	42
1985	66	67	91	67	83	75	78	70
1990	74	79	92	79	91	94	84	70
1995	92	96	92	83	94	89	88	72
2000	95	96	97	92	96	89	91	76
2005	92		97	92	95	90	91	77
Percent rise 1970–2005	91.2%	91.1%	89.3%	88.1%	87.8%	85.7%	83.9%	64.6%

Sources: Except Taiwan and Thailand, 2000 and 2005 from World Bank 2008a (for Indonesia and South Korea, 2005=2004). *Costa Rica:* 1960–1990: Mesa-Lago 2000a: 530 (1965=1964, 1970=1969, 1975=1977, 1990=1989). 1995(=1994): WHO/UNICEF 2001. *Chile:* 1960–1995: Mesa-Lago 2000a: 165. Chile and Costa Rica: national figure calculated from separate urban and rural figures using proportion rural in each year from World Bank (2001). *Argentina:* 1970(=1969): PAHO 1970: 169; 1985(=1983): PAHO 1986a: 233; 1995(=1998): PAHO 2000a. *Brazil:* 1970(=1969): PAHO 1970: 169; 1985(=1983): PAHO 1986b: 233; 1995(=1998): PAHO 2000a. *Taiwan:* "Percentage of population served of tap water." 1960(=1961): Taiwan. CEPD 2001: 303; 1965–2005(=2004): Taiwan. CEPD 2007: 303. *South Korea:* "Percentage of houses with piped water." 1960–1965: World Bank 1979: 523 (1960=1962; 1965=1966). 1980, 1985: Korea 1982: 172 ("piped water supply ratio"). 1990: Korea NSO 1994: 215. 1995: Korea NSO 1998: 255. *Thailand:* Wibulpolprasert ed. 2005: 110, 121 (2005=2003). *Indonesia:* 1970(=1971): Iskandar 1997: 224 ("access to clean drinking water"). 1980: Betke 2001, Annex 1. 1985–1995: WHO/UNICEF 2001, from Demographic and Health Surveys 1987, 1991, 1994 (source not a river, spring, or unprotected well).

TABLE A12. *Percent of Urban Population with Access to Improved Sanitation,*
1960–2005

Year	Thailand	Argentina	Chile	Brazil	Costa Rica	Indonesia
1960	1				69	
1965	6		25			
1970	20	34	31	25	86	47
1975	34		44			
1980	43		67		94	52
1985	47	93	75	33	94	46
1990	74		81		97	46
1995	96	89	85	74	92	46
2000	98	91	90	83	89	52
2005		92	91	83	89	55
Percent rise 1970–2000	97.5%	86.4%	85.5%	77.3%	21.4%	9.4%

Sources: 2000 and 2005 from World Bank 2008a, except Thailand (for Indonesia, 2005=2004).
Costa Rica: 1960, 1970, and 1980 ("population with feces disposal"): Rosero-Bixby 1996: 168.
1985, 1990(=1989): Mesa-Lago 2000a: 530. 1995(=1994): WHO/UNICEF 2001. *Chile:* 1960–
1995(=1993): Mesa-Lago 2000a: 165. *Argentina, Brazil:* 1970(=1969): PAHO 1970: 169;
1985(=1983): PAHO 1986a: 233; 1995(=1998): PAHO 2000a. *Thailand:* Wibulpolprasert ed.
2005: 110, 121 ("percent of households with access to sanitary latrines"). *Indonesia:* 1970
(=1971): Iskandar 1997: 224 ("houses with latrines"). 1980: Betke 2001, Annex 1. 1985–
1995: WHO/UNICEF 2001, from Demographic and Health Surveys of 1987, 1991, and 1994;
national figure calculated from separate urban and rural figures using proportion rural in each
year from World Bank (2001/02). *South Korea, Taiwan:* no information. Percent rise in urban
sanitation 1970–2000 formula: (san00-san70)/(100-san70).

TABLE A13. *Proportion of the Total Population Malnourished, 1970–2005*

Year	Indonesia	Costa Rica	Brazil	Chile	Thailand	Argentina	South Korea
1971	47	21	23	6	29	3	3
1981	24	11	15	7	23	3	3
1992	9	6	12	8	30	3	3
1997	6	5	10	5	23	3	3
2004	6	5	7	4	22	3	3
Percent decline 1971–2004	87.2%	76.2%	69.6%	33.3%	24.1%	0%	0%

Sources: World Bank 2008e. Percent of total population with inadequate dietary energy intake
based on FAO food balance sheets, survey estimates of inequality of food access, and average
calorie requirements. No information for Taiwan. Formula for percent decline of malnourishment 1971–2004: (%malnour71-%malnour04)/(%malnour71).

TABLE A14. *Proportion of Under-5 Children Malnourished, 1960–2005*

Year	Costa Rica	Chile	Argentina	Brazil	Thailand	Indonesia
1960		5.9				
1965	13.5					
1970		3.5				
1975				18.4		
1980	6.3	1.6				
1985					25.8	40
1990	2.8	0.3		7.0		38
1995	2.2		6.6	4.5	15.4	32
2000		0.3				25
2005			2.3	3.7	9.3	28

Proportion of under-5 children more than two standard deviations below the normal weight for age.

Sources: *Costa Rica* (under 6): 1965: Costa Rica. Ministerio de Salud 1980: 28–30. 1980(=1982), 1990, 1995(=1994): WHO 2008b (1994 figure restricted to children attended by the primary care program). *Chile* (under 6): Monckeberg 2003: Table 2.2. *Argentina* 1995(=1995–96): WHO 2002 (from health center data). 2005(=2004, aged 6 months to 5 years): WHO 2008b (from National Nutrition and Health Survey). *Brazil*: 1975 and 1990(=1989): WHO 2002. 1995(=1996) and 2005(=2002–03): WHO 2008b. *Thailand*: 1985(=1986), 1995: Heaver and Kachondam 2002: 49. 2005: Thailand. NSO 2006: Table 6. *Indonesia*: 1985(=1987): WHO 2008b. 1990(=1989), 1995, 2000, 2005: Atamarita 2006. *South Korea, Taiwan*: no information.

Table A15. Health Care Spending, 1960–2005

PANEL A15.1. Public health care spending as a percent of GDP

Year	Costa Rica	Chile	Argentina	Brazil	Taiwan	South Korea	Thailand	Indonesia
1970			3.6			0.4		
1975			4.7					
1980	7.2	2.1	3.6	2.4			1.1	
1985	5.0	1.9	4.2	2.2			1.5	
1990	6.7	2.0	4.3	3.2	2.1	2.1	1.2	0.6
1995	6.0	2.4	5.0	3.4	1.9	2.1	1.7	0.6
2000	5.4	3.2	4.7	3.1		2.9	2.0	0.8
2005	5.4	2.8	4.5	3.5		3.1		1.0

PANEL A15.2. Total health care spending as a percent of GDP

Year	Costa Rica	Chile	Argentina	Brazil	Taiwan	South Korea	Thailand	Indonesia
1970			7.7			2.5		
1975						3.0		
1980	9.4	5.5	6.4	6.2	3.3	4.0	3.8	
1985	7.4	5.3	6.9	6.1		4.8	5.6	
1990	9.0	5.5	7.8	7.9	4.2	5.2	5.7	1.1
1995	8.3	5.6	11.3	9.1	5.2	5.1	5.4	1.3
2000	7.0	6.3	11.2	7.6	5.6	4.5	6.1	1.8
2005	7.1	5.4	10.2	7.9	5.9	5.9		2.1

PANEL A15.3. Total health care spending per capita

Year	Costa Rica	Chile	Argentina	Brazil	Taiwan	South Korea	Thailand	Indonesia
1970			756			64		
1975						102		
1980	657	367	699	420	197	180	103	
1985	452	304	618	398		295	188	
1990	571	392	639	540	472	499	277	32
1995	603	555	1194	627	789	678	363	48
2000	567	735	1298	540	1074	727	395	69

Panels A15.1, A15.2: *Costa Rica, Chile, Argentina, Brazil*: 1980–1995: PAHO 2003 (public includes "social insurance's health spending"). 2000, 2005: World Bank 2008a (2000=2001 in Costa Rica, Chile, and Brazil; Argentina figures for 2000(=1999) from PAHO 2003). *Argentina*: public spending, 1960–1975: Lo Vuolo 1995: 34 (includes social insurance through the *obras sociales*); total spending, 1970: González García 1997: 189. *Taiwan*: public spending calculated from Chow 2001: 31; total spending from Chiang 1997: 227 (1980), Chow 2001: 31 (1990), and Taiwan. Department of Health 2008 (1995–2005). *South Korea*: 1970: Park 1980: 111. 1975–1985: Kwon 1993: 324. 1990–1995: World Bank 2001c. 2000(=2001)–2005: World Bank 2008a. *Thailand*: Wibulpolprasert ed. 2005: 323 (public spending calculated from public as a share of total health spending). *Indonesia*: 1990–1995: World Bank 2001c; 2000(=2001), 2005: World Bank 2008a. Panel A15.3: Total health spending as a percent of GDP (Panel A15.2) times GDP per capita (Table A1).

Appendix Tables

TABLE A16. *Proportion of Births Attended by Trained Health Staff, 1960–2005*

Year	Costa Rica	Chile	Argentina	Brazil	South Korea	Thailand	Indonesia
1960		67				20?	
1965		74					
1970	74	81					
1975	83	87			36		
1980	92	91			69	41	
1985	95	97			77	69	37
1990	95	98	95	72	98	91	36
1995	98	100	95	88	100	94	41
2000	98	100	98	96	100	96	64
2005	99	100	99	97	100	97	72

Sources: *Costa Rica*: Costa Rica. MIDEPLAN 2008: Table 5–9. *Chile*: 1960–1990: Chile. Banco Central 1989: 424 ("Percent of births with professional care," 1990=1988). 1995–2005: World Bank 2008a ("Births attended by skilled health staff (% of total)," 2000=2001; 2005=2004). *Argentina*: 1990, 1995: PAHO 1998a: V.1, 272. 2000(=2001), 2005: World Bank 2008a. *Brazil*: World Bank 2008a (1990=1991, 1995=1996, 2000=2001, 2005=2003). *South Korea*: 1975(=1977), 1980(=1982): Mehrotra, Park, and Baek 1997: 277. 1985(=1986): World Bank 2001c. 1990, 1995(=1997), 2000, 2005(=2003): World Bank 2008a. *Thailand*: Haynal (1959: 2–3) estimated that in the late 1950s, when 90 percent of Thais lived in rural areas (World Bank 2001c), traditional midwives without formal medical training attended 85–90 percent of rural births. 1980(=1983), 1985(=1987): Mikhanorn 1991: 128. 1990, 1995: Thailand. NESDB 2004b: 71. 2000(=1999): UNRC-Thailand 2002: 6. 2005(=2006): World Bank 2008a. *Indonesia*: 1985(=1987), 1990(=1991), 1995(=1994): Bell, Curtis, and Alayón 2003: 14. 2000(=2001), 2005(=2004): World Bank 2008a. *Taiwan*: no data.

TABLE A17. *Proportion of Children Immunized, 1960–2005*

PANEL A17.1. *Three doses of the antigen for diphtheria, tetanus, and pertussis (DTP3)*

Year	Costa Rica	Chile	Argentina	Brazil	Taiwan	South Korea	Thailand	Indonesia
1980	86	93	44	37		61	49	1
1985	90	99	66	66		76	62	27
1990	95	95	87	66	93	74	92	60
1995	85	94	85	84		99	96	69
2000	88	91	83	99	95	97	97	75
2005	91	91	92	96	92	96	98	70

PANEL A17.2. *Measles containing vaccine (MCV)*

Year	Costa Rica	Chile	Argentina	Brazil	Taiwan	South Korea	Thailand	Indonesia
1980	60	94	61	56		4	5	6
1985	78	92	54	67		89	26	26
1990	90	97	93	78	69	93	80	58
1995	91	97	99	90		93	91	63
2000	82	97	91	99	90	95	94	72
2005	89	90	99	99	96	99	96	72

Proportion of 12–23 month-olds inoculated.

Source: WHO 2008a, except Taiwan: 1990(=1989), 1995(=1996): Chen and Liu 2005: 308. 2005(=2007). *Taiwan Journal* 2008 ("percent of infants and children receiving both primary and booster doses" of each antigen).

TABLE A18. *Democracy in Eight Societies, 1960–2005*

	Costa Rica	Chile	Argentina	Brazil	Taiwan	South Korea	Thailand	Indonesia	Mean
1960	10	5	-1	6	-8	8	-7	-5	1.0
1961	10	5	-1	5	-8	-7	-7	-5	-1.0
1962	10	5	-1	5	-8	-7	-7	-5	-1.0
1963	10	5	-1	3	-8	3	-7	-5	0.0
1964	10	6	-1		-8	3	-7	-5	-0.3
1965	10	6	-1	-9	-8	3	-7	-5	-1.4
1966	10	6	-9	-9	-8	3	-7	-6	-2.5
1967	10	6	-9	-9	-8	3	-7	-7	-2.6
1968	10	6	-9	-9	-8	3		-7	-2.0
1969	10	6	-9	-9	-8	3	2	-7	-1.5
1970	10	6	-9	-9	-8	3	2	-7	-1.5
1971	10	6	-9	-9	-8	3	-7	-7	-2.6
1972	10	6	-9	-9	-8	-9	-7	-7	-4.1
1973	10	-7	6	-9	-8	-8		-7	-3.3
1974	10	-7	6	-4	-8	-8	3	-7	-1.9
1975	10	-7	6	-4	-7	-8	3	-7	-1.8
1976	10	-7	-9	-4	-7	-8	-7	-7	-4.9
1977	10	-7	-9	-4	-7	-8		-7	-4.6
1978	10	-7	-9	-4	-7	-8	2	-7	-3.8
1979	10	-7	-9	-4	-7	-8	2	-7	-3.8
1980	10	-7	-9	-4	-7	-8	2	-7	-3.8
1981	10	-7	-8	-4	-7	-6	2	-7	-3.4
1982	10	-7	-8	-3	-7	-6	2	-7	-3.3
1983	10	-6	8*	-3	-7	-6	2	-7	-1.1
1984	10	-6	8	-3	-7	-6	2	-7	-1.1
1985	10	-6	8	7	-7	-6	2	-7	0.1
1986	10	-6	8	7	-7	-6	2	-7	0.1

1987	10	-6	8	7	-1		2	-7	1.9
1988	10	-1	8	8	-1		3	-7	3.3
1989	10	8	7	8	-1	6	3	-7	4.3
1990	10	8	7	8	-1	6	3	-7	4.3
1991	10	8	7	8	-1	6	-1	-7	3.8
1992	10	8	7	8	7	6	9	-7	6.0
1993	10	8	7	8	7	6	9	-7	6.0
1994	10	8	7	8	7	6	9	-7	6.0
1995	10	8	7	8	7	6	9	-7	6.0
1996	10	8	7	8	8	6	9	-7	6.1
1997	10	8	7	8	9	6	9	-7	6.3
1998	10	8	7	8	9	8	9	-5	6.8
1999	10	8	8	8	9	8	9	6	8.3
2000	10	9	8	8	9	8	9	6	8.4
2001	10	9	8	8	9	8	9	6	8.4
2002	10	9	8	8	9	8	9	6	8.4
2003	10	9	8	8	9	8	9	6	8.4
2004	10	9	8	8	10	8	9	8	8.8
2005	10	9	8	8	10	8	9	8	8.8
Mean	10.0	2.5	1.2	1.4	-2.0	0.8	2.0	-4.6	1.4
Mean (n yrs)	10.0 (106)	2.2 (105)	-0.1 (102)	-0.3 (100)	-3.1 (57)	0.0 (68)	-3.3 (99)	-3.5 (61)	0.8 (698)

Source: Marshall and Jaggers 2006. Figures are "polity" (democracy minus autocracy) scores, which vary from +10 (most democratic) to -10 (most autocratic). Mean: mean polity score, 1960–2005. Mean (n yrs): mean polity score 1900–2005 (no score in years of regime transition or colonial rule; South Korea includes Korea 1900–1910). Argentina 1983 is miscoded +8; the military ruled from January to November 1983. Costa Rica 1917–1919 is miscoded +10; General Tinoco exercised authoritarian rule from February 1917 to August 1919.

Works Cited

See McGuire 2009 (Web Appendix E1) for expanded versions of each citation.

Abrantes Pêgo, R., Almeida, C. (2002). "Ámbito y papel de los especialistas en las reformas en los sistemas de salud." Working Paper 299, Kellogg Institute, University of Notre Dame.

Achmad, J. (1999). *Hollow Development*. Canberra: The Australian National University.

Acuña, C., Chudnovsky, M. (2002). "Salud: Análisis de la dinámica político-institucional y organizacional del área materno infantil." Buenos Aires: Fundación Gobierno y Sociedad. http://www.udesa.edu.ar/Faculty/Tommasi/cedi/cedi.htm (retrieved Mar 9, 2004).

Acuña, C., Kessler, G., Repetto, F. (2002). "Evolución de la política social Argentina en la decada de los noventa." Working Paper, Center for Latin American Social Policy, University of Texas, Austin. http://www.utexas.edu/cola/insts/llilas/claspoesp/documents/ (retrieved Feb 20, 2004).

Adams, D.K., Gottlieb, E.E. (1993). *Education and Social Change in Korea*. New York: Garland.

Adams, F.G., Davis, I. (1994). "The Role of Policy in Economic Development." *Asian-Pacific Economic Literature* 8, 8–26.

Adelman, I. (1996). "Social Development in Korea, 1953–1993." Working Paper, Dept. of Agricultural and Resource Economics, University of California, Berkeley. http://are.berkeley.edu/~adelman (retrieved Nov 8, 2003).

Ahmad, O.B., Lopez, A.D., Inoue, M. (2000). "The Decline in Child Mortality." *Bulletin of the World Health Organization* 78.10, 1175–1191.

Alden, D., Miller, J.C. (1987). "Out of Africa." *Journal of Interdisciplinary History* 18.2, 195–224.

Alesina, A., et al. (2003). "Fractionalization." *Journal of Economic Growth* 8.2, 155–194. Associated data: http://www.anderson.ucla.edu/faculty_pages/romain.wacziarg/papersum.html (retrieved Mar 15, 2008).

Alesina, A., Perotti, R. (1996). "Income Distribution, Political Instability, and Investment." *European Economic Review* 40.6, 1203–1228.

Alesina, A., Rodrik, D. (1994). "Distributive Politics and Economic Growth." *Quarterly Journal of Economics* 109.2, 465–485.

Alexander, R.J. (1978). *The Tragedy of Chile*. Westport, CT: Greenwood.

Allende Gossens, S. (1939). *La realidad médico-social Chilena (sintesis)*. Santiago, Chile: Ministerio de Salubridad, Prevision y Asistencia Social.

Altimir, O. (2001). "Long-Term Trends of Poverty in Latin American Countries." *Estudios de Economía* 28.1, 115–155.

Altimir, O., Beccaría, L. (2001). "El persistente deterioro de la distribución del ingreso en la Argentina." *Desarrollo Económico* 40.160, 589–619.

Alves, D., Belluzzo, W. (2004). "Infant Mortality and Child Health in Brazil." *Economics and Human Biology* 2.3, 391–410.

Ameringer, C.D. (1978). *Don Pepe*. Albuquerque: University of New Mexico Press.

Aongsomwang, S. (2005). "The Impact of Bilateral Free Trade Agreements on the National Health Coverage Scheme." In FTA Watch, ed., *Impact of Thai FTAs*. July, 1–9. Bangkok: FTA Watch. http://www.twnside.org.sg/title2/FTAs/General.htm (retrieved Dec 15, 2006).

Aráoz Alfaro, G. (1936). *Por nuestros niños y por las madres*. Buenos Aires: Libreria del Colegio.

Araújo, J.L.A.C. Jr. (1997). "Attempts to Decentralize in Recent Brazilian Health Policy: Issues and Problems, 1988–1994." *International Journal of Health Services* 27.1, 109–124.

Arce, H., Katz, J., Muñoz, A. (1993). "Morfología y comportamiento del sector de salud de la República Argentina." In Katz, J., ed., *El sector salud en la República Argentina*. Buenos Aires: Fondo de Cultura Económica, 331–362.

Arellano, J.-P. (1985a). "Social Policies in Chile: An Historical Review." *Journal of Latin American Studies* 17.2, 397–418.

— (1985b). *Políticas sociales y desarrollo: Chile 1924–1984*. Santiago, Chile: CIEPLAN.

— (2005). "Políticas sociales para el crecimiento con equidad en Chile, 1990–2002." *El trimestre económico* 72.286, 409–449.

Argentina. DGE [Dirección General de Estadística] (1947). *Sintesis estadística mensual de la República Argentina*. Año 1, No. 4. Abril. Buenos Aires: Dirección Nacional de Investigaciones, Estadística y Censos.

Argentina. INDEC [Instituto Nacional de Estadística y Censos] (2006). "Evolución de las tasas de mortalidad infantil por 1.000 nacidos vivos, según provincia de residencia de la madre. Total del país. Años 1980–2004." http://www.indec.gov.ar/principal.asp?id_tema=66 (retrieved Jun 7, 2006).

Argentina. INDEC (2008a). "Incidencia de la pobreza y la indigencia en el total de aglomerados urbanos y regiones estadísticas. Semestre de octubre de 2007 a marzo de 2008." http://www.indec.gov.ar (retrieved Jul 20, 2008).

Argentina. INDEC (2008b). "Síntesis de coyuntura." http://www.indec.gov.ar (retrieved Jul 20, 2008).

Argentina. MASSP [Ministerio de Asistencia Social y Salud Pública] (1966). *Política sanitaria y social. 12 de octubre de 1963–31 de diciembre de 1965*. Buenos Aires: Ministerio de Asistencia Social y Salud Pública.

Argentina. MBS/SESP [Ministerio de Bienestar Social, Secretaría del Estado de Salud Pública] (1974). *Public Health in the Argentine Republic*. Buenos Aires: MBS/SESP.

Argentina. MBS/SESP (1978). *La atención primaria de salud en la República Argentina*. Prepared for the Conferencia Internacional Sobre Atención Primaria de la Salud, Alma Ata, USSR, September 6–12, 1978. Buenos Aires: MBS/SESP.

Argentina. Ministerio de Salud (2001, 2004, 2005). *Estadísticas vitales: Información basica.* 2000, 2003, and 2004 eds. Serie 5, Nos. 45, 47, and 48. Dirección de Estadísticas e Información de Salud. Buenos Aires: Ministerio de Salud. http://www.bvs.org.ar/indicador.htm (retrieved Jul 15, 2008).

Argentina. Ministerio de Salud (2007). *Estadísticas vitales: Información basica – 2006.* Dirección de Estadísticas e Información de Salud. Serie 5, No. 50. Buenos Aires: Ministerio de Salud. http://www.deis.gov.ar/ (retrieved Jun 30, 2008).

Argentina. MSAS [Ministerio de Salud y Acción Social] (1985). *Argentina: Descripción de su situación de salud.* October. Buenos Aires: Ministerio de Salud y Acción Social, Organización Panamericana de la Salud, y Organización Mundial de la Salud.

Argentina. MSPyMA [Ministerio de Salud Pública y Medio Ambiente] (1983). *Estadísticas vitales y de salud.* Serie Histórica, Estadísticas Demográficas, Años 1944–1970. Serie 5, No. 22. Buenos Aires: Ministerio de Salud Pública y Medio Ambiente.

Arretche, M. (2005). "Toward a Unified and More Equitable System: Health Reform in Brazil." In Kaufman, R.R., and Nelson, J.M., eds., *Crucial Needs, Weak Incentives.* Baltimore, MD: Johns Hopkins University Press, 155–188.

Arriagada, I., Aranda, V., Miranda, F. (2005). "Políticas y programas de salud en América Latina: problemas y propuestas." Santiago, Chile: Comisión Económica para América Latina y el Caribe. December. www.cepal.org/publicaciones/xml/7/23777/sps114_lcl2450.pdf (retrieved Jul 16, 2008).

Ascher, W. (1984). *Scheming for the Poor.* Cambridge, MA: Harvard University Press.

Aspalter, C. (2002). *Democractization and Welfare State Development in Taiwan.* Aldershot: Ashgate.

Astorga, P., FitzGerald, V. (1998). "The Standard of Living in Latin America During the Twentieth Century." Queen Elizabeth House Development Studies Working Paper 117, University of Oxford, U.K.

Atamarita (2006). "Analisis Antropometri Balita, Susenas Tahun 1989–2005." Updated April 2006. http://www.gizi.net/download/all-prov-sus%2089-05.pdf (retrieved Aug 13, 2008).

Atwood, A. (1990). "Health Policy in Brazil." In Graham, L.S., Wilson, R.H, eds., *The Political Economy of Brazil.* Austin: University of Texas Press, 141–163.

Avelino, G., Brown, D.S., Hunter, W. (2005). "The Effects of Capital Mobility, Trade Openness, and Democracy on Social Spending in Latin America, 1980–1999." *American Journal of Political Science* 49.3, 625–641.

Ayala, N. (2007). Personal interview, San José, Costa Rica, February 2. Lic. Ayala from 1994 to 1998 coordinated the Comprehensive Basic Health Care Teams program for the Caja Costarricense de Seguro Social.

Azevedo, A.C. de (1981). "Otimização das ações de saúde a nivel nacional." *Revista de Administração Pública* 15 (ed. extra), 57–91.

Baker, T.D., Perlman, M. (1967). *Health Manpower in a Developing Economy: Taiwan.* Baltimore, MD: Johns Hopkins University Press.

Bamber, S. (1997). "The Thai Medical Profession and Political Activism." In Hewison, K., ed., *Political Change in Thailand.* London: Routledge, 233–250.

Ban, S.H., Moon, P.Y., Perkins, D.H. (1980). *Rural Development.* Cambridge, MA: Harvard University Press.

Bangkok Post (2006). "Free Universal Medical Project Approved." October 31, 2006. http://www.bangkokpost.com/breaking_news/breakingnews.php?id=113905 (retrieved Nov 24, 2006).

Baraka, J. (1999). "Does Type of Degree Explain Taiwan's Gender Gap?" Research Program in Development Studies Paper 189. Woodrow Wilson School, Princeton University. http://www.wws.princeton.edu/rpds/papers.html (retrieved Oct 22, 2006).

Barclay, G.W. (1954a). *Colonial Development and Population in Taiwan*. Princeton, NJ: Princeton University Press.

(1954b). *A Report on Taiwan's Population to the Joint Commission on Rural Reconstruction*. Princeton, NJ: Office of Population Research, Princeton University.

Bark, S.I. (1994). "Social Costs of Economic Restructuring in the Republic of Korea." In UN Economic and Social Commission for Asia and the Pacific, ed., *Social Costs of Economic Restructuring in Asia and the Pacific*. Bangkok: UNESCAP, 406–450.

Barlow, R., Vissandjée, B. (1999). "Determinants of National Life Expectancy." *Canadian Journal of Development Studies* 20.1, 9–29.

Barrientos, A. (2000). "Getting Better after Neoliberalism." In Lloyd-Sherlock, P., ed., *Healthcare Reform in Latin America*. London: Institute of Latin American Studies, University of London, 94–111.

(2002). "Health Policy in Chile." *Bulletin of Latin American Research* 21.3, 442–459.

Barro, R.J., Lee, J.-W. (2000). "International Data on Educational Attainmment." CID Working Paper 42, Center for International Development, Harvard University. Data Tables (Panel Format). http://www.cid.harvard.edu/ciddata/ciddata.html (retrieved Jun 20, 2001).

Barros, A.J.D., et al. (2005). "Brazil: Are Health and Nutrition Programs Reaching the Neediest?" In Gwatkin, D.R., Wagstaff, A., Yazbeck, A.S., eds., *Reaching the Poor with Health, Nutrition, and Population Services*. Washington, DC: World Bank, 281–306.

Bastos, N.C. de B. (1993). *SESP/FSESP: evolução histórica, 1942–1991*. Recife: Comunicarte.

Bauer, A.J. (1975). *Chilean Rural Society*. Cambridge: Cambridge University Press.

Becker, R.A., Lechtig, A. (1986). *Brasil: Evoluçao da Mortalidade Infantil no Periodo 1977–1984*. Brasília: Centro de Documentação do Ministério da Saúde.

Bell, J.P. (1971). *Crisis in Costa Rica*. Austin: University of Texas Press.

Bell, J., Curtis, S.L., Alayón, S. (2003). "Trends in Delivery Care in Six Countries." DHS Analytical Studies 7. Calverton, MD: ORC Macro. http://www.measuredhs.com/pubs/pub_details.cfm?ID=482&srchTp=advanced (retrieved Aug 14, 2008).

Belmartino, S. (1991). "Politicas de salud en Argentina." *Cuadernos Médico Sociales* (Rosario, Argentina) 55, 13–33.

Belmartino, S., Bloch, C. (1994). *El sector salud en Argentina*. Publicación 40. Buenos Aires: Oficina Panamericana de la Salud.

Bengelsdorf, C. (1994). *The Problem of Democracy in Cuba*. New York: Oxford University Press.

Ben-Porath, Y. (1980). "Child Mortality and Fertility." In Easterlin, R.A., ed., *Population and Economic Change in Developing Countries*. Chicago: University of Chicago Press.

Berman, P.A. (1984). "Village Health Workers in Java, Indonesia." *Social Science and Medicine* 19.4, 411–422.

Berman, P.A., Sisler, D.G., Habicht, J.-P. (1989). "Equity in Public-Sector Primary Health Care." *Economic Development and Cultural Change* 37.4, 777–803.

Bermann, S., and Escudero, J.C. (1978). "Health in Argentina under the Military Junta." *International Journal of Health Services* 8.3, 531–540.

Bertone, A.A. (2002). "As idéias e as práticas: a construçao do SUS." Masters Thesis, Instituto de Medicina Social, Universidade do Estado do Rio de Janeiro. http://dtr2001.saude.gov.br/bvs/publicacoes/monografia_revisada_Arnaldo.pdf (retrieved Jul 17, 2006).

Betke, F. (2001). "The 'Family-in Focus' Approach." Innocenti Working Paper 83. Florence: UNICEF Innocenti Research Centre.

Bevan, D., Collier, P., Gunning, J.W. (1999). *Nigeria and Indonesia.* New York: Oxford University Press.

Bhalla, S.S. (1997). "Freedom and Economic Growth." In Hadenius, A., ed., *Democracy's Victory and Crisis.* New York: Cambridge University Press, 195–241.

Bidani, B., Ravallion, M. (1997). "Decomposing Social Indicators Using Distributional Data." *Journal of Econometrics* 77.1, 125–139.

Biesanz, M., Biesanz, R., Biesanz, K. (1999). *The Ticos.* Boulder, CO: Lynne Rienner.

Birdsall, N., Bruns, B., Sabot, R.A. (1996). "Education in Brazil." In Birdsall, N., Sabot, R., eds., *Opportunity Foregone.* Washington, DC: Inter-American Development Bank, 7–47.

Birdsall, N., Ross, D., Sabot, R. (1995). "Inequality and Growth Reconsidered." *World Bank Economic Review* 9.3, 477–508.

Bloch, C. (1988). "Atención primaria de salud en Argentina." In Spinelli, H., et al., eds, *Segundas Jornadas de Atención Primaria de la Salud.* Buenos Aires: Asociación de Médicos Residentes del Hospital de Niños Ricardo Gutiérrez and Comisión Argentina de Residentes del Equipo de Salud.

Blofield, M.H. (2001). "The Politics of 'Moral Sin'." Santiago, Chile: FLACSO-Chile. http://www.unc.edu/~blofield/Flacso%20publication.pdf (retrieved Jul 14, 2003).

Bloom, D.E., Canning, D., Graham, B. (2003). "Longevity and Life-cycle Savings." *Scandinavian Journal of Economics* 105.3, 319–338.

Bloom, D.E., Canning, D., Malaney, P.N. (2000). "Population Dynamics and Economic Growth in East Asia." *Population and Development Review* 26 (Supplement), 257–290.

Bollen, K.A., Jackman, R.W. (1985). "Political Democracy and the Size Distribution of Income." *American Sociological Review* 50.4, 438–457.

Bombardieri, M. (2002). "Bangkok Offers First Class to 'Medical Tourists'." *Boston Globe*, July 14, Travel Section, p. M7.

Bongaarts, J. (1987). "Does Family Planning Reduce Infant Mortality Rates?" *Population and Development Review* 13.2, 323–334.

   (2006). "How Long Will We Live?" *Population and Development Review* 32.4, 605–628.

Boomgaard, P. (1986). "The Welfare Services in Indonesia." *Itinerario* [Leiden, Netherlands] 10.1, 57–82.

   (1987). "Morbidity and Mortality in Java, 1820–1880." In Owen, N.G., ed., *Death and Disease in Southeast Asia.* Singapore: Oxford University Press, 48–69.

Booth, J. (1998). *Costa Rica: Quest for Democracy.* Boulder, CO: Westview.

Booth, J.A., Seligson, M.A. (1979). "Peasants As Activists." *Comparative Political Studies* 12.1, 29–59.

Bortman, M. (2002). "Indicadores de salud: ¿Mejoró la equidad? Costa Rica 1980–2000." San José, CR: Ministerio de Salud, PAHO-Costa Rica Office. http://www.cor.ops-oms.org/TextoCompleto/configuredList.asp (retrieved Sep 27, 2006).

Borzutzky, S. (2002). *Vital Connections*. Notre Dame, IN: University of Notre Dame Press.

Bos, E., Saadah, F. (1999). "Indonesia: Childhood Mortality Trends." *Watching Brief* 4. Washington, DC: World Bank, East Asia and the Pacific Region.

Bowie, A., Unger, D. (1997). *The Politics of Open Economies*. Cambridge: Cambridge University Press.

Boyer, W.W., Ahn, B.M. (1991). *Rural Development in South Korea*. Newark: University of Delaware Press.

Brasil. Ministério da Saúde (1972). "30 Anos de Atividades em Saúde Pública, 1942–1972." Rio de Janeiro: Ministério da Saúde, Fundação Serviços de Saúde Pública.

Brasil. Ministério da Saúde (2000a). "Programa Agentes Comunitários de Saúde." Brasília: Secretaria Executiva, Ministério da Saúde.

Brasil. Ministério da Saúde (2000b). "Programa Saúde da Família." Brasília: Secretaria Executiva, Ministério da Saúde.

Brasil. Ministério da Saúde (2002). "Desafios e conquistas do PSF." *Revista Brasileira de Saúde da Família* [Brasília] 2.5, 6–24.

Brasil. Ministério da Saúde (2003). *Sistema de Informação da Atenção Básica – SIAB. Indicadores 2000*. 3° ed. atualizada. Série G. Estatística e Informação em Saúde. Brasília: Ministério da Saúde. http://dtr2001.saude.gov.br/bvs/publica-coes/SIAB_2000.pdf (retrieved Jul 14, 2006).

Brasil. Ministério da Saúde (2006). "Atenção Básica: Saúde da Família." Brasília: Ministério da Saúde. http://dtr2004.saude.gov.br/dab/atencaobasica.php (retrieved Jul 6, 2006).

Brasil. Ministério da Saúde e Ministério da Previdência e Asistência Social (1981). *Programa Nacional de Serviços Básicos de Saúde, PREVSAÚDE, 1981–1986*. Brasília: Ministério da Saúde and Ministério da Previdência e Asistência Social.

Brasil. TCU [Tribunal de Contas da União] (2003). *TCU Evaluation of the Family Health Program*. Brasília: TCU.

Brennan, J.P. (1994). *The Labor Wars in Córdoba*. Cambridge, MA: Harvard University Press.

Bresnan, J. (1993). *Managing Indonesia*. New York: Columbia University Press.

Brett, M.T. (1984). "Primary Care and the Pattern of Disease in a Rural Area of the Argentine Chaco." *Bulletin of the Pan American Health Organization* 18.2, 115–126.

Britos, S., et al. (2003). "Programas alimentarios en Argentina." Buenos Aires: Centro de Estudios Sobre Nutrición Infantil. http://www.cesni.org.ar/libros_cesni.php (retrieved May 26, 2004).

Brundenius, C. (2002). "Cuba: The Retreat From Entitlement?" In Abel, C., Lewis, C.M., eds. *Exclusion and Engagement*. London: Institute of Latin American Studies, University of London.

Bryce, J., et al. (2003). "Reducing Child Mortality." *Lancet* 362, 159–164.

Bucciarelli, M., González, A., Scuri, M.C. (1993). "La provincia y la política." In Bandieri, S., Favaro, O., Morinelli, M., eds., *Historia de Neuquén*. Buenos Aires: Plus Ultra.

Bulatao, R.A., Ross, J.A. (2003). "Which Health Services Reduce Maternal Mortality?" *Tropical Medicine and International Health* 8.8, 710–721.

Cabello, O. (1956). "The Demography of Chile." *Population Studies* 9.3, 237–250.

Caldwell, J.C. (1986). "Routes to Low Mortality in Poor Countries." *Population and Development Review* 12.2, 171–220.

(1997). "Population and Human Resources." In Jones, G.W., Hull, T.H., eds., *Indonesia Assessment*. Singapore: Institute for Southeast Asian Studies, 59–66.

Caldwell, J.C., Caldwell, P. (1993). "Women's Position and Child Mortality and Morbidity in Less Developed Countries." In Federici, N., Oppenheim Mason, K., Sogner, S. eds., *Women's Position and Demographic Change*. New York: Oxford University Press.

Callison, C.S. (2002). "Social Protection Programs: Components, Priorities, Strategic Choices and Alternatives for Indonesia." Report PEG 92, 7 October. Jakarta: U.S. AID. http://www.pegasus.or.id/Reports/92)%20Social%20Protection.pdf (retrieved Apr 9, 2003).

Cameron, D. (1984). "Social Democracy, Corporatism, Labor Quiescence, and the Representation of Economic Interest in Advanced Capitalist Society." In Goldthorpe, J., ed., *Order and Conflict in Contemporary Capitalism*. New York: Clarendon.

Campos, A.L.V. de (1997). "International Health Policies in Brazil: The Serviço Especial de Saúde Pública, 1942–1960." PhD Diss., University of Texas at Austin.

(1998). "The Institute of Inter-American Affairs and Its Health Policies in Brazil during World War II." *Presidential Studies Quarterly* 28.3, 523–534.

Campos, J.E., Root, H.L. (1996). *The Key to the Asian Miracle*. Washington, DC: Brookings.

Cardoso, E., Helwige, A. (1994). "Populism, Profligacy, and Redistribution." In Dornbusch, R., Edwards, S., eds., *The Macroeconomics of Populism in Latin America*. Chicago: University of Chicago Press, 45–70.

(2000). "Import Substitution Industrialization." In Frieden, J., Pastor, M., Tomz, M., eds., *Modern Political Economy and Latin America*. Boulder, CO: Westview, 155–164.

Casas, A., Vargas, H. (1980). "The Health System in Costa Rica." *Journal of Public Health Policy* 1.3, 258–279.

Castañeda, T. (1984). "Contexto socioeconomico y causas del descenso de la mortalidad infantil en Chile." Documento 38. Santiago, Chile: Centro de Estudios Económicos.

(1992). *Combating Poverty*. San Francisco, CA: International Center for Economic Growth.

Castañeda, T., Beeharry, G., Griffin, C. (2000). "Decentralization of Health Services in Latin American Countries." In Burki, S.J., et al., eds., *Annual World Bank Conference on Development in Latin America and the Caribbean 1999*. Washington, DC: World Bank.

Castro, C. de M. (2000). "Education: Way Behind but Trying to Catch Up." *Dædalus* 129.2, 291–314.

Cavarozzi, M. (1984). "Los partidos y el parlamento en la Argentina." In Sábato, H., Cavarozzi, M., eds., *Democracia, orden político y parlamento fuerte*. Buenos Aires: Centro Editor de América Latina.

CCP-UCR [Centro Centroamericano de Población – Universidad de Costa Rica] (2009). "Tasas demográficas básicas de Costa Rica 1950-." http://ccp.ucr.ac.cr/observa/CRindicadores/tasas.htm (retrieved Apr 29, 2009).

CEDI [Centro de Estudios para el Desarrollo Institucional] (2002). "El functionamiento del sistema de salud Argentino en un contexto federal." Documento 77. Buenos Aires.

CEPAL [Comisión Económica para América Latina] (2002). *Panorama Social de América Latina 2001–2002*. Santiago, Chile: CEPAL.

Cesaltina, A. (2004). "Conferências: palco de conquistas democráticas." *Revista CONASEMS* 2 (19 January). http://www.walkinmedia.com.br/conasems/mostraPagina.asp?codPagina=48&codServico=36 (retrieved Jul 17, 2006).

Cesar, J. A., et al. (2005). "Saúde infantil em áreas pobres das regiões Norte e Nordeste do Brasil." *Cadernos de Saúde Pública* 21.6, 1845–1855.

Chan, H.-S., Yang, Y. (2001). "The Development of Social Welfare in Taiwan." In Aspalter, C., ed., *Understanding Modern Taiwan*. Aldershot: Ashgate, 149–167.

Chandarasorn, V. (1990). "Implementation of Primary Health Care Policy in Thailand." *Thai Journal of Development Administration* 30.3, 39–59.

Charoenparij, S., et al. (1999). *Health Financing in Thailand*. Boston, MA: Management Sciences for Health.

Chaudhury, N., et al. (2006). "Missing in Action." *Journal of Economic Perspectives* 20.1, 91–116.

Chen, C.-S., Liu, T.-C. (2005). "The Taiwan National Health Insurance Program and Full Infant Immunization Coverage." *American Journal of Public Health* 95.2, 305–311.

Chen, C.-S., Liu, T.-C., Chen, L.-M. (2003). "National Health Insurance and the Antenatal Care Use." *Health Policy* 64.1, 99–112.

Chen, L.-M., Wen, S.-W., Li, C.-Y. (2001). "The Impact of National Health Insurance on the Utilization of Health Care Services by Pregnant Women." *Maternal and Child Health Journal* 5.1, 35–42.

Chen, X., et al. (2004). *Regression with Stata*. Web Book, UCLA Academic Technology Services. http://www.ats.ucla.edu/stat/stata/webbooks/reg/ (retrieved Aug 17, 2005).

Cheng, T.-M. (2003). "Taiwan's New National Health Insurance Program." *Health Affairs* 22.3, 61–76.

Chernichovsky, D., Meesook, O. A. (1986). "Utilization of Health Services in Indonesia." *Social Science and Medicine* 23.6, 611–620.

Chi, C. (1994). "Integrating Traditional Medicine into Modern Health Care Systems." *Social Science and Medicine* 39.3, 307–321.

Chiang, T.-L. (1997). "Taiwan's 1995 Health Care Reform." *Health Policy* 39.3, 225–239.

Chile. Banco Central (1989). *Indicadores económicos y sociales*. Santiago, Chile: Banco Central.

Chile. CNVR [Comisión Nacional de Verdad y Reconciliación] (1993). *Report of the Chilean National Commission on Truth and Reconciliation*. Notre Dame, IN: University of Notre Dame Press.

Chile. FONASA [Fondo Nacional de Salud] (2008). Problemas de Salud AUGE. http://www.fonasa.cl/prontus_fonasa/antialone.html?page=http://www.fonasa.cl/prontus_fonasa/site/edic/base/port/auge.html (retrieved Jul 18, 2008).

Chile. INE [Instituto Nacional de Estadísticas] (2002). *Anuario de Estadísticas Vitales 2000*. Santiago, Chile: INE.

Chile. MIDEPLAN [Ministerio de Planificacion y Cooperación] (2003). "Indicadores económicos y sociales 1990–2000: Gasto social." http://www.mideplan.cl/sitio/Sitio/indicadores/htm/indicadores_gastos.htm (retrieved Jul 7, 2003).

Chile. Ministerio de Salud (2008). "Mortalidad infantil y sus componentes, Región Chile: 1990–2005." Departamento de Estadísticas e Informacion de Salud. http://www.minsal.cl (retrieved Jun 30, 2008).

Chile. ODEPLAN [Oficina de Planificación Nacional] (1975). *Mapa extrema pobreza.* Santiago, Chile: ODEPLAN.

Chile. ODEPLAN (1977). *A Social Development Experiment in Chile: Report.* Santiago, Chile: ODEPLAN.

Chin, H.-Y. (1998). "Colonial Medical Police and Postcolonial Medical Surveillance Systems in Taiwan, 1895–1950." *Osiris* 13, 326–338.

Cho, N. H., Seo, M. H. (1992). "Recent Changes in the Population Control Policy and Its Future Directions in Korea." In Korea Institute for Health and Social Affairs and Taiwan Provincial Institute for Family Planning, eds., *Fertility Control Experiences in the Republics of Korea and China.* Taipei: Maternal and Child Health Association of the Republic of China, 17–43.

Choe, M. K. (1987). "Sex Differentials in Infant and Child Mortality in Korea." *Social Biology* 24. 1–2, 12–25.

Cholil, H. A. (1997). "The Mother Friendly Movement in Indonesia." Paper presented at "Safe Motherhood Matters," Colombo, Sri Lanka, 20 October 1997. http://www.popcouncil.org/pdfs/aneorta/pdfs/indo/fr/infr23.pdf (retrieved Sep 21, 2002).

Chomitz, K. M., et al. (1997). "What Do Rural Doctors Want?" Policy Research Working Paper 1888. Washington, DC: World Bank.

Chou, S.-Y., et al. (2007). "Parental Education and Child Health." NBER Working Paper 13466. http://www.nber.org/papers/w13466 (retrieved Jul 30, 2008).

Chow, P. C. Y. (2001). "Social Expenditures in Taiwan (China)." Washington, DC: World Bank Institute. http://www.worldbank.org/wbi/publications/wbi37167.pdf (retrieved Jul 17, 2002).

Chung, Y. I. (1979). "Transition in the Substance of Poverty in Korea." *The Philippine Economic Journal* 18.4, 493–540.

Chutikul, S. (1986). *Malnourished Children: An Economic Approach to the Causes and Consequences in Rural Thailand.* Working Paper 102. Honolulu: East-West Population Institute.

Cifuentes, M. (1991). "Sector Salud." In Larroulet, C., ed., *Soluciones privadas a problemas públicos.* Santiago, Chile: Libertad y Desarrollo, 51–91.

Ciocchini, F. J., Molteni, G. (2007). "Medidas alternativas de la pobreza en el Gran Buenos Aires, 1995–2006." Documento de Trabajo 16, Departamento de Economía, Pontificia Universidad Católica Argentina. http://www.uca.edu.ar/esp/sec-feconomicas/esp/page.php?subsec=d-economia&page=investigacion/docs_trabajo (retrieved Aug 21, 2008).

Clark, M. A. (2001). *Gradual Economic Reform in Latin America.* Albany, NY: SUNY Press.

——— (2004). "Reinforcing a Public System." In Kaufman, R. R., Nelson, J. M., eds., *Crucial Needs, Weak Incentives.* Baltimore, MD: Johns Hopkins University Press, 189–216.

——— (2005). "The Medical Profession, the State, and Health Reforms in Costa Rica." Prepared for the 46th annual meeting of the International Studies Association, Honolulu, March 1–5, 2005.

Cohen, J. (2006). "Brazil: Ten Years After." *Science* 213.5786, 484–487.

Cohen, P. (1989). "The Politics of Primary Health Care in Thailand." In Cohen, P., Purcal, J.T., eds., *The Political Economy of Primary Health Care in Southeast Asia*. Canberra: Australian Development Studies Network, 159–176.

Colitt, R. (2003). "Pensions 'Time Bomb' Tops Hit List as Lula Wins Over Governors." *Financial Times*, Europe edition 1, February 26, 8.

Collier, D., Brady, H., Seawright, J. (2004). "Sources of Leverage in Causal Inference." In Brady, H., Collier, D., eds., *Rethinking Social Inquiry*. Lanham, MD: Rowman and Littlefield, 229–266.

Collier, D., Mahoney, J. (1996). "Insights and Pitfalls." *World Politics* 49.1, 56–91.

Collier, R.B., Collier, D. (1991). *Shaping the Political Arena*. Princeton, NJ: Princeton University Press.

Collins, C., Araújo, J., Barbosa, J. (2000). "Decentralising the Health Sector." *Health Policy* 52.2, 113–127.

Collins, J., Lear, J. (1995). *Chile's Free-Market Miracle*. Oakland, CA: Institute for Food and Development Policy.

Constable, P., Valenzuela, A. (1991). *A Nation of Enemies*. New York: W.W. Norton.

Consumers International (2005). "Health for All in Thailand." *Asia Pacific Consumer* 41.3, 32–34.

Cordeiro, H. de A. (1980). *A Industria da saúde no Brasil*. Rio de Janeiro: Edicões Graal.

   (1982). "Politicas de saúde no Brasil." In IBASE [Instituto Brasileiro de Análisis Sociais e Econômias], *Saúde e trabalho no Brasil*. Petrópolis: Ed. Vozes, 83–90.

Cornwall, A., Shankland, A. (2008). "Engaging Citizens." *Social Science & Medicine* 66.10, 2173–2184.

Costa Rica. CCSS [Caja Costarricense de Seguro Social] (1986). "Desarrollo de un nuevo modelo de atención ambulatoria en Costa Rica." San José, CR: CCSS.

Costa Rica. CCSS (1998). "Hacia un nuevo modelo de atención integral de salud." San José, CR: CCSS.

Costa Rica. CCSS (2004). "Estadísticas generales de los servicios de atención de la salud, CCSS. 1980–2004. Cap. V: Salud Reproductiva." http://www.ccss.sa.cr/germed/dis/diess/salrep04.htm (retrieved Sep 17, 2006).

Costa Rica. MIDEPLAN [Ministerio de Planificación Nacional y Política Económica] (2008). Sistema de Indicadores sobre Desarrollo Sostenible. http://www.mideplan.go.cr/sides/social/ (retrieved Jun 27, 2008).

Costa Rica. Ministerio de Salud (1976). *Programa de salud para comunidades rurales de Costa Rica*. 3rd ed. San José, CR: Dirección General de Salud, Departamento de Salud Rural.

Costa Rica. Ministerio de Salud (1980). *Encuesta Nacional de Nutrición 1978*. December. San José, CR: Ministerio de Salud, Departamento de Nutrición.

Costa Rica. Ministerio de Salud (1989). *Programa de Salud Integral en Costa Rica (SILOS)*. San José, CR: Serie Política y Legislación Sanitaria, Representación OPS/OMS.

Costa Rica. Ministerio de Salud (2002). *Analisis Sectorial Costa Rica 2002*. San Jose, CR: Ministerio de Salud. http://www.netsalud.sa.cr/seccion1.pdf (retrieved Jun 27, 2003).

CRLP [Center for Reproductive Law and Policy] (1999). "Women's Reproductive Rights in Chile: A Shadow Report." New York: CRLP. http://reproductiverights.org/en/archive/publications (retrieved Mar 21, 2009).

CRLP (2001). *Women of the World: Laws and Policies Affecting Their Reproductive Lives. Latin America and the Caribbean*. New York: CRLP. http://reproductiverights.org/en/archive/publications (retrieved Mar 21, 2009).

Croll, E. (2001). "Amartya Sen's 100 Million Missing Women." *Oxford Development Studies* 29.3, 225–244.

Cutler, D., Deaton, A., Lleras-Muney, A. (2006). "The Determinants of Mortality." *Journal of Economic Perspectives* 20.3, 97–120.

Da Matta, R. (1991). *Carnivals, Rogues, and Heroes*. Notre Dame, IN: University of Notre Dame Press.

Dahl, R.A. (1989). *Democracy and Its Critics*. New Haven, CT: Yale University Press.

(1998). *On Democracy*. New Haven, CT: Yale University Press.

Dal Bo, L.A. (2000). "Reforma Hospitalaria." *Revista de Hospital Privado de Comunidad* 4.1/2, 87–91. http://www.hpc.org.ar/pdf/v4p87.pdf (retrieved Jan 28, 2004).

Dal Poz, M.R. (2002). "Cambios en la contratación de recursos humanos." *Gaceta Sanitaria* [Barcelona] 16.1, 82–88.

Dal Poz, M.R., Viana, A.L. (1999). "The Family-Health Program as a Strategy for Reforming Brazil's Health System." For IADB/IDRC seminar on "Reformas a la Política Social en América Latina: Resultados y Perspectivas," Washington, DC, May 11–12. http://www.idrc.ca/lacro/foro/seminario/dalpoz_pb.html (retrieved Aug 18, 2001).

Danielson, R. (1979). *Cuban Medicine*. New Brunswick, NJ: Transaction.

Dasgupta, P. (1993). *An Inquiry into Well-Being and Destitution*. New York: Oxford University Press.

David, B., et al. (2000). "II Relatório de Andamento do Projeto Mão de Obra, Emprego e Demanda por Reforma Agrária." http://www.dataterra.org.br/Documentos/relatorio2/relatorio2frame.htm (retrieved Jun 22, 2001).

De Haas, J.H. (1939). "Infant Mortality in Batavia for the Years 1935 and 1936." *Indian Journal of Pediatrics* 6, 12–45.

Deininger, K., Squire, L. (1996). "A New Data Set Measuring Income Inequality." *World Bank Economic Review* 10.3, 565–591.

(1998). "Measuring Income Inequality: A New Database." Washington, DC: World Bank. http://www.worldbank.org/research/growth/deisqu2.zip (retrieved May 8, 2001).

Denton, C.F. (1971). *Patterns of Costa Rican Politics*. Boston, MA: Allyn and Bacon.

Deyo, F.C. (1992). "Imperatives of Development and the Formation of Social Policy." In Brown, R.H., Liu, W.T., eds., *Modernization in East Asia*. Westport, CT: Praeger.

Dhanani, S., Islam, I. (2002). "Poverty, Vulnerability and Social Protection in a Period of Crisis." *World Development* 30.7, 1211–1231.

Djamin, A., Kertonegoro, S. (1998). "Social Security Profiles in ASEAN Countries." Jakarta: Indonesian Human Resources Foundation. http://www.asean-ssa.org/sspac.pdf (retrieved Apr 9, 2003).

Dorner, P., Thiesenhusen, W.C. (1990). "Selected Land Reforms in East and Southeast Asia." *Asian-Pacific Economic Literature* 4.1, 65–95.

Dow, W.H., Schmeer, K. (2003). "Health Insurance and Child Mortality in Costa Rica." *Social Science and Medicine* 57.6, 975–986.

Draibe, S. M., Guimarães de Castro, M. H., Azeredo, B. (1995). "The System of Social Protection in Brazil." Democracy and Social Policy Working Paper 3, Kellogg Institute, University of Notre Dame.

Drèze, J., Sen, A. K. (1989). *Hunger and Public Action.* Oxford: Clarendon.

  (1995). *India: Economic Development and Social Opportunity.* Oxford: Clarendon.

Durán-Valverde, F. (2002). "Anti-Poverty Programmes in Costa Rica." ESS Paper 8. Geneva: International Labour Office. http://www.ilo.org/public/english/protection/socsec/download/esscostarica.doc (retrieved Jun 24, 2003).

Easterlin, R. A. (1996). *Growth Triumphant.* Ann Arbor, MI: University of Michigan Press.

  (1999). "How Beneficent is the Market?" *European Review of Economic History* 3.3, 257–294.

  (2000). "The Worldwide Standard of Living Since 1800." *Journal of Economic Perspectives* 14.1, 7–26.

Easterly, W., Levine, R. (1996). "Africa's Growth Tragedy: Policies and Ethnic Divisions Dataset." http://go.worldbank.org/K7WYOCA8To (retrieved May 8, 2001).

Eberstadt, N., Banister, J. (1992). "Divided Korea." *Population and Development Review* 18.3, 505–531.

Eckert, C. J., et al. (1990). *Korea Old and New.* Seoul: Ilkochak.

Eckholm, E. (2007). "In Turnabout, Infant Deaths Climb in South." *New York Times,* April 22, 2007, A1.

Economist (1995). "Thailand: The Needy and the Greedy." May 13, 36.

Economist (1996). "South-East Asia's Wealth Gap." April 13, 29–30.

Economist (2002). "A New Order: A Survey of Thailand." March 2.

Economist (2006). "Brazil: Lula's Leap." March 4, 33.

Edmonds, R. L. (1996). "Taiwan's Environment Today." *The China Quarterly* 148, 1224–1259.

Eibner, C., Evans, W. N. (2005). "Relative Deprivation, Poor Health Habits, and Mortality." *Journal of Human Resources* 40.3, 591–620.

Elson, R. E. (2001). *Suharto: A Political Biography.* Cambridge: Cambridge University Press.

English, B. H. (1971). *Liberación Nacional in Costa Rica.* Gainesville: University of Florida Press.

Epstein, E. S. (2000). "Labor under Neoliberalism." Prepared for the annual meeting of the American Political Science Association, Washington, DC, August 30–September 3.

Escudé, C. (1976). *Aspectos ocultos de la salud en la Argentina.* Buenos Aires: El Coloquio.

  (1989). "Health in Buenos Aires in the Second Half of the Nineteenth Century." In Platt, D. C. M., ed., *Social Welfare, 1850–1950: Australia, Argentina, and Canada Compared.* Houndmills: Macmillan, 60–70.

Escudero, J. C. (1981). "Democracy, Authoritarianism, and Health in Argentina." *International Journal of Health Services* 11.4, 559–572.

  (2003). "The Health Crisis in Argentina." *International Journal of Health Services* 33.1, 129–136.

Espinel, E., et al. (1998). "Transformaciones del sector salud en la Argentina." Publication 48. Buenos Aires: PAHO. http://www.ops.org.ar/FuentesInfo/PublicacArg/Publicacion48.pdf (retrieved May 5, 2004).

Esrey, S. A. (1996). "Water, Waste, and Well-Being." *American Journal of Epidemiology* 143.6, 608–623.

Etchemendy, S., Palermo, V. (1998). "Conflicto y concertación." *Desarrollo Económico* 37.148, 559–590.

Evans, P. (1995). *Embedded Autonomy*. Princeton, NJ: Princeton University Press.

Fagen, R. (1969). *The Transformation of Political Culture in Cuba*. Stanford, CA: Stanford University Press.

FAO [Food and Agriculture Organization] (1999). *Perfiles Nutricionales por Países: Costa Rica*. Rome. http://www.fao.org/Regional/LAmerica/prior/segalim/accalim/costar/COS.pdf (retrieved Jun 29, 2003).

Faria, L. R. de (1995). "Os primeiros anos da reforma sanitária no Brasil e a atuação da Fundação Rockefeller (1915–1920)." *Physis: Revista de Saúde Coletiva* [Instituto de Medicina Social, UERJ] 5.1, 109–127.

Ferreira, F. H. G., Leite, P. G., Litchfield, J. A. (2006). "The Rise and Fall of Brazilian Inequality: 1981–2004." World Bank Policy Research Working Paper 3867.

FGV-EPOS [Consórcio Fundacão Getúlio Vargas – EPOS Health Consultants] (2001). "Determinacão do Custo do Programa de Saúde da Família – PSF. Relatório Final." 1.3. Versão Revisada. Brasília: Ministério da Saúde. http://dtr2004.saude.gov.br/dab/caadab/estudos.php (retrieved Jan 9, 2007).

Fields, G. S. (1992). "Living Standards, Labor Markets, and Human Resources in Taiwan." In Ranis, G., ed., *Taiwan: From Developing to Mature Economy*. Boulder, CO: Westview.

Figueres Ferrer, J. (1973). *La pobreza de las naciones*. 3rd ed. San José, CR: Imprenta Nacional.

Filmer, D., Hammer, J. S., Pritchett, L. H. (2000). "Weak Links in the Chain." *World Bank Research Observer* 15.2, 199–224.

(2002). "Weak Links in the Chain II." *World Bank Research Observer* 17.1, 47–66.

Filmer, D., Pritchett, L. (1999). "The Impact of Public Spending on Health." *Social Science and Medicine* 49.10 1309–1323.

Fiszbein, A. (1999). "Institutions, Service Delivery and Social Exclusion." Prepared for the Decentralization Colloquium, Department of Political Science, Yale University, January 28, 2000.

Fogel, R. W. (2004). *The Escape from Hunger and Premature Death, 1700–2100*. Cambridge: Cambridge University Press.

Ford, N., Koetsawang, S. (1991). "The Socio-Cultural Context of the Transmission of HIV in Thailand." *Social Science and Medicine* 33.4, 405–414.

Foreit, K. G., Koh, K. S., Suh, M. H. (1980). "Impact of the National Family Planning Program on Fertility in Rural Korea." *Studies in Family Planning* 11.3, 79–90.

Foxley, A., Raczynski, D. (1984). "Vulnerable Groups in Recessionary Situations." *World Development* 12.3, 223–246.

Frankenberg, E. (1995). "The Effects of Access to Health Care on Infant Mortality in Indonesia." *Health Transition Review* 5.2, 143–163.

Frankenberg, E., Suriastini, W., Thomas, D. (2005). "Can Expanding Access to Basic Healthcare Improve Children's Health Status?" *Population Studies* 59.1, 5–19.

Frankenberg, E., Thomas, D. (2001). "Women's Health and Pregnancy Outcomes." *Demography* 38.2, 253–265.

Freedman, R., et al. (1994). "The Fertility Transition in Taiwan." In Thornton, A., Lin, H.-S., eds., *Social Change and the Family in Taiwan*. Chicago: University of Chicago Press, 264–304.

Freedman, R., Takeshita, J.Y. (1969). *Family Planning in Taiwan*. Princeton, NJ: Princeton University Press.

Freedom House (2007). "Freedom in the World Country Ratings 1972–2006." http://www.freedomhouse.org/template.cfm?page=5 (retrieved Apr 22, 2007).

Freeman, R.B., Medoff, J.L. (1984). *What Do Unions Do?* New York: Basic Books.

Friedman, B.L., Hausman, L. (1993). "Poverty and Social Protection in Korea." In Krause, L., Park, F.K., eds., *Social Issues in Korea*. Seoul: Korea Development Institute.

Friend, T. (2003). *Indonesian Destinies*. Cambridge, MA: Belknap.

FRS/RSMLAC [Foro-Red de Salud y Derechos Sexuales y Reproductivos-Chile/ Red de Salud de las Mujeres Latinoamericanas y del Caribe] (2003). "Atención Humanizada del Aborto Inseguro en Chile." Santiago, Chile: FRS/RSMLAC. http://www.forosalud.cl/forosalud/revista/uploaded/atencion_%20humanizada.htm (retrieved Jan 8, 2006).

Galiani, S., Gertler, P., Schargrodsky, E. (2005). "Water for Life." *Journal of Political Economy* 113.1, 83–120.

Gall, N. (1972). "Births, Abortions and the Progress of Chile." *American Universities Field Staff Reports*, West Coast South America Series 19.2. http://www.norman-gall.com/chile_art1.htm (retrieved Jul 5, 2003).

Gallup, J.L., Gaviria, A., Lora, E. (2003). *Is Geography Destiny?* Stanford, CA: Stanford University Press.

Gallup, J.L., Mellinger, A., Sachs, J.D. (2001). "General Measures of Geography." http://www2.cid.harvard.edu/ciddata/Geog/physfact.csv (retrieved Jan 16, 2002).

Gallup, J.L., Sachs, J.D. (with Mellinger, A.). (1999). "Geography and Economic Development." Working Paper 1, Center for International Development, Harvard University (April). http://www2.cid.harvard.edu/ciddata/geodata.csv (associated data retrieved Jan 15, 2002).

Gardiner, P., Oey, M. (1983). *Morbidity and Mortality in Java 1880–1940*. Yogyakarta: Population Studies Center, Gadjah Mada University.

Garnier, L., et al. (1997). "Costa Rica: Social Development and Heterodox Adjustment." In Mehrotra, S., Jolly, R., eds., *Development with a Human Face*. Oxford: Clarendon.

Gasparini, L. (2004). "Poverty and Inequality in Argentina." CEDLAS-The World Bank. http://www.depeco.econo.unlp.edu.ar/cedlas/monitoreo/default.html (retrieved Feb 18, 2008).

Gauri, V. (1998). *School Choice in Chile*. Pittsburgh, PA: University of Pittsburgh Press.

(2002). "Brazil: Maternal and Child Health." World Bank Report 23811-BR. Washington, DC: World Bank.

(2004). "Social Rights and Economics." *World Development* 32.3, 465–477.

Gauri, V., Khaleghian, P. (2002). "Immunization in Developing Countries. *World Development* 30.12, 2109–2132.

Gauri, V., Lieberman, E.S. (2004). "AIDS and the State." Prepared for the annual meeting of the American Political Science Association, Chicago, September 2–5, 2004.

(2006). "Boundary Institutions and HIV/AIDS Policy in Brazil and South Africa." *Studies in Comparative International Development* 41.3, 47–73.

Gaviria, A., Panizza, U., Wallack, J.S. (2003). "Economic, Social and Demographic Determinants of Political Participation in Latin America." *Latin American Journal of Economic Development* [Universidad Católica de Bolivia] 3, 151–182.

http://www.geocities.com/upanizza/Participation_2004_GPS.doc (ms. version retrieved Aug 14, 2006).

Geddes, B. (1990). "How the Cases You Choose Affect the Answers You Get." *Political Analysis* 2.1, 131–152.

(1994). *Politician's Dilemma*. Berkeley: University of California Press.

Gelb, A., et al. (1988). *Oil Windfalls: Blessing or Curse?* New York: Oxford University Press.

Gereffi, G., Wyman, D.L., eds. (1990). *Manufacturing Miracles*. Princeton, NJ: Princeton University Press.

Gerring, J. (2001). *Social Science Methodology*. New York: Cambridge University Press.

(2007). *Case Study Research*. New York: Cambridge University Press.

Gerring, J., et al. (2005). "Democracy and Economic Growth." *World Politics* 57.3, 323–364.

Gerring, J., Seawright, J. (2007). "Techniques for Choosing Cases." In Gerring, J., *Case Study Research*. New York: Cambridge University Press, 86–150.

Gerring, J., Thacker, S.C. (2001). "Political Institutions and Human Development." Prepared for the Northeast Universities Development Consortium Conference, Boston University, Boston, MA, September 28–30. http://www.bu.edu/sthacker/papers.html (retrieved Mar 15, 2002).

Gerring, J., Thacker, S.C., Alfaro, R. (2005). "Democracy and Human Development." Prepared for the annual meeting of the American Political Science Association, Washington, DC, September 1–4.

Ghai, D., ed. (2000). *Social Development and Public Policy: Some Lessons from Successful Experiences*. New York: St. Martin's.

Ghobarah, H.A., Huth, P., Russett, B. (2004). "Comparative Public Health." *International Studies Quarterly* 48.1, 73–94.

Ghuman, S.J. (2003). "Women's Autonomy and Child Survival." *Demography* 40.3, 419–436.

Giaconi Gandolfo, J., Montesinos B.N., Schalchli, V.A. (1988). "Rural Health Care in Chile." *The Journal of Rural Health* 4.1, 71–85.

Gold, T.B. (1986). *State and Society in the Taiwan Miracle*. Armonk, NY: M.E. Sharpe.

Goldenberg, B. (1964). *Los sindicatos en América Latina*. Hannover: Verlag für Literatur und Zeitgeschehen.

Goldstein, M.S., Donaldson, P.J. (1979). "Exporting Professionalism." *Journal of Health and Social Behavior* 20.4, 322–337.

González García, G. (1997). *Mas salud por el mismo dinero*. Buenos Aires: ISALUD.

González Jansen, I. (1986). *La Triple-A*. Buenos Aires: Contrapunto.

González Rozada, M., Menéndez, A. (2002). "Public University in Argentina." *Economics of Education Review* 21.4, 341–351.

González Vega, C., Céspedes, V. (1993). "Costa Rica." In Rottenberg, S., ed., *The Political Economy of Poverty, Equity, and Growth: Costa Rica and Uruguay*. New York: Oxford University Press.

Goodman, R., Peng, I. (1996). "The East Asian Welfare States." In Esping-Anderson, G., ed., *Welfare States in Transition*. Thousand Oaks, CA: Sage, 192–224.

Gore, F. (2000). Subsecretario de Salud, Provincia del Neuquén, Argentina. Personal communication by email, November 28, 2000.

Gorosito, J. (2000). Ministro de Gobierno, Educación y Justicia, Provincia del Neuquén, Argentina. Personal communication by email, December 29, 2000.

Goulart, F. A. de A. (2002). "Experiências em Saúde da Família." PhD Diss., Fundação Oswaldo Cruz, Rio de Janeiro. http://desterro.tripod.com/documentos/tese_doutorado (retrieved Jul 6, 2006).

Graham, C. (1994). *Safety Nets, Politics, and the Poor.* Washington, DC: Brookings Institution Press.

Grassi, E., Hintze, S., Neufeld, M. R. (1994). *Políticas sociales, crisis y ajuste estructural.* Buenos Aires: Espacio Editorial.

Green, A. (2000). "Reforming the Health Sector in Thailand." *International Journal of Health Planning and Management* 15.1, 39–59.

Grindle, M. (2004). *Despite the Odds.* Princeton, NJ: Princeton University Press.

Gunawan, S. (2001). "Jayawijaya Women and Their Children's Health Project." Jakarta. http://papuaweb.org/dlib/lap/watch/2001-gunawan.pdf (retrieved May 13, 2003).

Gupta, S., Verhoeven, M., Tiongson, E. R. (2003). "Public Spending on Health Care and the Poor." *Health Economics* 12.8, 685–696.

Gutiérrez Góngora, J. (2007). Personal interview, San José, Costa Rica, February 1. Dr. Góngora was a member of the Board of Directors, Caja Costarricense de Seguro Social, 1970–1978.

Gutiérrez Sáenz, R. (2004). "La Facultad de Medicina y universalización de los Seguros Sociales." In Miranda Gutiérrez, G., and Zamora Zamora, C., eds., *La construcción de la seguridad social.* San José, CR: Editorial Universidad Estatal a Distancia, 201–232.

Haggard, S. (1990). *Pathways from the Periphery.* Ithaca, NY: Cornell University Press.

Haggard, S., Kaufman, R. R. (2008). *Development, Democracy, and Welfare States.* Princeton, NJ: Princeton University Press.

Hakim, P., Solimano, G. (1978). *Development, Reform and Malnutrition in Chile.* Cambridge, MA: MIT Press.

Haliman, A., Williams, G. (1983). "Can People Move Bureaucratic Mountains?" *Social Science and Medicine* 17.19, 1149–1455.

Hall, A. (2006). "From Fome Zero to Bolsa Família." *Journal of Latin American Studies* 38.4, 689–709.

Halstead, S. B., Walsh, J. A., Warren, K. S., eds. (1985). *Good Health at Low Cost.* New York: The Rockefeller Foundation.

Han, L.-W. (1956). *Taiwan Today.* 3rd ed. Taipei: Hwa Kuo.

Hanzich, J. (2005). "A Man on a Mission." *Harvard International Review* 27.2, 28–31.

Harpelle, R. N. (1993). "The Social and Political Integration of West Indians in Costa Rica: 1930–50." *Journal of Latin American Studies* 25.1, 103–120.

Harris, B. (2004). "Public Health, Nutrition, and the Decline of Mortality." *Social History of Medicine* 17.3, 379–407.

Harrison, L. E. (1992). *Who Prospers?* New York: BasicBooks.

Hatt, L., et al. (2007). "Did the Strategy of Skilled Attendance at Birth Reach the Poor in Indonesia?" *Bulletin of the World Health Organization* 85.10, 774–782.

Haynal, A. P. (1959). *Thailand's Rural Health Program and the Role of U.S. Assistance in Its Recent Development.* Bangkok: United States Operations Mission Thailand.

Heaver, R., Kachondam, Y. (2002). "Thailand's National Nutrition Program." HNP Discussion Paper 25551. Washington, DC: World Bank. http://www.worldbank.org/reference/ (retrieved Nov 21, 2006).

Heclo, H. (1978). "Issue Networks and the Executive Establishment." In King, A., ed., *The New American Political System*. Washington, DC: American Enterprise Institute, 87–124.

Heller, L. (2006). "Access to Water Supply and Sanitation in Brazil." Human Development Report Office Occasional Paper 2006/24. New York: United Nations Development Programme. http://hdr.undp.org/en/reports/global/hdr2006/papers/ (retrieved Jul 24, 2008).

Henderson, G. (1968). *Korea: The Politics of the Vortex*. Cambridge, MA: Harvard University Press.

Henshaw, S.K., Singh, S., Haas, T. (1999). "The Incidence of Abortion Worldwide." *International Family Planning Perspectives* 25, Supplement, S30-S38.

Hernández Valle, R. (2006). "Regulación jurídica de los partidos políticos en Costa Rica." In Zovatto, D., ed., *Regulación jurídica de los partidos políticos en América Latina*. Mexico: Instituto de Investigaciones Jurídicas, Universidad Nacional Autónoma de México, 367–411.

Herrán, C.A., Rodríguez, A. (2001). "Secondary Education in Brazil." Inter-American Development Bank Report BR-014. Washington, DC: Inter-American Development Bank. http://www.iadb.org/int/DRP/Ingles/Red4/educationdocs.htm (retrieved Jul 6, 2001).

Hertzman, C. (2001). "Health and Human Society." *American Scientist* 89.6, 538–545.

Heston, A., Summers, R., Aten, B. (2002). Penn World Table Version 6.1. Center for International Comparisons, University of Pennsylvania, October 2002. http://pwt.econ.upenn.edu (retrieved Oct 20, 2002).

(2006). Penn World Table Version 6.2. Center for International Comparisons, University of Pennsylvania, September 2006. http://pwt.econ.upenn.edu (retrieved Jun 22, 2007).

Hewison, K. (2004). "Crafting Thailand's New Social Contract." *Pacific Review* 17.4, 503–522.

Hicks, A., Swank, D. (1984). "On the Political Economy of Welfare Expansion." *Comparative Political Studies* 17.1, 81–119.

Hill, H. (2000). *The Indonesian Economy*. 2nd ed. Cambridge: Cambridge University Press.

Hill, K. (1991). "Approaches to the Measurement of Child Mortality." *Population Index* 57.3, 368–382.

Hill, K., AbouZahr, C., Wardlaw, T. (2001). "Estimates of Maternal Mortality for 1995." *Bulletin of the World Health Organization* 79.3, 182–193.

Hill, K., et al. (1999). *Trends in Child Mortality in the Developing World: 1960–1996*. New York: UNICEF.

(2007a). "Estimates of Maternal Mortality Worldwide Between 1990 and 2005." *Lancet* 370.9595, 1311–1319.

(2007b). "Epidemiologic Transition Interrupted: A Reassessment of Mortality Trends in Thailand, 1980–2000." *International Journal of Epidemiology* 36.2, 374–384.

Hirschman, A. (1987). "The Political Economy of Latin American Development." *Latin American Research Review* 22.3, 7–36.

Hirschman, C., Guest, P. (1990). "The Emerging Demographic Transitions of Southeast Asia." *Population and Development Review* 16.1, 121–152.

Hobcraft, J.N. (1993). "Women's Education, Child Welfare and Child Survival." *Health Transition Review* 3.2, 159–175.

Hochman, G. (1998). "Great Hospital, Vast Backlands." Prepared for the 1998 meeting of the Latin American Studies Association, Chicago, September 24–26.
　(2005). "Reformas, instituições e políticas de saúde no Brasil (1930–1945)." *Educar em Revista* [Universidade Federal do Paraná] 25, 127–141.
Hojman, D. E. (1989). "Neoliberal Economic Policies and Infant and Child Mortality." *World Development* 17.1, 93–108.
Horn, J. J. (1985). "Brazil: The Health Care Model of the Military Modernizers and Technocrats." *International Journal of Health Services* 15.1, 47–68.
Horowitz, D. L. (1985). *Ethnic Groups in Conflict*. Berkeley: University of California Press.
Hsu, S.-C. (1970). "Family Planning in Taiwan, 1949–1970." *Industry of Free China* 34.6, 7–17.
　(1972). "Nutrition in Taiwan." *Industry of Free China* 38.1, 2–20.
Htun, M. (2003). *Sex and the State*. New York: Cambridge University Press.
Huber, E. (1996). "Options for Social Policy in Latin America." In Esping-Andersen, G., ed., *Welfare States in Transition*. London: Sage, 141–191.
Huber, E., et al. (2006). "Politics and Inequality in Latin America and the Caribbean." *American Sociological Review* 71.6, 943–963.
Huber, E., Stephens, J. D. (2001). *Development and Crisis of the Welfare State*. Chicago: University of Chicago Press.
Hughes, D., Leethongdee, S. (2007). "Universal Coverage in the Land of Smiles." *Health Affairs* 26.4, 999–1008.
Hugo, G. J., et al. (1987). *The Demographic Dimension in Indonesian Development*. Singapore: Oxford University Press.
Hull, T. H. (1987). "Fertility Decline in Indonesia." *International Family Planning Perspectives* 13.3, 90–95.
　(1989). "The Hygiene Program in the Netherlands East Indies." In Cohen, P., Purcal, J. T., eds., *The Political Economy of Primary Health Care in Southeast Asia*. Canberra: Australian Development Studies Network, 140–148.
Hume, D. (1978 [1740].) *A Treatise of Human Nature*. 2nd ed. Oxford: Clarendon.
Hunter, W. A. (1997). *Eroding Military Influence in Brazil*. Chapel Hill: University of North Carolina Press.
Hunter, W. A., Power, T. J. (2007). "Rewarding Lula." *Latin American Politics and Society* 49.1, 1–30.
Hytrek, G. (1995). "Labor and Social Development." *Journal of Third World Studies* 12.2, 73–102.
IADB [Inter-American Development Bank] (2000). *Development Beyond Economics*. Washington, DC: IADB.
IADB (2003). "Costa Rica: Innovation Loan for Health Sector Development." Proposal CR-0114, approved January 30, 2003. Washington, DC: IADB. http://www.iadb. org/exr/ENGLISH/PROJECTS/cr1451e.pdf (retrieved Jun 28, 2003).
Idiart, A. (2002). "Neo-Liberal Experiments, State Reform, and Social Policy in the 1980s and the 1990s." PhD Diss., Emory University.
　(2004). "Institutional Factors and Neo-Liberal Trends." Prepared for the 16th annual meeting of the Society for Socio-Economics, Washington, DC, July 8–11, 2004. http://www.sase.org/conf2004/papers/idiart_alma.pdf (retrieved Jun 12, 2006).
ILO [International Labour Office] (2002). Laborsta database. http://laborsta.ilo.org/ cgi-bin/brokerv8.exe (retrieved Dec 4, 2002).

Indonesia. BPS [Badan Pusat Statistik-Statistics Indonesia] and ORC Macro (2003). *Indonesia Demographic and Health Survey 2002–2003.* Calverton, MD: BPS, ORC Macro.

Indonesia. CBS [Central Bureau of Statistics] (1995). *Indonesia Demographic and Health Survey 1994.* Calverton, MD: CBS, Macro International. http://www.measuredhs.com/pubs/pdftoc.cfm?ID=104 (retrieved Jun 10, 2005).

Indonesia. MoH [Ministry of Health] (2000). *Indonesia Health Profile 1999.* Jakarta: Ministry of Health. http://www.depkes.go.id/english/Statistics/index.htm (retrieved Apr 16, 2003).

Ipsen, C. (1996). *Dictating Demography.* New York: Cambridge University Press.

Iskandar, M.B. (1997). "Health and Mortality." In Jones, G.W., Hull, T.H., eds., *Indonesia Assessment.* Singapore: Institute for Southeast Asian Studies, 205–231.

Isuani, E.A., Mercer, H. (1988). *La fragmentación institutional del sector salud.* Buenos Aires: Centro Editor de Américal Latina.

Isuani, E.A., Tenti, E. (1989). "Una interpretación global." In Isuani, E.A., et al., eds., *Estado democratico y política social.* Buenos Aires: Eudeba.

Jankilevich, A. (2003). *Historia de la Seguridad Social Argentina.* Buenos Aires: Asociación Argentina de Historia de Hospitales y Organizaciones de Socorro. http://www.hospitalycomunidad.com.ar/Anterior/default.htm (retrieved Jan 28, 2003).

Jara Vargas, A. (2002). "Médicos y Seguridad Social En Costa Rica durante las décadas de 1950 y 1960." Prepared for the Mesa de Historia Cultural, VI Congreso Centroamericano de Historia, Universidad de Panamá, July 22–26, 2002. http://www.historia.fcs.ucr.ac.cr/hca/cong/mesas/cong6/docs/HistCult/ajara.doc (retrieved Sep 19, 2006).

Jarvis, L.S. (1985). *Chilean Agriculture under Military Rule.* Berkeley: Institute of International Studies, University of California.

Jatene, A. (2001). "The Structure of Primary Care." In Molina, C.G., Nuñez del Arco, J., eds., *Health Services in Latin America and Asia.* Washington, DC: Inter-American Development Bank and Johns Hopkins University Press, 111–118.

Jenkins, R. (1991). "The Political Economy of Industrialization." *Development and Change* 22.2, 197–231.

Jiménez, J., Romero, M.I. (2007). "Reducing Infant Mortality in Chile." *Health Affairs* 26.2, 458–465.

Johannes, L. (2007). "Output-based Aid in Health." *OB Approaches* 39608, Note 13. Washington, DC: The Global Partnership on Output-Based Aid. http://www.gpoba.org/publications/approaches.asp (retrieved Jul 15, 2008).

Johnson, C. (1987). "Political Institutions and Economic Performance." In Deyo, F.C., ed., *The Political Economy of the New Asian Industrialism.* Ithaca, NY: Cornell University Press, 136–164.

Johnson, L.J. (1967). "Problems of Import Substitution." *Economic Development and Cultural Change* 15.2, Part 1, 202–216.

Johnston, W. (1995). *The Modern Epidemic.* Cambridge, MA: Council on East Asian Studies, Harvard University.

Jones, G.W. (2003). "Strategies and Achievements in Expanding Lower Secondary Enrollments: Thailand and Indonesia." Asian MetaCentre Research Paper Series 13. Asia Research Institute, National University of Singapore. http://www.populationasia.org/Publications/Research_Papers.htm (retrieved Nov 13, 2006).

Jones, G., et al. (2003). "How Many Child Deaths Can We Prevent This Year?" *Lancet* 362.9377, 65–71.

Jones, G., Hagul, P. (2001). "Schooling in Indonesia." *Bulletin of Indonesian Economic Studies* 37.2, 237–232.

Jones, M.P. (2005). "The Role of Parties and Party Systems in the Policymaking Process." Prepared for the Inter-American Development Bank Workshop on "State Reform, Public Policies, and Policymaking Processes," February 28–March 2. Washington, DC: IADB. http://www.iadb.org/res/publications/pubfiles/pubS-310.pdf (retrieved Aug 31, 2005).

Joo, J. (1999). "Explaining Social Policy Adoption in South Korea." *Journal of Social Policy* 28.3, 387–412.

Jost, J.T., Banaji, M.R., Prentice, D., eds. (2004). *Perspectivism in Social Psychology.* Washington, DC: American Psychological Association Press.

Ju, J.S. (2000). "Nutrition in the Republic of Korea." *British Journal of Nutrition* 84 Supplement 2, S195-S198.

Katakura, Y., Bakalian, A. (1998). "PROSANEAR: People, Poverty, and Pipes." Working Paper, UNDP-World Bank Water and Sanitation Program. http://www.wsp.org/pdfs/working_prosanear.pdf (retrieved Jul 9, 2001).

Katz, P.R. (1996). "Germs of Disaster." *Annales de Demographie Historique*, 195–220.

Kaufman, R.R., Nelson, J.M. (2004). "Conclusions." In Kaufman, R.R., Nelson, J.M., eds., *Crucial Needs, Weak Incentives.* Baltimore, MD: Johns Hopkins University Press, 473–519.

Kaufman, R.R., Segura-Ubiergo, A. (2001). "Globalization, Domestic Politics, and Social Spending in Latin America." *World Politics* 53.4, 553–587.

Keefer, P., Khemani, S. (2005). "Democracy, Public Expenditures, and the Poor." *World Bank Research Observer* 20.1, 1–27.

Kennedy, B.P., Kawachi, I., Prothrow-Stith, D. (1996). "Income Distribution and Mortality." *British Medical Journal* 312, 1004–1007.

Khoman, S. (1993). "Education Policy." In Warr, P.J., ed., *The Thai Economy in Transition.* New York: Cambridge University Press, 325–354.

(1995). "Thailand's Industrialization." In Krongkaew, M., ed., *Thailand's Industrialization and Its Consequences.* New York: St. Martin's Press, 289–323.

Kim, K., Moody, P.M. (1992). "More Resources Better Health?" *Social Science and Medicine* 34.8, 837–842.

Kim, Y.B. (1980). "Education and Economic Growth." In Park, C.K., ed., *Human Resources and Social Development in Korea.* Seoul: Korean Development Institute, 234–273.

King, G., Keohane, R.O., Verba, S. (1994). *Designing Social Inquiry.* Princeton, NJ: Princeton University Press.

King, G., Tomz, M., Wittenberg, J. (2000). "Making the Most of Statistical Analyses." *American Journal of Political Science* 44.2, 347–361.

King, P.J. (1989). "Comparative Analysis of Human Rights Violations under Military Rule in Argentina, Brazil, Chile, and Uruguay." In Wilkie, J.M., Ochoa, E., eds., *Statistical Abstract of Latin America*, Vol. 27. Los Angeles, CA: UCLA Latin American Center.

Kinugasa, T., Mason, A. (2007). "Why Countries Become Wealthy." *World Development* 35.1, 1–23.

Kiranandana, T., Tontisirin, K. (1992). "Eradicating Child Malnutrition." Innocenti Occasional Papers EPS 23. http://ideas.repec.org/s/ucf/iopeps.html (retrieved Mar 22, 2009).

Kirby, E. S. (1960). *Rural Progress in Taiwan.* Taipei: Chinese-American Joint Commission on Rural Reconstruction.

Kittikanya, C. (2005). "State Hospitals Left Behind in Race." *Bankok Post, Economic Review, Year-End 2005.* http://www.bangkokpost.net/yearend2005/page52.html (retrieved Nov 23, 2006).

Kleinman, A. (1980). *Patients and Healers in the Context of Culture.* Berkeley: University of California Press.

Klieman, A. S. (1981). "Indira's India." *Political Science Quarterly* 96.2, 241–259.

Knodel, J. E., Chamratrithirong, A., Debavalya, N. (1986). "The Cultural Context of Thailand's Fertility Decline." *Asia-Pacific Population Journal* 1.1, 23–48.

Korea, Republic of (1982). *The Fifth Five-Year Economic and Social Development Plan, 1982–1986.* Seoul: Government of the Republic of Korea.

Korea, Republic of, NHIC [Republic of Korea, National Health Insurance Corporation] (2002). "Outline of the National Health Insurance Program." http://www.nhic. or.kr/wbe/wbeb/2002/11/19/207,250,0,0,0.html (retrieved Jan 3, 2004).

Korea, Republic of, NSO [Republic of Korea, National Statistical Office] (1994). *Korea Statistical Yearbook 1994.* Seoul: NSO.

Korea, Republic of, NSO (1998). *Korea Statistical Yearbook 1998.* Seoul: NSO.

Kristiansen, S., Santoso, P. (2006). "Surviving Decentralisation?" *Health Policy* 7.3, 247–259.

Krongkaew, M. (1982). "The Distribution of and Access to Basic Health Services in Thailand." In Richards, P., ed., *Basic Needs and Government Policies in Thailand.* Singapore: Maruzen Asia, 33–65.

Krongkaew, M. (1995). "Contributions of Agriculture to Industrialization." In Krongkaew, M., ed., *Thailand's Industrialization and Its Consequences.* New York: St. Martin's Press, 289–323.

Kruk, M. E., et al. (2007). "Health Care Financing and Utilization of Maternal Health Services in Developing Countries." *Health Policy and Planning* 22.5, 303–310.

Ku, Y.-W. (1997). *Welfare Capitalism in Taiwan.* New York: St. Martin's Press.

Kuo, W.-H. (2002). "Building Practical Statehood for an Authoritative Regime." Prepared for the International Conference on the History of Science in East Asia, Shanghai, August 20–23, 2002.

Kurzman, C., Werum, R., Burkhart, R. E. (2002). "Democracy's Effect on Economic Growth." *Studies in Comparative International Development* 37.1, 3–33.

Kuznets, S. (1955). "Economic Growth and Income Inequality." *American Economic Review* 45.1, 1–28.

Kwon, H.-J. (1999). *The Welfare State in Korea.* New York: St. Martin's Press.

Kwon, S. (1993). *Social Policy in Korea.* Seoul: Korea Development Institute.

(2003a). "Healthcare Financing Reform and the New Single Payer System in the Republic of Korea." *International Social Security Review* 56.1, 75–94.

(2003b). "Health and Health Care." *Social Indicators Research* 62–63.1–3, 171–186.

(2003c). "Payment System Reform for Health Care Providers in Korea." *Health Policy and Planning* 18.1, 84–92.

(2003d). "Pharmaceutical Reform and Physician Strikes in Korea." *Social Science and Medicine* 57.3, 529–538.

Kwon, S., and Reich, M. R. (2003). "The Changing Process and Politics of Health Policy in Korea." Center for Population and Development Studies, Harvard University. Revised June 24, 2003.

Kwon, T.-H. (1986). *The Trends and Patterns of Mortality and Health in the Republic of Korea*. Bangkok: UN Economic and Social Commission for Asia and the Pacific.

Kwon, T.-H., et al. (1975). *The Population of Korea*. Seoul: The Population and Development Studies Center, Seoul National University.

La Porta, R., et al. (1998). "The Quality of Government." National Bureau of Economic Research Working Paper 6727. http://www.nber.org/papers/w6727 (retrieved Feb 27, 2002).

Lai, T.-H., Myers, R.H., Wou, W. (1991). *A Tragic Beginning*. Stanford, CA: Stanford University Press.

Lake, D.A., Baum, M.A. (2001). "The Invisible Hand of Democracy." *Comparative Political Studies* 34.6, 587–621.

Landsberger, H.A., MacDaniel, T. (1976). "Hypermobilization in Chile: 1970–1973." *World Politics* 28.4, 502–541.

Lane, R.E. (2003). "Rescuing Political Science from Itself." In Sears, D.O., Huddy, L., Jervis, R., eds., *Oxford Handbook of Political Psychology*. New York: Oxford University Press, 755–793.

Larrañaga, O. (2001). "Distribución de ingresos: 1958–2001." In French-Davis, R., Stallings, B., eds., *Reformas, crecimiento y políticas sociales en Chile desde 1973*. Santiago, Chile: CEPAL, 295–328.

Lasswell, H.D. (1936). *Politics: Who Gets What, When and How?* New York: McGraw Hill.

Lavín, J. (1987). *Miguel Kast: Pasión de vivir*. 3rd ed. Santiago, Chile: Zig-Zag.

Lee, C.Y., Kim, E. (2002). "Case Study: Republic of Korea." In Brodsky, J., Habib, J., Hirschfeld, M., eds., *Country Case Studies on Long-Term Care*. Volume 1: Developing Countries. Geneva: World Health Organization. http://www.who.int/chronic_conditions/casestudies/en/ (retrieved Jan 7, 2004).

Lee, H. (2000). "Poverty and Income Distribution in Argentina." In World Bank, *Poor People in a Rich Country*. Vol. 2. Washington, DC: World Bank, 2000.

Lee, J.-C. (2003). "Health Care Reform in South Korea." *American Journal of Public Health* 93.1, 48–51.

Lee, J.-C., Kee, C.-D. Kee (1996). "The Rise of Western Medicine and the Decline of Traditional Medicine in Korea, 1876–1910." *Korean Journal of Medical History* 5.1, 1–10. http://medhist.kams.or.kr/abstract.asp?body=199606 (retrieved Nov 5, 2006).

Lee, M.-L. (2001). "Health Care in Taiwan – Past, Present and Future." Speech, 54th World Health Assembly, Geneva, 14 May. http://www.gio.gov.tw/taiwan-website/4-oa/politics/hct20011205.htm (retrieved Jan 12, 2007).

Lee, Y.-J., Parish, W.L., Willis, R.J. (1994). "Sons, Daughters, and Intergenerational Support in Taiwan." *American Journal of Sociology* 99.4, 1010–1041.

Leinbach, T.R. (1984). "Rural Services Delivery in Indonesia." In Lonsdale, R.E., Enyedi, G., eds., *Rural Public Services: International Comparisons*. Boulder, CO: Westview, 297–314.

Leonfanti, F.L., Chiesa, M.E. (1988). "Neuquen, Argentina: Provincial Health Policies and Their Results." *Journal of Rural Health* 4.1, 59–70.

Levcovitz, E., et al. (2000). "Brazil: Restructuring Local Healthcare Systems, Finance, and Delivery: The Case of Camaragibe." For a forum on "The Challenge of Health Reform," San José, CR, May 24–26, 2000. http://wbln0018.worldbank.org/LAC/LACInfoClient. nsf/49a0102c9b95cf028525664b006a17a4/c18a0c3de46a38f5852568d50052 5f47/$FILE/BRAZIL+Fam+engl.pdf (retrieved Jul 21, 2001).

Levitsky, S., Murillo, M. V. (2008). "Argentina: From Kirchner to Kirchner." *Journal of Democracy* 19.2, 16–30.

Lewis, J.P., Kapur, D. (1990). "An Updating Country Study: Thailand's Needs and Prospects in the 1990s." *World Development* 18.10, 1363–1378.

Lewis, P.H. (2004). "The 'Gender Gap' in Chile." *Journal of Latin American Studies* 36.4, 719–742.

Lieberman, E. S. (2005). "Nested Analysis as a Mixed-Method Strategy for Comparative Research." *American Political Science Review* 99.3, 435–452.

Lieberman, S., Marzoeki, P. (2000). "Health Strategy in a Post-Crisis, Decentralizing Indonesia." World Bank Report No. 21318-IND. http://siteresources.worldbank. org/INTINDONESIA/Resources/Human/Health.pdf (retrieved Sep 21, 2002).

Lima, N. T. (2007). "Public Health and Social Ideas in Modern Brazil." *American Journal of Public Health* 97.7, 1168–1177.

Lin, K. (1994). "Taiwan's Health Care Reform in Comparative Perspectives." Department of Sociology, Yale University. http://twrf.formosa.org/kuoming/ PAPER1.htm (retrieved Sep 11, 2003).

Litsios, S. (2002). "The Long and Difficult Road to Alma-Ata." *International Journal of Health Services* 32.4, 709–732.

Liu, C.-T. (1998). "Health Care Systems in Transition II. Taiwan, Part I." *Journal of Public Health Medicine* 20.1, 5–10.

Liu, E., Lee, J. (1998). "Health Care Expenditure and Financing in Taiwan." Document RP08/PLC. Hong Kong: Legislative Council. http://www.legco.gov.hk/yr97–98/ english/sec/library/08plc.pdf (retrieved Jul 16, 2002).

Livi-Bacci, M. (2001). *A Concise History of World Population*. 3rd ed. Malden, MA: Blackwell.

Livingstone, M., Raczynski, D. (1974). "Análisis cuantitativo de la evolución de algunas variables de salud durante el periodo 1964–1972." CEPLAN Documento 40. Santiago, Chile: Universidad Católica de Chile, Centro de Estudios de Planificación Nacional.

Lloyd-Sherlock, P. (1997). "Policy, Distribution, and Poverty in Argentina Since Redemocratization." *Latin American Perspectives* 24.6, 22–55.

(2000a). "Failing the Needy." *Journal of International Development* 12.1, 101–119.

(2000b). "Healthcare Financing, Reform and Equity in Argentina." In Lloyd-Sherlock, P., ed., *Healthcare Reform and Poverty in Latin America*. London: Institute of Latin American Studies, University of London, 143–162.

(2004). "Ambitious Plans, Modest Outcomes: The Politics of Health Care Reform in Argentina." In Kaufman, R.R., Nelson, J.M., eds., *Crucial Needs, Weak Incentives*. Baltimore, MD: Johns Hopkins University Press, 93–123.

(2005). "Health Sector Reform in Argentina." *Social Science and Medicine* 60, 1893–1903.

(2006). "When Social Health Insurance Goes Wrong." *Social Policy and Administration* 40.4, 353–368.

Lo Vuolo, R. (1995). "The Welfare State in Contemporary Argentina." Democracy and Social Policy Working Paper 2, Kellogg Institute, University of Notre Dame.

Lobato, L. (2000). "Reorganizing the Health Care System in Brazil." In Fleury, S., Belmartino, S., Baris, E., eds., *Reshaping Health Care in Latin America*. Ottawa: International Development Research Centre. http://www.idrc.ca (retrieved Apr 12, 2001).

Lobato, L., Burlandy, L. (2000). "The Context and Process of Health Care Reform in Brazil." In Fleury, S., Belmartino, S., Baris, E., eds., *Reshaping Health Care in Latin America*. Ottawa: International Development Research Centre. http://www.idrc.ca (retrieved Apr 12, 2001).

Londoño, J.L., Székely, M. (1997). "Persistent Poverty and Excess Inequality." Working Paper 357, Office of the Chief Economist, Inter-American Development Bank. http://www.iadb.org/res/publications/pubfiles/pubWP-357.pdf (retrieved Feb 3, 2004).

Loveman, B. (1979). *Chile: The Legacy of Hispanic Capitalism*. New York: Oxford University Press.

Low, S. (1985). *Culture, Politics, and Medicine in Costa Rica*. Bedford Hills, NY: Redgrave.

Lu, J.-F.R., Hsiao, W.C. (2003). "Does Universal Health Insurance Make Health Care Unaffordable? Lessons From Taiwan." *Health Affairs* 22.3, 75–88.

Lucas, R. (1993). "Making a Miracle." *Econometrica* 61.2, 251–272.

Lynch, J.W., et al. (2000). "Income Inequality and Mortality." *British Medical Journal* 320.7243, 1200–1204.

Lyttleton, C. (2000). *Endangered Relations*. Bangkok: White Lotus.

MacEwan, A. (1999). *Neo-Liberalism or Democracy?* London: Zed.

Macinko, J., et al. (2007). "Going to Scale With Community-Based Primary Care." *Social Science and Medicine* 65.10, 2070–2080.

Macinko, J., Guanais, F.C., Marinho de Souza, M.F. (2006). "Evaluation of the Impact of the Family Health Program on Infant Mortality in Brazil, 1990–2002." *Journal of Epidemiology and Community Health* 60.1, 13–19.

MacIntyre, A.J. (1994). "Business, Government, and Development." In MacIntyre, A.J., ed., *Business and Government in Industrializing Asia*. Ithaca, NY: Cornell University Press, 1–28.

Maddison, A. (2001). *The World Economy: Historical Statistics*. Table 3, Per Capita GDP. Database file updated 2001. http://www.eco.rug.nl/~Maddison/Historical_Statistics/horizontal-file.xls (retrieved Jul 12, 2005).

(2007). "World Population, GDP and Per Capita GDP, 1–2003 AD." Updated August 2007. Faculty of Economics, University of Groningen. http://www.ggdc.net/maddison/ (retrieved Apr 2, 2008).

Mainwaring, S.P. (1999). *Rethinking Party Systems in the Third Wave of Democratization*. Stanford, CA: Stanford University Press.

Malloy, J.M. (1977). "Social Security Policy and the Working Class in Twentieth-Century Brazil." *Journal of Interamerican Studies and World Affairs* 19.1, 35–60.

(1979). *The Politics of Social Security in Brazil*. Pittsburgh, PA: University of Pittsburgh Press.

(1991). "Statecraft, Social Policy, and Governance in Latin America." Working Paper 151, Kellogg Institute, University of Notre Dame.

Mamalakis, M.J., ed. (1980). *Historical Statistics of Chile*. Vol. 2. Westport, CT: Greenwood.

Mansilla, C.R. (1983). *Los partidos provinciales*. Buenos Aires: Centro Editor de América Latina.

Marcel, M., Solimano, A. (1994). "The Distribution of Income and Economic Adjustment." In Bosworth, B.P., Dornbusch, R., Labán, R., eds., *The Chilean Economy*. Washington, DC: Brookings Institution Press, 217–256.

Marín Camacho, D. (2006). "El EBAIS que viaja con las olas." *Infocaja* 7 June 2006. http://www.ccss.sa.cr/ (retrieved Sep 17, 2006).

Marín, F. (2007). Personal interview, San José, Costa Rica, February 5. Vice Minister of Health, Costa Rica, 1994–1998.

Marmot, M., Wilkinson, R.G. (2001). "Psychosocial and Material Pathways in the Relation Between Income and Health: A Response to Lynch et al." *British Medical Journal* 322.7296, 1233–1236.

Marshall, M.G., Jaggers, K. (2000). "Polity IV Project: Dataset Users Manual." College Park: Center for International Development and Conflict Management, University of Maryland. December 1. http://www.bsos.umd.edu/cidcm/inscr/polity/index.htm (retrieved Nov 30, 2001).

(2006). "Polity IV Project: Political Regime Characteristics and Transitions, 1800–2004." p4v2006. http://www.systemicpeace.org/polity/polity4.htm (retrieved Oct 7, 2007).

Marshall, T.H. (1950). "Citizenship and Social Class." In Marshall, T.H., *Citizenship and Social Class and Other Essays*. Cambridge: Cambridge University Press, 1–85.

Martin, M.P. (2000). "Integration and Development." In Toloza, C., Lahera, E., eds., *Chile in the Nineties*. Stanford, CA: Stanford University Libraries, 309–347.

Martine, G. (1996). "Brazil's Fertility Decline, 1965–95." *Population and Development Review* 22.1, 47–75.

Martínez Franzoni, J. (1999). "Poder y alternativas." *Anuario de Estudios Centroamericanos* [Universidad de Costa Rica] 25.1, 159–182.

Martz, J.D. (1967). "Costa Rican Electoral Trends, 1953–1966." *The Western Political Quarterly* 20.4, 888–909.

Mason, E.S., et al. (1980). The Economic and Social Modernization of the Republic of Korea. Cambridge, MA: Harvard University Press.

Mason, J.B., et al. (2006). "Community Health and Nutrition Programs." In Jamison, D.T., et al., eds., *Disease Control Priorities in Developing Countries*. Washington, DC: World Bank, 1053–1074. http://www.dcp2.org/pubs/DCP (retrieved Aug 16, 2006).

Mata, L. (1985). "The Fight Against Diarrhoeal Diseases." In Vallin, J., Lopez, A.D., eds., *Health Policy, Social Policy, and Mortality Prospects*. Liège: International Union for the Scientific Study of Population.

(1990). "Health and Social Development Programme (HSDP), Costa Rica." In Jennings, J., et al., eds., *Managing Successful Nutrition Programmes*. Nutrition Policy Discussion Paper 8, United Nations Administrative Committee on Coordination – Subcommittee on Nutrition. http://www.unsystem.org/SCN/Publications/NPP/nutpolicypapers.htm (retrieved Aug 16, 2006).

(1991). "Reduction of Infant Mortality in Costa Rica and Possibility for Further Improvement." Prepared for the National Council for International Health (NCIH) workshops on Rural Health and Infant Mortality in the United States, Durham and Boston.

Mathews, T. J., MacDorman, M. F. (2008). "Infant Mortality Statistics from the 2005 Period Linked Birth/Infant Death Data Set." *National Vital Statistics Reports* 57.2, 1–32. Hyattsville, MD: National Center for Health Statistics.

Mauldin, W. P., et al. (1974). "A Report on Bucharest." *Studies in Family Planning* 5.12, 357–395.

McGreevy, W. P., et al. (1984). *Política e financimento do sistema de saúde Brasileiro.* Brasília: Instituto de Planejamento Econômico e Social.

McGreevy, W. P., Piola, S., Magalhães Vianna, S. (1989). "Health and Health Care Since the 1940s." In Bacha, E. L., Klein, H. S., eds., *Social Change in Brazil, 1945–1985.* Albuquerque: University of New Mexico Press, 311–343.

McGuire, J. W. (1995a). "Development Policy and Its Determinants in East Asia and Latin America." *Journal of Public Policy* 14.2, 205–242.

(1995b). "Interim Government and Democratic Consolidation." In Shain, Y., Linz, J.J., *Between States.* Cambridge: Cambridge University Press.

(1996). "Strikes in Argentina." *Latin American Research Review* 31.3, 127–150.

(1997). *Peronism without Perón: Unions, Parties, and Democracy in Argentina.* Stanford, CA: Stanford University Press.

(1999). "Labor Union Strength and Human Development in East Asia and Latin America." *Studies in Comparative International Development* 33.4, 3–34.

(2001). "Social Policy and Mortality Decline in East Asia and Latin America." *World Development* 29.10, 1673–1697.

(2005). "Democracy, Social Service Provision, and Under-5 Mortality." Prepared for the 2005 annual meeting of the American Political Science Association, Washington, DC, September 1–4. http://condor.wesleyan.edu/jmcguire/ (retrieved Mar 22, 2009).

(2006). "Basic Health Care Provision and Under-5 Mortality." *World Development* 34.3, 405–425.

(2009). Web Appendices for this book on the Cambridge University Press website at http://www.cambridge.org/us/catalogue/catalogue.asp?isbn=9780521515467

McGuire, J. W., Frankel, L. B. (2005). "Mortality Decline in Cuba, 1900–1959." *Latin American Research Review* 40.2, 84–116.

McGuire, W. J. (1999). *Constructing Social Psychology.* New York: Cambridge University Press.

McKeown, T. (1976). *The Modern Rise of Population.* New York: Academic Press.

McNicoll, G. (2006). "Policy Lessons of the East Asian Demographic Transition." *Population and Development Review* 32.1, 1–25.

Measham, A. R. (1975). "Latin America 1974: An Overview." *Studies in Family Planning* 6.8, 281–282.

Médici, A. (2002). "La desregulación de las Obras Sociales." Washington, DC: Inter-American Development Bank. http://www.iadb.org/sds/doc/Desregulacion.pdf (retrieved Mar 8, 2004).

Mehrotra, S. (1997a). "Social Development in High-Achieving Countries." In Mehrotra, S., Jolly, R., eds., *Development with a Human Face.* Oxford: Clarendon, 21–62.

(1997b). "Health and Education Policies in High-Achieving Countries." In Mehrotra, S., Jolly, R., eds., *Development with a Human Face.* Oxford: Clarendon, 63–110.

Mehrotra, S., Jolly, R., eds. (1997). *Development with a Human Face.* Oxford: Clarendon.

Mehrotra, S., Park, I.-H., Baek, H.-J. (1997). "Social Policies in a Growing Economy." In Mehrotra, S., Jolly, R., eds., *Development with a Human Face.* Oxford: Clarendon, 264–296.

Meller, P. (2002). "El cobre chileno y la política minera." Documento de Trabajo 142, Centro de Economía Aplicada, Universidad de Chile. http://www.cea-uchile.cl/ pags/publicaciones/index.html (retrieved Jul 2, 2003).

Mellington, N., Cameron, L. (1999). "Female Education and Child Mortality in Indonesia." *Bulletin of Indonesian Economic Studies* 35.3, 115–144.

Meltzer, A. H., Richard, S. F. (1981). "A Rational Theory of the Size of Government." *Journal of Political Economy* 89.5, 914–927.

Mena, I., Belleï, C. (2000). "The New Challenge: Quality and Equity in Education." In Toloza, C., Lahera, E., eds., *Chile in the Nineties.* Stanford, CA: Stanford University Libraries, 349–391.

Merrick, T. W. (1985). "The Effect of Piped Water on Early Childhood Mortality in Urban Brazil, 1970 to 1976." *Demography* 22.1, 1–23.

Mesa-Lago, C. (1978). *Social Security in Latin America.* Pittsburgh, PA: University of Pittsburgh Press.

(1985). "Health Care in Costa Rica." *Social Science and Medicine* 21.1, 13–21.

(2000a). *Market, Socialist, and Mixed Economies.* Baltimore, MD: Johns Hopkins University Press.

(2000b). "Achieving and Sustaining Social Development with Limited Resources: The Case of Costa Rica." In Ghai, D., ed., *Social Development and Public Policy.* New York: St. Martin's, 277–322.

(2008). *Reassembling Social Security.* New York: Oxford University Press.

Midré, G. (1992). "Bread or Solidarity? Argentine Social Policies, 1983–1990." *Journal of Latin American Studies* 24.2, 343–373.

Mikhanorn, J. (2003). Personal interview, College of Public Health, Chulalongkorn University, Bangkok, January 9. Dr. Mikhanorn was a leader of Thailand's Rural Primary Health Care Expansion Project (1978–1986).

Mikhanorn, J., ed. (1991). *Report of the Evaluation of the First Decade of Primary Health Care in Thailand (1978–1987).* Bangkok: Ministry of Public Health, Office of the Primary Health Care Committee.

Milevcic, C. (2002). Personal interview with L. Oster, a research associate of the author, Santiago, Chile, May 2, 2002. Ms. Milevcic was at this time the Executive Director of the Fundación Miguel Kast in Chile.

Miller, E. D. (1993). "Labour and the War-Time Alliance in Costa Rica 1943–1948." *Journal of Latin American Studies* 25.3, 515–541.

Mills, A. (1991). "Exempting the Poor: The Experience of Thailand." *Social Science and Medicine* 33.11, 1241–1252.

Miranda Gutiérrez, G. (1995). "Development of the Social Security Institute." In Muñoz, C., Scrimshaw, N., eds., *The Nutrition and Health Transition of Democratic Costa Rica.* Boston, MA: International Foundation for Developing Countries, 33–59.

(2003). "La seguridad social costarricense." In Bustamante, X., Alfaro, B., eds., *100 años de salud: Costa Rica, Siglo XX.* San José, CR: Ministerio de Salud/PAHO, 244–267.

(2007). Personal interview, San José, Costa Rica, January 29. Dr. Miranda from 1970 to 1990 was a leader of Costa Rica's Caja Costarricense de Seguro Social.

Miranda, E., Scarpaci, J.L., Irarrázaval, I. (1995). "A Decade of HMOs in Chile." *Health & Place* 1.1: 51–59.

Mirzaee, M. (1979). "Trends and Determinants of Mortality in Taiwan, 1895–1975." PhD diss., University of Pennsylvania.

Mishima, S.M., et al. (1992). "Agentes Comunitários de Saúde: Bom para o Ceará. bom para o Brasil?" *Saúde em Debate* 37, 70–75.

Mississippi. SDH [State Department of Health] (2008). "Vital Statistics: Mississippi, 2005." http://www.msdh.state.ms.us/phs/stat2005.htm (retrieved Aug 23, 2008).

Mitchell, B.R. (1981). *European Historical Statistics 1750–1975.* 2nd ed. New York: Facts on File.

Mohs, E. (1983). *La salud en Costa Rica.* San José, CR: Editorial Universidad Estatal a Distancia.

——— (1995). "Health Policies and Strategies." In Muñoz, C., Scrimshaw, N.S., eds., *The Nutrition and Health Transition of Democratic Costa Rica.* Boston, MA: International Foundation for Developing Countries. http://www.unu.edu/unupress/food2/UIN05E/UIN05E00.HTM (retrieved Aug 16, 2006).

——— (2002). "Un mundo posible." *Revista Panamericana de Salud Pública* 11.2, 69–71.

Molina Jiménez, I., Lehoucq, F. (1999). "Political Competition and Electoral Fraud." *Journal of Interdisciplinary History* 30.2, 199–234.

Molina Silva, S. (1972). *El proceso de cambio en Chile: la experiencia 1965–1970.* Santiago, Chile: Editorial Universitaria.

Molina, N. (1989). "Propuestas políticas y orentaciones de cambio en la situación de la mujer." In Garretón, M.A., Cox, C.D., eds., *Propuestas políticas y demandas sociales.* Vol. 3. Santiago, Chile: Facultad Latinoamericana de Ciencias Sociales, 61–80.

Monckeberg, F. (2003). "Prevención de la desnutrición en Chile." *Revista Chilena de Nutrición* 30.1, 160–176.

Monsalvo, J. (2003). "A 25 años de Alma Ata." Unpublished paper, Sociedad Argentina de Medicina Antropológica. http://www.sama.org.ar/25.htm (retrieved Feb 10, 2004).

Montlake, S. (2002). "Developing Nations Watch Thailand's Bold Healthcare Plan." *Christian Science Monitor,* August 14, 2002, Section 2, 7.

Moon, B.E. (1991). *The Political Economy of Basic Human Needs.* Ithaca, NY: Cornell University Press.

Moon, C.-I., Yang, J.J. (2002). "Globalization, Social Inequality, and Democratic Governance in South Korea." In Tulchin, J., Brown, A., eds., *Democratic Governance and Social Inequality.* Boulder, CO: Lynne Rienner.

Moreno, E. (1979). "La mortalidad infantil en la Provincia de Neuquén, Argentina." In Organización Panamericana de Salud, ed., *Condiciones de salud del niño en las Américas.* Washington, DC: Organización Panamericana de Salud.

Morgan, L.M. (1987). "Health without Wealth? Costa Rica's Health System under Economic Crisis." *Journal of Public Health Policy* 8.1, 86–105.

——— (1989). "Health Effects of the Costa Rican Economic Crisis." In Edelman, M., Kenen, J, eds., *The Costa Rica Reader.* New York: Grove Weidenfeld, 213–218.

——— (1990). "International Politics and Primary Health Care in Costa Rica." *Social Science and Medicine* 30.2, 211–219.

——— (1993). *Community Participation in Health.* New York: Cambridge University Press.

Morley, S.A. (2001). *The Income Distribution Problem in Latin America and the Caribbean.* Santiago, Chile: CEPAL. http://www.eclac.cl/publicaciones/xml/3/7213/lcg2127i.pdf (retrieved Apr 7, 2007).

Morris, M.D. (1979). *Measuring the Condition of the World's Poor: The Physical Quality of Life Index.* New York: Pergamon.

Morsch, E., et al. (2001). "The Effects of the Family Health Program on Child Health in Ceará State, Northeastern Brazil." *Archives of Public Health* 59, 151–165. http://www.iph.fgov.be/aph/pdf/aphfull59_151_165.pdf (retrieved Jul 14, 2006).

Mosley, W.H., Chen, L.C. (1984). "An Analytical Framework for the Study of Child Survival in Developing Countries." *Population and Development Review* 10 (Supplement), 24–45.

Muangman, D. (1987). "Prince Mahidol: Father of Public Health and Modern Medicine in Thailand." *Asia Pacific Journal of Public Health* 1.4, 72–75.

Muller, E.N. (1988). "Democracy, Economic Development, and Income Inequality." *American Sociological Review* 53.2, 50–68.

Munck, G., Verkuilen, J. (2002). "Conceptualizing and Measuring Democracy: Evaluating Alternative Indices." *Comparative Political Studies* 35.1, 5–34.

Munck, R. (1998). "Mutual Benefit Societies in Argentina." *Journal of Latin American Studies* 30.3, 573–590.

Muñoz Retana, C., Valverde, J.M. (1995). "Problems and Challenges of the Health Sector During the 1980s." In Muñoz, C., Scrimshaw, N.S., eds., *The Nutrition and Health Transition of Democratic Costa Rica.* Boston, MA: International Foundation for Developing Countries. http://www.unu.edu/unupress/food2/UIN05E/uino5eoo.htm#Contents (retrieved Jun 28, 2003).

Murphy, K.M., Schleifer, A., Vishny, R.W. (1989). "Industrialization and the Big Push." *Journal of Political Economy* 97.5, 1003–1026.

Murray, C.J.L. (1988). "The Infant Mortality Rate, Life Expectancy at Birth, and a Linear Index of Mortality as Measures of General Health Status." *International Journal of Epidemiology* 17.1, 122–128.

(2007). "Towards Good Practice for Health Statistics." *Lancet* 369, 862–873.

Murray, C.J.L., Yang, G., Qiao, X. (1992). "Adult Mortality: Levels, Patterns, and Causes." In Feachem, R.G.A., et al., *The Health of Adults in the Developing World.* New York: Oxford University Press, 23–110.

Murthi, M., Guio, A.-C., Drèze, J. (1995). "Mortality, Fertility, and Gender Bias in India." *Population and Development Review* 21.4, 745–782.

Muscat, R.J. (1990). *Thailand and the United States.* New York: Columbia University Press.

(1994). *The Fifth Tiger.* Armonk, NY: M.E. Sharpe.

Musgrove, P. (1996). "Public and Private Roles in Health." Discussion Paper 339. Washington, DC: World Bank Health, Nutrition and Population Division. http://www.eldis.org/static/DOC11001.htm (retrieved Jul 28, 2004).

Nash, N.C. (1993). "Chile Advances in a War on Poverty." *New York Times* (April 4), A14.

Navarro, V. (1974). "What Does Chile Mean?" *Milbank Memorial Fund Quarterly* 52.2, 93–130.

Negri, B. (2000). "Primary Health Care: Fewer Diseases, More Life." In Ministério da Saúde, Secretaria Executiva, *Priority Actions in Primary Health Care.* Brasília, DF: Ministério da Saúde. http://dtr2001.saude.gov.br/bvs/publicacoes/capa_priority.pdf (retrieved Jul 14, 2006).

Nelson, J.M. (1992). "Poverty, Equity, and the Politics of Adjustment." In Haggard, S., Kaufman, R.R., eds., *The Politics of Economic Adjustment*. Princeton, NJ: Princeton University Press.

(2004a). "External Models, International Influence, and the Politics of Social Sector Reforms." In Weyland, K., ed., *Learning from Foreign Models in Latin American Policy Reform*. Washington, DC: Woodrow Wilson Center Press, 35–52.

(2004b). "The Politics of Health Sector Reform: Cross-National Comparisons." In Kaufman, R.R., Nelson, J.M., eds., *Crucial Needs, Weak Incentives*. Baltimore, MD: Johns Hopkins University Press, 23–64.

(2007). "Elections, Democracy, and Social Services." *Studies in Comparative International Development* 41.4, 79–97.

Neri, A. (1982). *Salud y política social*. Buenos Aires: Hachette.

Neri, M.C., et al. (1999). "Brasil." In Ganuza, E., Sauma, P., León, A., eds., *Gasto público, gasto social y servicios sociales básicos en América Latina y el Caribe*. New York: United Nations Development Programme. http://www.undp.org/rblac/documents/poverty/gastosoc/bra.pdf (retrieved Jul 4, 2001).

Neumann, N.A., et al. (1999). "Desempenho da pastoral da criança na promoção de ações de sobrevivência infantil e na educação em saúde em Criciúma." *Revista Panamericana de Salud Pública* 5.6, 400–410.

(2002). "Impacto da Pastoral da Criança sobre a nutrição de menores de cinco anos no Maranhão: Uma análise multinível." *Revista Brasileira de Epidemiologia* 5.1, 30–40.

Neuquén (Provincia del). Consejo de Planificación, Comité Permantente (1968). "Diagnostico preliminar de la situación de la provincia del Neuquén y fundamentación del plan de trabajos públicos 1968." Tomo 1 (Relación General). Ms., Marzo 1968.

Neuquén (Provincia del). DPEC [Dirección Provincial de Estadística y Censos] (2008). "Tasa de mortalidad infantil, neonatal y postneonatal registradas según año. Provincia del Neuquén. Años 1980–2006." http://www3.neuquen.gov.ar/dgecyd/flash/indexflash.htm (retrieved Jul 14, 2008).

Neuquén (Provincia del). Ministerio de Salud Pública (1990). *Estado, sociedad, salud: Neuquén (1944–1972). Investigación histórica sobre el Plan de Salud Neuquino. Primera Parte*. Neuquén, Argentina: Ministerio de Salud Pública de la Provincia del Neuquén, Departamento de Historia de la Universidad Nacional de Comahue.

Neuquén (Provincia del). SS/MDS [Subsecretaría de Salud, Ministerio de Desarrollo Social] (2000). Unpublished data on birth rates and mortality rates in Argentina and in the Province of Neuquén, 1941–1999, kindly provided by Fernando Gore, Subsecretario de Salud, Provincia del Neuquén, as an email attachment on November 29, 2000.

Newhouse, J.P. (1977). "Medical-Care Expenditure: A Cross-National Survey." *Journal of Human Resources* 12.1, 115–125.

Nitayarumphong, S., et al. (2001). *Macro-Economic Adjustment Policy, Health Sector Reform and Linkages with Accessibility, Utilization, and Quality of Health Services in Thailand*. Ottawa: International Development Research Consortium. http://www.idrc.ca/mimap/maphealth/pdf/Thailand.pdf (retrieved Jul 22, 2002).

Nooruddin, I., Simmons, J.W. (2004). "Institutions, Constituencies, and Public Services Spending." Prepared for the annual meeting of the Southern Political

Science Association, New Orleans, LA, January 2004. Revised March 3, 2004. http://www-personal.umich.edu/~irfann/research/humandev.pdf (retrieved Sep 24, 2004).

Nugent, J.B. (1991). "The Demise of Economic Development in Latin America and Its Implications for Other Developing Countries." *Journal of Economic Development* 16.1, 7–35.

Nunn, A. (2009). *The Politics and History of AIDS Treatment in Brazil*. New York: Springer.

Nunn, F.M. (1970). *Chilean Politics 1920–1931*. Albuquerque: University of New Mexico Press.

Nussbaum, M. (2000). *Women and Human Development: The Capabilities Approach*. Cambridge: Cambridge University Press.

Nyerere, J. (1969). "Socialism and Rural Development." In Svendsen, K., Teisen, M., *Self-Reliant Tanzania*. Dar es Salaam: Tanzania Publishing House, 246–266.

Oconitrillo, E. (1981). *Un siglo de política costarricense*. San José, CR: Editorial Universidad Estatal a Distancia.

O'Donnell, G. (1978). "State and Alliances in Argentina, 1955–1976." *Journal of Development Studies* 15.1, 3–33.

(1984). "¿Y a mi que me importa?" Working Paper 9, Kellogg Institute, University of Notre Dame.

(1988). *Bureaucratic Authoritarianism: Argentina, 1966–1973*. Berkeley: University of California Press.

Oey-Gardiner, M. (1997). "Educational Developments, Achievements and Challenges." In Jones, G.W., Hull, T.H., eds., *Indonesia Assessment*. Singapore: Institute for Southeast Asian Studies, 135–166.

Olshansky, S.J., Carnes, B.A., Cassel, C. (1990). "In Search of Methuselah: Estimating the Upper Limits to Human Longevity." *Science* 250.4981, 634–640.

Olshansky, S.J., Carnes, B.A., Désesquelles, A. (2001). "Prospects for Human Longevity." *Science* 291.5508, 1491–1492.

Omestad, T. (1988). "Dateline Taiwan: A Dynasty Ends." *Foreign Policy* 71, 176–198.

O'Neill, B.C., Balk, D. (2001). "World Population Futures." *Population Bulletin* 56.3, 3–40.

Oppenheim, L.H. (1999). *Politics in Chile*. 2nd ed. Boulder, CO: Westview.

Oxhorn, P.D. (1995). *Organizing Civil Society*. University Park, MD: Penn State Press.

Pachanee, C.-A., Wibulpolprasert, S. (2006). "Incoherent Policies on Universal Coverage of Health Insurance and Promotion of International Trade in Health Services in Thailand." *Health Policy and Planning* 21.4, 310–318.

PAHO [Pan American Health Organization] (1970). *Las condiciones de salud en las Américas 1965–1968*. Washington, DC: PAHO.

PAHO (1986a). *Evaluation of the Strategy for Health for All by the Year 2000*. Seventh Report on the World Health Situation. Vol. 3: Region of the Americas. Washington, DC: PAHO.

PAHO (1986b). *Health Conditions in the Americas, 1981–1984*. Vol. 2. Washington, DC: PAHO.

PAHO (1988). *Los servicios de salud en las Américas: Análisis de indicadores básicos*. Cuaderno Técnico 14. Washington, DC: PAHO.

PAHO (1998a). *Health in the Americas*. 1998 ed. 2 Vols. Washington, DC: PAHO.

PAHO (1998b). *Health Statistics from the Americas*. 1998 ed. Washington, DC: PAHO.

PAHO (2000a). *Situación de salud en las Américas: Indicadores básicos 2000.* Washington, DC: Programa Especiál de Análisis de Salud, PAHO.

PAHO (2000b). *Roll Back Malaria in Meso America.* Document PAHO/HCP/ HCT/181/01. http://www.paho.org/English/HCP/HCT/MAL/rbm-mesoamerica. htm (retrieved Jun 28, 2003).

PAHO (2003). *PAHO Health Accounts Data Spreadsheets.* http://www.iadb.org/sds/ specialprograms/lachealthaccounts/CreatingHA/data_sources_en.htm (retrieved Jun 30, 2008).

PAHO (2007). *Health in the Americas.* 2007 ed. 2 Vols. Washington, DC: PAHO.

Pak, S. (2004). "The Biological Standard of Living in the Two Koreas." *Economics and Human Biology* 2.3, 511–521.

Palermo, V. (1988). *Neuquén: la creación de una sociedad.* Buenos Aires: Centro Editor de América Latina.

Palloni, A., Rafalimanana, H. (1999). "The Effects of Infant Mortality on Fertility Revisited." *Demography* 36.1, 41–58.

Palmer, S. (2003). *From Popular Medicine to Medical Populism.* Durham, NC: Duke University Press.

Pannarunothai, S., Patmasiriwat, D., Srithamrongsawat, S. (2004). "Universal Health Coverage in Thailand." *Health Policy* 68.1, 17–30.

Park, C.K. (1980). "The Organization, Financing, and Cost of Health Care." In Park, C.K., ed., *Human Resources and Social Development in Korea.* Seoul: Korean Development Institute, 97–168.

Park, C., Kim, M. (1998). "Current Poverty Issues and Counter Policies in Korea." Seoul: Korea Institute for Health and Social Affairs and United Nations Development Programme.

Park, J.H. (1998). *The Saemaul Undong Movement.* Seoul: Korea Rural Economics Institute.

Parsell, D.P. (1998). "Maternal Death Rate Tough to Reduce." *The Indonesian Observer* (April 12), Focus, 3.

Pastoral da Criança (2000). Untitled document. http://www.rebidia.org.br/pastoral/ ingles/index.html (retrieved Jun 26, 2001).

Pastoral da Criança (2006). "Razão de Mortes de Crianças menores de 1 ano por mil nascidos vivos na Pastoral da Criança – CNBB, Brasil – 1991/2003." http:// www.pastoraldacrianca.org.br/htmltonuke.php?filnavn=resultados/razao_mort_ menores_1ano.html (retrieved Jul 11, 2006).

Paus, E. (1994). "Economic Growth through Neoliberal Restructuring?" *Journal of Developing Areas* 28.1, 31–56.

Pautassi, L.C. (2001). "Equidad de género y calidad en el empleo." Comisión Económica de América Latina, Unidad Mujer y Desarrollo, Serie Mujer y Desarrollo 30. Santiago, Chile: CEPAL. http://www.eclac.cl/publicaciones/UnidadMujer/6/ LCL1506P/lcl1506e.pdf (retrieved Mar 26, 2004).

Peabody, J.W., Lee, S.-W., Bickel, S.R. (1995). "Health for All in the Republic of Korea." *Health Policy* 31.1, 29–42.

Peliano, A.M. (1992). "Os programas de alimentação e nutrição para mães e crianças no Brasil." In Monteiro M.F.G., Cervini, R., orgs., *Perfil estatístico de crianças e mães no Brasil.* Rio de Janeiro: Ministério da Economia, Fazenda e Planejamento / Fundação Instituto Brasileiro de Geografia e Estatística, 111–127.

—— (1993). *O mapa da fome.* 3 Vols. Instituto de Pesquisa Económica Aplicada. Documentos de Política 14, 15, 17. Brasília: IPEA.

Pérez Yrigoyen, C. (1989). "Política pública y salud." In Isuani, E., et al., eds., *Estado democratico y política social*. Buenos Aires: Eudeba.

Perrone, N. (2000). Former Subsecretario de Salud, Provincia del Neuquén, Argentina. Personal communication by email, December 18, 2000.

Persson, T., Tabellini, G. (1994). "Is Inequality Harmful for Growth?" *American Economic Review* 84.3, 600–621.

Pessino, C., Andrés, L. (2002). "Argentina and Brazil: A Comparison of Poverty Profiles and Socioeconomic Outcomes in Volatile Economies." Prepared for the Inter-American Development Bank. 3rd Draft, September. http://home.uchicago. edu/~luis/research.html (retrieved Feb 7, 2004).

Peterson, C.E. (2000). "The 1993 Indonesian Family Life Survey: Appendix E, User's Guide." Document DRU-1195/6-NICHD/AID (February). National Institute for Child Health and Human Development; Agency for International Development Labor and Population Program. http://ftp.rand.org/software_and_data/FLS/ iflsi/IFLSdocs/DRU1195.6/DRU1195.6.appc.pdf (retrieved Oct 2, 2002).

Phongpaichit, P., Baker, C. (2002). *Thailand: Economy and Politics*. 2nd ed. New York: Oxford University Press.

Pinto, V.G. (1984). *Saúde para poucos ou para muitos*. Brasília: Instituto de Planejamento Econômico e Social.

Pitanguy, J. (1994). "Feminist Politics and Reproductive Rights: The Case of Brazil." In Sen, G., Snow, R.C., eds., *Power and Decision*. Cambridge, MA: Harvard University Press, 101–122.

Plank, D.N., Sobrinho, J.A., Xavier, A.C. (1996). "Why Brazil Lags Behind in Educational Development." In Birdsall, N., Sabot, R.A. eds., *Opportunity Foregone: Education in Brazil*. Washington, DC: Inter-American Development Bank, 117–146.

PLN (1973). "Documento de trabajo para la definición de la política de salud durante el periodo del gobierno 1974–1978." Comisión de Salud, Planes y Programas.

PLN [Partido de Liberación Nacional, Costa Rica] (1968). "Patio de Agua: Manifiesto Democrático para una Revolución Social." http://www.pln.or.cr/docs/patio.htm (retrieved Sep 9, 2006).

Pongpanich, S. (2003). Personal interview, College of Public Health, Chulalongkorn University, Bangkok, January 9, 2003. Dr. Sathirakorn Pongpanich was on this date a faculty member in the College of Public Health.

Porapakkham, Y. (1986). *Levels and Trends of Mortality in Thailand*. Asian Population Studies Series 77. Bangkok: United Nations Economic and Social Commission for Asia and the Pacific.

Potter, J.E. (1988). "Does Family Planning Reduce Infant Mortality?: Comment." *Population and Development Review* 14.1, 179–187.

Potter, J.E., Schmertmann, C.P., Cavenaghi, S. (2002). "Fertility and Development: Evidence From Brazil." *Demography* 39.4, 739–761.

Prawiro, R. (1998). *Indonesia's Struggle for Economic Development*. New York: Oxford University Press.

Pritchett, L., Summers, L.H. (1996). "Wealthier is Healthier." *Journal of Human Resources* 31.4, 841–868.

Programa de Economía del Trabajo (1992). *Series de indicadores económico sociales. Series anuales 1960–1991*. Santiago, Chile: Programa de Economía del Trabajo.

Przeworski, A., et al. (2000). *Democracy and Development*. New York: Cambridge University Press.

Raczynski, D. (1983). "Reformas al sector salud: Dialogos y debates." *Colección Estudios CIEPLAN* 10.70, 5–44.

(1991). "Social Policy and Economic Change in Chile, 1974–1985." *International Journal of Health Services* 21.1, 17–47.

(1994). "Social Policies in Chile." Democracy and Social Policy Working Paper 4, Kellogg Institute, University of Notre Dame.

(2000). "Overcoming Poverty in Chile." In Tulchin, J.S., Garland, A.M., eds., *Social Development in Latin America.* Boulder, CO: Lynne Rienner.

Raczynski, D., Oyarzo, C. (1981). "¿Por que cae la tasa de mortalidad infantil en Chile?" *Colección Estudios CIEPLAN* 6.55, 45–84.

Rajkumar, A.S., Swaroop, V. (2002). "Public Spending and Outcomes: Does Governance Matter?" World Bank Policy Research Working Paper 2840. Washington, DC: World Bank.

Ramachandran, V.K. (2000). "Human Development Achievements in an Indian State." In Ghai, D., ed., *Social Development and Public Policy.* New York: St. Martin's, 46–102.

Ramesh, M. (1995a). "Social Security in South Korea and Singapore." *Social Policy and Administration* 29.3, 228–240.

(1995b). "Politics of Illiberal Capitalism." In Dixon, J., Scheurell, R.P., eds., *Social Security Programs: A Cross-Cultural Perspective.* Westport, CT: Greenwood.

Ramesh, M., with Asher, M.G. (2000). *Welfare Capitalism in Southeast Asia.* New York: St. Martin's.

Ramírez Rodríguez, E. (1992). *Evolución Socioeconómica de Costa Rica, 1975–1989.* San José, CR: Escuela de Economía, Universidad Nacional, Ministerio de Planificación Nacional y Política Económica.

Randolph, R.S., Thompson, W.S. (1981). *Thai Insurgency.* Beverly Hills, CA: Sage.

Rao, M.G. (1998). "Accommodating Public Expenditure Policies." *World Development* 26.4, 673–694.

Raper, A.F. (1953). *Rural Taiwan: Problem and Promise.* Taipei: Good Earth Press.

Rattanabirabongse, V., et al. (1998). "The Thailand Land Titling Project." *Land Use Policy* 15.1, 3–23.

Reese, T.H., Soedarmadi, Suyono, H. (1975). "The Indonesian National Family Planning Program." *Bulletin of Indonesian Economic Studies* 11.3, 104–116.

Reich, M.R. (1994). "The Political Economy of Health Transitions in the Third World." In Chen, L., Kleinman, A., Ware, N.C., eds., *Health and Social Change in International Perspective.* Boston, MA: Harvard School of Public Health.

Reichard, S. (1996). "Ideology Drives Health Care Reforms in Chile." *Journal of Public Health Policy* 17.1, 80–98.

Reisman, D.A. (1999). "Payment for Health in Thailand." *International Journal of Social Economics* 26.5, 609–641.

Repetto, F. (2000). "Gestión pública, actores y institucionalidad." *Desarrollo Económico* 39.156, 597–618.

Repetto, F., et al. (2001). "Transferencia de recursos para programas alimentarios en las provincias." Documento 54. Buenos Aires: Centro de Estudios para el Desarrollo Institucional – Fundación Gobierno y Sociedad y Fundación Grupo Sophia.

Reynolds, J. (1973). "Costa Rica: Measuring the Demographic Impact of Family Planning Programs." *Studies in Family Planning* 4.11, 310–316.

Rice-Márquez, N., Baker, T.D., Fischer, C. (1988). "The Community Health Worker: Forty Years of Experience of an Integrated Primary Rural Health Care System in Brazil." *Journal of Rural Health* 4.1, 87–99.

Ricklefs, M.C. (1993). *A Modern History of Indonesia Since c. 1300.* 2nd ed. Stanford, CA: Stanford University Press.

Riggs, F.W. (1952). *Formosa under Chinese Nationalist Rule.* New York: Macmillan.

Ripoll, C.M. (2002). "Evolución historica de la lucha antichagásica en la provincia de Jujuy, Argentina." Organización Panamaericana de Salud, Document OPS/HCP/HCT/216/02, 94–104. http://www.paho.org/spanish/hcp/hct/dch/xi-incosur.htm (retrieved Feb 20, 2004).

Roberts, K.M. (2007). "The Crisis of Labor Politics in Latin America." *International Labor and Working Class History* 72.1, 116–133.

Roberts, W.T. (2006). "Demographic Regimes and the Democracy-Economic Growth Relationship." Ms., Department of Sociology, Colorado College.

Robinson, J., Baland, J.-M. (2005). "Land and Power: Theory and Evidence." Paper 16, Economic History Seminar, University of California, Berkeley. http://repositories.cdlib.org/berkeley_econ211/spring2005/16/ (retrieved Jan 12, 2006).

Rock, D. (1987). "Political Movements in Argentina." In Peralta Ramos, M., Waisman, C.H., eds., *From Military Rule to Liberal Democracy in Argentina.* Boulder, CO: Westview.

Roddick, J. (1988). *The Dance of the Millions.* London: Latin America Bureau.

Rodríguez Aragones, A.R., Mohs Villalta, E., Evans Meza, R. (1971). "Consideraciones acerca del Programa de Salud Rural del Ministerio de Salubridad Pública." San José, CR: Ministerio de Salubridad Pública.

Rodríguez Herrera, A. (2006). "La reforma de salud en Costa Rica." Serie Financiamiento del Desarrollo 173. Santiago, Chile: CEPAL. http://www.eclac.org/publicaciones/ (retrieved Feb 26, 2007).

Rodríguez, F. (1976). "Estructura y características del sector salud en Chile." In Raczynski, D., ed., *Salud pública y bienestar social.* Santiago, Chile: CEPLAN, 65–82.

Rodrik, D. (1994). "King Kong Meets Godzilla." In Fishlow, A., et al., eds., *Miracle or Design? Lessons From the East Asian Experience.* Washington, DC: Overseas Development Council, 13–53.

Roemer, M.I. (1991). *National Health Systems of the World.* Vol. 1. New York: Oxford University Press.

Rogers, G. (2003). "Argentina Puts Health First as it Gets Back on Its Feet." *The Lancet* 362 (July 12), 134.

Rohter, L. (2006). "As Brazil Prepares to Vote, Scandal's Taint Seems to Fade." *New York Times* September 25, 2006, A8.

Rojroongwasinkul, N. (2004). "Income, Income Inequality, and Mortality in Thailand." PhD Diss., Department of Demography, Mahidol University, Bangkok. http://www.ipsr.mahidol.ac.th/content/Publication/onlinelib.htm (retrieved Nov 24, 2006).

Romero, Hernán (1977). "Planificación familiar en Chile." *Revista Médica Chilena* 105.10, 724–730.

Rosenberg, M.B. (1979). "Social Security Policymaking in Costa Rica." *Latin American Research Review* 14.1, 116–133.

——— (1981). "Social Reform in Costa Rica: Social Security and the Presidency of Rafael Angel Calderón." *Hispanic American Historical Review* 61.2, 278–296.

Rosenberg, M.B. (1983). *Las luchas por el seguro social en Costa Rica*. San José, CR: Editorial Costa Rica.

Rosero-Bixby, L. (1985). "The Case of Costa Rica." In Vallin, J., Lopez, A.D., eds., *Health Policy, Social Policy, and Mortality Prospects*. Liège: International Union for the Scientific Study of Population, 341–370.

——— (1986). "Infant Mortality in Costa Rica: Explaining the Recent Decline." *Studies in Family Planning* 17.2, 57–65.

——— (1990). "Socioeconomic Development, Health Interventions and Mortality Decline in Costa Rica." *Scandinavian Journal of Social Medicine*, Supplement 46, 33–42.

——— (1996). "Adult Mortality Decline in Costa Rica." In Feachem, R.G.A., et al., *The Health of Adults in the Developing World*. New York: Oxford University Press, 166–195.

——— (2004a). "Spatial Access to Health Care in Costa Rica and Its Equity." *Social Science and Medicine* 58.7, 1271–1284.

——— (2004b). "Evaluación del impacto de la reforma del sector de la salud en Costa Rica mediante un estudio cuasiexperimental." *Revista Panamericana de Salud Pública* 15.2, 94–103.

Ross, J.A. (2001). Futures Group International Family Planning Effort Scores for 1982, 1989, 1994, and 1999. Kindly provided by Dr. John Ross on October 9, 2001, as an email attachment.

——— (2008). Constella Group Family Planning Program Effort Scores for 2004. Kindly provided by Dr. John Ross on February 24, 2008, as an email attachment.

Ross, J.A., Mauldin, W.P. (1996). "Family Planning Programs: Efforts and Results, 1972–94." *Studies in Family Planning* 27.3, 137–147.

Ross, M.L. (2006). "Is Democracy Good for the Poor?" *American Journal of Political Science* 50.4, 860–874.

Rossi, M.T., Rubilar, A.N. (2007). "Breve reseña histórica de la evolución de los sistemas de salud. El caso argentino." *Revista de la Asociación Médica Argentina* 120.3, 18–39.

Rudra, N., Haggard, S. (2005). "Globalization, Democracy, and Effective Welfare Spending in the Developing World." *Comparative Political Studies* 38.9, 1015–1049.

Ruffino-Netto, A., Azevedo Figueiredo de Souza, A.M. (1999). "Reforma do setor saúde e controle da tuberculose no Brasil." *Informe Epidemiológico do SUS* 8.4, 35–51. http://www.funasa.gov.br/pub/iesus/pdfs/ies843551h.pdf (retrieved Jun 16, 2001).

Ruiz-Tagle, J. (2000). "Balancing Targeted and Universal Social Policies: The Chilean Experience." In Ghai, D., ed., *Social Development and Public Policy*. New York: St. Martin's, 323–360.

Rungpitarangsi, B. (1974). *Mortality Trends in Thailand: Estimates for the Period 1937–1970*. Working Paper 10. Bangkok: Institute of Population Studies, Chulalongkorn University.

Sáenz, L.B. (2007). Personal interview, San José, Costa Rica, February 6. Dr. Sáenz in the mid-1990s directed the Proyecto de Modernización of the Caja Costarricense de Seguro Social, as well as the Equipos Básicos de Atención Integral de Salud (EBAIS) program in Costa Rica.

Salas, A. (2007). Personal interview, San José, Costa Rica, February 6. Dr. Salas served the Caja Costarricense de Seguro Social as Director of Technical

Services (1990–1994), Executive President (1994–1998), and Director of Health Information (2005–2008).

Sandiford, P., et al. (1991). "Why Do Child Mortality Rates Fall? An Analysis of the Nicaraguan Experience." *American Journal of Public Health* 81.1, 30–37.

Sauma, P., Trejos, J.D. (1999). "Costa Rica." In Sauma, P., Ganuza, E., León, A., eds., *Gasto público en servicios sociales básicos en América Latina y el Caribe.* Santiago, Chile: PNUD, CEPAL, UNICEF. http://www.undp.org/rblac/documents/poverty/gastosoc/index.html (retrieved Sep 17, 2003).

Scarpaci, J.L. (1985). "Restructuring Health Care Financing in Chile." *Social Science and Medicine* 21.4, 415–431.

Schattschneider, E.E. (1960). *The Semisovereign People.* New York: Holt, Rinehart, and Winston.

Scheper-Hughes, N. (1992). *Death Without Weeping.* Berkeley: University of California Press.

Schneider, R.M. (1991). *"Order and Progress": A Political History of Brazil.* Boulder, CO: Westview.

Schultz, T.P. (1993). "Returns to Women's Education." In King, E.M., Hill, M.A., eds., *Women's Education in Developing Countries.* Baltimore, MD: Johns Hopkins University Press, 51–59.

Schumpeter, J. (1975 [1942]). *Capitalism, Socialism, and Democracy.* New York: Harper Colophon.

Schwartz, B. (2004). *The Paradox of Choice.* New York: Ecco.

Schwartzman, S. (2000). "Brazil: The Social Agenda." *Dædalus* 129.2, 29–56.

(2005). "Education-Oriented Social Programs in Brazil." Prepared for the Global Development Network conference on "Research for Results in Education," Prague, Czech Republic, March 31 to April 2, 2005. http://www.schwartzman.org.br/simon/pdf/bolsa_escola_eng.pdf (retrieved Jun 30, 2006).

Schwarz, A. (1994). *A Nation in Waiting: Indonesia in the 1990s.* Boulder, CO: Westview.

Scully, T.R. (1995). "Reconstituting Party Politics in Chile." In Mainwaring, S., Scully, T.R., eds., *Building Democratic Institutions.* Stanford, CA: Stanford University Press.

Segundo Foro Social de Salud (2003). "'Salud para todos ya'." *La fogata digital.* http://www.lafogata.org/forosalud/foro10.htm (retrieved Feb 15, 2004).

Seligson, M.A. (1978). "Development and Participation in Costa Rica." In Booth, J.A., Seligson, M.A., eds., *Political Participation in Latin America.* Vol. 1. New York: Holmes & Meier, 145–153.

(1980). *Peasants of Costa Rica and the Development of Agrarian Capitalism.* Madison: University of Wisconsin Press.

(2002). "Trouble in Paradise? The Erosion of System Support in Costa Rica, 1978–1999." *Latin American Research Review* 37.1, 160–185.

Sen, A.K. (1981). "Public Action and the Quality of Life in Developing Countries." *Oxford Bulletin of Economics and Statistics* 43.4, 287–319.

(1985). *Commodities and Capabilities.* Amsterdam: Elsevier.

(1990). "More Than 100 Million Women Are Missing." *New York Review of Books* 37.20, 61–66.

(1993). "Capability and Well-Being." In Nussbaum, M., Sen, A.K., eds., *The Quality of Life.* Oxford: Clarendon.

(1999a). *Development as Freedom.* New York: Alfred A. Knopf.

Sen, A.K. (1999b). "Assessing Human Development: Special Contribution." In United Nations Development Programme, *Human Development Report 1999.* New York: Oxford University Press, 23.

Sepúlveda, C. (1994). "The Right to Child Health: The Development of Primary Health Services in Chile and Thailand." Innocenti Occasional Papers Child Rights Series 7.

Serra, J. (2001). "Addressing Health Inequalities in Brazil." Transcript of presentation at the World Bank seminar on "Addressing Health Inequalities: The Brazilian Experience." World Bank, Washington, DC, April 10, 2001.

    (2002a). *Ampliando o possível.* Rio de Janeiro: Editorial Campus.

    (2002b). *O sonhador que faz.* Rio de Janeiro: Editora Record.

    (2003a). Author's interview with Dr. Jose Serra, Cambridge, MA, May 9, 2003. Dr. Serra was Brazil's Minister of Health from 1998 to 2002.

    (2003b). Public lecture delivered at the Massachusetts Institute of Technology, Cambridge, MA, May 8, 2003.

Seth, M.J. (2002). *Education Fever: Society, Politics, and the Pursuit of Schooling in South Korea.* Honolulu: University of Hawai'i Press.

Shandra, J.M., et al. (2004). "Dependency, Democracy, and Infant Mortality." *Social Science and Medicine* 59.2, 321–333.

Shankar, A., et al. (2008). "The Village-Based Midwife Programme in Indonesia." *Lancet* 371.9620, 1226–1229.

Shen, T.H. (1970). *The Sino-American Joint Commission on Rural Reconstruction.* Ithaca, NY: Cornell University Press.

Shiffman, J. (2002). "The Construction of Community Participation: Village Family Planning Groups and the Indonesian State." *Social Science and Medicine* 54.8, 1199–1214.

    (2003). "Generating Political Will for Safe Motherhood in Indonesia." *Social Science and Medicine* 56.3, 1197–1207.

    (2007). "Generating Political Priority for Maternal Mortality Reduction in 5 Developing Countries." *American Journal of Public Health* 97.51, 796–803.

Siamwalla, A., Setboonsarng, S., Patamasiriwat, D. (1993). "Agriculture." In Warr, P.J., ed., *The Thai Economy in Transition.* New York: Cambridge University Press, 81–117.

Silva, E. (1996). *The State and Capital in Chile.* Boulder, CO: Westview.

Silva, M.V. da (2000). "Programa de alimentação escolar no Brasil: Evolução e limitações." *Archivos Electrónicos de Nutrición* No. 1. http://www.slan2000com/html/SLAF01F.htm (retrieved Jul 2, 2001).

Simms, C., Rowson, M. (2003). "Reassessment of Health Effects of the Indonesian Economic Crisis." *Lancet* 361.9366, 1382–1385.

Singh, S., Sedgh, G. (1997). "The Relationship of Abortion to Trends in Contraception and Fertility in Brazil, Colombia and Mexico." *International Family Planning Perspectives* 23.1, 4–14.

Skidmore, T. (1988). *The Politics of Military Rule in Brazil, 1964–85.* New York: Oxford University Press.

Smith, W.C. (1989). *Authoritarianism and the Crisis of the Argentine Political Economy.* Stanford, CA: Stanford University Press.

Smith-Nonini, S. (1997). "'Popular' Health and the State: Dialectics of the Peace Process in El Salvador." *Social Science and Medicine* 44.5, 635–645.

Snyder, R. (2001). "Scaling Down: The Subnational Comparative Method." *Studies in Comparative International Development* 36.1, 93–110.

Somoza, J. L., Dehollain, A., Salvia, F. (1962). "Examen crítico de algunas estadísticas de población de la Argentina." *Desarrollo Económico* 2.2, 85–141.

Son, A. H. K. (1998). "The Construction of the Medical Insurance System in the Republic of Korea, 1963–1989." *Scandinavian Journal of Social Welfare* 7.1, 17–26.

——— (1999). "Modernization of Medical Care in Korea (1876–1990)." *Social Science and Medicine* 49.4, 543–550.

——— (2003). "The Extension of Entitlement to Health Insurance in South Korea and Taiwan." *Economic and Industrial Democracy* 24.3, 455–478.

Sparrow, R. (2008). "Targeting the Poor in Times of Crisis: The Indonesian Health Card." *Health Policy and Planning* 23.3, 188–199.

Spence, J. D. (1990). *The Search for Modern China*. New York: W. W. Norton.

Stallings, B. (1978). *Class Conflict and Economic Development in Chile*. Stanford, CA: Stanford University Press.

Stark, R. (1985). "Lay Workers in Primary Care." *Social Science and Medicine* 20.3, 269–275.

Stepan, A. (1988). *Rethinking Military Politics*. Princeton, NJ: Princeton University Press.

Stepan, N. (1976). *Beginnings of Brazilian Science*. New York: Science History Publications.

Stillwaggon, E. (1998). *Stunted Lives, Stagnant Economies*. New Brunswick, NJ: Rutgers University Press.

Stover, E. (1987). *The Open Secret: Torture and the Medical Profession in Chile*. Washington, DC: American Association for the Advancement of Science.

Streeten, P., Burki, S. J. (1981). *First Things First*. Oxford: Oxford University Press.

Stycos, J. M. (1982). "The Decline of Fertility in Costa Rica." *Population Studies* 36.1, 15–30.

Suárez-Berenguela, R. M. (2000). "Health System Inequalities and Inequities in Latin America and the Caribbean: Findings and Policy Implications." Prepared for the Health and Human Development Division of the Pan American Health Oganization-World Health Organization. http://www.paho.org/English/HDP/HDD/suarez.pdf (retrieved Aug 25, 2006).

Sugiyama, N. B. (2008). "Theories of Policy Diffusion: Social Sector Reform in Brazil." *Comparative Political Studies* 41.2, 193–216.

Suh, S.-M. (1985). "Impact of Adjustment and Stabilization Policies on Social Welfare: The Korean Experiences During 1978–84." Working Paper 8504. Seoul: Korea Development Institute. http://www.kdi.re.kr/eng/db/search/search.jsp (retrieved Nov 30, 2003).

Sullivan, J. (1972). *A Review of Taiwanese Infant and Child Mortality Statistics, 1961–68*. Taipei: Institute of Economics, Academia Sinica.

Suryahadi, A., Sumarto, S., Pritchett, L. (2003). "The Evolution of Poverty during the Crisis in Indonesia." SMERU Research Institute Working Paper (March). http://www.smeru.or.id/ (retrieved Apr 23, 2003).

Svitone, E., et al. (2000). "Primary Health Care Lessons from the Northeast of Brazil." *Pan American Journal of Public Health* 7.5, 293–302.

Taeuber, I. B. (1944). "Colonial Demography: Formosa." *Population Index* (current item) 10.3, 147–157. [No author in source; Barclay (1954a: 267) identifies author as Taeuber].

——— (1958). *The Population of Japan*. Princeton, NJ: Princeton University Press.

Taeuber, I.B. (1961). "*Population Growth in a Chinese Microcosm: Taiwan.*" *Population Index* 27.2, 101–126.

Taghreed, A., et al. (2005). "Cost Effectiveness Analysis of Strategies for Maternal and Neonatal Health in Developing Countries." *British Medical Journal* 331.7525, 1–7.

Taiwan Journal (2008). "The Immunization Rate for Infants and Young Children." *Taiwan Journal* 25.23. http://taiwanjournal.nat.gov.tw/ct.asp?xItem=44067&CtNode=122 (retrieved Jul 1, 2008).

Taiwan. AREC [Administrative Research and Evaluation Commission, Executive Yuan] (1972). *A Review of the Administration of the Republic of China.* Taipei: Executive Yuan.

Taiwan. CDC [Center for Disease Control] (2000). "History of Vaccination in Taiwan." http://203.65.72.83/En/di/ShowPublication.ASP?RecNo=480 (retrieved Jul 31, 2002).

Taiwan. CEPD [Council for Economic Planning and Development] (2001). *Taiwan Statistical Data Book 2001.* Taipei: Council for Economic Planning and Development.

Taiwan. CEPD (2007). *Taiwan Statistical Data Book 2007.* Taipei: Council for Economic Planning and Development.

Taiwan. Department of Health (2008). *Health Statistics in Taiwan, 2006.* http://www.doh.gov.tw/EN2006/DM/DM2.aspx?now_fod_list_no=9377&class_no=390&level_no=2 (retrieved Jul 1, 2008).

Taiwan. DGBAS [Directorate-General of Budget, Accounting and Statistics] (1975, 2001, 2002, 2007). *Statistical Yearbook of the Republic of China.* Taipei: Republic of China, Executive Yuan, Directorate-General of Budget, Accounting and Statistics.

Taiwan. EPA [Environmental Protection Administration] (2006). "Background." http://www.epa.gov.tw/english/offices/g/background.htm (retrieved Oct 22, 2006).

Taiwan. GIO [Government Information Office] (2002). *The Republic of China Yearbook 2002.* Chapter 15: Public Health. http://www.gio.gov.tw/taiwan-website/5-gp/yearbook/chpt15-3.htm (retrieved Apr 21, 2002).

Taiwan. GIO (2003a). *Taiwan Yearbook 2003.* Chapter 16: Public Health. http://www.gio.gov.tw/taiwan-website/5-gp/yearbook/chpt16.htm (retrieved Sep 19, 2003).

Taiwan. GIO (2003b). "Public Health in Taiwan – Past, Present and Future." http://www.taiwan.com.au/Polieco/Policies/WHO/report02.html (retrieved Sep 22, 2003).

Taiwan. Ministry of the Interior (2005). "An Outline of Interior Affairs, 2005." Chapter 8: Construction and Planning. http://www.moi.gov.tw/stat/english/download.asp (retrieved Oct 23, 2006).

Taiwan. Ministry of the Interior (2008). "Life Expectancy at Birth and at Ten-Ages-Specific-Males [Females] in Taiwan Area, 1952–2006." http://www.moi.gov.tw/stat/english/index.asp (retrieved Aug 22, 2008).

Tang, K.-L. (2000). *Social Welfare Development in East Asia.* New York: Palgrave.

Tangcharoensathien, V., et al. (2002). "Universal Coverage and Its Impact on Reproductive Health Services in Thailand." *Reproductive Health Matters* 10.20, 59–69.

(2007). "Achieving Universal Coverage in Thailand." Paper commissioned by the World Health Organization Health Systems Knowledge Network. http://www.

who.int/social_determinants/knowledge_networks/add_documents/en/index. html (retrieved Aug 8, 2008).

Taucher, E. (1984). "Mortalidad infantil en Chile." Prepared for the Organización Panamericana de la Salud Taller Regional sobre Estrategias de Atención Primaria y Mortalidad del Niño, May 7–11, Mexico, DF.

——— (1996). "The Impact of Fertility Decline on Levels of Infant Mortality." In Guzmán, J. M., et al., eds., *The Fertility Transition in Latin America*. Oxford: Clarendon, 291–309.

——— (2002). Personal interview with L. Oster, a research associate of the author. Santiago, Chile, June 10, 2002.

Taucher, E., Jofré, I. (1997). "Mortalidad infantil en Chile." *Revista Médica de Chile* 125.10, 1225–1235.

Tendler, J. (1997a). *Good Government in the Tropics*. Baltimore, MD: Johns Hopkins University Press.

——— (1997b). "Ceará vs. Kerala." In McGuire, J. W., ed., *Rethinking Development in East Asia and Latin America*. Los Angeles, CA: Pacific Council on International Policy, 109–122.

——— (2003). "The Fear of Education." Background paper for *Inequality and the State in Latin America and the Caribbean* (World Bank). http://www.oecd.org/ dataoecd/43/40/2489865.pdf (retrieved Jun 2, 2004).

Terra de Souza, A., et al. (1999). "Variations in Infant Mortality Rates among Municipalities in the State of Ceará, Northeast Brazil." *International Journal of Epidemiology* 28.2, 267–275.

Thabrany, H. (2000). "Managed Health Care in Indonesia." *The Electronic Journal of the Indonesian Medical Association* 2.1, 1–12. http://www.e-jima.com/pdf/ edt01_v01_no2.pdf (retrieved Sep 21, 2002).

——— (2006). "Human Resources in Decentralized Health Systems in Indonesia: Challenges for Equity." *Regional Health Forum* [WHO South-East Asia Region] 10.1, 75–88. http://www.searo.who.int/LinkFiles/Regional_Health_Forum_Volume_10_ No_1_RHF_Vol.10_No.1.pdf (retrieved Aug 15, 2008).

Thailand. IHPP [International Health Policy Program] (2006). "Universal Health Care Coverage: Experience Sharing from Thailand." Presentation at the Interregional Meeting on Implementation of the Strategy on Health Care Financing, Ulaanbaatar, Mongolia, 29 August 2006. http://164.115.5.20/ihpp/journal.html (retrieved Dec 5, 2006).

Thailand. MoPH [Ministry of Public Health] (1988). *Mini Health Profile*. Bangkok: MoPH.

Thailand. MoPH (2000). *Thailand Health Profile, 1997–98.* http://eng.moph.go.th/ ContentDetails.asp?intContentID=34&strOrgID=001 (retrieved Mar 22, 2004).

Thailand. MoPH (2007). "Health Policy in Thailand 2007." Bangkok: Bureau of Policy and Strategy, Ministry of Public Health. http://bps.ops.moph.go.th/ HealthPolicy7.pdf (retrieved Aug 7, 2008).

Thailand. NESDB [National Economic, and Social Development Board] (2004a). "Thailand's Official Poverty Lines." Prepared for the 2004 International Conference on Official Poverty Statistics: Methodology and Comparability, Manila, 4–6 October. http://www.nscb.gov.ph/poverty/conference/papers/ default.asp (retrieved Feb 18, 2008).

Thailand. NESDB (2004b). *Thailand Millennium Development Goals Report.* Bangkok: Office of the National Economic and Social Development Board. http://

www.searo.who.int/en/Section1243/Section1921/Section1924/Section2086.htm (retrieved Aug 18, 2008).

Thailand. NSO [National Statistical Office] (2001). *Statistical Yearbook Thailand.* No. 43. http://www.nso.go.th/syb2001/syb2001.htm (retrieved Jun 27, 2002).

Thailand. NSO (2006). *Thailand Multiple Indicator Cluster Survey December 2005-February 2006, Final Report.* Bangkok: National Statistical Office. http://www.childinfo.org/mics3_surveys.html (retrieved Aug 6, 2008).

Thiesenhusen, W.C. (1995). *Broken Promises: Agrarian Reform and the Latin American Campesino.* Boulder, CO: Westview.

Thompson, A.A. (1985). "Estado, sindicatos y salud." *Cuadernos Médico Sociales* 33, 35-53.

Thornton, A., Lin, H.-S. (1994). *Social Change and the Family in Taiwan.* Chicago: University of Chicago Press.

Tien, H.-M. (1992). "Taiwan's Evolution toward Democracy." In Simon, D.F., Kau, M.Y.M., eds., *Taiwan: Beyond the Economic Miracle.* Armonk, NY: M.E. Sharpe.

Tinsulanonda, P. (1995). "Thai Experience in Combating Insurgency." Speech before the commanders of the Armed Forces of the Philippines, Manila, March 4. http://www.generalprem.com/Speech4.html (retrieved Dec 5, 2006).

Titaley, C.R., et al. (2008). "Determinants of Neonatal Mortality in Indonesia." *BMC Public Health* 8.232, 1-15.

Titelman, D. (1999). "Reformas al financiamiento del sistema de salud en Chile." *Revista de la CEPAL* 69, 181-194.

Tobar, F. (2001). "Economía de la reforma de los seguros de salud en Argentina." Buenos Aires: Isalud. http://www.federicotobar.com.ar/economia.php (retrieved Jul 16, 2008).

Tomz, M., Wittenberg, J., King, G. (2001). CLARIFY: Software for Interpreting and Presenting Statistical Results. Version 2.0. Cambridge, MA: Harvard University. http://gking.harvard.edu (retrieved Aug 6, 2002).

Torcal, M., Mainwaring, S. (2003). "The Political Recrafting of Social Bases of Party Competition: Chile, 1973-95." *British Journal of Political Science* 33.1, 55-84.

Towse, A., Mills, A., Tangcharoensathien, V. (2004). "Learning from Thailand's Health Reforms." *British Medical Journal* 328.7431, 103-105.

Treisman, D. (2002). Data associated with "Defining Decentralization: A Global Perspective." Unpublished Paper, Department of Political Science, University of California, Los Angeles. Data set kindly provided by Dr. Treisman as an email attachment on January 17, 2006.

Trejos, J.D. (1995). "Costa Rica: The State's Response to Poverty." In Raczynski, D., ed., *Strategies to Combat Poverty in Latin America.* Baltimore, MD: Johns Hopkins University Press.

— (2002). "La equidad en la inversion social 2000." *Octavo informe sobre el estado de la nación en desarrollo humano sostenible.* San José, CR: Programa Estado de la Nación. http://www.estadonacion.or.cr/info2002/nacion8/Po-equidad/ (retrieved Sep 28, 2006).

Trirat, N. (2001). "Two Case Studies of Corruption in Medicine and Medical Supplies Procurement in the Ministry of Public Health." Civil Society and Governance Programme, Institute of Development Studies, University of Sussex. http://www.ids.ac.uk/ids/civsoc/final/thailand/tha1a.doc (retrieved Jul 12, 2002).

Trussell, J. (1988). "Does Family Planning Reduce Infant Mortality?" *Population and Development Review* 14.1, 171–178.

Tsurumi, E. P. (1977). *Japanese Colonial Education in Taiwan, 1895–1945.* Cambridge, MA: Harvard University Press.

Turner, J. E., et al. (1993). *Villages Astir.* Westport, CT: Praeger.

Ugalde, A., et al. (2000). "Conflict and Health: The Health Costs of War: Can They Be Measured? Lessons From El Salvador." *British Medical Journal* 321.7254, 169–172.

UNAIDS/WHO Working Group on Global HIV/AIDS and STI Surveillance (2004). "Epidemiological Fact Sheets on HIV/AIDS and Sexually Transmitted Infections: Thailand. 2004 Update." http://data.unaids.org/Publications/Fact-Sheets01/thailand_EN.pdf (retrieved Nov 21, 2006).

UNAIDS/WHO Working Group on Global HIV/AIDS and STI Surveillance (2008). "Epidemiological Fact Sheet on HIV and AIDS: Thailand. 2008 Update." http://www.unaids.org/en/KnowledgeCentre/HIVData/Epidemiology/epifactsheets.asp (retrieved Aug 7, 2008).

UNDP [United Nations Development Programme] (1993, 1994, 1996, 1999, 2001, 2002, 2003, 2005, 2006). *Human Development Report.* New York: Oxford University Press.

UNDP (1998). *Una mirada al PROMIN. Programa Materno Infantil y Nutrición.* Misión de revisión y análisis externo. Buenos Aires. In Acuña and Chudnovsky 2002: 59–72.

UNDP (2007). *Human Development Report 2007/2008.* New York: Palgrave-Macmillan.

UNDP-Indonesia (2001). *Indonesia Human Development Report 2001.* Jakarta: BPS-Statistics Indonesia, Bappenas, and UNDP Indonesia.

UNESCAP [United Nations Economic and Social Commission for Asia and the Pacific] (2003). *Economic and Social Survey of Asia and the Pacific 2003.* New York: United Nations.

UNESCO [United Nations Educational, Scientific, and Cultural Organization] (2001). World Education Indicators. http://unescostat.unesco.org/en/stats/statso.htm (retrieved Jul 5, 2001).

UNESCO Institute for Statistics (2008). "National literacy rates for youths (15–24) and adults (15+)." http://stats.uis.unesco.org/unesco/ReportFolders/ReportFolders.aspx (retrieved Jun 25, 2008).

UNFPA [United Nations Fund for Population Activities] (1982). *Republic of Korea: Report of Mission on Needs Assessment for Population Assistance.* Report 47. New York: UNFPA.

Unger, D. (1996). "Organizing Workers in Thailand." Prepared for the 92nd annual meeting of the American Political Science Association, San Francisco, CA, August 28 to September 1, 1996.

(1998). *Building Social Capital in Thailand.* New York: Cambridge University Press.

UNICEF [United Nations International Children's Education Fund] (1996, 2001). *State of the World's Children.* http://www.unicef.org/sowc/ (retrieved Mar 23, 2009).

UNICEF et al. [UNICEF, the UN Population Division, WHO, and The World Bank] (2007). "Levels and Trends of Child Mortality in 2006: Estimates Developed by the Inter-Agency Group for Child Mortality Estimation." Working Paper. http:// www.childinfo.org/mortality_174.htm (retrieved Jul 4, 2008).

UNICEF Office for Thailand (2007). *2007 Multiple Indicator Cluster Survey of Women and Children in Thailand: Summary Report.* Bangkok: UNICEF Thailand. http://www.childinfo.org/mics3_520.htm (retrieved Aug 6, 2008).

United Nations (1952, 1961). *Demographic Yearbook.* New York: United Nations Department of International Economic and Social Affairs.

United Nations (1992). *Child Mortality since the 1960s.* New York: United Nations, Department of Economic and Social Development, Population Division.

United Nations (2008). Millennium Development Goals Indicators. http://mdgs. un.org/unsd/mdg/Data.aspx (retrieved Jan 15, 2008).

United States. Bureau of the Census (2008a). *Statistical Abstract of the United States 2006.* Washington, DC: Government Printing Office.

United States. Bureau of the Census (2008b). "State & County Quick Facts: Sharkey County, Mississippi." http://quickfacts.census.gov/qfd/states/28/28125.html (retrieved Aug 24, 2008).

United States. MSMC [Mutual Security Mission to China] (1956). *Economic Development on Taiwan, 1951–1955.* Taipei: International Cooperation Administration.

UNRC [United Nations Resident Coordinator] – Thailand (2002). UN Common Database for Thailand. Bangkok: Inter-Agency Support Unit, Office of the United Nations Resident Coordinator. Issue 1. http://www.un.or.th/Resource_Centre/ UN_Database/un_database.html (retrieved Oct 3, 2003).

USOM [United States Operations Mission in Thailand] (1969). *A Brief History of USOM Support to Public Health Programs in Thailand.* Bangkok: United States Operations Mission.

Valdés, T. (2002). Personal interview with L. Oster, a research associate of the author, Santiago, Chile, June 27, 2002.

Valente, M. (2005). "Argentina: Defying Vatican, Kirchner Fires Rightist Army Bishop." IPN – Inter-Press Service, 18 March 2005 (retrieved Jun 13, 2006 from Lexis-Nexis).

Vallin, J., Lopez, A.D., eds. (1985). *Health Policy, Social Policy, and Mortality Prospects.* Liège: International Union for the Scientific Study of Population.

Van de Walle, D. (1994). "The Distribution of Subsidies through Public Health Services in Indonesia, 1978–87." *World Bank Economic Review* 8.2, 279–309.

Varavarn, S., H.S.H. Prince (2000 [1930]). "Public Health and Medical Service." In Executive Committee of the Eighth Congress of the Far Eastern Association of Tropical Medicine, *Siam in 1930: General and Medical Features.* Bangkok: White Lotus, 185–244.

Vargas [González], W. (1995). "Development and Characteristics of Health and Nutrition Services for Urban and Rural Communities of Costa Rica." In Muñoz, C., Scrimshaw, N.S., eds., *The Nutrition and Health Transition of Democratic Costa Rica.* Boston, MA: International Foundation for Developing Countries. http://www.unu.edu/unupress/food2/UIN05E/uin05e00.htm#Contents (retrieved Jun 28, 2003).

Vargas González, W. (1977). "El programa de salud rural de Costa Rica." *América Indígena* 37.2, 353–365.

Vasconcelos, E.M. (1999). "A priorização da família nas políticas de saúde." *Saúde em Debate* [Rio de Janeiro] 23.53, 6–19.

Vergara, P. (1990). *Políticas hacia la extrema pobreza en Chile, 1973–1988.* Santiago, Chile: Facultad Latinoamericana de Ciencias Sociales.

Viana, A.L.D., Dal Poz, M.R. (1998). "A reforma do sistema de saúde no Brasil e o Programa de Saúde da Família." *Physis: Revista de Saúde Coletiva* [Instituto de Medicina Social da Universidade do Estado do Rio de Janeiro] 8.2, 11–48.

Viel, B., Campos, W. (1987). "Historia Chilena de mortalidad infantil y materna, 1940–1985." *Perspectivas Internacionales en Planificación Familiar* (Special Issue), 24–28.

Vilches, J.R., Ibáñez, F. (1993). "El sector salud de la provincia de Salta." In Katz, J., ed., *El sector salud en la República Argentina.* Buenos Aires: Fondo de Cultura Económica de Buenos Aires, 111–155.

Villegas de Olazábal, H. (2004). "Atención integral de salud en Costa Rica." In Miranda Gutiérrez, G., Zamora Zamora, C., eds., *La construcción de la seguridad social.* San José, CR: Editorial Universidad Estatal a Distancia, 235–253.

(2005). "Atención primaria de salud y Salud para Todos: Costa Rica y Centroamérica." In Ministerio de Salud de Costa Rica et al., eds., *Atención Primaria de Salud en Costa Rica: 25 años después de Alma Ata.* San José, CR: Organización Panamericana de la Salud y Organización Mundial de la Salud, 21–58. http://www.cor.ops-oms.org/ (retrieved Feb 16, 2007).

Wade, R. (1990). *Governing the Market.* Princeton, NJ: Princeton University Press.

Wagstaff, A. (2003). "Child Health on a Dollar a Day." *Social Science and Medicine* 57.9, 1529–1538.

Waisman, C.H. (1987). *Reversal of Development in Argentina.* Princeton, NJ: Princeton University Press.

Waters, H., Saadah, F., Pradhan, M. (2003). "The Impact of the 1997–98 East Asian Economic Crisis on Health and Health Care in Indonesia." *Health Policy and Planning* 18.2, 172–181.

Wells, H. (1970–71). "The 1970 Election in Costa Rica." *World Affairs* 133, 13–28.

Wen, S.W., et al. (2002). "The Impact of Missing Birth Weight in Deceased versus Surviving Fetuses and Infants in the Comparison of Birth Weight-Specific Feto-Infant Mortality." *Chronic Diseases in Canada* 23.4, 146–151.

Wennemo, I. (1993). "Infant Mortality, Public Policy, and Inequality." *Sociology of Health and Illness* 15.4, 429–446.

Western, B. (1995). "Concepts and Suggestions for Robust Regression Analysis." *American Journal of Political Science* 39.3, 786–817.

Weyland, K. (1995). "Social Movements and the State: The Politics of Health Reform in Brazil." *World Development* 23.10, 1699–1712.

(1996). *Democracy without Equity: Failures of Reform in Brazil.* Pittsburgh, PA: University of Pittsburgh Press.

(1997). "'Growth with Equity' in Chile's New Democracy." *Latin American Research Review* 32.1, 37–67.

(1999). "Economic Policy in Chile's New Democracy." *Journal of Interamerican Studies and World Affairs* 41.3, 67–96.

(2005). "The Growing Sustainability of Brazil's Low-Quality Democracy." In Hagopian, F., and Mainwaring, S., eds., *The Third Wave of Democratization in Latin America.* New York: Cambridge University Press, 90–120.

(2006). *Bounded Rationality and Policy Diffusion: Social Sector Reform in Latin America.* Princeton, NJ: Princeton University Press.

Weyland, K., ed. (2004). *Learning from Foreign Models in Latin American Policy Reform*. Washington, DC: Woodrow Wilson Center Press/Johns Hopkins University Press.

Whang, I.-J. (1985). "Delivery System of Public Health Services in Rural Areas: The Korean Case." Korea Development Institute Working Paper 8509. December. Seoul: KDI. http://www.kdi.re.kr/eng/db/search/search.jsp (retrieved Nov 30, 2003).

WHO [World Health Organization] (1980). *Sixth Report on the World Health Situation 1973–1977*. Part II. Geneva: WHO.

WHO (1993). *World Health Statistics Annual*. Geneva: WHO.

WHO (2002). WHO Global Database on Child Growth and Malnutrition. WHO, Department of Nutrition for Health and Development. http://www.who.int/nutgrowthdb/p-child_pdf/index.html (retrieved Jul 12, 2002).

WHO (2003). WHO Estimates of Health Personnel. http://www3.who.int/whosis/health_personnel/health_personnel.cfm?path=whosis,health_personnel&language=english (retrieved Aug 11, 2003).

WHO (2004). "WHO/UNICEF Estimates of National Immunization Coverage, 1980–2003." Database updated September 24, 2004. http://www.who.int/vaccines-surveillance/StatsAndGraphs.htm (retrieved Jun 3, 2005).

WHO (2008a). "WHO/UNICEF [Immunization] Coverage Estimates for 1980–2006, as of August 2008." Updated January 2008. http://www.who.int/immunization_monitoring/data/data_subject/en/index.html (retrieved Jun 27, 2008).

WHO (2008b). "WHO Global Database on Child Health and Malnutrition." http://www.who.int/nutgrowthdb/database/en/ (retrieved Jun 29, 2008).

WHO/UNICEF (2001). "Access to Improved Drinking Water Sources." Geneva: World Health Organization; New York: UNICEF. WHO/UNICEF Joint Monitoring Programme for Water and Sanitation, Coverage Estimates for 1980–2000. http://www.childinfo.org/eddb/water/database.htm (retrieved Sep 2002 to May 2003).

Wibulpolprasert, S., ed. (2002). *Thailand Health Profile 1999–2000*. Nonthaburi: Bureau of Policy and Strategy, Ministry of Public Health. http://www.moph.go.th/ops/thealth_44/index_eng.htm (retrieved Oct 3, 2003).

—— (2005). *Thailand Health Profile 2001–2004*. Nonthaburi: Bureau of Policy and Strategy, Ministry of Public Health. http://www.hiso.or.th/hiso/HealthReport/report 2004–2007ENG.php?manu=3 (retrieved Jul 2, 2008).

Wibulpolprasert, S., Pengpaibon, P. (2003). "Integrated Strategies to Tackle the Inequitable Distribution of Doctors in Thailand." *Human Resources for Health* 1.12, 1–17.

WIDER [United Nations University – World Institute for Development Economics Research] (2007). World Income Inequality Database Version 2.0b, May 2007. http://www.wider.unu.edu/research/Database/en_GB/wiid/ (retrieved Jan 21, 2008).

Widjojo, N. (1970). *Population Trends in Indonesia*. Ithaca, NY: Cornell University Press.

Wiley, J. (1995). "Undocumented Aliens and Recognized Refugees: The Right to Work in Costa Rica." *International Migration Review* 29.2, 423–440.

Wilkie, J. W., Alemán, E., Ortega, J. G., eds. (1999). *Statistical Abstract of Latin America*. Vol. 35. Los Angeles, CA: UCLA Latin American Center Publications.

Wilkie, J. W., Reich, P., eds. (1978). *Statistical Abstract of Latin America*. Vol. 19. Los Angeles, CA: UCLA Latin American Center Publications.

Wilkinson, R. G. (2001). *Mind the Gap*. New Haven, CT: Yale University Press.

Wilson, B. M. (1998). *Costa Rica: Politics, Economics, and Democracy*. Boulder, CO: Lynne Rienner.

Winckler, E. A. (1984). "Institutionalism and Participation on Taiwan." *The China Quarterly* 99, 481–499.

Wong, J. (2004). *Healthy Democracies*. Ithaca, NY: Cornell University Press.

Woo, J. H. (1991). "Education and Economic Growth in Taiwan." *World Development* 19.8, 1029–1044.

Wood, C., Carvalho, J.A.M. de (1988). *The Demography of Inequality in Brazil*. Cambridge: Cambridge University Press.

World Bank (1979). *Korea: Policy Issues for Long-Term Development*. Coord. Hasan, P., Rao, D. C. Baltimore, MD: Johns Hopkins University Press.

World Bank (1980). *World Development Report*. New York: Oxford University Press.

World Bank (1988). *Argentina: Social Sectors in Crisis*. Washington, DC: World Bank.

World Bank (1993a). *World Development Report 1993*. New York: Oxford University Press.

World Bank (1993b). *The East Asian Miracle*. New York: Oxford University Press.

World Bank (1994). "The Organization, Delivery and Financing of Health Care in Brazil: Agenda for the 90s." Report 12655-BR. Washington, DC: World Bank.

World Bank (2000a). *World Development Report 2000*. New York: Oxford University Press.

World Bank (2000b). *Poor People in a Rich Country: A Poverty Report for Argentina*. Vol. 1. Washington, DC: World Bank.

World Bank (2001/02). Health, Nutrition, and Population database. http://devdata. worldbank.org/hnpstats/ (retrieved Oct 2001 to Feb 2002).

World Bank (2001a). "An Assessment of the Bolsa Escola Programs." Report 20208-BR. Latin America and the Caribbean Regional Office. wbln0018.world-bank.org/External/lac/lac.nsf/4c794feb793085a5852567d6006ad764/ed5eeaaed 4101b9385256a53007492a4/$FILE/Bolsa+Escola.pdf (retrieved Jul 16, 2001).

World Bank (2001b). "Poverty Reduction in Indonesia: Constructing a New Strategy." Report 23028–IND. Washington, DC: World Bank.

World Bank (2001c). *World Development Indicators on CD-ROM*. Washington, DC: World Bank.

World Bank (2002). *World Development Indicators on CD-ROM*. Washington, DC: World Bank.

World Bank (2003a). "Implementation Completion Report (CPL-36540; SCPD-3654S) on a Loan in the Amount of US $22 Million to the Republic of Costa Rica for a Health Sector Reform Project." Washington, DC: Latin America and the Caribbean Regional Office. http://www.worldbank.org (retrieved Feb 25, 2007).

World Bank (2003b). Indonesia-Health Workforce and Services. Project Information Document PID10698, Project ID P073772. Prepared March 25, 2003. http:// www-wds.worldbank.org/servlet/WDS_IBank_Servlet?pcont=details&eid=000 094946_0110120434064 (retrieved Apr 9, 2003).

World Bank (2003c). "Program Document for a Proposed Provincial Maternal-Child Health Sector Adjustment Loan in the Amount of US$750 Million to the

Argentine Republic." Report 26527-AR. Washington, DC: World Bank. http://www-wds.worldbank.org/servlet/WDS_IBank_Servlet?pcont=details&eid=000112742_20031111095049 (retrieved Feb 23, 2004).

World Bank (2004a). *World Development Report 2004*. New York: Oxford University Press.

World Bank (2004b). *Brazil: Equitable, Competitive, Sustainable*. Washington, DC: World Bank.

World Bank (2005). "Improving Indonesia's Health Outcomes." Indonesia Policy Brief. February. http://siteresources.worldbank.org/INTEAPREGTOPHEANUT/Resources/health.pdf (retrieved Oct 9, 2006).

World Bank (2006a). "Project Appraisal Document on a Proposed Loan in the Amount of US$300 Million to the Argentine Government for the Provincial Maternal-Child Health Investment Project in Support of the Second Phase of the Provincial Maternal-Child Health Program." Report 37702-AR. Washington, DC: World Bank. http://www-wds.worldbank.org/external/default/WDSContentServer/WDSP/IB/2006/10/17/000090341_20061017113406/Rendered/PDF/37702.pdf (retrieved Jul 15, 2008).

World Bank (2006b). "Country Assistance Strategy for the Argentine Republic, 2006–2008." Report 34015-AR. Washington, DC: World Bank. http://siteresources.worldbank.org/INTARGENTINA/Resources/1CASAr.pdf (retrieved Jul 15, 2008).

World Bank (2006c). "The Impact of Intel in Costa Rica." Washington, DC: World Bank/MIGA. http://www.fdi.net/investing_in_development/intelcr (retrieved Feb 20, 2007).

World Bank (2007). "Status of Projects in Execution – FY07: Argentina." Washington, DC: World Bank, Operations Policy and Country Services. www1.worldbank.org/operations/disclosure/SOPE/FY07/LAC/Argentina.pdf (retrieved Jul 15, 2008).

World Bank (2008a). *World Development Indicators Online*. Washington, DC: World Bank (retrieved Mar 15, 2008).

World Bank (2008b). *Realizing Rights through Social Guarantees*. Report 40047 – GLB. Washington, DC: Social Development Department, World Bank.

World Bank (2008c). Country Data Sheets. Reports and databases providing the underlying data used to produce consensus estimates of infant mortality and under-5 mortality. http://go.worldbank.org/6BXP1CUWX0 (retrieved Jul 31, 2008).

World Bank (2008d). "Investing in Indonesia's Health." Health Public Expenditure Review 2008. Washington, DC: World Bank. http://go.worldbank.org/T1U1VY0060 (retrieved Aug 15, 2008).

World Bank (2008e). *World Development Indicators Online*. Washington, DC: World Bank (retrieved Aug 2, 2008).

World Bank Thailand Office (1999). "Coping with the Crisis in Education and Health." *Thailand Social Monitor*, Issue 2. http://www.worldbank.or.th/social/index.html (retrieved Jul 24, 2002).

World Bank Thailand Office (2000). "Thailand's Response to AIDS: Building on Success, Confronting the Future." *Thailand Social Monitor*, Issue 5. http://www.worldbank.or.th/monitor/social/2000nov.shtml (retrieved Feb 18, 2004).

World Bank Thailand Office (2001). "Poverty and Public Policy." *Thailand Social Monitor*, Issue 6. http://www.worldbank.or.th/social/index.html (retrieved Jun 14, 2002).

Yang, B.-M., Prescott, N., Bae, E.-Y. (2001). "The Impact of Economic Crisis on Health-Care Consumption in Korea." *Health Policy and Planning* 16.4, 372–385.

Yang, J., et al. (1965). "Fertility and Family Planning in Rural Korea." *Population Studies* 18.3, 237–250.

Yashar, D. (1995). "Civil War and Social Welfare." In Mainwaring, S., Scully, T. R., eds., *Building Democratic Institutions.* Stanford, CA: Stanford University Press.

(1997). *Demanding Democracy.* Stanford, CA: Stanford University Press.

Yen, C.-H. (1973a). "Public Health in Taiwan, Republic of China, 1921–1971." Part 1. *Industry of Free China* 39.2, 6–17.

(1973b). "Public Health in Taiwan, Republic of China, 1921–1971." Part 2. *Industry of Free China* 39.3, 25–35.

Yen, Y. T. (1971). "Health Stations in Taiwan." *Canadian Journal of Public Health* 62.2, 161–164.

Yeon, H.-C. (1981). *Primary Health Care in Korea: An Approach to Evaluation.* Seoul: Korea Development Institute. http://www.kdi.re.kr/eng/db/search/search.jsp (retrieved Nov 30, 2003).

(1988). "Role of International Cooperation: An Approach to Developing Primary Health Care in Korea." Prepared for the Third Takemi Symposium on "International Cooperation for Health Policy in Developing Countries," Tokyo, July 1–3, 1988. Seoul: Korea Development Institute. http://www.kdi.re.kr/eng/db/search/search.jsp (retrieved Nov 30, 2003).

(1989). "Social Development in the Republic of Korea." Seoul: Korea Development Institute. http://www.kdi.re.kr/eng/db/search/search.jsp (retrieved Nov 30, 2003).

Yi, I. (2003). "The National Patterns of Unemployment Policies in Two Asian Countries: Malaysia and South Korea." Working Paper 15, Stein Rokkan Centre for Social Studies, Bergen University Research Foundation, Bergen, Norway. http://www.ub.uib.no/elpub/rokkan/N/N15-03.pdf (retrieved Nov 8, 2006).

Yip, K.-C. (2000). "Malaria Eradication: The Taiwan Experience." *Parassitologia* 42.1–2, 117–126.

Zankel, S. (2003). Personal interview, Village No. 7 (Ban Pong), Tambol Inthakhil, Mae Taeng district, Chiang Mai province, Thailand, January 14, 2003. From 1977 to 1980 Dr. Zankel was a health information officer for the Rural Primary Health Care Expansion project. From 1981 to 1990 he was the Project Coordinator for the Hill Tribe Health and Family Planning Program.

Zweifel, T. D., Navia, P. (2000). "Democracy, Dictatorship, and Infant Mortality." *Journal of Democracy* 11.2, 99–114.

Index

Made in the USA
Charleston, SC
03 September 2013